INVENTING
THE
MIDDLE AGES

INVENTING
THE
MIDDLE AGES

THE LIVES, WORKS, AND IDEAS OF THE GREAT MEDIEVALISTS
OF THE TWENTIETH CENTURY

NORMAN F. CANTOR

WILLIAM MORROW AND COMPANY, INC.
NEW YORK

Library of Congress Cataloging-in-Publication Data

Cantor, Norman F.
    Inventing the Middle Ages : the lives, works, and ideas of the
great medievalists of the twentieth century / Norman F. Cantor.
        p.   cm.
    Includes bibliographical references (p.442) and index.
    ISBN 0-688-09406-6
    1. Middle Ages—Historiography—History—20th century.   I. Title.
D116.C35   1991
940.1'072—dc20   91-22748
                                                            CIP

Printed in the United States of America

BOOK DESIGN BY M'NO PRODUCTION SERVICES, INC.

For Max

PREFACE AND ACKNOWLEDGMENTS

———— ◆◆◆ ————

This book is the story of the founding era of medieval studies from 1895 to about 1965, through the lives, works, and ideas of the great medievalists, and is an evaluation of their continuing impact, into the 1980s, on how the European Middle Ages are interpreted.

From my own personal acquaintance with seven of the twenty master medievalists on whom this book is primarily focused, from a variety of biographical and autobiographical sources, as well as from accounts passed along to me, I have tried to construct in each instance a life narrative along with an assessment of ideas and an analysis of the continuing impact of these medievalists' interpretations.

I wish to thank the following:

Sir Geoffrey Elton, Robert Hanning, Kate Ludwig Jansen, Darlene Levy, Margaret Jennings, Ann Rabinowitz, and Richard Schneider for recently providing important information. They have not read this book in manuscript and are in no way responsible for what I have done with the information provided.

The Houghton Library of Harvard University, for permission to quote from the unpublished letters of Charles Homer Haskins.

The Office of the Dean of the Faculty of Arts and Science of New York University and particularly Dean Ann Burton for providing secretarial assistance.

My secretary, Nelly Fontanez, for careful handling of a difficult manuscript and her skill in the word processing of several drafts.

Peter Lang Publishing of Bern, Switzerland, and the *Oxford Magazine* for allowing me to adapt a half dozen pages that I previously published in articles in respectively *Einheit in der Vielfalt, Festschrift für Peter Lang zum 60. Geburtstag* (1988) and the magazine's issue of November 1987.

My students at Columbia University in 1964; Brandeis University in 1966; State University of New York at Binghamton in 1973; New York University in 1982, 1987, and 1990; and Tel Aviv University in 1988, with whom the ideas and material that constitute this book were discussed in courses. I have benefited from their comments and suggestions.

Sidney Burrell and Charles Dellheim, who read an earlier draft of the book and made many valuable suggestions.

Joan Raines, for her encouragement and advice.

Elisa Petrini and Randy Ladenheim-Gil, for editing of the manuscript and making it more readable.

Mindy Cantor, who has shared with me over the years her insightful impressions of the great medievalists whom we have jointly met. Mindy has also suggested to me several critical relationships between modernism and medievalism.

Greenwich Village, New York City

CONTENTS

———◆———

CREDO

Like dwarfs standing on the shoulders of giants, we see farther than they.
                    —Bernard of Chartres, northern France, c. 1130

I shall not pass over silently that certain people . . . don't want to presume to go beyond their venerable predecessors. But having thus covered up their inertia, they dawdle about lazily and deride, ridicule and mock the industriousness shown by others in the quest and discovery of truth. But he who dwells in heaven shall ridicule them; the Lord shall mock them.
                    —Richard of St. Victor, northern France, c. 1160
                    (Trans. M. D. Chenu, J. Taylor, and L. K. Little)

That learned man [St. Jerome] knew . . . how obscure truth is, how deep it lies buried, how far from mortal sight it has plunged into the depths, how it will admit only a few, by how much work it is reached, how practically no one ever succeeds, how it is dug out with difficulty and then only bit by bit.
                    —Andrew of St. Victor, northern France, c. 1170
                    (Trans. M. D. Chenu, J. Taylor, and L. K. Little)

CREDO

INVENTING
THE
MIDDLE AGES

CHAPTER ONE

THE QUEST FOR THE MIDDLE AGES

I

BETWEEN ROME AND RENAISSANCE

In France, Germany, and Italy they still call it the Middle Age. In English-speaking countries since about 1840 it is generally referred to in the plural—the Middle Ages—signifying the several distinct sub-eras during one very long epoch. Whether called by the singular or the plural, the medieval era in Western civilization is the millennium that stretched from the fall of the Roman Empire in Europe (about A.D. 450) to the Italian Renaissance of the late fifteenth century. The question that has engaged the lifetime interest and work of thousands of historians, literary critics, art historians, philosophers, theologians, and archaeologists in modern times is, What happened between Rome and the Renaissance? What was the nature of the European medieval world, and what is its connection to our own?

Interest in the meaning and relevance of the Middle Ages stretches far beyond academia. Books about King Arthur and his Round Table, both fiction and nonfiction, constitute a thriving cottage industry. In 1978 Barbara Tuchman, a distinguished historian although not an academic, published a best-selling medieval book, *A Distant Mirror*, that demonstrated to almost universal satisfaction similarities between the troubled fourteenth century in Europe and the more depressing moments of the twentieth century. In 1990 no fewer than three Hollywood film companies almost simultaneously announced they were going to produce a new movie about Robin Hood, to replace the jovial 1938 film that starred Errol Flynn and Olivia De Havilland, and a new blockbuster film about the mythic medieval hero is now actually in production. Perhaps on a more exalted level of discourse, the papacy in 1987 prohibited a professor of theology at

17

the Catholic University of America in Washington, D.C., from teaching about sexuality in a manner that sharply departed from allegedly authoritative medieval Catholic tradition. *Hagar the Horrible*, the rambunctious Viking, is a favorite comic strip. Every summer tens of thousands of middle-class Americans climb into tour buses in London, Paris, Frankfurt, Rome, and Vienna and spend a week or two visiting medieval cathedrals and the remains of medieval castles. Curiosity is thereby stimulated about the people who created the world of castle and cathedral.

In 1984 the English translation of a novel by an Italian professor of medieval literature, *The Name of the Rose* by Umberto Eco, surprised the New York publishing world by becoming a phenomenal best seller. The popularity of Eco's highly cerebral novel was helped by its being cast in the form of a detective story. Yet the setting was the fourteenth century, and the story is placed in the context of one of the more dramatic conflicts within the medieval church: between the papacy and the radical, or Spiritual, wing of the order of Franciscan friars over the nature of the church and its role in society.

Asked to explain the phenomenal success of his novel, Eco modestly attributed it "to a period of renewed interest in the Middle Ages . . . both in Europe and America." Another comment by Eco puts it more sharply: "[T]he fact is that everyone has his own ideas, usually corrupt, of the Middle Ages." The huge popular success of Eco's and Tuchman's medieval books gave new attention to the ideas held about the Middle Ages by the leading academic medievalists of the twentieth century, whose research and insight the two best-selling authors had freely drawn upon. Specifying parallels between the agonies of the fourteenth and twentieth centuries or setting a brilliant detective story within the conflict between the papacy and the Spiritual Franciscans was only a small sliver of the medieval European experience that stretched for a millennium beyond the fall of the Roman Empire. Which additional interpretations or fascinating data loom strongly out of the work of three generations of medievalists since 1900? Which were the colossal personalities and dramatic crises that the medievalists had revealed? What further parallels or contrasts could be drawn between the Middle Ages and our own culture and society? How do the medieval sensibility, imagination, and faith relate to our own set of assumptions and perceptions? These were subjects broached by sophisticated literary agents and editors as they took luncheons in two-star restaurants with academic medievalists, seeking to find at least one who, like Tuchman (but certainly not Eco), wrote suburban middle-class prose.

Out of this talent search came a 1987 book by an academic medievalist that indeed gained a wide audience: the persuasive and crisply written biography of the late fourteenth-century English poet Geoffrey Chaucer by Stanford University literature professor Donald R. Howard. "The readers who made Barbara Tuchman's *A Distant Mirror* a best seller have another treat in store for them," enthused the reviewer in the Chicago *Tribune*.

Barbara Tuchman never had more than a B.A. from Radcliffe College and was proud of being a self-taught, nonacademic historian. Eco and Howard were literature professors at major universities. But in all three instances their popular books were based not only on their own reading and research but also on the vast corpus of mainline scholarly work in the twentieth century on the European Middle Ages. Much of this scholarly work is too technical to be accessible to the general college-educated reader. But it is the base upon which highly readable accounts of the medieval world are constructed.

Scrutiny of the work of the leading academic medievalists, such as that attempted in this book, reveals a condition that prevails generally in the university humanities. The medievalists' work is obviously divisible into distinct groups or schools of interpretation, and they differ among themselves, sometimes vehemently, on the essential character and the precise development of medieval civilization. To outsiders, such academic debate can seem to be hairsplitting chatter of cloistered professors. But a closer look reveals much that is at stake in these debates, because during their course hypotheses are tested, ideas refined, and ultimately a consensus is reached. Academic medievalists constitute the interpretive community to which the popular writers about the Middle Ages, like Tuchman, Eco, and Howard defer in their highly imaginative writings.

In spite of perceptual variety and debate, we can assert the basic facts about the Middle Ages in a manner that reflects a broad, if not universal, consensus among academic medievalists. The magnificent Roman Empire in Western Europe went into irrevocable economic, political, and military decline sometime after the middle of the fourth century. The effective political leadership the Romans had enjoyed for many centuries now became rarer, the best managers possibly being siphoned off to rule the church. But the main problem was that there was a sharp decrease in the size of the population, at least

exacerbated, if not entirely caused, by the spread of the bubonic plague
and venereal disease. Population decline meant a diminution in agricultural and industrial production, a shrinking of the government's
tax base, and a weakening of the military capability of the Roman
Empire. Rome could no longer defend in the fifth century its long
eastern frontiers on the Rhine and Danube rivers against the German
invaders or protect Britain from incursions of the Scandinavian kin
of the Germans from Denmark and what is today northwest Germany. The Germans were drawn into the Empire by its great wealth,
now prey to theft, and its richly cultivated lands, now open to an-
nexation by Germanic peoples. The latter were further pushed into
the Roman Empire by the penetration behind them into the Danube
basin of Central Asian warrior groups such as the Huns, ethnically
akin to the people of Mongolia.

The once-great Roman Empire, its beautiful cities, its capable government and lawcourts, its deeply learned schools and libraries, descended into the twilight of the Dark Ages of the sixth and seventh
centuries, in which literate civilization survived only in a handful of
ecclesiastical centers, mostly walled Benedictine monasteries. Western Europe was further cut off from the vibrant economic and intellectual life that still prevailed in the eastern Mediterranean, centered
on great cities like Constantinople (today Istanbul in Turkey) and
Alexandria, by the explosive and completely unanticipated expansion
of Muslim Arabs in the late seventh century. The Arabs had conquered—with the aid of newly converted groups to Islam from the
old societies of the Mediterranean coastline—North Africa, Sicily,
and most of Christian Spain by the mid-eighth century.

At that point something creative stirred in the northern half of
Germanic France. A heroic warrior family emerged to exercise leadership over the other Germanic chieftains. This family's lands lay in
the Seine Valley, where high productivity of oats fed the horses be-
longing to the family's armored cavalry. The Muslim advance into
France was halted in the 730s, and the Arabs were driven back to
Spain. Out of this one warrior family came the emperor Charlemagne, who reigned from 768 to 814. He gathered at his court in
Aachen in the Rhine Valley the most learned churchmen from not
only France but also England and northern Italy, and there was an
intensive recovery of classical Latin learning and remarkable progress
in all the arts.

This new Carolingian civilization of Western Europe was politically too fragmented to withstand a renewed Scandinavian invasion

in the ninth century. Charlemagne's great empire slowly split apart after his death into a myriad of feudal principalities. But both west and east of the Rhine River in the tenth century an aristocratic family persuaded the church to designate it the holder of the title and privileges of sacred kingship. Thereby the memory of the ambitious Carolingian experiment of a unified political system was preserved into the new era of population growth, economic expansion, improved literacy, and stabilized political and social order that marked the late tenth century. Herein, in this space and time—northern France, southern England, the Rhine and Rhône valleys, and northern Italy around the year 1000—lies the crucible of medieval Europe.

By the year 1000 European society was relatively stable and successful—at least in comparison with the chaos and disintegration of 600. Western Europe was growing, economically and intellectually; technological resources increasingly were integrated with the social structure, and the elite class of landed nobility was self-confident and reasonably efficient. The population was still thin, but it had started to increase rapidly for the first time since about A.D. 400. No one has fully explained why the population was static for six hundred years, but historians blame disease, the meager food supply, and the chronic violence of European society. There always is an unknown factor in demography, but it is generally true that populations grow in times of economic prosperity, such as the late tenth century. The population of Western Europe in 1000 is estimated at ten million people, close to what it was in the Roman Empire.

The environment was still primitive and underdeveloped, and perhaps half of Western Europe was still useless for agriculture. Large parts of Germany, northern France, and central England were covered with huge, uninhabited forests, while some areas facing the North Sea in the Low Countries, northern Germany, and eastern England were unusable marshlands. These coastal lands have been fruitful since the seventeenth century; but at the end of the tenth century nobody in Europe knew anything about drainage, and the shoreline was in many places much farther inland in 1000 than it is today. Between the fourth and the eighteenth century, no one in Europe knew how to build good roads, and apart from a few Roman survivals there were no real roads in eleventh-century Europe. Europe was fortunate, however, in its extensive river system, especially involving the Rhine, which made long-distance travel and commerce possible. The Danube was too far east for all except Vikings and Slavs and a few intrepid merchants, but there was heavy traffic on the Rhine, the

Seine, the Rhône, and the estuary of the Thames. Centers of population grew up near rivers, and the noticeable emptiness of most of central France can be ascribed to the absence of useful rivers.

Western Europe remained technologically backward in 1000, but its agricultural situation had been improved around 800 by the coming into general use of a heavy, wheeled plow. Farmers began at last to get fairly good yields from their hard soil, which required a deep furrow. The light plows of the Romans, which scratched the thin surface of the Mediterranean soil, were not effective in northern Europe, and this partly explains why the Romans did not settle far from a few centers of civilization in the north. It took several centuries for northern Europeans to develop their own equipment and techniques, but with the increasing stability of life after 900, the food supply began to grow—an essential factor in the progress of society and civilization. With the production of varied and abundant crops, including grapes as well as grains and high-protein foods like beans, European civilization began to move forward after 900.

Despite its emperors and popes and kings, tenth-century Europe had a patrimonial, nucleated society based on the domination by great aristocratic families over everything (even the church) within their own territorial domains. Bastard sons and younger brothers of the local lords became bishops or abbots of local churches and monasteries. Religion, as well as government and economy and law, was dominated by the great families. Everything belonged to the lords, who became more and more greedy and aggressive—particularly on their own estates—as the years went by. By 1000 they were depriving their peasants even of the right to keep pigs or hunt in the forest, which, like everything else, belonged to the lord. As far as we know, however, there was no peasant dissent and no rebellion. Because they were either too content or too effectively repressed, tenth-century peasants did not protest; the lower classes of rural society were (and remained for a long time) politically inert.

Change came to the stable society of 1000, but it did not originate at the bottom of the social pyramid. Rather, it began at the top, among the great aristocracy. The main characteristic of European social history is its constancy, the aristocratic, high familial domination of society that continued even past the Industrial Revolution. It was an effective system, and thus its persistence is not surprising. The nobility produced not only warlords but scholars, poets, artists, and religious leaders.

The ecclesiastical buildings of A.D. 1000 in the Romanesque style

were much more imposing than anything built in Europe in the preceding five hundred years. Some of these fortresslike stone structures, with marvelously elaborate sculptures, still stand, particularly
in the Rhineland and southern France. These were expensive structures, for piety was fashionable in 1000; the European nobility liked
priests and monks and were willing patrons of ecclesiastical architecture and clerical pursuits.

Tenth-century churchmen were highly honored and well rewarded, but religious enthusiasm is only one explanation for the increase in their number during the late tenth and eleventh centuries.
The demand for clerical services increased very rapidly because
churchmen were still almost the only literate people in Europe and
thus immensely useful in any task requiring writing. They drew up
the wills and charters and tax documents and letters without which
aristocratic households and royal courts could not function. "Chapel"
and "chancery" were interchangeable terms, and the identification of
the religious class with the intellectual class (which included an educated bureaucracy) gave a unique character to medieval civilization.

By 1000 this elite and growing group of educated churchmen had
developed an extremely complex theological system that was in many
respects unlike the religious beliefs of the common people. There was
gross superstition and heathenism within popular Christianity in the
tenth century, and many beliefs that formed no part of the faith of
educated men were tacitly accepted by the church. Under the leadership of Pope Gregory the Great at the end of the sixth century, the
church had decided to accommodate and accept the prevailing popular religion with its magic, devils, and fertility cults. Contemporary
leaders realized that the conversion of the heathen Germans would
have to be gradual, that drastic excision of their ancient paganism was
neither possible nor desirable. Nineteenth-century Protestant scholars used to denounce the medieval church for its laxity and tolerance
of superstition, but it seems probable that Gregory made a wise decision and that the church would not have survived with a different,
more stringent attitude.

However, pagan superstition was not part of official theology—a
rich and complicated network of traditions from many sources. The
Old and New Testaments and the patristic writings (St. Augustine
was the most influential of the Church Fathers) were central strands
in medieval Christianity, but other strands were derived from the
classical culture of Greece and Rome and from the mystical neo-Pla-
tonism that developed in Alexandria in the third century A.D.

Orthodox tenth-century Christians believed in one God in the three persons of the Trinity: God the Father, God the Son, and God the Holy Ghost. No one could define exactly how God existed in three persons (after all, faith is beyond reason), but people were convinced that He did. God the Father was a combination of a Roman emperor and the tribal god of Israel, a rewarder and punisher in this world and the next. The Old Testament, with its emphasis on the power and majesty of God, played a much larger role in the tenth-century image of God than did the tender and emotional words of the New Testament. God the Son was regarded as a vehicle or an instrument of salvation, and His personality was not much considered. Medieval artists did not even begin to portray Jesus as an infant until the eleventh century, when certain artists in southern France and northern Spain depicted his childhood in their sculptures—but with Jesus as a miniature grown man, not as a baby. Before that time Christians could not conceive of Jesus as a child at all in any emotional or personal sense; in 1000 he was appreciated primarily as the mechanism of human redemption and the supreme judge and emperor.

Medieval Christians believed that God had to create Jesus to appear in human form and to suffer because man was too corrupt to be saved by his own merit. Some men and women were better than others, but all would be damned without the intervention of Jesus. Tenth-century theologians adhered to the Augustinian doctrine of the corruption and depravity of the human will. The sin of concupiscence (physical greed) begins when the infant suckles at the mother's breast. Greed, lust, and selfishness are born with people, who would have to suffer eternal damnation unless part of God accepted punishment of human sin. Jesus Christ took on humanity's suffering by His own choice; salvation is an act of "grace," undeserved and freely given. People can join in the sacrifice and participate in the merits of Jesus through the sacrament of the mass, which gives to each communicant an infinitesimal, but efficacious, share of the glory of Christ. The wafer and wine of holy communion are miraculously transformed in substance into the body and blood of Christ, who is present at the altar.

Medieval Catholicism was based on a difficult and complicated theological system, but it was well suited to high ceremony as well as to intellectual argument. The sacrament of communion was performed most impressively in medieval churches, where illiterate peasants and knights who could not have understood Augustinian dogma could appreciate the incense and music and vestments of the mass. Tenth-century Christianity was a mysterious, sacerdotal, sacramental religion capable of profound appeal to the emotions as well as the mind. Unlike Judaism, it tended to generate art and poetry and music even while it remained open to intellectual refinement—to thought, preaching, and interpretation.

The third face of the Trinity was the Holy Spirit—God's shadow on the world whose institutional form was the church, the earthly embodiment of a heavenly ideal. This concept was derived from the Platonic notion of pure idea, represented in appearance by something less pure. The tenth-century church, however, seemed to contemporaries to be as nearly pure as an earthly institution could be; it represented God, making physical and visible the spirit that moved people in their hearts. To deny the authority of the church was to deny God, and the greatest sinner was the heretic who flouted its teaching. The church used every instrument of culture and communication to put across its indisputable message. Art and reason contributed to the mixed-media happening that was medieval Catholicism, where each mass was a miracle and men and women waited for the shadow of God to fall across their hearts. Some people in the Western Europe of the year 1000 imagined the finish of the world and the Second Coming of Christ with the end of the millennium. Instead they were left to continue their economic and cultural progress.

The Mediterranean world, with its successor civilizations to ancient Rome, became aware of the new European consciousness, wealth, and power in the First Crusade of 1095–99. Then aristocratic chain-mailed, mounted French Crusaders leading peasant rabble in their crimson wake, fired by the subtle and seductive preaching of a wily monastic pope, burst upon the quiet hilltop cities of the Rhine Valley. The crusading army headed half-blindly but stubbornly toward jeweled Constantinople on the Bosporus and beyond to fabled Anatolia and through luxurious Lebanon to liberate Christ's Jerusalem from the Turks. The Muslim rulers of the Middle East had allegedly repelled Latin pilgrims and frustrated Christian missionary tours of the Holy Land as they docked in Jaffa and Acre with their love boats of saints and prostitutes. The Crusaders aimed to punish Muhammad's legions.

Now in 1096 above the Rhine gorges, in the ghettos of the crooked little urban enclaves overlooking the magical great river, the French Crusaders beat upon the caftaned, defenseless Jewish townspeople as the Latin lords and knights proceeded along their boisterous way to the brilliant and effete East. The French Crusaders regarded the Jews as sharing the Muslim status of enemies of Christ.

In many past centuries the armed, ignorant lords and knights of Roman Catholic and Germanic Europe had huddled, embarrassed and fearful, in their swampy, forested, and mountainous redoubts to escape from the magnificent, inscrutable caliphs and stern mullahs and incessantly disciplined Muslim armies of the south. In their smoky, putrid northern halls, the Franks had long gossiped about the southern riches, aching to add Arab booty to their looted capital accumulation. They fervently imagined the sunny, sexy wonders of the Mediterranean climes. Now these wild and subliterate Frankish warriors had at last been organized and channeled by a handful of great kings and dukes from their castellanies in the river valley of the north. Zealous Latin-mouthing priests, chatting persuasively about reviving the glorious Roman Empire, had given them a simple but more elevated self-image. The aristocratic Frankish women—with whom the lords and knights diurnally copulated in the high-ceilinged wooden feasting halls among the packs of dogs and heaped garbage bones of countless red meat roasted dinners—if only to save themselves from constant pregnancies and early deaths in the roulette experiences of perilous childbirths, had begun to urge their masters and sons to fabled and valiant deeds of heroic romance in distant exotic climes.

Now, in the First Crusade, the French nobles cried, "God wills it!" as they in 1096 sifted sloppily and drunkenly down the Rhine-Danube valley chute that the Caesars had created many centuries before, toward the mother of civilization, the vast warm inland sea. Now the Franks sought too-long-delayed revenge upon Muhammad's mysteriously wealthy and literate myrmidons.

Medieval civilization came of age in the First Crusade. This was the breakthrough moment. From within their metal helmets and woolen cowls, clean-shaven Frankish faces now imbibed the warmth and inhaled the sea-salted air of the Mediterranean. They came home again, after so long hiding in the northern dragon lairs, to the heartland of classical nations and ancient cities. In 1099 the French Crusaders broke the walls of Jerusalem. In King David's golden city on the fertilized plateau high above the arid Palestinian plain, God willed the Franks victory over the momentarily confused and divided Muslims. Now the commingled blood of Arab and Jew—peaceful, compatible citizens then—rose in a flash flood to the knee joints of the Europeans' feudal chargers.

Christ's city, the undoubted center of the world, was theirs for now, these Crusaders of the Latin West, and they felt good in their simple theory of history and exulted in their triumph. They believed Divine Providence, proceeding chronologically along a teleological straight line from Creation through Incarnation to the Last Judgment, was very much on the side of aristocratic families from Normandy, the Loire Valley, and Toulouse. Quickly and securely European-centered historical destiny would now accelerate the Second Coming of the Lord, a clean-shaven, tall, blond, lithe, French-looking nobleman in a gold-trimmed white silk shirt. Jesus' image in the minds of the French Crusaders was identified with the shining image their courtly grandsons were to hold of Lancelot, who lay with Queen Guinevere.

The First Crusade of 1095–99 inaugurates the era of the high Middle Ages of the twelfth, thirteenth, and early fourteenth centuries. This was the time when Western Europe exhibited unprecedented creativity in literature and the visual arts and remarkable advances in theology, philosophy, popular piety, government, and law, as well as a population boom and commercial and urban expansion. The precise character of these achievements of the high Middle Ages, the causes of their development, and the varied side effects that accompanied them have been the subject of intense scrutiny and ongoing debate among medievalists in this century.

On the one side the medievalists have sought to reveal and celebrate the ideas and institutions of the high Middle Ages. On the other side they have sought to evaluate dispassionately and critically the long-range significance of these manifestations of creativity, spirituality, management, and prosperity. The one conclusion that everyone can agree to is the great complexity of high medieval culture, society, government, law, economy, and religion. Each facet of life in the twelfth and thirteenth centuries was intertwined with many other facets. Each movement forward generated new issues and countervailing tendencies. Every great personality that we can discern turns out to be a very complex and frequently mysterious man or woman indeed.

The Victorians were sure of the relative simplicity of the medieval world and were confident in making opinionated assessments of it. Partly because of the depth of our learning and partly because of different intellectual assumptions we employ about human behavior, we are more impressed with the ambivalence and ambiguity about things medieval. That quality of complexity and contradiction makes the medieval world much closer to our own than was even dimly imagined a century ago. It also allows medievalists to find in the Middle Ages the mirror image of themselves or parallel manifestations to trends and happenings in the twentieth century. Our profound learning about the high Middle Ages has provided the opportunity for provocative image making of a medieval past that conforms to our current emotional and public needs.

There is greater agreement about the era from the mid-fourteenth to the mid-fifteenth century as a time of catastrophe in the form of disease, war, climatic deterioration, and political decline as well as of descent into long economic depression in several parts of Europe. Debate among medievalists resumes when the late fifteenth century, particularly in northern Italy, is reached. Is Italian Renaissance culture a culmination of medieval thought and learning or a break away from them? Has the dawn of a new era begun in Florence around 1450 or the last brilliant moments of an old one manifested themselves? There is no consensus whatsoever on these issues.

II

DISCOVERY AND LEARNING

At least half our present knowledge of the classical and other ancient worlds was a legacy of the nineteenth century. Whether it was discovering Troy or the Egypt of the pharaohs or interpreting the career of Julius Caesar, the Victorian contribution to understanding the ancient world was grandly accomplished and is still highly significant. But medieval studies were very largely a twentieth-century phenomenon. Victorian culture made its contribution to discovery of the medieval world by the founding of research institutes, by the building up of libraries and the organization of archives, and by the publication of medieval records. This was important work, but it was preliminary to actual historical reconstruction of the Middle Ages. It was not the creative work of perception, imagination, and narrative itself.

We owe to the historians, poets, and artists of the romantic era of the early nineteenth century the alteration of the image of a "Middle Age" of barbarism, ignorance, and superstition that allegedly constituted an age of persistent decline between the twin peaks of classical Rome and the Italian Renaissance at the end of the fifteenth century. This was the negative view of medieval culture that had been invented by the fifteenth-century Renaissance Italian humanists themselves as the historical theory to accompany and give narrative depth to their claim that they were engaged in the salutary postmedieval revival of ancient learning and classical Latinity. The romantics of the early nineteenth century replaced this negative view of the Middle Ages with the shining image of a Gothic culture steeped in idealism, spirituality, heroism, and adoration of women.

But the romantics lacked the scholarship, the learning and instruments of research, to go beyond the most superficial kind of inquiry into the medieval past. Both the Renaissance denigration of the Middle Ages and the romantic acclamation of medieval culture were almost exclusively based on mere ideological projections. The romantics liked the Middle Ages because they thought they saw in that world the beliefs and behavior that contrasted vividly with the rationalism of the Enlightenment, the mechanism of the Industrial Revolution, and the centralizing bureaucracy of the national state, which they found repulsive and conducive to dehumanization. After the 1840s, Victorian culture superseded romantic idealism with nationalism, deterministic organicism, and racist social Darwinism and imposed these conditioning perceptions on further interpretation of the Middle Ages. This did not improve the understanding of the realities of medieval life and thought. Assertion of these dogmatic Victorian modes precipitated a decline from the naive but occasionally inspiring Gothic image embraced by the earlier romantic advocates of the Middle Ages.

Did the nineteenth-century historians misunderstand the Middle Ages because they were early pioneers who worked with a very narrow data base? Or was there something about the Victorian mind— its love of huge entities, vulgarly simple models, hastily generalized and overdetermined evolutionary schemes—that made it unsuitable for doing lasting work in interpreting the Middle Ages? We may say that both conditions were at work in fostering the Victorian misconstruction of the Middle Ages.

All the nineteenth-century medievalists wrote about human relationships before the revolutionary cultural consequences of the emergence of social, behavioral, and psychoanalytic sciences in the modernist culture of the early twentieth century. Therefore, not only is their work obsolete, but it offends against our assumptions about human behavior, psychological structures, and institutional functions. After Durkheim, Boas, and Freud, historians had to contemplate human beings and social actions in radically different ways.

Medieval studies in the twentieth century have not only enjoyed the benefit of novel insights into human nature and society but also cultivated vast collections of informative material. We in the twentieth century are capable of knowing much more about the medieval world than about classical and other ancient civilizations primarily because of the much greater volume of written records that have survived. In total, there survives between ten and twenty times more written material from the medieval than from the Greco-Roman world. The survival rate of source material is extremely thin for the period between 400 and 800. By 1100 it has become substantial. By 1200 it is incomparably superior to the record available to us of any ancient society, even the Roman Republic and Empire. Medievalists who deal with law and government or university learning by 1300 are wearily overwhelmed by the stupendous and unmanageable volume of unpublished material surviving in European archives and libraries.

So much more has survived of the literate heritage of the Middle Ages than of the classical world both because more was originally written down and because the ravages of time and social disorder have taken a less heavy toll on medieval manuscripts. There is a special reason for the greater volume of medieval cultural survival: the nature of the material on which writings were made. More than half the writings of the classical world were done before A.D. 300 on paper that slowly decomposed in the moist climate of most of Western Europe, whereas after about 700 and until about 1400, the medievals mostly wrote on parchment, derived from stretched and bleached lambskin or calfskin, which can survive indefinitely.

For the era down to about 1250 almost everything of value in the documentary and literary heritage of the medieval world has been published in modern editions. The existence of medieval history as a field in which scholars can work from published material for the period to 1250 means that the research in the earlier medieval era can be done as effectively at Harvard or Princeton, wherever there is a great medieval collection, as at Oxford or Munich. Definitive modern editions exist of all major works of medieval literature. The Index of Christian Art at Princeton University is a readily usable catalog of all modern photographs of medieval art.

For the period after 1250 there is a vast amount of unpublished material in European archives, in such places as London, Paris, Barcelona, Munich, Toulouse, Florence, Rome, and Palermo. There are many philosophers or theologians of the late Middle Ages of whom we know little because their treatises exist in lengthy but seldom studied or completely unread manuscripts.

There exist in the Public Record Office in London, appropriately near the lawcourts on Chancery Lane, stenographic records of the major English central courts in the fourteenth and fifteenth centuries, term by term, case by case. Only a handful of these plea rolls have been published. Most have not been read since the day they were filed by the court clerk. Each runs to about four hundred pages, in the jargon of law French and in hasty secretarial handwriting. It is not surprising that few scholars, even those with the requisite technical backgrounds, have chosen to devote decades-long labor to making sense out of what was going on in these trials.

Italian libraries and archives are stuffed with medieval manuscripts. Only after several decades of scrutiny by scholars from several countries have the vast Florentine archives begun to yield their rich information, not only about the public finance and politics of the medieval republic but about the inner history of the great urban families. The medieval records in the Vatican Archives in Rome are so voluminous they have never been systematically cataloged. No one is sure exactly what is there, and in any case the discreet cardinals have kept some series of records closed or given access only to a very few privileged clerical researchers. A microfilmed copy of perhaps a third of the Vatican medieval collection is available in St. Louis, Missouri, thanks to the generosity of the Knights of Columbus. The Hill Monastic Manuscript Library in Collegeville, Minnesota, contains microfilms of seventy-three thousand medieval books, including the collections of seventy-six Austrian and thirty Spanish libraries.

European libraries and archives are so replete with late medieval writings that it is hazardous to assert dogmatically that any work of that period of which there is mention somewhere will not be found eventually if only bound surreptitiously at the back of some other treatise or cut up into strips for the binding of another volume. All the surviving records of the classical world have been published, but extensive publication of the records of late medieval Europe would be such an expensive, long, and exhausting task that it will probably never be systematically pursued.

Before the Second World War American medievalists had little in the way of research support to work in the rich European archives. Like the Harvard medievalist Charles Homer Haskins, they spent family capital. Haskins, in the first decade of this century, resembling a character in a Henry James novel, spent years wandering from European archive to archive, leisurely retracing the steps and reconstructing the political and administrative institutions of the Norman French nobility. Or these medievalists made terrible personal sacri-

fices. My favorite early American hero of medieval studies research
was James Willard, professor of medieval history at the University of
Colorado in Boulder, who died there in 1935 after three decades of
teaching and fervent boostering of the college football team (he suffered a heart attack while watching a college football game and died
three days later). A classroom building at Boulder is named after Willard, who was of the same pioneering generation as Haskins. Willard
got his Ph.D. in 1902 at the University of Pennsylvania, studying in
the fine library that the banker-scholar Henry C. Lea had collected
and left to the university. Nearly every summer in the Age of Hard-
ing, Coolidge, and Hoover, Willard made his way by train and boat
to London. Also using up his sabbaticals and with a single small grant
from the newly established American Council of Learned Societies,
he researched in the Public Record Office the rise of parliamentary
taxation in late-thirteenth-century England, a subject of major importance in the history of medieval government. Willard's magnificent
monograph on the subject was published two years before his death.
Clear, comprehensive, confident, it has been redone recently by an
Oxford don but has not been significantly improved upon.

What was it like in 1931, as the Depression set in and the Dust
Bowl threatened, for Willard to leave his beloved Colorado mountains, about which he eventually wrote a book, to chug eastward across
the breadth of America and then across the Atlantic, to endure a bed-
sitter in Kensington, and to arrive promptly each morning in coat
and starched shirt to work in the archives on the exchequer and other
administrative rolls and the parliamentary writs of summons? Somewhere in the intersection of Colorado cultural history, the American
Protestant tradition of calling, and the psychopathology of masochistic behavior lies the explanation for Willard's motivation in the heroic
age of medieval research. Since 1950 American medievalists have been
assisted in their research trips to Europe by the generous availability
of grants from private foundations and public endowments.

The groups and agencies that set about publishing medieval records were diverse, from austere Belgian monks in the seventeenth
century to bumbling Anglican country vicars, right out of a Trollope
novel, in the Victorian era. The people who did it right were the
Germans. The Institute for Research on the German Middle Ages,
usually referred to as the Monumenta, from the title of its publication
series, was founded in the early nineteenth century. By the 1870s,
drawing on the textual editing methods developed by German clas-
sicists, it had become a highly professional organization. Located in

Berlin and generously supported by the Prussian and, after 1871, the German imperial governments, the Monumenta was a consummately authoritative scholarly operation, whose editions of medieval records and texts are models of the art.

Among its other services the Monumenta provided employment to each new generation of young German Ph.D.'s in medieval history and gave them postdoctoral training of extraordinary quality. Another positive feature of the Monumenta was that it construed the geographical scope of its operation very broadly. Since medieval German emperors spent large segments of time contending against popes, the documentary history of the papacy until 1250 was one of its priority areas. Since the German emperors had deep involvements in Italy, the history of the Italian cities down to the age of Dante was also pursued by Monumenta scholars, under the supervision of a subsidiary institute located in Rome. In its long history—since 1945 the Monumenta has been in Munich—the German institute has published more than 250 impeccable folio volumes of medieval sources.

In accumulating records and texts, students of the Middle Ages greatly benefited from the nineteenth-century era of modern national entities. National governments all over Western Europe emulated the Germans in subsidizing the publication of medieval records to demonstrate their countries' origins, even when such evolutionary organicism was farfetched. For example, the Belgian monarchy, which came into existence at a diplomatic conference in 1830, engaged a distinguished scholar, Henri Pirenne, to write a five-volume history of medieval Belgium, although it is not easy to trace Belgian national consciousness back to either the lords or the bourgeoisie of medieval Flanders and contiguous feudal principalities.

In Britain the crown spent lavishly to emulate the Germans in publishing medieval records and got a mixed bag of volumes (the *Rolls Series*) in return. William Stubbs, then an obscure country curate, did the best work and gained the distinction of being paid at a level that would be very generous for rewarding humanistic scholarship even by twentieth-century standards. Stubbs's editions of medieval chronicles eventually got him the senior history chair at Oxford. Some of the volumes turned out by obscure vicars and schoolmasters for the *Rolls Series* were, however, an appalling botch.

The publication of medieval records in France under government auspices attained a level of quality in the nineteenth century somewhere between the consistent professionalism of the Germans and the idiosyncratic amateurism of the English. The best value the French got out of this state project was the founding in Paris of a university-level school and institute for historical archives, L'École des Chartes ("the school of documents"). After this school had come under the direction of a great medievalist, Ferdinand Lot, early in the century and remained under his tutelage for the next four decades, the quality of medieval research in France rapidly escalated because of the training there of several generations of skillful researchers.

Editing medieval texts presented several problems that Victorian schoolmasters, vicars, and priests, blithely drawing on their classical Latinity, did not anticipate. In the first place, medieval Latin has subtle differences, not so much grammatically as stylistically, from the ancient Roman form, and a vast number of new technical words, whether for warfare or for philosophy, entered the vocabulary after 1150. Reading Cicero fluently does not necessarily prepare one to read the late-thirteenth-century Oxford Franciscan philosopher Duns Scotus, who anticipated a good deal of Wittgenstein's linguistic philosophy.

Secondly, there was the problem of paleography—that is, reading the handwriting in medieval manuscripts. Movable type that made printing possible was a medieval invention but only after 1470. Until then books were produced laboriously in individual hand copies on parchment or (after 1350) also on rag paper. In addition to formal books (codices), there were the innumerable rolls of governmental or business documents that continued to be executed in handwriting until the common use of the typewriter in the late nineteenth century.

Most medieval books were the products of writing and copying offices sustained by governmental institutions in church and state or in the late Middle Ages by corporations (guilds) engaged in book production as a business for the market. Considering the slowness and difficulty of this handicraft production, the volume of medieval book productivity exceeds any reasonable expectation. Of course, under these conditions the price of books was very high by our standards. You had to be a wealthy man to leave your heirs a library of fifty volumes.

For the long stretch of the Middle Ages, from 800 to 1250, the handwriting in Latin documents closely resembles Roman script or modern book print and is not hard to read. During this era of the central Middle Ages the standard medieval script was Carolingian minuscule. It is called that because it was inaugurated by monastic scribes of the Carolingian Empire around 800 and because while imitating ancient Roman script, it used lowercase (minuscule) as well as capital letters (the Romans before A.D. 350 used only capital letters). Carolingian minuscule is so clear and simple a script that the proprietors of the early printing presses in the late fifteenth century found it easy to transpose it into movable type. Modern book print is thus a derivation from Carolingian minuscule, as revived about 1470, and anyone picking up a twelfth-century Latin manuscript, after mastering a few commonly used abbreviations, will have no trouble reading it. After 1250, especially in the stenographic hands of overworked governmental and ecclesiastical clerks, there were radical departures from Carolingian minuscule (it was too slow for stenography and the rapid production of documents). Reading these late medieval hands in which Latin documents were written requires special training and long experience. There is the additional problem of distinctive hands in vernacular (non-Latin) texts when these appear in great numbers after 1150.

Another problem in studying medieval manuscripts arises from the many important texts—such as philosophy, canon law, and imaginative literature—existing in multiple or even dozens of copies. Some minor variation between copies of the same text was inevitable, by the inconstancy of the act of copying it. But sometimes there are major differences—whole sections of the work altered or added or subtracted. How can we establish what is the Ur-text, the text the author himself would have recognized as the standard one? Sometimes the author would have been troubled to make such a determination because he or she over time altered the work. If trying to establish what is the standard text of James Joyce's *Ulysses* has recently generated a fierce controversy on two continents, one can imagine the difficulty of deciding what is the canonical version of a medieval work that exists in fifteen manuscripts from three different countries, which the author himself, an assistant, or an epigone altered over time.

All the problems of reading and comprehending the accumulated writings and records of the Middle Ages notwithstanding, the medievalist can have an immediate, tactile experience that the classical scholar cannot. Except for a very few accidental fragments, no actual manuscripts survive from the European Roman world. Only stone inscriptions endure from Rome. The texts of Cicero or Vergil or Horace come down to us only in medieval copies. Catullus survives only in a single fortunate manuscript made by a monk somewhere who had a taste for erotic poetry. But anyone who can read Latin can go to a major European archive and actually breathe upon and turn the pages of writings made in the twelfth or thirteenth century, sometimes an "autograph" made by the author himself or at least a copy made during or shortly after the author's lifetime. In examining the legal and fiscal and other administrative records of the English and French monarchies around 1300, we can scrutinize the actual day-to-day business writing on parchment of judges, tax collectors, or royal councillors or their secretaries. This is not a historian's report but the active living record of events as they occurred. There is almost nothing of such live manuscript recordings extant from the ancient world.

The medieval world thus comes back to us on sheets of pumiced lambskin parchment in a very direct and existential way. And when some manuscripts are also brilliantly illuminated by exquisite miniature paintings that took months or years to execute and cost a great deal in labor and materials, we know how precious the individual manuscripts were to medieval people as well as to us.

To understand why the Middle Ages are the invention of the twentieth rather than the nineteenth century, one must also look to the thousandfold increase in the number of university positions in medieval studies since 1900. Whatever their provenance, medievalists exhibit the traits of other academic humanists. They are people who, for whatever combination of psychological and sociological circumstances, become fascinated in childhood or early adolescence with language and the historical past. They abstain from the common pursuit of wealth and power in the interest of the acquisition of learning and the opportunity to teach. A small minority of academic humanists have private means or gain affluence through special treatment by their universities in recognition of their distinguished reputations. But most actually live on their modest professorial salaries, usually at sacrifice to their families. The academic humanists' most productive and creative years are generally in their forties and early fifties. Most burn out in their late fifties and stop doing important intellectual work, although they may continue to shine in the classroom. Normally, academic medievalists, like other university humanists, do not write well or at least well enough to address a wide audience of readers.

Even when the focus of their research is narrow, continuing a pattern forced on them in their doctoral training, medievalists as a rule are interested in the relationship and interaction of medieval and modern cultures. For example, Umberto Eco in 1974 boldly proclaimed "The Return to the Middle Ages." He drew close parallels between medieval alternative cultures and disempowered groups on the one side and the counterculture and student radicalism in the United States in the 1960s on the other.

We cannot interpret medieval culture or any historical culture except through the prism of the dominant concepts of our own thought worlds. When we look back later, some of these interpretive concepts have become stale and out of date, and we're embarrassed then by our own reflexive trendiness; but there was a time when these concepts were productive and stimulating and were appropriately relished in their application.

Nevertheless, the accumulation of data, the reading of texts and archival research, and the advancement of learning make a very great difference. The problem with the Victorian perception of the Middle Ages was not only that it involved the imposition of nineteenth-century concepts that no longer convince us, such as evolutionary organicism, but that the Victorians simply didn't know much about the Middle Ages. The research work had not yet been done. Any bright American college sophomore who today takes a good survey course on medieval history has a better understanding of the components of the medieval world than anyone who wrote before 1895. That superior insight is not the result of vanguard concept formation by American college students. It is due to their benefiting from the accumulated learning of twentieth-century scholarship and the research labors, as well as interpretive insights, of three or four generations of twentieth-century academic humanists.

Yet the ideas of this century, its concept formations in philosophy, literary, and artistic criticism and social and behavioral science, are not embarrassments. Trendy as they may be, quickly as they may become worn down, they do give great insights into the Middle Ages or any past or present culture and are to be taken full advantage of and not wasted.

Intellectualization does take its toll. Twentieth-century ideas imposed on medieval interpretation in retrospect raise challenging questions and claims of vulnerability. It may be said with plausibility that the great German medievalist generation of the 1920s too easily wore the seductive mantle of philosophical idealism, thereby blinding it to conditioning factors of a social and material nature and making it also relatively insensitive to the impact of individual personality upon art and literature. It is not hard to make a case for the assertion that the American medieval historians of the once-dominant Harvard-Princeton institutional school too readily applied the bleak assumptions of pragmatic instrumentalism and transferred the hegemonic mind-set of American exceptionalism to their image of Anglo-Norman and French medieval state building. Not infrequently in the 1980s the French mandarin school of social history flaunted intellectualization like a boulevard weapon of self-promotion and succumbed to dancing the seven veils of post-Marxism on the tables of the Left Bank cafés to court the younger Parisian generation.

What was wrong was not the application of powerful modern ideas to interpreting the Middle Ages but the lack of the self-critical temperament to recognize their limitations and to reexamine assumptions periodically. What was wrong was not too much intellectualization in medieval studies but too little. It is well-nigh inevitable that once a group of scholars has gained success working with a set of intellectual assumptions and, following from the work using these ideas, has advanced to positions of comfort and power within the academic establishment, self-criticism wanes, and the ideas and assumptions that once were novel inspirations, held tentatively, harden into orthodox academic dogma, which the next generation is supposed to parrot.

This establishmentarian cyclicity in medieval studies, as in any field of the academic humanities, will be corrected and superseded by two systemic conditions, however. The appropriated ideas will in time become tired and obsolete and lose credibility within the culture, as in the case of German idealism and American instrumentalism and exceptionalism. And a new generation will come along, the more ambitious and brilliant of which, seeking to make its mark, will rebel and consciously apply novel twentieth-century ideas to understanding the medieval past.

The Middle Ages as we perceive them are the creation of an interactive cultural process in which accumulated learning, the resources and structures of the academic profession, the speculative comparing of medieval and modern worlds, and intellectualization through appropriation of modern theory of society, personality, language, and art have been molded together in the lives, work, and ideas of medievalists and the schools and traditions they founded.

Since 1960 generally the most original and suggestive work in medieval studies has been not by historians but by scholars in literature departments, and that trend persists. These critics and literary expositors have fastened not on the soft marginality of the medieval world but on an incredibly vibrant and complicated centrality of medieval culture that connects directly across the centuries to the philosophy, art, psychology, and literature of the twentieth century. It speaks of linguistic affiliations and archetypal structures and deconstructive, revelatory readings of traditional meanings. There is something here that gives off flashes of creativity and discovery beyond conventional historical concerns.

The twentieth-century quest for the Middle Ages, like the medievals' quest for the Grail, is perilous and never-ending. It has led through many byways and is conditioned by many adventures and unanticipated happenings. As in the medieval romance, the perilous quest for the Middle Ages often doubles back on itself. It becomes a psychological exploration of intimate experience and then resumes a chartable course. Nor, as in the Grail legend, is the goal all that clear, the object pursued with so much thought and labor all that sharply defined. But there is an asymptotic, never fully defined perception that the end is brilliant and immensely satisfying.

Sometimes the quest proceeds in pessimistic realization of human limitations and final shortfall:

> Drawn heavenward by divine accord
> I had seen and heard more mysteries yet;
> But always men would have and hoard
> And gain the more; the more they get.
> So banished I was, by cares beset,
> From realms eternal untimely sent.

[*Pearl*, XX, English midlands, late fourteenth century; transl. Marie Borroff.]

And sometimes in the quest there is that optimistic conviction of simple and unmediated triumph such as the first Crusaders enjoyed, when the joy is greater because the expectations are undefined:

> Dawn was conquering the morning hour
> which fled before it, so that from afar
> I recognized the shimmering of the sea.

[Dante, *Purgatory*, I, 115–17, northern Italy, early fourteenth century; transl. George Holmes.]

III

THE MEDIEVAL MIND

The Middle Ages are especially interesting and instructive to us because the medieval people had to deal in their literature and theory with the fundamental fact of human life: the relationship and the tension between the spiritual and the material, the intellectual and the physical. The intriguing circumstance is they had to do this, at least before the thirteenth century in France and England, without systems of law and public administration to set down rules of behavior that channel and precondition, as they do for us, a large segment of behavior, programmatically establishing the interfacing of the spiritual and material sides of life and the intellectual and physical aspects of the human personality.

The medievals had to work out the solution to the human condition for themselves. Until well into the Middle Ages and then only fitfully and in certain places, they were not routinized into behavior patterns dictated by a technologically powerful law and government that predetermined the behavioral relationship of the two spheres of human experience, the spiritual and the material. There is, therefore, a naive autonomy and a persistent choice making about medieval people that we find fresh and exciting. That the great clerical thinkers of the Middle Ages were clear-sighted on the great split, the conflict between spirit and matter, idea and force, there is no doubt: "The heavenly city . . . while in its state of pilgrimage on earth avails itself of the peace of earth. So far as it can without injuring faith and godliness, the heavenly community desires and maintains a common agreement regarding the acquisition of the necessaries of life, and makes this earthly peace bear upon the peace of heaven [St. Augustine, *The City of God*, Book XIV, Tunisia, c. 425, transl. Marcus Dods]."

Bishop Augustine of Hippo, good Roman that he was, thus looked to the state to paper over the conflict between the spiritual and the carnal will and to maintain a measure of social stability so that the church's work of conversion could be pursued. In a much later era, between the collapse of the Roman state and the rise of the medieval one, St. Bernard of Clairvaux lays out the conflict within human personality more sharply and pessimistically than Augustine: "You have not the power to banish, by the mere purity of your spirit, and to rise entirely out of the reach of, the inrushing and thronging crowd of material images and ideas [St. Bernard, *Sermons*, France, c. 1145, transl. S. J. Eales]."

St. Bernard argues, however, for a solution to this bifurcation of human nature. For a happy few, the conflict between the spiritual and the material is transcended in a mystical experience, "the sweet inpouring of Divine Love." St. Bernard is inconveniently vague about how this exalted mystical condition is to be gained. In the *Divine*

Comedy Dante agrees with Bernard's mystical resolution. But in another work, *Monarchy*, Dante simply depicts the divided self—"the beatitude of this life" governed by the "teachings of philosophy" and the "beatitude of eternal life" directed by "spiritual teaching." The split endures.

There were no easy solutions for the medievals, and there are none for us. The early Freud of depth psychology agrees with St. Bernard that not even the putative purity of life frees us from the inrushing of material (that is, sexual) images. We—saints as well as sinners—experience always the return of the repressed. But in a weary late book, *Civilization and Its Discontents* (1930), Freud is trying to find a mediating position between Eros and social stability and comes to something like an Augustinian position. The view of the divided self propounded by the phenomenological and deconstructionist theorist of our time, Yale's Paul de Man, accords with the medieval view of personality: "The poetical act (in the general sense that includes all the arts) is the quintessential historical act: That through which we become conscious of the divided character of our being, and consequently, of the necessity of carrying out and fulfilling the divided character in the present, instead of suffering it in the afterlife."

Those two congenital thirteenth-century optimists St. Francis of Assisi and St. Thomas Aquinas thought they had clear and radical solutions to the condition of human conflict. St. Francis, the prototypical counterculture holy man, sought to create in his community of friars a society of love. If the spiritual and material are thoroughly fused in action, there is no conflict. "Those who presented themselves to observe this kind of life distributed all they might have to the poor. We loved to live in poor and abandoned churches and we were ignorant and submissive to all. And when they do not give us the price of our toil, let us resort to the table of the Lord, begging our bread from door to door [*The Will of St. Francis*, northern Italy, c. 1220, transl. Paul Sabatier and L. S. Houghton]." This is also the ethos of New Left communes of the 1960s and the Woodstock generation. It is a solution to the problem of the divided self but only for a few and at a special moment. It endures not. St. Thomas Aquinas, the Neapolitan aristocrat turned Dominican friar and Paris professor, tried the liberal solution suggested by Aristotle: "Law must concern itself properly with the order directed to universal happiness [Thomas Aquinas, *Summa Theologica*, France, c. 1265, transl. A. C. Pegis]."

In the New Deal tradition, which harks back to Thomism, with the American Civil Liberties Union and those fine liberal lawyers in Washington, we are told that we have nothing to fear but fear itself. But what if law concerns itself with power and privilege, not universal happiness? St. Thomas Aquinas did not have a practical meliorative response to this situation. Neither do we.

There were even those, like the young Peter Abelard, who tried the radical neo-Freudian approach of high eroticism (copulation makes you free) à la Wilhelm Reich, Norman O. Brown, and Herbert Marcuse: "No degree in love's progress was left untried by our passion, and if love itself could imagine any wonder as yet unknown, we discovered it [Peter Abelard, *History of My Calamities*, France, c. 1135, transl. H. A. Bellows]."

After Abelard's girl friend's uncle had castrated him, he thought differently. None of these solutions to the tensions and ambivalences of human life—the great split—worked very well in the Middle Ages or work in our century. We can therefore say of the medievals that we empathize with them because we have met the medievals and recognizably they share our sensibilities and anxieties. The medievals, however, did not sink under our burdens of the bureaucratic-juristic-technological state that closes in upon and conditions and regulates us along predetermined lines graciously delineated for us at Ivy League law schools, although after 1200 there were plenty of Bologna and Montpellier law graduates petitioning befuddled kings to let them try the same kind of draconian rationalization.

IV

RECOGNITIONS AND FORMULATIONS

Because the insights and anxieties of the medieval mind are so close to our own, the discovery of the Middle Ages is an extensive and continuing process. The determination of the meaning and relevance of the Middle Ages for the twentieth century has been probed and shaped by the medievalists who are the subject of this book. The twentieth century, with its elaborate tools of research, its unlimited learned resources, and its capacity for persistent and organized analysis, has generated disparate visions of the Middle Ages and has discovered individual segments of the medieval experience that have not only illuminated the medieval past but stimulated the interaction of medieval and modern cultures.

The great medievalists who are the focus of this book, like all creative thinkers and artists, fashioned their interpretations of the Middle Ages out of the emotional wellsprings of their lives, and these lives were in turn conditioned by the vast social and political upheavals of the twentieth century, especially during the dark times from 1914 to 1945. The twentieth century invented for itself a medieval mosaic that was significantly patterned by its own agonizing experiences between the soundings of the guns of August 1914 and the last piercing cries of the Holocaust in the fetid, mortal spring of 1945. Creating a medieval world picture and projecting themselves into it were one therapeutic recourse by which sensitive and benign twentieth-century people sought to regain their sanity and get control of their feelings in the evil times of slaughter and madness.

The therapeutic value of imagining the Middle Ages was substantial, and in the more peaceful times since 1945 we have continued to draw upon the medieval sources for comfort and inspiration and direction in our lives, as was done before 1914. In that regard, twentieth-century medieval studies resemble the utility of the Middle Ages to the romantics of early nineteenth century, for whom the Middle Ages were a refuge against satanic industrialism and militarism. The difference lies in the incomparably greater capacity of twentieth-century learning to discover and represent the real world of Charlemagne, St. Francis, and Chaucer.

As we approach the end of the second Christian millennium, many of the cultural goals and intellectual assumptions that have molded the twentieth century run down into entropic nothingness, and a new set of ideals will have to be integrated into guidelines for survival and happiness in the twenty-first century. As this transition occurs, as the familiar ideological signposts of the twentieth century fade away into the enigmatic silence of the superseded past, the time-tested spiritual and social ideals speaking directly to us from the Middle Ages will move ever more centrally on to the horizons of culture and thought.

We are only partway toward a confident recovery of the medieval world and its symbiotic interaction with our hopes and expectations. As this upheaval proceeds, the mosaic of the Middle Ages fashioned by the great medievalists of the twentieth century will come under ever closer scrutiny and project yet sharper iconic messages for new times.

I agree with Umberto Eco that everyone has an idea of the Middle Ages, but I would not say with him that these ideas are "usually corrupt." I would instead say: Everyone carries around a highly personal view of the Middle Ages. For most people this is extremely vague or grossly simple and dogmatically crude, although not thereby to be held in contempt. Most people's idea of the Middle Ages, gained from dim recollections of what they were taught in school or saw in a film like *Ivanhoe*, while meaningful to each of them and constituting part of the set of assumptions on which they sometimes act in daily life, is of an intellectually very low-voltage variety. Some people have had the benefit of college courses in which they read a standard textbook, such as an older one by the American Joseph R. Strayer, or one of more recent vintage, for example, the overview of medieval civilization by the French guru Jacques Le Goff. People who have enjoyed a course in college in which they read (normally in translation) works of medieval literature or took a course in medieval art history have a solid basis for persuasively articulating an idea of the Middle Ages and its significance to them and our culture in general.

The people I write about in this book went infinitely further than that, both in terms of deep knowledge, gained from their own research, and in terms of their thinking about the Middle Ages as the central concern of their profession. Their work superseded the interpretations of the Middle Ages previously offered by some fertile minds, such as Edward Gibbon in the eighteenth century and Jules Michelet and Henry C. Lea in the nineteenth century. No book written about the European Middle Ages before 1895 or so is still worth reading except for curiosity's sake because the data base was inadequate and because the phantasmagoric screen of now-obsolete Victorian assumptions shaped perceptions of the past that are too remote from the understanding of the late twentieth century to be worth bothering about.

Even such a work as Henry Adams's *Mont-Saint-Michel and Chartres*, completed in 1913, reads today as naive and idiosyncratic, in a way that his great history of early-nineteenth-century American politics does not. Although Adams taught medieval history at Harvard in the 1870s and appears to have done not a bad job there, all things considered, he never mastered the complexity of twelfth-century ecclesiastical culture sufficiently or asked tough enough questions about it to make his book useful today as other than an emblem of an artificial neoromanticism in early-twentieth-century Boston culture. Whatever insights Adams had to offer pale alongside the great book on twelfth-century sensibility published by R. W. Southern in 1953. Yet in spite of the vast learning of the twentieth-century medievalists I consider, and in spite of their thinking within a frame of intellectual reference that is approximately our own in the early 1990s, there were still profound disagreements about the development and significance of the Middle Ages among these prominent scholars and writers, particularly with reference to the explosively creative era from the late eleventh to the middle of the fourteenth century.

What interests me most of all is how the life experiences and cultural milieus of these medievalists became integrated into their conscious reflections on the medieval world. In writing and reading history, we are visibly creating a psychoanalysis in which our own anxieties, hopes, loves, fears, and disappointments become interactive with the learned discoveries and data bases that academic research proliferates.

Anyone can sing an operatic aria, and some with good natural voices and a little training can do a pretty good job for it. But nobody is going to regard such singing for private satisfaction as authoritative constructions or readings of Mozart, Wagner, or Verdi. We pay good money to go to a major opera house and listen to the master singers. Their interpretations of particular arias or whole operatic roles always marginally and sometimes radically differ. So it is with humanistic scholars when they try to construct for us an image of the past. They, too, do a highly professional job. The ideas of the Middle Ages articulated by the master medievalists vary substantially one from another. The libretto and score they are working from—the data of historical fact—are the same. The truth, therefore, is ultimately not in the textual details but in the interpretations.

We cannot in these demotic times, when cultural egalitarianism is mandated by holders of power in government, the universities, and the media, say out loud that these academic medievalists' ideas about the Middle Ages are better than those of the high school student quickly forgetting Western civilization or world history or of the college graduate who has superimposed upon a fading memory of Strayer's textbook a recent reading of Tuchman and Eco. We can say that the medievalists' books are more authentic, subtle, elaborate, more worthy of our time and money, just what we would say about an opera diva's performance as we exit Lincoln Center or La Scala. We can affirm that medievalists' learned and imaginative creation of a Middle Ages offers recognitions of reality that constitute art and formulations of paradigms that constitute science.

Recognitions and formulations of the European Middle Ages are almost infinite in number. But certain great issues loom large in the work of the twentieth-century medievalists. As we try to make sense out of the massive data derived from the millennium between Rome and Renaissance, some questions predominate, giving shape to understanding the politics, society, and culture of the Middle Ages.

What were the factors of strength, creativity, and growth that sometime between A.D. 800 and 1100, after four hundred years of decline, fragmentation, and enfeeblement, set Western Europe on its phenomenal rise, which has never been fundamentally reversed or halted for a significant length of time and thereby distinguishes the West from all other civilizations among humankind?

How in the midst of a violent society did there emerge in fewer than two centuries a novel judicial system of such completeness that in all fundamentals of concepts and procedures it is still at the heart of American law today?

How did medieval kings for a long era exercise leadership and command loyalty without the personnel and techniques of modern bureaucracy, using tribal, ritual, and heroic bonds and images, and then later and suddenly delineate the institutional foundations of the modern state?

How did the labor and aspirations of peasant communities integrate with the ambitions and bellicosity of a warrior aristocracy, and the feelings and pieties of the common man gain respect and authenticity within the elaborate and proud culture of the nobility?

How did the strong perpetuation of the linguistic, intellectual, and religious structures of antiquity and the late Roman Empire precondition the philosophy, art, and literature of the high Middle Ages yet permit the exercise of personal sensibility and boisterous creativity?

How did the church's rapid paradigm shift from focus on God the Father-Emperor to God the Loving Son, the role model for human behavior, occur, and how did his Mother affect belief and existence?

How could the church function within the tensions aroused between hierarchic authority on the one side and evangelical groups and individual piety on the other?

These are prime questions of medieval history, researched, contemplated, and debated among the leading medievalists of this century. The artistic recognitions of reality and the scientific formulations of explanatory paradigms they developed in response to these persistent and complex questions about the European Middle Ages came neither quickly nor easily. The answers emerged out of the depths of their hard-earned learning derived from decades of personal research and the work of others and out of the experiences of their own lives and cultural contexts that helped them illuminate the past.

These prime questions about the Middle Ages appear in recent years to be increasingly significant to American college students, to judge from the burgeoning enrollments in medieval studies courses. The current surge of interest in the Middle Ages is a cyclic phenomenon within the culture of modern American higher education. It was present in the 1920s, necessitating the appointment of dozens of new college teachers in medieval studies and the rapid deployment of doctoral programs to train them. The popularity of medieval studies was again evident in the decade 1955–1965, and another such era of heavy enrollments in medieval courses began in the mid-1980s.

There are two ways that medieval studies can be didactically justified as of central and persistent importance in education and culture. First, we can say the medieval heritage is very rich today in a prominent set of ideas and institutions, such as the Catholic Church, the university, Anglo-American law, parliamentary government, romantic love, heroism, just war, the spiritual capacity of little as well as elite people, and the cherishing of classical literatures and languages. That this heritage ought to be consciously identified, cultivated, and refined is commonly asserted. Secondly, we can say less conventionally that medieval civilization stands toward our postmodern culture as the conjunctive other, the intriguing shadow, the marginally distinctive double, the secret sharer of our dreams and anxieties. This view means that the Middle Ages are much like the culture of today, but exhibit just enough variations to disturb us and force us to question some of our values and behavior patterns and to propose some alternatives or at least modifications. The difference is relatively small, but all the more provocative for that.

The medievalists who are the focus of this book have been chosen for both the reasons that the Middle Ages are important to us—as heritage and as other. Their works most convincingly and dramatically give us the knowledge and concepts to consider the Middle Ages from both of these challenging perspectives.

CHAPTER TWO

———— • ◦◦◦ • ————

LAW AND
SOCIETY

FREDERIC WILLIAM MAITLAND

I

A DEATH IN THE CANARY ISLANDS

In 1906 Frederic William Maitland who was born in 1850 and was the Downing Professor of the Laws of England at Cambridge University, died suddenly at Las Palmas in the Canary Islands, where the university had allowed him to retreat each winter for several years because of the fragility of his health. There in the hot climate of a sleepy seafront Spanish village, attended by his wife—the cousin of Virginia Woolf—and his two young daughters, Maitland had continued his prolific historical work. In addition to teaching law and legal history at Cambridge and writing the outstanding work of legal narrative in the English language, he was the principal founder and general editor of the publications of the Selden Society, established to publish the records of English legal history, especially of the medieval period.

Using transcripts or photographs of documents or often actual manuscripts that easygoing archivists in that genteel era had allowed him to borrow, Maitland continued his frenetic pace of skillfully editing and translating these records while sitting in the sun of the Canary Islands. He died at the pinnacle of his career. He was buried in the oceanside town where he died, a strange, distant resting place for the finest historical mind his country had yet produced.

Maitland was admired by historians as much as or more than by lawyers. Among the latter in his lifetime he was probably most revered at the Harvard Law School, then the singular citadel for the academic study of Anglo-American law in the United States that was in course of transforming the American legal profession.

Yet peculiarly Maitland's last years were a series of major steps not taken. He declined the regius professorship of history at Cambridge, the senior chair, when it became vacant, on ostensible grounds of health. Regarded as a deity at Harvard, he never visited the United States, although Arizona or Southern California would have done as much for his Edwardian weak lungs as the Canary Islands could, and in the United States he would have had some good medical attention, which he could not obtain in the Spanish resort. Maitland was in delicate health for the last ten years of his life, but none of his biographers clearly knows the nature of his problem, and his surviving letters strangely do not tell us. Probably it was tuberculosis, the English intellectual's disease, possibly complicated by diabetes. Nevertheless, it is pretty clear that his premature death in 1906 was simply the result of bad medical practice. He got influenza on shipboard going south and then, in the Canary Islands, died of pneumonia that resulted from it.

Maitland's death was greeted in both England and Cambridge, Massachusetts, with effusive outpourings that a genius and saint had gone. Nobody had a critical word to say about him or his work. His brother-in-law H. A. L. Fisher, a young Oxford historian (and later a famous college master), rushed a hagiographical biography into print. No other biography was published until 1966, when a cautious legal historian at Oxford, C. H. Fifoot, produced a longer and much more circumstantial but not very different account. The only other substantial study of Maitland's work is a concise book published in 1986 by the formidable Sir Geoffrey Elton, regius professor at Cambridge.

It is easy to adulate Maitland as a medieval historian, humanist, legal scholar, and a secular saint. He did everything right, from developing vast interpretations to editing records to writing textbooks. In 1971 a published letter, theretofore hidden away in a Glasgow archive, showed that Maitland was not entirely free from the social anti-Semitism that was then starting to engulf the Anglo-American academic world. But this blemish means very little compared with what he did and said in feverish bouts of prolific work (he didn't start as a historian until he was about thirty-five).

Maitland had a photographic memory. He relied a great deal on it. If he had stopped to take extensive notes, he would have accomplished only a small part of what he achieved. Historians like Maitland who work from their memories rather than extensive notes are prone to make a plethora of small errors. It is astonishing how extremely few such errors Maitland made in his work.

He was indeed a secular saint—a quiet, decent, fair, generous person. He suffered fiscally and professionally at the hands of Sir Frederick Pollock in their awkward collaboration on *The History of English Law* from 600 to 1272, but he did not complain. He even paid Pollock a fifth of the royalties on this monumental work, even though in terms of Pollock's actual contribution, the latter merited at most 1 percent of the royalties. When the first treasurer of the Selden Society embezzled all the funds and committed suicide, Maitland's concern was for the man and his family, and uncomplainingly he went right to work and found new benefactors for the society. Maitland was a keen supporter of letting women take degrees at Cambridge. He also assiduously furthered the career of a young woman medievalist, Mary Bateson, who unfortunately died a few months before he did.

Maitland's personality equipped him to be the hero in a Shaw play. There is an eyewitness account, written down some years after the event, of Maitland addressing a faculty meeting at Cambridge in 1894:

> He looked at that time a youngish man, though he was nearing fifty; but his face was covered with a network of minute lines, too fine and delicate to be called wrinkles, and contributing not a little to the general impression of intellectual power and intensity of purpose. No single feature of his face ever seemed to be still. Every emotion expressed in his speech was reflected equally clearly in his countenance—contempt followed enthusiasm; intense conviction succeeded persiflage; humour, sweet reasonableness, pity, detestation, were as plainly visible as they were audible. But after a little time even his features faded—at least from the notice of one observer—and all that one could see, or at any rate, note, was his wonderful eyes. All that one was conscious of was the flow of epigram, argument and even invective—and the eyes.

Photographs of Maitland show a slim, athletic, handsome figure with intense eyes. A typical Edwardian don—a *Chariots of Fire* person, that peculiar English combination of strength and sensibility.

Reading Maitland's book, lectures, and letters is still a heartwarming experience. He always says the right thing, and says it right in epigrammatic form. We could call these quotes the sayings of Chairman Frederic. Maitland is in a class by himself—the standard by which others are judged. He is a visionary whose sayings resonate in all sorts of directions; his legacy is a complex and ambiguous one:

> If we speak, we must speak with words; if we think, we must think with thought. We are moderns and our words and thoughts can not but be modern. (1898)

Our one hope of interpreting [medieval English law] . . . seems to lie in an effort to understand the law of Angevin times [1154–1272], to understand it thoroughly, as though we ourselves lived under it. (1891)

The only direct utility of legal history . . . lies in the lesson that each generation has an enormous power of shaping its own law. I don't think the study of legal history would make men fatalists. I doubt it would make them conservatives. I am sure that it would free them from superstition and teach them they have free hands. I get more and more wrapped up in the Middle Ages, but the only utilitarian justification [is] that . . . if history is to do its liberating work, it must be as true to fact as it can possibly make itself; and true to fact it will not be if it begins to think what lessons it can teach. (1896)

In my judgement no discussion of [legal institutions] that does not deal very much thoroughly with the history of legal ideas is likely to do much good. (1893)

A Natural History of Institutions is a fascinating ideal, but we must have a care or our Natural History will bear to real history the relation that Natural Law bore to real law. Exploration in foreign climes may often tell us what to look for, but never what to find. (1898)

Englishmen do not love lawyers, and the law they love they do not think of as lawyer's law. (1892)

Lawyers have written a great deal of nonsense in all ages: The Middle not excepted. (1899)

If these remarks were made today by a visiting speaker in the weekly colloquium on legal history that flourishes at the New York University School of Law, they would not startle anyone by their originality, but they would be well received. They would still fit in very well with current discourse; they would not sound antique or obsolete. What Maitland said in the 1890s is integral in concept and language with the cultural mode of a century later—an astonishing originality.

Compare now the Oxford constitutional historian William Stubbs around 1870, only a few decades before Maitland: "The polity developed by the German races on British soil is the purest product of their primitive instinct.

"How was English liberty won? . . . It is a work of very fallible men, a result brought out of weakness by the strength of the Wise Ruler, King of kings. . . . The constitution was written by men who had no personal ambition, but abundant patriotic honor and moderation. Their works abide, while edifices of men who have had but their own aggrandisement at heart perish."

   This belongs to a very different mind-set and historical field of
vision from Maitland's. Stubbs's perception of the Middle Ages is
filtered through a thick prism of Victorian organicism, teleology, piety,
and cant. Stubbs is not playing the same game as we are. Maitland
is, and therefore, he is the earliest master of medieval studies whom
we can still read with pleasure and enlightenment, not simply out of
curiosity.

   What happened in the quarter of a century between Stubbs and
Maitland that should make the assumptions and rhetoric of their works
so different? How do we account for the great breakthrough that
resulted in the modern imaging of the Middle Ages at the turning of
the century? Maitland had all the characteristics of a genius, an un-
expected man who cannot by a significant margin be fully accounted
for by his background and ambience, any more than Einstein, Freud,
or Joyce can be thus accounted for. But we can see in his life and
times, like theirs, certain inspirations and reinforcements for an intellectual revolution.

II

MEDIEVALISM AND MODERNISM

Maitland was an austere, very private person. But there is just enough
biographical material to indicate how his mind developed. In 1884
Frederic Maitland was an attorney in London, specializing in conveyancing—that is, land law. The English legal profession was in the
midst of serious discussion about streamlining and simplifying the old
land law, with its complex medieval procedures and archaic formularies that no longer were needed and made practice in this excruciatingly conservative field difficult and slow. The Americans had
modernized their land law, derived from the same medieval heritage,
in the first half of the nineteenth century. Now it was England's
turn.

   Substantial labor and subtle legal reasoning were involved in the
updating and simplifying of English conveyancing. The reform was
carried out between 1890 and 1920, and Maitland welcomed this development, as the reforming liberal rationalist that he was. But he
wondered how and why these bewildering and inexplicable forms of
action had come into existence in the first place. Now they were
musty and irrational, often mere Latinate mumbo jumbo and worthy
of Charles Dickens's scornful pronouncement that the common law

was an ass or Jeremy Bentham's remark around 1780 that Blackstone's defense of the old common law was nonsense on stilts. But once these now-obtuse and unnecessary judicial complexities must have had a purpose, Maitland assumed. People do not intentionally create a system of legal mystification. The law becomes a mystery over time if unreformed because social relationships change. But when these actions were inaugurated, they were meaningful, they were reasonable, they performed critical functions in the society of that time, and they rationally served the immediate interests of particular social groups and political forces.

So thought Maitland. In so doing, he was coming on to the way of twentieth-century sociological thinking called functionalism that a young professor of education at the University of Bordeaux, Émile Durkheim, was also developing at the same time in more theoretical form and that Durkheim, the son of a Paris rabbi, the first professor of sociology at the University of Paris, was to propound in the early years of the new century. Maitland in the mid-1880s was thinking along these functionalist lines and applying that to medieval law and society: Everything in the old land law, the first part of English law to mature into a full-fledged system, had once served a rational social purpose. Where, when, and why?

Maitland had time to pursue these new historical interests of his because he was not very busy as a lawyer. Indeed, his brother-in-law was to say after his death that Maitland had very few clients and slipped into scholarship and historical research as an alternative.

So, his law practice being quiet, Maitland made his way to the British Museum library and the Public Record Office and other archives and began to read medieval law cases in the plea rolls, the earliest of which survive from the 1190s, when the great legal revolution that Henry II and his judges like Glanvill had instituted was only three decades old. These early rolls were in Latin, the handwriting resembled modern book print, and Maitland, with a good English secondary school education, had no trouble with them. He soon realized, however, that a hundred years later most of the plea rolls were written in a French jargon, and the handwriting—the quasi stenography of hard-pressed clerks who were often translating oral Latin or English simultaneously as the case went along—was frequently very hard to read. Maitland taught himself law French and wrote the first, and still the only, treatise on the subject, and he mastered medieval handwriting without ever attending a class in this arcane subject.

In the dark afternoons in Bloomsbury in the mid-1880s, on the steps of the ornate British Museum and over tea and pastries in a restaurant nearby, Maitland met two remarkable men, one his age, one ten years older, who had already been doing research in English legal history for some time and were already learned in the subject. They were both from continental Europe, and at the time they knew infinitely more about the origins of the common law than any Englishman did. That they were continental Europeans did not trouble Maitland. Before he took up legal practice, he had traveled much on the Continent, especially in Germany, where he had strayed as an adolescent for months on end, and he spoke and read German very fluently. (Of all the eminent British-born medieval historians of the twentieth century before 1970, only David Knowles and Geoffrey Barraclough, in addition to Maitland, were fluent in German.)

The older of the two scholars with whom Maitland chatted in Bloomsbury as the carriages and horse-drawn tram cars rolled by, and newsboys hawked papers with accounts of General Gordon at Khartoum, the discovery of gold in the Transvaal, or the hanging of the French-Indian rebel Louis Riel in Canada, was a Berlin Jew, Felix Liebermann. His well-tailored clothes, trim beard, and gold-rimmed glasses and his courteous manners showed Liebermann off as a scion of a wealthy German Jewish family. He had a Ph.D. and had already begun to publish the result of his pioneering research on Anglo-Saxon law. His three-volume edition of *The Laws of the Anglo-Saxons* (1903–17) is still the edition we use today, flawlessly professional in the best German mode and one of the great achievements of late-nineteenth-century scholarship. But because of anti-Semitism, then on the rise in imperial Germany, Liebermann (like Freud in Vienna a couple of decades later) had no hope of a regular university professorship. Through thirty years of monumental research and meticulous dedication, Liebermann worked as a "private scholar." He held no university position and lived off his family's comfortable income.

When he first met Liebermann in the 1880s in Bloomsbury, Maitland was in awe at how deeply this disciplined, cheerful German Jew had mastered the manuscript texts of English law from the earliest dooms, or law codes, around 600 down to the early twelfth century. Liebermann, in course of traveling all over England, was examining and transcribing manuscripts, and he revealed to Maitland how incredibly prolific English archives and libraries were in the law codes and court rolls of the Middle Ages. By lucky accidents, and as a result of long centuries without invasion and few civil upheavals,

England had a much more extensive written judicial heritage than any European country. It was characteristic of the Age of High Modernism (1890–1920) that behind just about every intellectual breakthrough—physics, philosophy, psychology, sociology, anthropology—there loomed a European Jewish mind. Felix Liebermann was a pioneer in the analysis of the documentary record of medieval law. He was Maitland's Jewish shadow.

The other European whom he met in the 1880s had an even greater influence on Maitland. This was a Russian of his own age, Paul Vinogradoff, who taught in St. Petersburg and was well recognized and rewarded as a prominent scholar by the Russian imperial government, even though he was a constitutional liberal and not sympathetic to czarist repression. Vinogradoff was in England to research a study of English peasant communities and manorial law in the eleventh century.

Vinogradoff talked enthusiastically about the mountains of medieval plea rolls and judicial treatises available in London, about what could be gained by reading them, and Maitland saw that this was the main route to answering the questions stirred in his mind by the current talk of reforming the land law. By reading these plea rolls (medieval court cases), Maitland hoped to establish how the common law had emerged and how it had functionally developed its actions and structure in response to social and cultural contexts. This was the project that was to take up the rest of his life, the results of which are laid down in Pollock and Maitland, the first great interpretive work on medieval history.

Liebermann and Vinogradoff pointed the way, and while Maitland could do nothing for Liebermann—a Jewish professor of humanities was as great an anathema in Britain at the end of the nineteenth century as in Germany—he did repay his debt many times over to Vinogradoff when the latter could no longer stomach czarist tyranny and sought permanent refuge in Britain. One of Maitland's many acts of generosity was shortly before his death to find a chair for Vinogradoff at Oxford, where Vinogradoff taught until he died in 1925. Both his books and lectures were mostly instructible to Englishmen, except for his last publication, a short book on Roman law in the Middle Ages, which is still the best introduction to the subject.

Maitland's family was solidly middle-class, comfortable, professionally ambitious, and increasingly secular. His grandfather had been an archivist and a published amateur historian of some reputation. His father was a lawyer who died when Maitland was a child. There was enough money in the family to give him an excellent secondary school and Cambridge education, which was intended to prepare him for study at the Inns of Court and a career at the bar. He did indeed become an attorney, but that was certainly not his first choice of a career on graduating from Cambridge. Originally Maitland wanted to be what we now call an academic political scientist. There was a graduate fellowship available for competition at the university that would have opened up this kind of academic career for him. He competed and submitted a thesis to support his candidacy. It wasn't very good, and the award went to someone else.

The two luminaries at Cambridge who greatly influenced Maitland were Henry Sidgwick, the political theorist, and Sir Leslie Stephen, the historian and biographer. They were the humanistic face of the new Cambridge, then moving away from centuries-old traditions of Protestant theology and puritanical fervor toward the natural and social sciences, toward rationalism, data gathering, quantitative analysis, and liberal reform.

As he completed his undergraduate studies, Maitland wanted to stay on and be part of this exciting, horizon-expanding, radical intellectual, and highly innovative academic world. He couldn't find a place there for himself. So he went to London, to return in triumph to Cambridge in 1888 as the first holder of a new chair in law. Meanwhile, he had married Leslie Stephen's niece and begun to move in the intellectual and social circles of the Cambridge-London axis that around 1900 became visible as the Bloomsbury group. Its first luminaries were Stephen's daughters, the novelist Virginia Woolf and the artist Vanessa Bell, their husbands—Leonard Woolf, the political commentator, and Clive Bell, the art critic—and an economist from another old Cambridge family, John Maynard Keynes. A milieu that Maitland moved within in the last two decades of his life was thus one of the two circles of intellectuals and artists that fostered modernism in Britain (the other circle was headed in London by two American expatriates, T. S. Eliot and Ezra Pound). Maitland's work in medieval legal history—especially the first edition of Pollock and Maitland's work published in 1895, and the second definitive edition of 1898, with Pollock's meager contributions almost entirely excised—was among the early expressions of the modernist cultural revolution.

Maitland knew where he was going and knew where he came from. The last book he published was a biography of the recently deceased Stephen. He wrote its first draft propped up in a sickbed in the Canary Islands. Had he lived another ten years, his name would now figure prominently in biographies of Virginia Woolf and Maynard Keynes. But even in his own university, his role as a founder of modernism has been forgotten. Virginia Woolf and Vanessa Bell would have known. He was their revered father's greatest disciple, by far.

In 1910 Woolf remarked that an exhibition of French postimpressionist painting that her brother-in-law, Clive Bell, had organized in London was the beginning of a new intellectual era. So was the publication of Pollock and Maitland in 1895.

The essence of modernism, whether in art, literature, philosophy, or the social and natural sciences, was to take the object studied out of linear and referential schemes and to concentrate on the thing itself, deriving maximal meaning from this in-depth, intensely focused examination. The modernist temperament is called self-referentiality, textuality, objectification, analysis. It is at work in Eliot's poetry, Kandinsky's paintings, Wittgenstein's philosophy, Einstein's physics. It also characterizes Maitland's method of history and medieval studies. It is that more than anything that separates Maitland from his Victorian predecessors and his Edwardian contemporaries as well. The result is to get behind the procedures and actions of the law to the social behavior and mind-set that shaped judicial institutions. Maitland is the discoverer of medieval society—not a medieval society that nineteenth-century ideologies wanted to find there but a society analyzed functionally within its self-referential operations. Through this modernist sociology, Maitland intended that we come to know medieval law "as though we ourselves lived under it." The intellectualization he brought to his medieval studies is not Victorian teleological whiggery, not even his personal proclivity for the radical wing of the Liberal party; it is a Durkheim-like structural and functional sociology.

Maitland's masterpiece, the Pollock and Maitland work, was written with phenomenal speed. The joke in Cambridge common rooms was that he wrote so fast to forestall the slow-starting Pollock from writing any significant part of the work and thereby ruining it. Maitland drew upon his astonishing memory and addressed an audience well beyond academic medievalists. He aimed at the transatlantic legal profession in the English-speaking world and much of the educated public in general. Here he writes with fire and abandon on the making of the forms of civil (property) action in the late twelfth century and the rise of the trial by jury in the late twelfth and early thirteenth centuries and the social relations involved. There is warmth and humor; he writes to make us feel we are there. He writes from the inside; his modernist functionalism clicks like a high-powered engine. It is an astonishing achievement, one of the truly great pieces of historical literature of all time, these chapters of Pollock and Maitland.

Maitland became involved with Pollock in an entrepreneurial publishing venture blessed by the Cambridge University Press (CUP), whose director salivated over the pounds sterling the press was going to make by the collaboration of Maitland with the much-better-known Oxford professor of jurisprudence and luminary of the bar Sir Frederick Pollock. He was indeed learned in the law, reviewing authoritatively each year major cases for the legal profession and writing impressive books on Spinoza and other philosophers. But as soon as Maitland saw the few pages Pollock had drafted in Anglo-Saxon law, he knew there was a terrible mismatch, for Pollock was premodernist, linear and referential, and very Edwardian. Maitland did not hide his disappointment. Pollock, gentleman that he was, offered to withdraw, but with visions of a fiscal coup, the CUP would not revise the contract. Pollock and Maitland it had contracted for, and that is what it insisted on. It cared not that Maitland wrote more than 99 percent of the two volumes. Pollock admitted in a gracious line in the preface that his contribution was minimal. The press did not even put Maitland's name first, in order to serve its marketing purposes.

Maitland's problems with Pollock and the Cambridge University Press did not detract from the quality of his work. On the contrary, not only did he write with phenomenal speed, but the bothersome edge of the contractual and collaborative problems drove his imagination and his writing to a level that was unique even for him.

III
PRESENT AT THE CREATION

Pollock and Maitland's two volumes go back to the era before the Norman Conquest of 1066. But the volumes primarily deal with the legal revolution that occurred in the reign of Henry II (1154–89), William the Conqueror's great-grandson, and the working out of the implications of this legal revolution down to 1272. This was the founding era of what has come to be called the common law, the judicial system that still prevails in England and Wales (but only partly in Scotland) and in the United States, the English-speaking provinces of Canada, and many other countries that were once part of the British Empire. No one knows for sure the origin of the term "common law." Either it means royal law—law common to the whole of the English kingdom, as distinct from local customs—or the term stands for secular law as distinct from church law. Henry II got into a furious conflict with his archbishop of Canterbury, Thomas Becket, formerly the king's friend and chief official, over the marginalization of ecclesiastical (termed canon) law in the interests of the great expansion of royal law, as well as over the property of the church. Even before Becket was removed in 1170 by assassination at the hands of four of the king's overeager courtiers, the archbishop was losing the fight to restrain this advance of the common law over every aspect of English life except marriage, divorce, blasphemy, and adultery. How and why this legal revolution happened, making English law very different from Continental European law, is the main theme of Pollock and Maitland.

The Angevin government of Henry II, as described by Maitland, arrived at its momentous reforming judicial decisions in the 1160s for reasons of both expediency and profit. Expedient was a low-cost judicial system that at the same time enhanced royal power over landed society. The profit came mainly from the cost of obtaining a royal writ to start a civil suit (as it does today) and the seizures by the crown of a felon's movable property. If the expansion of the jury system was an institutional innovation that was bound to be favored by the gentry who would staff the juries and find their participation in the process of the common law enhanced, thereby stiffening their loyalty to the crown, this was a happy side effect. Maitland stresses that we are witnessing not the preparation of a fully elaborated, predetermined structure but a great many functional contingencies and experiments at work. The judicial outcome could have been different if one or more components were variant or absent. The role of the crown was crucially important, but there were many other factors at work, including the need for landlords to settle property disputes and the desire of peasant villagers to control crime. Dozens of contingencies had to fall into place and interact for the common law to compose itself in the way it did.

The founding and shaping of English common law between 1160 and 1270 are among the half dozen most important events of the Middle Ages because it created the only alternative to Roman law in Western civilization. But the creation of this new legal system was based not on well-defined ideology or predetermined organic forces, as Victorians believed, but on the choices, ambitions, and decisions of many people, each suiting his own interest. This was the story that Maitland had to tell. It was not easy to do so; it required great narrative art.

By the early thirteenth century a variety of legal mechanisms, called assizes, assured that all property disputes between and within landed families were litigated in the royal courts. The centuries-long English identification of property and litigation was fully in place by 1220. Instituting civil actions by securing writs and defending against these actions were the judicial texture of the life of landed society.

In the thirteenth century the royal itinerant justices sent to preside at the shire courts were given commissions of general eyre, or circuit, which imposed upon them a great variety of important political and administrative as well as judicial functions. The meeting of the shire courts under the presidency of the justices in eyre (the circuit-riding judges) became the prime means by which the crown imposed its will in county society. Through the common law's procedures, the king and his ministers communicated their program to the aristocracy and the gentry and made demands upon them in face-to-face confrontations.

Maitland used all the skills of his narrative art to try to get us to visualize a general eyre in the thirteenth century. The coming of the justices in eyre to a county town was a terrifying experience for many attending the shire court. It was a supremely serious moment, when not only all felonious malefactors but also everyone who owed some obligation to the king would be called to account. We are not surprised to learn under these circumstances that whole villages in the more outlying and violent regions like Cornwall took to the woods when they heard the king's justices were about to descend upon them. The entry of the circuit judges to a county town was appropriate to the seriousness of their tasks. Maitland's account conjures up a clear and circumstantial image for us. With a flourish of trumpets and a waving of royal banners, accompanied by the sheriff and the keeper of the pleas (the coroner) of the shire and followed by an armed bodyguard, the justices rode through the main streets of the town, which was jammed to overflowing with magnates and knights who had been summoned from every part of the county. With all the juries and litigants who had been summoned in land cases, with the felons who had been apprehended on the oaths of the indicting grand juries, required or forced to be in attendance, the population of the county town on these court days swelled to several times greater than the normal numbers of the native burgesses. There was no room in either the inns or the holding jails.

After the panel of justices, usually four in number with at least one cleric as the chief of the panel, had suitably refreshed themselves, the business of the court commenced. The articles of the general eyre in the king's commission were read, and the justices went through a long list of administrative and financial matters of interest to the crown before turning to the strictly judicial proceedings. All matters affecting the royal demesne and the king's position as liege lord were dealt with. The judges were extremely busy, hard-pressed men who could stay only a week or two in the county before they had to move on to another shire or back to Westminster. They did not have time to concern themselves deeply with the question of whether justice was being done to an accused criminal in any particular instance, and this was especially true if the accused had little wealth or status in society. In criminal suits the judges wanted "jail delivery." All the accused were to be taken out of the holding jails and dealt with in one way or another. Similarly, in civil suits the judges wanted the jurors to respond to the precise points asked of them in the writs that started the lawsuit whether the plaintiff was indeed unlawfully and without judgment dispossessed of his estate or whether the plaintiff was indeed the legitimate heir of the recent possessor of the land.

Initially the common law was devoted to narrow routines of "formal" (rigidly routinized) pleading partly because of the heavy schedule under which the judges operated and partly because of early medieval tradition. The judges wanted no long discussions in court. In criminal suits there was to be a formal appeal (complaint) by an individual accuser or a formal indictment by the grand jury; then the defendant was to make his formal denial and immediately be subjected to proof of guilt or innocence. In civil suits the plaintiff made his complaint; the defendant, his formal denial of the truths of the complaint; the jury, thrust before the court by the sheriff, made its precise recognition of the facts; and the justices rendered immediate judgment.

As we read the court rolls of the 1190s and the next couple of decades, we may begin to believe that the judges wanted no trial, whether civil or criminal, to endure more than five minutes, and most of them did not, proceeding in the most routinized and austere manner. Medieval justices always seemed to have foremost in their minds the pressure of the king's business in the next county and the warm fire and good dinner waiting for them back at the inn. Nothing irritated the justices more than juries that failed to give indictments or recognitions when they were asked to. This slowed up the regular and quick procedure of the court, and inevitably the justices would punish the community by fining the shire court. A hung jury was sometimes dealt with by piling the jurors into a cart and dragging them from court to court after the justices until they reached a unanimous decision.

Although by the fourteenth century the common law was—and is even today—notorious for the slowness of its procedures, compared with the Roman law process, this was not the case in the last two decades of the twelfth century. The Roman judges would be slowed up by having to study carefully written briefs presented by plaintiffs and defendants and by having to make a careful inquisition themselves on the facts of each case. It was undoubtedly an attractive prospect to the Angevin king and his justices that they did not have to take these pains. All the pleading was oral, and the common law judges had to make no preparation before the trial began. The hard work of investigation had furthermore been done for them by the juries of indictment and recognition, which were self-informing panels (the juries did all the investigative work, without pay). Between lunch and dinner the justices could therefore run through dozens of civil and criminal pleas and return to Westminster after a couple of months on the road with the satisfaction that they could inform the king they had cleared up all the lawsuits in no fewer than five counties. Under Roman law procedure, the equivalent number of trials would have occupied five panels of learned inquisitor-judges for perhaps a whole year.

As it crystallized in the early thirteenth century, common law became committed to the adversary system of judicial procedure. Whereas in the Roman law that came to dominate on the Continent the judges took the leading role in directing the course of the trial, the bench in common law acted as impartial arbitrator, as it were, enforcing the rules and handing down the judgment, while allowing the contending parties—plaintiff and defendant in civil suits, community and defendant in criminal pleas—to struggle judicially against each other. This adversary system placed judges in an elevated position and served to entrench the belief that the actual trial was a function of communal, popular institutions. This impression was enhanced by the circuit-riding judges' peculiar position as social aliens in the shire, momentary (although necessary) interlopers in the ordinary life of county society. The judges' impartiality should not be confused with reticence or nonintervention. The judges took an active voice in the course of the trial, defining the law and establishing the issue for the jury. Especially in civil actions, the judges' determination of the issue for the jury's decision was critical for the outcome of the trial.

Common law procedure in property disputes is the womb from which the profession of attorneys emerged. The adversary system and increasing complexity of pleading generated an increasing need for legal counsel, especially in civil actions. Whether you won your civil suit in common law was much more conditioned by the quality of counsel than in Roman law, where the judges dominated the trial. The gentry were centrally involved in the change after the middle of the thirteenth century in the composition and education of the legal profession. The most important change was the decline of the clerical lawyer, usually educated in France or Italy, and the rise of the lay lawyer, educated in London. The last great ecclesiastical lawyer in English history was Henry de Bracton in the 1240s; after him they all were laymen from the gentry class. A corporate, entirely indigenous legal profession was formed. Entry into it was tightly controlled: A lawyer had to have certification; he had to be called to the bar. All these formalities and restrictions emanated by 1300 from one little place—the Inns of Court in London. The Inns became the controlling body, they provided legal education, and they drew students and members almost exclusively from the ranks of the gentry. (The odd cases—sons of merchants, for instance—were quickly absorbed, and they, too, became gentlemen.)

Law belonged no longer to the church but to the knightly class, the landed gentlemen of England. The Inns of Court were their university. As a rule, after 1300, the gentry did not send their sons to Oxford, unless they were meant to be theologians—something as rare then as it is now—or clerics. Even if they did not become lawyers, young gentlemen spent a year or so at the Inns; they learned the law, the basis of their way of life; then they went back to the county and managed their family estates. More and more the gentry learned to identify their way of life with the operations of the common law.

The most dramatic changes of the thirteenth century were in criminal law procedure. In 1215 the church forbade clerical participation in the ordeal as a method of proof of guilt, thus making it impossible to continue the practice of relying upon God to demonstrate guilt or innocence. In the ordeal of cold water, for example, a defendant bound and thrown into a pond was guilty if he floated, because water as a holy element would not receive a guilty person.

Maitland wrote a particularly brilliant account of the next six or seven decades, during which the English judges sought a method of proof to replace the ordeal. The judges went on with the grand jury that indicted felons. It already provided a viable method of starting a criminal trial. Now, as they searched for a method of proof, they kept the grand jury in mind, and eventually they worked directly with it. They developed the petty jury, the jury of verdict. After news of the abolition of ordeals reached England in 1217, the judges were at first not very confident about relying on the final verdicts of men, although the judges had already become disenchanted with the ordeal and its capricious outcomes. The first juries of verdict after 1217 often consisted of forty-eight men—twelve from each of the four points of the compass. But it was not very practical to summon forty-eight men to the county seat. Some of them were likely not to appear, and the royal judges were not patient men. By the 1250s and 1260s it was normal to impanel a second jury of twelve men to decide on the truth of an accusation made by a grand jury. Twelve, the number of the apostles, was a lucky number in the Middle Ages.

This new jury procedure was astonishingly efficient. Both juries were selected from the same neighborhood people, and the grand jury indictment was usually confirmed. This suited the judges. Even though the Roman law principles they sometimes quoted told them they should be seeking justice, they were mainly eager to settle cases, hang felons, seize the chattels of felons for the crown, and move on to the next county.

Royal justices around 1230 did not lie awake at night wondering if justice was being done by the new petty jury of verdict. They were not men known for their tender consciences. In the twelfth century they had relied on the opinion of local society to a great extent; in the thirteenth century they took it all the way. There was nothing a royal judge liked less than indecisiveness in criminal actions. It meant that the case had to be carried over, and this involved a whole other set of problems. The defendant himself was the biggest. Jailbreaks seem to have been an everyday occurrence in medieval England; obviously there was nothing hard about them. So the judges were pleased to get quick convictions through the jury of verdict, which replaced the ordeal as the method of proof in criminal cases in the shire courts.

There was a procedural problem in introducing trial by jury. The defendant had, first of all, to agree to abide by the judgment of the petty jury—to "put himself on the country." Here was a new procedure without legislative sanction, a risky, untried method, and the defendant had in the 1240s the nominal option of deciding whether or not he would submit to it. He feared that the jury of verdict would not find contrary to the indicting grand jury. Why would one group of his neighbors disagree with another group? No wonder defendants were not eagerly clamoring to come before the jury of verdict; trial by jury was far from being conceived as a sacred constitutional right. But a defendant who refused to put himself on the country was a nuisance. If he could not be prevailed upon by sweet reason, he was subjected to *peine forte et dure*, a charming method of persuasion. Weights would be piled on top of his chest until he accepted jury trial or died. This is the closest that English common law got to the use of torture, which was a central method of proof in Continental Roman law. If the defendant put himself on the country, he faced the imminent prospect of the gallows, but he did have the privilege of choice. By the second quarter of the fourteenth century the defendant was no longer asked his choice; he was automatically put on the country—that is, subjected to jury trial.

In the course of eight or nine decades the judges thus brought about the greatest single change in criminal law procedure that has ever taken place in the common law. The jury of verdict came to be a definitive part of common law procedure. But the story of trial by jury is one of rapid rise and decline. No sooner was trial by jury fully developed than resistance to it appeared in the plea rolls. Maitland noticed in the mid-thirteenth century the rise of what today is called jury nullification of the law. Juries were reluctant to convict the very young, women, the senile, or first offenders with good reputations. A 1980 study shows a conviction level of indicted people—not much higher than in New York City today—of only 35 percent in about the year 1320. In response, judges did what criminal justice officials in New York do today. They began to resort to plea bargaining. If defendants for whom sympathy by juries was likely "fessed up," judges discharged them without the formality of a trial or promised that after trial and conviction the bench would seek a royal pardon. Soft treatment thitherto provided to churchmen as benefit of clergy was then accorded to other groups in society. As late as the mid-eighteenth century women and first offenders were able to "plead their clergy" (plea-bargain a light sentence or a conditional discharge). Another recent study of criminal justice in late medieval England shows that in one year in the early fifteenth century, during wartime, the overwhelming majority of indicted criminals were released without trial if they joined the king's army.

Soon, too, organized criminal gangs took advantage of a vulnerable and overloaded criminal justice system. They suborned juries and threatened judges, and the criminal justice system started to leak profusely. The crown resorted to novel expedients. Panels of gentry in each county were appointed justices of the peace to hear misdemeanors and reduce the police burden on overworked sheriffs. The justices of the peace were authorized vigilantes drawn from landed society. Steely-eyed special commissions of judges on horseback with heavy bodyguards were also impaneled and sent out on gang bashing to use their powers as special prosecutors against organized crime and to stiffen the spines of fearful jurors. It didn't help much. These kinds of special commissions to pursue criminals still have little permanent effect.

The criminal justice system Maitland describes as being in effect in late-thirteenth-century England exists in the New York of 1990 (in Britain the grand jury was abandoned several decades ago, and it has been superseded in California by indicting magistrates). It had defects then. It doesn't work well now. But it is still around. Maitland tells us precisely how trial by jury came into existence and how it functioned. His account is without illusion. He does not sentimentalize trial by jury. For him it was a functional response to a particular social and judicial situation, not a glorious stage in the history of civil liberties. His dispassionate, realistic account of the beginning of trial by jury within the context of medieval society ought to help us recognize the contingent nature of the common law criminal justice system and after seven centuries to amend or supersede it at last.

IV

THE REACH OF THE COMMON LAW

Maitland's interpretation of the making of the common law made all previous accounts completely obsolete and was unchallenged until the 1960s. Since then two major criticisms of Maitland's version of the judicial creation have appeared, and the debate continues.

The first critique was offered by R. C. van Caenegem, who holds the venerable chair of medieval history at the University of Ghent in Belgium. Van Caenegem argued that Maitland did not give sufficient attention to the implications of the slim evidence that indicated that the Anglo-Saxons had the grand jury ("twelve leading thegns") around 1000. Far from this being a temporary and abortive experiment, as

Maitland believed, the grand jury continued to be used here and there in local communities for the century after the Norman Conquest, Van Caenegem contended, until it was reinstituted on a national level by Henry II and his judges. Generally, what Van Caenegem argued for was the vesting of the common law in the continuing mind-set and practice of local communities, and he saw Maitland's account as giving too much importance to the creative efforts of the royal government. This was essentially a neo-Victorian, neo-Stubbsian viewpoint that was also suggested in the 1950s by Helen Maud Cam, who taught at Cambridge and Harvard.

Maitland had a very strong distaste for the communalist view of the founding of the common law. It sounded to him premodernist, sentimental Victorian romanticism about the imaginary democratic instincts of medieval people. His response to neocommunalism would be that it is not sustained by the records. Cam worked backward from late-thirteenth-century local records in which communality was certainly prevalent. But this judicial corporatism of local society, Maitland would say, was the *consequence* of the actual impress of the common law and jury system for more than a hundred years, not the force that made the common law in the first place. Cam, a sturdy 1920s feminist, who was right out of a Dorothy Sayers novel, had confused the social outcome of the common law with its causes, Maitland would point out. The common law *created* judicial communities, not vice versa. Maitland would have respected Van Caenegem's painstaking researches in eleventh- and twelfth-century documents, but he would say that the evidence is so sparse and the documents involved are so corrupt as to make the case without merit.

S. F. C. Milsom, the Cambridge legal scholar writing in the 1970s and 1980s, also believed that Maitland gave too much legitimacy and impact to the planning efforts of royal government in the making of the common law. Like Van Caenegem and Cam, Milsom wanted to see the common law as not in any way the creation of an autocratic regime, initially imposed from the top on society. However, in Milsom's interpretation, it was not the perpetuation of the communal feelings of local democracies but the exclusive interest of feudal landed society and the highly autonomous judicial practices of these baronial and knightly families that drove the shaping of the common law.

The difference between Maitland and Milsom is perhaps more one of emphasis than of sharp disagreement, but Milsom drew the differences in interpretation dialectically. Maitland viewed the common law in civil procedure, the land law, as *initially* the creation of the royal government to serve both the power and wealth of the crown and the needs and interests of landed society, particularly the knightly or gentry class. He also saw this development as a very rapid legal revolution, largely achieved in one generation. Then the exclusive interest of the gentry and the guildlike independence of the legal profession took over and further developed the complex edifice of the common law. Milsom made the role of the central government extremely marginal from the beginning, compared with the autonomous capacities of the landed families as a group, both nobility and gentry, to work out slowly over several decades a system of litigation in land law suitable to their situation. Milsom thought Maitland was still suffering from Victorian tendencies to overpoliticize legal history. He was critical of Maitland's assumption that the new common law civil procedure worked against the reserved interests of the great barons and represented some kind of comity of interest between royal government and the gentry.

To put it simply, Maitland saw the common law initially, in the twelfth century, forged by an alliance between king and gentry. For Milsom this was a residual Victorian anachronism. He claimed that the land law was almost entirely a product of the joint interests of baronial and gentry families. The burden of change was driven by litigation over an extended period, and the royal government was only peripherally involved, if at all. The debate between the supporters of Maitland and Milsom continues on both sides of the Atlantic.

Maitland's impact on the legal profession and judicial culture has been greater in the United States than in Britain. He has been at least intermittently a very real presence in leading American law schools and, through them, the mind-sets of lawyers trained there. His impact on English legal culture in this century has been comparatively marginal, at least before the 1970s. There are three reasons for this sharp difference in Maitland's influence on transatlantic lawyering. First, the legal profession in England declined in the twentieth century both in numbers relative to the global size of the population and in impact on society. In the year of Maitland's death the Liberal party, which he strongly supported, came to power in Britain and began the introduction of the welfare state, to be much expanded by the Labour party government of the late 1940s. With the coming of the welfare state there was created a host of bureaucratic authorities and arbitration boards that dealt with problems of working conditions, public welfare, environmental control, health, transportation, and education that previously—and still in the more market-oriented United States—

were often addressed by litigation. The need for lawyers and their visibility on the national horizon therefore diminished in Britain. Compared with the position of the legal profession in England in the age of Blackstone and Dickens, it was a constricted profession, still affluent and respected but not as central and vibrant. Declining professions have no zest for expanding their intellectual frontiers. Legal history in general and Maitland's work in particular found modest resonance in England's stodgy, quiescent legal profession.

The legal profession in the United States underwent three eras of dynamic expansion: the industrial and financial capitalist boom at the beginning of the century; the New Deal's introduction of the regulatory state in the 1930s, which, unlike Britain's welfare state, enhanced lawyering by leaving a great many issues to be resolved by litigation; and the most recent wave of corporate expansion, which began in the 1950s.

By the 1980s the size of the American legal profession relative to population was more than three times England's and was in absolute number ten times. It admitted to the bar each year a number of new attorneys that approximated the prevailing size of the whole English legal profession. It was attracting to itself in the 1980s at least three quarters of the top 10 percent of college graduates in the humanities and social sciences. This gargantuan, supremely self-confident profession rolled like a Moloch across American society, absorbing everything in its wake, including culture and ideas, and it maintained a persistent interest in Maitland's work and his sociological approach to the law.

The second reason for Maitland's American presence, compared with his impact in Britain, was in the great difference in legal education between the two countries. Until the 1970s, when there was some modest sign of a boom in legal education in British universities and polytechnics, British law schools were very modest operations, with very little intellectual vitality and academic quality and with consistently small and overworked faculties. Legal education in the United States, beginning with the model Harvard Law School early in the century, was again very different. Before 1950 there were always a half dozen American law schools that were genuinely centers of legal scholarship, research, and theory, and by 1980 there were at least twenty such type A American law schools. Their faculties included professors who had the leisure, training, and capacity for a highly intellectual and heuristic approach to the law, and Maitland's presence loomed large in this affluent and learned ambience.

The third reason for Maitland's impact in the United States was that his modernist, sociological, functionalist approach to law fitted in perfectly with the pragmatic, relativist, antiformalist attitude, called in the 1930s and 1940s legal realism, that dominated the top law school faculties from the early years of the century and the Supreme Court as well after Roosevelt's legal revolution of 1937–41. The recent new wave of Marxism in the elite law schools like Harvard and Stanford, called critical legal studies, has been able to find affinity with Maitland as well.

In his own country and time, Maitland had to look over his shoulder at the formalists, organicists, and traditionalists and be concerned about getting too far out in front of them. That was not the problem in America. Here the most radical, deconstructive, functionalist core of Maitland's work found persistent echo, even in his own day. There were three times and places when his American influence was especially consequential. The first was again at the Harvard Law School between 1895 and 1917, the Harvard Law School of Oliver Wendell Holmes, Jr., Roscoe Pound, and Louis D. Brandeis. There a dynamic and richly structured legal culture was put together out of disparate elements: post-Civil War Yankee expansionary capitalism; Boston Anglophilic devotion to the transatlantic continuity of the common law; the voluntarist pragmatism of Charles Saunders Peirce and William James; New York and southern German Jewish intellectuality; and Wilsonian progressivism. With a Harvard Law School culture so constituted, Maitland's work was not only compatible but a stimulant and vehicle of advocacy. His conviction that the common law grew out of the interaction of a thousand interests and much luck and serendipity over many centuries, that there was nothing organically necessary about the common law, that it could have come out very different and might still do so in the future, were just what Roscoe Pound and the legal realists and partisans of Roosevelt's Supreme Court revolution wanted to hear.

A specific impact of Maitland in American legal thought occurred in the new school of American legal history that was founded at the University of Wisconsin in the 1940s and 1950s by J. Willard Hurst, the intellectual heir of midwestern progressivism. Hurst was consciously trying to do for American legal history what he thought Maitland had done for medieval English common law—get away from teleology, formalism, and organicism and focus on the sociological dynamics of the legal history. Hurst's viewpoint is succinctly stated in his *Law and the Conditions of Freedom in the Nineteenth-Century United States* (1956): "The substance of what business wanted from law was the provision for ordinary use of an organization through which entrepreneurs could better mobilize and release economic energy. . . . It was natural to its buoyant optimism and its confidence in the release of energy that nineteenth century law coupled concern for vested rights with a high record for keeping open the channels of change [resulting in] . . . preference for dynamic rather than static property, or for property put to creative new use rather than property content with what it is." This is pure Maitland, but filtered through the prism of the American neo-Victorian taste for schematization and ideology. Hurst inspired and in some instances personally trained a productive generation of American legal historians.

The full implication of Maitland's work is only now in the course of crystallizing. This may be called the theory of common law structuralism. It sees the common law as a deep cultural structure not only in the Middle Ages—as Maitland perceived—but continuously in the Anglo-American world, so that this deep structure was present in American law. Many issues are still being sorted out and debated within this broad rubric of common law structuralism, but it is taking shape as the legal theory of the 1990s.

From the contributions of an array of legal and social analysts, a post-Maitland structuralism in legal history has emerged. Within wide and vague parameters sustaining social order and civic virtue, there is in the common law an intrinsic cultural bias toward market economy. This is what the common law adversary system and property formulation fundamentally affirm. The adversary system, writ process, and pleading of the common law constitute the structural foundation of market capitalism, a vibrant core within an indeterminate but existing ethical context.

Whatever the role of the monarchy in the founding of the forms of action, by the early fourteenth century, after the establishment of the Inns of Court and the creation of a native lay legal profession, the common law operated autonomously, outside the dictates of the royal family and administration. Between Edward I's land law legislation (1275–95), which in any case was probably drafted by the leaders of the legal profession at the behest of landed society, until the legislation of Henry VIII in the late 1530s and early 1540s on trusts and wills, there is only one English statute that has a significant relationship to judicial change. That was the statute in the mid-fourteenth century on the justices of the peace, and we know that these officers were in operation for several decades before the statute, which was only confirmatory, not creative.

Why the legal profession should have functioned so autonomously we do not know for sure. It may have had something to do with the pluralist guild corporatism of the late Middle Ages. It may have been the consequence of the monarchy's overinvolvement in overseas wars through most of this period. In any case, the common law was left to develop not only its forms of land law action but whole new branches of private law, such as tort or liability for personal injury. These new areas of the common law were developed in collaboration between the judges and the senior barristers, from whose ranks the bench was drawn. They also developed an elaborate form of adversarial pleading that might look to later generations of the nineteenth and twentieth centuries as rigidly overformalized and as sacrificing the law as substance to judicial procedures but that, as Maitland insisted, were indeed intrinsically functional and rational if the cases are closely read.

What this elaborate legal and structural assemblage also engendered was a cast of mind, a cultural mentality that was carefully communicated in the Inns of Court and the many years of apprenticeship required before entrance to the bar. Whatever else the common law fostered, it created a durable culture, an identifiable way of looking at human behavior that was perpetuated down through the centuries and spanned the Atlantic. The main qualities of the common law mentality were a high degree of autonomy from governmental dictates and royal politics; proclivity to adversarial competition; the protection of wealth and access to legal redress only for those who could afford the steep fees or retainers; a reluctance ever to close a civil action completely, always leaving open the at least marginal opportunity to recover from adversity at the bar; a veneration of property as the basis not only of wealth but of status; a determination to pass on through many family generations both wealth and status; a perception of government not as a sacred authority but as an instrumental facility to provide a level playing field in juristic competition; a general disdain for clerics and professors and a diurnal obliviousness of the sufferings and impotence of the poor, yet not so inflexibly as to drive these underprivileged groups outside the procedural defenses of the law into oppositional communities. These qualities are clearly identified in Pollock and Maitland.

We can see here as early as the beginning of the Hundred Years' War—fought by kings and nobles with a hyperaristocratic temperament and value system—the culture of capitalism and affluent individualism. When eventually in the 1630s monarchy and church appeared to turn aggressively against the culture of the common law, the disciples of Sir Edward Coke, the leader of the bar, believed they had no alternative but to rally other disaffected groups—evangelical Protestants, small farmers, impoverished gentry, and artisans, with whom they did not normally associate—to obstruct and oppose the royal administration. Out of the ensuing commotion in the House of Commons (1640–42) came the English Revolution.

That well-known story is not as important for American law as the relatively unruffled revival of the culture of the common law in the late seventeenth century and its transmission to British North America. Although in the polemical outburst that preceded the American Revolution, the colonists and their supporters in Britain sometimes claimed to be the true successors of Sir Edward Coke and the common law, in fact, the American Revolution was ideologically much more inspired by an alternative culture immediately arising out of Scottish philosophy and the French Enlightenment. This alternative culture can be distinguished from common law traditions of historical continuity and adversarial competitiveness. It stemmed from the civic humanism emerging out of the Italian Renaissance of the early sixteenth century and focused on the neoclassical idea of republican civic virtue. The historian of this intellectual tradition, which competed with the common law culture in the mind-set of the American Revolutionary era, is John G. A. Pocock, a brilliant New Zealander who has taught at Johns Hopkins University for two decades. Pocock's first book on common law mentality in early-seventeenth-century England was directly inspired by Maitland. But his more recent, celebrated work has tried to unravel the implications of the "Machiavellian moment" of civic humanism and republican virtue in early modern Europe. Following Pocock, we can perceive an alternative tradition to that of the common law—a cohesive, cooperative, consensual mode of public discourse among a well-dedicated egalitarian elite instead of the common law's contextualization of adversarial competitiveness, social hierarchy, protection of property rights, and devotion to old forms of judicial actions. In the 1760s and 1770s the neoclassical ideal of republican civic virtue, immediately transmitted to America through Scottish philosophy and French Enlightenment, slowly heated up into revolutionary utopianism.

Thus, while the leaders of the American Revolution claimed they were going to war to protect the good old common law from tyranny, in fact the foundations of their radical thought lay more in the alternative culture ultimately derived from Renaissance humanism. This alternative culture fostered a temporary retreat from English political historicism. Confidence in the benign continuity of English law and Parliament for half a generation was replaced by a universalist rationalism and apocalyptic meliorism. It is the interim rupture from English historicism that made a revolutionary temperament possible for a decade or so in British North America.

The structural force of the common law mentality rapidly reasserted itself after the Federal Union was established, and it already exercised some influence on Madison and the framers of the Constitution in 1787, with even more impact on the First Ten Amendments of 1791. The common law's proclivity to an inherited English tradition of national centralism, its insatiable love of property (in a country pursuing the greatest land grab in history), its incomparably subtle intertwining of procedure with juristic substance, its bias toward the affluent without totally depriving the rest of society, and its grant of the flexible power of innovation to bench and bar—all these characteristics of the common law culture, structurally perpetuated from the Maitland's Middle Ages, were contextually functional in the early American Republic. An immensely powerful cultural heritage, that of the common law, would in any case have worked deconstructively on the rationalist and egalitarian legacy of the American Revolution, but the social circumstances of the time enhanced and facilitated the common law revival.

Maitland showed us that the common law was a complex and unique judicial and cultural structure. Its language and concept formations retained a residual public ethic—at times quite visible, at other times almost subliminal—of medieval order and moral restraint at the same time as it served as the incubus of competitive market capitalism that constantly stretched and tested the confines of a traditional code of behavior. In the past quarter of a century we in the United States have become acutely conscious of this ambivalence and polarizing tension central to a social existence shaped by common law mentality and critically dependent upon the legal profession for problem solving, collective stability, and individual security.

To put it another way, Maitland created for us a functioning model of civil society, the distinctive quality of Western civilization, particularly in the English-speaking world. Others have found the foundations of civil society in the classical or Thomist philosophical traditions. Maitland did not entirely exclude these sources, but he posited the base of civil society in the mentality and institutions of the common law. By "civil society" is meant a legal order that allows the mainly free operations of a myriad of corporations and communities, as well as individuals, within the framework of the state. The authority of the state over these subpolitical institutions and the populace is greatly limited by the due process of law and the power of bench and bar, and it is to the latter that corporation, community, and individual turn for normal security of life, liberty, and property. The social and economic condition of England and its successor states abroad, particularly the United States, lies, therefore, mainly in a lawful rather than in a political order. This is the Western idea of civil society that the countries of Central and Eastern Europe, burdened by long histories of successive centralizing and overly privileged authorities, are now groping toward.

What Maitland was able to do was to extract from the Middle Ages a view of legal order and the role of the judiciary and the legal profession that has remained a widely perceived theory of common law juristic functions and, more broadly, the foundations of the theory of civil society. No medievalist of the twentieth century succeeded in putting his invention of a segment of the medieval world to more practical and continuing social use. In retrospect, Maitland fully achieved his ambition when he was a Cambridge undergraduate of making an enduring contribution to political science.

As a master of sociological jurisprudence and as a functionalist interpreter of politics Maitland, if he were alive today, would approve the insights into the workings of the higher levels of British government offered in the popular TV comedy program *Yes, Prime Minister*, mainly written by Antony Jay, a veteran political television producer and journalist. Maitland's study of how Parliament functioned in the year 1306 was fully in accord with the perception of Parliament now offered in *Yes, Prime Minister*. Parliament was a tool of the king's ministers, Maitland believed, an instrument for the better functioning of centralized law and administration rather than in any way an autonomous body and the legislative voice of the people.

Maitland was the first historian to examine closely a record of a medieval parliamentary session and analyze the business of what was done there. Previous writers on early Parliaments, like William Stubbs, had used only the writs summoning representatives of the county courts and the borough councils as well as individual invitations from the king to members of the nobility. Stubbs hypothesized from there, imagining the actual business of a parliamentary session and stressing the legislative function of Parliament and its supposed necessary constitutional role in approving new royal taxes on income and personal property. Maitland's examination of the parliamentary record of 1306 showed, however, no consent to taxation and no significant legislation by the representatives of county and town. Furthermore, "Parliament" began before these gentry and burgesses got there and continued after they went home two or three weeks later. Parliament, Maitland concluded, was merely a special meeting of the King's Council, composed of his chief ministers and judges, and its business was normally judicial and administrative. The knights of the shire and the burgesses, who after about 1350 consolidated into the House of Commons, were allowed before they went home to present petitions to the chancellor reflecting the interest of their constituents. These petitions were the origin of parliamentary legislation, but the issues they dealt with were nearly always local and mundane: grant a pardon, repair a bridge, etc.

Maitland's image of Parliament again involved, as did his account of the creation of the common law, the projection of himself into the midst of the lawyers who were prominent in the King's Council and into the mentality of these busy attorneys. They were using a special, augmented meeting of the King's Council to get done some unusual business for the crown. There was nothing political, consensual, or even dramatic in the Parliament of 1306. Stubbs had envisaged the Parliament of 1295, for which the writs of summons extensively survive, as a "Model Parliament" embryonically anticipating the great Commons of the Age of Gladstone and Disraeli. Maitland's judicial and sociological insights demolished this anachronistic mythology.

The difference in perceptions of the history of Parliament offered by Stubbs and Maitland reflected their backgrounds. Stubbs was a moderately devout Anglican priest (and later bishop) with a keen sense of long-range tradition that was central to the culture of the Church of England. Transferring this discourse to the political sphere, he had to see Parliament from medieval times as much the same institution as it was in Victorian times: a national legislature and debating society focused on ideological pronouncements and party conflict. There is a powerful nationalist and moralizing flavor to Stubbs's view of Parliament in the later Middle Ages. Maitland came at Parliament the way any good lawyer approaches any institutional operation. He reads the records carefully and tries to unravel how the institution and its principal participants are operating at a particular moment, skeptically putting aside long-range traditions, nationalist sentiment, and moral and ideological assumptions. Maitland's tough-minded modernist propensity to close reading and detailed analysis reinforced his lawyerly deconstruction of the Stubbsian parliamentary legend.

Since Maitland's day and especially since the 1930s there has been a noisy conflict between two views of the history of the English Parliament: those, like Stubbs, who see it as a popular national assembly and those who followed Maitland in seeing it as primarily an instrument of the legal and administrative officers of the crown to get done certain business efficiently and quickly. *Yes, Prime Minister* affirms what the roll call of historians also signals: Maitland's view has prevailed by a decisive margin. In the confirmation of Maitland's theory of Parliament, he has been assisted by a formidable array of political historians, including two British political historians of genius, descended respectively from Vilnius's and Prague's greatest rabbis, Sir Lewis Namier and Sir Geoffrey Elton. Namier's and Elton's talmudic temperaments spontaneously endorsed Maitland's lawyering skepticism about the democratic imaginings of parliamentary constitutionalism.

There is further meaning, however, to the triumph of Maitland's theory of Parliament as an administrative and judicial instrument of the crown rather than as an expression of national popular will, and that is a foreshadowing of the political consensus that runs from Washington through London, Paris, and Berlin to Moscow in the closing decade of the twentieth century. The valuable function of government, we know now, is not to be an arena for irreconcilable ideological polarities and an outlet for passionate debate. The state is there to make the lives of ordinary people secure and comfortable, to maintain a civil society through the rule of law, to provide a framework for what St. Augustine called the peace of men, or, as we would say, personal happiness and creativity. Now with all political passion spent, government everywhere falls into the hands of those who can administer the instruments of state frugally for the common welfare, and this means the necessary power of public-spirited, well-educated bureaucrats and lawyers largely free of ideological fanaticisms. This is what Maitland saw in the meeting of Parliament in 1306—a functional tool for national order and public efficiency in the hands of the great ministers and judges of the crown. And it is what we know the state to be, and should be today. Speeches of ideological fury in parliaments and Congress and the convoluted machinations of fractious political parties, these peculiar phenomena that, in baleful legacy of the unfortunate English Revolution of 1642 and the calamitous French

Revolution of 1789, so fascinated a Victorian like Stubbs and led him to project them back anachronistically into the England of 1300 we know will do nothing for economy, for the arts, for science, for family, for the good things we live by. And Maitland, the man without illusions, the modernist analyzer of how politics really functioned, the cool-eyed social scientist, perceived this truth, too, in the very early years of this century.

CHAPTER THREE

THE NAZI TWINS

PERCY ERNST SCHRAMM AND ERNST HARTWIG KANTOROWICZ

I

OLD HEIDELBERG

It was a warm summer day in 1925 in Heidelberg, the dreamy university town above the banks of the Neckar River in central Germany. In a café near the walls of a seventeenth-century fortress, shaded by trees that may have been as old as the fortress itself, high above the river and the university town below, sat two young and precocious medieval historians drinking Moselle wine. They were Percy Ernst Schramm (1894–1970), always called Percy Ernst in academic circles, and Ernst Hartwig Kantorowicz (1895–1963), always called Eka (he signed his books Ernst H.) by his intimates. They both were handsome men, a little above average in height, thin, hair cropped close, and extremely well groomed. Each wore a nicely tailored coat with a crisp white linen handkerchief carefully displayed in the breast pocket and a tie. Schramm had a small Prussian mustache, carefully trimmed. Kantorowicz always looked as though he had just stepped out of an expensive barbershop, and he probably had.

Percy Ernst and Eka had grown to know each other well in the previous six months. They were entering a friendship and collegial relationship that outlasted Hitler and endured until the day Kantorowicz died in Princeton, New Jersey, in 1963, while Schramm was still living in Göttingen, about 150 miles west of Hamburg, where he had come to the university in 1929. On that dreamy summer day they compared notes on the books they were writing, the seminal works in medieval history in the German language within this century. In Schramm's case it was a study of the reign of the Saxon emperor Otto III, who died in 1002. Kantorowicz was writing a biography of the Hohenstaufen emperor Frederick II, "the Wonder of the World," who died in 1250. Their books exploded like rockets on the staid world of German scholarship and catapulted both of them into full professorships at—for Germany—phenomenally early ages. Kantorowicz's study of Frederick II was published in 1928, Schramm's book on Otto III in 1929. By 1931 they both were tenured professors—Kantorowicz at Frankfurt, Schramm at Göttingen. Of course, Kantorowicz, a Jew, had to leave his chair in 1935 because of the exclusionary Nuremberg laws, but beginning in 1939 at Berkeley, he was to have a glorious career in America, while Schramm became the ornament of the Göttingen humanities faculty and the dean of German medievalists.

Percy Ernst and Eka had a lot in common. They both came from very wealthy families. Schramm's family had been merchants in and around Hamburg for nine generations. In the nineteenth century the Schramms became very wealthy—even more affluent and influential than the family (his own) that Thomas Mann chronicled in *Buddenbrooks*. (Mann's family was located in another great northern port, Lübeck, which descended, like Hamburg, from the medieval Hanseatic League.) Kantorowicz, despite his elegance, was very Jewish-looking. With a prominent nose and his Slavic name there was no disguising the fact that he was descended from Jews on the eastern border of Germany, between Prussia and Poland. His family were the Bronfmans of eastern Germany, very big in the liquor trade. They did not practice their religion, but he thought of himself as a Jew and hated the Catholic Church. Once a year, at Passover, he was moved to comment on this particular holiday of freedom and what it meant to him. Even though Kantorowicz was a Jew and Schramm a Protestant, Eka's personal social status was then a little higher than Percy Ernst's. Schramm's family members were great merchants, very high bourgeois, but Kantorowicz had been brought up in Prussia with the Junker aristocracy. Count This-and-that, Margrave In-and-zu here and there were his adolescent friends. He moved with easy familiarity in the highest ranks of aristocratic society—like another Jew, Marcel Proust, in Paris.

What had brought both men to Heidelberg, a pretty but sleepy university town with a student population in 1925 of about three thousand, 95 percent male, were two formidable medievalists there, Karl Hampe and Friedrich Baethgen, respectively the senior and junior tenured professors of medieval history. Hampe was the grand old man of medieval German imperial history. His textbook on the Ger-

man emperors under the Salian and Hohenstaufen (or simply Staufen) dynasties, early eleventh to mid-thirteenth centuries, was canonical
writ in German colleges and secondary schools. This authoritative
and readable textbook was to go through no fewer than seven editions, the last produced posthumously after World War II by Friedrich Baethgen, whom Hampe had handpicked from among the brilliant
young men at the Monumenta institute in Berlin to be his junior
colleague and ultimate successor. Baethgen never produced the great
book everyone expected him to write, but his omnivorous knowledge
of the sources of late medieval political history not only in Germany
but throughout Europe, and his total recall of the history of the medieval German Empire, virtually hour by hour made him both revered and feared by the younger generation emerging in the 1920s.
If you made a mistake, whether large or small, about the medieval
German monarchy, Baethgen knew it immediately. But Hampe and
Baethgen were relatively friendly, easygoing, paternalistic men who
delighted in having rich young geniuses around them to teach and
guide.

Hampe and Baethgen were thus the magnets that drew Schramm
and Kantorowicz to Heidelberg in the mid-twenties. It was a very
pleasant medieval university town, inexpensive to live in, but far from
the intellectual and political dynamism of Berlin. Yet there was no
one in Berlin in medieval studies to match these two. Paul Kehr at
the Monumenta was engrossed in his institute administrative duties
and had very little time for teaching. The medieval history chairs at
the University of Berlin were held by Erich Caspar and Albert
Brackmann. Caspar, a great scholar (half Jewish and later dispossessed by the Nazis), was remote and withdrawn as he worked on
the very early Middle Ages, engaged in writing his monumental history of the papacy to the death of Pope Gregory the Great (604).
Schramm and Kantorowicz wanted to work on a much later era, the
central and late Middle Ages, and on the First German Empire. The
professor in this field in Berlin was Albert Brackmann, a pale mediocrity, compared with Hampe and Baethgen, and a vain, difficult
person as well, so the two upper-class academic dynamos made their
way to Heidelberg.

Schramm pursued the normal academic route. He wrote his Ph.D.
thesis—a short and insignificant document in German universities,
more like an American M.A. thesis. The Ph.D. entitled its holder to
be only a high school (gymnasium) teacher, a civil servant, or an
archivist. If you wanted a university post, you had to produce and

publish a lengthy (four-hundred-page or more) second dissertation, called a *Habilitationsschrift* ("appointment work"), and this was what Schramm was doing with his study of the reign of Otto III.

Kantorowicz's career was less orthodox. He had a Ph.D.—in Oriental economic history. Now he was writing his biography of Frederick II not as an academic exercise but rather as a popular manifesto. He intended it for the general reader. He would not submit it for academic habilitation. Indeed, in 1928 he published it without footnotes—(even in America today many would think that an unscholarly style). He was not hoping for a chair. He wanted to communicate a message to all educated Germans (the book did sell ten thousand copies in its first two years, a runaway best seller by German standards of the period). He was in Heidelberg, supporting himself from his lavish family resources, to use the library and to get occasional advice on difficult problems of textual analysis from the old master Hampe and the new master Baethgen. In any case, it was the two Heidelberg masters, along with Brackmann in Berlin, who would make the academic judgment on his biography of Frederick II. By talking to Hampe and Baethgen in Heidelberg while he was finishing the text of his seven-hundred-page book, Kantorowicz might anticipate some of their objections. Brackmann was a conventionally conservative political appointee, who hated Jews; no point in Kantorowicz's hanging around Berlin to see him.

Schramm and Kantorowicz reinforced and encouraged each other. Both worked in the tradition of German *Geistesgeschichte*—"spiritual" (cultural and intellectual) history, drawing upon the long tradition of Hegelian idealism in German humanistic circles. But both wanted to put original twists on the old *Geistesgeschichte*. The word *Geistesgeschichte* has no equivalent term in English. It stands for the dominant tradition in the learned humanities in Germany from the 1890s until 1933. It means placing in one's foreground past ideas, theory, and the literary and visual arts and making these spiritual and intellectual refinements, rather than material and social forces, the central concern of the historian. *Geistesgeschichte* is a manifestation of German philosophical idealism and the assumption that ideas and learned traditions that perpetuate ideas have a durable reality and a human value separate from any other aspect of society.

It is in this dominant school of *Geistesgeschichte* that both Schramm and Kantorowicz were trained. Both were interested in the liturgy and court ideology of kingship. Both wanted to make innovative use of art history as source material. Both had an interest in historical personality, trying to find the dynamic person behind the ideas. This was true especially of Kantorowicz, but Schramm also sought to do this. Both had a proclivity to synthetic history, big subjects treated in the grand manner and written in a neo-Victorian mode with verve and eloquence. They had come to these vanguard positions in historical writing by association with two of the vibrant intellectual circles of postwar Weimar Germany—principally the art history school of Aby Warburg, in Schramm's case, and the circle of the poet and visionary Stefan George, in Kantorowicz's.

Aby Warburg was a scion of the old Jewish banking family. He made a cash settlement with his brothers, withdrew from the family business, and set up in Hamburg the first great institute and library for the study of *Kunstgeschichte* ("art history"). Every major art history department in Britain and the United States is today the dual intellectual and professional descendant of Warburg's institute and his method of iconology, looking for the symbolic and topical meanings in medieval pictures and relating these artistic images as precisely as possible to literary sources, especially the Bible, the Church Fathers, and the Latin classics. While still a high school and novice college student, Schramm had studied in Warburg's institute and used his magnificent library, and he imbibed from that ambience a bold sensitivity to the historical value of medieval artistic images.

Schramm was also influenced by Walter Goetz, a medieval historian in Leipzig and one of the few remaining disciples of Karl Lamprecht, who before the First World War had antagonized the humanistic establishment by a call for a more materialistic, environmentally sensitive, social science-oriented kind of history. Not only ideas and political institutions but dress, diet, and other conditions of daily life were, in Lamprecht's view, worthy of historical consideration. Vehemently opposed by the formidable intellectual conservative Friedrich Meinecke in Berlin, Lamprecht and his students had been shunted to the margins of German academic life. Goetz was one of the few Lamprecht disciples ever to get a chair. Lamprecht's materialism and behaviorism clashed with the traditions of idealistic *Geistesgeschichte*, as Meinecke had thundered in crushing Lamprecht. But Schramm saw something worth preserving in the Lamprecht tradition, through Goetz. It led him to a concern with the dynamic symbols of power, a kind of anthropology of medieval rulership through close reading of coronation liturgy and study of pictures and royal artifacts. Schramm wanted to get beyond the humdrum minutiae of political and administrative history to the emotional texture that fostered and shaped loyalty to rulers in the medieval world. He wanted to communicate the actual image of monarchy in the medieval mind. Kantorowicz had the same interest but in a more emotional and polemical way. He sought to reconstruct the excitement that a great medieval king generated among the populace.

Drawing upon the new insights of Warburg and Goetz and the learned mastery of Hampe and Baethgen, Schramm gave humanistic *Geistesgeschichte* a new lease on life. His book on Otto III was an intellectual revolution in medieval studies, and it is as exciting and original today as the day it was published (it has never been translated into English). He never, in the huge array of books he produced over the next four decades, quite reached this peak again. Perhaps Kantorowicz's friendship and direct influence in the mid-1920s gave Schramm an emotional edge he could never recapture.

The Stefan George circle in which Kantorowicz had moved along with some of his high aristocratic friends was much tighter than Schramm's networks and went beyond vanguard learning. George was a flamboyant lyric poet and visionary, who gathered around him a group of rich, well-educated young men (the homosexual tone, whether latent or explicit, was up-front) to cultivate German national traditions and explore high horizons of culture and political revival through great leadership. The leadership principle was strongly prevalent with George and his disciples. This was one of the intellectual foundations of nazism, although the George circle, several members of whom were Jewish, would not in the end be satisfied with the vulgar corporal from Vienna. They were thinking of apocalyptic figures like the great Staufen emperors of medieval Germany. Along with poetry, the George group went in for the writing of romanticized biographies to put models of charismatic leadership before the beaten, confused, and impoverished postwar German people so that the *Volk* would rise again under some Nietzschean and Wagnerian heroic figure.

This is how Kantorowicz came to be in Heidelberg. He was assigned by George to write the biography of the most apocalyptic of medieval German figures, Emperor Frederick II. He was doing it to satisfy his master, George, and to stir the German people to national renewal under some new wonder of the world. This project was sentimental, trendy, even a little idiosyncratic, but not ridiculous or useless in the German ambience of the 1920s.

George's message was an amalgam of Greek classicism with pris-

tine Germanic heroism: "A people is dead when its gods are dead."
Out of the materialism, corruption, and disorder of the Weimar era
a "Secret Germany" of cultured supermen will emerge and take over
power from the unaware lumpen masses, George proclaimed. It is
never easy to translate late romantic German poetry into English, and
George is particularly elusive (or feverish), but this gets close to the
original:

> Who then, who of you brothers
> Doubts, unshocked by the warning,
> That what most you acclaim, what
> Most you value today is
> Rank as leaves in the fall-wind.
> Doomed to perdition and death!
> Only what consecrated earth
> Cradles in sheltering sleep
> Long in the innermost grooves,
> Far from acquisitive hands,
> Marvels this day cannot grasp,
> Are rife with the fate of tomorrow.
> [Transl. O. Marx and E. Marwitz, 1949.]

Whatever we may think of this is colored for us by what happened
in the 1930s. Whether the triumph of nazism was a fulfillment of
George's vision or a grotesque perversion and betrayal of it has been
debated since the thirties, and there is no resolution to this issue. To
the young Kantorowicz, George was the guru who saw the truth and
foretold the future. If George wanted a biography of Frederick II as
part of his visionary program of German renewal, Kantorowicz would
do what he was told and produce it and write it in accordance with
the leadership principle and the late romantic excitement that George
generated.

What is important for medieval studies is that Kantorowicz read
all the voluminous published sources on Frederick II, mastered all
the modern literature on the Staufen dynasty, and used modern
scholarly research on the medieval empire and papacy. He applied
his incredible linguistic ability and his deep knowledge of the Middle
East and the Orient to put some new angles into the old Staufen
story. He then wrote the most exciting biography of a medieval monarch produced in this century. It has aged very well. It still has power
to stimulate the mind and stir the blood. Its learning and insight are

phenomenal. If Kantorowicz were alive today to do a new edition (there has never been an American paperback), and if he stuck with the assumptions and goals he had in mind in 1925, he would have very little to do in bringing out a revised edition—maybe change about seventy-five of the seven hundred pages.

Schramm and Kantorowicz were medievalists of unsurpassed erudition. But they were not antiquarians. They were very present-minded. They were trying to communicate something highly relevant to the Germany of their day. They did this with great style and confidence, which derived from their wealth, the supportive intellectual networks they belonged to, the fortunate scholarly association with Hampe and Baethgen, and especially the encouragement and strength they gave each other as they worked away in old Heidelberg and drank white wine under the walls of the old fortress on quiet summer days.

II

IN HITLER'S SHADOW

The German professors had long prided themselves on their academic freedom, their separation from the vulgar world of politics. There had always been an element of false supposition in this consciousness of academic freedom. The German universities were thoroughly state-funded institutions, and the minister of education in each territorial state had the prerogative of making the final selection for each tenured chair out of three candidates proposed by an academic committee. In practice this academic system meant the virtual exclusion, before the era of the postimperial liberal Weimar Republic in the 1920s, of even the moderate left. It also meant rigid prejudice against appointment of Jews, especially in the humanities faculties, although again in the 1920s some change in that direction was visible. But even in the 1920s the German professors were overwhelmingly Christian (Protestant or Catholic, depending on the religious majority in the territorial state where each of the two dozen universities was located) and rightist or centrist in politics. There was no complete freedom from politics, but a tenured German professor, who had the salary and social status of a Cabinet minister (his wife could put on airs, calling herself Frau Professor Dr. Schmidt), was usually not involved in or very interested in politics. This freedom from politics central to the old tradition of German academic freedom became much harder to sustain in the 1920s as a new political tide slowly engulfed the campuses.

First there was the issue of the liberal democratic but unstable Weimar Republic itself, hastily created in 1919 after the kaiser abdicated and fled and a Communist revolution in Berlin and Munich had been suppressed. (The capital was still intellectually vibrant Berlin. It was called the Weimar Republic because it was in Goethe's provincial city that the new liberal constitution was drawn up in 1919.) Most German professors were hostile to the republic. Friedrich Meinecke, Lamprecht's antagonist, was a conservative humanist as a scholar. He was, however, one of the few outspoken supporters of the Weimar regime. He called himself "a republican of the head"— that is, there was no choice; it was reasonable to support the Weimar Republic. But most of the German professors regarded the new republic with disdain. They thought it tawdry, unstable, impoverished, a product of betrayal and failure in the war, its politicians corrupt and vulgar. It was held to be alien to the historic German spirit. The professors longed for the return of the glory days of Bismarck's empire in the 1870s and 1880s (there was in fact a flurry of laudatory Bismarck biographies published in the 1920s). The academics felt humiliated by the British, undermined by the French, threatened by the Soviets. They wanted the return of heroic leadership or at least strong leadership to restore Germany's destined greatness. The twentieth century was supposed to have been Germany's century. In 1914 German science, humanistic scholarship, medicine, and technology were the best in the world. Now the century was turning out bad. There was an inevitable yearning for the glories of the imperial past.

This, then, was the dominant mood among the German professors in the 1920s. When the Nazis became the largest party in the national parliament in 1931, there was concern but also hope in academic ranks. Perhaps strong leadership would come now. Even if Hitler was not exactly what was wanted in the way of a leader, he was better than that motley crew of liberals, socialists, Jews, and alleged adventurers who made up the Weimar governments. When old President Paul von Hindenburg calamitously made Hitler chancellor in 1933 and the Nazis, through their control of the Ministry of Justice and the secret police seized power and proceeded to eliminate their opponents and declare a new thousand-year Reich, the great majority of German professors either applauded or stood mute and waited to see what would happen.

Some were delighted, others embarrassed that Jews were quickly booted out of faculties, and Jewish professors and doctoral students fled en masse into exile—to France, Britain, Palestine, and, especially after 1936, to the United States. Hitler's New Order was accepted as readily in the universities as elsewhere in German life. As guardians of the national spirit professors turned out to be nothing special. There was some concern, even in Nazi governmental circles, that so many physicists and mathematicians turned out to be Jews and suddenly departed. In spite of all the blabber about Einstein's "degenerate" Jewish physics, the loss of him and the exclusion of other Jewish scientists obviously hazarded harm to German technological and military potential. But there was confidence that this would be rapidly overcome. As for Jewish humanists—historians, philosophers, art historians, literary critics—they shouldn't have been given chairs in the first place, it was widely affirmed. As Jews they could not reach the true German spirit from within; they were, after all, rootless cosmopolites. Nobody ever took a poll of German academics, but in 1935 at least 85 percent might have assented to this view, although some with inner misgivings. In all German academia only one Nobel physicist who was a Gentile left of his accord—Erwin Schrödinger, who went to Dublin. And even he returned—to Austria—for a while. Among all the historians only one who had no Jewish blood or Jewish spouse chose to leave in protest against Hitler—young Theodor Mommsen, Kantorowicz's friend and holder of a great name. Mommsen's grandfather of the same name had been Germany's greatest Roman historian. Young Mommsen, who was also a nephew of the sociologist Max Weber, went to the United States.

All the other exiled German historians left between 1933 and 1936 because of racial laws, not voluntarily: Kantorowicz, Wilhelm Levison, Hajo Holborn, Felix Gilbert, Hans Rosenberg, Hans Baron—a very distinguished group indeed. It was anti-Semitism, not, in fact, their political commitments, that made most Jewish professors in German universities anti-Nazi. This is not, of course, what they said when they reached Britain or the United States. And many of them rolled back into Germany in 1945 as American intelligence officers assigned to denazify the German universities! No wonder no German professor from 1945 to 1947 was purged by the American army.

The German professoriat as a whole was sucked into the vortex of nazism partly for ideological reasons but mostly because its members were too unworldly, naive, timid, lazy, and selfish to resist the Nazis. Even Meinecke, who could have obtained a chair in any country in the world, did not budge from Berlin. Late in 1945 he published a book on nazism called *The German Catastrophe*. That wasn't hard to do when the British and American armies already occupied West Germany. He had said nothing in public during the twelve-year Hitlerian Reich, not even against the Holocaust.

The second way in which the surrounding political tide engulfed the German universities in the late 1920s was through the students. There are strong parallels between the 1960s in German as well as American universities and the 1920s in the Weimar era campuses. In both eras, highly organized groups of politically active students—in the 1960s on the left but in the 1920s on the far right—exercised a severe impact on the educational scene. In the Weimar universities, well-funded, well-organized groups of students carried out propaganda and terror, making life miserable for the small minority of liberal and Jewish professors. Historians still dispute how many students really belonged to these Nazi campus organizations; estimates range widely from 15 to 40 percent of the student body. (There is a similar mystery about how many members campus leftist organizations really had in the 1960s, in both the United States and West Germany.) In any case the Nazi students powerfully affected the university ambience, just as the leftist groups did in the sixties. Professors were afraid of them; rectors sought to appease them with compromises—we know the scenario well. Militant students created an environment in which far-right and racist groups engaged in recruiting for Nazi organizations on the campus. Politicization along Nazi lines then crept slowly into scholarship and teaching. As in the 1960s, ideologically committed or simply opportunist or fearful professors supported the student militants.

As soon as the Nazis came to power, academics of distinction— the famous philosopher Martin Heidegger at Freiburg, the historians Albert Brackmann at Berlin and Adolf Rein at Hamburg—leaped into the fray, making pro-Nazi speeches and giving courses infected with Nazi propaganda. Probably Heidegger soon regretted what he had done, but Rein and Brackmann persisted in their nazification of the historical curriculum, Rein giving laudatory and expectant courses on German imperialism and Brackmann talking enthusiastically about the tradition of medieval German *Ostpolitik* ("Eastern policy") to justify the invasion of first Poland and then Russia.

There is no substantial study in any language of the intellectual and social nazification of the German professoriat (though there are good books in both German and English on the Nazi student movement). Afterward it was thought best not to delve into this sensitive subject in a detailed and circumstantial way, naming names. If you go nowadays to the splendid historical museum in Hamburg, you will see dramatic displays on all periods of German history from the eleventh century down to 1933. Then the exhibition abruptly skips to the 1950s and Hamburg's rebuilding after it was half destroyed by British bombing in 1943 and 1944. The whole Nazi era is commemorated in one small display cabinet stuck in a corner that shows . . . Hamburg under Royal Air Force incendiary bombs. That is the memorial of the whole Nazi era in Hamburg's historical museum! The history of German universities in the Nazi period has not done much better. Even in the 1980s it apparently took courage for a rector or senior professor even to give a public lecture stating there *was* a Nazi period in the German university. Detailed historical accounts of the nazification of the German university are avoided.

The two young German medievalists who in 1925 were preparing their masterpieces for publication, Schramm and Kantorowicz, both were far-right in outlook, and this despite Eka's being very visibly a Jew. Hitler's shadow fell upon them ideologically and politically. They were swallowed up in the demonic turmoil, as were so many others. This was the dark, almost inexplicable moment of the German soul. These two learned, sensitive humanists became involved fundamentally, centrally in the Hitlerian story. Kantorowicz in the end was lucky to get out with his life. Both he and Schramm got out with their reputations and careers intact, although Schramm had a few anxious months when the British army occupied Göttingen in 1945.

Göttingen in 1933 had probably the most distinguished physics and mathematics faculties in Germany. Since close to half of them were Jews, there was a radical diminution of quality in the next three years. Schramm said nothing, nor did he protest when Aby Warburg's prime disciple in art history, Erwin Panofsky, was evicted from his position at the recently founded University of Hamburg and had to seek refuge at New York University, where the prestigious Institute of Fine Arts is today Panofsky's memorial. We don't know how regretful Schramm was even at the sight of Warburg's great institute and library moving to London in 1931. There is no sign that Schramm grieved over the Hitlerian scourge upon German science and humanistic learning. Instead he devoted himself to writing a history of the medieval English coronation, and in 1937, when the new king, George VI, was crowned, he presented it obsequiously to the royal family and the British aristocracy in a hastily arranged-for English translation. It is Schramm's weakest book, the only one that is sloppy and error-ridden. Later, when two American medievalists pointed out these errors, Schramm with characteristic gentility and rectitude politely acknowledged their contributions.

The History of the English Coronation shows that Schramm was one of many German academics and upper-class people who hoped that the New European Order would not renew the devastating confrontation of the two alleged Aryan/Nordic peoples but rather that world power could peacefully be divided between Germany and Britain at the expense of other countries. This is what Hitler indeed offered Churchill in June 1940 after he let the beaten British army escape— without its weapons—at Dunkirk. Peace with honor and pieces of the French Empire is what Hitler offered the new British prime minister, Winston Churchill. It is to Churchill's eternal credit that although his fiscal advisers told the aristocratic prime minister that to continue the war against Germany would mean the elimination of Britain's financial reserves and would occasion second-class status after the war, even if Hitler were defeated, Churchill fought on. It was Britain's finest hour, the highest moral sacrifice of a nation in modern history.

Schramm was disappointed at Churchill's intransigence, as were many Anglophilic upper-class Germans. He had visions of another book perhaps, pointing out the close family ties between the medieval Plantagenet rulers of England like Henry II and the Welf (Guelph) dukes of Saxony. But he had not much time to grieve over this historical disappointment. When war came in 1939, Schramm did not avoid being recruited as an officer attached to the General Staff, the executive command group of the Wehrmacht. How he must have exulted over the German army's victories in France and elsewhere in the spring of 1940! The highest glories of the medieval Empire were now re-created. Major Schramm had a variety of high-level assignments in Berlin that brought him into contact with the generals glowing in victory and with Hitler himself. He had plenty of opportunity to begin close scrutiny and judgment of the Führer.

On January 1, 1943, Major Percy Ernst Schramm commenced a scholarly assignment of the highest importance in the German war effort. He was made the official historian of the General Staff of the Wehrmacht, the keeper of its daily diaries of command decisions and oversight of events. Unfortunately his appointment coincided with the defeats of the eastern front and the slow decline of Germany's military fortunes. It turned out that he was to be an official historian of the downfall of the Third Reich, but he nevertheless pursued the job with his usual scrupulous care. Since Hitler had taken over personal command as head of the army, Schramm spent several months at Hitler's army headquarters bunker in East Prussia. Schramm was in Hitler's presence almost daily and able to jot down the leader's table talk remarks, as Martin Luther's eager disciples had taken note of the great pastor's religious and scatalogical table talk in the sixteenth century.

In retrospect, Schramm cannot be condemned for not joining the resistance alongside the pathetic White Rose student rebellion in Munich in 1943; the theologian Dietrich Bonhöffer, who in 1940 gave up a position at the Union Theological Seminary in New York to return to death at the hands of the Gestapo in 1945; Count von Stauffenberg and a dozen or so aristocratic army officers who tried and failed to assassinate Hitler on July 20, 1944, and ended up on the Gestapo's meat hooks; and even Schramm's own sister-in-law, who died as a member of the resistance. The historical record, however, shows Schramm at the other extreme from the resistance martyrs. Whatever his secret reservations about Nazi behavior may have been, they did not inhibit him from providing key service to Hitler and his generals and personal attendance upon the Führer. This makes him a prominent Nazi accomplice and in effect a war criminal. There is essentially no difference between him and Albrecht Speer, Hitler's architect and minister of war production, who was convicted at Nuremberg and imprisoned for several years.

It is not surprising that in the summer of 1945, back in Göttingen, Major Schramm, now again a professor, was worried that the occupying British would purge him from his chair. Indeed, he was suspended from teaching for a semester while British intelligence launched an investigation into his wartime career and Nazi affiliations. Schramm wrote hastily to Kantorowicz in Berkeley, asking his old friend to intervene and give Schramm a favorable reference to the British army. Kantorowicz complied, but it wasn't necessary. First the Soviets, then the French and Americans let all the Nazi professors back into their chairs, and the disappointed British officials, who really wanted a careful political review of German professors, let Schramm and others who should have been purged—or even imprisoned—back into their academic positions. By 1946 Schramm had fully resumed his role as dean of German medievalists.

But Schramm could not forget about Hitler. Percy Ernst, the authority on medieval rulership, had sat for many hours in the presence of the most extraordinary political leader of modern Germany, the most dynamic and demonic leader of the twentieth century. He felt he had an obligation to give his impressions of Hitler, to publish a memoir in 1963. This publication created a furor in West Germany because of its ambivalence. By no means was it the usual formal condemnation that now dropped so automatically from the lips of German professors. One would have to say that Schramm was courageous to publish this account (translated into English in 1971 by Donald S. Detweiler under the title *Hitler: The Man and the Military Leader*), knowing the fuss it would kick up in Germany. Was he being faithful to his historical calling to put his recollections before the public, or was he still a devoted Nazi who refused to accept the emptily pious, often insincere condemnations that his colleagues now reflexively engaged in? Was Schramm so driven by guilt that he put himself in some danger in order to punish himself? These explanations for his sensational publication are not mutually exclusive; they all were probably at work in his psyche. It is not surprising, moreover, that a public lecture on Schramm in 1987 by the president of Göttingen, Norbert Kamp, passes over Schramm's wartime experience in one sentence and the book on Hitler in a footnote.

Schramm did provide early in his book a two-page list of German war crimes, including the Wannsee Conference "initiating the deportation of the Jews to the East and beginning their systematic annihilation." And Hitler was ultimately responsible for all these crimes, he notes. But Schramm is not interested in the details of the Holocaust and other crimes. He wants to give us a close-up picture of the leader, and admirable traits are readily evident. Schramm's Hitler is no monstrous psychopath. He is a very human figure:

Hitler kept himself very clean. He washed his hands often. . . . He bathed daily. . . . Hitler required only a minimum of sleep. . . . With his excellent memory, Hitler had an uncommon ability to recognize people. . . . Hitler generally weighed important decisions at length, consciously turning them over and over in his mind in rational terms. In the last analysis, however, he invariably depended upon what he called "instinct"—a word synonymous in his mind with political shrewdness. . . . Hitler saw his particular strength in an ability to simplify complex problems and to think consistently. . . . Hitler never told off-color stories, let alone dirty jokes. . . . He did not want to be better than German soldiers at the front. Since he did not smoke, avoided both coffee and alcohol, and subsisted solely on vegetarian fare, he felt he could look any soldier in the eye in respect to diet. . . . Hitler was not only inland oriented; he was completely rooted within the cultural boundaries of the old Roman Empire. He clung to the civilization of the Mediterranean world and took no part in his followers' grotesque glorification of the Teutons. . . . Hitler hated lawyers. . . . Hitler was inclined to regard financial experts as rogues and villains.

No raving maniac mass murderer here, but a man of admirable traits and intelligent disposition. So what went wrong? Schramm does not explain that. He tells us why Hitler ultimately failed as a military leader—too rigid, not sufficiently willing to take good advice from his generals—but he does not explain Hitler's criminality, except to say that the Führer acted upon pseudo-Darwinist illusions that he picked up from the culture of the early twentieth century. At the end of his candid book Schramm claims that "Adolf Hitler could become the most disastrously fateful figure in German history because there were so many levels to the being behind the opaque mask. . . . The fact of Hitler's historical existence will remain a disconcerting, extreme case of human individuality. Generations to come will reflect on the grim history of the frightful man who for twelve years determined the fate of Germany, and for five brought the earth to tremble."

Schramm does not discuss the complicity of himself and millions of other Germans of his generation in the grim history of that demonic man. Nor does he detail what that catastrophic history was. It is altogether a sanitized, upbeat assessment of Hitler. Schramm could have been writing about a medieval German emperor. Indeed, at times Schramm's memoir of Hitler is uncannily reminiscent of the life of the medieval emperor Charlemagne that his monastic secretary Einhard wrote in the early years of the ninth century. The treatment that Schramm accords to Hitler subtly parallels Einhard's method of depicting Charlemagne—the same dispassionate perspective sprinkled with a few intimate details, the same ambivalence, the same kind of ultimately enigmatic picture. Assuredly Schramm knew what he was doing, what model he was following. He probably got a kick out of doing an Einhard type of biography of Hitler. Maybe the whole thing was supposed to be an elaborate academic joke, a medieval parody, except nobody in the 1960s got the point.

In the summer of 1938, while Neville Chamberlain was preparing to fly to Munich and betray the Czechs, that distant country about which the British knew so little, and Herr Professor Percy Ernst Schramm was waiting to be offered an army commission if and when war broke out, Ernst Hartwig Kantorowicz was living quietly in a small but comfortable apartment in central Berlin, pursuing his research and writing on medieval kingship. Three years before, he had had to leave his chair at Frankfurt, into which he had been sensationally promoted after publication of his best-selling biography of Frederick II in 1928 and the stormy aftermath. In 1930 Albert Brackmann had denounced Kantorowicz in the leading establishment history journal as a mythmaker, a nonscholar who made things up, a romanticizer who did not do honest *Kleinarbeit* ("detailed research"). As best they could, Hampe, and particularly Baethgen came to Kantorowicz's defense. They didn't always agree with what he said, but they both believed that this flamboyant George disciple, this *outré* Jewish aristocrat was not a fake but a man of very deep learning and capable of important insights. Then, in 1931, Kantorowicz delivered a missile that crushed Brackmann. He published an *Erganzungsband*, an appendix volume to his biography, in which for three hundred pages of incredibly dense and often obscure learning he backed up his unfootnoted, popular biography. Whether or not he really could sustain all his statements in *Frederick II*, Kantorowicz demonstrated that he was a scholar of astonishing breadth and depth of learning. He was offered a tenured chair at Frankfurt University; the proposal was like Will Durant or Barbara Tuchman's being offered a full professorship at Harvard. Unlike the fearful, conservative Americans, German academics were not afraid to do unconventional things once in a while. Kantorowicz's far-right political associations helped, too, of course, once an academic committee had put him on a short list before the state minister of education.

Even though he had to leave Frankfurt in 1935, the Nazi government saw to it that Kantorowicz continued to draw his professorial salary. He lived quietly in Berlin, untouched by the Gestapo. This was possible because except for the misfortune of being a Jew (it must be said that when I later got to know Kantorowicz quite well, I never heard him bewail this fate of birth) he was the ideal Nazi scholar and intellectual. Many of his aristocratic friends, Count This and Freiherr That, were now high up in the German government, and even the number two Nazi, Hermann Göring, was an admirer of his book and a friendly acquaintance. The Nazi big shots worked to protect him into the summer of 1938.

Kantorowicz's Nazi credentials were impeccable on every count except his race. He had returned in 1919 from the First World War, in which he had been a very young captain in Turkey, giving advice to the Turks in their successful resistance to the British invasion at

Gallipoli. He found Communists attempting revolution in Berlin and Munich. He forthwith joined the Free Corps, a proto-Nazi terrorist group of far-right officers who engaged in street fighting and assassinations of Reds. Then followed his key membership in the George circle, the most illustrious proto-Nazi intellectual group, and his best-selling biography of Frederick II, which was published with a swastika on its cover. It is true that this symbol, beloved of the George group as well as of Hitler and the National Socialist party, had traditions as an old peace symbol in the Orient, and later, in the 1950s, Kantorowicz was eager to explain away its appearance on the cover of his book in those apologetic terms. But in 1928 everyone in Germany knew that the swastika had become the special Nazi symbol.

And then there was that wonderful book, the most brilliant and fortunate piece of propaganda that Hitler's cloddish and violent followers could imagine, as Kantorowicz expatiated on "German world-rule and world greatness, resting on the qualities of a single man and not upon the people." Who could say this in 1928 in divided, turbulent Weimar Germany and not know that he was feeding the leadership principle and glorifying Hitler? And then the concluding passages of the long book, romantic, lyrical beyond rational analysis, and almost untranslatable even in the hands of Kantorowicz's skilled British translator in 1931:

The weary Lord of the Last Day has naught to say to the fiery Lord of the Beginning, the seducer, the deceiver, the radiant, the merry, the ever-young, the stern and mighty judge, the sage who leads his armed warriors to the Muses' dance and song, he who slumbers not nor sleeps but ponders how he can renew the "Empire." The mountain would today stand empty were it not for the son of Barbarossa's son [Frederick II]. The greatest Frederick is not yet redeemed, him his people knew not and sufficed not. "Lives and lives not," the Sibyl's word is not for the Emperor, but for the German people. [transl. E. O. Lorimer.]

This is a perfect complement to George's visionary poetry. *Frederick II* constituted a tocsin for militant nationalism and faith in the great leader. Despite his personal distaste for Hitler as inadequate for the role of reborn leader, how could Kantorowicz have not known that he was providing a frenzied feast for Hitler's followers, that he was making a mighty contribution to the Nazi onslaught on middle-class liberalism and the democratic Weimar Republic? Perhaps he thought, as many Jewish professors and businessmen still hoped in 1928, that militant anti-Semitism was just a vulgar intermediary instrument for the Nazis and would burn away. Then he would get his suitable reward and eminence in the Hitlerian regime. Perhaps he was so intoxicated with Stefan George's far-right humanistic mentality that he recklessly didn't care.

Ten years later he knew better. The racism would not burn away in the Nazi regime. It was getting much worse. But he stayed on in Berlin until he was visited in the summer of 1938 by an English friend, the Oxford poet and classical scholar Maurice Bowra, who told him this high-risk nonsense couldn't last. War would come soon. Anti-Semitism could turn into mass murder. Not even Göring could protect him much longer. Kantorowicz packed a couple of bags, left behind his marvelous private library and art collection, and quietly got on the train out of Berlin with Bowra, holding the British visa that Bowra had quickly arranged for him.

Bowra also got Kantorowicz a one-year visiting appointment at Oxford. The year did not go well. The Oxford dons were offended by the German's aristocratic arrogance, enraged by his highly intellectualized kind of history, disturbed by his combining disparate subdisciplines like German, Byzantine, and English history. Brackmann types of claims of fakery and underlying subtle anti-Semitism exploded into hostility and contempt. Leading the critics at Oxford was a young Balliol College don, Richard Southern, the protégé of Frederick Maurice Powicke, the senior professor of medieval history and the head of the history faculty. Among the characteristics that bothered the Oxford dons was the German's persistent overdressing, as if he were always going to have tea with a duchess, rather than the sloppy tweed jacket and baggy flannels that were a don's uniform. Every time he opened his mouth they burst out laughing. His singsong way of speaking seemed ridiculous. It was a German aristocratic affectation—imitating a Chinese mandarin singsong intonation—just as a stutter was the privileged speech affectation of the British aristocracy.

As the days shortened, the rain fell, the long British winter descended on the unheated Oxford rooms, Bowra had to admit to his German friend, whom he so greatly admired, that there was no place for him at Oxford or probably anywhere in Britain. Kantorowicz was for the first time in his life facing money problems. His salary had been stopped when he fled Berlin, and his family's vast business had been confiscated by the Nazis. He took to reading the employment ads in the *Times* of London. There one day he found a small announcement that the University of California at Berkeley was looking for an associate professor in medieval English constitutional history. Kantorowicz was an authority on medieval German history. Medieval England was a field about which he knew almost nothing. But he answered the ad anyway and made claims that he was currently researching the subject of the English constitution and could easily teach it. Fortunately the appointment lay mostly in the hands of a senior professor at Berkeley who was one of Charles Haskins's many Ph.D.'s from Harvard of the 1920s. The Harvard man at Berkeley had never published a line but had the largest private collection of classical phonograph records in the San Francisco Bay Area. He was delighted to receive Kantorowicz's job application. Getting to Berkeley the brilliant and controversial German medievalist was a boon—a target of opportunity, as the entrepreneurial dean said in approval.

Five weeks after he sent the application, Kantorowicz got a cable that he was appointed and should turn up early in September prepared to teach. It was then late in July. After booking a place on a Cunard liner to New York, he headed straight for Blackwell's on Broad Street in Oxford. "I want the best book ever written in English constitutional history," he told the clerk. The clerk could very well have given him Stubbs's *Constitutional History*, still the favorite Oxbridge textbook, but he was a bright young man. He handed Kantorowicz the two volumes of Pollock and Maitland's *History of English Law*. The German took them with him on the boat. He sat on the deck day after day reading, astonished by Maitland's subtlety, learning, grandeur of thought. This man Maitland was very, very good. Why hadn't we appreciated him in Germany? By the time the Cunard liner passed the Statue of Liberty, Kantorowicz knew he would have no trouble with English constitutional history. He arrived in Berkeley in the first week of September 1939, just as the Second World War broke out, and began teaching a week later. He was immediately a smashing success. The California students loved his singsong way of talking, his romantic gestures, his elegant Continental clothes, his astonishing erudition in a dozen languages. And he loved Berkeley. They were made for each other.

Berkeley in the war years was a delightful and cheap place. Kantorowicz found a house overlooking the bay and furnished it with locally manufactured rattan porch furniture, which he retained until the end of his life, incongruously using it in his Princeton house down the street from Einstein's in the 1950s. He discovered jugs of California white wine that were ridiculously cheap and almost as good as the vintage Moselle he used to drink with Schramm under the walls of the old Heidelberg fortress. The Berkeley library was astonishingly good. Haskins's student, the senior medievalist with the immense phonograph record collection, didn't publish, but otherwise he did all the right things, including building up the library's medieval collection. And the students—the girls, blond and tanned, and beautiful young men stripped to the waist walking across campus. Germany was far away now. While Schramm sat at Hitler's table in the East Prussian military bunker, Kantorowicz became a Berkeley prince.

In the late 1940s he gathered around him a remarkable group of graduate students, whom he treated as though they were the members not just of a doctoral seminar but rather of a new Stefan George kind of intellectual circle. They sat around his house for hours in the evening, drinking wine and listening to the master explicate medieval Latin texts, word by word. He used each phrase as a signifying key to very complex traditions that stretched back from thirteenth-century Europe to sixth-century Constantinople, to the Roman Empire, to ancient Asia, to a whole international discourse that floated across Asia and Europe over two millennia. No medievalist on this continent had ever given such a dazzlingly dramatic performance. In this way, talking incessantly, showing off a lot, he took a whole year to get through Dante's *Monarchy*, a treatise of a mere 120 pages.

During the first five years after World War II, as American academia resumed its normal pace and rhythm, Kantorowicz worked hard to legitimate himself within the ranks of American medieval historians, who were still mostly Haskins's students from the 1920s, supplemented by a sprinkling of émigré German Jews from the 1930s. Kantorowicz knew that the Haskins establishment would not approve the flamboyant kind of work that had gone into *Frederick II* and that had so angered Albert Brackmann in 1928 and the Oxford dons in 1939. He put his great book behind him, never cited it in his subsequent scholarship, and, if it ever came up in conversation, even with students, absurdly pretended it was a preacademic work of superseded youth. He never even tried to interest an American paperback publisher in a new edition of *Frederick II*. It was finally reprinted in a limited edition by an academic reprint house in 1957.

Kantorowicz believed that the road to academic legitimation in America, even though he was now a tenured full professor at Berkeley who needed no one's good opinion of him, was for him to be as dull as everyone else in the profession. He did not succeed at that, but it was not for lack of trying. He never gave up his elegant way of dressing, and he also retained his aristocratic singsong pseudo-Chinese way of speaking. But he set to work and published a boring standard monograph on some aspects of the liturgy of kingship. The kind of learning that in 1931 he had effortlessly encoded into two or three pages of his appendix volume to *Frederick II* was now excruciatingly expanded into a two-hundred-page scholarly monograph with the usual forest of murky footnotes. He went around to meetings of the genteel Medieval Academy of America in Cambridge, Massachusetts, and Madison, Wisconsin, and read long, dense papers on Roman and canon law. He was after the highest honor of the Medieval Academy, the Haskins Medal, and eventually he got it.

Then a strange thing happened. Kantorowicz suddenly lost his job at Berkeley, became an overnight hero of the American liberal left (what would Stefan George and Hermann Göring have thought of that?), and gained a better job at the Institute for Advanced Study at Princeton—all in a matter of a few months in 1950 and 1951. This was an outcome of the famous loyalty oath controversy at the University of California. The year 1950 was part of the era of the postwar Red scare, the so-called Joe McCarthy era. The legislators of the state of California had lavishly funded the campuses of the state university for half a century and seen them grow during that time from boondock colleges in orange groves and desert crossroads into the finest public university system in the country and, in the case of the Berkeley campus, into an institution that had by 1950 more Nobel prizewinners on its faculty than existed in the whole of British higher education. In the cold war ambience of 1950 the California legislators naively decided that they wanted to make sure their students were not being corrupted by Red teachers, and they imposed an anti-Communist loyalty oath on the faculty. A half dozen faculty members at Berkeley (most probably fearing prosecution for perjury, as in the Alger Hiss case) refused to sign and were fired. Kantorowicz, who was the most prominent, said he was not a Communist. In fact, he honestly insisted that in 1919 he had shot Communists, but signing a loyalty oath, he claimed, was a violation of academic freedom and would set the universities on the downward slope toward what had happened in Germany. A skillful Berkeley chancellor could have easily finessed this unusual situation, but Berkeley's chancellor at the moment was inept, and Kantorowicz lost his tenured professorship and paradoxically, for a former Free Corps assassin of Reds and a proponent of proto-Nazi ideology, found himself the darling of every leftist-dominated faculty club from coast to coast.

As a matter of fact, he was never in danger of unemployment. By law of the new Federal Republic of Germany, Kantorowicz could recover his chair at Frankfurt anytime he wanted, and the German government owed him all his back salary since 1938. But he didn't want to go back to Germany, where he was such a controversial figure and where his ambivalent role in the rise of nazism was well remembered. He had a better prospect right in the good old United States. From 1939 to 1941, Kantorowicz's first two years at Berkeley, Robert Oppenheimer was a professor of physics there. An American who was trained in Germany in the 1920s, Oppenheimer was an aesthete, an amateur philosopher, a flamboyant character in whom Kantorowicz could well recognize a kindred spirit when they encountered each other in the Berkeley faculty club, a Japanese teahouse the size of a football stadium. Now, in 1951, Oppenheimer, after directing the famous atom bomb project, was the director of the Institute for Advanced Study in Princeton. Oppenheimer was urged to bring Kantorowicz to Princeton by Erwin Panofsky, the Aby Warburg disciple who had been ejected from his Hamburg chair in the Nazi era and was also now at the Princeton institute. That Kantorowicz was a close friend of Percy Ernst Schramm, and Panofsky and Schramm both were disciples of Aby Warburg, strengthened Panofsky's attachment to Kantorowicz. Secret conversations on the terms of his removal to Princeton had already been held when the loyalty oath crisis broke. Kantorowicz would likely have ended up at the institute in any case in 1952 or 1953. Suddenly his migration was accelerated and he arrived wearing the unaccustomed halo of academic freedom, the days when he had published a far-right book with a swastika on the cover quietly forgotten.

One who did not forget was the professor of medieval history and the chairman of the history department at Princeton University at the other end of Tigertown from the institute, Haskins's prime protégé, Joseph R. Strayer. He hated everything about Kantorowicz—his Nazi past, his style, his mannerisms, even his current Roman-canonical scholarship, which Strayer early saw was something of a racket. But as usual Strayer sucked on his cigar and said nothing. He tried to avoid having to meet Kantorowicz, and if they happened to be in the same company, after a formal greeting and a frozen smile, Strayer headed to the other side of the room. Kantorowicz noticed this; it hurt him a bit, but after all, what difference did it make?

After being consigned to oblivion by R. W. Southern and the Oxford dons in 1939, he was not going to be depressed by anyone.

Although often erroneously regarded by the media and the public as part of Princeton University, the Institute for Advanced Study is an entirely different institution. The only comparable places in the Western world are the Collège de France in Paris and All Souls College in Oxford—very affluent, completely autonomous institutions that have faculties but normally no students. All three are research institutes devoted to supporting presumed academic geniuses, most of them quite mature, but with a handful of younger ones on the rise. The Institute for Advanced Study in Princeton was founded in 1932 as a refuge for Einstein and other eminent German Jewish scientists with money from the Macy's department store family.

Just about the time the Second World War started in Europe the institute added to its science faculty a division in the humanities—mainly classics, medieval history, and art history. The luminaries in the "historical" faculty were first Panofsky and then Kantorowicz, who, by the time he settled in at Princeton, was fifty-five years old and had only a dozen years to live, although it was not until about 1960 that ill health began to overtake him. He bought a house just down the street from Einstein, furnished it in bizarre fashion with his rattan collection from Berkeley, and lived a quiet, reclusive life of intense scholarship, trying to complete a massive study he had begun at Berkeley on the "theology of medieval kingship."

Most of his circle of handsome young men from Berkeley turned up in Princeton in one guise or another for a year or two at a time. But Kantorowicz made no effort to create a new circle of disciples in Princeton. He had an old friend in the Princeton history department, Theodor Mommsen, who, after spending the war teaching Latin at Groton, was hired by the department chairman, Joseph Strayer in 1946, precisely because Mommsen and Strayer agreed on absolutely nothing about the Middle Ages. Mommsen had worshiped Kantorowicz for thirty years. As far as Mommsen was concerned, it was still 1928 in Weimar Germany and *Frederick II* had just sent the old establishment figures scurrying for cover. It was really the old Kantorowicz, not the new one, whom Mommsen revered. Mommsen occasionally invited Eka and a group of university doctoral students to his apartment, and Kantorowicz, as in the old California days, put on a dazzling display explicating Dante's *Monarchy*. But this was a rare happening and done mainly to feed Mommsen's nostalgia. Kantorowicz was not looking for young disciples anymore.

III
THE IMPERIAL DESTINY

The main focus of the work of Schramm and Kantorowicz was on the ideology of medieval kingship and, beyond that, upon the personality of great kings who functioned within the structure of the medieval theory of kingship. This is what their first, and best, books were about: Schramm's study of kingship in the reign of Otto III, *Kaiser, Rom, und Renovatio* ("emperor, Rome and renewal"), and Kantorowicz's *Frederick II*. All their subsequent works—in the case of Schramm more than a dozen volumes, in the case of Kantorowicz three—were further explorations of medieval kingship.

Why did they concentrate upon the implications of the ideology of kingship rather than upon some other great longitudinal theme in medieval history? For a number of reasons: because they themselves were social and political elitists who wanted to study medieval civilization from the top down; because they lived in the 1920s in a society that had suddenly lost its monarchy and was bereft of its stability and seemed on the verge of chaos, so that the history of kingship satisfied impulses of both nostalgic longing and social healing; and simply because since early in this century kingship and its relationship to papal monarchy and the struggle for order and dominance between kings and popes had become the number one subject among German medieval historians. There had been a pioneering and classic study of the ideology of early medieval kingship published in 1914 by Fritz Kern (translated into English as *Kingship and Law in the Middle Ages*), and Karl Hampe and Friedrich Baethgen had continued these monarchical studies; Schramm and Kantorowicz in their masterpieces of 1928 and 1929 brought this line of inquiry to new significance in works of high humanistic art.

It is possible to see that the conditions of the Second German Empire under Prussian Hohenzollern rule created by Bismarck in 1871 set the course for the traditions of German interpretation of the Middle Ages. This Empire had almost equal populations of Protestants and Roman Catholics, and out of the ensuing tension came in the 1880s a great Kulturkampf (cultural controversy) over the relationship between church and state in imperial Germany and particularly which institutions should control the educational system. Projected back into the Middle Ages, this dispute inspired a study of the emotional pull of kingship in society, of the theoretical justifications for royal leadership in society, and of the way that medieval kingship, especially in the First German Empire, from the late tenth to the mid-thirteenth century, used religious ideas to assert its sovereignty over the clergy and the church's intellectual and cultural resources.

This was the intellectual and political tradition in which Schramm and Kantorowicz were educated. They explored that tradition deeply and brought new insight to it, but they did not fundamentally alter it. They saw no need to do that. For them the problem of kingship was the central problem in medieval history. It also offered a highly attractive alternative to the liberal democratic republic in which they lived from 1919 to 1933, for which they had no respect, and to the communism they detested with all their beings. In terms of twentieth-century political ideology, Schramm and Kantorowicz assumed that the great threat to Western civilization was Soviet communism, which stood for barbarism and materialism as well as alien invasion, and they believed the West had to find a political principle to countervail the Communist threat. If they had grown up in the successful liberal republic of post-1948 Western Germany, they might have seen things differently. There is evidence that in the 1950s Kantorowicz did see things differently, or at least *said* he did, drawn from his American experience. There are no data that indicate that Schramm substantially changed his political views. Back in the 1920s and 1930s both he and Kantorowicz believed that a medieval monarchy, and the idea of the German Empire, were a tradition that, if fostered in terms of modern rulership, could prevail against the Soviet threat.

Both wrote about medieval kingship and the German Empire at the moment of crisis—around the year 1000 in the case of Otto III, the period 1220–50 in the case of Frederick II. There was inspiration to be gained, there were lessons to be learned from these critical periods that could be applied to the era of the Weimar Republic.

The specific traditions of medieval kingship, as perceived by Schramm and Kantorowicz, were those of Rome, Christianity, and Germany. The Roman Empire had a well-formulated ideology and institutions of monarchy, and by the late Empire this was an absolute monarchy. Emperors could not always do just what they wanted to do, of course, but the system operated as though the imperial will were all-powerful; no constitutional mechanism existed to frustrate or modify it. In any premodern absolute monarchy, effective limitations were set by primitive communications networks and by the small size of the civil service, which frequently made it impossible to implement the royal will even when it was accepted as law. The ideology of absolute monarchy was developed out of a Roman law, based on

Hellenistic and Oriental traditions, that held that the people had sur-
rendered their natural powers to the monarch and could never revoke
the surrender.

The greatest contribution of Rome to political thought was the
concept of office. Romans believed in obedience to the office without
regard to the person of the officeholder and that the emperor held the
sovereignty of the state whether he was a good or bad man (or an
effective or an incompetent leader). With the first Christian emperor,
Constantine, A.D. 312, the emperor became the earthly reflection or
image of God, as close to God as a human could possibly be. To
question or resist the Christian emperor was a sin as well as a crime.

The Christian tradition of kingship was ambiguous. It tended to
favor the power and authority of kings, but statements or concepts
that would deny or limit the royal power could be found in the Scrip-
tures. The royalist tradition was based on sacred history, particularly
on the Old Testament story of Samuel's anointing Saul by rubbing
holy oil on his head. Then it became an extremely influential image,
and anointment was a key constitutional ceremony in Latin Europe
after about A.D. 750. David refused to resist Saul when the king be-
haved badly, on the ground that Saul was the anointed of the Lord,
and his refusal was a powerful example to medieval men. The sacred
authority of anointed kings was a self-evident proposition, like the
force of gravity, and resistance to kings was unnatural.

In the New Testament St. Peter said, "Obey God rather than
men," and this text was sometimes used to justify resistance to a king
who went against God. An atheistic king had to be resisted, of course—
but an atheistic medieval king would be hard to discover! A king who
abused the church or clergy might be resisted, however, and indeed,
there was very little opposition to medieval kings that was not sanc-
tioned by some churchman. Alongside Peter's pronouncement that
could be cited to justify resistance to kings, medieval Christian kingship also retained the legacy of St. Paul, with his belief that "The
powers that be are ordained of God." (It is unlikely that this was
intended as a general political statement, but it was usually interpreted as such: Paul was warning the Christians in Rome not to attract persecution by becoming conspicuous.) In general, out of these
contradictory apostolic texts, Christian teaching sanctified kingship
unless a king flagrantly violated God's will. A king who was a violent
person or a war leader was not likely to be treated as a hopeless
sinner, unless his violence was directed against the church itself.

Alongside Roman and Christian ideas of rulership, there was

the heroic tradition of early Germanic kingship. A German king was the equivalent of a chief, a war leader, the best fighter of a group. The epic poem *Beowulf* (c. 800) gives the fullest picture of a Germanic king. Beowulf was a strong fighter who parceled out the booty after a battle. He was the ring giver, or booty giver, for the tribe. The people's survival depended on his strength. When the hero Beowulf was slain, the people's future became a gloomy prospect.

Medieval people achieved a synthesis of these three traditions of kingship suitable to their needs and to their understanding. The medievals never got away from the idea that the core of kingship was personal and that the good king was the best fighter among the people; military skill remained the most important attribute of an effective or respected king. Even the famous Charlemagne, who ruled from 768 to 814, won wide loyalty primarily because he was a great warrior who could give his followers much booty. When he grew older (and less terrifying), his hold over his people began to slip.

After the mid-eighth century medieval kings also followed the Christian tradition of anointment. Society was then being Christianized, and Christian ideas were taken very seriously. Anointment gave stability to the reigning monarch, who was regarded as a priest and thus fairly safe from assassination. Kings tried hard to impress the sacred, priestly qualities of their office upon their people. The Christian tradition was useful, too, in the transference of kingship from one dynasty to another. When a satellite family of great nobles grew in wealth, it could get moral sanction for taking over the kingship through the ceremony of anointment. The church favored royal anointment, which gave churchmen some power over the selection of the monarch and made the church indispensable to royalty. On the opposite side, however, it was almost impossible to oppose a king, once anointed. The church exerted its maximum control when a king died or lost the support of the nobility and it could threaten to transfer its allegiance to a new family, forcing the king to obey its will.

The Roman tradition of kingship, in spite of or because of its sophistication, had little influence until the eleventh century, largely because Roman government had depended on a system of law and a strong bureaucracy that early medieval kings did not have. Early medieval men simply could not conceive of public authority, of a state apart from personal leadership. To the Romans, the will of the emperor had the force of law because the power of the state was behind it, but this was not intelligible in the early Middle Ages.

Insofar as the Roman tradition was maintained in early medieval kingship, it was perpetuated through the monks who guided their royal masters. Being educated in classical history and rhetoric, monks knew that Roman emperors had aimed at grander ventures than mere conquest. They revealed to their kings the image of the Christian emperors Constantine or Theodosius the Great, who were more than war leaders. Considering the conceptual level of the period and the conditions of social life, that was all of the Roman tradition that could be perpetuated in the early Middle Ages. The potential for change in the aristocratic-dominated social system of late-tenth-century Europe came from the elite class itself, particularly from certain great noblemen who wore crowns. Toward the end of the tenth century kingship began to become an important distinction among members of the aristocratic class, even between certain great aristocrats and their cousins or brothers. In 950 kingship involved not much beyond ceremonial vestiges of the Roman style, but kings and emperors soon became more ambitious. Inspired by their clerical advisers' tales of Roman majesty, they discovered that ancient rulers had led large armies, collected taxes, and lived more grandly than ordinary men. The "Roman" emperors of Byzantium still lived in palaces and expected obeisance from their subjects. Very little had yet happened in Europe to make meaningful the concept of majesty. Now ambitious ideas and pretentious claims began to appear, often in advance of actual accomplishment.

The most pretentious of the European monarchs, the ruler with the fanciest title, was the "Roman emperor" of Germany. Challenging the emperor in Constantinople, the German ruler claimed that his title succeeded from the ancient emperors of Rome. In the year 1000 the German emperor happened to be a young man whose Byzantine mother had brought him up on her own ideas of what imperium should mean, and he was not content merely to enjoy better food and wine and clothes than his aristocratic neighbors. Imperium demanded something more substantial.

This, then, in Schramm's account in *Kaiser, Rom, und Renovatio*, was the first importance of the reign of Otto III (983–1002), the Saxon child-king with a Byzantine mother, who spent most of his reign in Rome. Under the guidance of a French cleric, Gerbert of Aurillac, who had previously studied the newly revived Greek philosophy and science in Muslim Spain and whom Otto III and his mother, Theophano, made Pope Sylvester II (taking the name of Constantine's companion pope in the fourth century), an activist monarchy was instituted. It had reforming ideals, this Empire of Otto III; it wanted to change things. This led to the second importance of Otto III's imperial ideal, a harmonious cooperation between pope and emperor, an integration of church and state so as to achieve the universal Christian commonwealth. A third part of the imperial program of renewal was to draw upon the learning of the Muslim world to foster the rise of philosophy and science in Christian Europe.

The Empire of Otto III also stood for unity and peace in Europe. A fourth aspect of the Ottonian-Gerbertian program was to forestall conflict between Germans on the one side and Hungarians and Slavs on the other, such as had already marked the reign of Otto I the Great, Otto III's grandfather, when the Germans began their historic *Drang nach Osten* ("push to the East"). Otto III, Theophano, and Sylvester II wanted not only peace with the Greeks in Constantinople (which Otto II's marriage to a Byzantine princess had been designed by Otto I to foster) but peace on the eastern front. There was to be a universal federated empire, centered on Rome, with the Hungarians and Slavs allowed to live in peace with the Germans, whose ruler, Otto III, they were to recognize as their overlord and to whom they paid tribute. Schramm made effective use of the iconological method that he had learned from Aby Warburg to explain the illuminations in an imperial court edition of the Gospels, in which blazing colored miniatures in the Byzantine style show the kings of Hungary and Poland bringing tributary gifts to the emperor and avowing their fealty. In these pictures the crowned and robed emperor sits on his throne in the Byzantine manner, flanked by German warriors on one side and German and Italian clerics on the other, thereby also symbolizing the cooperation of church and state under the rule of the emperor-priest.

Alas, this noble dream came to naught. Otto III died young, carried off by the malaria from the fetid Roman swamps, followed in a couple of years by Pope Sylvester II. Otto III's successor was his German cousin, a typical warrior chieftain of the North, who abandoned Rome and with it the whole program of renewal and world peace. All the tragedies that Gerbert (famed in the Middle Ages as a magician, for anyone who knew a little bit of algebra A.D. 1000 might be expected to be regarded as such) had foreseen came rapidly to pass: the official schism between the Latin and Greek churches in 1059 (still not repaired); the great "investiture conflict" and war between the German emperor and the papacy that began in 1075 and endured for half a century and flared up again and again in succeeding eras; and the centuries-long duel for survival in East-Central Europe between Teuton and Slav that stopped, perhaps only temporarily, only in 1945.

Thus Schramm's masterful book is a study in great ideals and their failure, of hope and expectations precociously raised and immediately quashed, of good roads not taken. In the fall of 1940 Major Percy Ernst Schramm speculated that as the swastika flew in triumph from Warsaw to Paris, the new order of European unity and cooperation that Otto III and Gerbert of Aurillac had envisioned was now in this unanticipated, wonderful, apocalyptic moment coming to pass. It was true that Hitler was not the ideal ruler, but then neither had been, for other reasons, Otto III. It was up to Major Schramm and other intellectuals and academics in Wehrmacht and Gestapo uniforms, as it had been up to Pope Sylvester II, to moderate the ruler's simple and violent instincts and impose noble humanistic ideals upon society. The great medieval renewal of the European order under a universal monarch could be accomplished at last. Hitler was not the end of European history. He was only a temporary ruler who, having united the lands from the Channel to the depths of Russia, would eventually pass from the scene and leave imperial power in more benign hands. This was Schramm's hope. Alas, the news from the eastern front was bad. Great hopes failed again. Now European renewal and unity died in the ice and blood of Stalingrad.

Frederick II in 1197 inherited a domain infinitely more complex than that held by Otto III. Frederick at the age of three became the potential heir to two of the imperial jewels of medieval civilization, Sicily and Germany. Finally, in 1218, initially with the assistance of his self-appointed guardian, Pope Innocent III, he entered into both his inheritances, at which point the cardinals in Rome soon backtracked and went into a panic that the emperor would become too powerful for the papacy. From his father, the dour political fanatic Henry VI, and his grandfather the majestic Frederick I Barbarossa, Frederick II derived the German imperial crown and the vast Staufen dynastic lands in what is today central Western Germany and Switzerland and even a few pieces of eastern France. From his mother, of the French Hautevilles who had ruled in Palermo since 1016, the Norman Sicilian heiress Constance, Frederick II gained Sicily and southern Italy (then called Apulia), where a mixed Christian, Muslim, and Jewish population lived in rich trading cities and where the grainfields of Sicily, which the Romans had planted, still produced their surplus crops. It was only after Frederick II's death that, in the next three centuries, a succession of French and Spanish rulers mismanaged and exploited the bountiful Sicilian kingdom and slowly turned the jewel of the Mediterranean into desiccated poverty and Mafia-ridden criminality (there is a tradition, still disputed among historians, that the Mafia had its origin in an underground association of freedom fighters devoted to Frederick II's memory who led a successful uprising against the hated French government that replaced the Staufen dynasty).

When Frederick II effectively came into his inheritance around 1220, he had enemies in every direction. The papacy, turning political with voracious ambitions of its own, wanted to rule Italy itself and needed to prevent the emperor from doing so. The northern Italian Lombard cities feared that the emperor would subjugate them, and they provided the money and mercenaries to their papal ally in a great war against Frederick. (How many army divisions had the pope? As many as the Lombard capitalists would give him.) The German princes at home were intent on enfeebling the Empire, making it into an administrative and judicial nullity and, if possible, stripping the crown itself from the Staufen dynasty. So Frederick had a three-front war going for three decades. And all four parties—the imperial court, the Lombard communes, the papacy, and the German princes—unleashed a propaganda war that dredged up every theological, political, legal, and moral argument to support their positions. Experts in Roman and canonical law found ready employment by each party, and it is this maelstrom of propaganda that has been drawn upon so eagerly by recent historians of the Roman and canon law tradition, which is like writing the history of the United States from the television commercials of the Democratic and Republican parties.

The conflicts and debates of Frederick II's era were colored and thickened by the apocalyptic and millenary visions of the southern Italian abbot Joachim of Fiore and the counterculture ruminations of the central Italian guru St. Francis of Assisi and their freaked-out followers. The heavily charged atmosphere of struggle for dominance of Italy and Germany stimulated these apocalyptic and millenary visionaries, and in turn, the propagandists on all sides drew upon the popular speculations and religious fantasies of the Joachimists and Franciscans.

These messianic speculations became attached to Frederick II himself, a handsome, immensely wealthy, powerful and controversial figure. But Kantorowicz sees it in another way: that these apocalyptic millenary and messianic speculations were already circulating in Italy at the time of Frederick's birth and childhood and were then already focused on him and deeply affected his image of himself and his mature behavior. Messianic speculations inspired and molded young Frederick as much as he and his ministers used these mystical thunderbolts to shape the highly charged speculative ambience of thirteenth-century Europe. The messianic prophecy of great renewal through a birth to the house of Caesar that Vergil had put into his *Fourth Eclogue* and that Christians had always regarded as a prophecy of Jesus' birth in the reign of Tiberius Caesar was now turned back into a sibyline prophecy of Frederick's birth. The papacy believed this reinterpretation of Vergil's vision of the great renewal through a royal birth to be not only blasphemous but politically dangerous. Since Empress Constance was forty years old when Frederick was born, miraculous implications of his delivery into the world were not surprising. Since life expectancy was only thirty-five, and menopause came at thirty, for a forty-year-old woman, especially of the upper class, to conceive and deliver a child was as astonishing in the medieval world as those strange events described today in supermarket tabloids.

Frederick acted out his messianic role not only in his political activity but in his brilliant court, where Muslim and Jewish scholars participated and helped him cultivate his own interest in the rudiments of science. He wrote a treatise on falconry that has never been superseded. Kantorowicz gives us an unforgettable portrait of Frederick's drawing into himself and exhibiting all the dynamic cultural forces of his age, raising wild expectations not only in his Empire but all over Europe—even in the mind of Matthew Paris, an English monk writing a history of his era in a monastery fifty miles northeast of London—that a messianic figure and an apocalyptic moment had emerged.

In the end, as in the case of Otto III, Frederick II's story is one of great hopes unfulfilled. Frederick was carried off by dysentery just when he seemed on the verge of triumph over his most durable enemies the Lombard cities. His sons, legitimate and illegitimate, collapsed under the force of the foes of the Staufen house. Twenty years after Frederick's death the Empire had disintegrated and his family line was all but extinct.

But Kantorowicz would not let it rest there. He envisioned a new messianic figure who would take up the great renewal, the apocalyptic moment again. Leni Riefenstahl's film of Hitler at a Nuremberg party rally, *Triumph of the Will* (1936), was a coda to Kantorowicz's call for political messianism. It wasn't the messiah he wanted, but when you call for a messiah, you cannot write out careful prescriptions. The volatility of the thing means you have to live with what you have conjured. The popes of the mid-thirteenth century, with all their mischievous selfishness, saw this danger clearly enough. Kantorowicz did not see it until too late.

Thus Schramm's Otto III and Kantorowicz's Frederick II are parallel works, studies in the ideals of political renewal, and renewals that would each have created a new European order. This is what they both passionately wanted in the late 1920s to replace the materialism, decadence, and democracy of the Weimar Republic and the post-World War I settlement in general. They wanted a revived imperial Middle Ages in their own time. A new European order did emerge by 1940, not exactly what they hoped for, but novel, different, apocalyptic, messianic, triumphant nonetheless. Schramm got on board this demonic flying machine and took his chances. Kantorowicz would have, too, if the accident of his birth to a Jewish family and the Nazis' stubborn persistence in aggravated anti-Semitism had not prevented him. When it was all over, when the messianic movement disappeared in rubble and the apocalypse turned into the fire raids on Hamburg, Berlin, and Dresden, they walked away from it all and went back to more sober-toned academic studies of medieval monarchy. But their inspired books on Otto III and Frederick II remain as products of a special awful place and time. They are singular books. No one has written better on the Middle Ages. We need the inspiration of a disturbed ambience, as well as deep learning, to write such great history.

IV
THE LOST WORLD OF GERMAN IDEALISM

The last important works of Percy Ernst Schramm and Ernst Kantorowicz, as had been the case with their early seminal works, appeared at almost the same time: Schramm's three-volume *Herrschaftszeichen und Staatssymbolik* ("signs of rulership and state symbols," 1954–56) and Kantorowicz's *The King's Two Bodies* (1957). These books may be regarded as the end of an era in the humanistic tradition of Central Europe, the last products of the culture of German idealism in medieval studies.

It is easy enough to condemn and deride the traditions of German idealism, stretching from Goethe and Schiller, Kant and Hegel into the generation of Schramm and Kantorowicz. You can say that this view of the world, this temperament, was abstract, unrealistic, class-privileged, extremely conservative and backward-looking, self-indulgent, and without care for the poor, the downtrodden, the unlearned. There is merit, of course, in such an indictment of the culture of German idealism, but it is a one-sided and unsubtle assessment. German idealism is now a lost world, a superseded culture that had small impact even on the West Germany of the 1970s and 1980s, with its harsh materialism and competitive individuals and its worship of technology and democracy and the art of the deal. But we have to look also at the actual strengths and accomplishments of German idealism and its sociological functions within a time and place to appreciate it. The works of Schramm and Kantorowicz represent a confluence of medieval and modern German idealism.

Schramm's three-volume work on the symbols of rulership is a vast analytical catalog of the physical objects of monarchy, the liturgical, literary, and artistic representations of it, and the theory behind these objects and projections. It is not a task that will have to be done again; it is not likely that anyone will want to try to do so. It teaches the lesson that medieval kingship was a very thick culture—complex, integrated, drawing upon vast and diverse learning and expressed not only in abstract terms but in very specific, tactile, objectified artifacts. Schramm has given us a descriptive anthropology of medieval monarchy. He admires it obviously but leaves us free to make our own judgment. We cannot, however, say that medieval kingship was other than grounded in learning, art, and theory of a very distinctive and elaborated kind. It was the obverse of being otiose, decadent, or effete. It was organically alive and forever flourishing in its creative capacity. It drew upon Roman, Germanic, Christian, and Byzantine sources and incessantly explored, recombined, and expanded these legacies. Any other culture we can think of is not more elaborate, vital, objectively tactile, specifically defined, original, spontaneous in its creativity at the margin while holding on to a persistent and highly functional core.

Kantorowicz's book, which he began at Berkeley in the forties and completed at the Princeton Institute for Advanced Study in the mid-fifties, is similar in its cultural message, although different in its particular purpose from Schramm's encyclopedia of kingship. Kantorowicz begins with Maitland's identification of the English constitution with the idea, articulated in so many words finally in the sixteenth century, that the king has two bodies, a natural body (i.e., a personal one, Elizabeth Tudor), and a political body (Elizabeth, queen in Parliament). Where and how does this idea arise and develop? Essentially Kantorowicz's thesis is that it comes out of theorizing about ecclesiastical forms. Long before the king had two bodies, the bishop had two, his personal and official. But that is not the main burden or value of the book. Kantorowicz wants to show that the common law constitutionalism that we in the United States of America live upon as much as the British comes not from the thin, largely unintellectual judicial stream out of the Inns of Court and the British legal profession but out of the vast panoply of Continental culture, out of Roman, Byzantine, scholastic, and humanistic traditions. What happened was that a simple point of common law was grounded and represented in that thick culture of infinite learning and ecclesiastical and humanistic imagination that made Continental kingship.

English lawyers and politicians, insofar as they were churchmen, directly participated in the culture of the Latin Church, and even if English law separated from Continental Roman law, their residual cast of mind and way of understanding judicial actions still drew heavily on this other Continental culture. After 1300, with the founding of national lay law schools in London, the Inns of Court, nearly all English attorneys and judges were laymen, and the numbers of royal ministers who were churchmen also significantly declined. But through their secondary education in Latin Christianity and through the language and concept formation of the literate culture in general, the Continental traditions of social validation still remained integral to English thinking. Kantorowicz's point has much merit. He argued that the divine right of kings and its ostensible opposite, the English common law idea of the separation of the king's political and personal bodies, arise from the same linguistic and cultural context. This is medieval idealism in extended impact—not vague but concrete, objectified, specific, tactile in its derivations from millennia of learned heritages of the Mediterranean world.

Modern German idealism has the same qualities. Idealist culture was universal and objective. It allowed for a measure of controlled personal creativity but within well-defined boundaries. It speaks a universe of discourse. It does not allow for relativism and autonomous individualism. It is more communal and group-oriented than personal and individualistic. Idealism was learned and highly literary. It stressed cultivation and education (in German *Bildung* and *Erziehung*). It stressed the long view, a great effort to sustain intellectually longitudinal culture stretching over many centuries and in diverse climes.

Idealism was against any kind of radical change and especially was hostile to political upheaval because that could lead to the politicization and corruption of culture and education. While conservative, it was not immobile. Idealism was not a facade for self-indulgence and moneymaking, not at all. Idealism appreciated money for art, education, travels, research, and personal cultivation and for the effective operation of institutions. The purpose of money was to foster intellectual and spiritual glow. Idealism did not believe that the rich are better and that the powerful are necessarily wise. The demands of custom and the obligations to society were paramount over personal satisfaction. Tradition was legitimation. It had prescriptive right and perpetuated social wisdom.

Today this idealism is greatly weakened in Germany's technocratic and materialistic world and similarly is in steady decline elsewhere in Europe. This leaves mediations in culture and social decisions to advocacy groups of the left or right or to charismatic leadership. To an extent, the charismatic option was exercised by Schramm's Pope Gerbert the Magician and Kantorowicz's Frederick, Wonder of the World. But they were restrained by the cultural envelope in which they functioned, comprising everything from the family and responsibilities they had to serve to the institutions of state and church they had to work within.

German idealism, like medieval idealism, kept civilization on prescribed rails and within well-defined boundaries to protect against political conflict and charismatic idiosyncrasy. That this kind of cultural conservatism could not hold back the Nazi combination of terror and charisma may be attributed to the singular crisis in Germany of the post-World War I era. It is a fact that the papacy in the 1230s and 1240s looked upon Frederick II of Hohenstaufen as a similar combination of the forces of evil charisma and unpredictable terror and used every resource it had, both material and moral, to withstand his pursuit of hegemony in Italy. The popes were successful but at cost to the institution of the papacy that sent it into a crisis and decline from which it never recovered. There was no comparable institution or group in Germany in 1930 that had the determination and resources to combat the rise of Hitler. The German professoriat might have been such a group, but it lacked the leadership nexus, collective institutions, and even a strong consensus to undertake this struggle.

Even the best of the academics, like Schramm and Kantorowicz, were too ambivalent about nazism, too intrigued by its penumbra, to focus their attention on this issue.

The cultural costs were incredibly high. West Germany recovered materially in the 1950s and 1960s from the twelve-year Reich, but it has not recovered morally and psychologically. Essentially the culture of German idealism was a victim of the Hitlerian era. It survived in severely attenuated form after 1945. Nor is it surprising that medieval studies, and the central place they played in the German humanities, also never recovered from the Hitlerian episode. Medieval studies today do not enjoy the pride of place they occupied in the German universities in 1930. Their place has been taken by contemporary studies. The German academics now are good at political science, literary theory, and economics, but their contribution to the study of the Middle Ages since the war has been far below the level of quality enshrined in the seminal works that Kantorowicz and Schramm published in the late twenties. The confidence and cohesion of German medieval studies represented by the focus on kingship and attaining its pinnacle in the work of Percy Ernst and Eka are no more.

German medievalism was integral to the inherited culture of German idealism. That was ruptured in 1933, and the lost ground has not been recovered. Nor is there any sign of great interest in trying to do so. The best humanistic scholarship is a fragile and special thing, tied to a particular place and time. Heidelberg is still there; it suffered no bombing in the war, and it looks much as it did when Schramm and Kantorowicz sat under the old fortress walls in 1925, drank Moselle wine, and talked about their forthcoming books. But everything else in Germany has changed.

Insofar as German idealism has found a transplanted home, it has been in the United States, although between 1968 and 1988 these humanist outposts were reduced by the onslaught of leftist doctrines of various sorts, usually of French provenance. The traditions of German idealist culture are best preserved in medieval studies by Karl F. Morrison, now the holder of a research chair at Rutgers University in New Jersey. Morrison was a scion of the Mississippi gentry, right out of Faulkner country, who found his way to Cornell University and was trained by Kantorowicz's friend Ted Mommsen.

Of the leading American medievalists of his generation, Morrison has remained closest to the traditions of the great German idealist school of the 1920s *Geistesgeschichte*, in a long series of thick books on medieval theology and social thought. In 1982 Morrison could still speak of *Geistesgeschichte* in enthusiastic terms that had long been blown away in West Germany by the succession of the Nazi calamity, postwar materialism, and the leftist orientation of the German humanists after about 1965. Morrison said that "the principles of *Geistesgeschichte* taught that the historian performed this task [of recovering the vital signs of a past culture] by re-living the aesthetic reactions that he was studying; that is, by an empathic recovery of, and participation in, the past. In this act of recapitulation, he could achieve a historical synthesis—a vision of. . . . 'the total system of ideas charged with emotion that explains an historical movement.' "

I confess that I do not see the *Geistesgeschichte* of Schramm and Kantorowicz and the other German masters in such a benign and positive manner. I look at them from a more sociological, less philosophical perspective, and I am more ambivalent about the German cultural heritage in medieval studies, as elsewhere. But I am genuinely glad to see the faith of German idealism preserved in Morrison's work and the great medievalist German tradition perpetuated through him to a new generation of American students. Possibly something very good will come of that.

CHAPTER FOUR

THE FRENCH JEWS

LOUIS HALPHEN AND MARC BLOCH

I
FLIGHT AND RETURN

June 14, 1940, was the worst day in modern French history. That was the day Hitler's army entered Paris triumphantly. The aged conservative general and new head of the French government Marshal Henri Pétain made a humiliating surrender. With the loss of only ninety thousand soldiers, the French Army had suffered total defeat. Hitler was the master of France, whether the officially occupied zone of the North and East or the so-called unoccupied zone in the South and West under Pétain's Vichy administration. Ten million French people fled before the Nazi armies to the unoccupied zone, where despite the Pétain government's close collaboration with the Nazis, they hoped they would be safer. Bordeaux, a city of two hundred thousand, ballooned in a few weeks to eight hundred thousand people. The roads, towns, and even farmland villages received these refugees with varying degrees of grudging hostility and discomfort.

Among those who fled south and west were large numbers of Jews. In 1940 there were about three hundred thousand Jews in France, fewer than 5 percent of the population. Two thirds of these Jews were French citizens who had gained citizenship during the French Revolution, and in many cases their families had been there for several centuries and were thoroughly assimilated into French culture. They intermarried frequently with Catholic and Protestant families and played prominent roles in commerce, banking, industry, the arts, and the learned professions, including science and the humanities. The other third of the French Jews were recent immigrants, since World War I, including refugees from Hitler, and most lacked citizenship. These noncitizen Jews were soon rounded up by the French

118

police, whether in the occupied zone or in the Vichy territory, and most of them ended up in Auschwitz. By 1943, when the Nazis took over direct control of the whole country, leaving the Vichy regime in place only as a puppet to the occupying power, French citizens from old Jewish families also fell victim to deportation eastward in cattle cars to the death camps. The exact figures are undetermined, but close to a third of French Jews perished during the German occupation.

Two Parisian Jews did not flee immediately when the Nazi tanks rolled into Paris in June 1940. They were the two most prominent medieval historians on the Sorbonne faculty of the University of Paris: Louis Halphen (1880–1950) and Marc Bloch (1886–1944). Halphen was the leading authority on the emperor Charlemagne and French history between 500 and 1000. Bloch held the chair of economic history, in which capacity he taught a variety of courses on world economic development, including a course on American economic history, but he was known mainly as France's expert on the medieval rural economy and on feudal society between 900 and 1250.

Halphen and Bloch were momentarily allowed to continue teaching by agreement of the French authorities and the German occupying power in recognition of their outstanding "scientific" services to the French people. But they, too, made their way south, first Bloch toward the end of 1941 and Halphen shortly thereafter. They relocated in southern universities, not without difficulty. These provincial universities were underdeveloped, poorly funded, already staffed, with little in the way of flexible resources to welcome the great names from Paris. In Bloch's case, his difficulties were compounded by the personal hostility toward him by the dean at Montpellier, where he relocated to teach. The dean was Augustin Fliche, a conservative Catholic medievalist, one of whose books Bloch, in characteristically outspoken fashion, had severely criticized. Halphen relocated in Grenoble, on the edge of the French Alps.

By 1943, as the Germans took over running the whole country and prepared for the inevitable Allied invasion with increasingly violent and repressive measures, Halphen and Bloch were gone even from these academic refuges, as uncomfortable as they had been. Halphen fled into the mountain fastness of the French Alps and hid there in a tiny village from the French police, who were relishing their job of finding Jews to send to Auschwitz. He did not return to Paris until November 1944, three months after the Allied liberation of the metropolis. Bloch's movements are harder to trace. He explored the possibility of emigrating to America, to which the Parisian anthropologist Claude Lévi-Strauss had already fled, through the French West Indies, to the New School for Social Research in New York. Bloch finally decided not to leave his country. Together with two other scholars of Jewish background, he issued a manifesto declaring the obligation of all French Jews to uphold "the value of the civilization to which we remain passionately attached. . . . The French people is our people. We do not value any other." Shortly before or after issuing this statement in 1942, Bloch made contact with the resistance. He became editor of a leading underground journal. By the latter part of 1943 he was actively at work in the resistance. Many French intellectuals and academics after 1944 claimed to be heroes of the resistance but actually joined late and did little. For instance, André Malraux, the novelist and art critic and later Charles de Gaulle's minister of culture, until early in 1944 relaxed in his mistress's villa on the Mediterranean and drank out the wine cellar. Simone de Beauvoir, the existentialist philosopher and feminist and paragon of the postwar French left, held a well-paying job during the German occupation in the Nazi-controlled Radio Paris. She later defended this collaboration by insisting she worked only on programs dealing with the Middle Ages. Bloch was very perilously involved in the resistance. He participated in the work of the Franc-Tireur, the most active non-Communist resistance group, which suffered periodically cruel losses by being penetrated by Gestapo informants. These betrayals were still an uncomfortable issue in France in the 1980s.

Bloch moved his family, now consisting of wife and four children (two older sons were already fighting abroad in De Gaulle's Free French Forces), to Lyons, where his wife died in the spring of 1944. Lyons, France's second city, was probably the most active center of the resistance organization. At least it has that reputation today, when much of the history of the underground is disputed and doubtful. About the time of his wife's death Bloch was living under an assumed name clandestinely in Paris, where he was arrested by the Gestapo. He was betrayed—so the postwar story, not reliable, went—by his landlady, who had noticed a radio transmitter in his room. Bloch was tortured by the Gestapo and was executed by firing squad along with twenty-five others in a field outside Paris on June 16, 1944, ten days after the Allied invasion of Normandy. A twenty-seventh victim miraculously survived and said after the liberation that in the truck transporting the doomed prisoners to be executed, Bloch had been calm and heroic to the end and had comforted the others.

Marc Bloch was the only prominent French academic to die a martyr of the resistance. This fact was to have a profound impact on French academic life as well as on the institutional context of medieval history in France after the war. The implications of his heroism and martyrdom are still felt not only in France but elsewhere, especially the United States. Bloch died at the height of his intellectual powers, but his death cast a shadow on the imaginative shaping of the Middle Ages that was probably even more profound than if he had returned to his chair at the Sorbonne. Like a great medieval churchman who was then canonized as a saint after his death for Christ, Bloch had a greater impact posthumously than in life. Perhaps he realized that would happen. He was an unorthodox, avant-garde thinker.

Until the tragic year of 1940 there were strong parallels between the biographies of Halphen and Bloch. Both came from the old French Jewish middle class. In Bloch's case there was a prime strand of Alsatian Jewry in his blood. Alsace, the disputed borderland between France and Germany, had been an important Jewish center since at least the twelfth century. It had become French again only in 1919, after having been German since 1870. This Alsatian background may have been one reason, but not the only one, why Bloch hated the Germans so much and risked his life to combat them when there was no external need for him to do so. Halphen's family was Parisian. Halphen and Bloch were both graduates of the École Normale Supérieure, the extremely selective and prestigious Parisian elite college from which the leaders of government, business, law, and academia were (and are) heavily drawn—like Oxbridge or the Ivy League, but perhaps even more preferential.

Halphen and Bloch, like most French professors, worked a great deal at home and built up large private libraries (which the Nazis later expropriated and shipped across the Rhine). Bloch especially hated to set foot in Paris's major library, the Bibliothèque Nationale, which he thought (rightly) was inefficient and badly administered. The current director of the BN, the historian Emmanuel Le Roy Ladurie, is in the direct line of intellectual progeny from Bloch. At the time Le Roy Ladurie took over in 1985, the Bibliothèque Nationale was not in much better shape than in Bloch's day.

Bloch and Halphen both came from academic families: Halphen's father was an eminent mathematician; Bloch's father was the prominent and powerful Parisian professor of ancient history Gustave Bloch. Both Halphen and Bloch were short and slight—about five feet six.

But Bloch especially was physically strong. He fought in the First World War for the whole duration of four years, was wounded in action, and won several medals, including the Legion of Honor. In 1940 he was an overage captain in the defeated French Army and wrote a bitter book about his experiences, severely and justly criticizing his inept and demoralized superiors. Halphen was never in the military.

In addition to this difference between the two academically prominent medievalist Jews, what separates their biographies are two things. Bloch, initially through his influential father, was always privileged in the academic world. Unfriendly colleagues called him the archbishop's son. He married the daughter of a wealthy engineer and was a man of considerable private means, which he used to travel a great deal, especially to England, Denmark, and Norway, countries whose political civility he admired. Until the great disaster of June 1940 Bloch lived in a penthouse apartment in one of the fashionable parts of Paris. When the Nazis came, the Gestapo, which later tortured and executed him, set up one of its headquarters in a hotel next door to his apartment. Halphen had no private means and lived modestly on his academic salary.

Aside from differences in their life-styles, Halphen and Bloch differed in temperament. Halphen could be stubborn, and he was ambitious and inner-directed, but he was outwardly a conformist, who made no waves. He was graduated from L'École des Chartes ("the school of documents"), which trained most French medievalists of his generation, and he worked quietly, precociously, and steadily to gain a reputation and ingratiate himself with the leaders of the academic profession. From 1910 to 1928 Halphen was professor of medieval history at Bordeaux, until he got a post in Paris and finally the same chair in medieval history at the Sorbonne previously occupied by his teacher, Ferdinand Lot.

Bloch was a rebel, a nonconformist, intellectually at odds with most of his colleagues. He was acerbically critical of the older generation of medievalists and saw himself as the savior of medieval studies. He built up around himself a coterie of brilliant graduate students and did not resist their turning toward hero worship and cult formation focused on him. He taught at the University of Strasbourg from the time it was reopened as a French university in 1919 and staffed with stars of the younger generation until 1931, when he transferred to Paris. He aimed high; twice he tried for a chair at the high-prestige

Collège de France, where, like Oxford's All Souls College and the Institute for Advanced Study in Princeton, there were only professors, no students, and the number of chairs was limited to the forty allegedly best academics in France drawn from all disciplines. Bloch's campaign manager at the Collège de France was the liberal Catholic historian of medieval philosophy Étienne Gilson, whom Bloch had known at Strasbourg. Bloch was rejected twice by the Collège de France, the second time in humiliating fashion. He settled for the chair of economic history at the Sorbonne, but his frustration, unhappiness, and resentment were highly visible.

It is curious that a major biography of this luminary of French academic life, the most influential French humanist scholar of his generation, this hero of the resistance, was published only in 1989 and by an American scholar, Carole Fink. Even the previously published best short biographical essay on Bloch (1982) was written not by one of his many stellar French disciples but by another American, a historian of modern France, Eugen Weber. One can only speculate on why Bloch's biography did not appear in Paris in the late forties or early fifties. One explanation may be that there was a much more complicated and controversial story involved in Bloch's betrayal to the Gestapo than his landlady's alleged perfidy. Many dark and ugly betrayals and deals happened in the resistance. Bloch's death could possibly have been traced back to one or more big names of postwar France if an industrious biographer had started to work on it shortly after the war. Another explanation for the lack of a major biography written in postwar Paris may be that his family didn't want it written, or rather wanted it written in such a way that would have affected unfavorably the buildup of the postwar Marc Bloch myth of martyrdom and sanctity, a cult that was personally very advantageous to certain of Bloch's colleagues and disciples.

In December 1960 I met one of Bloch's sons, a television producer, who was in New York for a few months to take some training at an American network. He did not speak of his father as a hero and martyr but as someone who had selfishly neglected his children and left them destitute and defenseless. He spoke not reverentially at all, but in bitter and hostile terms. A memoir of Bloch by another of his sons, published in 1987, is restrained; but the bitterness shows through. As a father Marc Bloch was not a great success, in the eyes of his son Étienne Bloch, who became an attorney in France and is today a judge:

I had a father. I was scarcely an adult when I lost him. . . . I loved
my father very much, but, because of his modesty about such feelings,
I did not know at the time if he truly loved me. . . . In his personal
life he encountered many of the problems of his contemporaries. The
paterfamilias par excellence, he was an authoritarian, occasionally ty-
rannical head of his family. Like all the bourgeois of his time, he was
accustomed to being served; though he never performed any domestic
task, even in this area he interfered constantly and directed everything.
He expected too much of his family and would have wished them to
share his strong sense of duty which he pressed on them to an extreme
degree. He was beset with a constant concern over his children, particularly the four older ones. For each of them he felt a profound af-
fection but in the expression of these sentiments he showed a certain
awkwardness and excessive shyness. He was even harsh and occasionally unfair, and he had very traditional, very narrow moral concep-
tions. . . . His children . . . were afraid of him; though aware of
being loved they were often struck by his reactions. One must say:
Our relations with him were rarely a joyful experience.

This downside of public heroism is not what the leaders of Parisian academic life wanted explored in Bloch's case, any more than the
monastic authors of medieval saints' lives dwelt on mundane and circumstantial things. Shortly after the war Bloch was memorialized at
Paris in two volumes of hagiographical tributes and memoirs. But it
was left to the American Carole Fink in the late 1980s to attempt a
detailed biography. Unfortunately, by then the biographical trail was
very cold, and in any case Fink pictured Bloch through the haze of
adulation that his disciples generated strategically after the resistance
martyr's death.

II

THE MANDARINS

In every country a small group of senior professors (between two and
ten people) at leading universities hold a disproportionate power within
a given discipline, whether it is physics, psychology, literary criticism, art history, or medieval studies. They have unimpeachable and
usually unchallenged prestige, and their books are universally praised
in the established academic journals, on whose editorial boards they
sit. They attract usually the brightest, the best-prepared, the most
ambitious, and the most industrious graduate students and so train

the academic stars of the younger generation who follow their ideas and interpretations unless Oedipal rebellion or a cultural revolution or a social earthquake (for example, the Great Depression of the 1930s) intervenes. This small cohort establishes a feudal network of job placements, in which these senior professors insert their students, who, because they are selectively so bright and hardworking, probably deserve the jobs anyway strictly on a merit basis.

Most of all, these senior professors in a given discipline are the controllers of patronage. Into their hands directly or indirectly flows the research support from learned foundations or government agencies without which it is rarely possible to undertake and complete a major research project. These funds go then entirely to them or their students by what is euphemistically called peer review. This senior cohort has a very strong influence with the major university publishers, and no prestige imprint will appear on a scholarly monograph that has not been approved of by two or three of them.

This feudal system is the basic sociology of power of the academic profession in every Western country. In France these academic power brokers are called mandarins (the term is also used for a coterie of reigning nonacademic intellectuals like Jean-Paul Sartre and his partner Simone de Beauvoir, in the Left Bank cafés) or grand patrons. In France the hold over academia by this group is more exclusive and formal, and less questioned, than in any other country except very small ones like Belgium or Holland, which in any case consciously follow the French model. A reason for this is that the prestige of the Parisian universities, colleges, and institutes of higher learning is so much greater than anything elsewhere in the country. The metropolitan professors immediately put anyone else in the country into the minor leagues as power brokers, no matter how well the provincial professors may have published and taught. France is culturally the most metropolitan, overcentralized country in Europe and has been so for many centuries, indeed since the thirteenth century. This condition of cultural overcentralization is itself a medieval legacy. Added to the compelling prestige of the Paris mandarin is his (and very rarely it is other than a male) proximity to government ministers, the editors of the more literate newspapers, the equally centralized legal, medical, and corporate leaders, and the supportive students and free-floating intellectuals in the Left Bank cafés. They accord his attitudes, favorite theories, and books an aura of legitimacy and authority that is irresistible and almost never questioned. To an extent that is less common in the United States, a senior Parisian professor is an emperor within his discipline, responsible only to himself, commanding learning, jobs, and research grants that determine the futures of the next generation of academics.

If the academic mandarin should turn out to be more productive and a little more avant-garde than most scholars, then the Parisian grand patron will be hailed on all sides as a genius. Not only will his lectures and seminars be oversubscribed, but students will take down every morsel of wisdom and knowledge that drips from the mouth of the master and publish it as gospel. Special issues of academic journals will be devoted to celebrating his ideas. Publishers will offer him attractive terms to write a popularized "high vulgarization" of his ideas, which, if written with style and verve, will win lucrative literary prizes. The front page of *Le Monde*, France's sober, upscale newspaper, will carry long, dense articles explicating his ideas.

Nowadays the Parisian mandarin will become a television star, easily enough when all television channels (three) are state-owned and the minister of education thinks that the lecture of the Paris mandarin is infinitely better for French civilization than a dubbed American sitcom. The master's fame spreads across the Atlantic. Three or four American departments become committed to propagating his ideas (and the American professors thereby win promotions or merit raises from the dean for bringing in light from the City of Light). American lecture tours are quickly and generously arranged. It doesn't matter that the French mandarin usually speaks English so badly that he is almost entirely incomprehensible to his adoring American campus audiences. He will still be idolized by the prexy's wife at the reception afterward, and female graduate students will offer him both their minds and their bodies. Finally (or perhaps much earlier) the heavyweight United States foundations like Ford or Rockefeller, devoted to enrichment of the trendy, will endow a new institute for the master in Paris, with a privileged satellite in an American campus.

This mandarinism has been the central fact of French academic life, especially in the humanities, since the beginning of the twentieth century. It has always operated this way, and in the personages of the philosopher and literary critic Jacques Derrida, the anthropologist Claude Lévi-Strauss, and the medieval historians Emmanuel Le Roy Ladurie, Georges Duby, and Jacques Le Goff, it still does. The proof of any academic system is not its political flavor, however, or behavior pattern but its intellectual outcomes. By this standard the French have done very well following this system, so well that even though the revolutionaries of 1968 denounced it and the French government promised to amend it, the changes have been mostly cosmetic and have left the system of grand patronage in existence. To change it fundamentally would require not only educational planning and reformation but a social and cultural revolution of shattering dimensions, which in the 1990s is improbable.

There were five mandarins or great patrons who strongly influenced the generation of French medieval historians of the 1930s and 1940s that Halphen and Bloch headed. These were the sociologist Émile Durkheim, the medievalists Henri Pirenne and Ferdinand Lot, the academic vulgarizer and popular educator Henri Berr, and the historical sociologist and geographer Lucien Febvre. Bloch owed a great deal, both intellectually and professionally, to all of them except possibly Lot, and Febvre was his special guru. Halphen was little influenced by the vanguard thinkers Durkheim and Febvre, but his career and his thinking were deeply affected by the other grand patrons.

Émile Durkheim was the prototype of the French academic mandarin in every way. His was one of the most original modernist minds of this century (he died in 1916), and he was a power broker of unsurpassed subtlety and ruthlessness. Durkheim was the son of a rabbi. He first made his reputation as a pioneering professor of education and exercised an influence on French secondary school teachers even greater than that exercised by John Dewey on their American counterparts. It was Durkheim who created the model lycée (secondary school) teacher: quite well paid, self-confident, left-wing, secular, anticlerical, superpatriotic, culturally chauvinist, and, not least, very learned (often the holder of an advanced degree and working on a doctorate, not in education but in a "real" subject). When he gained a chair at the Collège de France, Durkheim, who at Bordeaux had held the first professorship of sociology in France, gave himself the title of professor of sociology and education. He continued to prepare lycée teachers, but he now devoted himself to founding the modern discipline of sociology (as his great contemporary sociological theorist in Berlin Max Weber, a former professor of Roman history and law, did not).

Durkheim had two fundamental ideas in sociology. First, the field is a quantitative discipline, and small mathematical margins (e.g., the suicide rate in Sweden as against France's) make a crucial social difference. Secondly, every society is an enclosed system. Each side of this confined boxlike system is a function of (that is, conditioned by and interactive with) the other sides. Thus economics relates to politics, politics to the arts, the arts to social structure, etc. This system can be destabilized when anomie sets in, when there is a gap between ideas and the institutions of power, as in the United States in the Vietnam era. But the conservating, absorptive qualities of the functional societal system are so powerful that revolution is very rare. Rather, the system co-opts and adapts the discordant elements (e.g., Jane Fonda, the Vietcong queen, becomes a video exercise billionaire; Tom Hayden, the revolutionary, a moderate left California legislator). What most impressed Bloch and Lucien Febvre about Durkheim's sociology was not the quantification (that didn't come in French historiography until the late fifties) but the principle of totality—that all parts of a society are interactive with every other part and the system must be comprehended in its functional whole. Understanding the impetus toward totality requires drawing upon as many of social and behavioral sciences as possible, according to Durkheim's disciples Febvre and Bloch.

Henri Pirenne was a Francophone Belgian citizen and patriot. He was chosen by the Belgian crown and Royal Academy in the 1890s to write a five-volume history of Belgium, with concentration on the medieval era, when Belgium did not exist but could be claimed to have had a prehistory in the county of Flanders and other feudal principalities. Pirenne created the requisite national past of Belgium. Professor of medieval history at the University of Ghent for four decades, Pirenne, who died in 1935, was pro-French and fiercely anti-German. He was interned by the Germans during the First World War. In the late 1920s and early 1930s he was the most famous medieval historian in the Francophone world, the recipient of a bushel of honorary degrees and other academic recognitions. He became renowned for his two "theses." No doctoral student in medieval history in the 1950s would dare approach his comprehensive exams without mastery of the two Pirenne theses and the debate they generated. A prominent Italian economic historian, Yale's Robert Lopez, made his early reputation largely as a critic of Pirenne.

Pirenne's first thesis was on the origin of medieval cities. He claimed that urban entities were a creation in the tenth and eleventh centuries of merchants engaged in international trade, who huddled for protection under the walls of a fortress (burg—hence burghers and bourgeoisie, those who reside under the walls of the burg) controlled by a king, duke, or bishop. Eventually, as other merchants congregated, some involved in local trade and artisans to support these bourgeois families, this urban middle class built a wall around itself. There then

appeared other townspeople who lived outside the walls, in the sub-
urbs, until there were so many of them that fifty or a hundred years
later they in turn built a wall around themselves, and then a new
suburb started. And so medieval cities grew in concentric circles of
walled formations around central fortresses or cathedrals from the
tenth until the early fourteenth century, when the population stopped
growing and, after the Black Death of 1346–48, sharply declined. It
was a beautiful explanation of urbanization propounded by Pirenne
in several limpidly written books and then in the new American *Encyclopedia of the Social Sciences* in an inspired long article, which was
later reprinted as a separate book. The only problem is that it was
evident even in the 1930s that the Pirenne medieval cities thesis is
not closely applicable to Italy, where there was diminished but actual
continuity of many cities since Roman times. Pirenne's bourgeois thesis fits best with the Flemish towns like Ghent and Ypres, and if you
bother to look at Pirenne's sparse footnotes, that is where most of his
material is drawn from. Recently scholars have argued that not only
does Pirenne's thesis not fit many German Rhineland cities, but there
are problems even in his home territory of Flanders and northern
France, where urban foundations going back to the sixth century can
be discovered.

Archaeology has not been kind to Pirenne: It tends to show remarkable continuity of urban enclaves from Roman or early post-
Roman times. Just possibly the archaeologists are mistaken in the
way they read their fragmentary data. As for Pirenne's insistence that
the birth of cities was inspired by international trade, this was a weak
point from the start. It is obvious that strictly regional trade was
often the crucial factor and that towns, especially in southern England and in Germany east of the Rhine Valley, emerged as artisan
and local marketing enclaves to suit the needs of the lord and his
family and warriors or of the bishop and his clergy and retainers. My
guess is that perhaps a third of the people of the cathedral towns in
the eleventh century, before the pope cracked down on clerical con-
cubines, were actually bastard children of the resident clergy or descended from such. Pirenne's medieval cities thesis offers a beautifully
clear paradigm, but it does not hold up well empirically. Many medieval urban centers were simply continuous from Roman times. And
the economic interest of the burghers was frequently in local, not
international, trade. The provenance of the burghers was diverse.

Pirenne's second thesis, the "Mohammed and Charlemagne" one,
so called from his major book on the subject, is even more controver-

sial and is still debated. It was not the fall of the Western Roman Empire in the late fifth century that began the Middle Ages economically and culturally, contended Pirenne, but the Muslim expansion of the seventh and eighth centuries. By the early eighth century Western Europe was cut off from the Mediterranean, which had become "a Muslim lake." The center of European life moved inland, for the first time, to the underdeveloped north country, and "driven back on its own resources," Europe had to create a distinctive civilization, for the moment less wealthy and literate than the Mediterranean world, but the foundation for future greatness. Thus Muhammad made Charlemagne.

This paradigm has precipitated a half century of debate. Did Roman civilization survive in sixth-century France? Was Mediterranean trade really terminated by Arab conquests? Was there or was there not continuation of international commerce between religious blocs? This historical football has been kicked back and forth for half a century. If one had to state a consensus on where we are now, it would be: Something important happened in changing the posture of European civilization in the eighth century from the Mediterranean to the North, but it was only marginally the consequence of the Muslim expansion. While Roman culture continued in the sixth century, it had by then such a devastated culture as to be socially or culturally of marginal effectiveness.

What was most important about Pirenne was not what he specifically said or whether his two famous theses were right or not, but how he said it. It was his method and style that counted. He accumulated a very small body of material, enough to provide a modicum of respectable footnotes, and above the footnotes he speculated very broadly. Pirenne's message was that there was an audience for large-scale generalization in medieval history, and this audience was much larger than the thin array of professional medievalists. If you presented plausible interpretations of a sweeping nature about medieval economy and society, the learned world and, even to some extent, the educated world beyond universities would listen, and you would become famous, honored, and affluent. Think big, write boldly. This lesson was not lost on contemporaries, including Halphen and Bloch. Pirenne taught medievalists to dare to be bold and speculative. Indeed, he talked grandly of a comparative history of civilization, of a world history, such as that which Arnold J. Toynbee was beginning to write in England, such as Oswald Spengler in his *Decline of the West* had done in Germany in the early 1920s in a strictly imagina-

tive, poetic, unscholarly way. Pirenne himself never tried this comparative world history, but his son Jacques Pirenne took it up, with
modest results.

The legitimacy of Pirenne's methodology was reinforced by the
example of the work of Ferdinand Lot, the head of L'École des Chartes
for several decades and professor of medieval history at the Sorbonne. Lot was a master technician, perhaps the only scholar west of
the Rhine who could match the great Monumenta institute Germans
for technical expertise in handling and editing medieval documents.
But he also produced a work of synthesis that became a longtime
academic best seller, *The End of the Ancient World and the Beginnings of
the Middle Ages*. It is hard to believe that this was the same Ferdinand
Lot who took several years to produce an exquisitely detailed edition
of thirty sixth-century charters. In the end he really let go and produced the most readable book on the fall of the Roman Empire since
Gibbon. There are chapters on "corruption of public spirit" (ah, the
Third Republic!), the intrusion of Oriental ideas (vive the French
Empire!), the barbarian invasions, the impact of the church and an
unforgettable metaphor: He compares the culture of A.D. 450 with
200 as if a dreamer on waking had seen a different set of stars in the
sky—the Rip Van Winkle version of the late Roman Empire. It was
so good and so popular that when Lot's publishers asked him in 1950
to bring out, after three decades, a new edition, he disdained to change
a line in his own now-classic text. He merely added an appendix
reviewing with enthusiasm what others had said since 1920.

Lot's *End of the Ancient World* appeared in a series called *The Evolution of Humanity*, edited by Henri Berr. He was a marginal, raffish
figure in the French academic world for fifty years, trying again and
again unsuccessfully to get a chair, giving only occasional adult education courses at the university. But Berr became a publishing powerhouse. After founding a journal called the *Review of Synthesis*, which
gained only modest success, he had the bright idea of getting famous
professors, masters of their field, to come out of the archives and
seminars and write works of high vulgarization, as the French called
it, for students and the general reader. From about 1910 to 1950 in
the transatlantic world Berr, this king of synthesis and populariza-
tion, played an important role in bringing learning from the universities into the classroom and middle-class living rooms. Henri Berr
was a French version of Will Durant and Clifton Fadiman. He had a
very good eye for what closeted research professors could do with a
little persuasion and the incentive of a little money. He got not only

Ferdinand Lot to cover the fall of the Roman Empire but Louis Halphen to write about the Carolingian Empire and Marc Bloch to attempt a review of feudal society.

By 1930 Henri Berr was no longer an embarrassing night school
joke. He had become a power in French academic life and in publishing, even in the English-speaking world, as most of the volumes in
The Evolution of Humanity series were translated into English and did
quite well in the face (before 1945) of very little competition. Many
of the volumes in Berr's series look funny today: They start off mum-
bling about science, documents, archives, archaeological materials, deep
learning. They slide off into generalization; then they go berserk in
blue sky speculation.

Lucien Febvre was at the other end of the academic spectrum from
Henri Berr. Febvre was a deep thinker, a courageous vanguard historian, and the author of at least three major books, a scholar of superior capability in a variety of disciplines and very successful by
standard professional criteria. He ended up with a chair at the Collège de France. But there were some similarities between Berr and
Febvre. Both were committed to interdisciplinary studies and not afraid
to engage in polemics for that end. Both were academic empire builders and entrepreneurs, who never bypassed an opportunity to capitalize on the main chance.

As a history graduate student before World War I Febvre came
under the influence of the social geographer Paul Vidal de la Blanche,
whose work was supported by the French government because of its
value to French colonial government (just as British anthropology in
the first five decades of this century was subsidized by the British
Colonial Office for the same reason). Out of this came Febvre's first
book, a close study of a small region of sixteenth-century France in
terms of a total examination of the environment's impact on society,
politics, and culture. Febvre was also a pioneer in using quantitative
data in premodern European history. When he became established at
Strasbourg in 1920 (going on later to Paris), Febvre turned to the
Reformation and examined Lutheranism in a sociological manner, assessing the way that Protestantism suited the mentality of the rising
bourgeoisie. It was part Durkheim, part Marx, part Weber in orientation. Febvre's third great book, written while he was in exile in his
country house from 1942 to 1944, was a study of Rabelais as evocative of a still predominantly oral culture, anticipating to some extent
Walter Ong's and Marshall McLuhan's later communications theory.

While writing these seminal works, Febvre was training a generation of intellectually and politically radical graduate students, among them Fernand Braudel, and engaging incessantly in polemics against what he regarded as academic conservatism and narrow-mindedness. Febvre was essentially an antimodernist neo-Victorian. He condemned "the idolatry of the fact" and "the collection of events as others collect postage stamps and match boxes." History was a consideration of large-scale problems, to be answered by drawing upon the social and behavioral sciences. "No problems, no history." Good history was speculative, highly interpretive. It must not be dull.

Febvre aroused bitter opposition, fear, and hatred among academics, but he wrote very good books. He could not be resisted. He marched up the academic ladder. But that wasn't enough for this restless gargantuan personality. He sought institutional innovations that would disseminate his ideas and give him patronage power to slay the opposition and create an intellectual revolution. With his Strasbourg (and later Paris) colleague Marc Bloch, Febvre founded in 1929 the *Annales d'Histoire Économique et Sociale* (later, giving anthropology and literary criticism their due, it was called *Annales: Économies, Sociétés, Civilisations*) as the organ of the new behavioral history. Looked upon in the 1930s as marginal and gauche (indeed, many of the articles in the early issues are naive and silly), the *Annales* steadily advanced to the front rank. By 1970, as Braudel proudly noted, a historian could not inaugurate his professional career in France (or get a better job) without an article in the *Annales*. Some of the articles are still naive and silly, but they are rarely boring. Febvre, with Bloch's assistance, now had a journal to be the focus of an *Annales* "school" of interdisciplinary social history and to sustain the behavioral, problem-oriented Annalist historians.

But ever the empire builder and entrepreneur, Febvre wanted a physical embodiment of all this—an autonomous, well-endowed, state-supported institute of the new vanguard social history, with attendant mandarin patronage. He wanted the new School of Higher Study in the Social Sciences to take on tactile physical and institutional form. Febvre wanted not only colleagues and protégés but power and patronage. Thanks mostly to Bloch's martyrdom, Febvre was able to gain all of this after the war. Carole Fink has shown that the relationship between Bloch and Febvre was sometimes tense. From 1940 to 1942 they disputed whether to continue to publish the *Annales* in Nazi-occupied Paris. Febvre insisted on this, and he prevailed.

Postwar Parisian governments deferred to Febvre's ambitions in veneration of Bloch's memory as a martyr of the resistance. With merciless efficiency and ideological intensity, Febvre forthwith blew away all opposition, and when he died in 1956 at the age of seventy-seven, he was the Caesar of French historiography and the leading power broker in Parisian social and behavioral sciences as a whole. Bloch was more valuable to Febvre in death than in life.

A countervailing force had appeared on the horizon in Febvre's later years, the structuralist anthropologist Claude Lévi-Strauss. This son of a Belgian rabbi, student of Marcel Mauss, Durkheim's nephew, had fled Paris in 1940 and spent the war in modest circumstances lecturing to adults at the New School for Social Research and teaching freshmen at Barnard College in New York City. Lévi-Strauss (in America he had called himself Mr. Strauss so as not to be confused with the blue jeans manufacturer) returned to Paris in 1947 to occupy the newly created chair of social anthropology at the Sorbonne, and he soon demonstrated that here was a new mandarin, who, by the brilliance and boldness of his ideas, the vanguard quality of his publications, and the consistency of his ambitions for power and patronage, could become a match even for the old master Lucien Febvre. But Lévi-Strauss bided his time and deferred to the venerable Febvre. Only in the same year that Febvre died, with the publication of Lévi-Strauss's literary as well as theoretical masterpiece *Tristes Tropiques*, did Lévi-Strauss begin to make his move. Fernand Braudel, Febvre's designated heir, soon made way for him, and for the next twenty years they shared almost absolute control over the "human sciences" in Paris.

The great transformation of French academia and legitimization of total social history that Bloch had dreamed of and Febvre planned for before the war had been fully achieved by 1960. Bloch, the rebel and outsider, who had failed to get a chair at the Collège de France and been publicly humiliated while trying for this supreme prize, was now transformed into an intellectual deity whose shrine demanded worship by all the academic mandarins of postwar Paris.

At a certain time in academe, a particular name becomes a symbolic talisman, with a full panoply of significations. Thus today Marc Bloch has the highest possible positive rating. Bloch has all the virtues that appeal to the American academic mind. He was French, Jewish, left, a hero and martyr of the resistance. He advocated and practiced an interdisciplinary approach. He applied concepts from sociology and anthropology to interpreting medieval society. His work is easily accessible, and some of it can be assigned in college courses, in the form of the University of Chicago Press's two-volume paperback translation of *Feudal Society* (1961), which Bloch contributed to Henri Berr's series and which he sent to the publishers as World War II commenced. No wonder "Marc Bloch" is today a talismanic code for all the academic virtues. Citing him in a discussion of medieval society is intended to have the mesmerizing effect of referring to St. Augustine in a thirteenth-century scholastic debate or, perhaps even a closer parallel, of calling upon the Virgin Mary for divine intercession.

III
LORDS AND PEASANTS

Whatever else a French mandarin medieval historian does, he must illuminate a segment of his own country's history. So it was with Halphen and Bloch. The period of French history from the 730s until the end of the ninth century is known as the Carolingian era, after the ruling family. The major figure is Charles the Great, Karl der Grosser, Charlemagne, who ruled from 768 to 814. He reigned at least nominally not only over what is today France but also over large stretches of western Germany, northern Italy, including Rome, and at times pieces of northern Spain. His legendary image looms in the *Song of Roland*, the first great work of French literature, an epic poem that comes down to us from the late eleventh century. The historical incident that stands behind this epic and its hero, Count Roland, is Charlemagne's unsuccessful effort to conquer the northern part of Muslim Spain. The white-haired weary old emperor is a prime character in the poem, the distributor of justice, the leader of the French knights, the savior and protector of the people.

What was the real, historical Charlemagne like? How did he rule, and what did he accomplish? What was the reality of the Carolingian Empire, which steadily fell apart after Charlemagne's death, because of internecine wars among his grandsons and devastation by the invading Vikings and Hungarians that the later Carolingian rulers could not stem? They had to give way slowly to local feudal dukes and counts who could provide a modicum of peace and protection. Was Charlemagne merely a great warrior when young and a distant symbol propped up by the clergy when old, but never an effective ruler engaged in the diurnal tasks of government? Since 1950 this skeptical view of Charlemagne has been the predominant one, propounded by Heinrich Fichtenau in Vienna and J. M. Wallace-Hadrill in Oxford.

The book these revisionists have contended against is Louis Halphen's classic study *Charlemagne and the Carolingian Empire*, published in 1947 and begun in 1944, while Halphen was hiding out in the mountains from the Nazis.

Halphen had prepared through his whole career to write this book. He had begun to publish documents and close, technical studies of aspects of Carolingian history as early as 1907. He traveled around the archives of France and northern Italy and acquired an incomparable mastery of the sources of the long and ambivalent Carolingian era, particularly of the reign of Charlemagne.

The Carolingians should have appealed to Halphen as a French Jew because this was the happiest era for Jews in the French Middle Ages—from the time the Carolingian dynasty began to rule in the 730s (although they did not officially take the crown until 751) until the beginnings of attacks on the privileged status of the Jews by the archbishop of Lyons in the 840s. Even then the Jews in France continued to prosper, until the rise of Christian militancy in the early eleventh century and changed economic circumstances brought a rapid deterioration in their condition. As was characteristic of nearly all early medieval societies (England under William the Conqueror around 1080, Germany around 1170, Poland in the early sixteenth century), Jews were useful to rulers in an underdeveloped economy. They acted as bankers and moneylenders and as international merchants. With the appearance of Christian businessmen who could do these things, the Jews' value sharply declined, but until then they were indispensable to the Christian monarchs for providing fiscal liquidity. The Jews in Carolingian France were especially useful in their role of enhancing Mediterranean trade with the Muslim world. With one branch of a Jewish family in Cairo or Fez, Morocco, and another in France, they had personal contacts and credit instruments to conduct trade across the Mediterranean and between religious blocs.

It is not just coincidence that the leading German historian of the Carolingian era in the 1920s and 1930s, Wilhelm Levison (who had to seek refuge in the late thirties in England) was, like Halphen, Jewish. Thus the Carolingian dynasty, so friendly for such a long time to Jews, found its prominent historians of the interwar era among Jewish-born medievalists in both France and Germany.

Carolingian era Jews held land in southern France, particularly in the Narbonne region. They were big in wine cultivation long before the age of Manischewitz, and this old Jewish vintage wasn't so sweet. There is even a story of disputable authenticity, on which two generations of Jewish historians have cut their teeth, that a Jewish lord in the Narbonne area married a Carolingian princess. All this Jewish landholding became unthinkable in the late eleventh century in view of clerical hostility and feudal jealousy, and in any case by that time you couldn't hold land unless you took a Christian oath of fidelity.

But Halphen was not a Jewish chauvinist. His question was not, Is it good for the Jews? The prosperity of the Jews under Charlemagne was part of his general vision of the overall benign temper of justice and peace that in his view marked Charlemagne's policy. What more than anything else appealed to Halphen was the idealism of the Carolingians. In the midst of barbarian society after centuries of upheaval and indiscriminate violence, there was a world in which intelligence and public ethics were being imposed on the countryside, in Halphen's view. Yet Halphen's attribution of paramount value to learned intelligence's imposing itself upon society was central to middle-class Jewish liberalism of his generation.

The Western-educated Jewish middle class before the 1920s and in large part until the cultural revolution of the 1960s made their scions into Leninists and Maoists, stood with the political forces everywhere that imposed order, peace, due process of law, and meritocratic principles upon society. Of course, such an attitude was self-serving for the Jewish bourgeoisie, as their radical, proletarian-loving offspring relished telling them in the 1960s. But more than self-interest was involved. The educated Jewish middle class of the transatlantic world prized above all family life and the security and advancement of their expensively educated children. Family destiny could have only a fortunate outcome in a lawful order of peace and stability, recognition of talent, and reward for postponed gratification and hard work. The Jewish temperament of the early twentieth century (outside the fetid maelstrom of Czarist rule, where the cauldron of persecution and revolution was effecting radical changes and producing mutants like a Bronstein/Trotsky and a Grün/Ben-Gurion) offered passionate support for liberal rationality, for the imposition of humanistic culture on society. That is why Jews everywhere were such Anglophiles. They thought they saw this kind of benign, humanitarian politics in Britain, whether the Liberals or Conservatives were in power there. That is why they stood for the centrist "Radicals," the self-proclaimed heirs of 1789, in the Third Republic of France. That is why they lionized Woodrow Wilson (and he reciprocated by placing the first Jew on the Supreme Court, Louis D. Brandeis, who had been his intimate adviser). And that is one reason why, projecting backward, Louis Halphen loved the Carolingians and took a positive view of them, especially the Great Charles.

Halphen was not naive. To attribute to Charlemagne, he said, the capability of being a profound politician would be "a simple mirage." But Charlemagne did have "a strong personality and a very sure instinct" for what was possible in the circumstances. His successors lacked these personal qualities. In general, the Carolingian Empire was "a regime which concentrated everything in the person of the emperor and made his will the supreme law of the state." This exercise of power was idealistic and unselfish because the emperor followed the advice of his clerical advisers, like the English monk Alcuin. The Carolingian officials conceived of a Christian order, but not with the militancy and fanaticism of later centuries. Hence the Jews could live comfortably in this kind of Christian state, as they did in Muslim Spain before 1100.

Halphen's interpretation of the Carolingian Empire is, therefore, of an effective and idealistic monarchy: "Under the influence of the Church, the Carolingian ruler is conscious of the duties which fall upon him as the head of the community of the peoples under submission to the government. . . . There is no obligation for the king of the Franks more demanding than that of a life conforming to the teachings of the Catholic Church." These teachings, while drawing upon the traditions of Augustine and the other Church Fathers, were still soft-core rather than hard-core. The Carolingian lords and priests wanted law, peace, justice, prosperity. They were not trying to bring about the Second Coming. The Carolingian ethos was that mankind was tarrying in a comfortable oasis, not preparing for the imminent wrath of God. It is a civil religion, not an apocalyptic, millennial fervor. It was good for the Jews. It resembled the humanistic and liberal ethos of the bourgeois-dominated Third Republic. This was Halphen's Carolingian world.

This was not a mirage. There *was* a kind of order under Charlemagne, at least until the emperor became very old and feeble. There was improvement in the instruments of government as far as the vast distances of the Empire allowed, a superior discipline imposed on monasteries and parish clergy, a firm protection of the frontiers, and the famous Carolingian Renaissance. This meant a gathering of scholars from all parts of Europe, especially England and Italy, to work directly under the patronage of the emperor at his court in Aachen. There was a great activity in book production. We would now have very little of the Latin classics were it not for the labor and intelligence of the Carolingian scribes. In Halphen's account, the Carolingian Renaissance generated marvelous illuminated manuscripts. It meant poetry and history writing and vast collections of canon law. Halphen took a very positive view of this world. He was entirely comfortable with it. He regarded it as a critically important age of progress, reform, and greatly enhanced literacy upon which the rise of medieval civilization was based. While it is easy enough to say that Charlemagne was just a semiliterate warrior (he apparently could read but not write) and his clerks were narrow, dull pedants, that judgment doesn't look right in the end. Something very important and magnificently creative did happen in Charlemagne's Empire, as perceived and described by Louis Halphen.

After the debate about Charlemagne and the nature of Carolingian civilization that occurred in the late 1940s and 1950s, four decades later Halphen's judgment seems to be the sound one, rather than the disillusioned post-Nazi era anti-intellectualism of Heinrich Fichtenau (Hitler was a phony, so Charlemagne had to be a phony, too) and the sour British vulgarity of Wallace-Hadrill (they all were barbarians, and intelligence never prevails in history anyway). Summing up in 1983 the vast research on the Carolingian world since 1945, Pierre Riché—professionally more a disciple of Marc Bloch and the *Annales* group than of Louis Halphen—gives a picture of the Carolingians that is close to Halphen's. The anti-Halphen revisionists, Riché concludes, "badly judged" the work of the Carolingians. When all is considered, Riché claims, as Halphen believed, that in the Carolingian world is laid the foundation of the European nations.

Marc Bloch's education and training as a medievalist were as rigorous and conventional as Halphen's. Before he went into the army in 1914, Bloch was extremely well trained in traditional close reading of medieval documents and examination of archaeological materials. He always had the capacity to be a superb technician when he wanted to be. In 1933 he published a twenty-five-page paper on "The Problem of Gold in the Middle Ages" that is the basis for all subsequent research on medieval numismatics (the study of coinage) and has never been superseded. His doctoral dissertation on serfs on royal estates in the Île de France was the conventional, highly technical kind of institutional history. Bloch came out of the army after four years of fighting and carnage dissatisfied with this kind of dry, narrow historical inquiry. He had experienced great collective endeavors and unequaled violence, and through his army experience this Parisian high-bourgeois Jew had come to know for the first time what French peasants were really like. It might be said that Bloch encountered a durable peasant mentality in the army and set out to show how it had come into existence over long centuries.

There is something in that, but Bloch's actual intellectual development is more complex than that. What he worked on in the first half of the 1920s after he started teaching at Strasbourg was not rural society but the opposite end of the spectrum of medieval civilization—the rituals of kingship. He wrote a long book on thaumaturgical kingship, the power of healing accorded to English and French monarchs. At times he looks in this work as though he were trying to locate himself within traditional German intellectual history of medieval monarchy. Bloch's book on the royal touch is actually a mediocre performance compared with the work of Schramm and Kantorowicz and the great German historians of sacral kingship. One thing it does *not* do is apply Durkheim's sociology. Bloch does not pursue the question of what there was in the medieval mentality that demanded such miraculous powers from kings. The book was also uncharacteristically sloppy from a technical point of view on the English side, as Richard Southern pointed out in a very negative assessment.

Bloch by the late 1920s was facing a crisis in his scholarly career and in his intellectual development. He solved it by surrendering to the influence of his brilliant Strasbourg friend and colleague Lucien Febvre and taking up the banner of total history, geographical and anthropological history, and Durkheim's functionalist sociology. Yet it was probably the threat posed to liberal traditions and to Jews by the rise of nazism and the onset of the Great Depression, which began to affect France in 1930, that jarred Bloch into new ways of thinking, as much as Febvre's influence. Febvre showed him the intellectual road to follow, but the Nazi threat and the apparent decline of capitalism in the Great Depression pushed Bloch strongly to the left, as these traumas did for many middle-class liberals, especially Jews, of his generation. It was then that he joined Febvre in the publishing project that became the seminal journal *Annales* and, more important for him, led in 1931 to the publication of *The Original Character of French Rural History*. This book signaled both his new historical orientation and leftist political views. Some critics regard this as Bloch's best book (although it was not translated into English, under the flat title *French Rural History*, until 1966). Bloch, "the archbishop's son," the privileged, privately affluent academic, in the late twenties underwent an intellectual crisis and became the radical Marc Bloch known to posterity.

In 1941 and 1942, while he was in exile in Montpellier and had just begun to establish contact with the resistance, Bloch summed up his historiographical principles in a book called *The Historian's Craft*. He never finished it, but it was published after the war and then in an English translation. It had a great impact. It sets forth with characteristic polemical boldness and clarity the assumptions that lie behind his two major works in medieval history—*Rural History* and *Feudal Society* (1940).

Marc Bloch's incomplete treatise on historiography, *The Historian's Craft*, shaped the minds of a generation of historians. He intended *Craft* to replace the early-twentieth-century French handbook on historical method by Charles-Victor Langlois and Charles Seignobos and other such works of modernist or "scientific" history. Aided by the restless temper of the decade after 1945, Bloch accomplished his aim. He contended victoriously against everything that Langlois and Seignobos stood for: their assumption that sources can be closely read and rigorously analyzed in a universally observed manner; their conviction that verifiable detail, not generalization, advances historical knowledge; their love of narrative history; and their belief that social history consists of colorful vignettes drawn heavily from literary sources, as Langlois demonstrated in his account of fourteenth-century French society. Langlois had been one of Bloch's teachers before 1914.

Craft became the clarion call for a generation of transatlantic historians who gave free rein to the historical imagination, who used concepts from the social and behavioral sciences as vehicles of exploration, who disdained narrative history for structural analysis, and who wrote social history from data—some of them quantitative—that revealed patterns of human behavior. Bloch's influence in the United States was as great as in France.

There are three distinctive ideas in *The Historian's Craft*.

First, The historian encounters the "tracks" of people only in the past, not their immediate presence, and he must in consciousness reconstruct from these traces what the people were like. In this work of imaginative reconstruction, the concepts of the behavioral and social sciences are critically valuable. Secondly, The direction of a society is shaped by its physical environment, but not exclusively. Anthropological factors reflected in institutions, rituals, dress, diet are also at work. Material and social factors are actively blended in a "total" situation to constitute the conditioning environment. The pre-scription for social history advocated by Bloch is Marxism softened by anthropology. Thirdly: What is important is not temporality or narrative, how a society is generated and developed, pursuit of which should be of secondary interest and is perhaps not worth the effort. What is important is the basic structure or "original character" of a society that is durable over long stretches of time. In other words, structural history is to replace narrative history. What matters is what Bloch calls the synchronous whole, not diachronic narrative. (These jargonistic terms are derived from French anthropology.)

All these ideas of Bloch's *Craft* became central to the *Annales* school and the historiography of the postwar generation on both sides of the Atlantic. Obviously, much creative and valuable work was done un-der their aegis. The limitation of the concept of tracks in the past is, however, that it is true for relatively inarticulate groups whose be-havior we can trace only in data drawn from economic and legal rec-ords. For the elite of medieval society we have much more than their tracks. We are in their presence. We know in many instances the finest nuances of their thoughts. We can see their actual handwritings on pieces of parchment. We encounter them face-to-face. And we can be quite rigorous in developing methods to analyze their thought and behavior. We know many individuals as personalities, not just as shadowy groupings in statistical data.

On the subject of environmentalism, Bloch constantly struggles with himself. He tries to walk a line between Durkheim and Marx. He tries to avoid simply geographical determinism and advocates an-thropogeography, which indeed perceives societies as being condi-tioned by physical environments, but he cautions that "other perspectives" need to be considered for the analysis to be complete. Bloch exults that economic history, and, therefore, recognition of ma-terial and environmental factors in social developments, are beginning to establish themselves. Bloch's environmentalism is expressed as a theory of the total social situation, in which there is interaction be-tween physical environment and society. His introduction of anthro-pological as well as geographical factors into the conditioning environment was to be of cardinal importance to the *Annales* school. Environmental conditioning in the form of the interactive quality of society and physical environment, and consideration of anthropo-logical contexts as well as geography, are Bloch's most influential ideas.

Considered from the perspective of the intellectual history of the

1930s and early 1940s and characterized on an ideological scale, the theory of history that Bloch presented in those anxious times was an updated, broadened, and softened Marxist determinism. The material forces in history represented by economic factors and the physical environment were accorded dominant causal significance in the shaping of a society. But importance was also allowed, in Bloch's view, to social institutions as an anthropologist might view them.

What geography, economics, and anthropology tell us about the functional context in which a society operates then becomes that total social situation in which everything else in medieval Europe—its politics, religion, art, literature—should be understood. Bloch's theory is quite close to that of the Frankfurt school of critical theory, a neo-Marxist group that was led in the 1930s by Theodor Adorno and of which Walter Benjamin and Herbert Marcuse were members. The Frankfurt school's idea was that a material base determines the creation of an institutional and cultural superstructure, but the latter gains a certain measure of autonomy from the material base in its specific operations.

Bloch and Adorno did not noticeably influence each other. They both were products of a certain terrible moment in European history, and they came to similar, although not identical, theories of history. This fact was of small importance in Bloch's own lifetime. It became important in the 1960s and 1970s, when Adorno's eager disciples in the American New Left found Bloch's work easy to accommodate and endorse because of the intellectual compatability between the *Annales* theory of total social history and the Frankfurt school's critical theory.

The analytic limitation of Bloch's total social history is that it is frequently too gross a factor to account for specific aspects of medieval culture. For example, that the Gothic cathedral is the product of a particular material and institutional environment is true. But having said that, we know very little about Gothic cathedrals and how they got designed and built. To take another example, the most insightful section in Bloch's *Feudal Society* is on the medieval sense of time. Yet it helps little to say that this sense of time is a product of the physical and social environment. A host of clerical traditions, theological assumptions, Roman carry-overs, and social practices of the nobility as well as political and legal phenomena is involved in shaping the medieval sense of time.

Therefore, there are severe limitations to stipulating anthropogeography or the total social situation as a conditioning agent for the Gothic cathedral or the medieval sense of time. To use this causal explanation of Bloch's is to state a truism, but it does not help much in explaining the particular aspect of medieval culture. This amended environmentalism of Bloch's results in little better than a tautology when we come to explain the emergence of a particular cultural manifestation. Bloch wanted to avoid complete materialistic determinism. But his kind of anthropogeographical, total social situation environmentalism is too general and vague to be of much use in specific cultural instances. Totality is an overdetermined concept. It explains everything but in such a thin global fashion as to be of small use in explaining anything. Bloch's work suffers from sociology's numbing propensity to surface generalities.

The severest limitation of Bloch's emphasis on structure, the long duration of "original character," the synchronic approach, is the inability to account for the rapid, detailed changes in politics during the highly creative era 1050–1325. That is the greatest flaw of *Feudal Society*. It attempts a structural approach to feudalism but cannot thereby account for the histories of the feudal monarchies of the twelfth and thirteenth centuries in which the personalities and discretionary choices of kings and individual barons played a very great role.

Another problem arising from Bloch's structural history is that in moving away from narrative history, it departed from what made the historical profession popular and socially influential in the nineteenth century. The take-over of structural modes of thinking and writing has been coterminous with the decline of the social visibility of the historical profession. Halphen was not only a great scholar and master of the sources but also author of two narrative histories that gained the attention and adulation of all kinds of people. Bloch's bold structuralism sacrificed the social role of narrative history and the historian's influence exercised by narrative history.

Bloch's *Craft* was a revolutionary work that came to signify the vision and method of a generation of historians. It unleashed creative energies and stimulated much valuable writing. It inspired the single best medieval book of the *Annales* school, Georges Duby's *Early Growth of the European Economy* (1974), a concise masterpiece that is superior to any of Bloch's own historical works. Bloch's ideas became the oracle of one major journal, the *Annales*, and strongly influenced at least two other important ones, *Past and Present* (Britain) and the *Journal of Interdisciplinary History* (United States). Bloch's ideas attracted to medieval studies fresh minds with behavioral and social science orientations.

Bloch's *Craft* is a monument to a generation of historians who were deeply moved by the rise of the behavioral and social sciences. They were also stirred by the political upheavals of the century and the leftward transatlantic cultural revolution of the 1930s and again of the 1960s. In this context, the humanistic history inherited from the early years of this century, with its literary associations, precise set of critical principles, and devotion to telling a story in a narrative form, seemed woefully inadequate. Bloch propounded the ideas along whose lines the new history would move. Of the importance and excitement of *Craft* in Bloch's time and through the 1970s there is no doubt. That the application of his ideas in the practice of historical writing has not quite produced the monumental breakthroughs that were anticipated is also true. The problem may lie in leftist ideology inhibiting the intellectual reach of the social and behavioral sciences. If you already know the outcomes you seek, then new concepts will have only limited impact on learning and research.

This conflict between received ideology and new methodology is highlighted in Bloch's own work on medieval society. In *Rural History* Bloch proclaims his peasant populism: "Let us ignore the lords and burgesses, controlling their estates and collecting their rents from their city or small town residences. Strictly speaking, these people had no part in peasant society, which was composed of husbandmen living directly off the soil they cultivated [Transl. Janet Sondenheimer]."

Bloch's peasant thesis is not well grounded in the reality of the Middle Ages. His bold demotic statement provokes rebuttal. Lords had fully as much to do with rural economy as peasants, if not more. They invested in land, provided soil and resources to the peasants, protected the latter as best they could from nature and banditry. They provided for the priest and the village school. Peasant economy relied on the lord's management. And until the late seventeenth century most lords lived on the land. Peasant society was not separate from the nobility. But it is easy to see how Bloch's polemical statement about the autonomy of peasant society appealed to the new radical generation of the two decades after 1968. By that time his work had a ready-made audience of Marxist academics, who were inspired by Adorno and Marcuse.

Populism is compounded with romanticism in *Rural History*. Bloch appeals to French national sentiment: "And so the past continues to dominate the present. If we seek to explain the physiognomy of modern rural France, we shall find that the antecedents of nearly every feature receded into the mists of time." If this means anything beyond sentimentality, it speaks to the backwardness of the French economy in the 1930s, when a third of the population still lived on the land, the catastrophic consequence of turning the land over to the peasants in the French Revolution, resulting in a backward ruralism that France did not start to come out of until the 1950s. *French Rural History* is, from one perspective, a curiously reactionary book that celebrates the relative backwardness of French society in 1931. The long duration of medieval peasant society was, in fact, a tragedy, not a triumph, for France. But in the socialist left there was frequently a recessive yearning for the premodern world. Bloch played to that yearning.

Feudal Society, published as the Germans broke through the flimsy French lines in the Ardennes Forest and rolled across to the sea and then to Paris, is altogether a better effort, with a sense of balance and frequent sensitivity to complex social situations:

> The men of the two feudal ages [before and after 1100] were close to nature—much closer than we are. . . . Behind all social life there was the background of the primitive, of submission to uncontrollable forces, of unrelieved contrasts.
>
> In stormy skies people still saw phantom armies passing by: Armies of the dead, said the populace; armies of deceitful demons, declared the learned, much less inclined to deny these visions than to find for them a quasi-learned interpretation. . . .
>
> In the course of the second feudal age political authority, which up to that time was much subdivided, began everywhere to be concentrated in larger organisms. . . . Corresponding changes took place in the mentality of men. The cultural "renaissance," from the end of the eleventh century, had made it easier for them to understand the social bond—always a somewhat abstract conception—which is implicit in the subordination of the individual to the government. It had also revived the memory of the great well-ordered monarchic states of the past [Transl. L. A. Manyon].

There are two flaws prevalent in Bloch's articulation of feudal society. First, his feudal world is too primitive, ignorant, violent, and poor. We are seeing the feudal world from the level of the upper stratum of the peasantry or lowest stratum of the knightly order. The wonderful learning, wealth, and imagination of monastery, court, cathedral, and university never come closely into focus in Bloch's book, and therefore, it is a strangely underdeveloped and attenuated medieval world we get. The dazzling artistic and imaginative side of the life of the medieval aristocracy is only peripherally mentioned.

The second failure of Bloch's masterwork is his characteristic incapacity for articulating change, and that is not surprising because the dynamics of clergy, city, aristocratic court, and royal administration that were integral to medieval leadership is change he is only peripherally interested in. Note what Bloch says about the rise of medieval monarchies within feudal society. He doesn't understand what is most important in that development—not the size, which was fragile, or the "subordination," which was uneven and ephemeral in many instances and always problematic; not the memory of monarchy, which was mostly contrived propaganda. What is important is the diurnal *technique* of government and law derived from the personalities and private ambitions of the administrators and lawyers, the routines of office and judiciary; the pragmatic emergence of a bureaucratic temperament and administrative imagination—this is what is heading up the change. Talking about "changes . . . in the mentality of men" is too vague and abstract a term for something that was quite concrete and tactile.

Yet Marc Bloch was capable of very productive insights. In his brilliant, magisterial essay "The Rise of Seigneurial Institutions," published in 1941 in the *Cambridge Economic History* (Volume I), which is more insightful than *Feudal Society*, he envisaged a group of feudal vassals as an artificial extended family. The lord is a surrogate father of his knights. This kind of behavioral perception anticipated the fashionably speculative humanistic imagination of the 1960s and 1970s. Bloch did not hesitate to speak of the Middle Ages in a vanguard intellectual's wording. That was indeed a turning point in medieval studies. He legislated a larger range of concept formations and more provocative language by which the Middle Ages could be defined.

"The Rise of Seigneurial Institutions" may have been the last essay on medieval society that Bloch completed. It is a more subtle work than nearly all of *Feudal Society*, the book on which his reputation today largely rests among all but professional, academic medievalists. Bloch's best work on medieval society may very well have still lain ahead of him when he joined the French Army to fight the Nazis. It should be recalled that in 1940 he had been a social historian of the Middle Ages for only a decade. His previous work had been mostly on other aspects of the medieval world. It is quite possible that in time he would have transcended the traditions of French leftist sociology and become a much more complicated and subtle thinker about the medieval world.

IV
THE LONG DURATION

When famous medieval saints got ill and old, especially if they were males (the market value of women saints was greatly discounted), the bishops in whose dioceses they resided, the heads of the religious orders to which they often belonged, and even sometimes the kings or dukes in whose territories they lived began to make plans on how they might capitalize on the faithful's enthusiasm for the marvelous power of intercession with Christ or the Virgin Mary that the saint's posthumous spirits would possess. Careful planning, shrewd intercession at Rome to get a quick canonization (official recognition) of a saint's status, and close programming and manipulation of the saint's disciples could produce high fiscal returns, cultural prestige, and even political value.

So it was with Marc Bloch. There is something of the halo effect with many eminent medievalists, whose posthumous reputation has been effectively employed for the benefit of disciples or institutions with which they were connected. That is a normal penumbra in the world of humanistic scholarship. But the Marc Bloch heritage of sanctity, principally by the manner of his death, was something special and was exploited to build a power base for his Annalist colleagues and disciples. This base, managed with unwavering determination, expanded over the next four decades to control medieval studies and even large stretches of modern history in France and to spread its reach overseas, especially to the United States.

Lucien Febvre in the two years after the war negotiated with the Rockefeller and Ford foundations in New York and the Ministry of Education in Paris to provide the funding—in the case of the ministry a continuing state budget line—for the creation of a research institute. Until 1975 the Annalist institute officially bore the name of the Sixth Section of the École Pratique des Hautes Études, a doctorate-granting umbrella graduate school within the University of Paris. The Sixth Section came to have its own building—the glass and steel Museum (*Maison*) of the Science of Man—as well as lavish resources to support research by its senior members and the doctoral studies of younger colleagues. In 1975, in the course of the reorganization of French higher education, the Bloch memorial Annalist institute became known as the School of Higher Study in the Social Sciences, which now grants its own doctoral degrees. By 1970 no one who was not a product of the institute could get a university post in medieval history in France, and at least half the positions in other fields of history were also awarded to members of this group. An educational monopoly was created to support an intellectual revolution.

Beyond the exploitation of the memory of Bloch, there were other reasons for founding grants from the Ford and Rockefeller foundations and the continued funding by the Ministry of Education. In the late 1940s American foundations were trying to counter the threat of Communist intrusion into Western Europe, and a favorite cultural means of counterattack was to support academic and intellectual groups that might have been left of center but were non-Communist. This was known as the struggle for cultural freedom. In the case of the British highbrow monthly *Encounter*, the ultimate source of funding was later demonstrated to be the Central Intelligence Agency, which was only doing its proper job, and perhaps the CIA was also the disguised source for the Sixth Section's grants from America.

That Febvre wished to establish a research institute and training center to cultivate the ideas propounded by Bloch and himself was deliciously appealing to the American cold war impresarios. Here were highly honored Sorbonne professors and doctoral students who (for the most part, including Febvre) were non-Communist, even if they did not eschew Marxism. In the case of the Ministry of Education's lavish support, which continues to the present time, there was a mixture of motives: to support a radically left group in French academic life that had not done well enough in the 1930s in university circles; to win plaudits from the rabidly leftist students in the Left Bank cafés and assorted boulevard socialist intellectual journals (in other words, radical chic); to strengthen the position of the social and behavioral sciences in French universities, which had by 1940 run down from the eminence of Durkheim's day. Conjoining the social and behavioral sciences with a group of first-rate historians boosted the former but with the long-range effect of making the social and behavioral sciences in Paris overloaded in a historical direction. No Frenchman has yet won the Nobel Prize in economics, and French sociologists were very slow and late in using computer data bases in their analyses. This was an adverse consequence of absorbing the social sciences into Annalist history.

Perhaps also in early days, in the confusions and desperations of the late forties, some people high up in the ministry were paying off debts of conscience for being collaborators with the Vichy government and the Nazis. By endowing Bloch's memory, they possibly were assuaging personal guilt or even paying blackmail for having been double agents who directly or indirectly caused his martyrdom. In any case, it was the Bloch cult of sanctity and patriotism that was directly enshrouded in the Annalist Sixth Section in both glory and money.

Febvre was succeeded as director of the institute in the early 1950s by Fernand Braudel. He had spent the war in Algeria writing his enormous dissertation, under Febvre's direction, on the Mediterranean world in the reign of Philip II—an eleven-hundred-page panorama on the environment, commerce, cultural dimensions, and social groups in both the Christian and Muslim Mediterranean countries in the late sixteenth century. This was regarded at the time as the masterpiece of the *Annales* school, as the embodiment of what the masters had said about total history in the 1930s, the conjuncture of history and anthropology, the dominance of geography and the environmental studies, and the continuity of the ruralist European social structure over many centuries. This Braudel, an inveterate advertiser of memorable phrases, came to call the structural mentality of the long duration. Braudel for ten years after the war was appointed by the ministry to chair the history section of the national program of teacher certification, and he used this in the way Durkheim had used his involvement with schoolteachers: to make his view of history central to the school curriculum of secondary education. So Bloch and the *Annales* school triumphed at the grass roots, in the French schools, as well as at the university and institute levels in Paris. French lycée graduates did not have to be indoctrinated in Annalist history when they entered the university. They were not familiar with any other kind of historical thought.

In the quarter of a century after 1950 Fernand Braudel was along with Claude Lévi-Strauss one of the two greatest mandarins and controllers of patronage in French academic life. Although Lévi-Strauss detested history as meaningless details, as he made amply clear in *Tristes Tropiques*, Braudel accommodated himself to the other grand master and made the *Annales* school even more structural, durable, long-view, contemptuous of the particular events in history than ever before. "Eventual history" now became curse words in French academic life. "Structural history," "durable systems," "interdisciplinary mentalities" were the positive phrases that all members of the rising generation of historians had to espouse as a doxology, unless they didn't mind spending (at best) their careers as assistant professors in the distant provinces or instructing in some obscure Catholic college.

Along with accommodating Lévi-Strauss's structuralism at the price of being able to explain particular events and account for even large-scale changes, Braudel made another concession. He increasingly brought into his own work, and those of his students in the late fifties and sixties, hard-core Marxist ideology in order to win favor with the Red students in the cafés and the leftist intellectuals in the journals and publishing houses. In 1968 he went so far as to proclaim the triumph of the Revolution: "[T]he troubles of May and June 1968 changed everything," though in fact, they changed almost nothing. Braudel then published a new edition of his masterpiece on the Mediterranean world, accommodating a greater dose of Marxist dialectics, to the plaudits of left-wing academics and café intellectuals.

The wonder of the first edition (1953) of Braudel's study of the Mediterranean world in the reign of Philip II was its anthropological plasticity, its sensitivity to the fascinating complexity of social life, its perception of the importance of communications, language, food, dress. By 1967 in *Capitalism and Material Life*, Braudel preferred a more narrow formula that satisfied the Left Bank ideologues: "Marx is right: Who owns the means of production, the land, the ships, the businesses, the raw materials, the finished products and no less the leading positions? . . . This is going back to the language of Marx, and staying with him, even if one immediately rejects his exact words. . . . It is the inequalities, the injustice, the contradictions, large and small, which makes the world go round and ceaselessly transform its upper structures, the only really mobile ones [Trans. Miriam Kochan]."

The beautiful subtlety and humanity of Braudel's early work, the sheer fun of information about human beings, are fading away here. We have seen the same proclivity in Marc Bloch. What restrained Bloch somewhat was the political situation in which he found himself, in the university and the country at large. Braudel felt no embarrassment in meshing the *Annales* view of history with Marxist dogmas because he knew that from the Left Bank cafés and journals to the *New York Review of Books*, he would be applauded. By the early 1960s Braudel's Parisian audience as well as his more radical readers overseas demanded a continuing Marxist tilt, and he complied with this market demand, anticipating correctly that avowal of Marxist formulas would not inhibit largess from American foundations and the French ministry that he could turn into patronage and further satisfy his insatiable empire building.

Braudel's last major work, the three-volume *Structures of Everyday Life*, a product of the late seventies and early eighties, modulated the Marxist dogmas of *Capitalism and Material Life*, which had appeared in French in 1967 and in English in 1973. After the mid-seventies there was a sharp decline of enthusiasm for Marxism among Parisian intellectuals, or at least a young and noisy group of anti-Marxist polemicists and theorists emerged. By 1980 Braudel faced for the first time a countervailing ideological force in Parisian mandarin circles, the now anti-Marxist historian of the French Revolution, François Furet, who attacked the Marxist Annalist traditions in which he himself had been educated. Braudel, ever attuned to the direction of the political wind, toned down his Marxist theory and returned partway to the kind of anthropological details of his *Mediterranean World*. His final trilogy offers much more data about everyday life than interpretive structure. But meanwhile, the younger generation of Annalists had followed Braudel's Marxist program.

The two best *Annales* medievalists of the new generation, Georges Duby and Emmanuel Le Roy Ladurie, made much of Marx's concept of primitive capital accumulation in their respective works on medieval rural societies. The question arising from Marxist doctrine was: In a primarily rural economy of low productivity, how is enough capital accumulated to provide the basis for the next stage of dialectical social development, the age of commercial capitalism? Duby in his *Early Growth of the European Economy* (1974) pointed to the gaining of booty in the barbarian forays and feudal wars of the early Middle Ages as the foundation for capital accumulation. Le Roy Ladurie (a quondam Communist and the privileged son of a Vichy collaborator and government minister) in his *Peasants of Languedoc* (1966) provided a broad explanation that he backed up with a pioneering effort in quantitative history: The Black Death caused an enormous fall in population in the late Middle Ages, but by 1450 agricultural productivity had after the end of the Hundred Years' War recovered to its level of two centuries before, creating a class of wealthy peasants with steady capacity for capital accumulation. In the late 1970s and 1980s, both Duby and Le Roy Ladurie, handsome, articulate, well-groomed Parisians, became TV stars in the metropolis. No one in Paris questioned their perception of the Middle Ages. No one dared to.

The populist familiar style that Duby and Le Roy Ladurie cultivated goes back through Bloch to Henri Pirenne. Bloch was very impressed that when he and Pirenne arrived in a northern city to attend an academic conference, after checking into the hotel, they discussed what they should do first: Visit the museums or tour the sites of contemporary life and architecture. Pirenne insisted on the latter: Begin with the present and work backward. So it was with the Bloch of *Rural History* and subsequently, and this attitude became a hallmark of the *Annales* group, descending to Duby and Le Roy Ladurie, who gave it a gloss of their strong personal charisma.

When Duby first visited Columbia University in 1962, he insisted on visiting not the Cloisters but a jazz club in Greenwich Village. He didn't want to be found paying a ceremonial call on a second-rate Spanish monastery. In 1980 Le Roy Ladurie made a triumphal tour of the eastern United States. Tall, blond, thin, handsome, a Gallic star, he first brought personal happiness to many on the campus of Bryn Mawr College, as he broadly hinted at a ceremonial luncheon for him tendered by the dean at New York University, where he arrived to give a public lecture. At the lecture 400 people crowded into a room meant for 250. Le Roy Ladurie read from a prepared English manuscript in an impenetrable French accent. Thirty minutes into his talk, the public-address system failed and was not repaired for twenty minutes. All the while Le Roy Ladurie never stopped reading from his manuscript, even though only the people in the first two or three rows could hear him. But no one in the audience stirred. What they were moved by was not his particular comments on medieval society but his charismatic presence. He was the rock star of medievalists. Indeed, he looked like a middle-aged David Bowie. Le Roy Ladurie was later President François Mitterrand's choice to be the director of the Bibliothèque Nationale, a position even more important in French cultural life than heading the Library of Congress is in the United States.

The eventual successor to Fernand Braudel in the 1980s as head of the Bloch-Febvre institute was the medievalist Jacques Le Goff. He, too, was master of the populist mode. His favorite publication was a lengthy manifesto calling for an anthropological history. When Le Goff published a collection of these programmatic manifestos under the sparkling title *Time, Work, and Culture in the Middle Ages* (1980), the book was greeted with ecstatic applause, especially in the United States. The *New York Review of Books*, a veritable house organ of the

Annalist school, took the lead in praising Le Goff's book as the last word in medieval studies.

What the younger generation of French medievalists learned from Bloch through Braudel was the importance of communication. It was not only what you said but how you said it, the way you communicated, the style with which you delivered your thesis—in short, marketing—that was so important and persuasive. Thereby they made medieval studies accessible to a much larger educated public. The University of Chicago Press caught on to this early, after phenomenal success with a translation of Bloch's *Feudal Society*. The University of Chicago Press came to specialize in attractively packaged translations of the *Annales* medievalists. It had an astonishing success with Duby's *Three Orders* (1980, original French edition 1978). Here Duby propounds the interesting but conventional thesis that eleventh-century feudalism was in large part shaped by ecclesiastical ideology, that feudalism was the imposition of clerical hierarchical ideals on society. This conventional interpretation was hailed at the annual Kalamazoo conference of American medievalists by Jeremy duQuesnay Adams of Southern Methodist University as "one of the most important works of creative medieval scholarship published in any language since the Second World War."

That feudalism was rooted in ecclesiastical ideology was an old idea. It could not have been the idea but the way Duby presented it that produced such praise at Kalamazoo. Similarly, packaging accounts for the number one best-selling book among postwar Annalist medieval studies, Le Roy Ladurie's book of the early 1970s *Montaillou*, which was a smash hit in both France and in its English translation in the United States, where it continues to sell well in a paperback edition. Since the 1920s it was known that there was in the Vatican Library in Rome a lengthy inquisitorial record made by a bishop (who later became pope; that is why it ended up in Rome) in a mountain town in southwestern France in the early fourteenth century. The inquisitorial record was fascinating because it offered not only confessions of backwoods Catharist heretics but a series of confessions about sexual misconduct. Since the mountaineer peasants were under pressure to confess in order to avoid severe punishment (including the stake), they babbled on endlessly about their religious and sexual misconduct, telling the bishop exactly what he wanted to hear, so they would be absolved. Scholars had looked at it many times, but no one had done anything about this record because of its tainted source. This did not stop Le Roy Ladurie. He treated it as if it were an anthropological fieldwork record of native informers telling a visiting social scientist about their kinship connections. The result was a deliciously fascinating book. It was flawed methodologically, but who cared? Only a few old fogy non-Annalist medievalists. Le Roy Ladurie presented the story artfully to communicate the impression that peasant life had not changed since the fourteenth century; all peasants ever cared about were the pleasures of the table and bed.

Jacques Le Goff was equally adept in packaging and communication. He wrote a little book on medieval usury, published in 1988 in English under the snappy title *Your Money or Your Life*. It is a solid, straightforward account of this well-researched subject, interesting but offering nothing new. But Le Goff spiced up his little book on medieval usury by quoting (twice!) a poem by Ezra Pound on usury. Is that relevant? No, but it makes for more attractive packaging. A pre-Annalist historian like Louis Halphen would have never opened his old-fashioned mind to the prospect of glitzing up an account of medieval usury by quoting Ezra Pound.

This is what made Bloch's disciples so exciting. They knew how to gain attention, how to communicate, how to market their ideas. They made medieval studies more accessible; they expanded the audience for the Middle Ages. And they legitimated just about any form, any technique, any gimmick for selling the Middle Ages to the educated public. Twenty years from now, when the Marxist interpretation at the core of the Annalist work will have become redundant and effete, the communicative skills and marketing techniques of Bloch's disciples will still seem instructive and admirable.

In the short run, and still in the early 1990s, we are left with the situation that the transatlantic triumph of the Annalist school and its affiliates signified the prominence of left-leaning, essentially Marxist interpretations in medieval studies. In 1952, in the introduction to the English translation of Bloch's *Historian's Craft*, Princeton's Joseph Strayer, the dean of American medieval historians, calmly placed Bloch as a medieval historian below the top rung of French medievalists like Louis Halphen and Ferdinand Lot. By the mid-1960s this evaluation was already obsolete and insignificant because Bloch's image was carried so high by his triumphant Annalist disciples. His environmentally and materially determined and class-oriented perspectives, and his enthusiasm for what came to be called in the 1980s the alternative population of the peasantry, were very widely perceived as a liberation movement in medieval studies and the beginning of a new, much better era (better both intellectually and politically) in the interpretation of the Middle Ages.

The Annalist triumph was further reinforced in the 1970s with the rise of women's history and feminist doctrines. Medieval women were viewed, like the peasantry, as another alternative population contrasted with the elite male cadre of aristocratic society. Women of the medieval nobility would actually have been unhappy placed in an oppositional category allegedly contending against their fathers and brothers. They would have resented ascription of solidarity to them against male lords and alongside peasants, Jews, heretics, and gays. But within the ideological categories of the 1970s and 1980s, this kind of polemical medieval women's history was popular and persuasive. The Annalist school was quick to validate medieval women's history and thereby gained a new cadre of adherents. As Susan Mosher Stuard, a leading American feminist medievalist, pointed out in 1987, the masters of the Annalist school themselves disappointingly devoted little attention to medieval women. But the ideological affinity between the Annalists and the feminist historians was compelling and offered early expectations of an innovative focus on gender.

Considering the political and intellectual history of the Western world from the mid-1930s into the 1980s, a class-oriented approach to looking at medieval society, with overwhelming sympathy for the peasantry and other unempowered groups and a perspective on the medieval world from the assumed outlook and interests of the rural working class, was likely to come to the fore. The head of the history faculty at Moscow State University in the late 1940s and 1950s, E. A. Kosminsky, indeed put forward a straight-line Marxist-Leninist model of late-thirteenth-century English society. But this lacked the subtlety of expression and, more important, the academic legitimation that were provided by the Annalist school. After the failure of the transatlantic revolution of 1968, its partisans sought refuge and careers in the academic humanities and social sciences. These now became the most vociferous and determined advocates of the *Annales* school in both France and the United States. They saw in the heritage of Bloch and Braudel justification for their own positions.

If the intended outcome in the sixties and seventies was to form a cadre of well-placed leftist medievalists and other humanists within the rising campus generation, Bloch would not have forgone this rare opportunity. His image of himself was unquestionably that of a revolutionary within academia, as much as or more than that of a per-

petuator of the great traditions of comprehensive medievalist discovery.
Bloch would have endorsed the more intransigent leftist politicization
of humanistic interpretation since 1968. Louis Halphen would have
resisted it.

Halphen and Marc Bloch were only six years apart in age. They
belonged essentially to the same generation. They came from identical cultural and social backgrounds: upper-middle-class Parisian Jewish academic families. They had identical educations and pursued the
same career as medieval scholars, in both cases with great success.
They both were victims of Nazi repression but were able to escape
from it—until Bloch with fierce courage actively turned against the
Nazis, returned from exile, and blatantly risked martyrdom as a genuine hero of the resistance. Despite the identical cultural, social, ethnic, and religious backgrounds of Halphen and Bloch, they significantly
parted company in the 1930s. Halphen remained steadfastly loyal to
the old rationalist, humanistic culture of Western Europe to which
assimilated Jews had become so devoted in the nineteenth century.
He believed that the good that happens in history is mainly the consequence of the impact of learned intelligence on politics and society.
Bloch came to revere the peasant masses and to commit himself to a
radical, essentially Marxist model of history and society. This is the
seismic rift—between the liberal center and the radical left—that ran
through the lives of all educated middle-class Jews in the free world
in the 1930s and 1940s. Profound traces of that rift are still clearly
visible and in places like Paris and New York City continue to be of
high signification for both intellectual and political life. This is one
of the most important developments in the intellectual and social history of this century. We are a long way from outliving its consequences. It is a crossroads that the newly liberated intelligentsia of
Eastern Europe will encounter.

What happened in the mind of Marc Bloch that separated him
from the old Jewish humanistic culture to which Halphen, as well as
Bloch's father, the Parisian classicist, subscribed? We do not know
for sure. Perhaps it was the shattering experience of long service in
World War I. Perhaps it was pessimism about the future of liberal
capitalism stemming from the Great Depression and the rise of fascism. Certainly the magisterial influence of the Faustian devil Lucien
Febvre played a part. But one thing we do know: Bloch's reinterpretation of medieval history along Marxist lines was an event of critical
importance not only for the understanding of the Middle Ages but
for academic culture as a whole, with a politically polarizing and in-

tellectually provocative outcome we are just beginning to appreciate fully.

The two most influential and widely read books on medieval history published in the past half century were Bloch's *Feudal Society* and *The Making of the Middle Ages* by the Oxford don R. W. Southern. They both were departures from the modernist kind of medieval history (detailed political, legal, and administrative analysis) that had retained high respectability since the late nineteenth century. They both were therefore works of intellectual rebellion, a clarion call to the younger generation to break out of the old mold and attempt new things. After that, these two books were very different. They were indeed intellectually and emotionally in conflict with each other. Bloch's book communicated social collectivities and class conflict understood through the language of the behavioral sciences. It was also a large, sprawling, messy work that exhibited the aggressive self-confidence of French mandarin culture. Southern's book was concise and artistically careful, and it communicated a refined neoromantic sensibility and an appreciation of individuated personality, as well as Oxbridge disciplined reticence.

The institutional outcome of Bloch's and Southern's celebrities was also very different. Southern worked alone, pursued a traditional Oxbridge career, encouraged no cadre of disciples, and formed no institute. Febvre and other associates and disciples of Bloch did what he himself certainly would have wanted, which was to create an institute to solidify the results of his work and train successive generations in his concepts and methods. Creating such durable edifices was traditional in French academic culture. By the fact of Bloch's martyrdom and other contingencies, this institute became the greatest power center in French academic life since 1945 in the whole array of what the French call the human sciences. Its distinctive impact on interpreting the Middle Ages will be felt for a long time. The language, scope, and texture of medieval studies have been permanently affected by Bloch's heritage.

A prominent left-wing ("New Historicist" is the current euphemism) critic of medieval literature and head of the Medieval Studies Center at Duke University, Lee Patterson, wrote in 1987: "There is a Middle Ages of the Right and Left, and they entail allegiances that govern most if not all of the critical work at the present time." This is stated more categorically than I would prefer to do, but there is a core of truth in it. Marc Bloch and the *Annales* school constitute the best the left has to offer in medieval studies. The relative complexity and sophistication of their thought have saved us from having to tolerate harsh Soviet dialecticians of the Stalinist-Leninist tradition as exponents of the left's articulation of a Middle Ages.

As an ingredient of the liberalization of East European culture, the ideas of Bloch and the Annalists have belatedly come to be embraced or at least freely articulated in Communist countries. In 1986 Bronislaw Geremek, the parliamentary leader of Solidarity in Poland, published in Bloch's journal *Annales* a tribute to the master. It offers no new insight into Bloch's work and indeed is rather crude and simpleminded, but the article was presumably published by the suave Parisian editors to show the political significance of Bloch's ideas for the new tide of social democracy in the East. In 1988 the Cambridge University Press published *Medieval Popular Culture* by the current Soviet leading medieval historian, Aron Gurevich. Gurevich's book, which received the customary accolades in the West automatically accorded the more liberal Soviet intelligentsia, is largely derived from the works of Jacques Le Goff, for whom Gurevich professes his "very high regard," and Le Goff's colleagues and students.

Possibly nothing would have made Bloch happier than to see the triumph of his ideas and assumptions in the Soviet Union and Poland and the absorption of the work of his disciples into the newly developing liberal-left culture of Eastern Europe. Solidarity with the more intellectual and humanistic wing of the international European left and the incorporation of his interpretation of medieval society into this leftist culture were a vision that was central to Bloch's being, and now it is coming to pass.

The heritage of Marc Bloch (articulated and strengthened through Febvre, Braudel, and the Annalist school) constitutes a central chapter in the intellectual history of the transatlantic and European world in the twentieth century. It is peculiar how especially influential that heritage has been in the liberalized Soviet world and in the United States, while undergoing something of a decline in France itself in the 1980s, as Jacques Le Goff himself lamented in a wistful article in the *Times Literary Supplement* in 1989.

With respect to the United States, finally we can point to the peculiar publishing history of *The Poor in the Middle Ages*, by the Sorbonne professor and devout Bloch disciple Michel Mollat. From 1962 to 1976 Mollat conducted a seminar in Paris on this canonized leftist subject, and the original French edition of the relatively short book that summarized the results of this lengthy inquiry and dialogue appeared in 1978. The book enshrines the familiar leftist dogmas of the

1960s and 1970s. We are told that criminals and antisocial individuals are "rebels before their time," as was proclaimed by the fashionable liberal-left sociological cant of the era. And the well-worn Leninist thesis of false consciousness of the proletariat that fails to realize the cause and nature of its misery is enshrined by Mollat as the governing assumption for studying the medieval poor: "They and their spokes-men seem not to have had a clear idea of either their fate or their solidarity, because they did not know themselves." We can nostalgi-cally place such assumptions within the obsolete leftist culture of the sixties and seventies, along with the occupations of university presi-dents' offices by the Students for a Democratic Society, were it not for the strange fact that in 1986 the Yale University Press chose to bring out an unrevised English translation of Mollat's conventional book, with a commendation from the professor of medieval history at Yale John Boswell, the expert on medieval gays and child abusers, that Mollat's study of the medieval poor was "authoritative." Author-itative of what? Certainly of the liberal-left culture of the sixties and seventies and the immensely active and seemingly perpetual intellec-tual tradition of Marc Bloch and his followers.

CHAPTER FIVE

———————◆◆◆———————

THE FORMALISTS

ERWIN PANOFSKY AND
ERNST ROBERT CURTIUS

I
FORMALISM AS INTERPRETATION AND
IDEOLOGY

The understanding and perception of the Middle Ages in the twentieth century, after the basic historical context of political and social development had been established, has depended heavily on the progress of the disciplines of art history and criticism and literary history and criticism. This shift has taken place not only because of the intrinsic importance of imaginative subject matter within human culture but also because of the enormous volume of surviving visual and written material. It is through the study of literature, art, and philosophy of the Middle Ages that further code-breaking entry into the medieval mentality will primarily occur well into the twenty-first century. Conventional historical research is not likely to alter the contours of presently perceived medieval government, society, and economy.

The development of art and literary history in medieval studies has not been just a miscellany of learned reports. There has also been a strong element of intellectual cohesion. It has been shaped by an overriding set of assumptions and an interpretive mode called formalism. The two most influential figures in the history of the formalist interpretive movement were Erwin Panofsky and Ernst Robert Curtius. Both were Germans, although because of his exile on racial grounds by the Nazis, Panofsky spent the greater part of his career in the United States. Panofsky and Curtius—these are the two formalist masters whose profound influence is still felt today in understanding medieval literature and art.

At least 85 percent of the work in medieval art history since the beginning of this century may be designated as formalism. In the twenty years after World War II, it enjoyed a similar dominance in literature departments' focus on medieval studies. Since the mid-sixties the formalist view of the study of medieval imaginative literature has been challenged, and this challenge partly accounts for the continued vigor and invention in literary as opposed to art history tracks in medieval studies. But 70 percent of the publications on medieval literature today are still within the formalist tradition.

In art history, formalism is called iconography or iconology (in the 1930s there was held to be a subtle distinction between these terms, but since the late 1960s their meanings have been practically synonymous, and the terms are used interchangeably). "Iconology" is derived from "icon" (image) and therefore means a symbolic form in medieval art. In literary history and criticism, formalism is identified with a concentration or interpretation that has several names meaning the same thing: topology; typology; figural studies; formularies. This view claims that medieval literature as well as art is an unfolding not of original creations by individuals but of a set of standard motifs, themes, tropes, and formulas of representation. The "topos" (type) is what is central to medieval imaginative literature, just as the iconic image is central to art.

A definition of formalism in medieval studies might be the way of interpreting literature or art that stresses the heavy or exclusive dominance of traditional standard images or motifs, perpetual coded formulas of representation and description. The traditional, standardized images and motifs are privileged and centered in this view of medieval visual and literary art, while individual creativity and original discovery are marginalized or excluded altogether. Formalists regard medieval literature and art as overwhelmingly dominated by traditional sets of images and themes and individual creativity in literature and art as rare.

Formalist iconography and topology hold that the painter or sculptor (or, over very long stretches of time, the architect) or the poet or prose writer of the Middle Ages was aiming not at originality in idea but at continuation of the established tradition that told him (99 percent of the time it was a "him") the precise motif or image to employ. The visual or literary artist's quality was determined by his skill in applying the inherited motif or image, not in thinking up new ones. Literary and artistic styles and genres did change, but not the the-matic content of ideas in medieval art and literature. Ideas, themes, motifs followed traditional formularies.

Iconology and topology also speak to the conservative continuity and enduring unity of higher medieval culture. The great preponderance of images and motifs was inherited from Greco-Roman classical art and literature or from the thought world of the Church Fathers (patristic culture, fourth to sixth century), which in turn was a product of the interaction of biblical ideas with the classical traditions. In practice, therefore, the art or literary historians and critics who subscribed to the formalist interpretation of medieval culture are always looking backward from the ninth, twelfth, or fourteenth century to trace the image or motif to its emergence in classical or patristic art or literature.

In this highly traditional context very small changes in presentation of a motif or idea are likely to be significant. Art or literary historians look for any minute adjustments in the formularies in the present works they are studying and try to account for these very modest modifications at the margin. Sometimes the slight alterations are intentional and meaningful; sometimes they are merely fortuitous. Formalist art and literary historians must be very learned in classical and patristic culture and work with a library of these ancient works, all sorts of dictionaries and reference works, and photographs of these visual monuments, at their sides.

A formalist is engaged in the exposition of the classical and patristic traditions within the structure of not only early but also the high and late (1000–1500) Middle Ages. A formalist in medieval studies is committed to demonstrating the continuity of classical and humanist and Christian ideas in European civilization. In this last respect, formalism has obvious ideological implications. It is a facet of cultural conservatism in the twentieth century, a kind of traditional humanism that rejects the radicalism that stems alike from the left and extreme right of political culture. Ideologically the opposite of formalism is relativism, which claims that ideas and images lack intrinsic value and stability and are mere reflections of group will, state power, and personal psychology. Formalism both demonstrates empirically the generational and longitudinal perpetuation of conceptual, imagistic, and linguistic constructions and contends that this traditional quality in thought and learning makes for social happiness and personal satisfaction.

Formalism stands in solidarity with learned elitism and the unity and continuity of a high European civilization. It rejects and fears mass culture and popular innovations whether of the Marxist, capitalist, or fascist varieties. Social deterministic interpretations of art and literature as products of class interests and material forces are intensely disliked by ideological formalism, which insists that art and literature are products of something fundamental in human nature, beyond the relative conditions of time and place. Popular commercial music and art, advertising, and determination of ideas and styles by the marketplace and the state—these are regarded as the manifestation of vulgar simplification and state terrorism and are condemned by formalism, which hearkens to the vision of the refined humanism that is independent of these popular impulses and authoritarian operations.

Formalism sees the art and literature that are its subject matter and the humanistic heritage it reveres as the products of a deeply learned, historically minded, and affluent elite joined continuously over generations and centuries. This elite was normally part of a ruling class. The resources for the production of art and literature came from this empowered class and the state it controlled. The poets and painters were usually under the patronage of the ruling-class families and state institutions. The literature, art, and philosophy of Western Europe were the product of the aristocracy, or of writers and artists working under aristocratic patronage and guidance, or of particular scions of the middle class who had imbibed aristocratic culture and linguistic capability. This is formalism's historical dogma. It is claimed that this recognizable social situation does not intrinsically detract from the spiritual, creative character, the intellectual autonomy, and the exclusive continuity of the traditions that the formalists study and admire as synonymous with Western civilization. This belief is central to formalism. It is an ideology of cultural conservatism.

Formalist scholarship in medieval studies loves the small gesture, the marginal line, the precise derivation, the subtle, almost imperceptible echo of an enduring leitmotif in European culture. In classical antiquity and the early church, as refined and delicately elaborated over the centuries, lies the glorious center of Western civilization, the formalists believe. Making all the difference are an autonomous mentality and coded behavior pattern, not the dirt of material forces and noisy confusion of social change. The latter is merely the fertilized dross from which the delicate rose of European culture grows. Manure is not roses.

Formalism's capital centers lie in the German universities of the 1920s, in Oxbridge and Paris, and, especially since the 1940s, in the Ivy League universities (and their imitators, like Berkeley, Ann Arbor, and Chapel Hill) and the Institute for Advanced Study at Princeton. Formalism is a culture that was especially defined by the German (often Jewish) academic and intellectual groups of the Weimar era and was then driven westward by the Hitlerian dispersion to join up with and greatly reinforce the formalist citadels already existing in the United States, Britain, and France. The significance of American mass culture, especially after the advent of the rock era, was in practice almost totally ignored by formalism.

The great formalists were by no means oblivious of the world in which they lived. Formalism in art and literary history reached its apogee of confidence and influence in the humanities departments of American universities in the 1950s and 1960s. This zenith of formalism was therefore coterminous with the age of American political and economic hegemony and cold war liberalism. That was the era of American exceptionalist faith that the United States uniquely stood for an open society and the preservation of the best that had been thought and said in the world. The formalists are not embarrassed by the flowering of their critical interpretation in the heyday of American power. They do not assent to the Marxist claim that this coincidence signifies that formalism was a cultural manifestation of American imperialism. American power and prosperity, the formalists respond, simply provided the intellectual freedom and security for the intense cultivation of the European heritage.

Formalism meant ideologically a concerted and persistent effort to combat the culture of political despair, spiritual pessimism, and moral relativism in order to preserve the hard residue of humanistic values of Western civilization against the barbarian threats of nazism and Stalinism. In the minds of its advocates, formalism represented reason, learning, stability, consciousness, ethics, and intellectual freedom, as opposed to cynicism, simplification, vulgarization, and tyranny.

Within this ideological signification of formalism lies a gradation of analytical practice. Formalist interpreters of medieval art and literature know, of course, that illumination and text were the products of a specific social and cultural time and place, and this can be considered when iconological and topological study is pursued. There is some variation in the extent to which the social and cultural ambience is reflected in the ultimate formalist interpretation. Simplifying with crude quantification by way of hypothetical explanation, formalist recognition of the importance of the social circumstances in which an illumination or text was created varies between a 5 and 25 percent recognition factor of social ambience, but to the social determinist and Marxist the variance is between 75 and 100 percent. This is the practical interpretive outcome of the conflict in ideological assumptions.

Formalism involves psychology as well as history and ideology. Formalism believes that creativity in the visual and literary arts (at least before the mid-nineteenth century) is the outcome of artists and writers whose private insights are subordinated to the authority of cultural tradition. Great visual and literary art develops along the margin of psychological constraint. It derives from placing individual skill and personal feeling at the service of global traditions and cultural authority. Formalism thus views creativity in medieval culture as emerging out of the exploration of memory. But in Jungian fashion the memory is much more of a collective than a personal one.

Personal memory is constrained and conditioned within the typologies and configurations of collective memory. This doctrine is central to formalist analysis. Formalism is, therefore, the polar opposite of the ideal of the individualistic, rebellious bohemian artist, responsible only to his or her own feelings, that has been a cultural myth of the past two centuries.

Opposition to formalism in medieval studies since the 1960s has come primarily from literary historians and critics who see in their texts after 1100 the exercise of a self-conscious personal as well as collective memory. They believe that the collective repression and the tracking system of the figural collective memory could not hold back novel personal insights, idiosyncratic self-consciousness, and expressions of individual psychology. While on an ideological level the struggle in general academic culture occurs between the formalists (conservative humanists) and the social determinists (Marxists), in medieval studies the productive dispute is mainly between the formalist adherents to the overwhelming power of collective memory (tradition) and those who recognize the power of personal sensibility (individual expression). To be able to make their innovative statements, the individualist interpreters, like Robert W. Hanning of Columbia University and Peter Dronke of Cambridge, had to master the vast learning of the formalist school of the previous half century, and the individuation and individualism they perceive in medieval literature are still recognized within a fundamental context of formal tradition and collective memory. The revisionist expression of personal memory and individual consciousness is rarely more than a 25 percent segmentation away from the continuity and comprehensiveness of the iconographical and figural collectivity.

The great formalists took as their subject matter the nuanced application and cultivation in the Middle Ages of the collective typological memory derived from classical antiquity and the early church. This remains the indispensable disciplinary foundation for the study of medieval art and literature. Any other more recent interpretation is an amendment to the hard-core formalist position and cannot gain meaning or credibility without recognition of the central position of classic formalism in the interpretation of medieval art and literature.

Formalism had strong affinities but not complete identities with two other intellectual movements of the first half of the twentieth century; German *Geistesgeschichte* and transatlantic modernism. Formalism's affinity with *Geistesgeschichte* lay in historicism (the assumption that no work of art or literature could be understood outside a developmental context or interpreted outside longitudinal tradition), in elitism, in love of learning, and in a proclivity to see an inner spirit within external shapes. Formalism's resemblance to modernism lay in an obsessive eagerness to concentrate on particular works of art and literature rather than to talk generally and abstractly and in as intense and concrete an examination of these works as possible ("close reading" in modernist parlance), filling up many years or the better part of a lifetime in this thorough examination with every conceivable resource of erudite analysis. There is an obvious contradiction at work here, *Geistesgeschichte's* propensity to long-range historical perspective clashing with modernism's compulsion to concentrate on the immediate specific work of visual or literary art (textuality)—the large scale signified as against the small scale exhaustively examined. This conflict was not practically important in art history departments since these were so small and marginal when the great German émigrés arrived in the United States and Britain that the latter did what they pleased. But tension did bubble up occasionally in literature departments in the 1930s and 1940s. There was conflict between the German proponents of intellectual history and the aggressive British-originated variant of modernism that was represented by a dominant residual group.

Where a meeting ground could be found was that both humanistic movements and academic groups were devoted to deep learning, were essentially elitist and hostile to demotic impulses, and were culturally conservative. Both movements also loved classical texts, and its members on both sides frequently had a taste for patristic theology. The antagonism between the diachronic (historicizing) tendency of *Geistesgeschichte* and the synchronic (antihistorical, analytical) attitude of modernism did present something of a problem for the formalists in American universities in the period 1935 to 1960 since they were in emotional and conceptual league with both sides. But formalism in its greatest exponents managed to live with, and perhaps benefit from, this stimulating contradiction, from its affinities with both *Geistesgeschichte* and modernism. Eventually, in the 1960s and 1970s, this left formalism open to charges of inconsistency, contradiction, and intellectual slackness. But by then the giants of formalism had done their seminal explorations of iconic image and topological motif. Meanwhile, pleasant luncheons and bibulous late afternoons in the faculty club, as well as mutual enjoyment of the blessed condition of American academia in its halcyon era from 1945 to 1965, could discourage and moderate much theoretical argument.

Critics of formalism today might venture the opinion that in the long run this avoidance of intellectual resolution generated a leveling off in the dynamic quality of formalist interpretation, that the onset of routinization in the sixties and seventies in formalist interpretation was a consequence of the shutting out of fundamental conceptual issues that were there from the beginning. But the product of every school of humanistic scholarship is better than its theory. Formalist medieval studies in art and literary history and criticism involved a peculiar combination of the structural and the contingent, the general and the specific, the diachronic and synchronic. Unresolved programmatic issues there were: Should social ambience be given some marginal consideration or be almost exclusively ignored? Should the text or picture be considered almost entirely within its immediate frame or within a more general and longitudinal perspective? Behind the perpetuation of icon and topos, what kind of individual consciousness affected the literary or visual artist? These issues did not prevent the great formalists of the half century after 1920 from doing their monumental work. These were proud lions and the big bears of medieval studies.

II
THE RISE OF ICONOLOGY

Behind German iconology of the 1920s and 1930s, where the history of medieval art history properly begins, there lie two other movements of medieval art interpretation: the Anglo-American connoisseurs and the French iconographers. We may read their books today mostly for curiosity or convenience rather than for enlightenment, but they were certainly colorful characters.

Go to any American campus, and you will find that art history may be taught by a department of that designation or by something called the department of fine arts. The latter title is a vestige of the age of connoisseurship in art history, when it was a study pursued by self-taught gentlemen and occasionally also by refined ladies. A connoisseur is someone who has no systematic academic training or methodology of art history. He (or, less often, she) is an autodidact who travels around enough looking at pictures and monuments, until he acquires practical learning and a judicious eye and opinionated judgments about medieval or Renaissance art. He is nearly always a dealer, either openly or surreptitiously, or is in the pay of dealers. This species has almost disappeared since today even the museum curators and private gallery experts have now had a preparation in academic training up to a point, if not at the doctoral level. But in the first half of this century these self-taught connoisseurs, these well-informed and dealing amateurs, were common and influential on both sides of the Atlantic. Their prototype was an Italian expert on Renaissance painting in the 1880s named Giovanni Morelli. The last of the great connoisseurs was Kenneth Clark, an Oxford graduate in the humanities from a billionaire textile family who rose to be the director of the Tate Gallery in London and that same Lord Clark who lectured us on BBC and PBS TV in the 1960s on the history of civilization.

The most famous, financially successful (he made $8 million from his expertise, $150 million in 1990 dollars), and influential of the great connoisseurs was Bernard Berenson. He was an immigrant Jew from the slums of Boston, short and slim, who won a scholarship to Harvard and early established a clientage relationship with Isabella Stewart Gardner. She was a vivacious millionaire Boston matron, who sent him traveling to Europe to learn expertise and develop a sharp eye and build a collection of Renaissance masters for her, which are still hung in her house (now a museum) on the Boston Fenway. Berenson's elaborate villa in Florence now houses a Harvard institute of Renaissance studies.

Berenson, after several adventures, not all of them strictly ethical, joined up around 1910 with Joseph Duveen, a London and New York art and antiques dealer to American billionaires (the Duveens were Dutch Jews who emigrated to Britain). Together for the next thirty years Berenson and Lord Duveen, as he came to be, dominated the transatlantic private art trade in old masters of the late medieval and early modern eras. In the side streets and impoverished villas of Florence, Rome, Venice, and Siena, Duveen and his agents discovered paintings at knock down prices. Berenson authenticated them, dated them, and ascribed authorship to them. Most of the time, laborious research has since shown, he was honest in his attributions, although sometimes honestly mistaken. Once in a while, under Duveen's pressure, Berenson leaned in a direction he should not have.

Berenson became famous in the early twentieth century for publishing pioneering messy books on Renaissance Italian art. It has recently been shown that some of the best of these were coauthored or even primarily written by his brilliant wife, Mary Pearsall Smith, a Bryn Mawr graduate from the first age of Pennsylvania mainline feminism and Bertrand Russell's sister-in-law. Kenneth Clark was Berenson's disciple and fought hard, in the 1960s and before his death, to protect his master's reputation from investigative biographers. Colin Simpson's book on Berenson and Duveen, *The Partnership* (1987), using for the first time the confidential files of Duveen's company, has blown the cover-up. One delightful item that Simpson relates is that Berenson and Duveen sometimes used Yiddish words as secret codes in their slippery art-dealing communications. Thus *chodesh* ("new") was the code word for "fake."

Paris in the late nineteenth century also had its share of connoisseurs, but they were more important for early modern Baroque French monuments than for medieval and Renaissance art, nor were the French as sharp and unscrupulous as Berenson and Duveen as dealers, if such a differential can be measured. A significant iconographical school of medieval art history also developed in France in the later decades of the nineteenth century. This French study and elaborate photographic publication of medieval religious images grew out of a state-funded effort at archaeology and restoration (often bungled) that goes back to the 1840s and was in part inspired by Victor Hugo's sensational romantic novel *The Hunchback of Notre Dame*. The great and still-read exponent of the French school of iconography was Émile

Mâle, who in 1892 published his *Religious Art in Thirteenth Century France* (available in an abbreviated, indifferently translated American paperback as *The Gothic Image*). Eventually Mâle's work developed into a three-volume account of French iconography from about 1100 to 1500 (completed in 1922). Mâle was a high school literature teacher with little or no training in art history when he began this work. He aimed at and gained a very wide audience, the reason why his volume on Gothic art is still extensively used in American college courses. But Mâle's knowledge, except for his close observation of cathedral facades and sculptures and occasional dipping into accessible illuminated manuscripts, was shallow. He lacked systematic control of his material and the deep knowledge of literature and theology that distinguished the German school of iconography, which was just getting into high gear when Mâle completed his work.

Mâle was essentially an industrious connoisseur and public educator who knew what he liked. His work is descriptive rather than analytical, an example of glorious French vulgarization. In the late 1970s Harry Bober, a New York University art historian, and the Princeton University Press curiously tried to resurrect Mâle with a magnificent new edition and an accurate translation of his trilogy. But Mâle's work belongs essentially to the era of the *prehistory* of iconography, as a postscript to nineteenth-century good intentions and superficial thinking. (The other great name in French medieval art history, Henri Focillon, who published from the late thirties to the mid-fifties, was really an intellectual and church historian making heavy use of iconographical examples.) French iconography is enthusiastic and romantic, the post-Hugo effect, rather than persuasively analytical and theoretically well grounded. In medieval art history it was the great German formalists—principally Erwin Panofsky and his colleagues, building on the methodological guidelines laid down by Aby Warburg—and their American and British disciples and epigones who were responsible for the rise of iconology to its stellar place in the interpretation of the Middle Ages.

Preparation for the German school of formalist iconology was adumbrated in the seminal work of Heinrich Wölfflin of the University of Basel, *Principles of Art History* (1915), which remains an important and a highly controversial book. Wölfflin's interest was in accounting for changes in style: How does painting get from Renaissance to Baroque style? To answer this, he withdraws painting from the world of culture and the world of nature alike and gives it an inner, autonomous history, "a life of its own." Every painting has a formal structure, and "every form lives on, begetting . . . the effect of picture on picture as a factor in style." Here is a kind of formalism emerging. Wölfflin anticipates the theory of literary criticism propounded by the Yale guru Harold Bloom in the 1960s. But the elaboration of formalism into iconography was principally the achievement of Aby Warburg, and it is from his work in the early 1920s that art history as we know it today is directly derived.

Warburg invested his share of the family banking fortune in a newly created library and institute located in Hamburg. This northern metropolis, the Venice of Germany, had always looked outward to the North Sea, Scandinavia, and Britain. Hamburg's economic relations with British ports go back to the magical days of the Hanseatic League in the fourteenth century. There was always something liberal and cosmopolitan about Hamburg. It possessed a vibrant culture stimulated by its external relations and its flotation on a series of inlets, canals, and rivers. It was the ideal place for a vanguard institute committed to the history of the classical tradition and especially the perpetuation of classical imagery in painting, sculpture, numismatics, emblems, and all forms of visual arts.

Warburg himself was a prodigious scholar and very high-strung (nervous exhaustion afflicted him for long periods and interrupted his research). He had little knowledge of and no taste for the Middle Ages; his own research lay in the sixteenth and seventeenth centuries. In fact, he subscribed to an outmoded nineteenth-century belief in the cultural stagnation of the Middle Ages. But he was prepared to let others try to trace the heritage of classical antiquity in medieval art and to try to demonstrate the manifold qualities of medieval iconology. He thereby drew to himself brilliant young medievalists, one of whom, Fritz Saxl, together with Warburg's loyal associate Gertrude Bing, perceiving the Nazi threat, two years after Warburg's death in 1929 moved the Warburg library to London. There they gained new funding from the textile magnates of the Cortauld family, and the Warburg-Cortauld Institute is today the doctoral and research department of art history at the University of London and the only major art history program in Britain. Warburg's disciple Ernst Gombrich emerged in the 1940s as the director of the Warburg-Cortauld Institute for the next three decades. Gombrich was a psychologist (*Art and Illusion*) as well as historian of art. In the 1960s the most illustrious personage on the Warburg faculty was Frances Yates, who worked in late Renaissance and Baroque art (*The Art of Memory*). Among its faculty today is the renowned novelist Anita Brookner, whose professional interest is in modern French art in relation to literature.

It was Aby Warburg who in the half dozen years after World War I articulated the program of the German iconological school. Iconology resembled the "close reading" of texts that modernist literary critics advocated. "God is in the details," said Warburg. Beyond that iconology had a threefold focus: the continuity of images (iconography per se); the close relation to the systematically examined literary text (absolutely essential and thereby differentiating German iconography from freewheeling French impressionist art history); and, under the influence of Jacob Burckhardt, the revered nineteenth-century historian of Renaissance Italian civilization and friend of the classicist and philosopher Friedrich Nietzsche, the interaction of artistic image with cultural context. In Warburg's work, and that of his disciples, the third focus was much less developed than the first two, and the banner of Warburg-founded German iconology overwhelmingly comprised the study of continuity of images integrated with literary texts.

Warburg was good at programmatic statements and definitions. Art, he said, is founded upon a "cool and detached serenity which belongs to the categorizing contemplation of things," and the iconographic tradition involves the "complete realization of the images that fill the mind." This statement has Hegelian overtones and parallels the contemporary development of archetypical collective psychology in Zurich by Carl Gustav Jung. In Warburg's conception (and in Jung's) this typology is activist and creative. For Warburg iconography in art history means perpetuating images by an active memory that in turn is coded emotion: "We look for the mint which stamps upon the memory the expressive movements of the extreme transports of emotion, as far as they can be translated into gesture language, with such intensity that these engrams of the experience of the suffering passion survive as a heritage stored in the memory. They become exemplars, determining the outline traced by the artist's hand as soon as maximal values of expressive movement desire to come to light in the artist's creative handiwork [Pub. 1929, probably written several years earlier, transl. E. H. Gombrich, 1970]."

What Warburg is saying is that the iconographic image is stored, coded passion that is perpetuated in a kind of determining collective memory and very strongly conditions (or completely governs) the artist's depiction of a particular motif. Iconographic image, again says Warburg, is "the function of the maximal values of human expression handed down in a tradition for the minting of dynamic symbols [Pub. 1927, trans. E. H. Gombrich, 1970]."

Warburg's repeated identification of iconographic tradition with a minting process is meaningful. Typology exists in memory like numismatic casts in a mint, and images are stamped out from memory and reproduced in particular depictions of motif. I go to the bank and order a roll of quarters, and I get them with identical motifs struck on each one from a common die cast. Thus in the continuity of postclassical art are the same images struck again and again from tradition. There are epistemological, psychological, and historical problems with Warburg's conception, but we know what he is saying, and no one has done better in developing a theory of art.

III
FORTUNE'S CHILD

Along with E. H. Gombrich, Erwin Panofsky was Warburg's most prominent disciple and the one who applied Warburg's theory of iconography to medieval art. Panofsky (1892–1968) was not actually a student of Warburg's in a formal sense. He already had his doctorate and was teaching art history at the new University of Hamburg in 1920 when he discovered the existence of Warburg's fabulous library and vanguard institute, was welcomed there, and participated in it as Warburg's newfound prime protégé and spokesman. By 1930 Panofsky was already a visiting professor at New York University's nascent Institute of Fine Arts.

By 1933, after the Nazis had evicted him in accordance with anti-Semitic exclusionary rules, Panofsky had the first appointment in humanities in the School of Historical Studies at Einstein's Institute for Advanced Study in Princeton. Unlike nearly all his Princeton institute colleagues, Panofsky in the 1930s continued to teach at both New York University and Princeton University and to engage in academic leadership and program development on both campuses so that after World War II, both had by far the most distinguished departments of art history in the country.

It was not until the mid-forties that Panofsky, a person of manic energy, stopped teaching regularly and took advantage of his research chair at the Institute for Advanced Study, but he still delivered a prodigious number of public lectures at colleges all over the country through the 1950s. He became the unchallenged academic power broker in art history in the United States, and he was showered with honors. Seemingly by 1955 every time some pedestrian college president wanted to improve his image as a supporter of the humanities, he sought to give Panofsky an honorary degree. Nor did "Pan" (as he signed his letters, a pun associating himself with the Greek demigod) refuse many such offers. By the end of his life he had received no fewer than fifteen honorary doctorates and nine medals or similar citations for scholarly excellence in medieval and Renaissance studies.

This was an establishmentarian persona for someone who had started out as an artistic, bohemian type at Hamburg, as described in 1922 by his first doctoral student, Edgar Wind, later a professor at Smith College and Oxford: "Panofsky had in those days a distinctly romantic physiognomy. A thick moustache (almost Nietzschean) covered his upper lip, and long whiskers descended in front of his ears, throwing into prominence the luminous eyes and high forehead over which the black hair was pretty long though already receding." When I saw Panofsky in the 1950s, he was a well-dressed, clean-shaven, freshly groomed, Central European-looking person, with sparkling eyes and a frequent smile on his lips. He could have passed easily for a successful Manhattan publisher or theatrical producer. He was a brilliant lecturer, one of the most facile and skillful I have ever heard. He relished Latin tags, quotes from German poetry, Greek philosophical terms, and puns in several languages. He seemed a man very sure of himself and very pleased with himself. He solicited adulation and loved flattery. He had by all external standards a very happy family life. His wife of half a century, the much admired Dora, was herself a trained art historian who helped him with his work. His two sons were brilliant students who became academic scientists.

When Panofsky was a graduate student, one of his teachers, said that fortune had smiled twice on him, giving him private wealth and incredible capacity to find a literary text related to an artistic image. Panofsky came from a wealthy German Jewish family. He intended originally to spend his life (like Felix Liebermann, the Anglo-Saxon legal historian) as a "private scholar," not trying to struggle against the anti-Semitic current by seeking an academic post. But the collapse of his family's fortune in the early Weimar era led him to take advantage of the liberal democratic republic's momentarily widened access for Jews into the humanities faculties of German universities. Even then fortune continued to smile on Panofsky. He quickly became Warburg's protégé, and he gained a full professorship in 1925 at the early age of thirty-three. When the Nazis took over, his road

to academic success and power in the United States was well prepared because he had already been a visiting professor in America.
He did not have to scrounge desperately for a job but instead immediately became the dominant force in art history on the American scene.

Everything he touched turned into a triumph. An obscure American Catholic college asked him to lecture on Gothic architecture, and
the resulting lecture, when published, went through ten printings in
a decade. He had always enjoyed films, especially of the silent variety, and in the 1940s, when he published a pioneering essay on the
iconography of film, he gained adulation in yet a wider circle. Nowadays Panofsky's essay is often regarded as the beginning of cinema
studies on the American campus. He thus almost single-handedly
legitimated a new discipline. In the late 1940s he liked to go around
to New Jersey towns lecturing and showing a Buster Keaton silent
film and then explicating its imagery. Panofsky was the prototype of
the happy, highly visible professor.

For a German formalist to engage in film study might seem a radical departure from ideological elitist humanism. But it works the
other way around. Panofsky was not surrendering to popular culture.
He was appropriating film into the formalist tradition of iconology.

In his earlier programmatic and theoretical statements, made in the
1920s and 1930s, Panofsky was concerned to distinguish his art history, in Warburg's wake, from what was for him the mechanical,
routinized, and relatively unintellectual kind of iconography practiced by Émile Mâle and his imitators in Germany as well as France.
Panofsky said that he felt compelled to make art history as comprehensive and culturally oriented as possible. He wrote in 1920 that
"the systematic study of art . . . demands that the objects of its study
must be grasped with necessity and not merely historically." This is
code for stating that art history must be pursued intellectually, not
merely through a kind of mechanical iconography, merely comparing
one image with another. What art history needs is "an Archimedean
point outside its own sphere of being." This Archimedean point is
held to be a broad cultural perspective. To emphasize this program,
Panofsky distinguished iconology (intellectualized, culturally sited art
history) from iconography. But in practice what he was saying was
no more than Warburg. A "visual type" must be placed in a cultural
context by attaching it to a literary text, "the power of small print."
This is a way to look beyond the routinized image to meaning that
the artist wants to convey:

In a work of art, "form" cannot be divorced from "content." The distribution of color and lines, light and shade, volumes and planes, however delightful as visual spectacle, must also be understood as carrying a more-than-visual meaning.

Not only does the re-creative synthesis serve as a basis for archaeological research. But the latter in turn serves as a basis for the process of re-creation.

The more the painters rejoiced in the discovery and reproduction of the visible world, the more intensely did they feel the need to saturate all its elements with meaning.

This can sound like some bold program for a historical sociology of art, and there is evidence that in the 1920s and 1930s Panofsky occasionally contemplated such a speculative vanguard approach. But in the end, especially after he had moved to the United States, he abandoned such ambitions and concentrated on formalist text-based iconology, what he termed a commonsense approach: "We have to ask ourselves whether or not the symbolical significance of a given motif is a matter of established representational tradition; whether or not a symbolical interpretation can be justified by definite texts or agrees with ideas demonstrably alive in the period and presumably familiar to its artists; and to what extent symbolical interpretation is in keeping with the historical position and personal tendencies of the individual master."

The three valuable studies on Panofsky—by William Hecksher, his student, made very shortly after Panofsky's death, and by Michael Podro and Michael Ann Holly, both published in the 1980s—give us a similar intellectual biography: a steady development from vague, wide-ranging ambitions, never realized, to mainstream formalism in both theory and practice. The year before he died Panofsky acknowledged in a private letter that his famous distinction between iconography and iconology, which a generation of graduate students in art history had to commit to memory as a sort of canonical creed, no longer meant anything significant: The terms were virtually interchangeable. The grounding of picture in literary text is what it all came down to in practice.

Panofsky's earliest, some would say also his best, work was on Albrecht Dürer, the early-sixteenth-century Lutheran artist. He returned to Dürer several times in his career. But Panofsky made four specific contributions to medieval art history: a study of Abbot Suger (1946), the builder and supervising architect of St.-Denis, usually re-

garded as the first church in the new Gothic style; a comparative
study of medieval artistic and cultural renaissances (1952–60) that de-
lineates the cultural history of the Middle Ages; his tour de force
lectures on *Gothic Architecture and Scholasticism* (1957); and, along with
his work on Dürer, what is considered his masterpiece, *Early Netherlandish Painting* of the late fifteenth century (1953).

St.-Denis was the royal abbey of France as Westminster Abbey is
of Britain. French kings were not crowned there (the coronation and
anointing took place at the Cathedral of Rheims, which also had a
special historical association with the crown). But there was a very
close connection in terms of the politics of culture and the culture of
politics (or, it might be said, public relations and propaganda) between this abbey on the edge of Paris and the ruling kingly family.
This was especially the case in the early twelfth century, when the
abbot Suger of St.-Denis (d. 1151) was also the chief minister of Louis
VI, King Louis the Fat, and a very effective servant of the Capetian
dynasty. In the 1140s Suger undertook an expensive and elaborate
rebuilding of the monastic church. When it was finished, it was an
ungainly structure, but it had two elements that made it an innovator
in what became known as the French style or what has since the
fifteenth century been called Gothic. St.-Denis's Church now had a
raised clerestory to bathe the altar in natural light, and it had a large
rose window over the front portal. The high clerestory and rose window became central, indispensable characteristics of the large new
cathedrals that were built in northern France over the next century,
as the booming population required much larger structures than
before.

Panofsky tells us that Suger, who very closely supervised and largely
designed the revised Church of St.-Denis, "set the course of Western
architecture for more than a century." Panofsky aimed to find the
origins of the new style: What inspired Suger in this direction? Panofsky did not have to look far because Suger himself wrote a memoir
explaining how and why he carried out the reconstruction, and Panofsky provided an excellent translation of this treatise to follow his
own analysis. St. Denis, after whom the abbey founded in the seventh century was named, was allegedly the disciple of St. Paul and
was the apostle to the heathen Gauls who martyred him and his companions on the Hill of Martyrs (Montmartre) in Paris. In the eighth
century a neo-Platonic theological treatise falsely attributed to St. Denis
(it was actually written by a Syrian Greek-speaking monk around
500) was translated into Latin. It is the text of "this neo-Platonic light

metaphysics," said Panofsky, following Suger's own suggestion, that inspired the new architecture. Suger wanted to let divine light (God's spirit) into the church, and that accounts for what he did.

Here is a beautiful example of Panofsky's text-based art history formalism. No one can quarrel with it in this instance. You couldn't find a more explicit example, and the essay on Suger is carried off with delicacy and panache. It could be wished, however, that Panofsky had followed up on two suggestions he mentions near the end of his study but does not explore. He points to Suger's egotism: "Suger . . . came to divert to the Abbey the whole amount of energy, acumen, and ambition nature had bestowed upon him." The Gothic churches were perhaps as much as anything else monuments to the ambition and wealth of the aristocratic French bishops and abbots who built them. St. Bernard of Clairvaux, paradoxically because he was himself a dreadful egoist, saw this clearly from the start of the great Gothic building program and therefore criticized it severely.

An even more important suggestion by Panofsky was also not followed up: "To Suger, St. Denis meant France, and so he developed a violent and almost mystical nationalism as apparently anachronistic as was his vaingloriousness." I do not know what the word "anachronistic" is doing there. There was nothing anachronistic about the vainglory of a medieval bishop or prominent abbot. That was central to his mentality. Nationalism was also very much an ingredient of medieval culture, at times all the more intense or violent for not having much in the way of mediating institutions to absorb it. Just as important as the reflection of neo-Platonic metaphysics in St. Denis's new church was royalist nationalism. The new Church of St.-Denis, associated with the royal Capetian family, not only expressed wealth and power but also served as the focus of loyalty of Frenchmen, at least of the landed classes—an aim that was fully accomplished within a century of Suger's death, in the reign of St. Louis IX.

One could indeed argue that as the builder of the new proto-Gothic church Suger was acting more in his capacity as the chief minister of the crown than as the abbot of the great monastery. He wanted a highly visible sign of the new self-confidence, ambition, and effectiveness of the Capetian dynasty. Political ideology may have played a greater role as the intellectual foundation of St.-Denis than mystical Christian theology. Because Suger drags in the pseudo-Denis writings as justification, do we have to believe that this is what really inspired him to undertake this expensive and technologically somewhat risky project? Here is demonstrated the weakness of Panofsky's image-and-text formalism. When you have a neat match of image and text (in this case Gothic style and neo-Platonic light theology), you downplay everything else, even though Panofsky had all the necessary learning and insight to know that other explanations, perhaps less precise but more persuasive, were in play.

Panofsky's rather conventional view of the history of twelfth-century architecture may also be questioned. Yes, the clerestory and rose window are central to the new French style. But just as important was emphasis upon the vertical plane rather than on the horizontal plane, as in the previous Romanesque style. The shift was already appearing in what is called Norman Perpendicular, the style of the soaring churches, somewhere between Romanesque and Gothic, that the French bishops whom William the Conqueror imported to England in the 1070s began to construct. In this regard, the breakthrough church is not St.-Denis but Durham Cathedral, which the bishop of Durham, William of St. Calais, a hard-bitten political prelate, began to construct in the 1080s in that northern frontier city. We cannot find any neo-Platonic mysticism in this feudatory's mentality. Yet he is building a much larger structure than any Anglo-Saxon church and one that carries the eye upward. An architectural revolution was achieved in this bleak northern town several decades before Suger's rebuilding of St.-Denis. If Panofsky had traced the beginnings of the architectural revolution to Bishop William of Durham, he would have had to look at the political ambitions of a frontier prelate. The only literary text with which Bishop William is associated is a lengthy account of his trial for feudal treason against the king (William the Conqueror's son and successor) during a baronial rebellion. There are ways that this text can be related to Durham Cathedral, but not in the direct manner that Panofsky grounds Suger's St.-Denis in neo-Platonic theology.

Panofsky's *Gothic Architecture and Scholasticism* is a fragile jewel, so clever, so subtle that if you look at it closely, it begins to decompose. But that is good reason to appreciate it. It is a beautiful piece of speculative interpretation. Panofsky skillfully demonstrates how the structure of the thirteenth-century Gothic cathedral closely parallels the architectonic format of the syllogistic exposition of Thomist philosophy—the elaborate logical way in which St. Thomas Aquinas presents his arguments. This is what Panofsky calls the "postulate of clarification's sake" and the "acceptance and ultimate reconciliation of contradictory possibilities."

The questions then become: Granted this is true, what is the causal

connection? Were the architects of these cathedrals trained in scholastic disquisition and mode of argument so they (consciously? subconsciously?) applied this mind-set to their architectural drawings?
Or do we have at work a "spirit of the age" or cultural nexus argument, in which a mentality common to the culture of the era spreads
out in all directions—philosophy, architecture, painting, law, imaginative literature? Panofsky does not answer these questions. From his
delicately articulated account both explanations seem possible. It would
be unreasonable to ask for more. One thing that may be said is that
Panofsky is one of the very few scholars who have written on Gothic
architecture without being boring or obscure. The value of this book
cannot be fully appreciated until you see how it galvanizes discussion
in a college class.

Renaissance and Renascences in Western Art is a substantial, heavily
footnoted book intended for a very different audience from that of
Gothic Architecture. Here Panofsky is addressing art historians and all
professional medievalists presumably exercised by the debate on the
nature of the Italian Renaissance and earlier medieval renaissances.

The Swiss historian Jacob Burckhardt, Nietzsche's friend and
sometime colleague at the University of Basel, was the first to describe the Renaissance as the unified cultural and political expression
of a distinct historical period. In *The Civilization of the Renaissance in
Italy*, published in 1860, Burckhardt described the Renaissance from
the organic point of view that characterized much of German historiography in the nineteenth century. He believed that modern European culture began to take shape in Italy two centuries before it
developed in the rest of Europe. For Burckhardt, the essential outlook, or Weltanschauung, of the Italian Renaissance was the product
of the matrix of political and intellectual currents in Italy in the period between 1350 and 1550. Burckhardt emphasized the emergence
of a new outlook that glorified the individual; he stressed social and
psychological factors. In so doing, he departed from the more re-
stricted concept that fifteenth-century Italian humanists had of their
own times, a concept that emphasized the revival of classical antiquity as the essence of rebirth.

Burckhardt attempted to describe the fundamental characteristics
that shaped the world view of the Renaissance, freed Europe from
the presumed "faith, illusion, and childish prepossession" of medieval
society, and ushered in the modern world. For Burckhardt, the political milieu of the Italian cities provided an environment in which the
awareness of the individual human personality broke the bonds of

"race, people, party, family, or corporation." He viewed Renaissance humanists as a species of Nietzschean supermen. Freed from the alleged political and intellectual limitations of the medieval world, the creative individual found in the glories of classical antiquity the necessary guide to further advance. The men and women of the Italian Renaissance, like their predecessors of ancient times, explored the world within the human psyche and nature outside it and went on to exploit the creative powers of the individual. The Renaissance Italians laid the groundwork for modern civilization in political and social relationship as well as in the arts.

Burckhardt's powerful work of interpretation of the Renaissance soon became the standard that all other works on the subject had to emulate or attack. He himself showed caution in applying his model of Italian Renaissance civilization to all Europe, but the prevailing trend of later Renaissance scholarship amplified his thesis and extended his model to the rest of Europe. In the hands of popularizers like the Edwardian man of letters and gay activist John Addington Symonds, the Renaissance became a clearly defined period that marked the end of the Middle Ages for all Western Europe and ushered in a new world. The concept of the Renaissance was expanded to comprise the source of all that was modern, and its precise content to vary with the historian's ideas of the essence of modernity.

In the early twentieth century, as Catholic universities participated in modern historical science, clerical scholars sought to challenge Burckhardt's Renaissance thesis, which they regarded as a thinly veiled attack upon the church. Then secular medievalists turned their attention to Burckhardt's paradigm because it cast aspersions, it seemed, on the intellectual and cultural level achieved in the medieval world. As most reputable universities by the mid-1920s appointed professors of medieval history, literature, and art, a debate echoed between the supporters of Burckhardt's separation of the Renaissance and the Middle Ages and the medievalist claim that the intellectual and cultural development of fifteenth-century Italy was only a late flowering of medieval culture itself and that what was valuable and distinctive in Renaissance humanism and thought had already been anticipated in earlier medieval centuries. This medievalist response to Burckhardt was forcefully summarized in 1928 in *The Renaissance of the Twelfth Century* by Charles Homer Haskins of Harvard, the leading American medieval historian of his generation. Haskins's *Renaissance* was originally given as a series of public lectures in Harvard Yard to en-

thusiastic response from the Brahmin matron audience. In paperback
form it has been foisted on generations of reluctant American college
students. The point that Haskins makes over and over again is that
there were medieval cultural movements centering, like the Italian
Renaissance of the fifteenth century, on the rebirth of classical learning and humanistic ideals. In a great many ways, Haskins argues, the
widespread revival of Latin letters and Greek philosophy and science
in the century or so after A.D. 1100 was the critical turning point, the
most creative renaissance of all, and anticipated nearly everything of
value in Burckhardt's Italian Renaissance. So Haskins gives us an
annotated catalog of twelfth-century writers and thinkers.

The dispute between the partisans of the Middle Ages and the
Italian Renaissance heated up only after Haskins's tome had appeared. An NYU historian, Wallace K. Ferguson, capably summed
up the course of the debate, but did nothing to resolve it, in *The
Renaissance in Historical Thought* (1948). The anti-Burckhardt movement continued, led by Harvard's Douglas Bush, R. W. Chambers
at the University of London, and by E. M. Tillyard at Cambridge.

It was into this noisy debate that Panofsky's *Renaissance* volume
magisterially entered. There was certainly an element of power trip-
ping in Panofsky's book, published in 1960, which began as a series
of endowed lectures in Sweden in 1952. Panofsky, among other purposes, wanted to show that no one had a greater mastery of both
medieval and Renaissance culture than he did. This purpose was fully
achieved. And it is an illuminating work besides. It is the most subtle
analysis ever made of the great Renaissance issue. For heavy-handed
dialectics and shrill polemics and boring lists, Panofsky substituted
subtle insights and complex distinctions.

Panofsky believed that there *is* such a thing as a cultural era. Whether
the Renaissance of the fourteenth and fifteenth centuries is such a
new era or an extension of the Middle Ages, however, is moot. But
the Italian Renaissance, Panofsky remarks, was at least a cultural
movement of great significance that expanded from literature to painting
to other arts and then from the arts to the natural sciences. The idea
of renewal or rebirth thereby became a central cultural theory in late
medieval Italy. There is nothing startling in this view: It is middle-
of-the-road, sensible, consensual. It is applied specifically to art history and supported with a confident mass of data:

The art historian . . . will have to accept the basic facts that a first
radical break with the medieval principles of representing the visible

world by means of line and color was made in Italy at the turn of the thirteenth century; that a second fundamental change, starting in architecture and sculpture rather than painting and involving an intense preoccupation with classical antiquity, set in at the beginning of the fifteenth; and a third, climactic phase of the entire development, finally synchronizing the three arts and temporarily eliminating the dichotomy between the naturalistic and classicistic points of view, began at the threshold of the sixteenth.

This is a reasonable conclusion. But applied to other areas of culture—imaginative literature, philosophy, law—this clear pattern would be difficult to sustain. Nor did the development of even the visual arts north of the Alps follow so neat a pattern.

The significance of the earlier revivals is clearly articulated by Panofsky. His treatment of these earlier medieval renaissances is actually more original than his paradigm of the fifteenth-century Italian one. Panofsky's explanation of the Carolingian Renaissance (780–860) is subtle and careful. Yes, there was a strong element of neoclassicism in Carolingian art, he tells us, but then there were two other cultural streams at work there: "Celto-German" and Byzantine. He sees, like Schramm, that Byzantine influence is strong in the Ottonian Renaissance of 970–1000 and concludes that the art of the year 1000 "may be said to have been animated, in form as well as content, by a prophetic vision of the high-medieval future rather than by a retrospective enthusiasm for the classical past." Neoclassicism and millenarianism fused together in Ottonian culture. The idea of reviving the Roman Empire in the reign of Otto III was not only a cultural motif but part of a prophetic vision.

Panofsky's long discussion of the "proto-renaissance of the twelfth century" mainly uses art and architecture as material, but with some attention to Latin literature as well. It is one of his finest achievements. It is neither radical nor conventional in its approach and conclusions, and it illustrates why he was so much admired. There is nothing in this immensely learned, finely controlled exposition that may be said to be derivative and boring or, on the other hand, disturbingly novel. It is very hard to work at this intellectual level and within these parameters.

The distinctive quality of the twelfth-century Renaissance in the visual arts is the focus of its classicizing on the three-dimensional arts—i.e., sculpture and architecture—Panofsky claims. Secondly, "an intentionally classicizing style is found in the ecclesiastical rather than in the secular sphere"—in churches rather than in royal and aristocratic dwellings. Thirdly, as Gothic culture reached its high point in the mid-thirteenth century, while it had drawn heavily upon classical philosophy and literature, it tended to develop a distinctive "high medieval system of thought, imagination, and expression . . . and the linguistic form of Latin writings completely emancipated itself from classical models." Indeed, there are signs of anticlassical, Orientalizing reaction in Mediterranean cultures in the mid and late thirteenth century. While the twelfth-century Renaissance did, compared with the Carolingian revival, "penetrate many strata of society" and while it appropriated classical culture in a more usable, activist, and less superficial form than the Carolingian Renaissance, "in art as well as literature classical form came to be divorced from classical content." By 1300 there was "a relative or—in the Northern countries— absolute estrangement from the aesthetic traditions, in art as well as literature, of the classical past."

Therefore, Burckhardt was fundamentally correct after all. The Italian Renaissance in Panofsky's view *was* unique: "The Middle Ages had left antiquity unburied and alternately galvanized and exorcised its corpse. The Italian Renaissance stood weeping at its grave and tried to resurrect its soul." It was not, however, Italian Renaissance classicism but Gothic art and culture that were the high point of medieval culture: "The acme of medieval classicism was reached within the general framework of the Gothic style." What distinguishes Panofsky in the debate about renaissances was his calm and judicious effort to give both medieval and Italian Renaissance culture their due. This is where the issue still stands.

The limitation of Panofsky's study of renaissances follows from his formalist avoidance of sociological perspectives. If he had examined the Italian Renaissance of the fifteenth century and its North European outcomes from a social determinist point of view, he would have perceived its meaning in radically different terms. The emphasis would then have been not on the Renaissance iconology in art and literature but on educational theory and curriculum reform. The Renaissance humanists devalued the importance of universities and concentrated on the school curriculum for seven- to sixteen-year-old males. They envisioned a European-wide training program in classical Latin for the narrow elite of the emerging generation in any aspect of political, economic, and intellectual leadership. The ability to read, write, speak, and think in classical Latin would distinguish the European elite that the humanists envisaged. This elite would be devoted to the state, the arts, the family, and conventional morality. Perpetuated in the British public school, the French lycée, and the German gymnasium, the educational program of the Renaissance humanists has proved profoundly durable and still—with some modification in content, especially to allow for natural science—fosters the European elite of today. Since Panofsky himself was a product of the German classical gymnasium and accepted its aims and outcomes at face value, he could not stand back and see its sociological significance.

Panofsky's other major book of his later years, his massive work *Early Netherlandish Painting*, represents a return to his first interest, Albrecht Dürer and sixteenth-century German art, because in his study of Jan van Eyck, the Flémalle Master, Roger van der Weyden, and the other leaders of Flemish art of the fifteenth century, Panofsky was studying the background to Dürer and the German late Renaissance and Baroque. What he is interested in in the *Netherlandish* book is the techniques of the renewed naturalism, such as perspective, color, and landscape and the depiction of the human face and body. Beyond noting that this naturalism represents the development of a stylistic change of revolutionary importance that began in Italy and migrated northward and underwent modification there, Panofsky does not account for the cause of the great upheaval in painting style. Instead, he minutely examines its techniques. He completely ignores Johan Huizinga's effort at cultural sociology in *The Waning of the Middle Ages*, published forty years earlier, in which the new naturalism of Flemish art was regarded as signifying the incapacity of late medieval civilization to sustain a common symbolic identity.

Near the end of his book Panofsky mentions the very important subject of a new lay middle-class market for naturalistic paintings in Flanders at the end of the fifteenth century: "We can observe an enormous increase in the production of copies of the variations on the works of Jan van Eyck and the Flémalle Master, indicative of a popular demand which does not seem to have existed in the preceding half-century. . . . As far as the buying public is concerned, this phenomenon might be explained by the rise of a Northern humanism which, as had happened in Italy, was accompanied by the emergence of a novel sense of history with its concomitants of national and regional self-consciousness." But that is as far as he takes sociological significance of the new style. To have done more would have carried Panofsky away from the formalist tradition and into uncharted and hazardous waters, into a very different kind of art history. A Marxist or any kind of social determinist would say that Panofsky ends his study of Netherlandish painting about where he should have started it. But Panofsky does have a right not to get into all that murky thicket. His failure to confront Huizinga's elusive but stimulating kind of cultural history is more disappointing.

While Aby Warburg, Panofsky's mentor in the 1920s, was developing the formalist school in Hamburg, which then became standard in the United States and Britain, a group of art historians in Vienna was pursuing a very different approach: art as a social phenomenon and the social determinants of art. The work of the Vienna school of art history, before its dispersion by the Nazis in the late 1930s, is memorialized by Arnold Hauser's four-volume *The Social History of Art*, which so many people have used as an introduction to art history in its American paperback edition. Hauser sought refuge in Britain, where he never obtained a mainline position. His volume on the Middle Ages is at best amateurish; its data basis, in either art or general culture, is very weak.

The alternative to formalism in medieval art history was most intriguingly presented in the work of Meyer Schapiro at Columbia University from 1945 to 1970. An art critic very much involved with American modernism, a member of the *Partisan Review* group of socialist intellectuals in the 1930s, a Ph.D. in art history from Columbia, where he taught for forty years, Schapiro tried to walk a fine line between the Warburg-Panofsky formalist school and the Vienna social interpretation somewhat vulgarly represented by Hauser's popular work (which Schapiro warmly praised). The result, in my opinion, was neither here nor there. When I taught at Columbia in the early 1960s, I used to join the standing-room-only crowds at Schapiro's lectures, and I have read his collected papers. He always seemed to be on the verge of saying something very important, but somehow it was never quite articulated. His awareness of the limitations and problems of Panofsky's formalism was evident. But I do not think that Schapiro ever worked out an intellectual system or methodology as an alternative. Like other famous Manhattan intellectuals who came out of the same *Partisan Review* group of the 1930s (the New York University philosopher Sidney Hook, the Columbia literary critic Lionel Trilling), Schapiro was more interesting as a person than as a theorist, at least of the Middle Ages, and greater in potential than in accomplishment.

In the 1980s a vigorous transatlantic Marxist school of art history began to emerge, led by the Englishman T. J. Clark and the American Rosalind Krauss. They work, however, on modern art. The great

Marxist antiformalist, anti-Panofsky art historian of the Middle Ages has yet to appear. It is indeed much easier to criticize Panofsky than to supersede him.

The formalism that Panofsky applied to medieval art history was, in his words, a commonsense approach. It is easy enough, he said, to conceive of a social determinist interpretation in which the painting, sculpture, or building is viewed as expressive of sociological and ideological factors embedded in the artist's or architect's environment. He did not deny that this social and ideological derivation had, at times, a marginal impact on the particular work of art. But, he argued, with that characteristic glint in his eye and smile on his lips, when you got down to it and examined the artwork closely, you would find that the artist was predominantly inspired by a theme or idea derived from the past and found in an earlier theological or literary text. The history of art before 1880, certainly before 1700, is a dialogue with the past, not a quest through the present. Cultural perpetuation, not social interaction, is the burden of medieval art history. Research sustained traditionalist formalism empirically. Truly the social determinists are the fantasizers, and the formalists the sober realists. This, I surmise, is the way Panofsky would defend his work today.

Panofsky belonged to that generation of German Jewish humanists who envisioned themselves as connected to a chain of civility and learning that stretched back from Bismarckian and Weimar Germany through the millennia to the classical and biblical worlds that became fused in the Christian patristic culture of the fourth century A.D. Granted there was a measure of intolerance, militancy, and, indeed, anti-Semitism in this medieval Christian humanism, but for Panofsky these less attractive aspects of the mainline tradition were burned away over the centuries. From Dante to Goethe the great tradition glowed in the firmament of European aristocratic culture, and it was still meaningful and instructive. Nothing had superseded this blend of classical and Gothic culture.

What happened in the 1920s and 1930s was for Panofsky warning enough against the treachery of the demotic new: the uncontrollable narcotic of social determinism, with its ever-escalating dosages of extremist denunciations and anxious dictates. Following the mainline of formalism gives us instead security and stability, peace and continuity and guides us to a renaissance, as it did for medieval people. Panofsky would stand today with cultural neoconservatism, in my opinion.

IV

PRESERVING WESTERN CIVILIZATION

Panofsky was outspoken but by disposition not a polemicist or controversialist. No single work on medieval literature has ever had the immediate impact and generated the controversy (which still continues) as *European Literature and the Latin Middle Ages* by Ernst Robert Curtius (1886–1956). The first German edition was published in 1948 in Bern, Switzerland. The author was a German citizen and a professor of Romance languages and literature at the University of Bonn. Curtius did have a relish for polemics and controversy. Panofsky's temperament was aristocratic and dignified; Curtius's, bourgeois and embattled.

An excellent English translation of *European Literature* was published in New York in 1953 in a series endowed by the Bollingen Foundation, which was established principally to publish all the works of Carl Gustav Jung. The donor was a member of the Pittsburgh billionaire Mellon family who had developed a great admiration for the Swiss psychiatrist and his theory of collective archetypes in the human psyche. Some works that could be easily construed as having a similar outlook were also translated and published in the Bollingen series, and Curtius's book was one of them. (Another was a seminal work on comparative religious myths, another Jungian interest, by Mercia Eliade, a sometime Romanian Nazi and, after the war, a professor at the University of Chicago.)

Translations of *European Literature and the Latin Middle Ages* appeared in Spanish, French, and Portuguese within four years of the English translation. In the three years after the original German edition (and again after the English translation appeared) there was a flood of lengthy reviews in every major journal of literary history and criticism. The *Times Literary Supplement* spoke of Curtius's "immense erudition." Max Laistner of Cornell University, a German émigré and leading authority on medieval Latin literature, called the book a masterpiece. The *Modern Language Review* called it "one of the most important books of our time." Erich Auerbach, a German émigré who had spent the war in Turkey before coming to the United States, where he became the leading Yale professor of comparative literature in the early 1950s, wrote two separate reviews of Curtius's book, one in English and one in German. He stressed the book's ideological significance, as did many other reviewers.

Auerbach commented that the book represents a "radical rejection of all national or chronological isolation within European civilization." But Auerbach was not enthusiastic about Curtius's view of medieval literature and particularly about his treatment of formalist typology. Paul Oskar Kristeller, another eminent German émigré, who taught medieval and Renaissance philosophy at Columbia University and whose reputation on the American campus in the 1950s was almost as great as Auerbach's, generally praised Curtius's book but was distressed by its ideological affinities to Jung and—allegedly—Arnold Toynbee, the British conservative world historian. Leo Spitzer, the conservative German émigré theorist at Johns Hopkins University, saw in Curtius's book the "abandonment of all . . . modernistic tendencies." Similarly the prominent modernist poet and critic Charles Olson, writing in 1953, regarded in Curtius's work a dangerous return to premodernist universalist thinking: "We are in the hands of a huge propaganda office. It isn't the contents of this book alone, it is also that it is the 36th volume of the Bollingen Series." On the other hand, Gary Davenport, writing in the still modernist-oriented *Sewanee Review* (1974), drew parallels between T. S. Eliot and Curtius's doctrine: "His constant effort is not to erect barriers between a corrupt present and a golden past but to tear down those barriers and to synthesize the ancient and the modern into a dynamic and vital culture that serves the living."

In the case of any seminal, classic work of humanistic scholarship, not only are there strong differences of opinion about it, but over time people tend to see in it what they want to see. That is not a bad definition of a classic—a work that so touches the nerve that it reinforces or illuminates the perception that the reader brings to it. The same reader, even if a very learned scholar and prominent critic, may also see the book differently at various times. Thus Peter Dronke of Cambridge in 1970 published a lengthy and unfavorable criticism of Curtius's treatment of topologies in medieval literature, but in 1980 he took a much more benign view: "By means of an elaborate series of interrelations . . . the whole achieves a richness and density greater than the sum of its ingredients."

It may be plausibly argued that the importance of a work of humanist interpretation is not articulated in the comments of the scholar's own generation, the current reviews in learned journals, because it may be too revolutionary and challenging to the placidity of contemporaries' own work for them to recognize or to acknowledge frankly.

The true test of the seminal quality of a book in history or criticism is how it affects the next generation. By this test Curtius's *European Literature* is indeed a monumental work. No superior dissertation on medieval literature by the end of the 1950s was written other than in the shadow of Curtius's book and effectively engaging in dialogue with it.

It is paradoxical that a book of such impact in medieval studies was written by a scholar who, while he had written his doctoral dissertation in the medieval field nearly four decades earlier, had done all his scholarly publication since that time on modern French and English literature. He was also disparaged by many of his colleagues as a "journalist" because he extensively wrote reviews in newspapers and popular journals and had published as well a best-selling book on modern French civilization, of which many academics had inevitably taken a dim view as lightweight and unscholarly. Did Curtius later write the most important single book on medieval literature in the twentieth century *despite* or *because* of his mostly nonmedievalist background? I suppose the answer is yes and yes.

Unlike so many great medievalists, whose lives are told only in boiler plate panegyrics, Curtius is fortunate that his life is the subject of two concise but careful biographical studies, by Heinrich Lausberg (1970) and Earl Jeffrey Richards (1983); the latter has also provided a very useful bibliographical summary of the history of the reception of all of Curtius's books.

Like Marc Bloch, Curtius came from a family stemming from Alsace, that contested borderland between France and Germany. He was born in one of the German-ruled eras of Alsace. His grandfather, also named Ernst, was an archaeologist and a classicist of distinction. His father was a civil servant, but his mother was a countess. His family was Protestant, and he remained a Lutheran but was later known for his strong sympathies for Catholicism. Curtius's early career was uneventful. He took a doctorate at the University of Bonn in Romance philology and began teaching courses there in both medieval and modern French literature. Like many great medievalists, he fought and was severely wounded in the First World War. In 1920 Curtius received a tenured position at Marburg. Now he quickly became a highly visible maverick in the German academic profession. He was a Francophile, a supporter of the Weimar Republic, and well known for his leftist and strongly anti-Nazi views. He wrote and spoke prolifically on modern and contemporary literary and cultural subjects, earning the hatred and contempt of the majority of his colleagues both for his politics and for writing for a very wide, nonacademic audience.

As well as studies on modern French writers and his best-selling and highly controversial pro-Parisian book on French civilization, Curtius in 1929 published the first piece of serious criticism in German on James Joyce. He became a trans-European intellectual, knowing personally the French novelist and critic André Gide, who noted in his journal in 1927 his great spiritual affinity for Curtius; the leftist French philosopher Jean-Paul Sartre; the English poet and left-wing critic Stephen Spender, as well as the German liberal novelist Thomas Mann.

Curtius was a stocky, ugly man with a very determined expression on his face and a completely autonomous and courageous person. By the late twenties he was known internationally as a good European, a believer in a common Western culture and a hater of extreme nationalism. These views made him unpopular among his colleagues but fortuitously helped his career. When the chair of Romance literature at his old University of Bonn fell vacant, he was one of the three final candidates, but there was bitter opposition from the Bonn literature faculty, mostly on ideological grounds, although—ironically in view of his later fame as a medievalist—also ostensibly on the ground that he was ill equipped to teach medieval literature. The decision under German education law lay with the Prussian minister of education, at the time a dedicated liberal (and also a distinguished scholar on medieval Islam), Carl Becker; he was very happy to have the opportunity to choose a liberal supporter of the Weimar Republic and named Curtius to the chair, which he occupied until his retirement in 1951.

When the Nazis took over in 1933, Curtius's position was difficult. Whether he could have found a position in another country is uncertain. Despite his cross-European orientation, he never felt at home in another country, and he rationalized to himself that the good Europeans and anti-Nazis who weren't Jews or Communists among the German professors, and thereby immediately proscribed, should stay on and conduct a subtle resistance to nazism from within. But he was a marked man. As late as 1944 the Nazi political agent on the Bonn faculty was still filing confidential reports to Berlin on Curtius, stating that he was an unreconstructed anti-Nazi and "liberal." To take the heat off, in 1937 Curtius greatly reduced his teaching in modern French literature (a provocative subject in a German university in the

Nazi era) and concentrated on medieval Latin literature. Paradoxically, the Nazi menace thus drove him back to the Middle Ages, the
field he had long abandoned and the field in which his enduring reputation entirely rests.

While publicly trying to stay out of trouble, Curtius was engaged
in a secret maneuver of great danger that could have cost him his job
and possibly his life: He and a colleague hid a Jewish former secretary in the Romance department until the end of the war.

Immediately after the war Curtius was bitter, depressed, and disillusioned. He had lost faith in the European left and was deeply
concerned about the future of Western civilization and the German
humanist tradition in particular. Could Europe survive the catastrophe of the war and the postwar malaise of confusion and poverty,
and could the German enlightened classical traditions represented by
Goethe and Kant revive? Slowly, as he resumed normal teaching (and
got some good food and rest), his spirits lifted, his self-confidence
and determination came back, and he decided to draw upon his ten
years of Nazi-enforced study in medieval Latin texts to write a book
that would be a rallying cry for the things he loved: the humanistic tradition and the continuity of a broad-based European civilization.

We don't have to infer these intentions from the book; he explicates them in the Preface in his characteristically outspoken "journal-
istic" style that so annoyed his German academic colleagues: "My
book . . . grew out of a concern for the preservation of Western
culture. It seeks to serve an understanding of the Western cultural
tradition insofar as it is manifested in literature. It attempts to illuminate the unity of that tradition in space and time by the application
of new methods. In the intellectual chaos of the present it has become
necessary, and happily not impossible, to demonstrate that unity. But
the demonstration can only be made from a universal standpoint. Such
a standpoint is afforded by Latinity [Transl. Willard Trask]." It would
take a right-wing German nationalist or even a Nazi to question the
sentiment behind this statement of the purpose and theme of *European
Literature and the Latin Middle Ages*. Beyond that, however, everything
Curtius said in this programmatic preface is controversial: whether
there was indeed a European unity in the Middle Ages; if there was,
whether it is relevant to the twentieth century; whether it was expressed in Latinity; what exactly medieval literature does manifest;
and, above all, what are the "new methods" of studying literature,
the formalist focus on topology that he refers to. That didn't bother

Curtius; he was used to bitter opposition and hostile criticism, to being the outsider. He wrote to a friend as his book was being published that "it will anger the guild people."

Curtius received only two honorary degrees: one from Glasgow, the other from the Sorbonne. The latter represented a kind of vindication for him in view of his fight over many decades on behalf of French culture in Germany. No German university, in spite of the immediate substantial adulation for his controversial work, ever offered him an honorary degree. The ironies and paradoxes that shrouded Curtius's whole career continued after his death. Twenty years later he was revered in the senior ranks of the German academic profession as the ideal literary scholar, but he was by that time being demonized by a new generation of German Marxist critics as a conservative humanist, as a rightist reactionary thinker of the cold war.

Although in the Preface of his book Curtius speaks of his "new method," he is generous in citing the influence of others upon him. He admires Aby Warburg. He acknowledges similarities in his interpretation to the "spheres that the psychology of C. G. Jung has explored." He is dealing with the topoi, the conceptual formularies, the typological array in medieval literature, and this typology by which the world is imagined, constructed, articulated in the medieval mind is, in Jungian fashion, "rooted in the deeper strata of the soul. It belongs to the stock of archaic proto-images in the collective unconscious." Curtius also quotes with approval the perception of the Austrian poet and dramatist Hugo von Hofmannsthal (especially remembered today in the Anglophone world as Richard Strauss's librettist): "There is a certain timeless European mythology: names, concepts, figures, with which a higher meaning is bound up, personified forces of the moral or mythical order. Thus mythological firmament spans all the older Europe."

Here lies Curtius's basic thesis on the nature of European culture, particularly in the Middle Ages. There derived from classical antiquity and the early church an immensely complicated and vibrant system of literary topoi, standardized images and phrases, and this cultural structure is intensified and cultivated through the Middle Ages. Medieval Latin writers (and, he suggests—but, except for Dante, does not deeply explicate—vernacular ones, too) understand the facets of nature, human experience, social relations, sense and sensibility entirely within this coded system. That is what medieval literature is: the projection on a mental screen of elaborated topoi communicated continuously through a temporally extended culture. The writers of the twelfth century "still live by concepts which go back to . . . systems of ideas which appeared between 150 and 400." This is the fundamental thesis, and almost all of Curtius's five-hundred-page book is taken up with detailed evidence sustaining this thesis, showing the details of medieval expression that confirm his interpretation. He argues for the existence of a kind of "Medieval Mannerism," borrowing a term from the art history of the sixteenth century that refers to a highly routinized but very elaborate, indeed obsessive, expression of standard images. Curtius dismisses a view of medieval culture that values individual creative expression, originality of articulation, personal innovation.

Certainly there is deep feeling in medieval Latin literature, but in Curtius's view, it gets expressed in a standard code of inherited typological rhetoric. With respect to the "humanism of the twelfth century," a key era of individuated expression in the eyes of some other critics, Curtius concludes: "The richness of the world and of life is reflected for it in the treasures and springs of power of the literary tradition, its assimilation, continuation, and transformation." The transformation is only the deepening of the preexisting lines of imagery: "Metaphors from books and writings are now more numerous and bolder."

The case of Dante seems crucial to Curtius's argument. Is Dante not an original thinker, a most innovative and creative poet? In Curtius's view, there is the deepest of sensibility and most fecund powers of imagination at work in Dante's writings, but always within the continuity of traditional culture—a shining of it, a diamondlike hardening of it. Here late Curtius shifts into the feverish style reminiscent of early Kantorowicz:

> It is a leaven which Dante casts into the tradition of the medieval West. . . . Dante's mind and soul, his architectonic thinking and his glowing heat, the tension of his will, which demanded stupendous efforts of itself . . . —these are the powers which conjured ten silent centuries into form. . . . The most immense frame of reference is required. From every point of his mythically and prophetically amplified experience connections run to every point of a given matter. They are forged and riveted in material as hard as diamonds. . . . The world drama of the Latin Middle Ages is played for the last time in the *Commedia*— but transposed into a modern language.

So Dante for Curtius represents the end of the Middle Ages, but Dante still is working within the structure of medieval typological culture. Dante makes it glow, he hardens it into a diamond, but the structure is still there, Curtius insists.

What is the meaning of all this for the mid-twentieth century? Curtius, never reticent, pounds the meaning at us near the end of his book. He denounces the *Geistesgeschichte* of the 1920s and 1930s for its "decadence." At first sight this appears astonishing to us—read naively, Curtius's book itself could be categorized as an exercise in *Geistesgeschichte*—but from Curtius's point of view this is superficial and misses the point. The great exponents of *Geistesgeschichte*, like Schramm and Kantorowicz, while they saw plenty of continuity of culture in the Middle Ages, sought to highlight the intellectual conflicts and innovations within this broad tradition. They looked for the subtle gesture, the revamped phrase that revealed *new* ideas emerging, revolt and change pushing through. That is what Curtius means when he condemns the German school. What Curtius wants is affirmation of continuity and homogeneity of ideas in the Middle Ages and in European culture in general because without this affirmation of structural consistency over time, the way is open for the radicals of left and right to corrupt with treacherous ideas and devastate Western civilization. Curtius pulls no punches; he is very outspoken:

> Even in times of educational atrophy and anarchy the heritage of the European mind, which is bound up with language and literature, can be fostered, as was the case in the monasteries of the early Middle Ages under the assaults of the barbarians and Saracens. . . . Only in words does mind speak its own language. Only in the creative word is it in its perfect freedom: above concept, above doctrine, above precept. . . . Upon memory rests the individual's consciousness of his identity above all change. The literary tradition is the medium by which the European mind preserves its identity through the millenniums [*sic*].

Now we can understand fully what Curtius is driving at. He fears the kind of change and instability that afflicted Germany in the 1920s and produced Hitler. He loves cultural stability and absolute intellectual continuity. Culture is fragile and hard to preserve. The great threat in his lifetime was ideology: "doctrine . . . concepts." This seductive relish for ideology fatally led to Hitler. The overly clever, treacherous *Geistesgeschichte* scholars of the Weimar era, by legitimating doctrine, by validating ideology, by highlighting new ideas, opened the cultural door to Hitler. Now that descent into hell must be closed off. And the way to do it is the (alleged) medieval way: the perpetuation of an essentially unchanging literary tradition. The road to hell is paved with intellectual innovation because that way authenticates ideology, which in turn, under the meretricious banners of intellectual originality, leads to anticivilization. We must give up the temptations of intellectual innovation. Curtius is arguing in favor of the preservation of a continuous literary culture that will protect humanity from what happened in Germany in the 1930s. The railroad track to Auschwitz starts where formalism ends.

The message to contemporaries that Curtius delivers is similar to the theme of Allan Bloom's *The Closing of the American Mind* (1987). Bloom, a University of Chicago philosopher and classicist, fears the upheaval and corruption that come from leftist ideology and disassociation from traditional culture. That, too, was Curtius's fear, and by the late 1940s he, in fact, saw that the left was as dangerous as the Hitlerian right. Both Curtius and Bloom are saying: Let us absent ourselves from the specious felicity of intellectual innovation, speculative ideology, and newspeak jargon. Let us stay with the great traditions and language of literary humanism grounded in the classical heritage, which therefore has to remain the dominant core of our educational curriculum if we are to avoid conjuring up monsters like Hitler and Stalin. It is significant how much positive response in their time there was to both Curtius and Bloom, as well as how much bitter opposition in academic circles each aroused. Of course, they both were seen as wanting to put the majority of humanists and social scientists out of business, and that conclusion was not paranoid.

The contemporary argument propounded by Curtius, which may be called fundamentalist humanism, therefore lives on and was again emphasized in the late 1980s. Curtius in the current debate about the core curriculum of Western civilization, literature, would obviously stand with Bloom on the side of preserving the traditional canon of humanistic classics. But Curtius is an even more radical conservative than that: He wants not only to restrict the canon but to perpetuate exclusively traditional ways of reading the classical texts. It is questionable how far Bloom would go in that direction. Bloom's precursor in cultural conservatism, Leo Spitzer, had mixed feeling about Curtius. He considered Curtius anti-intellectual.

Curtius's methodological and typological focus has also in recent years been recentered through the influence upon literary criticism of the structuralist anthropologist Claude Lévi-Strauss, his spokesman in literary criticism, Roland Barthes, and their disciples in Yale and other American literature departments. This literary structuralism is not quite the same thing as Curtius, but there is a recognizable overlap. In both Curtius's typological formalism and Barthes's literary structuralism there is a conviction that self-perpetuating language codes are the main subject to be explored. The similarity is not accidental in view of the affinity between Lévi-Strauss's structuralist anthropology and Jung's theory of archetypes, which the French mandarin belatedly acknowledged in the 1970s.

So Curtius's views have in recent years enjoyed a partial revival with regard to both his ideology (Bloom) and his methodology (Barthes). His interpretation of medieval literature and culture remains as controversial as ever. Essentially the situation is as noted by the venerable German authority on medieval literature Paul Lehmann, in his review of the 1948 edition of Curtius's book. Curtius had summed up the continuities and homogeneities in medieval literature, but one could as easily write a volume of equal length, Lehmann said, summarizing the discontinuities and discordances, especially if one focused on the vernacular literatures after 1000, about which Curtius said little. Furthermore, even with regard to the "Latin Middle Ages," the continuities and standardized impress of the formularies, it may be argued, may not have been as overwhelming as Curtius's exposition aimed to demonstrate. No one has yet uncoded the voluminous Latin writings of the late-twelfth-century abbess Hildegard of Bingen, although most of her works have been in print since the seventeenth century and she was referred to by Goethe. Hildegard, who may be the most interesting Latin prose writer of the twelfth century, fits uneasily into Curtius's thesis. It is curious that he refers to her only once in his book, in a footnote. The apocalyptic writings of Hildegard's contemporary the Italian abbot Joachim of Fioré also overflow the banks of traditional formularies.

Generally, in addition to the separations of vernacular literature from his interpretation, Curtius may therefore be said to have not sufficiently examined the more visionary kind of Latin ecclesiastical writings. The rise of the individualist school of interpreting high medieval culture, which was given a big boost by R. W. Southern in the 1950s and today includes Robert Hanning, Peter Dronke, and Colin Morris, challenges Curtius's attribution of dominant weight to topology as overdrawn and one-sided. This was already foreshadowed in a couple of brief, insightful chapters in Erich Auerbach's *Mimesis*, which appeared in German two years before Curtius's book.

When Curtius and Auerbach met at a conference at Princeton in 1949, they were understandably cool to each other.

The overwhelming mass of biographical and narrative historical writing before 1150 and a substantial amount thereafter were highly typological, and therefore, the formalist view is well grounded. To that extent Curtius is absolutely correct, although I cannot share his enthusiasm for this highly idealistic and derivative kind of writing in which kings and monks are described as doing things that prototypes of kings and monks are supposed to do, rather than things that individuals actually did. Even after 1150 much of this typology continued. For example, some of the biographers of Thomas Becket, the Canterbury martyr (d. 1170), describe the archbishop as rising at 2:00 A.M. daily to wash the feet of thirteen paupers. This *could* indeed have happened, but it is no more plausible than George Bush or Margaret Thatcher's turning up every evening at a church to distribute soup and soap to the homeless. After his martyrdom Becket's biographers felt compelled to tell stories about him that made him a thoroughgoing saint, and this formalization remains common in medieval writing. Indeed, after approximately a century of a trend toward greater realism, there was something of a drift back to typology in the late thirteenth century.

So far Curtius is on the right track, although again one does not have to hypostatize this typology into the only way to preserve Western civilization. The problem, within the context of literary criticism, is that much of the best literature of the late twelfth and early thirteenth centuries, especially in the French and German vernaculars, does not fit securely into Curtius's formalist model. The romances of Chrétien de Troyes are obvious examples. Of course, the search for the Grail and other such perilous quests fit into an ancient topos of heroic journeys, as in the *Odyssey* and the *Aeneid*, but to say that does not get you very far into the spirit or even the subject matter of Chrétien de Troyes. His *Lancelot* (1180), for instance, treats the theme of heroic quest with ambivalence bordering on derision. The poem is really about the problematic, sadomasochistic relationship between the sexes. It is closer to modern realism than the ancient typology, to such an extent that when Chrétien recited a draft of it to the court of Champagne, he was probably told to forget about finishing it; he cut too close to psychological distress. That is not typology. As for the great German romance *Parzifal* by Wolfram von Eschenbach (1200), you can find plenty of typology in it, but that is not what makes it a great work of imaginative literature. The typologies are grotesquely distorted by fantasy into a sensibility well beyond tradition. The paradoxical judgment that may be made about Curtius's view of medieval literature is that he gets most of it right, but the boring, not the interesting, part.

The ultimate problem with Curtius's formalist interpretation of medieval literature was one of the weaknesses that Freud immediately identified in Jung's theory of archetypes: How does all that mythological stuff help the therapist deal with the singular complexity of an individual life? Even if there was an overcast of typology in much of medieval literature, how does that give more than superficial insight into the significance of a particular work of deep feeling and high imagination?

The heated contortions that Curtius has to go through to get Dante into the mainline typological tradition shows the problem. As one of the most learned men of all the medieval era, Dante could, of course, summon up any topos by pressing a mental button, and he does do that. But all that traditional jazz is not what makes Dante a great poet and seminal thinker, and for the more learned and literate of Dante's contemporaries, that fact was probably as evident as it is for us.

Perhaps the three most widely admired and emulated critics of medieval literature in American universities since the late fifties, Yale's E. Talbot Donaldson, Berkeley's Charles Muscatine, and Columbia University's Robert Hanning, have given post-A.D. 1100 medieval literature a much higher degree of creative autonomy than Curtius allowed. They have indeed found substantial conventionality in medieval literature, but this proclivity to make use of standardized conventions was not, in the eyes of this distinguished critical triumvirate, just a historicizing perpetuation of late antiquity but a complex, distinctive, and in many ways innovative amalgam. It was constructed out of many derivations from the twelfth century onward, and it reached its zenith in Chaucer in the late fourteenth century. Even the use of literary conventions was often highly conscious and crucially instrumental. The author knew he was using a literary tradition and subtly massaged it for his own purposes.

Generally, Donaldson was following pre-World War II's New Criticism (whose citadel was at Yale) in assuming the highly privileged integrity of a particular poetical text that is liberated from historical traditions—that is, the meaning is in the text itself, not in its historical derivation. Muscatine admired Erich Auerbach's insistence on the quasi-realistic capacity of medieval writers to manipulate and partly transcend typologies. Of Chaucer, Muscatine concluded in 1957, "he sees the courtly and bourgeois modes, idealism and practicality, in ironic juxtaposition." Focusing on twelfth-century literature in England and France, Hanning is close to the Donaldson and Muscatine interpretive post-Curtius program, while stressing the capacity of writers in both poetry and prose to express personal feeling and psychological insights.

In spite of all these reservations and limitations, Curtius's formalist interpretation of medieval literature captured the tone and texture of at least 60 percent of it and perhaps as much as 80 percent of the Latin component. That is a formidable achievement. But there is something more to his book, harder to assess. It has a quality that haunts the mind, that never can be set aside, that perpetually challenges anyone who wants to understand and speculate about the pattern of medieval culture. Curtius's book is a kind of topos of its own, an image of the Middle Ages that endures and disturbs. His formalist interpretation serves as a kind of Jungian archetype that actively impresses itself on all subsequent critical speculation about the meaning of the Middle Ages.

By the mid-1950s, once West Germany and other devastated and demoralized parts of Western Europe had recovered from the war and had begun to enter an era of prosperity and economic growth unprecedented since 1914, Curtius's *Latin Middle Ages* had become more meaningful and provocative on the American educational and intellectual scene than the European. The Europeans still had their marvelous secondary school education, whose curriculum in the humanities was still richly traditional and hence redolent of a spontaneous formalism. In the United States, at the college as well as at the high school level, centering literate learning on the great texts of Western civilization, which were either created or transmitted through medieval culture, was altogether a bolder and more controversial endeavor. This issue again boiled over in the 1980s with the dispute over the nature of the literary and philosophical canon.

In the 1950s and 1960s Curtius's most outspoken and skillful disciple on the American campus was Durant Waite Robertson, Jr., a professor of medieval literature in the Princeton English department. Conventionally trained at the University of North Carolina at Chapel Hill, which had strong medieval literature departments, D. W. Robertson, Jr., as he signed his many articles and books, adopted a severely formalist, Curtius-inspired interpretation of medieval literature.

In Robertson's version, it was the patristic, especially Augustinian, tradition that was the dominant intellectual force in medieval literature of any kind. Chaucer's ironies and personality portraits become mere allegories for Augustinian ethical and religious doctrines, as viewed by Robertson. To the indignation and, indeed, occasional horror of his more gentlemanly colleagues in the Princeton English department, Robertson insisted that Chaucer's poems, as well as clerical literature, were to be read entirely within the context of topology.

Robertson, like Curtius, saw himself engaged in a cultural struggle for preservation of Western civilization, not only as establishing the right way to read medieval literature. Robertson disdained "the rancid solipsistic pit into which the major tendencies of post-romantic thought have thrust us." Thereby he is saying that the easygoing admiration for individuality and personal privilege that conventional humanistic and academic liberalism inclined to threatened to dissolve the cement that held Western culture together. The road to be taken, Robertson and his exegetical disciples insisted, was that of medieval literature, which was "directed towards the establishment and maintenance of those traditional hierarchies . . . dear to the medieval mind." The medieval mode of thinking was universally and univocally the "tendency to think in terms of symmetrical patterns, characteristically arranged with reference to an abstract hierarchy." We should also seek a cultural harmony and social stability by pursuing the medieval mode of discourse—being "able to discuss the goal of personal effort, of social effort, and of religious effort in a single terminology, and to come to an agreement about the general meaning of that terminology." Thus Robertson stands as an aggressive traffic cop on the busy conservative intellectual highway that leads from Curtius to Allan Bloom.

An inspiring and dedicated teacher of graduate students, Robertson produced in the fifties and sixties a steady stream of very capable Ph.D.'s who preached his Augustinian version of the formalist tradition and carried it to English departments in colleges all over the United States and Canada. For the "Robertsonians," as for Curtius, studying the Middle Ages represented the polemical advocacy of cultural conservatism.

The Middle Ages, in the minds of the Robertsonian disciples of Curtius and Panofsky, signified something different from the medieval image held by Maitland, by Bloch and the Annalists, and even by the formalists' uneasy allies in cultural conservatism, Kantorowicz,

Schramm, and the adherents of German *Geistesgeschichte*. For Maitland and the modernist functionalists who admired him, medieval society lived on the margin of perpetual chaos, and its intellectual resources were modest. But "the felt necessities of time," in Oliver Wendell Holmes, Jr.'s splendid phrase, somehow congealed a stable legal order within a viscerally anxious and indeterminable context. Bloch and the Annalists, to turn around Freud's phrase, lived off the illusion of a future, the elimination of hierarchy and injustice that was prepared in their aggressive minds by cerebral manipulation and erosion of the inequalities of medieval society. To know intimately the democratic nightmare of medievalism prepared them, they assumed, both emotionally and rationally for a postmodernist society of universal social justice. This illusion, so fiercely cultivated since 1917, has sunk in 1990 but not irrevocably.

Schramm and Kantorowicz and their disciples envisaged a medieval culture focused on the exploitation of Latin Christian ideals by charismatic leaders bent on realization of some universal new order. But it was also intrinsic to their medieval vision that it be a tragic one in which the heroes never prevail in the end and the superhuman efforts of the medieval past have to be emulated in some kind of angry neomedievalist present composed of idealism, anxiety, and terror.

The formalists, finding their deep thinkers in Panofsky and Curtius and even more polemical advocates in the Robertsonians, vehemently rejected Maitland's picture of a disordered medieval world fortuitously brought into stasis by functional conditions and a million individual decisions; that was very far from the triumphal heritage of classicism and patristic Christian theology they wanted to cultivate. Bloch and the Annalists, from the point of view of the formalists, were mere radical ax grinders winning the revolution on the speciously imagined medieval landscape that they could not gain in the real world of the twentieth century. For the formalists, Bloch stood for a peculiar Parisian kind of regressive infantilism. Nor were the protagonists of *Geistesgeschichte* without a deep flaw. Schramm and Kantorowicz were as skillful as anyone in mastering and communicating the classical and patristic heritage and tracing it through medieval culture. But perversely they would not leave it at rest. They somehow wanted to turn this incomparable medieval ethos into a staging ground for the hazardous transformation of modern society.

The formalists wanted instead to project themselves entirely into medieval culture and to submerge modernity in a passive retromedi-

eval culture of uniform classicism and Christian theology. In a peculiar way, the formalists stood toward the *Geistesgeschichte* people as the
Italian Renaissance humanists stood toward the fourteenth-century
scholastic philosophers. The latter wanted to define the new truths
out of the classical and patristic canon. The Renaissance humanists
thought they had all the truth that was needed, or possible, in retro-
classicism. So did the formalists, following Curtius and Panofsky;
only it was now to be medievalism more than antique classicism that
was to generate all actionable assumptions and monopolize all education and the arts.

CHAPTER SIX

THE OXFORD FANTASISTS

CLIVE STAPLES LEWIS, JOHN RONALD REVEL TOLKIEN, AND FREDERICK MAURICE POWIEKE

I

SAVE THE BELOVED LAND

In the early forties, during the height of the war years, while a bomber moon shone down upon the deer park on the grounds of Magdalen College, Oxford, a half dozen dons and their friends, who were also writers and lived in or near Oxford, gathered on Tuesday evenings in the rooms of the Magdalen College tutor in medieval literature and political theory. The Magdalen tutor was C. S. Lewis—Jack to his friends. They drank beer and tea, smoked heavily in the British manner, throwing their cigarette ashes on the worn carpet, and read to each other from, and caustically commented on, written work in progress. The group came to call themselves the Inklings. One of this group in Jack Lewis's rooms was an editor of the Oxford University Press, the dramatist and novelist and Christian polemicist Charles Williams, who was relocated by the press in Oxford from London for the duration of the war. He died there in 1945. Another of the Inklings was a lawyer, Owen Barfield, later Jack Lewis's executor, which was eventually to be not a small job.

Another Inkling was the reclusive professor of Anglo-Saxon, John Ronald Reuel Tolkien, called Ronald. In the late twenties and early thirties he was renowned as an authority on Old and Middle English. He was the leading scholar on the subject of two precious fourteenth-century poems written anonymously in the Midlands, about seventy miles from Oxford, in the dialect of that region. These poems, *Sir*

Gawain and the Green Knight and *Pearl*, are now regarded, along with *Beowulf* (c. 800) and the works of Chaucer (late fourteenth century), as the greatest medieval poetry in the English language. There is no more beautiful poem in any medieval language than *Pearl*, an allegorical elegy for a dead child. Tolkien was responsible for the definitive text of *Sir Gawain*, published in 1925. For thirty years, off and on, he labored on a translation of *Pearl*; it was finally published posthumously, but it was soon superseded by a remarkable metrical translation made by Yale's Marie Borroff.

Despite his prodigious learning and early professional accomplishments, Tolkien's academic career in the early forties seemed on a downward trajectory. In the previous decade his only book publication was a children's fantasy, *The Hobbit* (1937), which had sold well. Tolkien's publisher clamored for a sequel, but as yet he had not produced it, although he desperately needed the money, having a wife and three children in a lower-middle-class suburb of Oxford. Tolkien had no private means, and he had to waste a month every summer picking up a few extra pounds grading examination booklets. Tolkien read to the Inklings miscellaneous sections of what seemed to be a disordered mythological fantasy addressed more to adults than children. Who would want to read this thing? Who would dare publish it? Jack Lewis's response to it was only intermittently enthusiastic.

Lewis in the war years was by far the best known of the Inklings group, both within the academic world and even more among the general public. He had established his reputation as a leading medieval literary historian with *The Allegory of Love* (1936), a pioneering and influential study of medieval romantic literature, which he had written one chapter at a time over a half dozen long summer vacations from his heavy Magdalen College teaching load. He was now rapidly gaining attention among the general public for his children's fiction, for science fiction novels and allegories with a Christian twist, and for a series of BBC lectures that were essentially soft-core sermons.

By 1943 Lewis was the best-known Christian polemicist in Britain, and he had begun to acquire a cult following in the United States. He lived in a fashionable house just outside Oxford with his brother, an army reserve officer and a nonacademic but very capable historian of Bourbon France in the Age of Louis XIV. They were bachelors. The household was dominated by a dragon housekeeper, the mother of Jack Lewis's best friend, who was killed in the First World War. With this difficult woman, Lewis had a bizarre, probably celibate, repressive, sadomasochistic relationship for three decades. Lewis was slowly becoming affluent from book royalties; he changed his lifestyle very little and gave away part of the money to relatives or to one charity or another.

Tolkien and Lewis were at least visibly good friends as well as colleague luminaries in Oxford's medieval language and literature faculty. Their friendship was always tense because their personalities were so different—Tolkien, reclusive, driven, querulous, unsatisfied; Lewis, calm, affable, outgoing, sociable. Underneath their surface friendship there was a deep rivalry between them, not so much in scholarship as in writing fantasy literature. Of all the medievalists of the twentieth century, Lewis and Tolkien have gained incomparably the greatest audience, although 99.9 percent of their readers have never looked at their scholarly work. They are among the best-selling authors of modern times for their works of fantasy, adult and children's. There are forty million copies of Lewis's work in print. The novel that Tolkien read bits of to the Inklings, with mixed response in the early forties, was finally published with trepidation by Allen and Unwin in three volumes in 1954 and 1955. It has now sold eight million copies in many languages, with about half the sales in an American paperback edition. This is *The Lord of the Rings*.

In the early forties, while Tolkien was grinding his way through his six-hundred-thousand-word fantasy, typing it all himself, with only marginal hope of ever finding a publisher, Lewis's fame grew steadily. In 1949 Jack Lewis's smiling face graced the cover of *Time* magazine, and he gained a huge audience in the United States. It tells you a lot about Lewis and Tolkien that although they shared a huge commercial success in the United States, greater than in their own country by a significant margin, neither ever set foot across the Atlantic. Today there is an institute devoted to Lewis's work at Wheaton College in Illinois, and the number of American doctoral dissertations written on Tolkien grows at a steady pace.

At the end of the war Lewis was the center of a popular transatlantic Christian cult, and his scholarly reputation also advanced steadily—eventually he published five scholarly books—but it is more likely that Tolkien, then regarded by many of his colleagues, possibly including Lewis, as a burnout case and a somewhat embarrassing failure who ought to resign his prestigious chair and give a younger and more productive man a chance at it, whose fame will be of infinite duration. It now looks as though *The Lord of the Rings* is one of the enduring classics of English literature and that a century from now, while Lewis's reputation will have flattened out, Tolkien will stand in the company of Swift and Dickens as a creator of imaginative fiction and in the lineage of fantasy writers going back to the author of *Pearl*, which he himself rescued form very deep obscurity.

When Rayner Unwin, Tolkien's publisher, was preparing *The Lord of the Rings* for publication in 1954, he asked Lewis to contribute a blurb for the dust jacket. Lewis complied, comparing Tolkien's novel with the writings of the Renaissance Italian poet Ariosto. Tolkien found this praise a bit overdone, and in fact, Lewis had mixed feelings about Tolkien's accomplishment. He did not anticipate the phenomenal popular success of Tolkien's fantasy of mythic quest. He did not expect that out of the shabby converted garage attached to Tolkien's modest suburban house would come a work of such international celebrity.

In terms of shaping of the Middle Ages in the popular culture of the twentieth century, Tolkien and Lewis have had an incalculable effect, and the story is far from ended. Their fictional fantasies cannot be separated from their scholarly writing. Their work in each case should be seen as a whole and as communicating an image of the Middle Ages that has entered profoundly and indelibly into world culture.

Whatever the tensions in their personal relationships, Lewis and Tolkien were important and good for each other. They did not so much influence each other along specific, calculable lines as they encouraged each other to pursue hazardous journeys of creation. For more than twenty years they emboldened, criticized, and reinforced each other. They legitimated for each other their singular careers, in which, while conscientiously fulfilling their teaching responsibilities, they took time (in Tolkien's case almost all of it) from their scholarly work to transmute their medieval learning into mythopoetic fiction, fantasy literature for a mass audience that communicated the sensibility of medieval epic and romance.

They were resented and envied by their colleagues, Lewis thereby failing to get the chair he wanted at Oxford and forced to find one at Cambridge (while continuing to live three days a week in his Oxford house), Tolkien losing much of his credibility in his colleagues' eyes. Strengthening each other's resolve, they persevered and transcended the academic world and became international media figures.

Their fantasy writing was a very serious undertaking. It was not done as a hobby or primarily as a moneymaking venture, although they both died well-off from it. They wanted to impart a sense of medieval myth to the widest audience possible. They wanted to represent to the public the impress of the kind of traditional ethic they derived from their devotion to conservative Christianity. But essentially they wrote as all creative writers do, from some compulsion within their beings, from something beyond the level of consciousness. Tolkien memorably described this obsession in 1953: "One writes such a story not out of the leaves of trees still to be observed, not by means of botany and soil-science; but it grows like a seed in the dark out of the leaf-mold of the mind; out of all that has been thought or seen or read, that has long been forgotten, descending into the deeps."

Lewis and Tolkien had very similar personal tastes and life-styles. They disliked French cuisine and liked plain English food. They did not relish travel abroad or driving motorcars. They were generally hostile to modern technology, although Lewis occasionally took in a film and came to appreciate sound recording. Lewis spoke also for Tolkien when he wrote in 1940: "I am conscious of a partly pathological hostility to what is fashionable." Like nearly all Oxbridge dons of their generation, they had little use for psychoanalysis, and neither ever had psychotherapy. They disliked dressing up and nearly always appeared in worn tweeds and baggy trousers. A brisk walk in the country followed by tea was a high point of each one's day.

They had no interest whatever in the United States and in American culture. They knew lots of people lived across the Atlantic because after their best sellers had appeared, they received innumerable letters from there, usually from women groupies. They courteously and carefully responded to such letters, but they never bothered to learn about the culture and society whence they came. For them the United States was just a colonial land with a thick and affluent population.

Both men were deeply affected by a nostalgia and a love for a rapidly disappearing England graced by the middle-class, highly literate Christian culture into which they had been born. They saw a continuity of this culture stretching back into the Middle Ages, when, in their perception, it originated. For them, these vibrant, imaginative, complex Middle Ages were in many essentials still activated in the donnish world of mid-twentieth-century Oxbridge and the English countryside, if not so much in London. Lewis and Tolkien wanted not only to preserve but to revitalize through their writing and teaching this Anglo-Edwardian retromedieval culture. In the mechanistic, capitalistic, aggressive age of Harold Macmillan and Margaret Thatcher, it looked as though their program of cultural nostalgia would have little long-range impact. In the 1990s we cannot be so sure of that.

The Lewis-Tolkien philosophy of history is lyrically summed up by Tolkien's quasi hero Frodo in *The Lord of the Rings:* "I tried to save the Shire, and it has been saved, but not for me. It must be often to be so, Sam, when things are in danger; some one has to give them up, lose them. So that others may keep them. But you are my heir: . . . and you will read things out of the Red Book and keep alive the memory of the age that is gone, so that people will remember the Great Danger and so love their beloved land all the more."

Lewis saw himself, Tolkien, and his other Oxbridge friends as spokesmen for an "Old European, or Old Western Culture," that was under siege. We know where Lewis and Tolkien would stand in the current dispute about the canon of literature. They were "dinosaurs," and it might be that "there are not going to be many more dinosaurs," said Lewis. But they were going to fight the last good fight. In Lewis's words, "The preservation of society, and the species itself, are ends that do not hang on the precarious thread of Reason: They are given by instinct. . . . We have an instinctive urge to preserve our own species. That is why men ought to work for posterity." This instinctive urge for preservation of humankind is not pursued through natural spontaneity but rather through highly literate discipline. Preservation is mediated through the literature and philosophy of the Middle Ages and the subsequent heritage deriving from and developing out of medieval humanistic culture. Their chief vehicle in this perilous journey of salvation was mythic fiction. As Lewis wrote of the sixteenth-century poet Edmund Spenser, they sought "to produce a tale more solemn, more redolent of the past, more venerable, than any real medieval romance . . . to hand on to succeeding generations a poetic symbol of the [Middle Ages] whose charms have proved inexhaustible."

Lewis (1898–1963) and Tolkien (1892–1973) differed in their personal lives in two significant respects. Tolkien fell in love when he was sixteen with a girl of his class five years his senior and married her five years later, just before he went to fight in France. He had three children and a stable, happy family life although his wife disliked Oxford for the forty years she lived there, feeling isolated and lonely. When Tolkien retired and had his first royalty checks from *The Lord of the Rings,* she made him move to a residential hotel in a plebeian seaside resort. One of Tolkien's sons also became an Oxford literature don.

Lewis was extremely repressed sexually. He did not marry until 1955 and did not consummate the marriage for several months thereafter. His wife was an ex-Communist New York Jewish groupie with two small sons who forced herself on him. She died of cancer in 1960. From the time he was a schoolboy, Lewis was affected by sadomasochistic fantasies of whipping, "something beautifully intimate and also very humiliating," he reported to a friend.

The other difference between Lewis and Tolkien was in their class background. Lewis came from a comfortably middle-class suburban professional family. His father was a successful lawyer. Tolkien's family was sliding into genteel poverty, greatly accelerated by the death of his father when he was four years old. He grew up in stringent economic circumstances and made it through prep school and college only on a series of scholarships. Lewis was therefore free and easy with money and generous to a fault. Tolkien was, not surprisingly, stingy and tight. He never hired a typist for the manuscript of *The Lord of the Rings*, and until it was set in type, there was only one copy. It was Tolkien's children who for the most part enjoyed the fiscal benefit of his best-selling smash in the last two decades of his long life.

But there were three ways in which the biographies of Lewis and Tolkien are very similar. First, they were outlanders, products of the Empire in its day of autumnal glow. Tolkien (whose family on his father's side came to Britain from Germany in the late seventeenth century) was born in South Africa and spent the first four years of his life there. Lewis was born into the Belfast Anglo-Irish and grew up in Northern Ireland. For them, therefore, England was a place to come home to and all the more to be cherished. At the same time they were at least in earlier years conscious of themselves as outlanders, as colonials.

Secondly, and most important, Lewis lost his mother when he was ten. Tolkien (who had already experienced his father's death) lost his mother when he was twelve. Lewis's father was very remote and unemotional, and Tolkien was a full-fledged orphan, with a local priest as his guardian. Each revered his mother's memory. Early loss of a parent, especially in the case of men, is a powerful stimulant for independence and creativity. It also stimulates a fantasy world of search for a happy time and land, a sublimated reunion with the absent mother.

Finally, Lewis and Tolkien were products of the era of British decline that occupied most of their lifetimes. They fought as officers in the First World War. Both witnessed scenes of indescribable carnage. From this experience they derived an appreciation of physical courage, an imaginative taste for violence, and a sense of the instability and fragility of life. The "Dark Power" is an ever-recurring threat. All these qualities are reflected in their fantasy novels. Lewis and Tolkien belonged to Britain's posthegemonic generation. The Empire was not lost until after World War II, but in the late thirties and forties, between Munich in 1938 and the abandonment of the raj ten years later, in spite of the dogged Christian heroism of the war, it was pretty clear that Britain's day of wealth and power was over. It was the time of Britannia's "sunset and evening star."

The response to economic and imperial decline was in the Britain of the forties a literary ambience of despairing resignation, suspicion of and incapacity to sustain an advanced technological society, and an intense but short-lived Christian revival. The leading British writers of the period—T. S. Eliot in poetry and drama, F. R. Leavis in literary criticism and cultural commentary, J. B. Priestley in fiction, Arnold Toynbee in metahistorical speculation—shared this temperament. It even affects the later writings, the satirical fantasies, of George Orwell. Translated into focus on the bureaucratic establishment, it is a theme also in C. P. Snow's novels.

Britain hadn't recovered psychologically before the sixties, possibly the eighties, perhaps never, from those miserable photos of February 1942, showing slim, diminished, embarrassed British officers in their little khaki shorts surrendering Singapore to exultant, masterful Japanese generals, or those heart-stopping photos of smiling young British bomber crews about to leave for their near-suicidal night missions over Germany in 1943 and 1944 and the loss of 59,000 air crews, the cream of a generation, at least half of them secondary school and college graduates. In addition to these irreversible traumas, there was after 1945 souring national austerity, fuel shortages, food asperity, a humiliating subordinate satellite relationship with the United States, and ignominious retreat from the tropical Empire, where nothing was recovered from centuries of prodigious effort and idealism.

This was the sad ambience, the bitter, depleted world in which Lewis and Tolkien wrote. They had, however, a more positive response to these conditions and events than the postimperial stoicism, cultural despair, and resigned Christian pessimism that were the common response of their British contemporaries. They were not prepared imaginatively and intellectually to withdraw and accept defeat. Out of the medieval Norse, Celtic, and Grail legends, they conjured fantasies of revenge and recovery, an ethos of return and triumph. As Chaucer said in *Troilus and Criseyde*, they aimed to "to make dreams truth and fables histories." A mythopoetic vision of medieval heroism was to be communicated to the masses through fantasy stories. "That something which the educated receive from poetry," Lewis wrote in 1947, "can reach the masses in stories of adventure, and almost in no other way."

II

THE MEDIEVAL IMAGINATION

Biographical studies of Lewis have slowly emerged. Most valuable are Humphrey Carpenter, *The Inklings* (1979), which, as the title indicates, is mostly focused on the 1940s scene in Oxford, and a 1988 book by George Sayer (*Jack: C. S. Lewis and His Times*) that is memoir as well as biography and is uneven but informed and insightful in places. To these highly sympathetic biographies there has been added a more hostile portrait (*C. S. Lewis: A Biography* [1990]) by the prolific British novelist and biographer A. N. Wilson: Lewis "was argumentative and bullying. His jolly, red, honest face was that of an intellectual bruiser. . . . He was frequently contemptuous in his remarks about the opposite sex."

In 1985 British television boldly presented a film, *Shadowlands*, depicting Lewis's relationship with Joy Davidman, the American to whom he was married for five years. A stage play derived from the TV film has since been presented in London and New York. In the TV film, Claire Bloom was miscast as Joy Davidman. The actor playing Lewis, Joss Ackland, although taller than he was, did facially resemble him. Lewis was a handsome man in that heavyset British manner. He came through in *Shadowlands* as a generally wise and generous person and as extremely kind to Davidman's two sons by a previous marriage (that was true), even paying for their attendance at an upscale boarding school.

Shadowlands communicates accurately that Jack Lewis brimmed with self-confidence. He had very firm opinions about everything, including the Middle Ages. For Lewis the quest for the Middle Ages was the pursuit of "the compulsive imagination of a larger, brighter, bitterer, more dangerous world than ours." In his view, this medieval imagination was the product of the tense interaction of three cultural traditions. One was the romantic tradition that attained its highest

development in the courtly literature, the love poetry of the aristocracy of northern France, southern England, and the Rhine Valley in
the late twelfth and thirteenth centuries—the world of "courtly love."
A second strand in medieval imaginative culture lay in the vast and
complex, often university-based, learned conception of a cosmic and
world order that came to fruition in the late thirteenth and fourteenth
centuries and is expressed both in academic treatises and in Dante's
Divine Comedy, which draws heavily upon this systematic learning.
Underneath these two cultural traditions, courtly love and the learned
structure of cosmic order, lies a third force, the pristine instinctive
feeling of a warrior society that became hedged about and largely,
but not entirely, submerged by the consciously developed other two
cultures.

This is the essential Lewis view of medieval literature and art.
When he began to propound it, in the mid-1930s, it was very much
a vanguard conception. No one in the English-speaking world had up
to then the learning, insight, and courage to attempt such a sophisticated definition of high medieval culture. There had been valuable
discussions of particular poets and treatises on philosophy and theology. But Lewis tried to define the essence of the twelfth-century literary imagination and did so in a formula that has withstood the
challenge of a half century of research and reflection: The world view
in twelfth- and early-thirteenth-century literature is the product of
the romantic courtly tradition interacting with a search for learned
order while to some extent perpetuating the underlying instinctive
feeling of a warrior society.

How does this medieval culture, so defined, relate to us? How
does it affect our consciousness? Medieval culture is both different
from ours and very much in communication with ours, Lewis believed. In this way there is an ambiguous, tensile, and creative relationship between the medieval heritage of literature and art and our
own way of thinking and seeing. To read medieval "literature aright
you must suspend most of the responses and unlearn most of the
habits you have acquired in reading modern literature." It is easy
enough to perceive that "in every way, if we have not outgrown, we
have at least grown away from, *The Romance of the Rose*," the French
romantic masterpiece of the late thirteenth century. On the other hand,
"such a view would be superficial. Humanity does not pass through
phases as a train passes through stations. Being alive, it has the privilege of always moving yet never leaving something behind. Whatever we have been, in some sort we are still. Neither the form nor

the sentiment of this old poetry has passed away without leaving indelible traces on our mind." So here is the second quality of medieval literature, after its tripartite foundations in romance, learned order, and primitive instinct: It is both separate from us and highly accessible to us and interactive with our own being. In the language not of Lewis but of Freud and Jacques Lacan, it is our other.

A third characteristic of medieval culture as seen by Lewis is its paradoxical combination of generalizing visions of unity with an intense concentration on the particular. Do medieval literature and art tend to be generalizing or do they concentrate on detail? Both, says Lewis, and this is their peculiar quality: "Medieval art attains a unity of the highest order, because it embraces the greatest diversity of detail."

This view exhibited compatibility with the contemporary principles of neo-Thomism, a theory about the Middle Ages developed in the 1930s and 1940s, originally under the influence of a group of theologians and cultural commentators on the liberal wing of the French Catholic Church. It had its greatest impact in France and the United States. Among its protagonists were Jacques Maritain, a philosopher who taught at the Sorbonne in Paris and after 1941 at Princeton, and Étienne Gilson, the historian of medieval philosophy, who held chairs in Paris and Toronto. In the United States neo-Thomism gained support not only in Catholic institutions like Fordham University, in New York, but also at the University of Chicago, where its spokesmen were the philosopher Richard McKeon and the educational theorist Mortimer Adler. It was embraced by the University of Chicago's activist and controversial president, Robert Maynard Hutchins. What neo-Thomism projected was an image of a medieval culture tending always on the side of synthesis and unity. Against the fractious, atomizing nature of modern culture and the disordered curriculum of modern education, medieval culture was held up as an ideal contrast of striving to bring everything together. St. Thomas Aquinas was particularly praised for his efforts to integrate Catholic theology with Aristotelian philosophy, the vanguard science of the day.

Lewis, too, affirmed that medieval man was "an organizer, a codifier, a builder of systems." He talked about "the essentially bookish character of their [medieval men's] culture, and their intense love of system." Lewis could therefore be appealed to, and was, by the neo-Thomists to support their point of view and confirm their program, which was to sustain traditional learned order ("the Great Books" in Chicago parlance) in the midst of the disturbing variety and instability of modern life. Lewis's phenomenal popularity in America in the 1940s and 1950s stemmed partly from the compatibility of his perception of medieval culture with neo-Thomist principles.

But Lewis saw more deeply into medieval culture than the neo-Thomists did. He knew there was another side entirely to medieval sensibility in contrast with system building, and this was a love of the particular, a propensity to concentrate on small facts and distinctive experience and to relish the individual and the concrete. In that respect, medieval culture had much in common with the modernism of the early twentieth century, in which Lewis, like others of his generation, was educationally reared and which had become inextricably intertwined with donnish Oxbridge mentality.

The medieval imagination, Lewis summed up near the end of his life, "is not a transforming imagination like Wordsworth's or a penetrative imagination like Shakespeare's. It is a realising imagination." Dante was obsessive about "extremely factual word-painting: the details, the comparisons, designed at whatever cost of dignity to make sure that we see exactly what he saw. Now Dante in this is typically medieval. The Middle Ages are unrivaled, till we reach quite modern times [here is an insightful reference to modernist foreshadowing in medieval culture], in the sheer foreground fact, the 'close-up.'" This statement encapsulates Lewis's lifetime consideration of medieval culture. It appears in *The Discarded Image*, a brief, reflective, subdued, almost depressive summing up, published in 1964, one year after he died, which was a final version of the lectures on the medieval imagination that he had been giving at Oxford and Cambridge for many years.

Lewis left a great many questions unanswered or even unasked about the nature of the Middle Ages, although what he had to say was persuasive and largely incontestable. There is an air of closure, of finality about *The Discarded Image*. The open-ended sociological, psychoanalytic, anthropological questions about medieval culture, not to speak of actual literary and linguistic issues, are for the most part resisted in this book. Lewis is here too much the legislator of the truth about medieval culture. It is the truth, by and large, but it is a somewhat narrow truth. It is unfortunate that Lewis did not spend a year or two at Yale or Berkeley, or at the Monumenta in Munich, or the Annalist institute in Paris. He might have been stirred out of his Oxbridge donnish proclivity, which *The Discarded Image* especially represents, to send postcard and command cable messages about the medieval world.

Yet Lewis was a great emancipator in medieval studies in the two other major scholarly works that he published: *The Allegory of Love* (1936) and *English Literature in the Sixteenth Century Excluding Drama* (1954). They are bold, original, seminal works that rocked the transatlantic Anglophone world of medieval studies and did a great deal of good. No one would recommend *The Allegory of Love* nowadays as an authoritative study of the immensely important subject of medieval romance. Lewis's book is now obsolete, pioneering but superseded by, in both learning and conceptualization, more recent works such as John Stevens's *Medieval Romance* (1973) and Lynette Muir's *Literature and Society in Medieval France* (1984). But Lewis's *Love* was a watershed in the invention of the Middle Ages because he legitimated the subject of the idea of love and gave academic authority to inquiry into romantic patterns within medieval literature. What heretofore had been only hesitantly and marginally considered was transformed by him into a sober-sided, central, crucial subject in medieval studies.

Lewis's account of nondramatic sixteenth-century English literature (it was for the multivolume, extremely uneven *Oxford History of English Literature* series, and someone else was unfortunately assigned Shakespeare and dramatic literature) is today very much worth reading because of his subtle and passionate argument that Renaissance literature, such as the poetry of Edmund Spenser, is still functioning within the language and concept formations of medieval culture. In other words, Lewis maintained vehemently that contrary to the viewpoint of the followers of Jacob Burckhardt, the Renaissance is only a late and special chapter in the history of medieval culture, not the dawn of a new era.

Lewis was not the only scholar of his generation to argue this emphatically at the time. It had already been done by E. M. W. Tillyard at Cambridge and Douglas Bush at Harvard. Indeed, in the 1950s the claim that the Renaissance constituted a new, secular postmedieval era ran up against conservative Christian sensibility in both Britain and America. In academic circles rebuttal of Burckhardt's conception of the Italian Renaissance as "the discovery of man and nature" occupied the time and attention of any critic or historian who was caught up in the short-lived postwar Christian reaffirmation. Lewis demonstrated, in great detail and with a quality of expository and critical writing he was never to attain again, the myriad ways in which the assumptions and expressive forms of English Renaissance literature perpetuated the medieval thought world and way of speaking.

The case against the applicability of the Burckhardtian view of the Renaissance to sixteenth-century England received its most persuasive articulation in Lewis's influential book. Of course, that did not terminate the debate. It only weighted the scales against the Burckhardtian idea for a decade or so.

There is an interesting proposal in the later chapters of Lewis's book that it was the rise of Puritanism in late Elizabethan England, the advancing tide of Calvinist theology and ethics in the last two decades of the sixteenth century, not the Renaissance literary movement of the early and middle decades of the century, that marked the real rupture with medieval culture. Even this watershed is problematical, however, since so much of Elizabethan Puritanism was itself a revival, in somewhat altered language and tone, of devotional attitudes that lie deep in the medieval past.

The defect of Lewis's *Sixteenth Century* does not lie at the empirical level. It may be conceded to him that the poetry of Henrician and earlier Elizabethan England is still heavily embedded in the thought world and language of medieval classicism and romanticism. It may be recognized also that the Puritanism of the later years of the century reflected some kind of seismic alteration in moral perceptions and personal expectations. The problem that Lewis ran up against is one of historical sociology or large-scale cultural analysis. What do we mean by an era, and what are the signs that it has ended? There is no way of shrugging off this issue. It is what the Germans call *Zeitwende*, the turning from one age to another. This is what Lewis is addressing in *Sixteenth Century*. The problem is that he does not address it directly and self-consciously enough. How do we gauge a change in mentality, a paradigm shift? Looked at from this global perspective, the fact that the poets of sixteenth-century England are still speaking within the referential discourse of the Middle Ages does not inevitably signify that they are still within the bounds of medieval culture. Precisely because Lewis's *Sixteenth Century* shows him in high gear, at his most learned and sparkling best, his book reveals the limitations of Oxbridge thinking at mid-century.

Jack Lewis never wrote the great book on medieval romantic culture and faith that he was capable of writing by virtue of his learning and insight. Instead, he applied these capacities to his fiction, which gained him an enormous audience. These books still sell well, remarkably in that their style now seems fustian Edwardian, out of touch with the later twentieth century. But to a certain kind of middle-class reader in the United States, specifically conservative Christians, in the Midwest and South, Lewis is still powerfully persuasive in terms of both his message and his low-key style. There is also a coterie of fanatical Lewis disciples among English Anglo-Catholics, who hold frequent cult meetings at Oxford. According to A. N. Wilson, this group dogmatically insists that Lewis never lost his virginity.

Lewis's best-selling and still most readable works of fiction fall into two groups. First are two polemical Christian novels: *The Screwtape Letters* (1942), which was appropriately first serialized in a newspaper, and *The Great Divorce* (1945). It was the transatlantic impact of these novels, plus the Christian trend within Time Inc., at that time under the influence of Clare Boothe Luce, the pious Catholic, sharp-tongued feminist wife of the publisher, Henry Luce, that landed Lewis on the cover of *Time* in 1949. This was also a moment in *Time*'s history when a senior editor was Whittaker Chambers, the former Soviet spy and eventual nemesis of Alger Hiss. Now a devout Quaker Christian, Chambers was keen on importing British conservative Christianity to American shores, and his favorite vehicles were Lewis and Arnold Toynbee.

Lewis's other continuing sale of books is from the seven-volume children's fantasy *Chronicles of Narnia* (1950–56), which is extremely uneven in quality—some pages read as though they were scribbled on the backs of envelopes on the train to London—but which also has strong sections. Into these nine volumes of fantasy fiction, Lewis put his medieval vision. Here he propounded more dramatically and clearly than in his scholarly writings the medievals' relevant message for us. The first of these messages is the reality of evil, personified by the devil and represented in the materialism, selfishness, corruption, and self-destructiveness of everyday life. Like medieval Catholics, Lewis preached a pessimistic, dualist view of the world as the scene of struggle between good and evil.

Pushed too far, this can result in the heretical Manichean doctrine of the existence of two gods, a god of light and a god of darkness. The devil is not a fallen angel; he is an antigod who slugs it out perpetually with Christ, the good god. Evil is not a perversion of God's good creation and a falling away from or "sinful" rebellion against God (the orthodox Catholic doctrine) but an antimatter, a stain of darkness covering the world and blotting out the sun. This gloomy but dynamic Manichean theology rose in Persia in the third century and penetrated the Latin-speaking part of the Roman Empire by 300. St. Augustine, before his conversion to the Christian Church, was a Manichee for ten years. Later Augustine was the chief theoretician and polemicist against Manicheanism, but there was always a residual palimpsest of dualism in Augustinian theology.

With the help of the Roman state, Manicheanism was repressed. But it filtered into the East Roman Greek-speaking Byzantine Empire in the ninth and tenth centuries directly from Persia and then into the Balkans, where the Manichee preachers were called Bogomils. Then, presumably following along Mediterranean trade routes, Manicheanism penetrated into southern France, where it was known as Catharism (the religion of the pure) or Albigensianism (after the fortress town of Albi near Toulouse, one of its strongholds). The Manichee or Catharist heresy was suppressed with enormous cost, difficulty, and violence in the thirteenth century by a royal French crusade at the behest of the papacy and by the interrogations and terrors of the Inquisition.

Yet in the seventeenth century, in obscure valleys of the French Alps, there were still Manichees over whom John Milton lamented when they were persecuted ("Avenge, O Lord, thy slaughtered saints . . ."). Manicheanism had an obvious appeal to a dour Calvinist like Milton. And like so many British intellectual progeny of Milton, Lewis, an Anglican with Catholic proclivities, had a temperamental disposition toward Manichean dualism, even though he knew that theologically dualism was unchristian. *The Screwtape Letters*, with its convincing embodiment of the devil, is tinged with Manicheanism, as is Milton's *Paradise Lost*, about which Lewis wrote a lengthy commentary, now little read.

In his private letters Lewis's medieval Manicheanism is at times unleashed and blatant. He wrote in 1946 in a private letter to a Catholic priest: "It seems to me that far the strongest card in our enemies' hand [a beautifully concise Manichean remark] is the actual course of the world: and that, quite apart from particular events like wars and revolutions. The inherent 'vanity' of the 'creature,' the fact that life preys on life, that all beauty and happiness is produced only to be destroyed [a very Manichean sentiment]—this is what stuck in my gullet." It also stuck in the gullet of the Catharist saints of thirteenth-century southern France. It is very much a strain in British Protestant culture as well.

The other medieval theme that emerges in Lewis's fantasy fiction is the antidote to evil: to maintain faith in the little imaginative things that grow out of the mundane and to be cheerful and laugh about it. British pessimism is to be alleviated by schoolboy-donnish delight in the little things and momentary experiences that make us feel good, whether tea and scones, tobacco, cricket, walks in the country, art, sherry, learning, or the brief encounter of heterosexual love. Essentially this is the message of medieval romance: the transformation of the realm of the mundane where the cloud bank of the reality of evil is ever-present, by projection of an imaginative faith out of the stimulations of particular uncostly things that make us feel good. This argument is what makes Lewis still so popular with the American middle-class reader. Smile your way to salvation. Feel good and be good.

Again and again Lewis propounds this idea (it resembles William James's psychological theory in *The Will to Believe* [c. 1897]) in his *Narnia Chronicles*. Thus, in *The Silver Chair* (1953), the witch tries to stop goodness by denying the possibility of putting a romantic shine on the mundane world: "Look how you can put nothing into your make-believe without copying it from the real world, this work of mine, which is the only world." But comes the response: "We're just babies making up a game, if you're right. But four babies [Inklings?] playing a game can make a play-world which licks your real world hollow." This sounds terribly schoolboy, but then Lewis thought that was his audience. The same kinds of schoolchildren who a few decades before had devoured G. A. Henty's and H. Rider Haggard's fictions of heroism in the Empire now read Lewis by the millions. Now the enemy was not Zulus in Africa or assassins in the Punjab but Manichean types of witches, antigods.

In some places in the *Narnia Chronicles*, Lewis evokes the medieval romance idea somewhat more eloquently: "When you listened to his song you heard these things he was making up: when you looked round you, you saw them [*The Magician's Nephew*, 1955]"; "The new one [Narnia] was a deeper country: Every rock and flower and blade of grass looked as it meant more [*The Last Battle*, 1956]." But the message is consistent, and it is a thoughtful one. Disillusionment, depression, and self-destruction, the reality of evil, come from abandoning faith in the small illusions that attach to the mundane realities of everyday life. This lack of faith in small imaginings leads to a breakdown of large-scale faith, to theological abandonment. When we look with faith, the simple becomes transcendent. The new Narnia looks superficially like the old one, but it has been transformed and ennobled by our vision.

This is the doctrine of an idealistic, well-meaning Oxbridge don of the 1950s that is today compatible with the conservative culture and New Age intimations of Middle America. The great medievals like Augustine, St. Bernard, St. Thomas Aquinas and Dante might have thought that it was not the ultimate in theology but that it was nevertheless good homiletics, a preaching to the common man. It is a theory that one might expect to prevail in the Britain of the 1940s and 1950s, a time and place of imperial and economic decline, when the struggle against evil and the sanctification of simple things in the Lewis mode was a ready displacement effect substitutive of empire building and getting on. This was a general trend, not surprisingly, in British culture at the end of the war. The David Lean–Noel Coward hit film *Brief Encounter* (1945) exhibits much of the same message of the golden glow of little things (romantic trysts in a dismal provincial train station coffee bar!) as Lewis advocates in his fantasy novels of the period. In this ambience even the Labour government of Clement Attlee ("a modest man," said Winston Churchill, "and he has much to be modest about") looked good.

Lewis thought that the goodness and beauty of common acts in everyday life, one of the messages of medieval romance, could comfort his troubled countrymen. The best life was following the call to high adventure. If that was no longer possible in postwar Britain, keeping the faith through intimate imaginings would preserve the community and provide a microcosmic heroism. This conviction, too, was an ingredient of medieval romance.

III
THE LONG JOURNEY

Tolkien's *Lord of the Rings* is much bolder, ambivalent, problematic, closer to the actual texture of medieval romance than Lewis's fiction. Tolkien's work had by the end of the 1980s generated a cottage industry of literary criticism, much of it from small colleges in the American Midwest and South. Two books of special interest, worth reflecting on, were published on Tolkien in Britain in 1983. One is T. A. Shippey, *The Road to Middle-Earth*. Shippey is an academic scholar and a medievalist of stature. His book on Tolkien (of which Tolkien read an early draft) is a suggestive, well-informed, and for the most part readable effort at a standard major work of literary criticism, such as one might attempt of any prominent novelist. The other volume, edited by Robert Giddings (*J.R.R. Tolkien: This Far Land*), is entirely different. It is a collection of idiosyncratic but often

interesting papers by a group of leftist teachers in British polytechnics (community colleges), writing under the influence of Britain's
leading Marxist literary critic of the older generation Raymond Williams (a Cambridge don who died in 1987) as well as the pioneering
student of popular culture the literary sociologist Richard Hoggart.

Shippey is highly sympathetic to Tolkien; Giddings and his colleagues are nearly all hostile. They are very upset by Tolkien's popularity. The sales figures of *The Lord of the Rings* are cited again and
again, as if they were a social crime committed by Reagan or Thatcher.
Roger King proposes that Tolkien's popularity *and* his thought world
fit into the era of "the privatization of cultural consumption" in the
late sixties and seventies. Instances of this trend are held to be
antiurban environmentalism, rock recordings that could only be stu-
dio-created and therefore could only be listened to privately (for example, the Beatles' *Sergeant Pepper's Lonely Hearts Club Band*), and
computer games. This world of suburban, affluent privatized fantasy
is identified as Tolkien's world and accounts for his notorious commercial success. Nigel Walmsley offers a similar explanation for the
explosive popularity of *The Lord of the Rings* and the renewed and
enhanced success of *The Hobbit* in the late sixties. These were literary
artifacts that fitted in with the era of psychedelic drugs and of communes in remote places. "*The Lord of the Rings* provided the alternative
course of cerebral atavism for those in Britain and America who did
not want to stray beyond the end of the block."

Obviously there is a measure of truth in what King and Walmsley
say, but there is also a great flaw. They help explain (but only in
part) the burgeoning popularity of Tolkien's work, what made it a
phenomenal best seller, but they do not explain or account for what
was in Tolkien's mind when he wrote these books, mostly in the
1930s and 1940s. He was not, of course, of the generation of rock
music, flower children, LSD, and computer games or of that cultural
ambience. There is nothing in Tolkien's letters to indicate that he
became attuned to or was even aware of the new youth culture. There
is, indeed, one window of connection between the pre-1914 world in
which Tolkien grew up and the youth culture of the late sixties and
seventies. In Edwardian and neo-Georgian England there was a group
of counterculture aesthetes, as they were called then, whose homo-
eroticism and opiate proclivities do remotely anticipate the culture of
the age of the Beatles. Walter Pater, Oscar Wilde, and Aubrey Beards-
ley are the obvious examples. But there is no empirical biographical

evidence that Tolkien—an orphaned, devoutly Catholic, provincial, immensely studious, introverted scholarship boy—ever was involved with this socially upscale Edwardian counterculture.

Shippey's concern is to ground Tolkien's work in his scholarly medieval interests: in his mastery of northern philology and Norse mythology. Yet Shippey does not re-create the psychological process by which this medievalist learning is drawn upon and transformed in *The Lord of the Rings*. In Shippey's valuable book the dynamic of creativity that inspired and shaped Tolkien's work is only partly exposed.

Tolkien's family-appointed biographer (and editor of his correspondence) Humphrey Carpenter does not dare try. His useful biography (1977) deals almost entirely with the pedestrian externals of Tolkien's life and offers very little about the imaginative process and literary psychology that went into it. It is curious that there are provocative passages in Carpenter's edition of Tolkien's letters (1981) that the biographer does not try to explicate in the narrative work that is based on the correspondence. Apparently this reserved approach suited Christopher Tolkien, an Oxford don and his father's literary executor and, in the case of the correspondence, a collaborator with Carpenter.

In some ways Tolkien is his own best critic. Rarely has an imaginative writer of renown so freely unburdened himself in his private letters to requests for explanations of the intention, meaning, and origin of his work. Tolkien was temperamentally incapable of not responding to a well-meaning and intelligent inquiry, although many of these replies, after being extensively drafted for several pages, never were mailed. They were, however, retained in his papers and published in his selected correspondence in 1981. Among such self-critiques, and one that he did mail, was a ten-page explanation of what *The Lord of the Rings* is all about that he sent in as a book proposal to Milton Waldman, a senior editor at Collins Publishers. Tolkien engaged in several years of frustrating and ultimately futile negotiations with Waldman until the book was finally taken by Rayner Unwin of Allen and Unwin, the publisher of *The Hobbit* in 1937 (as a ten-year-old boy in 1937, Rayner was also the chief reader for publication of that manuscript).

It is an ironic publishing story that Collins would probably have published *The Lord of the Rings* if Waldman had not chanced to go away on an extended vacation at a critical moment in the negotiations and disappeared into an inaccessible Italian village. It is also a nice piece of publishing gossip that Sir George Unwin and Rayner Unwin were so doubtful of the work's commercial possibilities that they tied

Tolkien to a cheapskate contract that paid no advance against royalties, only a share of the profits after the publisher's costs were recovered. In the end, of course, Tolkien made more money this way. *The Lord of the Rings* gave a condition of affluence to Allen and Unwin that it had not enjoyed since the 1920s. It was also a big boost to the American hardback publisher, Houghton Mifflin, and even more so to Ballantine, the American paperback publisher (after a brazenly pirated edition by a mass paperback outfit, Ace, had been forced off the market).

In 1938, in a public lecture a year after *The Hobbit* was published, Tolkien—aware of heavy academic eyebrows being raised at this kind of publication by the holder of one of the senior chairs in the Oxford English faculty—pithily and cryptically explained how he had come to write a children's fantasy: "A real taste for fairystories was wakened by philology on the threshold of manhood, and quickened to full life by the war." The excruciating experience in the trenches during World War I impacted, then, on an innate love of philology, the study of the structure of language, to generate a pseudomedieval fantasy; that is what Tolkien said. The key here is the love of philology, with which Tolkien became fascinated while still in school. As a scholarship student in the English faculty at Oxford he turned out not to be a first-rate literary critic but to have a phenomenal capacity for what was then called philology and what we would now call comparative linguistics, and this became his major undergraduate study. His mastery of this field (with very little instruction) got him his first job when he got out of a military hospital, working on the famous *Oxford Dictionary of the English Language on Historical Principles*. The language structure that Tolkien was devoted to was of a kind that has not been pursued since the 1940s. The historical approach that was inherited from the nineteenth-century German scholarship (the diachronic method so called) has now been replaced by an anthropological and psychological analysis of language (the synchronic method). Tolkien could be regarded as the last great representative of the science of historical philology that in the Anglophone world has passed out of the curriculum, to be replaced by Noam Chomsky's antihistorical transformational grammar.

Within his science of historical philology, Tolkien was mainly interested in the northern world of Old English, Old Norse, and Celtic languages. One of the skills he had was the ability to create a whole grammar and vocabulary of an early but extinct northern language from a very few fossilized fragments. This capability was, however, by no means unheard of among the old historical philologists; there were a half dozen scholars in Germany in the early twentieth century who could do likewise. What made Tolkien unusual as a philologist was that having created this previously extinct language, he could then imaginatively elaborate for it an epic literature such as may have once existed but had in the mists of time disappeared.

To put it another way, Tolkien regretted the disappearance of these pristine northern languages and their (assumed) literature and compensated by re-creating the literature. Even when a language survived, the literary remains were small. *Beowulf* was the only major work of pre-Christian (in Tolkien's view) Anglo-Saxon culture. So Tolkien set out to elaborate from nothing an imaginary epic and made the challenge even greater by doing it not in a surviving early northern language but one that had all but disappeared and he had first to reconstitute.

Tolkien claimed that he imagined first the language, then the story of long journey and quest (epic) in that language. Then he pretended that he was translating from that epic into modern English, retaining proper nouns and a few other key words—a triple-decker work of imagination. Obviously there were a few other historical philologists of his generation who had the scientific capability of doing this, but Tolkien produced not a few specimen pages of the pseudotranslated fantasy work but a six-hundred-thousand-word narrative that was published in three volumes as *The Lord of the Rings*. To do this, he needed not only science and literary imagination but also obsessive living in a personal fantasy world for more than two decades. Tolkien is a prime example of being what the British psychiatrist R. D. Laing called " a successful schizophrenic." This is what lies behind *The Lord of the Rings*. It is the most astonishing monument to the old historical philology ever developed and the most extended and difficult piece of pseudomedievalism ever imagined.

Tolkien explained his starting point to the poet W. H. Auden in 1955: "It has always been with me: the sensibility to linguistic pattern which affects me emotionally like colour or music . . . the deep response to legends (for want of a better word) that I would call the North-Western temper and temperature." In 1947 he defended his fantasying this way: "Fantasy remains a human right in our measure and in our derivative mode, because we are made; and not only made, but made in the image and likeness of our maker." So his medieval-like fantasy had divine sanction. On another occasion he explained the end product of his linguistic and imaginative endeavors by saying that his "typical response upon reading a medieval work was to desire not so much to make a philological or critical study of it as to write a modern work in the same tradition." *The Lord of the Rings* is thus a modern reconstruction of a fragment of medieval culture.

The narrative was to fit into the traditions of English culture as Tolkien perceived it: "I had in mind to make a body of more or less connected legend which I could dedicate simply: To England; to my country. It should . . . be redolent of our 'air' (the clime and soil of the North West, meaning Britain and the hither parts of Europe, not Italy or Aegean, still less the East), and while possessing (if I could achieve it) the fair elusive beauty that some call Celtic (though it is rarely found in [existing] Celtic things). It should be 'high,' purged of the gross, and fit for the more adult mind of a land steeped in beauty." Tolkien could become very annoyed when someone compared his work with Richard Wagner's—there is a ring involved in both stories, but that is all, he said—but it is clear from this statement that Tolkien shared with Wagner a faith in the elevated ethos of the Nordic peoples. That accounts in part for the popularity of *The Lord of the Rings*. It is genteel Nordic neoracism in the form of neomedievalism.

This Nordic ethos of reserved courage and unilateral dedication is the saving grace of Tolkien's quasi-hero Frodo in his long journey through and against the force of darkness. The landscape through which Frodo and his friends move in *The Lord of the Rings* is essentially a medieval environment. There are Germanic barbarian types of hordes. There are decayed cities. There are comfortable pockets of momentarily quiet and enclosed country. And there is war, threat of war, destruction of war, and memories of war:

> Horsemen were galloping on the grass. . . . From the heavens . . . ships put out to sea; and out of the East Men were moving endlessly: Swordsmen, spearmen, bowmen upon horses, chariots of chieftains, and laden wains. All the power of the Dark Lord was in motion.
>
> Fire glowed amid the smoke. Mount Doom was burning, and a great reek rising. . . . All hope left him. . . .
>
> All dead, all rotten. Elves and Men and Orcs. The Dead Marshes. There was a great battle long ago, yes, so they told him . . . when I was young. . . . It was a great battle. Tall Men with long swords, and terrible elves, and Orcses shrieking. They fought on the plain for days and months. . . . But the Marshes have grown since then, swallowed up the graves; always creeping, creeping.

This was the way it was in France around 1450, after the Hundred Years' War, or in France around 480, after the Germanic invasions. "High mounds of crushed and powdered rock, great cones of earth fire-blasted and poison-stained, stood like an obscene graveyard in endless rows, slowly revealed in the reluctant light."

Here is the medieval world at its most bellicose, destructive, and terrible moments: the Age of the Barbarian Invasions in the fifth and sixth centuries; the Hundred Years' War in the fourteenth and fifteenth centuries. This is imaginatively evoked, graphically described, but it is conventionally medieval, a given, a stock scene well constructed. What is surprising and original in *The Lord of the Rings* is not the power of darkness but the force for good led by Frodo. This departs from the medieval heroic image. Frodo is not physically powerful, and his judgment is sometimes erratic. He wants not to bring about the golden era but to get rid of the Ring, to place it beyond the powers of evil; not to transform the world but to bring peace and quiet to the Shire, to remove threats and promote stability and civility: These are the purposes of his long journey. It is not a romantic quest of nobility. It is the wish of the little people in the world. It is a common man's rather than an aristocratic ethos. The outcome of the incredible journey and perpetual struggle is not glory but weariness: "For the fleeting moment, could one of the sleepers have seen him, they would have thought that they beheld an old weary hobbit, shrunken by the years that had carried him far beyond his time, beyond friends and kin, and the fields and streams of youth, an old starved and pitiable thing."

Frodo, who, more than anyone else, is responsible for having saved the beloved land from darkness and war, is not hailed and rewarded at the end as the Once and Future King. He is treated more like the wounded veterans of the world wars (Tolkien included) who were ignominiously shunted aside by their ungrateful homelands. Modor is destroyed, the Shire is saved, but Frodo's wounds do not heal in Middle-Earth. He "dropped quietly out of all the doings of the Shire, and Sam was pained to notice how little honor he had in his own country." Resigned to "defeat," Frodo leaves the Shire. "It [the dream] is gone for ever, and now all is dark and empty."

There are two ways to interpret this pessimistic conclusion to the long journey and great struggle. Tolkien is saying that in the modern world there are no rewards for heroes. They do not become kings; they become ailing veterans on abysmal pensions and fade away in loneliness and poverty. If his philological capability had not rescued him by gaining for him first a job at the *Oxford Dictionary* in 1918 and then his first teaching job at the University of Leeds, that would have been Tolkien's as well as Frodo's fate. Or Tolkien may be saying that this is the way it really was in the Middle Ages: not the Arthurian heroism of golden knights but the wearying, almost endless struggle of the little people against the reality of perpetual war and violent darkness to find a hiatus of peace and security for their families and communities. *The Lord of the Rings* is thereby a medieval story, but a counterromance, telling it "like it really was," not the way the court poets told it to flatter their lords. These two interpretations are not mutually exclusive; Tolkien may be commenting on both the twentieth century and the medieval world.

In his remarkable ten-page book proposal to Milton Waldman of Collins Publishers in 1951, Tolkien addressed the meaning of *The Lord of the Rings*. Modern criticism has long denied to an author interpretive authority over his own work. Indeed, there has been a recent tendency to give greater legitimacy to "reader response" and "interpretive communities" of English literature professors than to authors. It is still, however, interesting how Tolkien, an eminent practitioner of criticism and literary history, explains his own work, even if it may be acknowledged that the meaning is thereby precariously shifted from the tale to the teller. The Ring, he tells Waldman, represents "the will to mere power, seeking to make itself objective by physical force and mechanism and so also inevitably by lies." Evil in the world is domination, and it is mechanistic domination; the enemy is the world of machines that strangle life and goodness, even when mechanization seeks to benefit humankind (obviously the flower children of the late sixties who embraced Tolkien were responding to this attitude): "The Enemy in successive forms is always 'naturally' concerned with sheer Domination, and so [is] the Lord of magic and machines; but [that is] the problem: That this frightful evil can and does arise from an apparently good root, the desire to benefit the world and others."

Tolkien violently objected when one of his admirers wrote him to comment that *The Lord of the Rings* reads like an allegory against communism. It is just a story, he said in response, not a message of contemporary significance. Tolkien may not have been intentionally writing a cold war allegory against the Soviets—that would be a very hazardous thing for an Oxford don to do in the late forties—but his book can be read, and was by himself, as an argument against the mechanistic state and society that commit evil even when their intentions are good. What more effective condemnation of socialist government or the regulatory and welfare state of late capitalism can be made?

Conjoined to this is the antiheroic theme, or rather the theme that heroism lies with ordinary people. Tolkien tells Waldman that his book teaches that salvation against the enemy occurs this way: "Without the high and noble, the simple and vulgar is utterly mean; and without the simple and ordinary, the noble and heroic is meaningless." Here is where *The Lord of the Rings* differs from the aristocratic Arthurian tradition. Tolkien agrees with Lewis in admiring the sensibility of the little people. In a letter of 1956 Tolkien affirmed that "Middle-Earth is just . . . the inhabited world of men." So in spite of Tolkien's professed distaste for allegory, *The Lord of the Rings* is a grand allegory, about both the Middle Ages and the twentieth century.

A year after its publication, Tolkien had another try at explicating its meaning. This time he was metaphysical in his interpretation: "I do not think even Power and Domination is [sic] the real center of my story. . . . The real theme for me is about something much more permanent and difficult: Death and Immortality: The mystery of the Love of the world in the hearts of a race 'doomed' to leave and seemingly lose it; the anguish in the hearts of a race 'doomed' not to leave it, until its whole evil-aroused story is complete." The theme in this interpretive version is very medieval. It would be instantly recognizable by Augustine, Bernard, and Dante: the ambivalence of human life, love and anguish, departure and return. It was a mystery central to medieval anxiety and passion, the never-ending human story before the Second Coming, as medieval intellectuals conceived it. *The Lord of the Rings* in this interpretation projects the tragedy of humanity without divine grace, grandeur without fulfillment, quest without finality. In December 1953, just as he was finishing the book, Tolkien described it to a Jesuit priest in this way: "*The Lord of the Rings* is of course a fundamentally religious and Catholic work; unconsciously so at first, but consciously in the revision."

The different ways in which Tolkien, in his day the holder of the senior chair in the Oxford English faculty, interpreted his own work are argument for those who would now fashionably divest an author of his own intellectual property, taking away his capacity to legislate on the meaning of his own work. *The Lord of the Rings* exists, apart from what Tolkien said at one time or another it was supposed to mean. It was largely a product of the realm of fantasy in the unconscious; that was its ultimate source. Therefore, what Tolkien later consciously thought about it is interesting, but not authoritative as to the work's meaning. I have to confess that I am not an enthusiast of *The Lord of the Rings*. I would not have been able to predict its phenomenal success during those ten years or more after the war when Tolkien was carrying his one copy back and forth on the train from Oxford to London in search of a publisher, reasonably afraid to put this single copy in the mails. *Rings* is one of the classic cases that demonstrate that great books are made great by the reading public, which finds something there that powerfully connects to its feelings. This is an inexplicable phenomenon that no one critic or publisher can anticipate.

The Lord of the Rings does in indelible fashion capture three salient aspects of medieval civilization. First, it communicates the experience of endemic war and the fear of armed bands that was a frequent condition of the period from 400 to the middle of the eleventh century and again from about 1290 to the late fifteenth century. The dark force of incipient terrorism in the form of armed invasion was a constant threat and fell particularly on village society, the common people. This is communicated in *Rings* in a dramatic fashion that no conventional historical exposition can come close to matching.

Secondly, *Rings* makes us feel the circumstances and conditions of a long journey undertaken not by a great nobleman with a powerful retinue but by an ordinary soldier with two or three companions. This kind of distant journeying by obscure people over long distances, for one reason or another, we know from stray references, was a much more common occurrence at all times in the Middle Ages, but especially after 1100, than we might a priori predict from the kind of primitive transportation system the medievals had access to. People of modest social status in surprising numbers traveled long distances, mostly on foot. This is a strange fact of medieval life, and *Rings* is centered on this event. Tolkien convinces us that the way this happened was that some local village leader got it into his head that he had to do something to help or save his people, something had to be carried a very long distance, some contact vaguely imagined had to be made, and off the person and two or three companions went on their incredibly long, footsore journey. These journeys were rarely documented for us in the Middle Ages and almost never in detail. Tolkien, by imagining such a journey, has graphically re-created an important but poorly understood facet of medieval social life.

Thirdly, Tolkien stresses for us what C. S. Lewis also believed:

that medieval heroism was not a special manifestation of aristocratic culture but something that existed among people of relatively humble social status. There is something very English about this conviction that the little people of the medieval world were heroic, too. However, not only is it a product of the Edwardian sentimental retromedieval imagination, but it has some documentation in the known realities of medieval English history. From 1194 onward, as Maitland was the first to demonstrate, there is available to us an increasingly detailed record of litigation in the county courts, and most of the "pleaders," as they were called, were strictly local people, small landowners, not the magnates, not the grand nobility. By the fourteenth century these records of litigation in the county courts allow us to look into the lives and feelings of the little people of the countryside—the lesser gentry and the yeoman class. They turn out to be highly articulate, self-conscious, ambitious, intelligent, the instigators of capitalist rationality. No other series of records from medieval Europe, before Florence of the fifteenth century, gives us such detailed insight into the minds of ordinary country or urban society. There are the Frodo types, socially. Thus Tolkien's reconstruction of the mentality of these kinds of people coincides with the evidence from the records of the common law. In this regard Tolkien is Maitland's successor as an archaeologist of medieval society. He also agrees with Bloch's admiration for the medieval peasantry.

Tolkien, like Lewis, made a concrete scholarly contribution to the study of the Middle Ages. Just as Lewis was a pioneer in legitimating the study of courtly love literature as central to medieval culture and had important things to say about the relationship between Renaissance literature and the Middle Ages, so Tolkien brought to the attention of the academic public some neglected masterpieces of medieval literature. Yet the importance of their work as medievalists does not lie primarily in these contributions. It lies in a much broader area, one harder to define. Tolkien and Lewis immersed the twentieth-century reader in medieval worlds and made that person a participant in the highly activated realm of the imagination that at the same time communicates how medieval people thought of themselves and gives us the opportunity to perceive ourselves as possible actors in a medieval place. This is a highly unusual achievement.

Another way of addressing the Tolkien and Lewis contribution is to say that, far beyond the level of being merely popularizers, they convinced us of a medieval world comprised not only of heroes but of little people who were sentient beings with anxieties, ambitions, and small triumphs we can fully empathize with. Lewis and Tolkien were essentially conservatives, romantics, fantasizers, rejecters of much of twentieth-century culture. They were very different by temperament and ideology from Maitland and Bloch. But they belong in company with those two as inventors of a medieval society we can believe in, project ourselves into, and enjoy.

IV
A PROUSTIAN DREAMWORLD

In 1946, while Jack Lewis, the fellow and tutor of Magdalen College, was turning out his best-selling Manichaean novels, and Ronald Tolkien, the Merton professor of English, was holed up in his garage writing endlessly about Frodo's journey, the regius professor of modern history Frederick Maurice Powicke (1879–1963)—peculiarly called Frederick for the first three decades of his life and then Maurice—was experiencing a crisis. His tenure as regius professor was ending, and the Labour government was engaged in an extensive and difficult search for a medievalist who was also a socialist to succeed him. "Modern history" at Oxbridge at that time still meant after the fall of Rome A.D. 476. Since the regius (royal) chair was established in the reign of George III, appointment to it had lain in the hands of the prime minister. Prime Minister Clement Attlee now had to be satisfied with Vivian H. Galbraith, the leading historical archivist in the Public Record Office. Galbraith looked and talked like a Yorkshire farmer and espoused the populist radicalism of a 1920s Communist. Powicke was not enthusiastic about his designated successor.

Powicke was sixty-seven in 1946 and being forced into retirement from his chair, which he did not wish to relinquish. As he sat in Oriel College in the dingy rooms allocated to the regius professor of history, finishing his enormous manuscript on the reign of Henry III, Powicke felt anxiety about what he would do when soon ejected from his chair and his Oriel rooms. He had been regius professor since 1929, when Stanley Baldwin, the pious, well-read Conservative prime minister had come upon a recently published lecture of Powicke's on "The Christian Life in the Middle Ages" and had been very favorably impressed by its learning, clarity, and subtle balance of admiration for medieval Catholicism with firm devotion to the Church of England. Baldwin rehabilitated Powicke, a native of the Lancashire North who had not done well as a student at Oxford. After this disappointment as a student Powicke had returned to the University of Manchester, whence he had come briefly on scholarship to Oxford. Baldwin had plucked Powicke from his professorship at Manchester, an institution sliding rapidly into mediocrity from its formerly vanguard position in British academic life, and made him regius professor at Oxford.

Powicke's second and long Oxford career as a professor was in some ways not much more successful than his first brief stay as a student. He had wanted to create a German type of graduate school and research library in medieval history at Oxford. The dons laughed at him, and he got nowhere, although he did recruit a handful of very good graduate students. Baldwin's bold choice for regius professor just didn't work out well because Powicke was not the Oxford type (he would have excelled and been much happier at Munich or Göttingen, or Harvard or Princeton). He also looked like one of Tolkien's hobbits or dwarfs. He was barely five feet tall, and as he got older, the disproportion between his large head and his shrinking body became even more remarkable. Powicke was a fierce, angry, determined man of the North, puritanical, mystical, with no love or even patience for the languid, decadent, aristocratic traditions of Oxford. If you searched all over Britain, you would not have found a distinguished medieval scholar who was temperamentally more at odds with the Oxford of *Brideshead Revisited*.

So Powicke's great project of creating a real institute of medieval history at Oxford having brought only frustration and derision upon himself (even his proposal for a modest change in the undergraduate history requirements was repeatedly voted down by the faculty), he retreated into his shabby Oriel rooms, into his religious introspection, and into the thirteenth century. Out of his pain, frustration, and displacement came the most ambitious work on medieval history written by an Englishman since Pollock and Maitland: *King Henry III and the Lord Edward*, duly published in 1947 by the elegant Clarendon division of the Oxford University Press in large type and on unusually fine paper. With its obsessively detailed index, it runs to 858 pages.

The Oxford University Press (OUP), expecting something very different, was astonished when in 1946 this huge manuscript landed on its doorstep. The press had contracted with Powicke for a survey volume on the thirteenth century (1216–1307), an introduction to the reigns of Henry III and Edward I, of about six hundred pages in its ongoing *Oxford History of England* series, a textbook series for British undergraduates and secondary school seniors. But Powicke had gotten only through the reign of Henry III, to 1272, in eight hundred pages, and what he had written was not a textbook. It was a Proustian dream vision of the politics and culture of the high aristocracy in the thirteenth century, a work very difficult and far too long for undergraduates to read and too imaginative and avant-garde for most of the pedestrian medieval historians of postwar Britain to endure. But no one was going to tell the regius professor with the fierce gaze and bristling little mustache and loud voice and imperious, angry manner that he had landed an unexploded bomb on the doorstep of the long-suffering OUP. It went ahead and published it with dignity and politely asked Powicke to try again to produce that badly needed textbook. He tried, and in 1953 it duly appeared. It was terrible. It went on for dozens of pages about obscure wars in the back valleys of Wales and said almost nothing about the beginnings of Parliament, which for textbook purposes should have been its main focus—the subject that the undergrads were mostly supposed to crib out of it for their weekly tutorials.

I talked with Powicke once for about ninety minutes, in November 1954. My supervisor Richard Southern, who was Powicke's student and, along with Beryl Smalley, his prime protégé, told me one day—in one of Southern's mischievous moods, which were not infrequent—to pay a courtesy call on the old gentleman and talk to him about my proposed research on church-state relations in early-twelfth-century England. I found Powicke across the street from Oriel College, in a set of flats owned by the college, where he had been moved after the new regius professor, V. H. Galbraith, the wild man socialist Clement Attlee had found hiding in the Public Record Office as an archivist, had arrived in Oxford. Powicke was in a small, very dark apartment, quite dingy and unpleasant. He was impeccably dressed: gray suit, white shirt, gray tie, looking like a Manchester traveling salesman of yard goods more than a casually dressed Oxford don. I began to describe to him my ill-fated research project. His gray eyes fixed on me intensely. It was clear he wasn't interested in what I had been saying, and suddenly he interrupted me. "Look what they have done to me," he shouted loudly across the room although I was sitting about three feet in front of him. I was bewildered. I said nothing. Then he launched into a tirade about how shabbily Oxford and particularly Oriel had treated him. Forced him to resign in the prime of his career. Replaced him by a Communist dunderhead who had never published a major book. Thrown him out with a miserable pension and subjected him to poverty. "After all I did for this place. It isn't a real university, you know. Not like Munich, or Paris, or even Harvard, or Manchester in the old days. They don't respect scholarship here. Don't know what it is. These dons . . ." He became speechless with rage.

I never mentioned the interview to Southern, nor did he ask me about it. He had, of course, known what would happen.

I saw Powicke once more, this time on a public occasion. He presided at a lecture given at Oxford by Cambridge's Helen Maud Cam. Sitting at the front of the room, Powicke and Cam made a dramatic contrast. She bore a distinct resemblance to Margaret Rutherford, now mostly remembered for her film performances as Agatha Christie's sleuth Miss Marple. But in 1947 Rutherford appeared in a delightful comedy called *Passport to Pimlico*, in which she played a jovial medievalist called in to authenticate recently discovered charters that made the working-class suburb of London an independent state. Rutherford's medievalist resembled Helen Cam in high gear too much to be just a coincidence.

Powicke's introduction of Cam was by no means boilerplate. He subtly got over the message that he didn't agree with what she was going to say but that he respected her and she was worth listening to. I thought it was both a clever and an honest performance as one seldom sees in the introduction of an academic speaker. There was a reception afterward. Powicke worked the room, talking in animated fashion with both dons and students. He was in good spirits and seemed now half a foot taller than when I had talked to him in the gloom of his modest flat. This was his world, a residual memory of a much happier time, when for more than a dozen years he had dominated medieval history at Oxford and substantially in the country at large, when he had been little loved but respected and greatly feared in the academic world.

There was one especially illuminating moment at the reception. He came up to Dorothy Whitelock, the accomplished Anglo-Saxon scholar and formidable social historian of early England. She was an elf, even shorter than Powicke. "And how are you, little lady?" Powicke said. There was something genuinely caring and wistful in his voice. At that point I wished I had known him in his glory days. Like me, this bourgeois, businesslike Puritan, was a visitor from another planet to Oxford. We would have had something in common. I also remembered that I had heard that in the mid-thirties, he had lost his only son in an automobile accident. I wondered if he had been different before that tragedy.

Later Powicke was given a knighthood—an honor that comes late in life in Britain to very distinguished humanists, as it does to actors, jockeys, and corporate speculators—and he called himself Sir Maurice. It didn't increase his bad pension or get him a better apartment, but perhaps his dignity assuaged the old man's wounds a bit. In 1938 Powicke went to the Newcastle-upon-Tyne campus of the University of Durham to deliver a set of the Riddell Lectures. These were annual public lectures that were supposed to have a religious and moral tone. When Powicke's contributions were published a year later, their cast of northern Puritanism, of Christian pessimism was not well received at Oxbridge, to such an extent that in Powicke's obituary notice in 1964 in the *Proceedings of the British Academy*, his foremost protégé, Dick Southern, quietly dismissed them as an embarrassment. The lectures are, it is true, not well written, but they do sum up Powicke's view of life and history and foreshadow his view of thirteenth-century culture that controls *King Henry III and the Lord Edward*, published a decade later.

Powicke acknowledged a sense of fatalism and of the insignificance of the individual in the totality of things: "History . . . gives us that sense of remoteness which we associate with fatalism. . . . I have seen the whole of human experience . . . as a great glacier moving imperceptibly, remorselessly. . . ." The meaning of it all, the macrocosmic dimensions on human history are beyond the historian's comprehension, indeed beyond the "judgment and understanding of the human mind." What we can understand and what the historian can narrate and explicate are the small-scale things, the finite, the microcosmic level. In a way, Powicke was here reflecting the modernist impulse of his generation to focus on the particular and the finite. The historian could and should do in discussing a segment of the past what Marcel Proust, James Joyce, and Virginia Woolf did in their novels: focus closely on the particular, on immediately perceived actions, and on shades of sensibility that lie behind these actions. Truth for the historian as for the novelist lies not in grand sweeps of meaning, but in the close detail, in a mosaic of individual action and personal sensibility. So in *King Henry III and the Lord Edward* we have a remembrance of the lost times of the thirteenth-century nobility, everything it did in politics and social relations, the infinite number of aristocratic actions, confusions, decisions, perceptions and misperceptions from 1216 to 1272.

What the nobility did outside court, council, Parliament, and battlefield was as important as these more visible political actions. To put it crudely, social history was as important as political history. As Powicke said in the Riddell Lectures, whenever there are grand ideas of reform, overriding programs of political change, "there is always something ludicrous, or pathetic, or far-fetched in beliefs of this kind. The means are out of all relation to the end. And so, throughout human history, man, in no spirit of laziness or weariness, has sought the relaxation in which he can be free to live his brief life and to reflect upon the mysteries of it, its beauty and its sorrow." Political history teaches the value of social history, the history of private life. Political life, grand ideas, and wide-ranging plans are attempted, but nothing much comes of these, or at least the shortfall between idea and action is overwhelming and disheartening. "This world is not created once and for all for us individually," Proust said in one of his last writings. "There are added to it in the course of our lives things of which we never had any suspicion." That comes very close to Powicke's pessimistic perception as well.

We are left with the importance of private life as against public life, the personal gestures and the interpersonal relations and intimate thoughts and aesthetic liminalities as the most durable and accomplished facets of human existence. This was Proustian modernism as reflected in the aristocratic temperament, which Powicke, the harsh northern bourgeois Puritan, did not himself exemplify but which he most admired. Proust goes beneath the political clamors of Paris of the Third Republic to explore the refined sensibility and private gestures of the very rich and wellborn. That is what Powicke is doing in his account of thirteenth-century aristocratic politics and culture in England.

This Proustian modernism was compatible with the British conservative ambience of the 1930s. In a world drenched with fanatical ideologies of left and right, British historians loved to fall back on, in their view, the social relations within the governing class that actually determined power and distributed offices, away from the crude polemical claims of party and leader. In the 1930s Lewis Namier wrote this way about eighteenth-century English politics, John Neale about the Elizabethan House of Commons, Ronald Syme about the Age of Cicero and Caesar in the late Roman Republic. This was the "British school of social politics," in which family connections and private clientage, rather than ideology or ostensible party groupings, were deemed the key to all political events. It was a neo-Burkean conservatism. In the Age of Hitler and Stalin this was a saving rationality. And Powicke tried to do for the thirteenth century what Namier,

Neale, and Syme, great historical eminences, did for their eras of concern.

The essential social fact of English politics in the first three quarters of the thirteenth century, as viewed by Powicke, was noble patrimonial lineage and the interaction of a very small number of great aristocratic families, and their myriad dependents, with the grandest noble family of all, the Plantagenet royal house. Everything else is relative and marginal to this core of social fact. The force for change was not political or legal ideas but the way in which the mentality of the great nobility was slowly but steadily changing in the thirteenth century. That, not the legacy of Magna Carta or the rise of Parliament, those grand but empty Victorian entities, is the focus of Powicke's Proustian dreamworld. What was happening was that the Christian discipline and personal piety were slowly spreading out from monastic houses and religious orders and reshaping the mind-set and behavior pattern of the great aristocracy:

> [There was] a diffusion of manners from the cloister to the court, of manners at table, in cleanliness and dress, in mutual behavior between superior and inferior and between equals. [This] helps to explain the sudden changes of temper [on the part of the great nobility], the apparent irresolution, the quick reconciliations which so often perplex us in the conduct of great men [in thirteenth-century] England, for these might be due not to caprice but to the restraint imposed by the recollection of a higher law, the law of Christ. This was the period in which the laity . . . emerged as a creative element in Christian society, not as barbaric intruder, but in virtue of the conscious appropriation, with the changes required by secular life, of a Christian discipline.

The two most imposing figures in thirteenth-century English politics were Simon de Montfort, earl of Leicester, the scion of a great French house who became the leader of the English barons' rebellion against the inept and luckless Henry III and after dramatic, short-lived success was defeated and killed, and his nemesis, the lord Edward, the heir to the throne and later King Edward I. Powicke makes clear which of these two empyreal leaders, Simon or Edward, he prefers and thinks thirteenth-century Englishmen preferred. Simon was too much the political idealist. He saw himself as the savior of the country at a time when "most Englishmen no longer wished to be saved. The spectacle of austere and arrogant constancy, the virtue which he most prized, began to divide men." (This could be a description of David Lloyd George or Winston Churchill, and assuredly Powicke was aware of this parallel.) So Earl Simon was brought down and died in battle against Prince Edward, who as king demonstrated that he "was a great man not in virtue of a subtlety or exaltation in his nature but because, an ordinary Christian gentleman, he could fill a great position."

Edward I represents for Powicke the pinnacle of medieval civilization, which was not political idealism or constitutional commitments but high birth, good education, steady work, Christian piety, and, above all, "fine habits" and "gracious manner." This was the meaning of nobility in the Middle Ages, and it still represented the best specimen modern Britain had to offer—the qualities of a Christian gentleman. The basis of successful politics lies in this kind of superior personal qualities and a well-mannered private life, whether in the reign of Henry III or the Age of Stanley Baldwin. This is Powicke's argument.

It is an argument that can be questioned. The counterclaim is that all the successful leaders of the thirteenth century were in fact not the even-tempered Christian gentlemen but the Simon de Montfort types, the extremists with an "austere and arrogant constancy." These were the people who changed things in the high Middle Ages. And they include Edward I, who was, in fact, very far from being ordinary. Whatever gracious manner he exhibited was merely a cover, a momentary role playing to hide his insatiable lust for power and wealth. The people of Wales and Scotland, which he invaded, crushed, and abused, would not have expatiated on his refined aristocratic habits. They thought of him as a freakish monster and a dark force.

Yet there was a core in what Powicke was arguing that was of great importance and incontestable. The life-style and mind-set of the West European aristocracy did experience fundamental change, and a kind of Christian piety was absorbed into their value system and affected their ambitions and actions. Private life was becoming not only more comfortable but more worthy of the time and attention of the great nobility. There are codas one can append to this conclusion that Powicke expostulated. It may be claimed that the turning point in the social history of the nobility came already in the later years of the twelfth century. And more significantly, one can claim that this process was not entirely as benign and progressive of civilization as Powicke thought. If Christian piety changed the nobility, the nobility in absorbing this piety also gained shaping control over Christian values, and the result was ambivalent. Christianity became much more of an establishment culture, and the church's capacity for criticism of aristocratic behavior was severely mitigated. The outcome was that those in the church who were not happy with the aristocracy's absorption and manipulation of piety and religious values in their own interests were driven into more radical opposition. Along with the rise of Powicke's Christian gentlemen, the late Middle Ages featured angry counterculture rebellion against a church socially ennobled and morally corrupted at the same time.

But none of this detracts from the freshness of Powicke's insight into the social politics of the thirteenth century. Charles Swann and the Parisian social elite that Proust wrote about may be viewed in a manner much more critical than the tone of *Remembrance of Things Past*. That does not reduce the persuasiveness of the dreamworld of sensibility that Proust created. So with Powicke and his thirteenth-century nobility.

In stressing the relative superficiality of politics and the importance of private life as the determining factor of the shift in aristocratic mentality, Powicke in the 1940s was moving toward the methodological program of Marc Bloch and the French Annalists. But he got there from precisely the other side of the political spectrum. They were adopting Parisian Marxism and leftist French sociology. He was ruminating on the implications of Christian pessimism and 1930s neo-Burkean conservatism. And he did not abandon the writing of political history. He still, unlike Bloch and his disciples, spent most of his time writing about politics, perhaps only because he had done this for thirty years and did not have an intellectual base in economics and social science to do otherwise. But what Powicke communicates in *King Henry III and the Lord Edward* is a not dissimilar message of the realities of feudal mentalities as against the traditional focus on the significance of explicit political ideas and constitutional crises. Certainly a very important thing that happened in England and France of the high Middle Ages was the absorption of Christian culture into social relations. It was left to Powicke's protégé Richard Southern, a more brilliant, subtle mind and a much better writer, to work out the implications of this message.

Writing away in his shabby regius professor suite at Oriel College in 1946, Powicke was just around the corner from Tolkien in Merton College and a few hundred yards from Jack Lewis at Magdalen. Surviving correspondence and biographies do not illuminate what Powicke thought of or said to the great fantasists or how they regarded him. There is no way to draw inferences of influence. He shared with them by the late thirties a point of view they had held much longer: that the realities of the Middle Ages have to be sought in the imaginative realm, in the feelings about God and beauty. This was a conviction that was professionally more difficult or even hazardous for a historian than for a student of literature. Most history dons at Oxbridge or elsewhere in Britain received this message from Powicke in stony silence—another cause for a grudge against this difficult, arrogant old dwarf. Now he was devaluing political history and deconstructing the conventional constitutional progressions on which the undergraduate curriculum in medieval history still was focused. He was threatening to put the medieval history teachers out of business. In 1948 Helen Maud Cam published a thunderous proclamation arguing that Stubbs's *Constitutional History* of the 1860s should still be the core undergraduate textbook! This reactionary attitude comforted the history dons. They could go on teaching the same old curriculum centered on alleged constitutional crises. What Powicke was implying by his Proustian tome on the age of Henry III was an intellectual and educational revolution, which, except for a maverick like David Knowles, the monastic historian, and his own disciples, Richard Southern and Beryl Smalley, was still unwelcome among medieval historians in British and American universities. Lewis and Tolkien did not have to face such an anti-imaginative resistance. Powicke was boldly endorsing, within the established ranks of historians, Lewis's and Tolkien's devotion to the imaginative world of the Middle Ages as being a very important key even to politics itself. Sir Maurice was asking the history dons to leave off their favorite themes of Magna Carta and the origins of Parliament and take a flyer into the Proustian dreamworld of aristocratic sensibility.

Yet there is a gulf between Lewis and Tolkien on the one side and Powicke on the other. There is in Lewis's and Tolkien's writings a strong sense of activism. They wanted to bring out of the Middle Ages in one way or another the ingredients for the reformation of the modern world, and when one thinks about the fifty million volumes that altogether are in print of their works and about the groupie cults they have generated, one realizes they had a measure of success in advancing this cultural revolution that is not negligible and that may grow as time goes on. Powicke, however, was at heart a pessimist and social conformist, who had no faith in cultural upheavals. His own bitter experience as a moderate educational reformer at Oxford only confirmed this pessimism and passivity.

The anti-intellectual conservatism of the British social politics history school of the 1930s, of Namier, Neale, and Syme, also served to reinforce Powicke's distaste for efforts at great upheaval. There is something apocalyptic, utopian about Lewis and Tolkien, indistinct and vague as they are on the precise program of liberation to be pursued. But Powicke did not believe that the Middle Ages could be revived. They could be understood and appreciated but not resuscitated where they lay. The best that could be hoped for was the continuing cultivation of the traditions of Christian gentility that he traced back to the nobility of the thirteenth century: "If . . . a true gentleman, just, cultivated, is also a Puritan, austere with himself and filled with a sense of God, he is the most civilized and free of all living things."

So Powicke wrote in 1938, while Neville Chamberlain, the quintessential Christian gentleman from Birmingham, flew to meet Hitler at Munich and to betray the Czechs, and Winston Churchill, the self-appointed aristocratic savior of Britain with his arrogant constancy, was still excluded from the government. Lewis and Tolkien would endorse Powicke's ideal of a Christian gentleman, but they were not content with it. They wanted something much more. There are moments in reading C. S. Lewis when one suspects that he wanted to found a new Manichean sect, to incorporate into its legions wild people like Clare Boothe Luce and Whittaker Chambers, and try to take over the world. Tolkien did not recognize the flower children of the sixties as his disciples, nor would he perhaps have appreciated as his progeny the Greens of the eighties, but there is with good reason an affinity between such provocative people and *The Lord of the Rings* they loved.

But Powicke, the ultimate traveling salesman from Manchester, just wanted to join a good London club where gentility and soft piety are served up with the rare roast beef and Yorkshire pudding.

Yet this strange, awkward, bitter little man whose books are no longer read had perceived something of immense importance in the Middle Ages. He had fastened on the emergence in the thirteenth century of an aristocratic culture that was composed of the social behavior and family interests of the higher nobility integrated with a new personal piety that was affecting all classes and of an aggressive political ambition expressed through persuasive ideas of consensual or constitutional government. Powicke thereby discovered the origins of the mentality of the West European nobility that were to endure as a central facet of European life until the Age of the French Revolution and in some countries, such as Britain and northern Germany, well into the twentieth century and that were to be the context within which all politics was set.

What Powicke realized was that along with the cultural formalism of classicism and patristic theology that lay at the center of the medieval ethos, there developed a more complex and subtle structure, the aristocratic mind-set and behavior pattern that was coexistent with the Europe that emerged out of the Middle Ages. Glossed up a bit around 1500 by refined language and a more rigid code of personal conduct that stemmed from the Renaissance humanists' improved system of secondary education, aristocratic formalism was the most persistent and vibrant intellectual and social tradition down into the nineteenth century and beyond. Not all the vast learning and intellectual breakthroughs of the twentieth century have found an easy substitute for the aristocratic tradition that crystallized in the Age of Simon de Montfort. Indeed, the best that the upper middle class of Western Europe could do in its renewed age of prosperity and confidence after 1965 was to imitate it.

CHAPTER SEVEN

AMERICAN PIE

CHARLES HOMER HASKINS AND
JOSEPH REESE STRAYER

I

THE WILSONIANS

While European views of the Middle Ages inevitably had a very strong impact in the United States, especially after the German émigrés began arriving in the mid-thirties, a distinctive American school of medieval history developed after Charles Homer Haskins (1870–1937) was appointed to a senior chair at Harvard in 1912. When the German émigré scholars in the 1930s found their bearings on the alien cultural shores of the United States, they found that most of the senior professorships of medieval history were held by Haskins's students or by contemporaries of his who were in full sympathy with his ideas and methods. The leading professional association for medievalists of any kind, the Medieval Academy of America, had been founded principally by Haskins in the early 1920s. Its offices were still in Cambridge, Massachusetts, as they are today. Furthermore, the rising star in medieval history in the 1940s was Joseph Reese Strayer (1904–1987), the chairman and senior professor of European history at Princeton, who not only was Haskins's student but consciously maintained the approach to the Middle Ages that Haskins had inaugurated in America. In addition, Haskins's and Strayer's distinguished and prolific publications were tightly situated in an American ideology, that of Wilsonian progressivism, called Democratic liberalism since the 1940s, and after 1968, cold war liberalism by leftist critics.

The Haskins-Strayer Wilsonian school of medieval history and its special concentration on the subject of royal administration, political rationalization and the "medieval origins of the modern state," to quote the title of Strayer's best-known book, dominated medieval history in the United States until the late 1960s. It viewed the Middle Ages from an entirely different frame of reference from German *Geistes-geschichte* or formalism, but it gave a place to the German intrusions, a dignified one intellectually but a subsidiary one in terms of academic power. It was only with the triumph of leftism on the American campuses after 1968 and the invasion of Frenchified social history of the Parisian *Annales* school and its ideological affinities to Marxism that the overwhelming hold of Haskins-Strayer Wilsonian administrative history substantially weakened in America.

Yet it has not passed away by any means. The professor of medieval history at Harvard today is Thomas N. Bisson, Strayer's student and giver of the memorial oration in the Princeton Chapel after Strayer's death in the summer of 1987. By both academic interest and personal temperament, Bisson is directly and unwaveringly in the Haskins-Strayer lineage. Haskins could come back to Harvard today, listen in on one of Bisson's lectures, and feel nothing had changed from the day in 1931 when he had a stroke and had to quit teaching. The tradition of Wilsonian ideology, as combined with and expressed through the administrative and political history of the Middle Ages, continues unabated on the banks of the Charles. At Princeton Strayer's student William C. Jordan, one of the two American black medieval historians (the fact that the other, Bennett Hill, at Georgetown University, is also Strayer's student speaks to Strayer's paternalistic liberalism), continues the same tradition in Tigertown. These people and their Wilsonian rationalist culture are as American and as durable as Grandma's recipe for apple pie, and as tasty.

The impact of Woodrow Wilson on American culture in the twentieth century probably exceeds that of any other man, including Franklin Delano Roosevelt. Wilson as a President and an international statesman had a very mixed record of accomplishment and can probably be viewed as a domestic political failure and internationally as a disaster. The record of positive legislation of Roosevelt's New Deal in the 1930s or that of Lyndon Johnson's Great Society in the mid-sixties was much greater than Wilson's. Nevertheless, it was Wilson who was the central figure in a kind of instrumentalist progressivism, a rationalist reformism, that permanently altered the way Americans thought about government, national destiny, and their role as citizens. Wilsonian progressivism is where modern America starts, and we are still groping to absorb, contend with, or fulfill the Wilsonian program of public service and international order or trying feebly to formulate an alternative cultural structure by which we can also live and respect ourselves. The literature on the subject of Wilsonian progressivism, which is the intellectual crust for the Haskins-Strayer American pie of medievalism, is substantial, although the definitive book on the subject has not yet been written.

Woodrow Wilson came from an old Virginia middle-class family. His father was a Presbyterian minister, and he himself was much inspired by a Calvinist sense of personal calling to do great things and by a rigid ethical code. Wilson obtained one of the first Ph.D.'s in the country in history and political science from The Johns Hopkins University in Baltimore, which had been newly founded to offer German-type graduate program. By the late 1890s Wilson was a famous teacher at Princeton, which was the favorite school for the scions of the southern gentry, and he was perhaps the best-known political scientist in the United States, with a pioneering book on the operations of the U.S. Congress. After his elevation to the presidency of Princeton, Wilson became immediately one of the three or four most activist and best-known American college presidents of his time. He aimed to change Princeton from a college for the wealthy and genteel into a real university with important graduate programs and research interests (in that regard he had only marginal success, and Princeton's full transformation into a major university occurred in the late 1940s and 1950s).

Wilson's greatest achievement at Princeton was in undergraduate education. He introduced the preceptorial system, a variant of the Oxbridge tutorial program, in which students met weekly in groups not larger than seven with an instructor for a free-flowing discussion. It was not so much this small-group tutorial focus as the complement of new instructors Wilson hired from the new graduate programs at Harvard and Yale to conduct the preceptorials that made the difference in Princeton education. They were a capable, well-chosen, and dedicated group of young professors who successfully balanced teaching and research responsibilities, and the blend distinguishes the Princeton faculty to this day.

By 1912 Wilson was the Democratic candidate for United States President and was elected as the result of a split in the Republican party. He was reelected in 1916 by the narrowest of margins after promising to keep the United States out of the war. Less than a year

later he persuaded Congress to declare war against Germany, ostensibly because of the draconian German policy of sinking neutral ship-
ping. The real reasons were the protection of American banks that
had overextended themselves in loans to the Allies and Wilson's ge-
neric Anglophilism, which meant the United States should not stay
neutral when it looked as though Germany would win the war.

The story of Wilson's activity at the Paris Peace Conference is well
known. He played a leading role in redrawing the map of Europe on
the basis of the application of the principle of political nationhood for
Central and Eastern European ethnic communities (for example, Poland, Czechoslovakia, Yugoslavia) created out of the ruins of the Austrian and Russian empires. But he could not prevent the British and
French leaders from imposing reparations on Germany that produced
such resentment and economic crisis there as to cripple the new liberal Weimar Republic and pave the way for a violent reaction. Nor
was the League of Nations Wilson devised an effective international
body for collective peacekeeping, especially when the U.S. Senate
rejected American membership in the League.

Judgment upon Wilson and assessment of his character are as divided today as they were in his lifetime. He was a bundle of contradictions. He was ideologically very much a liberal democrat, but his
own behavior was invariably authoritarian, impetuous, and oblivious
of the feelings and advice of others. This was partly due to his stern
Calvinist religion, which made him believe he had a personal line to
God, and partly the consequence of a high-strung disposition arising
from unresolved Oedipal feelings and repression of his sexual urg-
ings. This was the view of Wilson held by no less of a psychoanalytic
authority than Sigmund Freud himself. Wilson tolerated suitably assimilated Jews and courageously made Louis D. Brandeis, the Boston
lawyer and Harvard Law School guru, the first Jewish Supreme Court
justice against bitter opposition within Congress and without. Brandeis had been one of his closest advisers. On the other hand, Wilson
had a white Virginian's hostility to and contempt for African-Americans. Segregation in the federal government offices actually increased
during his presidency, and his mistreatment of a segregated black
army regiment in Texas was cruel and disgraceful. Wilson talked world
peace and the comity of nations but acted as a gross imperialist toward
Mexico. On the one hand, he wanted to regulate the untrammeled
robber baron style of capitalism that had developed in the late nineteenth century; on the other hand, he shrank from doing this effectively when he had the chance.

Wilson was so Anglophilic that he could not maintain rational judgment on America's relationship to the Great Powers. Nor did this disposition equip him to deal skillfully with the problems of Central and Eastern Europe. The Versailles settlement made stability and a long peace in Europe virtually impossible. It made the totally excluded Soviets hostile and searching for mischief. It created so many weak and unstable regimes in Central Europe as to generate incessant crises of one sort or another. Wilson can be and has been portrayed from his own day to our own as arrogant, bigoted, rash, fanatical, irrational in judgment, and ineffective in operation, a walking disaster for any institution he headed, whether a university, the United States, or an international peace conference.

Yet he was a man who (at least before America's entry into the war in 1917) won the unswerving loyalty and the firmest admiration of a great part of the academic, professional, and intellectual elite of the United States, which saw him as one of the two or three best-qualified Presidents in American history, which envisioned him as the inaugurator of a new era for both his country and humanity. Possibly they saw what they wanted to see. They projected onto Wilson their hope that the United States was coming of age, that the economic confusion and public chaos and social pathology produced by the huge industrial expansion of the late nineteenth century, the vast ill-digested inflow of immigrants from Eastern and Central Europe, the need for the advancement of learning and organized professions, and the expectation of a significant and benign role for the United States internationally would be met in the Wilson presidency.

Wilsonian progressivism signified an educated middle class seeking to gain power and extend its learning and code of rationality and efficiency to every walk of life. Wilsonianism's fundamental dogma was that centralizing power in the hands of an educated and professional elite was the salvation of the country. It had no qualms whatsoever about the corrupting tendencies or practical incapabilities of power. Science and humanistic learning could provide the answer for everything from slums, public health, sanitation, and crime in the cities to war and imperial control internationally—if only the right kind of people were in power.

There was certainly a WASP or at least Northern European flavor to progressivism. It believed in a view of history in which wisdom and righteousness belonged to the Protestant nations of Western Europe, with some tolerance for the Parisians and the Florentines. Catholic and Mediterranean cultures, the Slavic world, nonwhites, and

Jews had little or no intrinsic credibility. However, the progressives were committed to upward social mobility, and at least all Caucasians (there was dispute about African-Americans), if by education and behavior modification they adopted the ideas, appearance, and life-styles of the North European Protestants, especially the British (not the Irish, of course), could then be accepted into the elite.

It is easy to criticize and make fun of Wilsonian progressives, but considering the vast problems the United States faced, the need for order and strong leadership, good government and the imposition of standards of civic virtue, it was almost inevitable they would have these biases. The alternatives were not apparent. And, it may be argued, their cultural model, their ideals of what is right and not right have prevailed to the present day, with only a little softening at the edges. The stamp of Wilsonianism is still upon us.

It is not just that Charles Haskins and Joseph Strayer, by circumstances of their academic status and their adherence to the liberal wing of the Democratic party, were perpetuators of the Wilsonian heritage. Their character as Wilsonians goes much deeper than that. It is an affect of their biographies and their temperaments. They were Woodrow Wilson duplicated and reincarnated. Haskins and Strayer were not just Wilsonians who happened to be medievalists. Their interest in the Middle Ages and their construction of medieval government and administration were a projection of Wilsonian ideals onto the medieval European past as well as a reliving and justification of the Wilsonian program from the lessons of the medieval origins of the modern state. The medieval political experience, as they understood it, sustained the value and exclusivity of the Wilsonian program in twentieth-century America. The personal style and behavior pattern exhibited by Haskins and Strayer, their psychological profiles, closely resembled Wilson's.

Haskins came from an affluent family in Pennsylvania. He was a very precocious child and his father, a well-educated man, taught him Latin and Greek before he was seven years old. At the age of fifteen Haskins entered a local school, Allegheny College, from which he sought the next year to transfer to Harvard. The dean of Harvard College, not unwisely, thought he was too young. But Johns Hopkins University in Baltimore accepted him, and there he continued his precocious ways. At the age of twenty he had a Ph.D. in American history from the institution and department that had graduated Woodrow Wilson a few years earlier, and he taught at the University of Wisconsin in Madison for a couple of years. Then Haskins decided to become a medievalist and left for Europe to get training at L'École des Chartes in Paris.

The leading professor in American history at Madison in the 1890s was Frederick Jackson Turner, the inventor of the famous frontier thesis in American history: that the character of American civilization had been shaped by the open frontier that was in the early nineties in course of closing. By studying medieval history, Haskins was going to find how another frontier-conditioned society, medieval Europe, had developed. Specifically he was interested in administrative, governmental, and legal institutions and how they brought order and stability out of the fluid and frequently (in his eyes) chaotic conditions of a medieval society that, like the United States, long had open frontiers and cheap land for development. Haskins, and Strayer after him, saw strong parallels between medieval and American history. Through analysis of medieval administrative centralization, the American experience could be illuminated. The Wilsonian instrumentalist ideal of the application of learned intelligence to government in a hitherto disordered society could be studied and affirmed in the medieval context. The capability of an educated elite to transform a violent society through standards of civility and law would be highlighted. Haskins was going to use medieval history both to explain the American experience and to confirm what became the Wilsonian program for American reform and advancement.

Haskins was precisely Wilson's contemporary, and there was much that was identical in the two men: a self-confidence slipping into arrogance, a deep American patriotism subtly intertwined with unbounded admiration for the British constitution and political achievement, an unquestioning elitism and proclivity to see humankind in terms of superior and inferior races, yet a willingness to concede that the less fortunate people could learn from the more capable and advanced northerners—what might be called an open kind of hierarchic racism.

Haskins spent a half dozen years in France, England, and Sicily, first getting the tools of medieval research in Paris and then traveling to archives in London, Rouen, and Palermo to track the steps of the Norman French of the eleventh century. He exhausted his substantial private resources in this learning and research process. Haskins was convinced that the best thing that ever happened to England was the Norman Conquest of 1066, by which William the Conqueror's government and the peculiar kind of centralized Norman feudalism brought thitherto disordered and backward England a highly rational and effective political and judicial order. He put for himself the task of examining the formation of Norman institutions everywhere, and he studied the Sicilian situation as well as the English one because the Norman aristocracy had conquered that rich country after their invasion in 1016. Back and forth Haskins went, to the archives of France, England, and Sicily, building up his view of *Norman Institutions*, his definitive work on the subject, which he finally published in 1918. Later he gave a series of published public lectures at Harvard on the rise of the Normans, whom he called the "supermen" of the eleventh century. After the articles, which later were collected in the 1918 book, began to appear, he was in 1910 invited to teach at Harvard, and with the retirement of Harvard's professor of medieval history, Charles Gross (the first Jew to teach in the Harvard history department and the last until 1940), Haskins in 1912 gained the senior chair in European history on the banks of the Charles River.

Like Wilson's, Haskins's interest in government was not merely historical and theoretical. He wanted very much to be involved in the practice of administration, and he relished the personal exercise of power. For more than a decade he served with great distinction as the dean of the Graduate School of Harvard, elevating its prestige to the premium position in America, higher even than Johns Hopkins, Columbia, and the University of Chicago, which, when Haskins began at Harvard, were ahead of the old institution in Cambridge as centers of doctoral training.

Woodrow Wilson saw in Haskins a replication of himself in every way, and he took Haskins with him to the Paris Peace Conference in 1919 and 1920 as one of his three principal advisers. The other two were his longtime confidant and hatchet man Colonel Edward House and another Harvard professor, Robert H. Lord. It was Lord who advised Wilson on the re-creation of Poland out of the Russian Empire and pieces of eastern Germany. Haskins's main assignment was to study the situation in the Saar Valley mining region. He actively lobbied Wilson on behalf of the French claims to obtain the Saar.

Haskins seconded Lord as a leading architect of Czechoslovakia and Yugoslavia, two new states created by combining several smaller entities derived from the Austro-Hungarian Empire. The two eminent Harvard professors had a bold vision of a reorganized Central Europe, placing the American principle of public instrumentality ahead of Central European nationalism and ethnic, linguistic, and religious particularism. Giving independence to every ethnic minority in the Balkans would create small states that would not be economically viable or politically functional. Haskins's view was that the need of these small societies to find economic prosperity and political stability would in time lead them to repress their national heritages in the interest of fiscal progress and administrative unity within the larger multiethnic states of Czechoslovakia and Yugoslavia. The United States was a multiethnic society. Why could not such a state work in the Balkans? Czechoslovakia and Yugoslavia, in spite of many vicissitudes, still exist. Haskins can be given credit for that measure of political foresight.

In the short run, down to 1939, the Versailles Central European design, for which Haskins can claim a significant measure of authorship, worked poorly. Czechoslovakia had a great deal of industrial potential, but placing 3.5 million "Sudeten" Germans within this new state was a great risk, and Hitler took advantage of it to dismember Czechoslovakia in the late 1930s. He easily stimulated discontent among the large German minority in Czechoslovakia and then incorporated it into his Third Reich. At Munich in 1938 Hitler got Britain and France to recognize this take-over. As for Yugoslavia, it was an impoverished and backward country down to World War II, and its two largest constituents, the Serbs and Croats, disliked each other intensely (they still do). Ironically, it was the Communist takeovers in these two Versailles-created states at the end of World War II, more than the planning of Haskins and Wilson, that brought a measure of stability to these two countries. How much of a success Haskins was as a designer of modern states rather than as a historian of medieval ones is hard to assess. But in both instances Haskins followed the same principle: Politics was more important than culture.

Back in Cambridge, Massachusetts, Haskins in the early 1920s devoted himself to the founding of the Medieval Academy of America, the professional association for medievalists, and its establishment journal, *Speculum*. It was Haskins's belief that American medieval scholarship had come of age, as the United States itself had become a power second to none in the world, and it was time to demonstrate this in the Medieval Academy with its elaborate, excruciatingly formal annual meetings and its journal, which was to be the equal of any journal of medieval scholarship in Europe. To demonstrate this, *Speculum* was printed on thick high-quality paper, and its articles were to have footnotes whose length and opaque quality were second to none in the world. Around him Haskins gathered a group of eager students from all over the country, especially from Ivy League colleges. He put them through a very rigorous training, similar to L'École des Chartes and the German Monumenta institute. His graduate students were supposed to arrive in Harvard Yard already knowing the general course of medieval history and with mastery of Latin, French, and German. Haskins's seminar was a demanding regimen in the reading and interpreting of documents. His students had to be able to sight-read Latin documents, particularly administrative records, often in the form of photostats of manuscripts that Haskins handed out in his seminar.

If you couldn't do this, or you wanted a more speculative approach to the Middle Ages, you were gone. Haskins was an impatient and very demanding taskmaster, who liked to push his students to the limit of exhaustion and frustration. But if they survived, he found them good jobs in leading universities, where they imposed, through the course of generations, precisely the same regimen on their own students. At Princeton and Harvard today the scope and method of training in medieval history that Haskins was using at Harvard half a century ago continue unabated and undiluted.

At the same time, in the Wilsonian tradition of addressing a broad public by expounding humanistic ideals, Haskins loved to give public lectures and to write books addressed to a wide audience. His *Normans in European History* was published as "one who loves France and takes a special interest in helping people to understand her," he wrote in a personal letter. Haskins during his years of wandering through European archives on his own had developed an interest in the learning of the twelfth century, particularly in medieval science. It was now time to institutionalize this field as well. Haskins believed, as a good Wilsonian, that nothing should be left to personal idiosyncrasy but should receive a perpetuating institutional form. "In general, it seems to me," he wrote in 1922, "that we have reached a point in the United States, both in scientific and historical studies, when some more definite effort should be made toward advancing the history of science both as a field for investigation and as a scientific subject." Haskins's academic power broking was extended also in this direction, and he obtained funds to establish a chair in the history of science at Harvard. The first occupant of the chair was a very prolific French medievalist, George Sarton (the father of the novelist May Sarton). As in the case of *Speculum*, *Isis*, the new journal for the history of science that Haskins and Sarton started, eschewed speculative and highly interpretive articles and concentrated on publication of very detailed research reports based on archival study.

While wandering around European archives in the first decade of the century, Haskins had noticed a surprising number of manuscripts dealing with physics, cosmology, and mathematics. They were not simply derivations from the Greeks and the Arabs. They often involved close reasoning, mathematical formulations, and diagrams. There was a technical side to medieval science, as well as a speculative one. Haskins was a pioneer in studying this thick, technical side of medieval science. The only chapter in Haskins's anti-Burckhardt project *The Renaissance of the Twelfth Century* that is still worth reading is the one on natural science. The only problem with this kind of history of science is that it tends to separate the physical sciences from the rest of culture and thought. The general place of science in medieval intellectual life is hard to fathom from the kind of close, technical analysis of medieval science that Haskins inaugurated.

Haskins was an intense, dour, extremely hardworking man who succeeded completely in the program he set out for himself. He was an astute politician, avoided confrontations, and in that respect was more adept than his master Woodrow Wilson. He dominated medieval studies in the overwhelming manner symbolized by the naming of the Medieval Academy of America's highest prize, the Haskins Medal, after him. At academic conferences in the Mayflower Hotel in Washington, D.C., or similar conclaves in Cambridge, Massachusetts, or Madison, Wisconsin, he planted himself in the foyer and held court as his students and his students' students came to pay homage to the great man. He presided over a small enclosed world of determined middle-class WASPs, ruling unchallengedly (before the German immigration of the late 1930s) on the history of Roman Catholic Europe. American Catholic medievalists, a marginal and timid lot, dared not challenge him. But to give Charles Homer Haskins his due, he was a serious, idealistic man whose taste for power did not preclude a dispassionate recognition of good work by others. Nor did he use his position to gain material advancement for himself. He lived simply and died a man of modest means. The Calvinist strain in Wilsonianism ran strong in Haskins's temperament.

Haskins was very much typical of a certain kind of American academic of the first three decades of this century—the scholars and administrators who were mainly responsible for building the great graduate schools of arts and science that stretched from Cambridge, Massachusetts, through Chicago and Urbana, Illinois, and Madison, Wisconsin, to Berkeley, California. In 1900 there was very little in the United States to compare with the traditional European universities. Even Harvard wasn't much compared with Oxford, Berlin, or the Sorbonne. Madison was a cow college; Berkeley, an obscure training college set in a desiccated orange grove. By 1930 the American universities as centers of learning and research were starting to enter world-class status. This is one of the most phenomenal chapters in the history of Western culture, and aside from Laurence Veysey's splendid book on the period down to 1914, it is a story that has not yet been well told. Haskins played a leading role in this development and was typical of the great academic entrepreneurs who by force of stubborn will and manic energy as well as shrewd political judgment carried out this academic and intellectual revolution in the United States.

The problem is that when Haskins came to write in 1928 *The Renaissance of the Twelfth Century*, which is today his only widely read book, he interpreted the intellectual and educational history of twelfth-century Europe far too much in the context of the American experience of his own generation. His book is largely an annotated catalog of authors, theologians, philosophers, translators, and scientists. Just as Chicago, Madison, and Berkeley came out of nowhere to become major centers of thought and learning between 1900 and 1930, and Harvard rose to transatlantic prominence from being just an undergraduate college, so Haskins thought that persistently multiplying names of writers and intellectuals could persuasively communicate the continuous growth of twelfth-century thought. The American university of the 1920s was created by an act of will and steady multiplication of faculty and supportive resources. Haskins gives the impression that the twelfth-century Renaissance was a similar cumulative and straight-line expansionary development. Of course, it was in a sense, but that is a superficial, external history, one that misses the inner dynamic and extremely complex ideological and emotional conflicts that distinguished twelfth-century culture.

Haskins did not take this catalog approach to twelfth-century culture out of obtuseness or laziness. Rather, he did not want to delve into the inner tensions, conflicts, and turmoil that were even in his day clearly visible in twelfth-century thought and sensibility. A critical approach also raised too many disturbing implications for the American intellectual and social world of his time. The old American academic WASPs, of whom there is no finer example than Charles Homer Haskins, were happy with their formidable accomplishments in building centers of learning comparable with Europe's. They did not want to complicate matters by contemplating the ideological divisions and moral issues within American culture (the shock of the

Great Depression and New Deal shortly was to force this upon them), and Haskins projected this irenic, repressive reticence onto the intellectual life of the Middle Ages.

In 1928 (three years before a stroke incapacitated him) Haskins was happy to find a student who was in many ways a carbon copy of himself and would thoroughly continue his work. This was a Princeton graduate, Joseph Strayer. It was the Wilsonian Princeton legacy of high-minded humanistic scholarship and public service that Strayer represented, not the other Princeton of the riotous eating clubs on Prospect Street with their drunken brawls each Saturday night and the glamorous life enshrined in F. Scott Fitzgerald's *This Side of Paradise* (1920).

Joe Strayer came from a Pennsylvania Dutch family. His father was George Strayer, a professor at Columbia's Teachers College for thirty years. Joe Strayer very closely resembled his father physically. George Strayer was a close associate of John Dewey and represented the American philosophy of instrumentalism, a social rationalism applied to the programmatic and persistent solution of social problems—in George Strayer's case, school curricula. Joe Strayer grew up on Morningside Heights in New York and hated it. He was graduated from the Horace Mann School, one of the best metropolitan private schools and long a favorite with faculty parents at Columbia. It also had a long association with John Dewey and Teachers College. Strayer later never spoke of New York except with hatred and could not mention Columbia except in spiteful terms and with contempt. The contrast between the vanguard culture of Manhattan in the 1920s and the bleak Protestant rectitude of his family constituted a great strain for young Strayer and was resolved by his coming down entirely on the side of Wilsonian rationalism and elitism and against the new culture of the Jazz Age. Strayer in the 1950s was fond of telling his students that the Jazz Age was an idle myth; he said he had never experienced it. No doubt in a personal sense that was true.

The kind of work Haskins demanded of his graduate students was perfect for Strayer to shine in at Harvard: close reading of administrative texts for which only a limited Latin vocabulary was necessary (Strayer's command of Latin was always marginal; he probably could not read a philosophical or theological work written in ornate ecclesiastical Latin) and a patient inductive approach, elucidating the operations of government from tax rolls and bureaucratic memorandums. Strayer was not a fast thinker, and he would not have done well in a group where high-level rapid-fire speculation was the currency. He had no taste for art, music, or imaginative literature, and Haskins also had small interest in these things.

Strayer's Harvard dissertation, *The Administration of Normandy Under Saint Louis*, duly published by Haskins's Medieval Academy, was a continuation of Haskins's *Norman Institutions*. After the French reconquest of Normandy from the English crown in 1204, how did the French govern Normandy? More important, did the skillful institutions of Norman administration teach the zealous Roman lawyers of the French crown in the thirteenth century how to develop their own systems of administration and taxation? This was the subject of Strayer's dissertation. There was no clear answer to the second and more interesting question.

When Strayer started teaching at Princeton in the early 1930s, he found himself under the shadow of a much more quick-witted and speculative medievalist, Lynn White, who had done some important work on Italian monasticism and was now beginning his highly suggestive researches into medieval technology. The stirrup, which allowed a knight to hold and stab with a lance without falling off his horse, was one of the great inventions of all time, thought White. The windmill, coming into use in the twelfth century, was a similarly revolutionary breakthrough, and so forth. But fortunately for Strayer, in 1938 Lynn White suddenly went off to head a women's college in California, leaving Strayer as the senior medievalist at Princeton. During the staff-starved wartime he took over as the chairman of the history department, a position he retained for two decades.

In the years after the war Strayer rapidly built up the best department of European history in the country, perhaps in the world. It was also a department known for brilliant undergraduate teaching. This rare combination of great scholars and superb teachers was the fulfillment of Wilson's academic ideal, and the students responded accordingly. By the late 1950s the Princeton history department had more majors, including the artist Frank Stella, than any other department on the campus. The lectures of its classroom stars—E. Harris "Jinks" Harbison on the Reformation, Gordon Craig on modern German and diplomatic history, Eric Goldman (a former senior editor at *Time*) on recent United States history—were standing-room-only affairs.

As department chairman Strayer used not only the Wilsonian ideal but the Haskins method of intimidation: My way or the highway. Every year he brought in three or four new Ph.D.'s, usually from

Harvard, and in three years they were gone unless they gave exceptional promise of prolific publication and were superb in the classroom. Strayer listed the department mailboxes not only by rank but by what he currently thought of his colleagues, especially the nontenured ones. And there were not enough boxes for all the faculty. Each fall a couple of assistant professors would find their mail tossed on the floor under the mailboxes; they knew then it was time to seek other jobs. But in the spirit of Wilsonian paternalism Strayer would—if they had no jobs by January for the next academic year—pick up the phone and get them ones at good colleges. Ann Arbor especially became known as the Princeton farm club. Strayer's influence in the university as a whole loomed large. He was very close to the dean of faculty J. Douglas Brown, the economist and New Deal Democrat, who in 1935 had helped devise the Social Security system. Strayer attended all monthly faculty meetings but never spoke at them and was very annoyed if any of his younger faculty in the history department spoke up.

Strayer was about five feet ten inches tall, stocky, square-built, with a large, round face and sandy, straight hair. His was a very mid-American face. He was a very neat man, always clean-shaven and freshly scrubbed. He had large, powerful hands with thick fingers, but I never saw him shake hands with anyone. His office desk was meticulously clean, even though because he was chairman of a large department, dozens of administrative documents (besides his research materials) must have passed over it each week. During a seminar in his office, if he wanted to find a research document, he would open an old-fashioned wooden filing cabinet, pull out a file, and immediately find the document he was looking for. The walls of his office were lined from floor to ceiling with books, carefully placed by subject matter, never a slip of paper showing from any of them. When I knew him in the 1950s, Strayer was a very heavy chain smoker of cigars, and in addition, he would solicit an occasional cigarette from a student during the seminar. He had no small talk, and in his company several minutes of total silence could pass. The large tumbledown house that he rented from the university for a nominal sum was stocked with a miscellany of unfashionable, beat-up furniture and the kinds of pictures you can buy at K mart.

Strayer's approach to the governance of the history department was identical to that which his favorite medieval king, Philip the Fair of France (d. 1314), ruled his expanded domains. There was a facade of a meeting of the whole departmental faculty at the beginning of

each semester, like Philip the Fair's occasional meetings of the Es-
tates-General. The purpose was not discussion or approval but dissemination of information. Strayer wrote several articles arguing that
medieval representative assemblies, even the English Parliament, were
not deliberative bodies but occasions for the dissemination of information. The main information disseminated at history department
meetings was the preceptorial assignments to the nontenured faculty,
which were given out one day before the start of classes. There were
gasps of shock and horror as assistant professors found themselves
teaching in fields very far from their areas of expertise. Strayer thereby
tested their adaptibility and institutional commitment.

Strayer taught graduate students in the Haskins manner by intimidation and by concentration on narrow research study of administrative records. He spent two years (1951–53) doing nothing else in his
seminar but reading medieval tax rolls, first of England, then of France.
When I proposed that I do a report on the Thomist idea of kingship,
he told me I should consider transferring to the philosophy department. "Sure, that is part of medieval history," he said, glowering
through his inevitable cigar, "but the philosophers will never study
tax rolls. If we historians don't do it, nobody will, so we have to do
it." There was logic in this, after a fashion.

Once Strayer said to me, with unusual explicitness, "Cantor, in
three weeks you will do a report on how St. Louis raised the money
for his crusade." I worked night and day for three weeks, including
the intervening Easter vacation. I felt I was ready. "Well, Cantor,"
he said, rubbing his cheek with a pipe that he seemed to keep around
for that purpose, "how many documents on this subject did you find?"

"Five," I replied.

"Not very good," he said. "There are seven. Of course, one is
unpublished. I found it in a Parisian archive. But the other is published. You should have found it." It turned out the document was
published in southern France in 1893 in an obscure journal, long extinct. It was in the library, however; if I had really been a first-rate
researcher, I would have found the document.

Strayer never turned on the overhead lights in his office during a
seminar. The seminar met for three hours at 2:00 P.M. The office was
a long, narrow room with only one window. By 4:00 P.M. in winter
it was so dark that it was impossible to read one's notes. One day I
had the gall to ask Strayer why he didn't turn on the lights. "So you
dummies will not be able to bore us by reading your verbose notes
and will have to speak succinctly from memory." A good lesson.

Strayer's own approach to scholarship was peculiar. The seminar was devoted to the most excruciating minutiae of medieval administration, but he wanted us, after we had mastered this, to give only the significance, the general import of our research materials. He had a mania against proper names. "What's the difference," he said once in fury, "whether it was the damned earl of Leicester or the earl of Gloucester? How did the son of a gun pay his taxes?" When I started precepting for him—taking the discussion sections tied to his under-graduate lectures on the high Middle Ages—I was stunned by the brilliance and beautiful organization of his lectures. He was not, like Harbison, Craig, and Goldman, a showman, but each lecture was crystal-clear and thoroughly memorable. He made even the most complex things in medieval government and law come alive. His mania against proper names went to extreme length in his lectures. He went into contortions trying to avoid using more than one proper name per lecture. He would say "the French king," "an English lord," "an early-thirteenth-century pope" but would not use an actual name unless he was going to speak about that person for at least half of a lecture.

Having Strayer as a dissertation adviser was a unique experience. In the four years I worked on the thing, I talked to him about it a total of thirty minutes, twenty-nine of which occurred when I started. Eighteen months later I sent him two chapters from England. Three weeks later I got them back. On the top of the first chapter, he had written, "You must do better." That was all. After four years I brought him the 450-page manuscript. "What is this?" he said.

"My dissertation."

"I thought you submitted it last year. Well, I will take it home tonight and read it. Come back tomorrow morning, and I will tell you what I think."

When I told his secretary why I had come and she buzzed him, he did not invite me into his office but came out into the secretary's office and handed me back the dissertation. "It's OK," he said. "We will set up a defense." Then he turned around and went back into his office and closed the door. He never said another word to me about it.

In the 1950s Strayer fulfilled the Wilsonian ideal of public service and international commitments by working for the Central Intelligence Agency for several years. He was personally recruited by the CIA director himself, Allen Dulles, who was a Princeton alumnus. For at least five summers Strayer spent five days a week at CIA head-quarters in Langley, Virginia, and during the year he would go down whenever there was a crisis somewhere in the world. If there was upheaval in Lebanon or Pakistan or wherever, I would wait at home by the phone, and sure enough, at 10:00 P.M., Strayer would phone and say, "Ah, I have to go to Washington tomorrow. Please take my lecture and preceptorials." Then he would tell me the subject of the lecture. Usually that presented no problem; sometimes I had to stay up most of the night writing a lecture on an unfamiliar topic. When Strayer got back in a day or two, he would summon me to his office and ask me to repeat the lecture to him word for word. I once had the temerity to ask him what he was doing for the CIA and why it found the services of a medievalist so important. The response was that Allen Dulles knew medievalists were used to drawing conclusions from fragmentary evidence, and that is just what the CIA did. It was rumored that Strayer was one of Dulles's chief advisers. It was evident that Strayer read many intelligence reports on the Soviet Union because he was fond of mentioning the Soviet government in his lectures. Dictatorships and totalitarian regimes don't last very long, he said, no matter how fierce and oppressive they are. It is a very inefficient system, and eventually even the people on top get tired of it, and the system loosens up or falls apart entirely. He predicted that in time the Soviet system would change, that Stalinism would be superseded. Of course, he has been proved right in that prediction; it happened just the way he said it would.

Strayer's universe was one in which good administration and law made everything else possible. And the good political system was a highly centralized one in the hands of the learned elite. But it was not a closed system. It had to respond to change, to the needs and feeling of the people, and allow for a substantial degree of social mobility. This sounded like England under Henry II or France under Philip the Fair, and those were the medieval governments he most admired. Essentially they were a mirror of the New Deal and its successors—a group of well-educated, public-spirited, uncorrupted, but power-hungry bureaucrats who worked on behalf of society's welfare as they perceived it. It was directly in the Wilsonian tradition. Strayer was not a political conservative in the ordinary sense of the term. He always voted for Democrats; he held the Republicans in low esteem, even when under Eisenhower and Allen Dulles he was employed by a Republican administration. He had no quarrel with the welfare state. But he was paternalistic, elitist, authoritarian within certain bounds and restraints, mostly self-imposed.

Strayer represents a great generation in American life, the generation that followed the Wilsonian tradition in creating the regulatory and welfare state, in raising American universities to the highest level in the world, and in guiding the United States to world hegemony. We shall not see such giants again in this country. Among other impediments, the Vietnam disaster and the rise of the New Left eroded self-confidence in the United States as a special agency of history or God and as destiny's darling. Strayer belonged to the generation of unwavering faith in American exceptionalism. That now seems long ago. A chasm has opened with that Wilsonian past.

II
THE CONTOURS OF
MEDIEVAL GOVERNMENT

With rare clarity and skill in comparative analysis of different royal administrations, Haskins and Strayer showed the workings of medieval government. They explored the diurnal functioning of medieval administration and revealed how the clerics who were the royal bureaucrats until about 1200 and the lawyers who were the senior bureaucratic personnel normally thereafter, imposed the will of the crown upon baronial families, peasant societies, and urban communities. It would be wrong, of course, to suggest that the Haskins-Strayer American administrative school of medieval history did it all on their own. Maitland's kind of sociology of law was an inspiration and model for them, although they lacked Maitland's delicacy and subtlety. Since the Americans themselves worked on Europe west of the Rhine, they had to rely on the reports of Karl Hampe and Friedrich Baethgen and their students for information on the German Empire, as well as the work of Geoffrey Barraclough, a British historian of medieval Germany. Strayer thought these scholars greatly overrated the sophistication of medieval German administration, and a recent writer, Oxford's Karl Leyser, in a paradoxical way, confirms this view. Leyser's argument is that the German monarchy didn't need public administration because it had such strength from tribal bonds. The pioneering six-volume work of the Manchester historian Thomas Frederick Tout on the growth of English royal administration, published in the 1920s and 1930s, provided helpful information on how the king's household slowly took on public functions. Strayer benefited personally from research assistance and advice offered him by Robert Fawtier, the Sorbonne professor who worked on the thirteenth-century French monarchy but who failed to write the big book on Philip the Fair's government he long projected. It was Strayer who finally published this monumental treatise, in 1980. In the work of clarifying, comparing, systematizing medieval government operations and the highlighting of the contours of medieval royal administrative systems, Haskins and Strayer led the way.

In their view, the most important accomplishment of the twelfth century was the rationalization and centralization of government, which had been essentially a local, fragmentary affair until the mid-eleventh century. The great aristocratic families had provided whatever effective government or law existed; the king was generally a figurehead without power. Centralized royal government emerged first in England under the Norman kings, about the same time, with only partial success, in Germany, and finally—by the end of the twelfth century, and very aggressively—in France. The kings provided a political factor in European civilization that had been absent since the fall of Rome in the fifth century.

Government itself was radical in the twelfth century, when monarchs were attempting to impose a system of centralized social order upon the ancient baronial hierarchy. The radical, progressive quality of twelfth-century government and its dynamic impact as a meliorative social force were a cardinal principle of faith for the Wilsonians Haskins and Strayer. In their view, service to the crown became equivalent to dissent from the centrifugal feudal tradition, and it was often not the kings themselves (most of whom were interested only in money and personal power) but the ambitious graduates of cathedral schools and the new universities who consciously created the medieval state and worked out its basic mechanisms. Between about 1150 and 1200 civil servants did the actual work of the institutionalization of government, imposing rational principles on aristocratic society. Disenchanted clerics, erstwhile poets, and student radicals, as well as zealous lawyers fulfilled their individual ambitions and pursued their personal quests as administrators and judges for Henry II of England, the German emperor Frederick Barbarossa, and the French king Philip Augustus.

One of the major accomplishments of the centralized monarchy was the institution of the legal system centering on the crown. This was successfully begun in England in the twelfth century, in France by the latter part of the thirteenth, and eventually even in some of the smaller countries like Aragon in Spain. The Germans were much less successful in this sphere during the Middle Ages.

The new governments also required their subjects to pay taxes to support the royal courts and the bureaucracy, and they developed effective military machines based on mercenary armies instead of feudal levies. The feudal army was not abandoned ceremonially (or emotionally) until much later, but kings began to use professional mercenaries instead of vassals who fought as a social obligation, although they still were led by generals who fought for the old reasons: because they were noblemen and because war was their job. However, the rank and file of thirteenth-century armies were mercenary soldiers, partly because of the enormous growth of population. The population of Europe, particularly of England and France, exploded in the thirteenth century in a manner not seen again until the eighteenth, and many of the superfluous people became professional soldiers.

Like all governments before the late nineteenth century, the new monarchies concentrated on law, taxation, and defense (or aggression); they did nothing about social service, welfare, or education. Kings who were personally interested in education endowed schools and colleges, but the medieval state as such took no part in cultural matters. With great fanfare, kings distributed occasional largess to the indigent, but this was far from a war on poverty. The role of government in European life changed very little between about 1270 and 1870; its basic functions were delineated by the royal bureaucrats and lawyers of the thirteenth century.

By the middle of the thirteenth century the royal bureaucrats had instituted legal systems managed by civil servants and professional lawyers, systems that gave many people access to something resembling due process of law. Lords got more justice than peasants, of course, but there was at least a beginning of judicial order, and the little man could hope for more than the ancient personal methods of redress. Outside England the new laws were based on those of the Roman Empire, and the royal lawyers faced the challenge of making law operate in society by convincing or frightening people into following it. All this required intelligence as well as learning, and patience as well as energy, and by the late twelfth century a career as a royal lawyer or bureaucrat was a creative role that attracted the best and brightest young people. It was normally more socially useful and appealing to university graduates than working for the church, and the best jobs available in 1200 were in the governments of the kings of England and France. The old Roman laws were dug out of archives, introduced into the curricula of the new law schools at Bo-

logna and Montpellier and elsewhere, and eventually made the basis
of new national legal systems. In their efforts to apply the law in the
circumstances of feudal society, the lawyers devised techniques that
went beyond those of the Romans. Generally, when Roman law conflicted with traditional feudal practice, the lawyers applied the Roman law (which usually favored the crown).

The Roman law of the Continental countries was based on the
principles of equity, rationality, and absolutism. In practice this meant
that judges worked for the state (or for the king) and had complete
control over what happened in court. Their decisions were made according to general principles, and they used written codes, which
they altered if they appeared to conflict with justice in a particular
circumstance. Judges accepted written depositions from attorneys and
attempted to decide the case on the merits of these briefs, but it was
their duty to get the truth by whatever means they could find, including interrogation and torture of witnesses. This system tended to
work well in ordinary civil and criminal cases, but it could be perni-
cious if ideological questions such as heresy and treason were involved. If the judges were proponents of one ideology, and the
defendants of another, then there could be little hope of justice, and
that is exactly what happened in the ecclesiastical courts that comprised the papal Inquisition, which were run like any other Roman
court. England, as we have seen, developed its own unique system
of common law, which did not employ torture.

Despite delays and failures in justice, the new legal systems gave
many people a direct experience of royal government and of a state.
Citizens encountered the king through his courts, and almost everyone but the lowest peasants had occasion at some time to be involved
with royal justice. By the early thirteenth century the royal power
had begun to impinge upon the lives of ordinary people, and the
disposition of the monarch himself—whether he was energetic, just,
and well intentioned—made a real difference. The format and operation of the law were extremely important in the rise and fall of landed
and merchant families, and family fortunes were decided in litigation
as often as on the battlefield or in the marketplace.

Citizens also encountered the king and his servants through the
new systems of taxation. Taxation, which forces people to give up
some of their own property to someone else, is an unnatural condition, and the great achievement of the royal bureaucrats was to get
the principle of taxation accepted at all. To be sure, it was accepted
mainly because people were forced to accept it by pressure from above,

but also because the government did offer people something and made them see that they had to pay for it. The first benefit offered by government, of course, was defense. The defense could be imaginary as well as real. Edward I of England in the 1290s extorted money from his subjects with fanciful threats of aggression by the French.

But the government also had to develop some sanctions or institutional means or justification for its taxes, some mechanism of consent, and this was done in two ways. First, kings made use of their ancient feudal prerogatives as overlords. Secondly, in the thirteenth century they began to develop representative institutions to act for the country at large, summoning representatives of the estates to consent to their proposals. In England this system endured to be modified into Parliament in the sixteenth and seventeenth centuries, but on the Continent the early representative institutions did not functionally survive the fourteenth and fifteenth centuries.

In the twelfth and thirteenth centuries, then, the ablest young men found idealistic, well-paid, and satisfying work in government and law. It was one of the rare periods when young people could advance rapidly to positions of power—somewhat like the New Deal of the 1930s, which pacified young radicals out of Ivy League law schools by allowing them to participate in government. This parallel was very much in Strayer's mind. University graduates became much less revolutionary in the generation after 1180, and they moved on to spectacular achievements in the establishment of rationalized government and law. They set up the essentials of legal systems that exist to this day; they organized the transition from feudal to mercenary armies; they established long-term systems of taxation (which, in France, survived until the Revolution). They wanted the central government to be strong because they were part of it, and they were largely responsible for the creation of the mystique of monarchy and the development of a significant sense of national identity. Europeans began to identify their individual ideals and fortunes with their states and their kings and to look to the crown for public order. This process Strayer called the "laicization of medieval society." The term is disputable, but the process certainly occurred.

Probably much more could have been accomplished in the way of economic organization and social justice, but after about 1230 there was much less idealism and more professionalism in public life. Political systems usually become less creative and more corrupt when their primary goals have been achieved.

During the fourteenth and early fifteenth centuries there was actually a decline in the effectiveness of royal governments and political stability in Western Europe. Strayer perceived that the new powerhouse French and English administrations, with their laicized, functional spirit, did not realize that there were necessary moral restraints on the use of royal power. They were so taken with their effective instruments of taxation and law that they went to extremes. They crushed old families, made a mockery of urban self-government, destroyed the autonomy and dignity of the papacy, and, beginning in the 1290s, turned upon each other in an international conflict that went on intermittently and devastatingly for 150 years. This extremism on the part of royal governments produced disloyalty, cynicism, and disillusionment on the part of the societies they ruled. Revived aristocracies took their revenge by meddling in royal government and plundering its resources. The royal administrators did not know what to do with demobilized soldiers during intervals of truce, and these well-trained veterans turned into bandit gangs or mercenary armies employed by separatist lords, causing social and legal chaos. In addition, royal government in the fourteenth century faced sharp drops in tax income because of economic depression and the loss of population in the Black Death.

There were many years in both France and England between 1370 and 1450 when the royal government was highly dysfunctional. But its basic systems were so well defined and routinized that they survived war, depression, plague, colder weather, and ill-advised policies, and after 1450 the royal administrations rapidly recovered ground. By 1500 they were back where they had been around 1300, with one important alteration: The "new monarchies" of 1500, having been scorched by the upheavals of the fourteenth and fifteenth centuries, were more remote from the people they ruled than in 1300. They were more secretive, self-contained, authoritarian, and disinclined to consult with representative estates and parliaments, even for ceremonial and information-giving purposes.

III

THE NORTHERN SUPERMEN

Where did it all begin, the process of political rationalization that led to the medieval origins of the modern state? As seen by Haskins, the Norman Conquest of Anglo-Saxon England was not the invasion by alien autocrats of a peaceful and happy land devoted to liberal institutions, which had been the sentimental Victorian view. Rather, the dramatic events of 1066 constituted the rescue of a declining and disintegrating society by political leaders of great genius. The Norman Conquest made England part of Europe and saved it from being absorbed into the barren Scandinavian world and from turning into another Iceland. Here is indeed a liberation thesis, with England viewed as being liberated for Western civilization. This Normanist interpretation, as it may be called, considered Anglo-Saxon government hopelessly feeble and pre-Conquest culture insignificant. It attributed high value to the impact of French higher culture in transforming English civilization. All the important political and legal institutions of late-eleventh- and twelfth-century England were the work of the Anglo-Norman monarchy, just as the process of westward expansion in the eighteenth and nineteenth centuries incorporated Anglophone North America into European culture and British common law. Haskins and Strayer had no more respect for the Anglo-Saxons than the American frontiersmen and land speculators had for the Native Americans. Historical destiny demanded that these less developed peoples give way to political modernization.

For Haskins, the Normans were eleventh-century "supermen," geniuses at the art of government who took feudal institutions that had been agencies of decentralization and reshaped them into powerful centralizing institutions. Under feudal guise the Normans applied rationality and organizational skill to the problems of medieval government for the first time. Therefore, the beginnings of the modern bureaucratic state are to be found in late-eleventh-century England. That the Norman conquerors, in their contempt for the conquered people, destroyed hundreds of Anglo-Saxon illuminated manuscripts, among the most precious artistic treasures of the medieval world, was of small account when the destruction was set against political progress.

Haskins knew that it was not enough to deify the Normans as supermen; he actually had to explain what William the Conqueror and his associates were trying to do, why they tried to do these things, and how successful they were. Especially he had to explain why and how Normandy developed its distinctive kind of rationalized government out of tribal and feudal foundations. He spent nearly two decades working on this subject. Why should the duke of Normandy in 1066 have had the most centralized and rational government in western Europe? The first eight decades of the duchy of Normandy, after its founding in 911, gave no promise of this remarkable achievement.

The Normans were Scandinavian pirates who descended upon the French Carolingian Empire at the end of the ninth century. Their number was not great, probably not more than 20 percent of the population they came to rule. These marauders, led by a wild chieftain called Rollo, established their hegemony in the diocese of Rouen, which was not a particularly fertile or wealthy part of France. Rollo and his warlords accepted Christianity, but this nominal conversion did not lessen their inclination to perpetual blood feuds. Rollo and his successors became the nominal vassals of the kings in Paris but in fact ruled independently.

Until the last decade of the tenth century these Scandinavian warriors fought among themselves in a particularly bloody and anarchic fashion. Then, beginning with the reign of Duke Richard I in 990, there was a marked change as the ducal government became devoted to peace and centralization of authority in its hands. Although our sources of information are meager and confused, it appears that this new phase in the history of Norman society was inaugurated under the influence of highly intelligent and ambitious churchmen who came into the duchy, usually at the urging of the duke, from Flanders, the Rhineland, and northern Italy. Particularly in the Rhineland and northern Italy the great bishops and abbots were in very close alliance with the German emperor, to the mutual benefit of both monarchy and church. In the four decades after 990, a similar alliance was effected in the Norman duchy. During this period there was a conscious attempt to bring intelligent and literate men into Normandy. In Haskins's view, the dukes had a progressive vision and at least a vague idea that somehow good government was bound up with literacy and therefore inevitably with the church. Learned churchmen experienced in the problems of royal government were attracted only by generous offers of large endowments for the ecclesiastical institutions over which they would preside, and after the year 1000 these offers brought into the duchy several ecclesiastics of very great ability. These men founded centers of learning and piety, and they were also able to advise the duke on how to establish peace in his duchy and control the savage nobility. In addition, the churchmen did all the literate work of government.

The most visible symbol of the great changes taking place in Normandy after 1000 was the erection of several magnificent stone churches in what historians of architecture call the Romanesque style. It is unlikely that before 1000 there was a single stone building in the whole duchy beyond a few unimpressive fortresses, but now some of the greatest churches of eleventh-century Europe begin to rise on the Norman plains. To build a great stone church in the early eleventh century required someone who was well trained in geometry, and it also called for the effective organization of labor, which meant in practice guilds of stonemasons. The building of the Norman churches could not therefore have been achieved without skilled planning, and the kind of intelligent organization that was effective in architecture could be equally successful in governmental decision making. Rationality, order, control, the efficient use of resources—these tools would now be turned upon problems of political and social organization. Again the minds of churchmen would direct great enterprises. The duke was their great protector and patron. The stronger he was, the more influential and wealthy would the bishops and abbots become, so the duke commanded their unquestioned loyalty. The duke consulted his clerical advisers on how to transform the disordered heroic society dominated by the Scandinavian warlords into a centralized political and legal unit, and the duke used the ecclesiastics in executing the program they urged him to adopt. In this way was begun the great transformation of Norman institutions that by 1066 made the duke the most envied and feared man in Europe.

For a century after 990 the dukes of Normandy were usually intelligent, ambitious, and energetic when measured against the usual medieval rulers. This is Haskins's basic assumption. The churchmen who assisted the dukes were also, as a group, remarkably superior in learning and in their sensitivity to the problems of political life. The monks who came to Normandy from the Rhineland and northern Italy had in many instances received the benefit of study in the new schools of Roman and canon law that made their appearance in those regions in the early eleventh century.

Beyond these superior qualities of the elite group in Norman society, the rise of ducal power may be explained in terms of the peculiar social framework of the duchy. The traditions of the previous Carolingian government had been largely obscured by the Scandinavian invasions. The Norman lords had been interested only in the pursuit of primordial blood feuds and had never developed any sense of community. Therefore, once the duke and the churchmen allied to achieve a centralized authority, the other forms of loyalty in this society were unable to withstand the impact of the intelligence and energy of the new elite group. In Normandy, more easily than anywhere else in Western Europe, ecclesiastical recollection of the beneficent authority of the Christian Roman emperors could be realized in practice. But in an intensely rural and deurbanized society where the nexus of feudal institutions had already begun to crystallize in the previous Carolingian era, it was obvious that the rise of ducal power would have to be attained through manipulation and reconstitution of these feudal institutions. In this way, in the first three decades of the eleventh century the duke and his clerical allies arrived at their singular policy of achieving centralized authority through the medium of a reconstituted feudalism.

The most difficult task for the early-eleventh-century dukes was to destroy the power of the great lords, the descendants of Rollo's companions, and to turn them from tribal chieftains into cooperative agents, who in turn commanded absolute loyalty and strict service from their vassals. The transformation of Scandinavian tribalism into a tightly controlled feudal order was difficult to achieve; this was still a very simple and inchoate society, so that sheer force was the most effective tool in political centralization and the duke had to become personally more powerful than the lords. This end was attained in the first three decades of the eleventh century by drawing the greater part of the duke's army from ecclesiastical estates. Knights were settled on church lands, and the bishops and abbots became the vassals of the duke. By 1035 three hundred well-equipped and well-trained cavalrymen had in this way been settled on ecclesiastical lands, and the duke's ecclesiastical vassals placed this new army at his disposal for beating down the independent lay nobility. The duke himself could probably draw between sixty and a hundred knights from his own estates so that he could put into the field an armored force that was large by medieval standards.

By the 1020s the second stage of Norman feudalization was under way, and the duke was forcing strict vows of homage upon the lay nobility of Normandy, rewarding those who were willing to give him the loyalty and service he demanded, and systematically destroying the old families that resisted him. It was Haskins's main thesis that in Normandy feudalization was the instrument of political centralization. By this process a new aristocracy began to emerge in the duchy, strictly subservient to the duke's authority. With the advice of churchmen such as the monastic scholar Lanfranc, who had begun his career as a lawyer in his native northern Italy, Duke William the Bastard, later known as King William the Conqueror, made Norman feudalism a political and social system that transcended the original nature of feudal institutions, fundamentally inclined to decentralization.

William arrived at a governmental structure that placed all authority in his own hands. The feudal hierarchy became a political and social pyramid with the duke at the pinnacle. The leaders of the lay and ecclesiastical nobility held their lands from the duke by feudal contract, and their subvassals in turn had to take oaths of loyalty to the duke that in case of conflict preempted any obligations they had to their immediate overlords. It was this "liege-lordship" that made all free members of society directly subject to the duke's authority and precluded the situation that existed in other feudal states by which the subvassals were loyal only to their immediate lords and passed out from under the authority of the central government.

In addition, every churchman and layman knew precisely how many knights he owed in military service to the duke in return for holding his fief. In Normandy the knight service owed was distributed in multiples of five, roughly in accordance with the value of the vassal's holdings. Haskins devoted many years trying to prove this exceptionally rationalized quality of Norman feudalism. (Inevitably his quantification of Norman feudalism has been recently questioned.) Each of the duke's tenants in chief knew that if he defaulted in giving the service owed, he would be held to account in the duke's court and that if he were found guilty by his peers, he would have to forfeit his land and with it the status in society he and his family enjoyed. Similarly, no lord could build a castle or engage in a private feud without the duke's license on pain of forfeiture. The duke's local representative, called the viscount, operated as an effective regional agency of the central power, supervising the administration of the duke's demesne, keeping watch on the local nobility, and returning to the duke's treasury the income that accrued from various incidents of feudal taxation. All the great vassals of the duke were required to attend meetings of his court in order to be informed of his policy and to participate in the trials of those magnates who had violated their oaths of allegiance.

William the Bastard presided at councils of the Norman church and exercised as close a control over the bishops and abbots as over the lay nobility. In order to enter into their offices, the bishops and abbots had to be invested with the symbols of their office by the duke himself, and this allowed William in effect to designate the candidate to be elected as bishop by the cathedral clergy and as abbot by the monastic community. William was inclined to appoint his own relatives to the episcopacy and the monastic clerks who had served in his own chancery to head the great abbeys. In addition, William enthusiastically supported the church's program of the Peace of God, by which the lay and ecclesiastical magnates were supposed to form themselves into peace organizations to prevent and exclude the endemic violence characteristic of feudal society. The Peace of God movement was more effective in Normandy than anywhere else in Europe because William made himself its president in his duchy. Once he had established a tightly organized political and social system with himself in complete control of the feudal hierarchy, he had everything to gain from the promulgation of peace and the prohibition, or at least drastic limitation, of private feuds. By the 1060s a Norman lord who rebelled against the duke found himself facing the overwhelming military superiority of the duke's army, condemnation in the duke's court by the subordinated vassals, forfeiture of his patrimony, and, in addition, excommunication by the church.

By 1060 William, in Haskins's account, controlled, in the form of a highly trained feudal host of a thousand knights, a massive military machine that, because of the strictness of feudal contract in Normandy, could actually be called out and put into the field. Although Normandy was by no means a very wealthy land, the duke had so organized his resources that at least west of the Rhine he was the most formidable military power of the middle of the century. But now he had another problem: He had to provide a war for his military aristocracy. The highly skilled Norman knights were not supposed to fight each other, but they had no function in life other than a military one, and consequently, William had to find an opportunity abroad for his massive armored power. The Norman lords, although beaten down, had no great love for the ducal family. Dissatisfaction and insurrection were always just beneath the surface. The pressure on the duke's government to appease the military ambitions of the lay nobility was increased by the steady population rise among the Norman aristocracy that meant a frustrating shortage of land for the younger sons of the prolific lords. In the early eleventh century there was a steady stream of emigrants from the duchy to Sicily and southern Italy, where the younger sons of Norman nobility, landless, restless, and unhappy, could carve out new estates for themselves. To a government capable of rational planning, this emigration of some of the best soldiers in Europe seemed an unfortunate waste of the duke's resources. It was far more prudent to use the duke's military machine in an organized conquest of new territory that could both satisfy the bellicose energies and insatiable greed of the Norman nobility and increase William's wealth, authority, and reputation. Thus, because of the very nature of the warrior society William the Bastard and his predecessors had created, the duke after 1060 could not be satisfied with what he had achieved; he had to become William the Conqueror.

But where could he lead an army? The geopolitical situation made it inevitable that William should turn to England. Of course, England was also a risky choice; it was a wealthy and thickly settled country whose population was at least five times greater than that of Normandy in 1066. The Battle of Hastings, in which William completely triumphed thus represents a classic case of a confrontation between an old, feeble monarchy unable to control the resources of a large and wealthy country and a new ferocious military aristocracy under the command of an extremely able leader who was forced by social circumstances to expand his territory. The clash between China and Japan is a close modern parallel.

In 1066 all England, after William's triumph at Hastings, was *terra regis* ("king's land"). William the Conqueror owned the whole country, and he had the opportunity for systematic political and social planning on a scale that appears again only in the eighteenth and nineteenth centuries, when Britons seized control of vast overseas territories. More than any previous medieval European government, Anglo-Norman government was rational. The origins of the modern state we can with justification say was being born here. Although we cannot yet find the concept of sovereignty, which is a necessity in the modern world, the administrative methods and characteristic attitudes of the central government in modern society can be glimpsed in late-eleventh-century England. This was the first planned society since the Roman Empire. A very small group of aggressive and highly intelligent men, many of them well educated, were in control of the royal administration. There were many technological checks and restrictions upon what they could do. The mindless pressures of aristocratic society always lay heavily upon them, but within these limits they planned with a degree of intensity that has seldom been matched in human history.

We can see how closely Haskins's view of the Normans' role in medieval government resembled the Wilsonian program of his own day. A small group of highly educated and dedicated men were bent on bringing order and rationality into the chaos of a postfrontier society. This is the meaning of Wilsonian progressivism, and it is also what the government of the Norman supermen stood for, in Haskins's eyes. Of course, since Haskins's day his clear and comprehensive thesis has been challenged in a cross-Channel maneuver. It has been argued that Anglo-Saxon government was by no means backward and feeble, that feudalization in England was well under way by 1066, that William just happened to win a lucky victory at Hastings, not because he represented progressive and rational political forces against backward and irrational ones.

The anti-Haskins position was first clearly enunciated in 1938 by R. R. Darlington, an Anglo-Saxon scholar. Since 1960 a veritable legion of Anglo-Saxon lovers has been at work in Britain. The Anglo-Saxon lovers contend that there was nothing inevitable about the Norman French victory at Hastings, in spite of the fact that the English nobility archaically dismounted and fought on foot while the French used up-to-date armed cavalry. The battle, until a stray arrow killed the English king Harold Godwinson, was indeed a close affair. Furthermore, the English had won a great victory near York against invading Norwegians just a short time before Hastings, and Harold had to march his exhausted army the length of country when William's crossing of the Channel became imminent. Harold undoubtedly lost some of his best soldiers en route, since one great battle a year was enough for most medieval warriors.

The dispute between Haskins-Strayer Normanists and the resurgent Anglo-Saxonists may never be resolved because both sides are inspired by ideological concerns and emotional fixations. I believe that the weight of the evidence lies strongly with the American Wilsonian Normanists, but this will never convince the Anglo-Saxon lovers across the Atlantic, who furthermore had gained support from a Californian, Warren Hollister. The dispute comes down to feelings about power, reason, justice, community, entities so embedded in the subconscious as well as consciously articulated attitudes that we are dealing here with pyschoanalytic phenomena and primordial anticipations.

The Anglo-Saxon revival is part of a general revulsion against political modernization and imperial triumphalism since the 1950s. While Haskins and Strayer regarded themselves as the quintessence of liberalism, behind the revanchist claims of the Anglo-Saxon lovers is an emotional distaste for American power, even though some British historians, particularly David C. Douglas, strongly supported Haskins's Normanist position.

Since the proclivity of American radical feminism is to ally women victims of empowered males with all other depressed groups, it is no surprise that feminist medievalists have come to the support of vanquished Anglo-Saxon as against postconquest alleged macho mentality. In 1989 Susan Mosher Stuard, one of the two or three leading feminist medievalist historians, claimed that the Anglo-Saxons had freely accepted the wielding of power by women. There was a decline in this sexual equality after the conquest, she said, resulting by the thirteenth century in a consciousness of "manliness" as an organizing principle of social and historical thought in England. Perception of this transition was not unknown to the early-nineteenth-century romanticism, as readers of Sir Walter Scott's *Ivanhoe* will recognize. I can imagine how Joe Strayer would have reacted to this feminist enthusiasm for the Anglo-Saxons. He would have puffed on his cigar and fixed his steely smile through clenched teeth.

With respect to the other side of the Channel, it has been recently argued that Haskins's view of Norman institutions under William the Bastard was anachronistic and overschematized, that he read back the administrative and legal situation of the twelfth century into a much earlier era of the duchy. These are the kinds of disputes that professional medievalists engage in and the way intellectual dwarfs climb on the shoulders of giants. But Haskins did present a consistent and comprehensive vision of the political role of the Normans in European history, and no one has yet come up with an alternative paradigm for the great political turnaround of the late eleventh century, just as the Wilsonian vision that America's future lay in the hands of a university-trained bureaucratic elite has not been superseded. It was indeed greatly confirmed by the Roosevelt-Truman and Kennedy-Johnson administrations and was only eroded at the edges, but not at all supplanted, by Reaganite populist conservatism in the 1980s.

IV

COLD WAR LIBERALISM AND THE MEDIEVAL STATE

Haskins's Normanist thesis was broadened by Strayer to embrace the comparative political history of the high Middle Ages. Joseph Strayer published eight books and a long list of articles. Of the latter, the essay on laicization of European life, especially the political sector, in the late thirteenth century (1938) is still regarded as a classic. Among his books he published both an extended and a brief textbook. The former, known as Strayer and D. C. Munro, *The Middle Ages* (4th edition, 1959), is important for its brilliant summary of European political history from about 1050 to 1350. D. C. Munro was Strayer's teacher at Princeton in the 1920s. The book in its later editions has almost nothing to do with old Munro, but his name stays on it for pietistic or contractual reasons. *The Albigensian Crusade* (1972) is a concise and shrewd account of the take-over of southern France in the 1220s and 1230s by the Parisian monarchy and northern nobility under the pretext of a papal-sponsored crusade against the alternative church Catharists. It reads like a confidential report, by a very shrewd colonial administrator, of a European imperial conquest in Africa or East Asia in the late nineteenth century.

In the 1950s Strayer got involved in a monstrous project sponsored by the Medieval Academy of America. This was a three-volume study by various contributors, *The English Government at Work* in the early 1320s. Much of it is as dull and verbose as the work of T. F. Tout. Strayer, however, edited the second volume, on taxation, and wrote a long introductory essay on the history of royal taxation that shows him at his best: clear, concise, subtle, with a Maitland-like feel for functional operations. Its realism disturbed British reviewers, who were still worshiping at the shopworn shrine of William Stubbs and dreaming of constitutionalism allegedly generated by consent to taxation. With respect to the mechanism and political implications of royal taxation, Strayer sees little or no difference between France and England.

Strayer also became involved in another multivolume American project of the fifties and sixties, a history of the Crusades edited at the University of Pennsylvania. This series ended up as a showpiece of both the best and worst of American medieval scholarship. Among the best is Strayer's essay on the "political Crusades" of the thirteenth century, which the papacy launched first against the emperor Frederick II and then against the king of Aragón. The indirect result of the latter venture was the destruction of the medieval papacy in the first decade of the fourteenth century by the French monarchy. Strayer's anticlericalism and contempt for Roman Catholicism were never more convincingly presented than in this study. It also contains some of his most ironical writing and would make a good outline for a television miniseries.

The three books that are Strayer's most important legacy are *Feudalism* (1965), which succinctly summarized three decades of his research and thinking on that social phenomenon; *On the Medieval Origins of the Modern State* (1970); and *The Reign of Philip the Fair* (1980). *Origins* and *Philip* lie at opposite poles of the historian's craft and demonstrate, first of all, Strayer's unusual diversity of conceptualization and exposition. *Origins* is an 111-page overview of medieval government, an essay in political sociology that has been many times reprinted and has been translated into four languages. *Philip the Fair* is a 424-page treatise derived from thirty years of research in archival and published administrative records and from Strayer's reflections on how this most aggressive and successful of medieval French governments functioned. He had finished most of the research by the early 1950s and had then written a draft of most of the book. The long delay in publication came about not only because of his distraction by university administration and service to the CIA but precisely because he wanted to bring to bear his own experiences in government upon his effort to understand and explain Philip's policy and operations. Strayer perhaps waited too long to publish; he was ten years past retirement, and his health was beginning to fail when he wrote the final draft. One thinks that he must have cut some things at the last minute, like the propaganda war against the papacy that the French government waged, because he still couldn't make up his mind on these matters. Still, *Philip the Fair* is a monumental work, something that French historians, with all their skill in self-advertisement, had dreamed of doing for a century but had not yet been able to do.

There is a vast literature on the nature of feudalism, not a little complicated by the fact that it is not a medieval word. The term was invented in the eighteenth century and used for polemical purposes by radical French democrats to categorize the old regime they wanted to overthrow. "Feudalism" was further employed by Karl Marx in the mid-nineteenth century to stand for the precapitalist stage of history. But historians have persisted in using the term "feudalism" in the twentieth century, and a variety of definitions and explanations of feudalism has been offered. Strayer's position is clear and firm:

The basic characteristics of feudalism in Western Europe are a fragmentation of political authority, public power in private hands, and a military system in which an essential part of the armed forces is secured through private contracts. Feudalism is a method of government, and a way of securing the forces necessary to preserve that method of government.

This is not as narrow a definition as it seems. The possessors of political and military power will naturally mold their society to fit their own needs. They will manipulate the economy so that they get the greatest share of production; they will, as wealthy consumers, influence writers and artists; they will establish standards to which their

society must conform. Thus, it is perfectly legitimate to speak of feudal society, or a feudal age, if we remember that it was the political-
military structure which made the society and the age feudal.

On the other hand, if we try a wider definition, feudalism becomes
an amorphous term. The most usual attempt to broaden the definition
of feudalism stresses social and economic factors; in its simplest form
it would find the essence of feudalism in the exploitation of an agricultural population by a ruling group. That this occurred in the feudal
society of Western Europe is certainly true; it is equally true that it
occurred in many other societies as well, both before and after the
Middle Ages. Nor can we say that this situation is typical of all pre-
industrial societies, and that therefore the socioeconomic definition of
feudalism is useful in marking a universal stage of economic development. . . . A definition which can include societies as disparate as
those of the Ancient Middle East, the late Roman Empire, medieval
Europe, the southern part of the United States in the nineteenth century, and the Soviet Union in the 1930s is not much use in historical
analysis.

In the latter paragraph Strayer is disagreeing with Marc Bloch's
Feudal Society and the *Annales* school. And he exudes his hostility to
Marxist universalist theorizing, to which Bloch and the Annalists
subscribed. Strayer did not think Bloch was a first-rate medievalist.
He held Bloch's leanings toward Marxism in contempt. The problem
with Strayer's view of feudalism is not on the sociological but on the
cultural side. Feudalism became a way of looking at the world, a
model of existence blended in with (if it was not largely shaped by)
the church's hierarchical theories. Feudalism as a culture, a paradigm
of ecclesiastical perfectionism, a product of the artistic imagination, a
manifestation of personal sensibility, between 1000 and 1200, is not
given sufficient consideration in Strayer's analysis.

There is a similar problem with Strayer's splendid and much admired essay *On the Medieval Origins of the Modern State*. Strayer's other
books justified his gaining the presidency of the Medieval Academy.
It is this book that made him also president of the American Historical Association. Strayer says that the most important criterion for
the emergence of modern state building is "a shift in loyalty from
family, local community, or religious organization to the state and
the acquisition by the state of a moral authority to back up its institutional structure and its theoretical legal supremacy." The thesis is
vulnerable. The two sides of this statement do not jibe. The medieval

state *did* acquire a moral authority (of an uneven, unstable, and ill-defined kind, but let that pass) to back up its institutional structure and its theoretical legal supremacy. At the same time this moral authority did not succeed in making much of a shift from family, local community, or religious commitment. The two facets of political experience, the statist and the familial and communal ones, existed side by side, often in tension, sometimes in open conflict.

Indeed, a plausible argument may be made that the rise of the medieval state *increased* loyalty to family, local community, and religious organization in the thirteenth and fourteenth centuries. The novel power of the state and its reserved attachment to the crown and the royal family frightened major groups in society, which, in reaction to the threat of a sovereign, collectivizing state, accentuated their adhesion to family and local institutions and religious communities as a reactive means of security and salvation.

Ten years later, in *Philip the Fair*, Strayer actually came close to conceding this challenge to his thesis in *Origins*. He begins the last chapter of his book by acknowledging that "Philip accomplished much, but in so doing he put heavy strains on the loyalty of his subjects. . . . What was gained by force had to be preserved by force." Then Strayer backtracks and reverts to his familiar claim for a modernizing political revolution through the rise of a new secular religion of the monarchy: "The political leadership of the papacy had collapsed: the dream of a united western Christendom had vanished. . . . Though the arguments of political theorists reached only a few ears, there was general agreement that the king was responsible for the welfare and security of the realm."

There is much question begging here. It all depends what is meant by "welfare and security of the realm" and by "the king was responsible." There existed a consensus that the king was the natural leader of the people in war and responsible for defense of the realm. But even that traditional conception did not mean that there was widespread enthusiasm for the king's undertaking aggressive war that impinged on the lives of most of his subjects. Late medieval people, in the overwhelming majority in all social classes, wanted to live out their lives within their families, villages, communities, and châteaus. There is little evidence of their enthusiasm for the king's undertaking responsibility for their welfare and security in terms of daily life. They feared the king more than they loved or trusted him. The great majority of medieval people preferred the king to stay away from their lives. His involvement was always expensive and occasionally hazardous. Kingship as a vague idea was popular. But there was almost universal hostility to the actual intervention of the royal government in private, family, and communal existence.

To the end of his life Strayer could not shake off the elitist statism of Wilsonian progressivism, as confirmed and entrenched by the New Deal and as emotionally transformed into the highly polemical postwar cold war liberalism and its dream of American exceptionalist destiny. Cold war liberalism regarded the American state as virtuous. Strayer's limitation as a medievalist was a refusal to see that the bureaucratic state that he and his generation so much admired, while it did indeed make its beginnings in the Middle Ages, was powerfully resisted then by alternative cultures in European life—demotic, communal, emotional, personal, romantic, heretical, imaginative, liturgical. A great variety of alternative cultures resisted the rationalizing administration and law of the royal bureaucrats.

Strayer assumed the legitimacy, credibility, and winning capacity of the rationalizing statists in all times and places. Like Haskins, he projected back from the Wilsonian civil servants and lawyers to the royal administrators and attorneys of medieval France and England. They, too, were good guys. From 1935, the onset of the New Deal in its decisive formulation, to the mid-sixties, this was a dogma of Strayer's generation. There was much to support this optimistic political belief in the experience of his generation: the welfare and regulatory state, the victorious war, the postwar American hegemony and the world economic recovery under the aegis of the United States, and civil rights legislation. But the 1960s counterculture, the failure in Vietnam, the New Left, and then Reaganite antistatist conservatism—all showed that even in the twentieth century the tide does not always run with the statists and rationalizers and the palm of victory does not always come into their ambitious grasp.

The Wilsonian heritage was central in twentieth-century American life, but it was not the only voice, not the only culture, and after the Wilsonian establishment made a mess of Vietnam (as it had failed at Versailles), the way was open for expression of contrary voices first on the left and then on the right. Which of these contrary voices will ultimately prevail, if any, or whether the neo-Wilsonians will recover their composure and regain lost ground cannot be known in 1990. But in the later Middle Ages the resistance to statism, centralizing monarchy, legal and administrative systems, political imperialism, and judicial triumphalism was fierce and took the form of counterchurches, communal democracy, aristocratic ideology, mystical sensibility, and artistic creativity. Bureaucracy was often identified with classical tyranny and the reign of the antichrist.

Strayer's interpretation of the late Middle Ages was flawed by his resistance to recognizing the merit in the claim made by these enemies of statist rationalism. His contempt for the history of ideas prevented him from realizing the intense ideological opposition to both cold war liberalism and the medieval state.

Strayer could not see the alternative wind of the New Left blowing in his own history department, until all he worked to achieve as chairman for two decades was in shambles. He had quit the department chairmanship but was still around and highly influential when in 1963 he allowed his colleagues to give a senior chair to the Oxford social historian Lawrence Stone. Stone was a prominent British don and a scholar of formidable reputation. He was also a vehement disciple of the British Marxist historian and Labour party ideologist R. H. Tawney. Stone's wife happened to be the daughter of Robert Fawtier, the Sorbonne professor who had very generously assisted Strayer with his archival research on *Philip the Fair*. This weakened Strayer's resolve to oppose Stone's appointment. Once Stone became entrenched at Princeton, the department Strayer had so lovingly built up as the epitome of cold war liberalism applied to the past rapidly became a citadel of leftist ideology. Natalie Zemon Davis, whose interpretation echoed the doctrine of the Soviet theoretician of the Stalinist era Mikhail Bakhtin, was recruited from Berkeley.

In an academic profession steadily infiltrated by the 1968 generation that had failed at the barricades and instead determined to take over the university, Davis's celebrity carried her to the presidency of the American Historical Association. What especially distinguished her work on sixteenth-century France was her admiration for all manifestations of antistatist and socially irrational behavior, including juvenile delinquency, petty crime, and familial disorder, as structurally representative of antiestablishment, protomodern revolution. The boisterous behavior of young men at Carnival (Mardi Gras) time was viewed by Davis (as by Bakhtin) as social protest.

Coinciding with the teachings of neo-Marxist Frankfurt school of critical theory and also inspired by the leftist school of symbolic anthropology headed by Clifford Geertz, Davis broadened the Marxist Revolution into cultural and affective upheavals. She became one of the editors of the *Radical History Review*, the most far-left historical journal in the English language. Compared with her, Marc Bloch was a moderate. Then the appointment of a series of Brits finished the process of leftist transformation of the Princeton history department and its emergence as the American center of the Annalist school, as Fernand Braudel enthusiastically recognized in the mid-1970s.

In Strayer's perception of the Middle Ages, rationality and order are the cardinal values to be identified and praised. In Davis's view of the sixteenth century, irrationality, disorder, and delinquency are the focus of attention and the behavior patterns to be endorsed. Davis merited her academic celebrity. Hers was the most self-consciously deconstructive American mind ever to apply itself to the study of early European society. She was the great anti-Wilsonian historical thinker.

By the time Strayer published *Philip the Fair* in 1980, the Princeton history department was ideologically remote from the one that he had capped off building in the late fifties. If the winds of discourse can change so rapidly and unpredictably in Strayer's own academic community, how naive and blind it was for him not to see how vibrant and deeply rooted were the antistatist cultures and irrational ideologies of late medieval Europe. Just as cold war liberalism suffered a humiliating retreat after 1968, so did the rationalizing statism that Strayer and Haskins identified with medieval politics go into rapid late medieval decline. This decline was due not only to the rash overreaching on the part of the French and English royal administrations (Strayer conceded that much, but it was only part of the story) but also to widespread ideological and emotional rebellion against the rationalizing and centralizing political systems. The great defect of the Wilsonian mind was to assume the inevitable triumph of political rationality in history. Irrationalism, too, has its victories and its satisfactions.

Strayer's paradigm of the trajectory of the late medieval state may be applied to the fate of the Wilsonian rationalists in the American university. Just as the French and English monarchies suffered the consequences of reckless abandonment of moral limitations and lost credibility, so did arrogance of power also erode the effectiveness of Wilsonians like Joe Strayer in the 1960s. They had been in control of American universities for so long—ever since Haskins in the mid-1920s dominated the foyer of Washington's Mayflower Hotel during academic conferences—that they could not conceive of being supplanted by ideologues who were committed to an alternative, much more radical set of values. Strayer and Wilsonian rationalists let power slip away from them in the late sixties and seventies.

Strayer spoke for a generation of medievalists in the United States and Britain who were fascinated by what they regarded as the distinctive quality of Western civilization, which they saw rooted in the emergence of rationalism in the medieval world. Already in the 1920s Haskins's colleague at Harvard, the former collaborator with Bertrand Russell in mathematical philosophy, and now a pioneering philosopher of science in the American Cambridge, Alfred North Whitehead had found in the rationality of the twelfth- and thirteenth-century Latin scholastics not only the preservation of the peculiarly Greek way of thinking about the natural world but anticipations of the scientific revolution of the late sixteenth and seventeenth centuries.

Another transplanted European to the Untied States, Robert S. Lopez, at Yale, came to this modernization theory and European triumphalism from his studies in medieval commerce. The son of a proscribed socialist leader in Mussolini's Italy, Lopez completely on his own re-created himself from the hazardous career of radical left journalist to historian of the medieval economy and won a fellowship to the University of Wisconsin at Madison in 1938. By the mid-fifties he held a senior chair at Yale. In Lopez's view, principally in Italy in the late tenth century there occurred an economic takeoff that created a role model for all other societies that followed. Lynn White, who had been Strayer's professional rival at Princeton in the mid-1930s before undertaking the presidency of a California women's college, reemerged as a medieval historian at UCLA in the 1960s and stressed the rationality represented by the technological advances of medieval Europe. All these writers were simply applying in extended areas of the history of science, economy, and technology the primacy of rationality that Haskins and most eloquently Strayer perceived in medieval government, administration, and law.

The Haskins-Strayer focus on administrative history of the high and late Middle Ages has not lost its potential value. Intellectually, however, if the American tradition of administrative history is again to open new vistas on the medieval world, it has to embrace additional insights garnered from sociological theory and literary studies. A triumphant updating of administrative history was achieved by the British scholar Michael T. Clanchy in *From Memory to Written Record* (1979). This is an exciting account of the development of medieval English royal administration from the perspective of the transition from an oral to a literate society and with focus on the language, literate, and communicative capacity and on the writing styles and materials of medieval government. This approach had been suggested in 1950 in an overly modest and concise book that Strayer greatly admired, V. H. Galbraith's *Studies in the Public Records*. Clanchy's is an elaborate study in the grand manner of how the transition from orality to literacy shaped medieval government and vice versa. It is, therefore, a breakthrough kind of sociology of medieval government. Clanchy was an innovator in another way. In the mid-eighties he abruptly gave up his tenured position at Glasgow and moved to London, without an immediate job prospect, so that his wife could accept an attractive professional opportunity as head of a girls' school. This egalitarian frame of mind was as remote from the attitudes of Strayer's generation as the frenetic speculations of medieval millenarians and mystics from the secular instrumentalism of the Wilsonian school of medieval studies.

CHAPTER EIGHT

AFTER THE FALL

MICHAEL DAVID KNOWLES AND
ÉTIENNE HENRY GILSON

I

ABSOLUTIZING THE MIDDLE AGES

The Roman Catholic Church in the late nineteenth century—from the papacy and the College of Cardinals in Rome through the bishops and abbots in various countries of Western Europe and the Americas down to teachers and scholars in Catholic colleges and universities— faced the very difficult and complex question of how and to what extent it was going to absorb and legitimate modern secular learning and science. This problem was an unfortunate legacy of the French Revolution. Toward the Enlightenment of the late eighteenth century, churchmen in France and the papacy itself had developed an ambivalent but by no means negative attitude. Then came the French Revolution, the secularization of the church in France, the confiscation of its property, and the declaration of war between the Roman church and the revolutionary state. Napoleon Bonaparte patched up an accommodation with Rome, and the French church regained a large measure of its wealth and influence in national life after the temporary restoration of the French monarchy in 1815. But the Catholic Church in the nineteenth century—until the pontificate of the reforming pope Leo XIII in the last two decades of the century, the most important reformer in the modern church until Pope John XXIII in the 1960s—adopted hostile and reactionary attitudes toward modern liberal democracy and the learning and science with which it was associated. To put it colloquially but on the whole truthfully, for close to a century, from the 1790s until the 1880s, the papacy "stonewalled" modern culture. Occasional efforts to break ranks with this

287

negativism by Catholic scholars, especially in Germany in the middle decades of the century, were sternly condemned by Rome.

This Catholic negativism and anti-intellectualism, of course, meant that the church was not interested in the scholarly study of the Middle Ages. Indeed, it generally looked upon the newly developing historical sciences with suspicion and hostility. The papacy did not want to see itself as a historical institution—that is, one that evolved and changed over time. It wanted to see itself as created instantaneously by the designation in the Gospel of Matthew of Christ to Simon Peter, allegedly the first bishop of Rome: ". . . thou art Peter [the rock], and upon this rock I will build my church . . . and whatsoever thou shalt bind on earth shall be bound in heaven: and whatsoever thou shalt loose on earth shall be loosed in heaven." The study of history, particularly of the early and medieval eras of the church, could only raise awkward questions about this belief in the instantaneous creation and perpetually unchanging character of a papal-centered church.

Works on the Middle Ages written within this Catholic doctrinal code were therefore only dogmatic displays projected back into the past and envisioning an essentially unchanging medieval church and papacy. An exemplary effort of this kind was the history of the papacy by the German conservative Catholic professor at the Austrian Catholic University of Innsbruck Ludwig Pastor, whose multivolume history of the papacy in the late Middle Ages and early modern eras began to appear in 1886. Nobody, including Catholic scholars, would read it today for other than insight into the curious mind-set of premodern Catholicism. The post-Vatican II multivolume *History of the Church* under the editorship of the distinguished German Swiss liberal Catholic scholar Hubert Jedin in 1973 characterized Pastor's work, in its time applauded in Rome and today gathering dust on the shelves of Catholic colleges on both sides of the Atlantic, as intellectually and heuristically useless. Pastor, said Jedin and his colleagues, was "undisturbed by all intellectual developments around him, and unconcerned about the changes in historical theories."

The liberating mandate for Catholic historical studies, including the study of the Middle Ages, came with the principle enunciated by the reforming pope Leo XIII in 1883: "The first law for writing history demands that nothing false be said; furthermore that the truth not be hidden; and lastly that any suspicion of either favoritism or hostility to Rome be avoided." This charter of liberty for Catholic historians was, however, accompanied in Leo's mind by a conviction that an honest, factually grounded account of the medieval church and papacy would result in an overwhelmingly positive view, arising from the church's conversion of the heathen barbarian invaders, its preservation of the classical legacy, and the papal struggle against the menacing sovereignty of the medieval emperors. There were individual popes whose demerits could not be covered up, Leo XIII allowed, such as the notorious Borgia pope Alexander VI, at the end of the fifteenth century. But Pope Leo was highly optimistic that close study of the medieval church would and should be supportive of the church's salutary role in civilization as well as religion. Those cardinals who feared research in medieval studies he dismissed as "small minds."

The great reforming pope made another crucial contribution to the shaping of the Middle Ages in twentieth-century Catholic culture. Leo XIII legitimated the neoscholastic movement in the church—that is, the push, starting in France and Germany, to revive the scholastic theology and philosophy of the Middle Ages, particularly the doctrines of St. Thomas Aquinas, as central writings in Catholic higher and secondary education. Neoscholasticism before 1900 was still doctrinal rather than historical—that is, it initially made little or no effort to study the Thomist and other scholastic writings within the original medieval context, as part of the intellectual and cultural history of the Middle Ages, as part of a developing medieval mentality. But so long as the papacy gave its approval to widespread and earnest resumption of the study of Thomist and other scholastic writings in Catholic schools, this set the stage for a historical inquiry into medieval scholasticism. That in turn required an investigation into the curriculum and organization of medieval universities, which had been the institutional settings for Aquinas and the other Schoolmen. Particularly in German Catholic learned circles at the turn of the century, this kind of research into medieval academic life was beginning.

Like Pope John XXIII in the 1960s, Leo XIII took risks and roused more expectations and experiments than the church hierarchy felt comfortable with and the laity could easily absorb. After Leo XIII's death in 1903, there was (as was the case also after John XXIII's death in 1963) a reaction, a conservatizing, quasi-repressive turn in Rome's cultural policy that was not fully corrected until the Council of Vatican II in the early sixties. In France, Germany, Britain, and the United States (especially in Baltimore), in response to Leo's cultural liberalization of the church, there had been an explosive advance among a vanguard group of clergy and some laymen toward integrating Catholicism with modern thought. This controversial trend—termed modernism in church circles—inspired the start-up in Catholic colleges and other research centers of a critical study of the early church. This development in turn revived very old disputes, going back to the thirteenth century itself, on the nature and organization of the church of Jesus, his immediate Apostles, and the initial generations of Christians. It was evident soon enough that the straight-line projection of the triumphalist, papal-centered, bishop-dominated church back into the beginnings of Christianity was highly questionable.

This was not just a historical or scholarly issue. As in the Middle Ages, the image of a nonhierarchical, or less hierarchical, apostolic and early church raised questions about the authenticity and legitimacy of the way the church was now organized. This questioning had the very disturbing implication of giving comfort to liberal Protestants' hostility to the legitimacy of papal authority, and it raised the specter of bringing back late medieval demands for democratization of the church, to transform it from a hierarchy of authority (magisterium) into an egalitarian community of the faithful. The condemned spiritual Franciscans in the early fourteenth century had articulated such an image of religious democracy. Therefore, Leo XIII's successor, Pope Pius X, put on the brakes heavily to stop the incipient intellectual and spiritual revolution that was loosely called Catholic modernism. He condemned it as heresy in 1907. The work of the most distinguished Catholic historian of the early church, Louis Duchesne, was unembarrassedly put on the Index of Prohibited Books in 1912, even though Father Duchesne continued to hold a senior position in a clerical institution in Rome until his death in 1922. A chill descended on Catholic historical scholarship, and repressive intellectual guidelines were promulgated that were not extensively withdrawn until the 1960s. They have been partly reimposed, with respect to the teaching of theology and sexual ethics, under John Paul II in the 1980s.

As a result of these starts and stops in the modernization of Catholic culture, rigid codes readily emerged for the way Catholic scholars were supposed to interpret the Middle Ages. It had to be a very defensive approach to the church's role. An extremely positive view of the continuity of a benignly arrayed papal power was prescribed. Catholics could write about the Middle Ages, but only in ways that made the modern church and papacy, held to be the direct continuator of the medieval institution, look very good. Catholic scholars in their invention of the Middle Ages were not to say things that would bring the church and papacy at any time into disrepute or to raise questions about the absolute authority of the papacy or universal applicability of canon law, the merit of religious orders, or the wisdom and learning of medieval Schoolmen. In short, nothing bad about the Middle Ages was to be articulated so as to give comfort to critics of the Catholic Church.

Leo XIII's confidence that writing medieval history, or studying any aspect of medieval culture and society, would help the modern church now took on the cast of a prescriptive code. This prejudicial Catholic sententious approach to the medieval world, the Jedin-edited post-Vatican II liberal Catholic *History of the Church* in 1979 called "the absolutizing of the Middle Ages." Such absolutizing holds residual respect in Catholic medieval scholarship today.

The history of medieval studies since 1907 in Catholic circles is therefore focused on the questions of how, why, and to what extent this absolutizing, apologetic interpretation prescribed by ecclesiastical authority in the early twentieth century has been modified. It would, of course, be unfair to specify this without noting that similar absolutizing—prejudicial, propagandistic—interpretations are the core of the African-American studies, feminist studies, and Jewish studies that today flourish in our colleges, are pointed to with pride by university presidents, and are readily supported by the National Endowment for the Humanities and the great private foundations. It would also be unfair and lacking in subtlety and insight to divide all Catholic scholars into two polarized groups: those who absolutize (strongly defend and sentimentalize the medieval papacy and church) and those who take a more independent, complex, and sophisticated approach. Since the late 1960s the truly dogmatic Catholic absolutizers have been a relatively small group. Their publications list is short. The only work of old-fashioned absolutizing of the Middle Ages in recent decades to command a large audience is that of a French cleric, Henry Daniel-Rops. His anodyne survey of the medieval church was a best seller in France in the late 1950s and gained a significant audience and surprisingly serious attention in the United States. In the post-Vatican II upheavals and bewilderments, it was undoubtedly a nostalgic comfort for Catholic laity to read once again about the systematically wonderful medieval church under benign and firm papal leadership.

Instead of using a simple paradigm of Catholic interpreters of the Middle Ages as falling on the two sides of absolutizers and truth seekers, we should specify that what all Catholic inventing of the

Middle Ages has in common is a sense of "after the fall." There are three falls that Catholic historians are responding to within their imaginings of the medieval world. First, *The Fall of Man:* This consists of Adam's rebellion, the expulsion from Eden, and the mark of sin that falls on human nature. This means the impotence of man to merit salvation without God's grace, transmitted directly to the individual soul as well as through the church as the indispensable (but not exclusive) dispenser of God's gift of salvation. How is this theology to be turned into history? Certainly since St. Augustine, perhaps since St. Paul, Christian thinkers have ruminated on this question. They come out with a variety of historical judgments, ranging from the conventional one that the medieval church gave the means of cultural as well as sacramental salvation to its members to the more radical, far less optimistic opinion that the mark of sin, the flawed inheritance of Adam and Cain, so devastatingly corrupts human nature as to make human beings, including medieval men and women, incapable of durably creating and sustaining beneficial institutions. Following this theology, institutionalization, reform, doing social good are likely to be and were in the Middle Ages defeated by the innate defects of human nature.

The Fall of the Roman Empire: The disintegration of the Western Roman Empire and the loss of the imperial power of Rome over the Latin-speaking world in the fifth and sixth centuries provided the opportunity for the Catholic Church to undertake its missionary and educational work and become the crucible of medieval civilization. This is the standard Catholic view. But there are downsides, problems to this development, too, that are encapsulated in the polemical slogan of the third-century anti-Roman North African Christian leader Tertullian: "What has Athens to do with Jerusalem?" By preserving classical civilization, the Latin church perpetuated Roman hierarchy and slavery in the West and a propensity to regard imperial centralization (increasingly now through the Roman church) as a historical goal. Why was the social and political thought of the early medieval church so derivative from the authoritarianism and inequality of the Roman Empire? And why did the papacy of the thirteenth century reassert this Roman legal and political doctrine in the face of bitter opposition from many of its most idealistic members? Why did the church believe that preserving Roman despotism and inequality after the fall of Rome was central to its social mission? These are difficult questions for Catholic students of the Middle Ages.

The Fall of the Medieval Church: Every Catholic who writes about

the Middle Ages is haunted by the cataclysmic outcome of the history of the medieval church: the Reformation or, as the Germans also
call it in a better term, *die Glaubenspaltung* ("the division of faith").
The depressing outcome of medieval ecclesiastical history and late
medieval intellectual development was the separation of a third of the
German-speaking people of Europe, about 90 percent of the English-
speaking people, more than half the Swiss, and nearly all the Dutch
and Scandinavian peoples from the Catholic Church. Not only were
gross numbers and territories lost, but also many of the best-edu-
cated, affluent, and urbanized populations of Europe withdrew from
the authority of Rome and furthermore used their Lutheran, Calvinist, and Anglican religions as bases for distinctive cultures quite different from that of the Counterreformation Baroque world that stayed
with Catholicism. Why and how did this great disaster happen? How
deep into the religion and culture of the late Middle Ages are the
roots of the Reformation? Why did such fanatical hatred develop in
the separated countries among educated and affluent people toward
the popular culture of Roman Catholicism? These are grave questions
that Catholic medievalists had to confront, once they got beyond the
devils-Luther-Calvin-and-Henry-VIII-made-them-do-it thesis, which
was fashionable among Catholic intellectuals at the beginning of this
century. Since the 1960s or even earlier demonization has not been a
creditable avenue in the more ambitious Catholic universities to understanding the fall of the medieval church.

These three great falls were the parameters that all Catholic interpretation of the Middle Ages had to operate within. All writing in
medieval studies by committed Roman Catholics is conditioned by
these three falls within the general supervision over scholarship exercised by the church. Since the 1940s to an appreciable extent, and
certainly since Vatican II in the early 1960s, Catholic scholars have
enjoyed a very high degree of intellectual freedom. But this freedom
still takes place within the boundaries of an ultimately authoritarian
institution. Whatever Catholic scholars say about the Middle Ages
can still raise doctrinal conflict and disciplinary response within the
church. It is not so much that since the 1960s there is likely to be a
mandate from Rome to keep silent about or withdraw an interpretation. It is that the Catholic intellectual world is sharply divided into
ideological groups, and vanguard, unconventional opinions are likely
to draw negative responses or even harsh judgments from more conservative and traditional Catholic scholars, publicists, and officials.

Since 1929 a church-sponsored Institute of Medieval Studies has existed on the campus of the University of Toronto. It has drawn support from the church and private sources. A research and training center of medieval studies of clerical provenance located at a state university would likely be considered unconstitutional in the United States, but in Canada it is not only legal but politically popular. The Pontifical Institute (as it may be called since 1939, when it received a full license from Rome) is effective at training students to read ecclesiastical Latin and medieval handwriting. It has published carefully edited texts of medieval theology and hagiography. But its interpretive work—outside the noncontroversial field of economic history—has been relatively modest. A sensitivity prevails that the great issues of medieval culture are highly relevant to the church of today. It is not so much that censorship is imposed from without on the faculty and doctoral students of the Toronto institute as it is that they are naturally hypersensitive to the provocative implications of almost anything they may say about the great religious and cultural issues of the medieval world.

The Pontifical Institute from its start has been distinguished by its interdisciplinary orientations. Lately the institute has started to concentrate on the use of language and the levels of literacy in medieval Europe. This project is promising. But it remains to be seen how far it will go when it begins to reach beyond technical analysis to impinge on the more general and controversial questions of medieval culture. Because of the deterioration of doctoral programs in medieval studies in the United States during the great academic depression of the 1970s and 1980s, the Toronto institute, which has a distinguished faculty and superb library, has attracted superior American students in recent years, and its importance as a center of advanced training and research in medieval studies has significantly increased.

The other institute of medieval studies sponsored by the church in English-speaking North America has been located since the late 1940s on the campus of the most celebrated Catholic university in the United States, Notre Dame, in South Bend, Indiana. The history of the Medieval Institute at Notre Dame has been disastrous. The institute never succeeded in obtaining a distinguished Catholic scholar to serve as its director. Scholars find the atmosphere in South Bend too clerical, partisan, and confining. In the 1970s Notre Dame tried to get Bernard McGinn of the University of Chicago to take over the leadership of its Medieval Institute. McGinn, a former priest, and his wife went to Notre Dame for a year in a tryout and fled back to Chicago. Although both are very devout Catholics, they could not abide the Notre Dame ambience, and McGinn could not see himself happily continuing there his important work on medieval millenary religious movements. It was not the threat of actual censorship—although that could happen—but the choking impact of Irish Catholic culture that McGinn feared, even though he had emerged out of that same culture and in his younger days had served for several years as a diocesan priest and teacher in a parochial high school in Staten Island, New York.

Any Catholic scholar interpreting the Middle Ages therefore begins with a certain problem of working within the confines of institutionalized Catholicism and its residual investment in absolutizing the Middle Ages. This is certainly not a uniquely Roman Catholic problem. There are strictures on freedom of expression in other religious groups as well. A faculty member of a southern college, even a state university, has to be very careful what he or she says about evangelical or Pentecostal Christianity. We all know about Salman Rushdie's problem with the mullahs. In 1980 the chairman of the New York University board of trustees, the well-known media baron and liberal Democrat Laurence Tisch, vetoed the appointment as director of the Jewish studies program at New York University of Rabbi Irving Greenberg, the most exciting and innovative Jewish theological mind in New York City, on what can arguably be termed doctrinal grounds. Tisch construed Greenberg's theology as a threat to upper-middle-class Jewish culture and behavior. Perhaps only in the world of northern Protestantism and Anglicanism is there truly freedom of thought within religious groups and institutions. Why that should be is a very long, complicated, and perhaps still not fully explicable story.

But tension, confinement, and conflict over sectarian beliefs and closeness exercised by communal authorities have positive outcomes in terms of intellectual creativity that are not easy for total intellectual freedom to approximate. Repression has its cultural victories no less than liberty. It is precisely because the burden of the past is disseminated through the living church of today that any assertions about the Middle Ages by a Roman Catholic has doctrinal as well as historical significance. Any publication based on research and interpretation about the Middle Ages is of central value to Catholic education and spiritual counseling. The Middle Ages are for the church not just out there; they are very much in here. For the church, the Middle Ages are a contemporary issue as well as a historical image. Therefore, the Catholic inventing of the Middle Ages carries with it a sharpness, an immediacy, and an emotional evocation that are of a very distinctive quality. This condition of communal significance and personal relevance is prevalent in the work of all Catholic medievalists, but it is best represented in the life and ideas of David Knowles (1896–1974), who was an English Benedictine monk and priest and from the age of forty-four also a Cambridge University professor. From the early 1930s to the late 1950s Knowles wrote a four-volume history of the monastic and other religious orders that is the outstanding accomplishment in medieval studies by a Catholic in this century. It is also one of the enduring works of historical literature in the English language, placing Knowles in the pantheon with Gibbon, Macaulay, and Maitland.

II

THE REBELLIOUS MONK

On a hot Wednesday afternoon in the first week of July 1959, I was rushing on foot across London from a hotel in Bayswater, where I was staying with my wife and ten-month-old son, to the Institute for Historical Research at the University of London's campus in Bloomsbury. I was twenty minutes late for my appointment for tea in the lounge of the Institute with the regius professor of history at Cambridge, Dom David Knowles. ("Dom," from the Latin *dominus* ["master"], is a term of address used in Britain for Catholic monks and priests.) He was waiting for me. With his clerical collar, I had no difficulty finding him as soon as I entered the room.

The two photographs and a sketch from life that I have seen of Knowles do not do justice to his physical appearance. He was a short man with a thin, ascetic face and a sinewy, strong body. In his younger days he played a lot of cricket, and he loved long walks in the countryside. His body, while thin, was far from emaciated; it was the body of an athlete, and he walked quickly and vigorously. His face was dominated by wide, piercing eyes and a sensuous mouth. His physical appearance reflected the complexity of the man, the ambivalence, the polarity, between the status of being a withdrawn, disciplined monk of religious profession and the personality profile of aggressiveness and determination that bothered and frightened both his monastic and academic colleagues. Dom David Knowles inspired fear as well as love in his associates.

Knowles was not a wispy, withdrawn monk. He had a loud, clear voice, and he did not suffer fools gladly. He could become very aggressive and outspoken when aroused, a not rare occurrence. A cover story had been developed in Catholic Church and Oxbridge circles to hide the truth of the conflicts, passions, and upheavals of Father David Knowles's life and the curious circumstances of his domestic arrangements. I heard the cover story several times while I was a student at Oxford in 1954 and 1955, and it went like this: Knowles had been a monk at Downside Abbey, near Bath, the largest, oldest (two centuries), and most prestigious Benedictine abbey in England. He was the leading scholar and intellectual in the Downside community and the editor of its journal, the *Downside Review*, which under his aegis had become the leading Catholic intellectual journal in Britain (that part of the cover story was true). In 1940, the story continued, Knowles published his masterpiece, *The Monastic Order in England* (to 1216), and vaulted to the top rank of medieval historians in Britain (true). Then, according to the specious story, Knowles slowly had a falling-out with his abbot because of an offer of a teaching position he received from Cambridge in 1944. At first the abbot allowed Knowles to take leave from residence at Downside and teach at Cambridge. But when, in 1946, he was offered the chair of medieval history at Cambridge, the abbot demurred and insisted that Knowles decline the offer and return to the abbey. Knowles refused, and a clerical crisis developed since he was bound in his monastic vow to absolute obedience to the abbot. Father David, so the cover story went, appealed to Rome, and the pope dispensed with Knowles's vow of obedience to the abbot; he was able to stay in Cambridge, where in 1953 he was appointed regius professor by the prime minister, Winston Churchill, and became the head of the history faculty. A nice story, but a falsification of the time and cause of the split between Knowles and his monastic community and the bitter quarrel with the abbot (who was never, in fact, opposed to Knowles's teaching at Cambridge). Furthermore, the cover story completely hid the most important personal experience of the last thirty-five years of Knowles's life: His relationship with Dr. Elizabeth Kornerup, a Swedish psychiatrist living in London.

There are four accounts of Knowles's life. The first is by William Abel Pantin, the Oxford don who served as a research assistant on one of his major books. Pantin's account was published in 1963 on the occasion of Knowles's mandatory retirement from the regius chair in 1961 and the presentation to him two years later of a volume of his collected essays, *The Historian and Character*. To this volume every medievalist of standing in Britain and several in the United States subscribed ahead of publication, and Pantin produced a "Curriculum Vitae" as an introduction. Here the cover-up is handled in amnesiac fashion: The break with Downside is totally ignored. Secondly, there is the boiler plate obituary essay in the *Proceedings of the British Academy* following Knowles's death. It was written by his student and literary executor Professor Christopher Brooke of Cambridge (Brooke's wife, Rosalind, was also Knowles's student). It is a reticent piece of work, mentioning but not explaining the break with Downside. Elizabeth Kornerup's name appears in passing, but her relationship to Father David Knowles is not explained. So here are two of the leading British medievalists at Oxbridge judiciously covering up the circumstances of Knowles's stormy life. He himself left behind a manuscript autobiography. This Brooke suppressed. It will not be published before 2004, nor is access allowed to the manuscript. How Brooke can reconcile this suppression of biographical material sixteen years after the death of the subject with a Cambridge history professor's obligation to his discipline, I do not know.

Finally, in 1979, the truth began to emerge, at least in part. Dom Adrian Morey, a monk and medieval scholar at Downside, five years Knowles's junior, who knew him well in the early days and, after a break of twenty years, again in the last dozen years of his life, published a memoir that is more than that: It is a brief critical biography, making extensive use of the Downside Abbey archives and focusing on the break between Knowles and his community in the 1930s. Morey's book is written not without sympathy and admiration for Knowles, but mainly with a stress on partisan defense of the monastery and the abbots who had to deal with Knowles's psychological and ideological rebellion. The relationship with Elizabeth Kornerup gets more detailed treatment than in any other published source, but since it is based on the presumption that the relationship was "innocent" (a strange monastic word—Dom Morey means celibate, asexual) and is very hostile to her, its value is limited. Finally, in 1986, Maurice Cowling, a colleague in modern history at Peterhouse, the Cambridge college where Knowles worked and lived for twenty years, published an insightful, concise, and independent assessment that is in some ways quite hostile, while yet admiring of Knowles's ideas and scholarly accomplishments. For several years before he became a Cambridge don in 1953, Cowling was a London journalist, and there is (in refreshing contrast with the Brooke-Pantin boiler plate and cover-up) a certain direct honesty about Cowling's essay. For example:

"Knowles was obsessed by Elizabeth Kornerup. . . . For the remainder of his life, he was inseparable from her."

David Knowles was born Michael Clive Knowles, the only surviving child of an affluent mid-level Birmingham manufacturer, who produced, among other things, all the needles for the phonographs bearing the label of His Master's Voice, the best-selling English phonograph before the 1950s. Both his parents were converts from evangelical Protestant Christianity to Roman Catholicism. This is very important in Knowles's life and ideas. He did not come from an old Catholic English gentry family (such as is described by Evelyn Waugh in *Brideshead Revisited*) or from Irish immigrant stock. His family had converted to Catholicism (not a rare occurrence at the end of the nineteenth century) because of a genuine religious search for something indefinable. Sixty years earlier John Henry Newman made the same spiritual pilgrimage for the same reasons, in his case from Low Church Anglicanism. Such Protestant converts to Catholicism had a starry-eyed view of the Catholic Church and sought in Catholicism something more dramatic, charismatic, and personally inspiring than the somewhat ramshackle, poorly led, and undereducated Catholic Church in England could reasonably deliver. Newman was disappointed, but he kept his new faith and pilgrimed on and at last became a cardinal. Some of the same tension and disappointment, communicated to Michael Clive Knowles from his parents, may be seen as casting a great shadow on his life. He wanted the Catholic Church to live up to the highest conceivable level of spirituality and learning. But the personnel of the Catholic Church in England was not destined for this kind of perfection, nor did the church even have the material resources to fulfill these maximal expectations. That is the first major source of conflict in Knowles's life. It is as if a very bright son of a pharmacist in Des Moines ended up at Iowa State and was unhappy because it wasn't Harvard, Berkeley, or Amherst.

His mother so loved Michael Clive Knowles that using weak health as an excuse, she kept him at home until he was ten years old and had him educated (sloppily) by governesses. He had no siblings and no school friends and was isolated in a large house with his mother all day. When he came out of this arrested personal development and began to develop his social personality (as happened in his late thirties), the results were explosive. This emotional upheaval shook Downside Abbey to its foundations and generated a crisis that threatened to become an international scandal for the church. Before he went away to school, young Knowles read a large selection of English

literature and history. His early schooling was therefore largely autodidactic and developed in him a fine sensitivity to English literature
and its intrinsic style. In this respect, there was similarity between
him and the man who later appointed him to the regius chair, Winston Churchill, who was also deeply read in English literature through
his own youthful efforts, which likewise gave him a remarkable ear
for nuance of style.

Downside Abbey ran the best Catholic private school in England,
and this is where Knowles was sent at the age of thirteen. That he
had a very hard adjustment—not surprisingly—is indicated by his
staying home for several months after his first term on the excuse
that he had injured his knee. But Knowles in his adolescence was
emerging as a very strong person both physically and psychologically, with an unshakable conviction of his superior intellectual capacities (only slowly recognized by his teachers) and his special calling
by God—a not unusual outcome for the son of a devout family who
was lonely and reclusive. By eighteen, in 1914, he had—apparently
with his parents' approval, although none of his biographers discusses
this important point—taken his first vows as a monk at Downside.
As Dom Morey points out, such early taking of monastic vows would
never be allowed today. This was a reflection of the naiveté and disorder in the Catholic Church in England at the time and also of
Downside's peculiar status within the Roman Catholic Church in
England. It had asserted the right to become completely autonomous
in the original medieval Benedictine manner, formally subject only to
distant and rare supervision from Rome. It also was a hotbed of converts to the church from among middle-class Protestant families. Three
Downside abbots in succession in the late nineteenth and early twentieth centuries were converts. There was, therefore, a certain air of
privilege and preciousness about Downside Abbey, an ambience of
idiosyncrasy and extreme autonomy, that also influenced the shaping
of Knowles's mind and temperament.

If Knowles as a monk exhibited independence, autonomy, ambition, and contentiousness, these were qualities that also characterized
Downside's culture and could easily be reproduced in exaggerated
form in its most brilliant and admired brother. It is highly significant
that when Father David Knowles had his smashup with his order in
the mid-1930s, the abbot at the time was a novel outsider. He was
neither a convert nor even a Downside school old boy but had instead
been educated in religious life mostly in France. So the quarrel was
from one perspective a quarrel between Downside traditions of in-

dependence and idiosyncrasy and the more disciplined, ordered, and centralizing attitudes of Continental Catholicism.

It was the tradition for monks to take a new first name on their entry into religious life, symbolic of their spiritual rebirth. So Michael Clive became David, and it was under the name of David Knowles that his first books, including *The Monastic Order* in 1940, were published. Later, as a Cambridge professor in the 1950s, Knowles tried a compromise and for several years signed himself as "M. D. Knowles" before going back to his simple monastic name in the last dozen years of his life. The names people call themselves are symptomatic of their conception of themselves, so Knowles's naming history is significant.

Knowles did not serve in the First World War. Many Downside alumni in his class did and were killed in action. Knowles could have served as a noncombatant, for example, as in the ambulance corps. Instead he spent the war as a student at Cambridge. It is not clear why he did not serve. From his active participation in cricket and rugger games at Downside, he seems to have been physically robust enough. This failure to serve in the war, in which many of his friends died, placed a pressure of guilt upon him and with it the conviction that his service to God as a monk and priest had to be of a very special and burdensome kind to justify his survival unscathed from the war era.

Nowadays it is possible that an abbot might have seen in Knowles's early life the roots of many psychological problems, certainly cause for propensity to extremism. Any abbot today might have questioned whether the monastic life was appropriate for Knowles, whether he had a sufficiently stable psychological profile for the discipline, indeed the ostensible boredom of monastic life. But in the England of the second decade of the twentieth century, such questions were not asked, especially in intellectually conservative Roman Catholic circles.

Knowles did brilliantly at Cambridge, getting a first (highest honors) in both philosophy and classics as well as winning a prize in English literature. The first in classics was an especially remarkable achievement because he had not received a thorough secondary school training in Latin and Greek and he had to do a lot of remedial work on his own. Obviously he was a devout, idealistic, but very resourceful young man with an excellent mind and unusual writing skills. Nowadays, again, church officers might question whether early and continual residence in a cloistered monastery was good for this kind of person and whether the church could afford to sequester such an extraordinarily talented young intellect. Nowadays someone like Knowles, even if in a religious order, might be sent off for several years' study in theology toward a doctorate at the Gregorian University in Rome. Instead Knowles returned from Cambridge to Downside, was ordained a priest, and except for a few months' desultory study in theology at Rome, entered the normal life of the Downside community. He taught in the abbey school, which in the postwar years was steadily growing in size and fashionable reputation among affluent Catholic families as far away as Poland. He became the editor of the *Downside Review*, the journal of theology and church history published by the abbey. Under his aegis in the late 1920s and early 1930s—when he not only published his own essays but exhibited his remarkable skill as an editor—the *Downside Review* recovered recently lost ground and became the leading Catholic journal of serious opinion in England. Although Knowles would have preferred to be and should have remained a teacher in the school, he was instead given the important office of novice master—that is, made the spiritual counselor and intellectual guide of the youngest monks.

In 1926 Knowles published his first book, *The American Civil War*. This two-hundred page book found an elite publisher—the prestigious Clarendon division of the Oxford University Press—and it was certainly an accomplishment for an Englishman in the mid-1920s to write a coherent and for the time relatively well-informed narrative of the American Civil War. In later years, after he had become famous and a prominent professor at Cambridge, Knowles explained that he had written the book because of his interest in historical personalities. The American Civil War had some outstanding ones, so that he thereby practiced his skill in character description. This disingenuous explanation does not convince because as a matter of fact, the personality portrayals in *The American Civil War* are not well done compared with Knowles's later, mature depictions of medieval personalities. Why did he write the book? The answer is indicative of the coming storm. A leading Harvard professor, Admiral Samuel Eliot Morison, had been a visiting professor at Oxford for a year and during that time had gotten together and left behind a small working library in U.S. history. Writing the Civil War book gave Father David Knowles an excuse to be away from Downside and to spend time at Oxford working in the Morison collection. This grasping at an excuse for absence from the abbey, plus trips he made in the summer vacation with his parents to the Continent, indicates a monk who was not entirely happy with his vocation or at least with his community.

The American Civil War, if anyone at Downside had the interest or wit to read it carefully, showed by its text a similar restlessness. It is a very romantic book in which Knowles has projected onto the Old South a yearning for a time of gentility and beauty that he was having a hard time finding in the Benedictine community: "The South gave their [sic] all—*as no other people has done*, as the North did not— in what became a desperate and hopeless effort to preserve what they [sic] loved most passionately. They staked their all, and lost all, and their Dixie, *the Dixie of the past*, vanished like mist from the hands that would have held her, and was lost for ever [Emphasis added]." What the venerable and learned abbot Cuthbert Butler should have done after having read these lines was to have called in Father Knowles and told him that he was obviously restless in the religious life and that in view of his excellent academic accomplishments, perhaps he ought to withdraw to either Oxbridge or the Continent and take an advanced degree in history or theology and possibly then, with the approval of his community, seek an academic career in a Catholic college somewhere. But the abbot had neither the initiative nor the insight to dream of doing such a thing.

Knowles remained at Downside, growing increasingly discontented. This was clear again from his next book, *The Benedictine Centuries*, published in 1927. This polemical work reveals that Knowles had created in his mind the model of an ideal Benedictine community, which he attributed to the original Rule of St. Benedict, that would be absolutely autonomous within the church (a plausible proposition), papal authority being reserved but seldom exercised, and would be at the same time a community of thoroughly saintly people who would also be an intellectual elite (not St. Benedict's idea of a monastery). It was clear from this book that neither Downside nor any current Benedictine house fulfilled this ideal.

By 1933, Cuthbert Butler having died, and a new abbot, with whom Knowles got along poorly for both personal and doctrinal reasons, in place, Knowles was in visible conflict with his community. Two years later he was exiled as an insubordinate troublemaker from Downside to a shabby annex priory (a satellite community) in Ealing, a lower-middle-class suburb of London. There he refused to participate in the life of the community, whose membership was intellectually inferior to the main community at Downside, not even conversing at mealtime with the brothers. He took, however, to commuting almost daily to the Reading Room of the British Museum Library in Blooms-bury, rushing to complete a major book on the monastic order in medieval England to 1216. He filed appeals to Rome against the abbot's action against him and claimed that he had been treated in a most unethical and uncanonical manner. He even put in a personal appearance in Rome to plead his case. He gained some surprising support from Benedictines there, but as might have been expected, the papacy supported the abbot. After he had returned to England and with his lengthy manuscript already accepted by the Cambridge University Press (the editor asked that he cut a hundred pages, and he complied), one night in 1938 Knowles suddenly disappeared from Ealing Priory, leaving his clothes and books behind. After several weeks of inquiry and search it was discovered that he had taken a flat just over the one occupied by a certain Elizabeth Kornerup, a Swed-ish psychiatrist attached to the distinguished Travistock Clinic. Knowles had developed an intense personal attachment for Dr. Kor-nerup, who, he claimed, was a saint. By canon law, Knowles was now not only automatically suspended as a monk and a priest but subject to being excommunicated by the church for being a renegade monk.

The Downside community felt great compassion for what had happened to its formerly most brilliant member. The Frenchified ab-bot who had expelled Knowles had suddenly died, and the new abbot was again a Downside old boy and onetime close friend of Knowles. Then, in June 1940, the Benedictine order and the Roman Catholic Church were presented with a further problem when *The Monastic Order in England*, having been published by the Cambridge University Press, was hailed as a masterful work by Maurice Powicke and other professors, who regarded Knowles as a rising star in the academic world. How could the church acknowledge that its new scholarly superstar was at the moment a renegade monk and possibly an excommunicate? The abbot, pressed by Rome, desperately tried to hush things up and to make peace with Knowles before a scandal broke. This was not easy because nothing short of a confession of grave error and acknowledgment of injustice by Downside against him would satisfy Knowles. Furthermore, for a couple of years all communication with him had to pass through Dr. Kornerup, who proclaimed herself his therapist and said he was suffering from mild schizophrenia and could not be disturbed. The abbot made trips to London to seek a personal meeting with Knowles but was turned away. The cover story of a "nervous breakdown" seemed a possible route, and the abbot sought, and surprisingly gained permission, from Dr. Kornerup to have Knowles examined by two psychiatrists. The results were inconclusive. As is often the case with psychiatric examinations of brilliant and learned people, short-term diagnosis was very difficult.

Meanwhile, Knowles was living in London, through the blitz and the war, spending weekends and summer holidays at Dr. Kornerup's house in the country, where he performed mass for her daily. A scandal of great embarrassment for the church threatened to explode daily into the media. Between the abbot and Rome it was decided that Knowles should be allowed to be an "extra-cloistered monk," a rare but canonical status, in which a monk is given indefinite leave from his community and practically freed from communal residence and his vow of obedience to the abbot. The problem was that Knowles refused to apply for this status because in his mind such a petition was a confession of some wrong on his part while all the wrong, he insisted, lay on Downside's side. Finally, in 1944, when he was made a fellow of Peterhouse, Cambridge, and began college teaching there, the church unilaterally imposed this peculiar extra-cloistral status on him and restored to him his office as priest. He did not, however, perform a public mass (as distinct from his private masses for "Sister Bridget," as he now took to calling the "saintly" Swede) until 1957. His *Monastic Order* had been published with no ecclesiastical imprimatur (notice of a license to publish from a bishop certifying that nothing in the book was offensive to faith or morals), nor did any of his subsequent books carry this stamp. It was ironic that the four-volume history of medieval English religious orders was published without any official review, although it was written by a priest and (technically) a monk. The British academic establishment and media closed their eyes to the significance of this odd situation.

Knowles's appointment as a fellow and tutor of Peterhouse was pushed forward by another fellow of the college, the professor of modern history Herbert Butterfield. Of a Methodist family, Butterfield was one of the leaders in Britain of a Christian revival among the intelligentsia and educated middle class that not surprisingly began in the bitter and exhausting war years and continued for about a decade after, when it was swamped by technology, materialism, and renewed prosperity. Butterfield recognized in Knowles a kindred evangelical spirit but within the Catholic Church. When the master of Peterhouse returned in 1946 from his wartime duties, he was not

pleased to find this Benedictine monk oddly placed among the tenured dons of his college. When Knowles was given a university chair
of medieval history in 1946, the wily master of Peterhouse tried to
peddle Knowles back to Christ's College, of which Knowles was an
alumnus, but the dons there wouldn't take him, nor would any other
Cambridge college elect him a fellow. He remained at Peterhouse,
where a tradition of Christian fervor started by Knowles and Butterfield has been perpetuated and is now most visibly represented by
Maurice Cowling.

That the master of Peterhouse was unhappy about Knowles's election to a fellowship and that all the other colleges, even his alma
mater, refused him tell two things. This stern, outspoken monk was
not the kind of chap the dons wanted in their senior common room
(who could blame them?), and there was still in the Cambridge of the
1940s deep reservations about Catholic scholarship as being partisan
and propagandistic.

From 1953 to 1961 Knowles served as only the second Catholic to
become regius professor of history at Cambridge (the first, in the
1890s, was Lord Acton, a liberal layman, an Anglo-German aristocrat, and a bitter critic of Rome) and the first and—probably for all
time—only priest and monk. Why did Winston Churchill appoint
him? It was an astute political move, gaining or at least solidifying
Catholic votes for the Conservative party. By 1950 Catholics constituted more than 20 percent of the British electorate. Possibly also
Churchill recognized in Knowles a kindred maverick spirit and another master of narrative history, who had put the stodgy dons to
shame by the grand sweep of his historical opus written (or at least
well started) outside the academic establishment.

The church now basked in the reflected glory of Knowles's academic triumphs. This was a public relations triumph all the sweeter
as it was completely unanticipated and unplanned for by the papacy
or the British hierarchy. It was a gift of Providence. Avoiding, by a
near miss, revelation to the public of his conflict and temporary schism
with the church, the rebellious monk now became the very model of
a modern Catholic scholar and intellectual. Knowles's unusual relationship with Elizabeth Kornerup was well known to his colleagues.
She occasionally called for him at Peterhouse and acted as though she
were a solicitous academic wife. But the media respected his privacy.

Knowles's public image in the late forties and fifties was a glorious
one. He was transformed from the disgraced outcast of the late 1930s
into the "great Catholic medievalist," basking in a friendly joy of his

order and the adulation of the Roman Curia. A cover story, as we have noted, almost completely false, was invented to explain the tensions that had appeared to develop between him and the abbot of Downside. The abbot at the time (1940s) was only too glad to have Knowles continue in his professorship at Cambridge and to give him continued nonobedient, extra-cloistered status. All this abbot was interested in was avoiding public scandal that revealed Knowles's actual behavior in the late thirties and early forties and his association with Elizabeth Kornerup. As far as the abbot was concerned, Knowles could stay a priest and monk, although Knowles's actual conduct raised grave question about the propriety of his behavior within the bonds of his vows and status. The new abbot, the Catholic hierarchy in Britain, and the Roman Curia in the 1940s wanted to hide Knowles's conflict with his superior and its hazardous consequences from public view, and with Knowles's reluctant cooperation, they finally succeeded. It may be assumed that in bringing Knowles to Cambridge in 1944, Herbert Butterfield was inspired by his profound admiration for *The Monastic Order*, but it is not impossible that the Peterhouse fellowship for Knowles may have followed a request to Butterfield from someone in the hierarchy to help the church out of what could have been a devastating public relations problem.

It was not until 1979 that Dom Adrian Morey finally told, albeit from a partisan Downside point of view, what actually occurred in the 1930s and 1940s in the Knowles affair. The response of Knowles's student and literary executor, Cambridge Professor Christopher Brooke, was to express unhappiness with Morey's account, but still to refuse to publish Knowles's manuscript autobiography giving his side of the story.

The essentials of what happened in the Knowles-Downside affair are now quite clear. The questions remain: Why did they occur? What motivated Knowles? What precipitated the rupture between Downside's most brilliant and learned monk and his community? It was Morey's intention, in a skillful piece of character assassination, to show that the problem lay entirely with Knowles, who allegedly went off the religious rails, underwent a psychological breakdown of one sort or another, and acted in a manner that was unreasonable, compulsive, and bizarre. Morey's artfully developed indictment, drawn more in the nature of a legal brief than with a monk's charitable care of personality exploration, tells us that Knowles in the 1920s was under stress from overwork. Morey points to a bad automobile accident that Knowles had in 1929 (he was driving and smashed into a

truck), leading to serious injury and slow convalescence. It is suggested that the consequent psychological impact was important in explaining Knowles's subsequent behavior. The implication is that having
survived, he thought that Providence had saved him for some special
task, and this led to a new severity in his expectations of himself and
others and to extremism in his view of the monastic vocation.

Morey then tells us that in 1931 and 1932 Knowles suffered a great
disappointment (which Morey concedes could have been better handled by Knowles's superiors). Knowles was first told that he would
be made the new director of the residence for student monks at Cambridge University, Benet House, an ideal job for him. Then this offer
was withdrawn. Knowles blamed the new abbot for his disappointment, and Morey indicates that this lay behind Knowles's bitter hostility to the new abbot and contributed to the breaking point in their
relationship. Morey insists that Knowles was an elitist (he even digs
up a quote from a private letter that Knowles wrote thirty years later
in which he describes himself in these terms, an irrelevant document,
I believe) and that Knowles expected more from Benedictine life than
it can or should possibly deliver. Reading enthusiastically the writings of the late sixteenth-century Spanish mystic St. John of the Cross,
certainly an extremist in religious life, and of French monks of the
1920s with a similar proclivity stimulated Knowles in his hazardous
direction, in Morey's account. (In Maurice Cowling's 1986 essay, this
intellectual impact is given even greater importance. But Knowles
read constantly in the whole tradition of Catholic religiosity, and I
question placing so much causal influence on particular items on his
reading list.) Finally Morey gives a highly unsympathetic account of
Knowles's relationship with Elizabeth Kornerup, who comes through
as the Swedish bitch from hell and as quite unbalanced, extreme, and
compulsive. That she was affiliated with the leading psychiatric clinic
in Britain seems to cut no ice whatsoever with Dom Morey, who
dismisses her contemptuously on three grounds: She was a woman,
a foreigner, and a psychiatrist. (Cowling's account exhibits similar
donnish male and national chauvinism.)

In Morey's account, Knowles precipitated the break with his abbot
and community from 1933 to 1935 by making extravagant demands
that could not possibly be met and were entirely outside the stability
of monastic life. The abbot made no effort to accommodate Knowles,
and Dom Morey thinks the abbot's cold response was entirely appropriate. The demands that Knowles made come down at bottom to a
desire to go off with nine young monks, whom he had supervised as

novice master, and live with them in a new satellite community, with a view to eventual independence from Downside. Knowles thus wanted to create his own monastery with his own protégés, as Morey tells it, and there is no reason to deny that is what he sought to accomplish in the early 1930s.

It was the kind of project that illustrious medieval monks and friars had commonly sought to pursue—to break off from the mother house and establish a satellite and eventually independent community of younger and more zealous or learned members. Usually they were refused; sometimes they succeeded. Morey talks about Knowles's plans for a new community in the early 1930s as though it were scandalously almost unheard of in monastic history, and the abbot's sharp refusal were the only reasonable response. But that interpretation may be seriously questioned. Just as every distinguished professor in a major university wants his own institute, so many a charismatic monk wanted to found a new community. It may even be more upsetting a proposal in a religious order than in a university, but it is in part of the sociology both of Catholic religious orders and of the academic institutions that in the late Middle Ages grew out of them.

Downside Abbey had received some years previously a gift from an Australian benefactor to establish a daughter Benedictine community in that country, and when enough income from the endowment had accumulated, some years down the road, it was understood that an effort would be made to fulfill this responsibility. Knowles first proposed that the Australian community be established immediately, with him in charge and his nine disciples as its initial members. The abbot rejected this without discussion. It is curious that if Knowles had been allowed to do this, he would never have become a great medieval historian. Australia in the 1930s lacked a medieval research library in which he could have written *The Monastic Order*. Even if there had been one, the new monastery would have been likely located quite far away from it, and in any case, as head of the new community Knowles would not have had time for extended work in medieval studies and writing of big books. When the Australian project was declined, Knowles proposed that Downside use its own resources to establish a new satellite community in England for him and his protégés. This was not only flatly declined by the abbot but resented by the majority of the Downside community members because Knowles was proposing to withdraw resources from their abbey in the interest of his own project. Knowles and the abbot then exchanged a remarkable series of angry letters. It is astonishing that they did not sit down together and try to find a solution, but it is obvious that a bitter personal antagonism had developed. The outcome was that Knowles's young disciples fully submitted to the abbot and were welcomed back into the favor of the community, while Knowles was ignominiously exiled to the monastic bush league at Ealing Priory.

In Morey's partisan and official Downside version, Knowles showed a profound misunderstanding of the stability of monastic life, was arrogant, egoistical, and personally ambitious, and had likely become psychologically disturbed in a severe manner. Morey does not reflect on the significance of the fact that these years of tension and upheaval for Knowles in the 1930s were precisely the time when he completed his greatest book, *The Monastic Order*, and when he began work on his other masterpiece, which we know as the first volume of *The Religious Orders in England*. On the contrary, Morey concludes his skillful but overdetermined brief against Knowles by trying to use these books against him. Morey contends that they illustrate Knowles's elitism, excessive ethical censuriousness, and misperception of the mainline monastic vocation. To put it simply, Morey claims that Knowles loved monks and friars who were extravagant saints or brilliant philosophers or prodigious scholars, even if they presented difficulties for their communities and the hierarchy. He points to a tendency in these volumes for Knowles to assign ethical grades to particular monks and friars that he holds indicative of Knowles's tiresome penchant for arrogance and elitism. In Morey's portrayal, Knowles got it into his head that he was called by God to act as judge on all monks and friars past and present, and whatever the value of such an enterprise, it is not what the monastic vocation is all about. The response is that from a formalistic standpoint Morey has some weight to his argument but that it would raise doubts not only about Father David Knowles but about St. Columban, St. Bernard of Clairvaux, St. Francis of Assisi, St. Dominic, St. Ignatius Loyola, and just about every great name in the history of Catholic monasticism, not to speak of the founder, St. Benedict of Nursia himself. Dom Morey turned a paradox that lies at the heart of Catholic religious life into a personal criticism of Knowles.

Drawing upon Morey's account (which, whatever its limitations, is circumstantial and immensely valuable), the insightful essay by Maurice Cowling, my own conversations with Knowles in 1959 and 1968, and information provided by Geoffrey Barraclough, I would

construe the story of the Knowles-Downside affair in a manner somewhat at variance with Morey's indictment of Father David Knowles.

There can be no doubt that disappointment over cancellation of
his appointment as the director of Benet House at Cambridge was
one powerful ingredient in the conflict and upheaval in Knowles's life
that ensued in the early 1930s. He himself said, many years later,
that if he had received the Benet House directorship appointment and
gone back to Cambridge around 1933, things would have been different. Certainly they would have with regard to his order. His disappointment was exacerbated by the slovenly and hurtful way in which
the matter was handled by two abbots in succession. Obviously, if
Knowles had removed to Cambridge in 1933, he would have been
happy there guiding the studies of the Downside monks who had
been sent to the university to obtain their B.A.'s, and he would likely
have won admiration and attention among the dons. But if Knowles
had gone to Cambridge in 1933, while the rupture with this abbot
and community might have been avoided or at least postponed, it is
questionable whether he would have ended up at the university with
a chair in medieval studies and then the supreme honor of the regius
professorship. If Knowles had avoided the tension, conflict, and upheavals that marked his life in the 1930s and early 1940s, it is doubtful his two greatest works, *The Monastic Order* and Volume I of *The
Religious Orders*, would be the wonderful efforts they are or would
have been attempted at all.

Knowles's psychological stress and religious trials gave an edge to
his temperament in the 1930s that summoned up a spiritual ferocity
and highly personal insight that are only occasionally prevalent in his
many later works. These two books were written out of despair, anger, yearning for revenge, internal resourcefulness, a sense of personal calling that make them, chapter after chapter and especially in
their discussions of religious leaders and the overall cultural and ecclesiastical ambience, works of forceful passion and imaginative power
that have very rarely been equaled in writing about the Middle Ages
or the history of the Catholic Church.

We know little about the wellsprings of literary creativity, but certainly a gestation out of tension, conflict, anger, fear, loneliness often
serves as the trigger. In Knowles's case these conditions certainly give
a fiery glow to these two volumes that only fitfully glimmers from
later volumes—try as he would from the comfort of his later eminence as the most admired Catholic historian in the world and of the

regius professorship. The third volume of *The Religious Orders* (1959) again catches fire in considerable stretches by the force of the regret and anxiety that Knowles felt when he contemplated the fall of the religious orders and the dispersal and execution of the monks under Henry VIII, but even in this climactic volume the fervor was a bit forced. The reckless spontaneity and inspired aggressive vision that came with his marginalization, condemnation, and desperate working in the 1930s as an obscure and lonely figure in the vast rotunda of the British Museum Library (like that other outcast Karl Marx) were never his again for extended periods.

Along with his disappointment over the loss of the Benet House position in 1933 came his discovery of his sexuality through his close association with the young novices in the Downside community whom he spiritually counseled and educated. This is the subconscious and preconscious psychological force that drove his life in the early 1930s and conditioned his behavior. The recognition for the first time of his sexual being, the release from extreme repression shaped by retarded Oedipal maturation, affected Knowles's subconscious and preconscious mind, and to some extent his consciousness as well, during the late 1920s and early 1930s and induced a powerful reaction in his attitude and conduct. During his mid-thirties he almost inevitably became emotionally involved with these beautiful, refined young men to whom he gave spiritual and educational counseling as novice master. This homoerotic disturbance in his life, sweeping aside his overly developed superego and making its way into his ego personality, was manifested in the signification of his wanting to run away with the young monks and found a new monastic community. There is nothing novel or astonishing about such an outcome, the withdrawal and romantic flight motif in the history of monasticism. It is especially explicit, with precise homoerotic overtones, for instance, in the writings of Ailred of Rievaulx, the mid-twelfth-century English Cistercian abbot, with which Knowles was very familiar. It is explicit also in the lives of Bernard of Clairvaux, Peter Abelard, and St. Francis.

Frustrated in his efforts to act out in an acceptable social manner his newly discovered self-image, Knowles turned with explosive anger on the abbot who blocked his way. It was the shock of this experience that later made it so difficult for him to accept a new abbot's benign effort to heal the breach and impelled Knowles's insistence that the abbey impossibly humiliate itself and confess injustice done to him. Downside had prevented Knowles's spiritual (perhaps physical) consummation of his love for the beautiful young monks. The hatred lingered long after the abbey sought reconciliation with him. The stigma of erotic deprivation, once implanted in the subconscious, is a wound very difficult to transcend. Knowles wanted the abbey to assume all the guilt and blame for his psychological crisis.

Another motive for the upheaval in Knowles's life in the early 1930s was his increasing revulsion against the cultural configurations of Downside religiosity, what we today would call its culture and life-style. Whether Morey is right to stigmatize Knowles as someone who wanted more from the monastic vocation that it *could* deliver is moot, but he certainly wanted more from Downside than it *did* deliver. By 1930 Knowles believed that Downside was lacking in refinement and intellectuality. He was the son of converts from Congregationalism who looked upon Catholicism as necessarily a superior culture to the plebeian church they had left—or why make the jump? His father's idyllic expectations of Catholicism were almost annually reinforced for Knowles when he took summer vacations with his affluent parents on the Continent or at the English seaside and then felt guilty about this private privilege as skipping beyond the bounds of monastic austerity. What was Father David Knowles returning to when, pumped up with his family's high hopes and lyrical imaginings of beautiful, refined Catholicism, he came back from these vacations? It was to Downside Abbey, whose cultural and intellectual level, while moving upward after the war, had now leveled off and was becoming dismayingly petty bourgeois and excessively Irish in Knowles's eyes.

Knowles fastened his disappointment upon the recently deceased abbot, who had been his teacher, friend, and patron, a product of Edwardian Anglo-Irish Catholic culture, Dom Cuthbert Butler. This was publicly revealed in 1934, when Knowles published under his own name a long obituary essay on Abbot Butler in the *Downside Review* that chilled the hearts of the community and stunned the new abbot. Butler was a scholar of not inconsiderable attainment and an administrator under whose rule the abbey had flourished for most of his long tenure. Knowles was one of his favorites, supposedly his protégé. Yet Knowles, toward the end of his long essay, after carefully accounting for the details of Butler's life and career in conventionally respectful terms, suddenly turned on the old abbot and savaged his behavior, personality and life-style:

> [Dom Cuthbert Butler] undoubtedly was unsympathetic, almost unresponsive, to a whole range of aesthetic and intellectual interests generally accounted part of the possession of all educated men. . . . He

had grown to maturity untouched by the Thomist revival and remained curiously eclectic and agnostic, even on many of the deepest
questions of philosophy and speculative theology. . . . It may be
doubted whether he had the capacity of giving which is of the essence
of deep friendship, or the corelative capacity of receiving the impress
of another's personality [unlike Knowles's homoerotic feelings]. . . .
He lacked the qualities of force and initiative and self-assertion in the
face of determined opposition. . . . Abbot Butler was an extremely
ineffective public speaker and preacher. . . . [In his sermons] he would
spend several minutes translating simple Latin into faulty English. . . .
Abbot Butler was careless of external appearances. . . . Upon Abbot
Butler the best clothes seemed ill-fitting. . . .

Knowles goes on to express contempt even for Butler's weak
face-shaving skills! This Abbot Butler, the greatest figure in early-
twentieth-century British monasticism, comes through in Knowles's
astonishingly candid memoir as devout and high-principled but deeply
flawed: insensitive, uncouth, narrowly educated, an essentially obsolete, old-fashioned Edwardian Anglo-Irishman. It is a devastating, cruel, if persuasive, portrait. It shows that a prime source of
Knowles's unhappiness and restlessness was his disappointment and
embarrassment that Downside was not keeping up with the leading
edge of cultural and intellectual change even within European Catholicism. It is also astonishing that in the commemorative edition of
Knowles's best papers that was edited in 1963 by William Abel Pantin and presented to Knowles by just about every Oxbridge medievalist, this condemnation of Butler was resurrected and republished
without deletions, suggesting that the Oxford dons of the 1960s were
as obtuse and backward as Butler and the Downside community of
early 1930s or that they chauvinistically relished the savaging of the
Anglo-Irish abbot. Knowles was bemused to see this memoir that
signified his break with Downside reprinted without comment or excision.

Thus Dom Morey's denunciation of Knowles as an elitist within
the Downside community of the 1930s does not explain what the real
issue was. Knowles looked around him and saw the school at Downside steadily increasing in size and influence, and he sensed the danger of Downside Abbey's going the way of so many Catholic religious
institutions in the transatlantic world of the era (and today), in which
the monastic community became primarily a support vehicle for the

school. He wanted to go in a completely different direction, for which he had prepared the way by his upgrading of the *Downside Review* into the leading English Catholic journal of serious opinion and communication. He wanted Downside Abbey to be the intellectual and religious leader of the Catholic Church in Britain and the English-speaking world. He envisaged a community of brilliant, learned brothers; if not saints, then at least thoroughly exemplary and committed people. He wanted to make a quantum jump to the current cultural and religious vanguard from where the abbey had been at the end of the Cuthbert Butler's regime.

But this was only the first step in Knowles's eyes. Now he wanted to go much above the level of Butler's Irish-Catholic-Edwardian culture into something that would stand in favorable comparison with the most learned and zealous qualities of Continental Catholicism. His community was disturbed and frightened by this exalted vision. Most did not want to follow him in this steep ascent or did not believe they had the capacity to do so. That is a human response, and Knowles may possibly be seen as inconsiderate or impractical but not "elitist." A close parallel may be drawn from the American academic world of today. One of the most common stories on American campuses in the past forty years is that of the gung ho new department chairman or dean brought in from the outside to upgrade the unit who runs into bitter conflict and resentment as he "changes the rules of the game." This conflict usually ends in confusion, defeat, and even tragedy. Knowles's place in Downside and in the English Catholic Church in general in the 1930s was similar to this kind of visionary department chair or dean, with predictably stormy results. That does not mean he was in the wrong or even in the right. It was a sad conflict of ideals, perceptions, and self-images.

Stung by the loss of the coveted Cambridge position at Benet House, thrown into emotional upheaval by his newly discovered sexuality, distressed by Downside's lack of refinement and vanguard intellectuality, Father David Knowles in the 1930s developed a compelling image of himself as a religious reformer, a charismatic and providential leader, in conflict with unjust and inept authority and a retrograde cultural ambience. His assessment of St. Francis of Assisi, perhaps the most carefully written and exciting portrait in the first volume of *The Religious Orders*, is very close to his own self-image in the late 1930s and for some years thereafter. He understood St. Francis by thinking about his own experience:

Francis had the mind of Christ, he lived in him, and it was an agony and ultimately an *impossibility* for him to divide, to adapt, and *to accommodate for others the unity and fullness of his vision.* . . . [Francis] was one who, while intensely receptive of all beauty and sensitive to the needs of creatures around him, nevertheless had bread to eat which they knew not, and walked by a light other than theirs. . . . *He felt called to assert . . . that the right of the individual friar to follow the perfect way was indefeasible, and that obedience should not be given to commands running contrary to spiritual perfection, even if persecution at the hands of superiors should ensue.* [Emphasis added.]

Knowles was the kind of historian and biographer who relived his or her own experience through past lives and understood past lives out of the agony and passion of his or her own experience. When he wrote these lines about St. Francis in 1941 or 1942, he knew he was already winning his great conflict with his superiors. They were trying to reach a reconciliation and settlement with him. There is, therefore, an ingredient of triumphal irony in these lines.

By this time also he had the strength and comfort given to him by Dr. Kornerup. Far from being a busybody, a crank, and a baleful influence upon him, she was the best thing that ever happened to Knowles. She rescued him emotionally and practically at the moment of his greatest crisis and deepest despair and guided and sustained him for the rest of his life (she died a year after he did).

Kornerup was a Lutheran convert to Catholicism whom another priest had referred to Father David Knowles in London for spiritual counseling. He thought from the first that she was touched by a special holiness. She was certainly devout, wishing to make confession and participate in the mass daily. She was reputed to carry around with her—in medieval fashion—a consecrated Host (the wafer from the mass). But she was also a psychiatrist, and she could help Knowles come to terms with his personal problems and mid-life crisis. All indications are that she was a loving and caring person. They lived intimately as if they were husband and wife, sharing their lives completely. Did that include sexual intimacy? There is no reason to doubt that occurred. It is possible but unlikely that they could sustain such an integrated emotional and domestic relationship, at a time of overpowering release for Knowles, without sexual involvement. As both a psychiatrist and Catholic saint in his eyes Kornerup helped Knowles decisively in the placing of his sexual needs within the context of his religious vocation. He had every right to believe that she had been sent by Christ to be the means of his salvation. It speaks to the appalling male chauvinism of British academia and church that she is treated so negatively in the four biographical accounts that have been published about Knowles. Pantin ignores her entirely, Brooke mentions her in passing as if she were a housekeeper, Morey condemns her, and Cowling makes fun of her.

It is possible to look at Knowles from another standpoint, from a sociological rather than biographical perspective—within the framework of the development of the Catholic Church in the twentieth century. Knowles was an archrepresentative of a transitional generation in the church, midpoint between condemned reformist modernism, which he explicitly admired, and Vatican II, which his intentions and behavior in the 1930s and 1940s anticipated. It is true that as an old man in the late 1960s, Knowles expressed reservations about the outcomes of Vatican II, especially the liturgical changes (the shift to vernaculars from the traditional Latin liturgy). He also naturally felt a gulf between himself and the younger generation of clerics committed to applying and extending Vatican II. But he was a great forerunner of that liberating council's spirit nonetheless.

Knowles's career especially speaks to the continuing problem of the church from the dawn of this century to the present: how to accommodate its most brilliant thinkers and learned scholars within institutional discipline and doctrinal cohesion. Knowles's case was one of the more important in teaching the hierarchy and particularly the Roman Curia that simple repression was not likely to redound to the church's benefit. Accommodation had to be made especially for biblical scholars and medievalists. Otherwise the church could find itself in the midst of a public confrontation that produced loss of face externally and demoralization and confusion within. By his resounding victory over authority, effected with astonishing courage and in the face of tremendous odds, Knowles has to be regarded as a prime liberator of Catholic intellectuals and academics everywhere. Like the triumph of St. Francis, to whom Knowles compared himself, it was a victory dictated by the forces of the age and the intrinsic course of Catholic belief.

III

THE NEMESIS OF SANCTITY

David Knowles's four-volume history of the monastic and other religious orders in England is the single greatest work in medieval studies in this century in terms of a sustained, immensely learned, closely
and subtly perceived treatment of a continuous major theme in medieval civilization over a very long period—from about 940 to about
1540. The four volumes comprise some eighteen hundred pages of
beautifully written narrative prose. The first volume was published
in 1940 under the title *The Monastic Order in England*. A second edition
was announced as published in 1965, but the changes were extremely
minor; not even the bibliography was brought up-to-date. The other
three volumes appeared under the title *The Religious Orders in England*.
Volume I, published in 1948, covers the period 1216 to 1340; the
second volume, published in 1955, goes from 1340 to "the end of the
Middle Ages"—i.e., about 1500—while the third volume, published
in 1959 and subtitled *The Tudor Age*, actually deals with the dissolution of the monasteries up into the early 1540s.

There are several distinct characteristics of Knowles's four-volume
work. First, it is written almost entirely from published sources. That
is one reason why the second volume of *Religious Orders* is the weakest
of the three volumes by far. For this period of English church history
(1340–1500), many important sources are in unpublished manuscripts, and working only from published material provides an inadequate data base for this period. Another reason for the drop-off in
the quality of this volume, compared with the others, is that Knowles
could not make up his mind on what precise themes he wished to
develop. He was thrown off his confident pace by the fact that the
three late medieval writers he most admired—the theologian John
Wyclif, the poet Geoffrey Chaucer, and the poetic preacher William
Langland (or whoever was the author of the visionary work *Piers
Plowman*)—hated and intensely criticized the religious orders whose
side Knowles was supposed to be presenting. Another problem with
Volume II was that Knowles relied for this era heavily on the advice
of William Abel Pantin, the eccentric Oxford authority on late medieval monasticism. Pantin was indeed an extremely learned person,
in a kind of unsystematic, quasi-amateurish way, and a very devout,
if old-fashioned, English Roman Catholic. He was, however, a historian of mediocre judgment, and his unfortunate influence on Knowles
shows in the second volume of *Religious Orders:* the apologetic tone;

the indecisiveness and hesitancy; the reluctance to address the great issues head-on.

For the last volume of *Religious Orders*, Knowles could again derive full data from published sources. Here again he was sure of what he wanted to say. The quality and confidence pick up, compared with the second volume, and almost but not quite get back to the pace and insight of *The Monastic Order* and Volume I of *Religious Orders*. Writing about the dissolution of the monasteries, Knowles is treading on a churned-up polemical and scholarly battlefield. Francis Cardinal Gasquet, a former head of Downside Abbey, at the beginning of the century had presented a sickly-sweet sentimental view of the great dissolution and expatiated on what a tragedy for spirituality this putative state crime had been. In the mid-1930s, an anti-Catholic polemicist, Geoffrey Baskerville, in a brilliant, sarcastic volume had severely crippled Gasquet's sentimental ghosts. Baskerville, a good researcher, pointed out that there was little actual resistance to the dissolution from the abbots. Most of them were happy to receive settlements from the crown that allowed them to become country gentlemen, often using as their manor houses the now-secularized residences of the monks. As for the latter, they were pensioned off by the crown on not unreasonable terms. Later the sizes of these pensions shrank drastically because of the great sixteenth-century inflation. The people who truly suffered—aside from a very small number of monks who resisted the crown and were executed as traitors—were the nuns, who were sent back as spinsters to unwelcoming family hearths.

Knowles does not essentially dispute Baskerville's account, although he sets out to counter its tone. He acknowledges that Gasquet's capacity to report facts was not of a high order. Knowles pulls no punches. He admits that many monastic houses in the early sixteenth century were undistinguished for religious zeal. He sardonically tells us that Henry VIII's investigating commissioners, looking for salacious scandal to justify suppression of the monasteries, reported back that they could find very little sexual promiscuity but quite a lot of masturbation. The way Knowles responds to Baskerville's contempt for the monks is to look at the dissolution from the religious brothers' and sisters' own point of view in order to evoke the tragic rupture the dissolution represented in their lives. He also puts the dissolution in the long perspective of five centuries of English religious life and considers the significance of the upheaval for culture and society. He gives us in Volume III of *Religious Orders* neither the ersatz lament of Gasquet nor the mocking contempt of Baskerville but the long view and the quiet poetic dirge.

Knowles makes us feel the cultural change that the withdrawal of the monks and friars and their establishments from the British ambience represented. It is very subtly done, in that the reader comes away with no illusions that the dissolution cut off the English religious orders at a peak of feeling and creativity. Knowles makes clear that such absolutizing of the monks and friars is specious. But he still evokes regret that a passage in spirituality and civilization has occurred. Volume III of *Religious Orders* is not quite at the level of intensity and artistic triumph that mark *The Monastic Order* and Volume I of *Religious Orders*—neither Knowles nor the historical reality was at that level—but he still makes us sad about what happened. It is in some ways his most difficult undertaking, and the result is a tour de force that by and large succeeds.

Knowles felt compelled to devote about a quarter of the space of his four-volume work to institutional history—ecclesiastical organization, administration of religious houses and orders, demography, fiscal and economic matters. It was his way of fully establishing his academic legitimacy and credibility, so that Powicke and other mandarins could say: "Good stuff, old chap; you can do it; welcome to the fold." It is amazing how much work Knowles put into these institutional segments, and they are finely organized and clearly written. But they still make for relatively dull reading and are by now quite dated. There is one special quality to these institutional segments that distinguishes them, especially in *The Monastic Order*. In the 1920s, partly in consequence of Continental vacations with his parents, Knowles had learned to read German fluently, a rarity for a British medievalist of his generation. Therefore, he was able to draw upon the vast German historical literature on medieval ecclesiastical institutions and place the English story within the Continental context. When *The Monastic Order* was first published, it gained high visibility and immediate admiration among British medievalists precisely (in part) because it filtered into the non-German-reading British faculty clubs the perspective of a general nature on medieval ecclesiastical institutions that Knowles derived from reading Ernst Sackur (a precocious Jew who died at the age of thirty-nine) and other early-twentieth-century German institutional historians of the medieval church. That is not why Knowles would be read today, nor is it what constitutes the distinctive quality of his work, although it must be stressed that Knowles had a marvelous capacity for textbook writing, for taking other people's scholarship, often remote to his public, and turning it concisely into easily comprehensible and succinct English prose.

There are two distinctive qualities of Knowles's work that account for its enduring fascination and perpetual value. The first is his many portrayals of what he called character or what we now call personality. Knowles was a biographer of exceptional insight and narrative skill. He creates real, complex people within medieval religious life in rounded, thoroughly convincing sketches that become burned into our minds as memories of individuals. He had a novelist's skill. These are often second- or third-level people he describes, not necessarily the great religious leaders. By the late 1950s the Cambridge University Press, Knowles's publisher (which originally counted so little on the enduring popularity of his work that originally it printed only five hundred copies of *The Monastic Order* and immediately broke up the type), realized that it was these biographical studies that were the most durably popular aspect of Knowles's four volumes. Therefore, in 1962, with his cooperation, the CUP brought out an anthology of these personality studies under the title *Saints and Scholars: Twenty-five Medieval Portraits*. If an American publisher had done this, it would, of course, have been excoriated in the *Times Literary Supplement* as a meretricious example of capitalist greed. Whatever the motive for its publication, this collection of Knowles's "greatest biographical hits" constitutes a permanent addition to the corpus of twentieth-century literature. For the naive reader, the Middle Ages will become the scene of real people after he or she absorbs these biographical sketches.

The second distinctive quality of Knowles's four volumes is his exposition of intellectual history, particularly philosophy and theology (he does little with imaginative literature, although a fair amount of it was written by members of religious orders). Knowles had a very rare aptitude for explaining medieval theory in terms which the laity and undergraduate could immediately understand and find interesting and significant. I have examined American doctoral students in several universities for three decades, and no matter how many thick tomes I recommend to them on medieval thought, when it comes down to their oral comprehensive exams, it is almost invariably evident that they derive most of what they say about medieval philosophy and theology principally from Knowles. Knowles's splendid pages on theory in these four volumes led to another sidebar publication, *The Evolution of Medieval Thought*, published by Longmans, a commercial publisher, also in 1962. In an American paperback edition this book has dominated medieval history courses in U.S. colleges for a quarter of a century. Five years previously Knowles's own student Gordon Leff had attempted to serve the same market in a Penguin book on medieval thought. From a technical point of view, Leff's is the superior book. Recently Knowles's survey of medieval philosophy has been further rendered out of date by new analytical approaches that are splendidly summed up in the two slim volumes (1983–87) of the Cambridge don John Marenbon. But the probability is that while Knowles's textbook on medieval thought is now somewhat obsolete, it will continue to dominate the market because of its delightful readability and persuasive enthusiasm. Knowles made medieval thought, an arcane subject, accessible to anyone with a high school reading level. That is not the meanest of his accomplishments.

The four-volume history of English monastic and other religious orders has a grand, persistent theme, which may be called the nemesis of sanctity. There was profound sanctity in medieval religious life, intermittent and inconsistent, but very much existent at particular times and places, Knowles contends. This sanctity was always threatened by absorption into the world and perversion of its divine accoutrements to secular uses. Popular material and political forces sought to harness sanctity for their own purposes; they capitalized on it, exploited it, abused and corrupted it. Sanctity was the start of its own nemesis. The veneration in which individual saints were held, and the admiration with which a distinguished community of religious was regarded, almost immediately set in motion society's efforts to appropriate for mundane purposes, ethical or worse, the holy spirit reflected in religious individuals and communities. This is Knowles's grand theme.

It is the theme of "after the fall." He is recounting an inspired story that is essentially tragic, long before the final martyrdom and dispersal of the monks in the early sixteenth century. It is a cyclical story of religious vocation attaining the highest levels of human sanctity, followed by the world, even the better elements in society, closing in and perverting that sanctity to its own uses, sometimes with good intentions, sometimes maliciously. The nemesis of medieval sanctity means that holiness carries within it the seeds of its own destruction. Knowles's history is an account of a transcendent spirituality that cannot find stability without starting on the downward slope to routinizing socialization and miserable corruption. He has written a history of the failure of medieval Europe to achieve the effective socialization of the highest reaches of the spiritual life. It is a kind of Grail legend in which the Grail cannot come into secular hands without self-destruction.

Father David Knowles seems to be at heart a pessimist who doubts very much whether transcendent spirituality can ever be socialized, whether the saint and the holy community can ever be at peace and in harmony with the world. He wrote what is essentially an epic of failure, a very human history of the erosion and destruction of the best gestures and most refined feelings that human nature can achieve. There are parallels to Nietzsche and anticipations of Michel Foucault in Knowles's work. Knowles agreed with the manic German philosopher and the austere French mandarin about the universal impact of power even upon ostensible idealism and spirituality.

This theme of the social nemesis of sanctity is illustrated again and again in Knowles's four volumes. It is the leitmotif of his eighteen-hundred-page religious epic. But he never entirely articulates the theological meaning of what he is recounting for us. He never quite states that the stability of the highest religious life is inevitably beyond the reach of defective human nature after the fall. He blames instead particular factors: the weakness of personality; the treachery or incapacity of leadership; the ineffectiveness of institutions; the lust for power and wealth in society. Again and again he tells a story of conflict between sanctity and society. A new monastery or religious order is founded on the inspiration of sanctity, on the compelling impulse to spiritual perfection. But it has to function as an institution, and in so doing, given at least the passage of time, it deteriorates and is led astray from its rock of sanctity and its original spiritual impulse:

> When once a religious house or a religious order ceases to direct its sons [Knowles has almost nothing to say about nuns] to the abandonment of all that is not God, and ceases to show them the rigours of the narrow way that leads to the imitation of Christ in His Love, it sinks to the level of a purely human institution, and whatever its works may be, they are the works of time and not of eternity. The true monk, in whatever century he is found, looks not to the changing ways around him, or to his own mean condition, but to the unchanging everlasting God, and his trust is in the everlasting arms that hold him.

Thus Knowles in 1959 summed up his central theme. It may be said that this conviction provides the tension and ambivalence that drive his narrative and give it grandeur. On the other hand, it may also be said that if Knowles had dogmatically stuck to this theme, it would have resulted in a very long-winded sermon, an incessant scold, and made for dreary reading. In practice, reading Knowles makes for a great experience not because of his main theme but because he breaks away from concentration upon it to highlight individual personalities who are living ambivalently under the pressure of the tension between sanctity and society. Even if they don't handle the conflict in a way that Knowles considers fully in accordance with the ideal of sanctity—or precisely because they do not, giving a flavor of challenge and complexity to their lives and dispositions—the substance of his character studies makes for fascinating reading. Knowles's essentially gloomy assumptions also do not prevent him from explicating medieval philosophical and religious ideas in a comprehensible and persistently intriguing manner, and this also keeps us turning the pages of his magisterial and lengthy narrative. It is his personality studies and his expositions of thought and religious culture, not his faith-driven central idea, that make Knowles an unsurpassed, possibly an unequaled medieval church historian—that and the turmoil and passions of his own life that gave empathetic color and verve to his examination of the spiritual crises of medieval people.

You yourself need to have deep experiences of the soul to understand the experiential crises of medieval personalities, and Knowles certainly had such experiences. His life was fully as complex and conflicted in terms of religious psychology as any great medieval figure, and that ingredient gives to his four volumes a quality of persuasion, a ring of truth, a depth of vision that make it one of the half dozen greatest achievements of historical literature in the English language. That is why the passage of time, the additional layers of research, the piling up of new data and insights will never make obsolete at least three of the four volumes of his history, any more than new research on the politics of late medieval England has made obsolete Shakespeare's *Richard II* and *Henry V*.

The major empirical weakness of Knowles's four-volume work, as a historical exposition, is his incapacity to explain the sharp drop in the popularity of the monks and friars that set in during the closing years of the thirteenth century. He exults in describing how, after the decline in veneration for the cloistered monks in the late twelfth century and their loss of centuries-long leadership in Western thought and culture, the coming of the friars, the monastic brothers who worked in the world, raised the popularity of the religious orders in England—especially in the case of the Franciscans—to an unprecedented level of lay enthusiasm. The Franciscans rapidly took over the philosophy and theology faculties of Oxford University, as the Dominicans like St. Thomas Aquinas were doing in Paris, and moved Oxford to vanguard limits of medieval abstract thinking. Yet by 1300 the popularity of the friars had passed its peak. By the late fourteenth century they were condemned even more vociferously than the old cloistered monastic orders, and by that time the golden age of Franciscan Oxford had also passed away into intellectual turmoil and confusion, followed in the fifteenth century by academic stagnation. The last two volumes of Knowles's work agonize over the rise of laicization, hysterical anticlericalism and, finally, the Reformation and the expropriation of the monasteries by the crown and the suppression of the religious orders.

This final disaster, Knowles has to acknowledge, met with little resistance either within or outside the religious communities. Not even the martyrdom of a handful of Carthusian monks who resisted Henry VIII to the end and were savagely executed, can assuage Knowles's grief over this persistent and lamentable decline from the glory days of the Benedictines in the eleventh century, the Cistercians in the 1160s and 1170s, and the Franciscans in the 1260s and 1270s. Knowles has no clear and convincing explanation for the decline of the status of the religious orders in late medieval English society and cultures. He points to internal problems and changing social and political attitudes. He describes in detail what happened, but he does not explain globally why it happened. He fails to develop (as has everyone else) a historical sociology for the fall of the medieval church.

We are left with a romantic sense of loss and nostalgia. At the beginning of the sixteenth century, he says of the monks of Durham Cathedral, "whatever their life may have held of ease and mediocrity, the beauty of the setting remained, and the display on high days and holy seasons of the treasures of artists and craftsmen that the centuries had accumulated. . . . The glory had departed from Durham [after the dissolution], for the ark of God had been taken away." As for the Carthusian martyrs, "rarely indeed in the annals of the Church have any confessors of the faith endured trials longer, more varied or more bitter than these unknown monks. . . . They died faithful witnesses to the Catholic teaching that Christ had built his Church upon a rock." But it was a rock that could not save them.

In the end there was a monumental turning away from Catholicism, from medieval traditional sanctity, leaving only bare ruined choirs and nostalgic memories of what had been and was no more. Knowles knew from the bitterness of his own experiences in the 1930s that not even upon the rock of the church could the sanctity of medieval monasticism be resurrected. He himself tried, but he was rejected, cast out, and failed. He could only memorialize the medieval religious in his history. He could not existentially re-create a holy community. He never returned to Downside Abbey even for a visit.

IV

THE CHRISTIAN PHILOSOPHER

After David Knowles, the most influential Roman Catholic medievalist of this century was the French philosophy professor Étienne Henry Gilson (1884–1978). Writing in 1962 as an old man, Étienne Gilson reflected that "the Catholics who came to grips with these [intellectual] difficulties during the first half of the twentieth century retain from those days the feeling that they lived in the midst of extreme confusion." Gilson was capable of bluntly expressing the truth about difficult situations, and he certainly did so here. His next remark—"a key notion was lacking, that of theology"—is also typical of this world-renowned and immensely honored medievalist. It is hard to understand what he is talking about.

Gilson came from a modest middle-class, traditionally French Catholic family. He attended the best Catholic school in Paris and pursued his secondary education at the Lycée Henri IV, the most prestigious and highly selective state high school in the metropolis. With a very firm grounding in philosophy, he went on to take his doctoral degree in that subject at the University of Paris, slowly developing an interest in what was for that secular university a still-neglected subject, the thought of St. Thomas Aquinas. Perhaps the most important fact of Gilson's extremely long and very illustrious career is that he was a very devout Catholic, an advocate and explicator of Thomism—indeed, in his time and still today the most renowned and influential authority on Thomism—yet he pursued his professional career in France entirely in the secular, state-supported realm of higher education and research, outside Catholic universities and institutes. This meant that once he had established himself as a leading medievalist of his generation, as was certainly the case by the mid-1920s, he was untouchable by Rome. The similarity to Knowles in this respect is striking. The cardinals and the French clergy were not happy with Gilson's ideas and prolific writings, especially before

World War II, but his success in the highly competitive world of French academia meant that he brought great honor to the church and its intellectual reputation. To try to suppress him was unthinkable. The church, whether in France or at Rome, had to accommodate itself to him.

Gilson used his celebrity by repaying the church through enthusiastic accounts of medieval philosophy and theology. He made medieval philosophy highly respectable not only in the French secular universities but also at Toronto and Harvard and several other North American universities, where he taught or gave visiting public lectures. He had become world-famous by the 1930s and represented French Catholicism on the public stage of cultural politics. He was a prominent member of the French delegation to the San Francisco Conference that established the United Nations in 1945 and was one of the principal drafters of the plan for UNESCO at the London Conference of 1946, although he had justifiably deep reservations about the results. Always independent and outspoken, he expressed doubts in the early 1950s about NATO, American domination of postwar Europe, and cold war diplomacy and cultural polemics and thereby gained for a time a reputation on the political as well as clerical scene of being well left of center.

Gilson was the principal founder of the Institute of Medieval Studies at the University of Toronto in 1929, obtained official papal approval of it in 1939, and in the thirties, forties, and fifties held a joint appointment between the Collège de France and the University of Toronto. He was a visiting professor at Harvard several times, also stimulated medieval studies there, and turned down its offer of a chair in favor of the Toronto offer because the latter allowed him to continue his appointment in Paris. Gilson was thus a transatlantic intellectual figure of totemic prominence between 1930 and 1960. Altogether he made more than forty trips across the Atlantic, and while in the United States and Canada, he carried out elaborate lecture tours throughout the hemisphere, spreading his gospel all the way from Ontario through Indiana and Virginia to Rio de Janeiro.

Gilson was courageous, and generally liberal-minded. He fought hard, although unsuccessfully, to protect the accomplished Dominican medievalist M. D. Chenu from censure by Rome (the papacy thought Chenu was not deferential enough to ecclesiastical authority). Gilson was certainly a prominent forerunner of Vatican II. In the first four decades of the century he was particularly friendly with Parisian scholars of Jewish origin, more so in fact than with French

Catholic academics. He tried vigorously, although unsuccessfully, to get Marc Bloch a chair at the Collège de France. Gilson stayed in France through the German occupation and twice refused a formal invitation to collaborate with the occupying power. He did not restrain his young son and one of his daughters from dangerously exhibiting their contempt for the Germans.

In retrospect, Gilson's name is often coupled with that of the neo-Thomist philosopher Jacques Maritain. In the 1920s and 1930s Maritain and Gilson shared the controversial belief that it was time for the church to moderate substantially its resistance to modern thought and culture. Yet Gilson retained an ambivalent attitude to the neo-Thomist movement in French Catholic intellectual life. He found neo-Thomism, as articulated by Maritain, too doctrinaire, too unhistorical, and too eager to serve Rome. Gilson also had a strong personal antipathy against Maritain and even more against his wife (a poetess and a militant Russian Jewish convert to Catholicism). Where Gilson stood allied with the neo-Thomists was in pointing to St. Thomas Aquinas as a model for the progressive road that Catholic culture should take in the twentieth century. Just as Thomas had tried to integrate theology with the best science and philosophy of his day—Aristotle and his Arab and Jewish commentators—so should Catholicism now turn toward considered and careful integration with modern science, philosophy, and art. Beyond this fundamental policy, however, Gilson regarded Maritain and the neo-Thomists as too partisan, although in later years, in the sixties and seventies, he was more benign toward them. This may be attributed to loneliness and senility. It was also by now a different Catholic age. After Vatican II Gilson did not have to worry about the intellectual backwardness of the church and its embarrassing confrontations with modern culture.

There was very little wrong with Étienne Gilson as a man and as a teacher. He was admirable in every way. The problem arose with his interpretation of medieval thought and his understanding of Thomism and other medieval theories. Here, indeed, "extreme confusion" was not absent, and in general there was blindness as well as insight.

Gilson published dozens of books and hundreds of articles, in both academic journals and the more intellectual press, over half a century. His major books went through several editions, in which he often made major modifications. He changed as the cultural world, medieval studies, France, and the church changed, although not as much as those entities did. Therefore, it is not easy to pin down Gilson's exact position on many issues in medieval thought and culture. His industrious official biographer Laurence K. Shook, of the Toronto institute, does much better at recounting the innumerable dinner parties Gilson attended, the raft of honors he received from all quarters, and the massive income he generated from his public lectures than in explicating Gilson's intellectual positions. But obviously Gilson's constant inclination was to view medieval thought as integrationist and synthesizing. He tried to find the unity, the harmony, the consensus, the internal consistency in medieval thought and culture, rather than to point to the conflicts and the dialectical dynamics of change. He held this view not out of ignorance—no one has ever been more learned in medieval philosophy and theology—but out of a conviction that this is indeed "the spirit of medieval philosophy." He revered the Thomist mediating position in medieval thought. Gilson's faith in the medieval synthesis was also conditioned by his own peculiar role of a bridge builder between a still-conservative Catholicism (for the greater part of his career) and a secular academia that was often residually suspicious of Catholic higher learning as partisan and dogmatic, at least until the mid-1960s.

There lies at the center of Gilson's vision of the Middle Ages a utopian desire for a cultural integration, social stability, and political consensus in European life, somewhat similar to the vision of Ernst Robert Curtius. Gilson was in part inspired by the experience of World War I, in which he fought in the trenches and during which he spent two years in a German prison camp. In his integrationist vision of medieval culture there is the same yearning for peace and consensus that is communicated in Jean Renoir's magnificent 1937 antiwar film *The Grand Illusion*, which is set in a German prison camp. Peace and unity for Western Europe were the hope and expectation of a generation, and they were renewed, though with less utopian conviction, in 1945. It is not surprising that Gilson in the fifties showed resentment toward the cold war and gained a controversial reputation as a "third force" (as the term then went) neutralist. The third force intellectuals dreamed of an integrated Europe free from both Soviet and American domination. Their time has finally come at the beginning of the 1990s.

Gilson's visionary integrationist interpretation of medieval thought was also reflective of the hopes and expectations of many Catholic intellectuals of his generation, who believed that the universality and centralism of the Catholic Church constituted it a ready-made model for leadership in the unity of European culture. To make this thesis convincing, they contended that the church in the Middle Ages had already performed this integrationist, consensual, and peacemaking role and could do so again. In 1933 an English convert to Catholicism, Christopher Dawson, who was an autodidact of private means teaching adult education courses at Exeter University and in the 1950s held a chair of Catholic studies at Harvard for several years, had projected this unifying, synthesizing vision of the medieval church in a widely read book, *The Making of Europe*. On a more learned and specifically philosophical level, Gilson propounded much the same thesis as Dawson. Percy Ernst Schramm, in his *Kaiser, Rom, und Renovatio* (1929), attributed the same unifying and integrating capacity to the papacy and German Empire working together around A.D. 1000. One difference is that Schramm's work gives credit to the empire as well as to the church. Another difference is that in Schramm's account, the attempt at cultural synthesis and political unity tragically fails. But Gilson believed that Thomism had actually achieved in the thirteenth century this yearned-for cultural synthesis and that it had a long, durable prologue going back to St. Augustine.

This optimistic view of the centrality of synthesis in the Middle Ages still commands a core of faithful adherents. It is often routinely taught in Catholic colleges and in some secular ones, too. "The medieval synthesis" is a compelling way to signify Catholic Europe in the era of Thomas Aquinas, and a retroideal to be embraced persuasively today. Gilson articulated this view of the medieval heritage as well as anyone has done:

> The fourteen centuries of [medieval] history . . . were dominated by two distinct influences, Greek philosophy and Christianity. Every time educated Christians came in contact with Greek philosophical sources, there is a blossoming of theological and philosophical speculation. . . .
> This tradition is not a dead thing; it is still alive and our time bears witness to its enduring fecundity [in neo-Thomism]. There is no reason why this fecundity should come to an end. . . . The treasure of Christian philosophy in the Middle Ages exhibits an amazing wealth of still incompletely exploited ideas.

This is a highly optimistic view of both medieval culture and the twentieth century. This statement, in the conclusion of *History of Christian Philosophy in the Middle Ages* (1955), represents the essentials of Gilson's view of the Middle Ages. In some of his other writings he is even more utopian and enthusiastic. In 1956, nudged by his friendly rival Jacques Maritain, he declared St. Thomas Aquinas an existentialist, keeping up with the fashionable transatlantic intellectual trends, and concluded with this panegyric: "Thomism appears in all its beauty. It is a philosophy which creates excitement by means of pure ideas, and does so by sheer faith in the value of proofs and denials based on reason. . . . Because he serves reason so lovingly, St. Thomas becomes a poet, and . . . the greatest Latin poet of the Middle Ages. . . . Nowhere else, perhaps, does so demanding a reason respond to the call of so religious a heart. . . . [Thomism] is a philosophy that sets out to express in rational language the total destiny of the Christian man."

In the 1950s and early 1960s this view of Thomism and medieval Christianity gained wide adherence in the United States. Christopher Dawson, called to Harvard from the obscurity of teaching continuing education classes in a provincial British university, was propounding very similar interpretations in Cambridge, Massachusetts, from a chair that the pious Protestant Harvard president Nathan Pusey had created for him. In 1963 Time-Life Inc. launched a ten-volume series of books on the history of Western civilization and promoted and marketed them into a couple of million American homes. The author of the medieval volume was an undereducated Catholic journalist named Anne Fremantle, who regarded herself as Gilson's disciple and presented a further vulgarized version of Gilson's view of the centrality of Thomism in medieval culture, its vibrant relevance to today, and the way all medieval history led up to the medieval synthesis of the thirteenth century. Therefore, the interpretation that Time-Life Books transmitted to two million American suburban households was essentially Gilsonian. No medievalist could want a greater popular impact than that. Those were the golden days of Gilsonism. It is ironic that although Gilson kicked up quite a public fuss in Paris by his reservations about American cold war policy, his view of the Middle Ages and Thomism seemed to fit in tightly with the ambience of the cold war era. In time he realized this. Just as the Soviet bloc had a common ideology in Marxist-Leninism, so did the West have a common intellectual foundation in Thomism and the medieval synthesis.

Within medieval studies, Gilson's integrationist and synthesizing position focuses on three issues: combining medieval theology with philosophy; the continuing relation of Augustinianism and Thomism; and the late medieval crisis. There was such a thing as "Christian philosophy" in the Middle Ages, Gilson contends, as there still is today. This view was easy for polemical, campus-based humanists, such as Chicago's Robert Maynard Hutchins, Richard McKeon, and Mortimer Adler, and the other American neo-Thomists to endorse. It was ready-made for the middlebrow media in the forties and fifties to feed upon and praise. But it was always a highly controversial thesis among professional philosophers. Neither French and Belgian Catholic philosophers in the 1930s nor Anglo-American analytic philosophers in the 1980s found Gilson's vision of a Christian philosophy other than vague and confusing. In their perception, medieval philosophy was one thing, theology something else. In their perception, it is like putting oil and water in a bottle and shaking it vigorously. You get some degree of temporary superficial emulsion, but it goes against the laws of chemistry, and as soon as you stop shaking, in a little while the separation is evident again. This is what was wrong with Gilson's emulsion of Christian philosophy in the Middle Ages, its critics then and now contend. The anti-integrationists have been very dominant in the last twenty years as analytic philosophers (the disciples of Ludwig Wittgenstein) have gotten to work on medieval treatises. They have separated away the theology with surgical skill. In the 1920s and 1930s, Gilson contended against the Catholic scholars at the University of Louvain and the Parisian Catholic Institute precisely on this point. Now he seems to have lost the argument within academia, and his work seems curious and eccentric for professional philosophers, although not for the educated public.

Throughout his life Gilson agonized over the question of whether or not Thomism represents a break with the thought of St. Augustine. He shilly-shallied back and forth on this issue. Indeed, he said various things about it at different times. Whether Thomism is an intellectual revolution against Augustinianism or a reinterpretation of Augustinian doctrine in a new Aristotelian intellectual ambience and language remains one of the persistent conundrums of medieval studies. It is my view that Thomism was an almost clean break with Augustinianism and that Gilson leans much too far in trying to picture a continuity between these two great medieval intellectual and religious systems. This is still a particularly difficult issue for Catholic scholars to deal with because Rome wants continuity, not rupture, within the development of Catholic theology. Regarding medieval thought as conditioned by conflict between the Augustinians and the Thomists gives legitimacy to intellectual dissent within the Catholic Church today. That is the Roman conviction. Therefore, for all his vanguard liberalism as a Catholic thinker in his day, Gilson in retrospect appears as a Romanist-leaning conservative who did not appreciate the full extent of the intellectual upheaval of the twelfth and early thirteenth centuries.

Finally Gilson bewailed the breakaway from Thomism in the fourteenth century by the nominalist Oxford Franciscan William of Occam and his many English and German disciples. The nominalist doctrine separated religious faith and reason. It created two separate intellectual worlds (as we have today): the world of religion and the world of science. Gilson cannot deny that this happened, but he expresses deep regret for the devastating impact of Occamism on medieval Christian philosophy. What is deficient in Gilson's account, apart from his never admitting how much greater the adherence was to Occamism than to Thomism in the late Middle Ages, is that he does not explain the cultural, social, and psychological causes for the rise and triumph of Occamist nominalism and the doctrine of separated truth. Why was this the outcome of medieval philosophy? What compelled the most brilliant clerical minds of the fourteenth century to turn away from Aquinas's integrated system? Since Gilson hates the consequence of what happened, he cannot bring himself to focus on the how and why of what happened.

This raises the question of whether an integrationist belief in the compatibility of faith and reason is the most productive starting point for the study of medieval thought. A believer in conflict and incompatibility within medieval culture and theory would have an easier time than Gilson and give us more persuasive account of medieval thought after 1100. This is an ungrateful but unavoidable judgment on the prodigious effort of Étienne Gilson to write the history of medieval thought. His prolific writings are increasingly seen as more an insight into the French and Toronto Catholicism of the first half of this century than into the thought world of the Middle Ages. In reading Shook's breathless accounts of transatlantic forays, endless lecture tours, acquisition of innumerable honors, one wishes one could go back and tell the Gilson of 1935 to slow down, pull back, rethink the whole thing, and not spend the next forty years defending what is seen now as an essentially indefensible position.

Nevertheless, one has to acknowledge that Gilson's summing-up of his position in *History of Christian Philosophy in the Middle Ages* is one of the books that still stand in the front rank of narrative, comprehensive overviews of a major segment of medieval culture. There are many pages in it of subtle insight and evocative writing. It remains one of the seminal works in medieval studies. Gilson is always well organized. He writes for a wide audience, the whole academic world, and for the Catholic laity as well.

At the University of Paris in the decade before World War I, Gilson studied philosophy with a Jew with Catholic leanings, Henri Bergson, whom he idolized then and continued to revere for many decades. There are many similarities between Bergson and Gilson. They both were industrious and ambitious and great platform and classroom performers. The content of their thought was vaguely idealistic and had just the right progressive sound to it. They both were inspiring to many younger academics and tried hard to guide them in advancing their careers. But at the center of their thinking, Bergson and Gilson both are vague, mushy, impetuous, imprecise, wishful, and idiosyncratic. In spite of the gargantuan reputations they enjoyed in their lifetimes—membership in the Académie Française and all that—there was a built-in obsolescence to their work. However, the sheer learning that was involved in Gilson's historical work gives it a durable substance and allows it to age less rapidly than Bergson's philosophy, which seems vapid or even silly today in the reading. So do some of Gilson's more polemical writings, but the *History of Christian Philosophy in the Middle Ages* retains much of its monumental character.

Although the current authorities on medieval philosophy, like Cornell University's Norman Kretzmann and the concise and insightful writer John Marenbon of Cambridge University, with their professional skill in separating the hard-core philosophy from the religious casing of medieval theory, make Gilson look like an outmoded absolutizer of the Middle Ages, there is a fundamental point that Gilson argued for that merits consideration. Pick up the great treatises of the late twelfth, thirteenth, and early fourteenth centuries, and there is prevalent not only, as the analytical critics like Kretzmann and Marenbon believe, a layered segmentation of religious belief and philosophical discourse but also a recognizable degree of synergy between theology and philosophy. Gilson was not wrong to speak of a "Christian philosophy." It is just that there have yet to be fashioned a method and a set of historical and cultural assumptions, going well beyond Gilson's naive Thomist integrationism, to analyze and signify this medieval intellectual structure.

Gilson had the right goal and a great deal of the learning to reach that goal. He somehow lacked the intellectual equipment, the analytical concepts, to work effectively toward his goal. Gilson studied not only with Bergson but with another mandarin Jew, Émile Durkheim,

whom he did not like at all. He found Durkheim cold, oversyste-
matic, hyperanalytical, unhumanistic. Gilson much preferred the romanticized sociology of Lucien Lévy-Bruhl. Gilson should have listened
more closely to Durkheim. He badly needed a less engaged, less committed, nontheological, nonabsolutizing, more reserved and analytical
approach to the history of medieval philosophy.

Ironies abound when we compare Gilson and Knowles. Knowles's
great four-volume history of medieval religious orders, although written by a monk and cleric, carries no imprimatur (ecclesiastical license). Gilson's *History of Christian Philosophy in the Middle Ages* carries
an imprimatur even though Gilson taught in Paris in a secular institution (in Canada he taught in a peculiar clerical institute within a
state university). Knowles and Gilson have this much in common:
They were the most celebrated Catholic medievalists of their generation, but neither was loved in Rome. They were actually feared
there because of the huge reputations they gained in the secular world.
The cardinals had to go through the motions of praising them or
suffer a terrible embarrassment and loss of intellectual prestige for
the church. The lives and careers of Knowles and Gilson showed the
high degree of liberty Catholic scholars had before Vatican II, *provided* they held chairs in nonclerical institutions and were widely es-
teemed outside the church. A very fine scholar like the Dominican
friar M. D. Chenu, who worked in clerical circles, could be pushed
around by insensitive authorities with impunity, but not Gilson or
Knowles.

There was another marked similarity between Gilson and Knowles.
Both were inclined toward what we now call interdisciplinary approaches to medieval studies, to combining questions and data and
concepts and learning from a variety of disciplines. Neither had a
systematic way of going about this. Neither had a theory of cultural
history or sociology, for better or worse. But both were pioneers in
interdisciplinary commitments in their writings, and this partly accounts for the celebrity and continued popularity of their writings.

As far as one can tell from the biographical accounts, neither
Knowles nor Gilson ever turned down an invitation to give a funded
series of lectures somewhere. At the peaks of their careers they both
became overcommitted and gave lectures, later published, which are
intelligent and learned but are not fully developed and not at the level
of their best work. Perhaps they accepted all invitations as a response
to the hostility and criticism of them—often covert but well known
to them—in clerical circles. They aimed to show up those priests and

cardinals, and they did; but the books that resulted, while respectable, are often forced and underdeveloped. Gilson also accepted invitations to speak anywhere about anything because he wanted the money for his "daughters' dowries," as he said half-jocularly in a letter to his wife. No biographer has yet spoken of Knowles's fiscal interests, but it appears that he had no children to support.

Knowles's most ambitious effort at a set of invited and endowed lectures, *The Episcopal Colleagues of Thomas Becket*, derived from his Ford Lectures at Oxford, is a disappointment. The book contains some insightful pages on Gilbert Foliot, bishop of London, who, as an aristocrat and supporter of the king, was the most determined enemy of the Canterbury martyr, a bourgeois upstart who dared to withstand (for unknown reasons, possibly masochistic and suicidal) the juggernaut of the Angevin state. Aside from the attention Knowles gives to Gilbert Foliot, the book is flat—a good idea that is not developed. Gilson's endless parade of public lectures makes even sadder reading nowadays. It is not always easy to imagine these performances exciting large audiences between 1925 and 1955. Perhaps it was a simpler age, or did a clerical claque of smooth-cheeked Jesuits always hype the crowd?

Intellectually and temperamentally, Gilson and Knowles belonged to two different Catholic heritages from the Middle Ages. Knowles was by temperament a radical Augustinian—that is, he believed the doctrine that there is nothing good in the world other than a sanctified soul. Gilson was by temperament and intellect a liberal Thomist, that is, he believed in the good potential of organizations and institutions and insisted that structural ambiences could be created that were beneficial in their impact on individuals. In this regard, Gilson was more a traditional Roman Catholic than Knowles. Gilson's Thomism involves the conviction that the church does a lot of good morally and the Pontifical Institute of Medieval Studies a lot of good intellectually. Knowles held to a perception that has created endless problems for the medieval and modern hierarchy, the conviction that saints were all that ultimately counted in the history of human salvation. Everything else, in comparison with Christ, is dung and dross. In the thirteenth-century context Gilson would have ended up as a university rector and possibly a cardinal. Knowles in the Middle Ages would have ended as a canonized saint if he had died young and probably as a condemned heretic burned at the stake if he had lived long enough. Herein lie the dilemma and the grandeur of Roman Catholicism.

CHAPTER NINE

THE ONCE AND FUTURE KING

RICHARD WILLIAM SOUTHERN

I
THE CLAIM OF THE IDEAL

We know now that the most important development in medieval culture was not continuity with classical antiquity or perpetuation of the
theology of the Church Fathers but rather innovative trends in imagination and feeling in the period from about 1080 to 1230 that may
be called the romantic revolution and the discovery of the individual.
Late-nineteenth and early-twentieth-century writers were not oblivious of snatches of this cultural upheaval. They talked about courtly
love and the Virgin cult, but they could not get these phenomena
into a clear perspective and define them precisely. Before C. S. Lewis's *Allegory of Love* (1936), there was lacking a substantial credibility
and intellectual dignity in even pursuing the subjects of medieval romanticism, eroticism, and individualism, as if the people who studied
these phenomena were themselves considered marginal, gauche, bohemian, and not genuinely academic.

The situation in the 1970s and 1980s was entirely different. The
subject of twelfth-century romanticism and its literature was now academically mainline and was not only legitimate but was considered
central to the general study of medieval culture. Here is John Stevens, a Cambridge don, in 1973, writing in *Medieval Romance*, intended as a textbook for literature students: "There are good reasons,
I think we can now see, why romance should be the principal type
of medieval fiction, the major genre. It grew into being to express
'the claim of the ideal' in an age which needed to formulate a secular
idealism . . . and, doing so, to complement rather than (at first) to

challenge the traditional religious idealisms." Clear, concise, confident, right on target: The twelfth century was an era of new claim of the ideal, a new secular idealism, a cultural revolution, expressed in the literature of vernacular romance.

Similarly another British scholar, Lynette R. Muir, in 1985 in her *Literature and Society in Medieval France:* "One result of the stress on personal identity and problems [in the twelfth century] is that the national and religious fervour of the epics, group emotions, are replaced by more self-centered feelings of love and friendship. . . . This stress on emotion as well as action in the romances reflects the wider audience for whom they were composed and especially the greatly increased importance of women as readers and patrons." So the romantic cultural revolution is tied to a social change involving the liberation of aristocratic women. What are now the unblinking postulates of textbooks were in 1950 considered radical and suspiciously outlandish. One book principally changed all that.

The book that opened the way to these new perspectives and broader horizons on twelfth-century culture and fully legitimated the close reading of romanticism and individualism was *The Making of the Middle Ages,* published in 1953 by Richard William Southern, a Balliol College, Oxford don. Although Southern was born in 1912 and this was his first book—so he was a slow starter (the war had taken half a decade out of his career, and ill health also slowed him down)—*The Making of the Middle Ages* was the breakthrough book that legitimated analysis of the romantic revolution and opened the way for a much deeper and more complex understanding of the Middle Ages. Published in an American paperback by the Yale University Press, *Making* has now gone through thirty printings, and it is arguably, even more than Marc Bloch's *Feudal Society* and Ernst Robert Curtius's *European Literature and the Latin Middle Ages,* the single most widely read and influential book written on the Middle Ages in the twentieth century. Even today, when it has been in some respects rendered obsolete by Southern's own later prolific writings, and its portrayal of twelfth-century culture challenged, extended, and modified by the critical and historical literature that *Making* prepared the way for, the book is a powerful, deeply moving performance, the work of a great craftsman and a person of very deep feeling.

Southern's book, originally commissioned as a textbook for undergraduates by Hutchinson, an established educational publisher in London, is a little more than 250 pages long. Its conciseness contributed greatly to its impact. It is a direct and convincing statement that targeted the study of twelfth-century spiritual and secular sensibility as the most important development in that era of change. It is a work of both information and inspiration. Southern was a student and the prime protégé of Maurice Powicke. It is in *Making* that intimations and expectations of the Oxford fantasists were compressed and transformed into a format that can be imbibed by undergraduate students and the educated public and accepted as a starting line for further research and speculation by scholars.

This is what a seminal work of humanistic scholarship does, and that is why there are so few high-impact books of this nature. The requisite nobility of temperament, learning, insight, high seriousness, and passion is very rarely joined with clarity, concision, and literary art and communicated in such a way that not only is what is being said convincing and stimulating, but also the reader receives the secondary impression that much more lies behind the present picture: that this book is an invitation to or an interim report on a monumental and far-ranging segment of human experience. In Southern's case he authenticated the claims of the ideal in twelfth-century culture and opened the way for a rapidly developing exploration of the diverse and extremely complex facets of the romantic revolution of the Middle Ages.

If *The Making of the Middle Ages* had not been written by Sir Maurice Powicke's protégé and a don at the very pinnacle of the Oxbridge establishment, a fellow and tutor of Balliol College, would it have had the impact that it had? Probably not as great if *Making* had been published by a professor at Berkeley, Columbia, Liverpool, or Glasgow. If the author had taught at Iowa or Oberlin or Cardiff or Manitoba, it might have been largely ignored or widely condemned. These depressing conditions within the sociology of academia do not, however, detract from the value and quality of Southern's book. And the sociological argument can be turned around. It required greater courage for Southern to publish a vanguard book taking a positive view of twelfth-century romanticism than someone else in a less exalted position. By no means did even Southern escape unscathed. The review of *Making* in *Speculum*, the establishmentarian journal of the Harvard Haskins school-dominated Medieval Academy of America, was a sneer that completely missed the point and importance of the book.

Even if Southern's book can be challenged or faulted in significant ways from current knowledge, even if it seems too cautious and conformist now, this does not lessen the degree of insight and magnitude of courage or the fineness of inspiration and insight that shaped it. It was a book that, lacking Southern's self-confidence, boldness, privileged audience, and literary skill, others could have written but didn't. The book spoke for a generation of medievalists and raised the dam to unleash a flood of publication that transformed over the next three decades the cultural and intellectual history of the Middle Ages. The focus was to be now, and largely remains, on romanticism as the most creative movement in medieval culture.

We have seen Sir Richard Southern as the heir of the Oxford fantasists. The appreciation of the personal feelings and self-consciousness in Southern's view of the Middle Ages had also been anticipated, to a degree, in David Knowles's *The Monastic Order* and Volume I of *The Religious Orders*, and it could be construed that Knowles's portrayal of individuated religious sensibility both inspired Southern and established a legitimation context for *Making*. This is generally plausible, but actually there was no significant personal contact between Knowles and Southern, and Southern was not inclined to recommend Knowles's books to his own students. The publication of *Making* coincided with the decline in the shining quality of Knowles's continuing work. Certainly Southern, after *Making* had become an immediate educational best seller and his visibility and credibility had increased greatly and very rapidly, needed no dependence on anyone, not even Powicke, who had patiently and devotedly guided his intellectual development and career for fifteen years.

Looking back after four decades at the whole question of twelfth-century romanticism that Southern's *Making* brought to the foreground of thinking about the Middle Ages, we can see many subtopics and complex facets. First, granted that the romantic movement of the twelfth century augmented self-consciousness, to what extent did it articulate a concept of individualism, the appreciable autonomy of the individual? Is such a concept of individualism even possible within the parameters of formalist literary traditions and of twelfth-century theology and devotional practice? Secondly, can we separate a secular romanticism in twelfth-century culture from a much-enhanced spirituality in practical mysticism? A subsidiary question to this one is the determination of the precise role of St. Bernard of Clairvaux and the new Cistercian order in twelfth-century romantic culture. A further related issue is whether romanticism was the outcome of the impact of the new piety of the late eleventh century on Western sensibility. Or were there underlying social forces—the population boom, urbanization, the wealth and comfort of the life of the nobility, the growth of literacy and learning and vernacular language after 1150, the growing plethora of educated young clerics without easy access to suitable employment, a reaction against centralizing bureaucratic power systems in church and state—that inspired and shaped both spiritual and secular forms of romanticism in the twelfth century?

Thirdly, did twelfth-century culture depart from the heightened sensibility and self-consciousness that we usually identify with romanticism to attain a new naturalism in perceiving the physical world and to a psychological realism in assessment of heterosexual human relationships? Or are this naturalism and this psychological realism part of the whole romantic movement itself? A related question is to account for the proclivity of twelfth-century (as early-nineteenth-century) romantic culture to combine contextual fantasy with precise realistic analysis of intricate personal behavior, a peculiar encoded texture. This means that the setting and the story in romantic literature are often fantastic and highly sentimental, but interpersonal relationships are depicted in subtly realistic terms.

Fourthly, what specific aspects of ancient eroticism (Plato, Ovid, etc.) inspired medieval romanticism? How did the romantic movement draw upon, interpret, and absorb these aspects of the classical heritage? A parallel question is the use and influence of the patristic (fourth- and fifth-century, especially Augustinian) treatment of the mind-body problem and doctrines of sexuality. Another parallel issue is the Mediterranean (Arab, Byzantine, Jewish) influence on twelfth-century culture; there have been those who persist in saying that the European medieval romantic movement was the consequential impact of Spanish Arab culture on the North. Finally, there is the whole issue of the relationship between the rise of popular heresy and counterchurch movements and facets of spiritual and secular romanticism. Was radical religion a confrontational extension of romanticism or possibly a conservative reaction against it?

These are immensely difficult and complex questions of cultural history and are critical to our understanding the meaning of the Middle Ages and the shape of the development of medieval civilization. And we have not yet listed such particular and familiar topics as the Virgin cult, courtly love, the Arthurian tradition, and the origins of Gothic architectural style.

The Making of the Middle Ages is a book of such seminal and transcendental quality because it legitimated these questions. I went through two years of graduate courses at Princeton from 1951 to 1953 with very distinguished representatives of the regnant schools of *Geistesgeschichte*, American institutional pie, and formalism and never heard a serious discussion of any of them. Southern forced medievalists, particularly of the younger generation, to address these questions. It set up a new discourse in medieval studies.

Southern himself has devoted the remainder of his long life and illustrious career to considering many of the particular issues arising from medieval romanticism. A group of sometimes starry-eyed academic knights followed this bold King Arthur of medieval scholarship into enchanted forests of learning and intellect in pursuit of these fiery and thorny dragons. As in the Arthurian legend, these young knights of the new Round Table did not in the end always reverentially follow Dick Southern's leadership, and he could plausibly wonder if some were his followers or his betrayers. But without this "Once and Future King," they probably would have never got started on their own quests. If in the end Arthur disappointed apocalyptic expectations and didn't entirely fulfill his charismatic promise and glorious start, well, that is part of the Arthurian archetype and possibly an inevitable consequence of human nature.

There was a fair king once in those sunny, simple days of the Eisenhower era, who set up (we thought) his Camelot court at Oxford and summoned us from the distant isles and ombré forests and cold climes. We imagined he had sent us a trumpeted message in his luminous book: Come and build with me a Camelot of mind and learning, and we shall start something very real and take over the world. And we came, and after a while we saw there was no round table, and Camelot was our own projection onto him of our wish fulfillment, our own dreams and nightmares from the recess of our frustrations and unsatisfied experiences. And there was no once and future king, only Professor Sir Richard William Southern, fellow and tutor of Balliol College, Oxford, later Chichlele professor of history in Oxford University, president of St. John's College and all the other tawdry tired persiflage of Oxbridge academia. And we went away, sad, lonely and sometimes bitter. But we had been touched and we were never the same again. Romanticism drives hard and stains deep. When the ideal has made its claim upon us, we cannot return to what was before.

II

LOOKING FOR CAMELOT

On December 10, 1953, I came back to my rooms at the Graduate College of Princeton University ("Magdalen College, Oxford, as conceived by Cecil B. De Mille," it was described by a visiting Oxford don) and found a telegram from the head of the history department at the University of Manitoba and chairman of that province's Rhodes Scholarship Committee. He informed me that I had been selected Manitoba's Rhodes scholar of 1954. So it was Oxford, the Valhalla of all Canadian middle-class boys, for me. Above all, I would be studying with Richard Southern, whose book I had just read and was thrilled by.

Two weeks after I arrived in Oxford, when I had not yet become conditioned to the abominable college food, nor found the WC in the Bodleian Library (it was hidden behind a door marked "School of Oriental Languages"), I received a card from Southern to come see him at Balliol College. I was impressed by his elegant study and even more by the man's appearance. He was the most beautiful Englishman I had ever seen in the flesh, with piercing blue-gray eyes, sandy hair slightly graying, an unmistakable mellifluous voice. Except for a long nose, he resembled Laurence Olivier. He was tall and moved gracefully. He was well dressed for a don. Southern lived in a very handsome house provided by Balliol College. There he would invite students to tea. His wife put out an elaborate spread of sandwiches and cakes, but it was evident that a student was not supposed to still his growling stomach from this generous display. The teatime lasted exactly forty-five minutes.

In the fall of 1954 Southern and I did not hit it off well. I was too eager to get on with my dissertation rather than to explore and learn. Southern did not like my investiture controversy topic. He thought it too Germanic (Southern, I am convinced, did not read German to speak of). He said I was too Germanic and dialectical in my orientation; he wondered whether I should work with him. Somehow he assumed I was a fervent disciple of Ernst Kantorowicz, whom he despised. "I am only paid fifteen pounds a year to supervise you. It's hardly worth my while," he said. I was devastated. Southern saw the color draining from my face. He was a very kind man. "I tell you what," he said, "write me an essay on St. Anselm of Canterbury. Then I will decide whether I should supervise you." I went back to my bed-sitter at Oriel (it was a really nice suite of rooms, the best

Oriel could give its students). I cried for a half hour. Then I wrote for fifteen hours on the typewriter. Of course, I had been working for a year on Anselm; I had read all his works. I possessed a copy of the new edition of Anselm's works by Father Schmitt. The next afternoon I left the essay of some thirty pages with Southern's secretary. Two days later, he summoned me again. "Look," he said with that incomparable Laurence Olivier-Henry V smile, "you have gotten it all wrong. You really don't understand Anselm. But it's remarkable you could do all this work so fast. So I will take you on as a student." Southern had forgotten that I had told him I had been working on Anselm for a whole year. He accepted me as a student because of a misunderstanding.

In my two terms at Oxford I saw Southern perhaps six times. Most of the time we would walk together in the university park, which was near his home. He would ask me questions about German scholarship, books that I had read and he hadn't (Percy Schramm, for instance). One day he told me he had agreed to write an article for the *Times Literary Supplement* commemorating the seven hundredth anniversary of the death of the only English pope, Adrian IV (Nicholas Breakspear). But he had discovered that the major work on Adrian IV was in Norwegian (Breakspear had been papal legate in Norway before his election as pope). I told Southern that the Oslo professor who wrote the book had contributed an English summary to an obscure magazine published in Minneapolis. When Southern's essay appeared in the *Times Literary Supplement*, I was amused to note the heavy use of this Minnesota article.

Southern and I argued incessantly about the medieval church. Essentially he had a much more favorable view than I of the church because he focused on the devotional, liturgical, and intellectual side and didn't think the political side, especially papal politics, meant very much. I then took the opposite view, under Strayer's influence. Now I would say Southern was 75 percent in the right. As a matter of fact, in the following decade I moved over mostly to his position. My *Medieval History: The Life and Death of a Civilization*, which for nineteen years penetrated American middle-class households via the History Book Club, at ninety-nine cents a copy, is largely a gloss on Southern.

It would be easy to say, and not unreasonable, that I had gone to Oxford after three grueling years of overwork and no social or sexual life at then-monastic Princeton, that as a Canadian drenched in colonial Anglophilic culture I had developed an absurdly idealized view of Oxford, and that I had projected all my expectations of relief and happiness onto Dick Southern. I had romanticized Oxford into a Camelot, which in the harsh days of 1954 it certainly did not pretend to be, and I had imagined Dick Southern to be the Once and Future King, the charismatic liberator, whereas he was just another learned Oxbridge don, with more imagination and literary skill than most. Later Dick and I did develop an amicable relationship, and we still correspond occasionally.

It is certainly true that Southern's career until he published *The Making of the Middle Ages* was not extraordinary. He came from the grimy northern industrial town of Newcastle-upon-Tyne. His family was middle class, with no affluence. There was an excellent state-supported secondary school in Newcastle, and Southern went there and showed he was a brilliant student. He won a scholarship to Balliol College, Oxford, then perhaps intellectually the most prestigious of Oxbridge colleges, and was graduated in 1932 with first-class honors in history. Maurice Powicke, the regius professor, took Southern under his wing, and for the next five years Southern was supported in that peculiar private, unprogrammed study that Oxbridge gives to its most promising graduates who want academic careers. He sought no doctorate, which was still uncommon for an Oxbridge historian to seek, but spent three years as an autodidactic "research" fellow, then a year at Paris, and a few months in Munich, where he did not learn to read the language. In 1937, with Powicke's assistance, Southern became a fellow and tutor in history at Balliol, a position he was to retain until he got a university chair in 1961. He turned out to be a brilliant teacher both in undergraduate tutorials and—rare for an Oxbridge don—on the lecture platform. By 1940 he was an officer in the army. He spent the last two years of the war, from which he emerged with the rank of major, as an intelligence officer attached to the Foreign Office. He married the widow of an RAF hero and resumed his Oxford career. He lived in that handsome house, which the Balliol leased to him for a nominal sum. His family life with his wife, a mainstay of the socially prominent Oxford Bach Choir, and two sons was a happy one.

In postwar Oxford Dick Southern had two close friends among the medievalists. One was Richard Hunt, the dour Bodleian archivist, who published very little himself but who introduced Southern to many intricacies of twelfth-century rhetoric, philosophy, and theology. The other was Powicke's other prime protégée, Beryl Smalley, who had published a disorganized and underresearched but brilliant book, *The Study of the Bible in the Middle Ages*. After years of marginal existence and grinding poverty, Smalley had obtained a teaching position at one of the Oxford women's colleges, where she eventually became vice-principal. In another era, one more hospitable to women scholars (the 1920s, or the 1970s and 1980s), she might have developed into a very important medievalist. As it was, she was not negligible and certainly interesting.

Southern liked Beryl Smalley as both a scholar and a person, as he did gloomy Richard Hunt. He wrote necrologies for both of them in the *Proceedings of the British Academy*. Consciously or not, his biographical essay on Hunt is devastating, an account of a man of great talent who, because of some psychological morbidity, accomplished little of what he could have done. Hunt's life and career are a salutary lesson in how much the British have suffered from their antipathy to psychotherapy. On the other hand, Southern's obituary essay on Beryl Smalley is upbeat, subtle, delightful, one of the best things he ever wrote, a portrait of an inimitable British eccentric. It should have been published in *Encounter* or the *New Yorker* instead of being buried in the dusty volumes of the British Academy. He does overrate the quality of Smalley's scholarship, but so what?

In 1952 Southern took leave from teaching for a year to recover from tuberculosis. While sick, he wrote *Making*, which astonished Oxford, because his previous publications of any consequence consisted of three articles—a slim rate of productivity even for a forty-year-old Oxford don who taught eighteen hours a week in term. Hutchinson, incessant publishers of textbooks, decided to get two leading Oxford dons to produce survey books for undergraduates, J. M. Wallace-Hadrill of Merton College on the early Middle Ages, and Southern on the high Middle Ages. Wallace-Hadrill's book *The Barbarian West* is the textbook he was commissioned to write. It has its moments, such as the trashing of poor Charlemagne, but withal it is a conventional, competent effort. Southern's book is very different. Drawing upon twenty years of thinking and lecturing about the Middle Ages, relaxed by his release from heavy teaching, fired by his consumptive disease and prospects of a short life, he immensely exceeded his mandate. It is indeed an introductory book—it can still be read by the more literate American college freshmen and sophomores— but *The Making of the Middle Ages* is, of course, much more than that: a personal statement of breathtaking sensitivity about medieval culture. It fulfilled his prescription that "the first duty of the historian is to produce works of art."

Every seminal book is made as much by its audience as by its author; so far we can agree with the "reader response theory." The important books respond to a demand, usually lying just below the surface. They articulate what many people want to have raised to consciousness at that moment. Great books release feelings, express yearnings, respond to existing wishes and hopes. That was true of Southern's book: He articulated the intellectual rebellion and imaginative stretching of an emerging generation of medievalists, like myself, and humanists in general.

That is why I plead not guilty to making unrealistic demands on Dick Southern and projecting onto him my own neuroses. His life, career, friends, family were entirely conventional for a Balliol don. But he had transcended this context intellectually, rising very far above this ambience as a mind and writer. He was far too intelligent a man, far too great a historian not to know that he had lit the torch of academic upheaval and cultural revolution. Publishing a book, at least one intended for a wide audience, represents the drawing of a social contract with its readers. You cannot say, "Let's build Camelot," and then unilaterally say, "Forget it." In those days Southern drew to himself like a megaton magnet starry-eyed young graduate students who looked on him as more than the greatest medievalist since Maitland. They—we—looked on him as the founder of a new religion who would transform the transatlantic academic and humanistic worlds. *The Making of the Middle Ages* was much more than a very great book of historical scholarship. It was a revelation, the Gospel According to St. Richard, a liberation, an epiphany. He had articulated what we all felt but could not find the words or courage to say, which is what a revelation is, in any time or place.

But emotionally and domestically Southern was unprepared to be the leader of a cult, to embrace a group of dangerous, obscure, and awkward young people drawn from overseas Rhodes scholars and the teachers' common rooms of British secondary schools. He didn't want to be another Frank Leavis, the famous Cambridge literary critic and cultural guru of a major academic and intellectual cult. And Southern didn't have to be. Leavis was marginal at Cambridge; he never even got a chair. He was, in fact, despised by most of the Cambridge English faculty, so he naturally fell back on being the leader of a cult; he had nothing else to sustain him, poor chap, and his brilliant Jewish wife, despised even more than he at Cambridge, urged him on. But Southern's situation was very different. Not only was he in the peculiar position of having written the best book on medieval history by an Englishman since Maitland and, along with Percy Schramm's *Kaiser, Rom, und Renovatio*, the best single volume on medieval history in this century, but he was also (thanks to Powicke and his donship at Balliol) at the center of the establishment. Among the renowned dons, Southern was treated with deference. He was living in an elegant house provided by Balliol, and his wife was a visible person on the Oxford scene and not the kind of woman who was happy to see her husband lead a great split in the academic establishment (no Mrs. Queenie Leavis, she, to put it mildly). So Southern eschewed the possibility of being the Wyclif (the revolutionary fourteenth-century Oxford don) of his day. That his health was poor at the time certainly also affected his reluctance to become a cult leader and an antagonist of the academic establishment.

I was not the only one hurt, aggrieved, and bewildered by Southern's cool and distant attitude, naive and foolish as I was. Far from it. I remember in March 1955 sitting in a coffee shop on Broad Street in the middle of Oxford and listening for two hours as a young Englishman whom Southern had just dismissed as a doctoral student and told to go back to schoolteaching poured out his heart to me through cascades of tears and rage. This was not a unique occurrence.

Southern in the mid-1950s had a very difficult, delicate choice to make. He chose not to play St. Francis or Frank Leavis. I am sure Sir Richard's life has been calmer and happier for it. I am also sure that currently humanistic scholarship and medieval studies are much the worse for his decision not to challenge the academic world.

Southern's reserve and modest ambitions were pleasing to his friend the Bodleian master Richard Hunt and to the erratic regius professor in the 1950s and early 1960s Vivian Galbraith. Hunt and Galbraith had between them made an intellectual desert and called it peace, and Dick Southern was not going to disturb it. The British establishment likes occasional intellectual innovators and is likely to treat the prized ones with better psychic and tangible rewards than they would receive in the United States, at least until very recently. But intellectual innovators are severely rationed in British academia—one or at most two per academic discipline per half century. In this subtle way, the intellectual conservatism of the establishment is actually reinforced, since the grandees can point to a single unique innovator as the outcome of their own ambient wisdom and plasticity, and they then can go peaceably back for another generation to pouring the sherry before high table dinner and the port afterward. C. P. Snow, who was a Cambridge science don in the 1930s, articulated this theme in at least three of his novels. Oxbridge's nemesis, herself an Oxford graduate, Margaret Thatcher, knew what was going on in those hallowed halls and why Oxbridge must be shaken and its best humanities dons dispersed overseas if Britain was to awake from its long slumber.

The designated and privileged innovator at Oxbridge has to hold a proper attitude, which means that while operating at the forward margin of the discipline in his own work, he does nothing to alter the received and prevailing organization and power structure. Guided by his Svengali, Hunt, Southern played this role to perfection. He operated at the outer limits of medieval studies and speculated boldly and persuasively as an analyst of high medieval culture. But any suggestion from the young that he form an indentifiable school, institutionalize his ideas into a programmed institute, set himself as the head of a long-overdue academic revolution, he coldly rebuffed. The people he did gather around him, the students he accepted and maintained were, with perhaps one or two exceptions, an ordinary, conformist, anal-retentive lot that excelled in reintegrating Southern's ideas, where they were most radical and fertile, back into the anodyne, established view of the Middle Ages and making sure that horizons would be sparsely adorned but not expanded. This outcome can readily be seen from the Festschrift (honorary anniversary volume) presented to Southern in 1981 on the occasion of his seventieth birthday. It is a dull collection of conventional pieces, in a few instances superficially glitzed up a bit with Southern-like sensibility. If all we knew of Southern was this volume, if we did not have his own writings, no one could ever tell that he was ever a burning rocket against the night sky of medieval studies. If the students' essays reflect the teacher, then Southern from the evidence of this lamentably pedestrian volume, was only slightly above average in imagination and insight. That would be a gross falsification, but it was the image of Southern that Hunt and Galbraith wanted to be projected, and Southern was content, indeed eager to go along with this charade.

Southern has always seen himself as an individual scholar rather than as the creator of institutions. More than that, he was a distinctive, unpredictable individual. When I knew him in 1955, he insisted that for political reasons (probably under the influence of his Communist colleague at Balliol Christopher Hill, who now indeed occupies a lavishly endowed chair in New York City) he would never visit the United States. But in 1962 Southern turned up in New York on a lecture tour of the northeastern United States. I was taken by the ease with which he talked with a group of Barnard undergraduates after he had given his charismatic Laurence Olivier type of platform performance there. He was genuinely interested in the adoring Barnard groupies as persons. He was not soliciting adulation, as Erwin Panofsky would have done. In 1989, very deaf and in seclusion as well as retirement, Southern performed an act of astonishing generosity. He had been awarded a sixty-thousand-dollar all-European prize for distinction in the humanities. He donated the prize to an Oxford women's college to help found a new position in medieval studies. The donation was in honor of Vivian Galbraith, whose daughter was the head of the college. I do not know how Southern could be so generous. Some of his books had done well, but he was by no means a wealthy man, and he had children who undoubtedly could have used the money. Completely inner-directed, unpredictable Dick Southern walked his singular road, listening like an idiosyncratic medieval saint to the call of a private trumpet.

It would have been psychologically very difficult for Southern in the fifties and sixties to have used his celebrity to create a medieval institute at Oxford, as much as that was needed, especially by graduate students and recent Ph.D.'s from the English-speaking world. Southern had a profound distaste for the institutional ambitions of the French mandarins. His vision of himself and his advancement was a conventional Oxbridge one: a chair, a knighthood, the headship of an Oxford college (of course, he wanted Balliol, but eventually he was satisfied with the presidency of St. John's, a small, quiet college then more famous for its swans than its students). The thought of heading an institute, becoming responsible for droves of eager, uncourtly, sassy doctoral students, the prospect of quarreling with the academic establishment instead of joshing with them collegially at Oxbridge high table filled him with dread. He sensed the tremendous power that potentially was his in the mid-fifties and early sixties, and he turned away from using it, lest he act in a way unconventional for a British don.

Southern today professes not to regret for a moment the course he took. But I wonder if he doesn't sometime in the dark of night think differently. History teaches. The remarkable thing about the great medieval oppositionists, Joachim of Fiore, St. Francis, John Wyclif (or Winston Churchill in the 1930s), is not what they said— many, many others had the same perceptions—but that they *did* say it, after all, and faced the terrible consequences, the emotional strain and psychic stress and loneliness. They paid the price. But they did change the world. Southern chose not to. He made, in Dante's term, the "great refusal." Herein lies a great difference in the road taken by the young David Knowles and that taken by Dick Southern.

I grieve for the sad anomaly, devastating in its ironic and imbecilic contradictions, in the history of medieval studies in the twentieth century. Bloch's disciples have built vast power bases where they have done some good, but also much damage. Southern, who could have done an enormous amount of good if he had founded an institute in his own best intellectual image and used its patronage powers to transform the medievalist profession, turned away and made the "great refusal." Schramm and Kantorowicz were distracted from institute building, in different ways, by Hitler's shadow, although if Kantorowicz had stayed at Berkeley, something very important could have happened there (the rudiments of a great school were emerging when he played strange tricks in the loyalty oath business and accepted Oppenheimer's siren call to Princeton). Knowles was emotionally worn out by the time he achieved a position of power. The Holy Spirit had departed from him. Gilson built skillfully at Toronto, but his own intellectual limitations and the clerical freezing of the mind at the Pontifical Institute conspired to create a respectable but torpid place. Strayer had enormous power and influence, but a combination of intellectual blindness and psychological imbalance prevented him from using it effectively. So we are left today with Bloch's disciples dominating in Europe and America because of their resources and organization. It was Southern's inhibition that hurt the most. It was an Arthurian—and Shakespearean—denouement.

III
"FOR HE IS AN ENGLISHMAN"

Southern's most original book since *The Making of the Middle Ages* was published in 1986, several years after he had retired from the presidency of St. John's College, Oxford. The leisure afforded by his retirement from administration and teaching and the improvement in his health allowed him to explore a new subject and a new cultural era, that of the early thirteenth century. The result was *Robert Grosseteste: The Growth of an English Mind in Medieval Europe*. Grosseteste (d. 1253) was a philosopher and scientist and in his later years the

bishop of Lincoln, the diocese in which Oxford University was located. Grosseteste not only had an official supervisory role over the
university as bishop of Lincoln but was much involved in its intellectual development. Although not officially a member of the Franciscan
order, Grosseteste was also very much connected to the English
Franciscans, who in his later years were coming to play the dominant
role at the university.

Southern's study of Grosseteste's life and thought was a radical
break from all previous accounts of this prominent thirteenth-century
thinker and churchman. While previous writers assumed that Grosseteste had studied at Paris and was a product of the rising scholastic
movement, Southern claims that Grosseteste received his education
only in England and was not part of the vanguard Continental cultural and educational development. The subtitle of Southern's book
is therefore highly significant. Grosseteste is an *English* mind. Even
more important, Grosseteste in Southern's portrayal represents a different strand in the cultural history of the thirteenth century from
Thomas Aquinas or the Franciscans teaching at Oxford in the late
thirteenth century, like Duns Scotus. Grosseteste's culture is humanistic, softer, a more personal, traditional, demotic culture with "a
preference for insight rather than formal structure." Grosseteste's intellectual roots, as viewed by Southern's, lie in the freewheeling humanistic, philosophical, and scientific (including astrological) speculation
of the late twelfth century, rather than in the new highly disciplined
Aristotelian, obsessively structured world of Parisian Thomism.

All works of history are in a sense autobiographical, particularly
if the author is dealing with a historical personality that he finds
sympathetic. This was especially the case with Southern, who in the
earlier work that had made him famous projected himself onto twelfth-
century religious figures like St. Anselm of Canterbury and St. Bernard of Clairvaux. Now, in his seventies, Southern saw himself in
Robert Grosseteste. Southern sensed his own distinctiveness, his own
special identity in medieval studies, his character as an "English mind"
within the European and transatlantic study of the Middle Ages, going
his own way, following his own counsel.

Southern's comments on his great contemporaries among medievalists were acerbic and largely negative. His review of the first volume of Knowles's *Religious Orders* in 1949 was patronizing and de-
meaning. Knowles should have stuck to strictly monastic history,
Southern proposed. He had little enthusiasm for Knowles's efforts at
broad cultural and intellectual history. His review treated Knowles

as a monk who had strayed off the reservation, with very modest appreciation for the breadth and grandeur of Knowles's vision of medieval religious culture and small enthusiasm for Knowles's personality studies. Kantorowicz had been personally detested by Southern when he heard him lecture at Oxford in 1939. Southern's review of *The King's Two Bodies* in 1959 continues to exude hostility and extreme contempt for Kantorowicz's "mystification" and inability to grasp "reality." Marc Bloch on feudal society is "all surface." Dick Southern walks alone. Even his assessment of the work of his teacher and patron Maurice Powicke, in another British Academy necrology, is sparing in praise. He liked Powicke more as a man than as a medievalist.

Southern's own major works, aside from his first book, *Making*, and his most recent on Grosseteste, comprise a study of St. Anselm of Canterbury and his monastic circle in early-twelfth-century England (1963); *Western Views of Islam in the Middle Ages* (1962), his weakest book; an important collection of essays on twelfth-century thought and culture, especially humanism (1970); and a valiant effort in a commissioned Penguin book to provide an overview of the medieval church (*Western Society and the Church in the Middle Ages*, 1970).

Because of the depth of learning and subtlety of insight, but also because of the skill in writing which reaches moments of high literary art, Southern has shaped a generation's view of medieval culture as it existed particularly in northern France, southern England, and to a lesser degree northern Italy. That leaves out a lot of Europe but except for western Germany involves the main centers of European culture from 1100 to 1250.

In *The Making of the Middle Ages* Southern said he was ignoring Germany because it had fallen behind the vanguard trends of the twelfth century; it was intellectually backward. This is, of course, doubtful. One of the three greatest religious visionaries of the twelfth century (along with the French abbot Bernard of Clairvaux and the southern Italian abbot Joachim of Fiore) was Abbess Hildegard of Bingen, from the German Rhine Valley. One of the three or four most subtle historical minds of the twelfth century was Frederick II's granduncle Bishop Otto of Freising. And arguably the single finest work of romantic literature in the period was Wolfram von Eschenbach's *Parzifal* (c. 1200), the work of a Rhineland nobleman.

There are obvious additional limitations to Southern's work as a medievalist. He has little to say about art, and what he does say is banal. His use of literary texts does not always appreciate the complex irony and trends toward psychological realism in twelfth-century literature, as in the romances of Chrétien de Troyes. And his account of medieval heresy is distant and uninvolved and lacks appreciation of the often inseparable intertwining of heretical movements with more general popular devotion.

Sir Richard's Middle Ages are inclined to the benign and harmonious. He stands alongside Knowles, Gilson, and Curtius as an enthusiast for the Middle Ages. From Southern's pages it is hard to understand the dismay and disappointment hardening into hatred and fury that the papal bureaucracy staffed with Roman lawyers generated among idealistic churchmen as well as materialistic and self-serving kings and lords. The significance of the rise of militant intolerance and a persecuting society, beginning with Judeophobia as early as 1100 and culminating around 1250 in the outright intellectual terrorism of the Inquisition, is largely ignored in his work. Southern's twelfth century is a sunny place, and menacing indications of hatred, militancy, power frenzy, and ideological fanaticism, while not entirely discounted, are placed in a distant background and are not effectively assessed.

Southern is a medievalist whose limitations are glaring, but so are his accomplishments. He is indeed a singular "English mind" in European culture with peculiar blind spots that so often characterize an autodidactic Oxbridge humanist. But when he is in command of his material, even when his interpretations can in some instances be plausibly challenged, he is magnificent. Dick Southern has written some of the best pages ever penned about the Middle Ages.

Southern devoted two decades to studying St. Anselm of Canterbury (d. 1109) and the circle of French monks whom this Italian monastic aristocrat brought with him across the Channel from Normandy when he became archbishop of Canterbury. Southern convinces us of two important cultural phenomena that rose from this circle. First, Anselm's theology represented a radical change in the medieval conception of the Godhead and understanding of salvation. The paradigm shift from the Old to New Testament, from God the Judging Father to God the Suffering Son was decisively articulated by St. Anselm and his disciples. They communicated a much altered kind of Christianity, one of service, devotion, and love rather than triumph, power, and authority. The significance of the Incarnation was modified. Why does God become man? asks Anselm. The answer is: Not only to save mankind but to show mankind how to behave—in charity, in concern for others, in sacrifice and generosity. The message of the cross is educational as well as doctrinal. Not only did this critical alteration in the direction of medieval Christianity profoundly shape the subsequent development of medieval piety and theology, but its impact has continued until the present time.

The second change that Southern directly traces to Anselm and his circle is the articulation of the Virgin cult so that Mary becomes not only the weeping mother at the foot of the cross but also the Madonna holding the Child Jesus in her loving and protecting arms. Mary becomes for purposes of practical devotion part of the medieval Godhead itself, and this quasi-theological, homiletic trend becomes central to the practice of religion in European daily life that is still prominent in Mediterranean countries. The Virgin cult fired the imagination of artists and poets. It influenced the image and status of women, for the better, we think, and stimulated an ever-evolving congeries of emotional, popular, and social structures within the culture of the high and late Middle Ages. The psychological dimensions and social reaches of the Virgin cult we still only partly comprehend, but Southern was able to show it gaining its first clear expression in Anselm's circle. Southern's study also indicates the homoerotic quality of conversation and interpersonal relationship in Anselm's monastic circle, but he keeps this on a level absenting sexual physical contact. It was left to John Boswell to draw upon Southern's research and—wisely or not is moot—make this part of the history of gays' Middle Ages.

In Southern's interpretation of twelfth-century culture, St. Bernard of Clairvaux (d. 1153) continued the devotional and theological course that Anselm and the Canterbury monks had set. The Cistercian order of "white monks" (from the color of their habit) communicated to Western society as a whole, not just the clerical orders, a kind of popular mysticism that became situated in a faith of diurnal devotion and experience as well as in ritual and institutions. One of the outcomes of this Cistercian impact was paradoxically the enrichment of the church through the widespread founding of new churches, priories, and oratories or the expansion of older ones by much enhanced royal and aristocratic patronage. Another impact was the novel central role of preaching and highly evocative and existential kind of pulpit speaking in the church service. This change, incidentally, placed demands on the parish and cathedral clergy that the more conventional, routinized kind of priest had a hard time responding to, opening the way to religious orders that serve in the world, first the Augustinian canons, and later the Dominican and Franciscan friars.

From this religious sensibility rooted in Anselm and Bernard, appreciation of sentiment and legitimation of personal expression branched out into courtly, only partly secularized literature and inspired the vernacular romances and Arthurian cycle of the late twelfth century. Such is the course of sensibility in Southern's century.

Stepping back from intimate recognition and looking at the cultural movement of the twelfth century in the long-range perspective, Southern saw it as a kind of humanism, as a discovery of the natural world, and associated with classical learning, law, and government. Others—Knowles and Chenu in a book published in 1957—glimpsed this development, but it is Southern's particular formulation of this cultural revolution that has most deeply affected the understanding of the Middle Ages. In 1968 Southern summed up his vision of the twelfth century by saying that the new piety, emotional disposition, and consciousness of the individual belonged to a cultural movement that

in its broadest sense, represented an increased interest in the natural world—an attempt to look scientifically on the natural world, to discover its construction, its laws, and its main features. The natural world, necessarily, included man.

The movement existed and gained momentum in Western Europe from the early years of the twelfth century onward. In a broad sense it was a continuing movement in Western history down to the present day. The first phase came to an end, however, in the late thirteenth century with the creation of great theoretical structures like the *Summa Theologica* of Aquinas, which combined the scientific interests of the previous centuries with the great structure of revealed religion. This structure contrasted very strongly with the way of life and the intellectual temper of the period from the seventh to the eleventh century when supernatural channels of causation and authority were the only channels that were thoroughly understood and valued.

Why did this change occur in the early twelfth century? First of all, the new society that was rapidly growing in numbers and in complexity required a new type of government by men trained to think about practical problems and their solution. Hitherto, government had worked by appealing to supernatural authority, to supernatural modes of proof in legal cases, and so on. But now what was needed was elaboration of systematic law and practical expedients for enforcing it. This could only be carried out by men with some kind of academic training. Hence there was a growing demand for trained men, and this led to the rapid growth of schools and universities which were the center of all scientific progress.

The source of this natural understanding of men and the world was ancient thought and literature. By the end of the eleventh century that body of ancient learning had become thoroughly assimilated and could be purveyed to fairly large numbers of students in the schools. I look on various works of the early twelfth century . . . as expressions of the mastery of the Latin past. For the first time in five or six hundred years, people in western Europe could go on to develop in new ways the ancient methods of investigation and contemplation of the world as a natural organization. This tendency was given a tremendous impetus by the discovery of the texts of Greek science in the twelfth century. The translation of the scientific works of Aristotle, Galen, and Ptolemy introduced to the West a great and complex scientific view of the world. This was absorbed into the university curriculum and became part of the ordinary teaching of the schools in the thirteenth century.

The same kind of thing happened in the monastic life, where a similar spirit of scientific enquiry encouraged a new interest in man and his will. By the end of the eleventh century, monks felt oppressed by the weight of liturgical and formal religious observances. Why this occurred is not clear—I suppose that something which seems exciting when it is new and developing seems burdensome when it becomes an old routine. Perhaps it was nothing more complicated than this that caused monks in the late eleventh century to rebel against the weight of observances and to seek a new kind of personal freedom in the monastic life. The monastic movements of the late eleventh and twelfth centuries represented (at least in one of their aspects) a search for greater personal freedom within a monastic routine. When formalities and accretions are stripped away, man begins to investigate his own nature. In the eleventh and twelfth centuries this shift in emphasis from routine to the inner self was occurring throughout the monastic world. It is hard to say why it happened, but it is clearly connected with the general growth of scientific enquiry—the switch from ritual to reason—that I have described already.

This is vintage Southern from the year 1968: the breadth of developmental vision combined with precise definition of particular cultural phenomena, the confident magisterial assertion that knows where it should stop, the enthusiasm and lyrical sensibility that still remain under control of intellectual discipline. The Southern style in medieval studies is an enthusiastic yet very learned evocation of the more

emotional and intellectual dimensions of ecclesiastical and closely related secular culture. But this evocation, while it is itself romantic in
tone and directed to highlighting medieval romanticism, is at the same
time effected in a very controlled and disciplined manner. Personal
insight on Southern's part is embedded in a portrayal of medieval
culture that, while radical at the edge, still lies within a broad consensus. Considering that all this is accomplished with very fine writing that makes the more complex aspects of medieval thought and
culture accessible to the lay reader and the undergraduate, the Southern style is well-nigh inimitable. Its ingredients can be defined, but
it is almost impossible to duplicate precisely.

Intellectually there are many overlaps between Southern's work
and that of Schramm, Kantorowicz, Panofsky, Curtius, C. S. Lewis,
Southern's teacher Powicke, and Gilson, but the texture and conceptual cast of the work of these masters and those of Southern are quite
different. The Knowles of the 1930s and 1940s, of *Monastic Order* and
the first volume of *Religious Order*, is the closest in warp and woof to
Southern. Presumably Southern was so uncharitable to Father David
Knowles in 1949, when he reviewed Volume One of *Religious Orders*
precisely because Southern had not yet fully found his own voice and
produced his own masterwork, and consciously or subconsciously he
was anxious that Knowles not make Southern's contemplated work
seem imitative and derivative. There are pages, whole sections of
chapters, of Knowles's two inspired volumes that come close to the
Southern style in medieval studies. Therefore, back in the 1960s I
understandably coupled the two under the appellation of the "English
medievalist school of neoromanticism." That is not wrong, but it
doesn't quite fit the reality of their relationship.

Knowles was a clerical mind, a radical Augustinian, but a cleric
nevertheless. Southern could roam free in the best traditions of English romanticism. In any case, while the best pages of Knowles,
burning with expression of his personal struggle within the church,
approximate the Southern style, the calm placidity and magisterial
combination of passion and discipline that consistently characterize
Southern's writing is a voice that Knowles could not sustain or fully
command, or want to. In any case, after Knowles had made his peace
with his order and gained eminence at Cambridge, the fire went out
of his work and was never quite recovered from the declining embers
of his insight and feeling. There is only one Richard Southern in
medieval studies.

IV

KNIGHTS OF THE SOUTHERN ROUND TABLE

One of the intriguing aspects of the vast cycle of Arthurian literature of the last 350 years of the Middle Ages is that usually King Arthur is not himself the central or most heroic character in the poem. Among the members of this entourage, sometimes called the Knights of the Round Table, who are separately highlighted, are heroes like Lancelot, Parsifal, and Gawain. There is a typological, figural parallel between this literary situation and Richard Southern's place in medieval studies. He did great things and is the magisterial personage who opened up the pursuit of medieval sensibility and individuality to legitimation and exploration. But he only went so far, and in particular areas and genres others went beyond him or even corrected him. Although Southern created no institute and discouraged personal discipleship, his influence was enormous by the intellectual impact of his work. In the period since the mid-sixties, his example and influence have been critical, even though most of those writing in the tradition he channeled out had only occasional personal contact with him, such as attendance at a lecture or brief personal chat or limited correspondence. But the mark of Southern is upon them. How much they had imbibed his message, were inspired by his vision, and felt legitimated and encouraged by the example of his personal triumph is readily evident. Southern was King Arthur, and they were the young knights who carried his inspiration in further pursuit of the Grail, which in this case signified additional unraveling of the meaning of the Middle Ages.

Among Southern's own students the only one with substantial stature has been Maurice Keen, who succeeded him as fellow and tutor of medieval history at Balliol College. Keen wrote an interesting but inconclusive book on the Robin Hood legend and a comprehensive essay on chivalry that is somewhat reticent but is still a useful overview.

The first important knight of the Southern round table was Robert W. Hanning, an American at Columbia University whose field is medieval English and romance literature. He studied at Oxford as well as at Columbia and got to know Southern slightly. Hanning was a principal sponsor of Southern's first American tour in 1962, which was a great triumph. Hanning studied with W. H. Jackson and Roger Loomis, formalist giants in the medieval literature field at Columbia, but the influence on him of Southern, as well as of Erich Auerbach, the Yale literature comparatist, is evident.

Hanning's first book, *The Vision of History in Early Britain* (1968), shows how personal feeling and individual perception slowly work into the interstices and corners of standardized, formalist medieval historical telling, going from the eighth to the early twelfth century in England. Auerbach's *Mimesis* (1946, English translation 1953) had suggested in a couple of chapters how personal sensibility and individuation could turn around within the formalist typological structure of the medieval depiction of events. Hanning carries out this concept on a large scale, and Southern's *Making* obviously helped him do it. Hanning's later study, *The Individual in Twelfth Century Romance* (1974), is not as much an essay in Southern's wake as *Vision of History* had been. It goes beyond Southern in its probing of individuation and personality treatment in medieval romance literature. Hanning points to the extreme complexity of character formulation in these works, to the delicate use of irony that sets up deconstructive countercurrents to the surface idealistic motifs, and to the emergence of psychological realism in the romances' examination of interpersonal relations between the sexes. Looking back in 1988, Hanning was critical of Southern's treatment of twelfth-century imaginative literature: "Southern's argument suffers from a lack of specificity in its consideration of Chrétien's romances: He would have done better, one cannot but think, had he concentrated on one or two works and drawn more precise parallels with Bernard and contrasts with *Roland*. And his analysis, like that of many historians in dealing with literary texts, ignores the substantial amount of irony and play in Chrétien's presentation of both the life of literature and the language of the passions." It is this irony and play of passions that Hanning's *Individual* explicates for us. It is going beyond Southern, but Southern prepared the way for Hanning.

Southern did the same for the two radical British Morrises of the 1970s—Colin and John. The former produced in *The Discovery of the Individual* (1971) a more extreme and polemical view of twelfth-century culture than had been adumbrated in Southern's work. Colin Morris's book is a delight for undergraduates, but it might be considered vulgarized and overschematized Southernism. It makes twelfth-century individualism too sharp, too simple, too ideological. It begs the question of whether medieval theology and philosophy, while they allowed for departures from strict formalism and for expression of personal sensibility, could go so far toward a modern kind of individuality that Colin Morris perceives. He is left with the problem, which he does not resolve, of explaining why, if this ideological individualism developed, it did not turn into a liberal political revolution, in the eighteenth-century manner.

John Morris was a college administrator at the University of London who labored for decades on the murky and pitifully scarce fragments that can be construed to indicate a historical Arthur in the late fifth or early sixth century. We know enough to affirm, from literary and archaeological evidence that Arthur, whatever his name, was a Romano-British prince who withstood the Germanic invasion from the east, somewhere in west-central or southwestern Britain for a few years or decades around 500, until he was finally overrun. Arthur's followers, retreating into the Welsh mountains, kept his memory alive and embellished the stories about this Celtic hero, until a Welsh cleric, Geoffrey of Monmouth, studying at Oxford around 1135 and writing under the patronage of the bishop of Lincoln, put them into his legendary *History of the Kings of Britain* and inaugurated the Arthurian cycle. But out of these records and artifacts, John Morris created a five-hundred-page tour de force, *The Age of Arthur* (1972). Some reviewers pilloried poor John Morris as a greater fantasist than Geoffrey of Monmouth. Morris's reconstruction of the historical Arthur is one of those books you either like very much or hate; I am in the former camp. Of course, it is highly imaginative, but it is not a fantasy. It is grounded in the sources, although a lot of imagining has fleshed out the fragments. John Morris worked on this book for many years. If Southern had not legitimated imaginative history and given a certain credibility to a kind of neoromantic perception about the Middle Ages, it is unlikely that Morris would have had the courage to publish *The Age of Arthur* just before his death. Today *The Age of Arthur* is available only in three extremely expensive volumes from an obscure provincial British press. Like the Arthurian story in the early Middle Ages, it is sinking into the country, but in time it may come forth again. In any case, I definitely place this fascinating book in the Southern entourage and wake.

At the opposite end of the academic spectrum of respectability from John Morris was Peter Dronke, distinguished holder of the chair of medieval literature at Cambridge. His exhaustive two-volume study of medieval Latin lyric (1965) finds, like Auerbach and Hanning, a modicum of personal sensibility and individual expression within formal and durable traditions. Dronke's work may be placed intellectually in the Southern tradition of interpreting medieval culture. In

Poetic Individuality in the Middle Ages (1970), Dronke goes further and launches an attack upon Curtius's topological formalism. Dronke contends that a topos or traditional theme can be highly original in the way the traditional motif is rhetorically handled. This is again a Southern disposition.

In *Women Writers of the Middle Ages* (1980) Dronke, like Hanning, surpasses and corrects the Southern paradigm. He finds four women writers of skill and sensitivity, an aspect of medieval culture persistently ignored by Southern. More important, he devotes half of his book to a lengthy essay on Hildegard of Bingen, the only detailed treatment her writings have received in English and the best in any language. No one can read Dronke on Hildegard and agree with Southern that Germany lay outside the scope of vanguard twelfth-century culture. On the contrary, there is a boldness in Hildegard, a pushing on the intellectual envelope of clerical tradition, that along with Wolfram's *Parzifal*, makes one think that possibly the real avant-garde after all lay not in northern France and southern England in the later years of the twelfth century but in the German Rhineland. It is a different culture from the Anglo-French one and is not university-based. But it is visionary, speculative, fantastic, and original and perhaps rises to a notch of intensity and visionary insight beyond Champagne or Canterbury.

A more direct imitator of Southern than Hanning or Dronke is Peter Brown, an English historian of the culture of the transition era 300–700. Brown has spent the mature years of his career at Berkeley and Princeton. His work on late antiquity and the emergence of the Middle Ages is closely modeled on Southern's approach to the twelfth century. Biography of a great religious figure—in Brown's case of St. Augustine of Hippo (1965)—is blended into successive studies of the religious and the cultural ambience of Augustine's time and a little earlier and later. The theme is that of what French scholars in the early twentieth century called syncretism, the blending of cultures and interweaving of religious ideas in the late Roman Empire. Brown's principal thesis is that there emerged in the late Roman Empire a distinctive comprehensive culture in which Christianity, paganism, classicism, neo-Platonic mysticism, and a large dose of popular astrology, magic, and faith healing were inseparably integrated. Brown has been particularly concerned with demonstrating how the adoration of saints in the early Middle Ages is rooted in the shaman cults of late antiquity.

This syncretic culture of late antiquity is the foundation of Augustinian theology and Christian doctrine on the mind-body problem and sexuality, in Brown's account. His biography of Augustine is not the best personality study of the saint and theologian. That distinction belongs to John O'Meara, the Dublin scholar, in his much-underrated *The Young Augustine* (1952). But Brown has placed Augustine within an intellectual milieu that spans all the cultural and intellectual facets of the time, as Southern did with St. Anselm.

Brown's reputation, hyped by the *New York Review of Books* and other media of the cultural left, has become empyreal. In 1986, however, there appeared a monumental work by an Oxford don, Robin Lane Fox, *Pagans and Christians*, that directly challenges Brown's fundamental theme of religious and cultural synthesis in the fourth century. To some extent reviving a thesis expounded by conservative Christian scholars from about 1920 to 1960, particularly Charles Norris Cochrane, Norman H. Baynes, and Andreas Alfoldi, but making use of his fresh reading of all the textual literature, Lane Fox makes the Christians out to be a small, committed, heroic minority at war with late classical culture. According to Lane Fox, the conversion of the Roman Empire in the fourth century represented the political triumph of a counterculture, not the Brownist syncretic blending of multifaceted Mediterranean culture. Lane Fox is quite explicit that he is challenging Brown's thesis. Strangely, Brown, in a review of *Pagans and Christians* in the *New York Review of Books* (the house organ for the Princeton history department), praised the book to the skies without engaging the crucial issue of Lane Fox's devastating attack on twenty years of his own work. There is a tactic in scholarly debate, risky but sometimes workable, that if you laud your opponent uncritically, you reduce him to imbecility. That seems to have been Brown's method in this case. The important point relative to Southern, however, is that Southern's legitimation of speculative and imaginative cultural history prepared the academic ambience for Lane Fox as well as for Brown.

A knight of the Southern round table who deserves high recognition is Malcolm Lambert, who has been a professor at the University of Bristol for three decades. His *Medieval Heresy* (1977) is the best overview of the subject in any language. Lambert spent time at the Monumenta institute in Munich doing research there for his book, and his debt to postwar German historians of heresy like Herbert Grundmann is obvious and is freely acknowledged. But where Lambert belongs at Southern's round table (Lambert was a student at Oxford in the 1950s but characteristically was ignored by Southern) is in his persuasive sketches of individual leaders of the counter-churches and his group portrayals of the temperament and ambitions of the heretical sects. It is again a book that follows in the wake of *The Making of the Middle Ages*. But like other knights such as Hanning and Dronke, Lambert goes well outside what Southern himself has to say about heresy. For Southern, twelfth-century heresy is of limited importance and associated with the bourgeois ethos. Lambert shows that heresy was much more widespread than that. It is a condition of the culture of landed as well as urban society and lies not at the margin but in the mainstream of twelfth-century spirituality. This raises very complex questions about the nature of twelfth-century spirituality and whether Southern's optimistic view is not only emotionally one-sided but conceptually constricted.

Although Southern himself was only marginally interested in medieval women and their culture, the leading feminist medievalist of the 1980s, Columbia University's Caroline Walker Bynum, may be perceived as another scholar of the following generation who was inspired by the horizons opened up by *The Making of the Middle Ages*. (Bynum was also very much influenced by her mother, a tough-minded feminist descended from the Old South who was a college philosophy teacher, and she has acknowledged a special debt to Peter Brown.) Bynum's solution to the question of the degree and nature of individuality in twelfth-century culture is quite Southern-like: "The twelfth century regarded the discovery of homo interior . . . as the discovery within oneself of human nature made in the image of God." In my view, this is true in an abstract or formalist sense but existentially and empirically there are departures from this overriding doctrine, for example, in the romantic poetry of Chrétien de Troyes and in the ethical theory of Peter Abelard.

In Bynum's most celebrated book, *Jesus as Mother*, much loved in feminist studies courses, she finds convincingly the cross-gender quality of twelfth-century religious writing: "These authors appear to have supplemented their image of God with maternal metaphors because they needed to supplement their image of authority with that for which the maternal stood: emotion and nurture." This constitutes a straightforward and valuable supplement to Southern's great book.

All historical thinking is dialectical, and opposition books residually presuppose the point of view they are undermining. So it is with Frank Barlow's biography of *Thomas Becket* (1987), the Canterbury martyr. An experienced writer, well on in years, and previously the author of several dull books on political and administrative history, Barlow here suddenly jumped several notches above the quality of his previous work and gave us what may be called the great anti-Southern book on the twelfth century. There is no doubt that for three decades Barlow brooded in quiet revulsion against Southern's enthusiastic portrayal of the twelfth century. The mark of a great humanistic scholar is the animosity as well as the devotion and imitation he elicits. In a negative way, Barlow, too, worked in Southern's shadow and influence. He intensely devoted himself to deromanticizing Southern's sunny century through the life of Archbishop Thomas of London, as his contemporaries called him.

Barlow dredges up, and persuasively confirms, every piece of nasty ecclesiastical gossip in Becket's lifetime, and the result is a terrific put-down of a vision of an age of spirituality and sensibility. It comes out more like an age of lust and greed. Barlow points out that Becket was a dropout or flunkout at the University of Paris. In spite of strenuous efforts at adult education while first royal chancellor and then archbishop, he never mastered the ornate ecclesiastical Latin of his day, and all his official letters as archbishop were written for him by his learned clerks after he had given them essential instructions (in French). Becket's rival, Archbishop Roger of York, while an archdeacon, kept a young boy for homosexual purposes, and when the scandal broke, Roger brought trumped-up charges against the boy in an ecclesiastical kangaroo court and had the boy blinded and hanged. When the French county of Blois suddenly was inherited by an abbess in England, King Henry II got some kind of ecclesiastical approval for the abbess to be forthwith removed from her convent and married off to a French nobleman. When Becket was chancellor, although he was in ecclesiastical orders, he put on armor and led a feudal campaign in France, and also when he was chancellor, his physician recommended sexual intercourse as a remedy for the strains of overwork. Barlow is unsure about Becket's actual chastity on this and some other occasions; he may have had a liaison with one of Henry II's discarded mistresses. In 1166 the king became so frustrated with the querulous Becket that he had a temporary royal breakdown, taking off all his clothes in public and chewing straw. Pope Alexander III was constrained from giving more than marginal support to Becket because without Henry's II's support he would not have secured the throne of Peter against an imperial antipope; if Alexander had supported Becket in the extreme manner the archbishop wanted, Henry would have simply switched to the opposition pope.

Barlow reports that John of Salisbury, the most renowned human-

ist of the twelfth century and one of Becket's clerks and later a principal biographer of the martyr, negotiated secretly with the king behind
Becket's back for several years. If the king had only been a little more
generous, John might very well have betrayed the archbishop. So
much for the call of the ideal! When the four royal knights broke into
the cathedral to kill Becket, John of Salisbury ran away. When one
of the knights ran up to assault Becket, the archbishop called him a
pimp. The punishment imposed on the four assassins of Becket by
the pope was ostensibly fourteen years on Crusade, but at least one
of them appears to have died a wealthy landowner in England. Because of his six years' exile in France, Becket acquired so many habits
of the French that when he was fatally assaulted, he commended his
soul not only to God and the Blessed Mary but also to St. Denis.

Barlow falls short of explaining convincingly what caused Becket's
erratic and self-destructive behavior. Barlow seems to prefer a social
explanation. Becket, a merchant's son of modest education, lived in a
very high aristocratic world of unlimited greed, ambition, and lust;
therefore, "he had all the failings of a typical parvenu." It should be
noted that this unattractive aristocratic ambience in England was also
the source for patronage of the Cistercian order and the audience for
Arthurian literature.

From the information Barlow provides, there are two other possible explanations for the Becket crisis. First, there appears to have
been a deep psychosexual tension between Becket and Henry II
(fourteen years his junior). It is significant that the prime obstacle to
a peaceful resolution of their quarrel, after two years of negotiation,
was Henry's refusal to give Becket a kiss of peace (on the mouth).
Secondly, Becket exhibits all the qualities now diagnosed as severe
manic depression or pathological mood swing. If he could have had a
dose of lithium each morning, there might have been no Canterbury
martyr.

Barlow brings out forcefully Becket's failures as archbishop and
the hatred on almost every side, both ecclesiastical and lay, that he
generated. "His rule as archbishop can be viewed as disastrous for all
concerned." His reputation altered radically when the blood of the
Canterbury martyr turned out to have almost incomparable curative
qualities for every known disease. Soon the selling of vials of water
with an alleged tincture of his blood became a prime industry. He
himself never drank water; it bothered his stomach; he preferred the
very best French vintage wine.

Barlow's devastating account of the world of Thomas Becket makes it hard to believe we are in the same country and the same century as St. Anselm and his monastic circle or the religious culture and mentality depicted in *The Making of the Middle Ages*. Barlow does not disprove Southern, of course, but he reminds us that there were many Middle Ages, that as the medievals would say, my father's house has many dwelling places, and that we tend to discover the past we set out to find. This is not because the past is a willfully imagined fiction but because it is such a complicated and multifaceted reality.

There is another way of looking at Barlow's disparagement of Southern's golden century. It illustrates the deconstructionist theory of the current French mandarins Jacques Derrida and Michel Foucault. Derrida tells us that every text deconstructs itself, that behind every statement there lurks deep in the interstices of words another, conflicting message. In the current postmodernist jargon, "the logo-centric and univocal are undermined by a subconscious negation that lies in the text itself and activates its oppositional conflict from within the unstable and intrinsically rebellious nature of language." Foucault gives us a Nietzschean nightmare in which any political, social, or cultural system, no matter how ethical the professed intention of its creators and leaders, is an expression of self-interested power. The facade of justice crumbles to reveal the privilege of dominance, and this is true not only of conventionally ambiguous political authority but of movements of idealistic reform: the insane asylum in the seventeenth century, the penitentiary in the eighteenth century, and feminism and women's liberation in the twentieth century. All are tainted at their core by the zeal for power. It is not hard to see Barlow's world of greed, lust, and horror as the inevitable deconstructive dimension of Southern's paradigm of a culture committed to learning, spirituality, and reason.

The common sense judgment would be that all history is selective and no society is free from disreputable manifestations of viciousness in individuals and the self-interest of groups and classes. That such immoral and ugly manifestations occurred in the sunny twelfth century should cause no surprise, and Barlow has performed a service in reminding us of their persistence. But that does not detract from the reality of the spirituality, sensibility, idealism, and beauty that Southern evokes for us, and these positive manifestations take on a deeper and more persuasive hue when they are considered in the context of the surrounding dirt and gloom.

Another way of looking at the Barlow response to Southern is to consider that it is not impossible, but it is hard, to write history over a lifetime's career and to undertake a large subject, without substantial projection of idealism, of positive value, into the time and place and the people and structures that the historian is describing. Romanticism generated modern historiography, and romantic projection remains at the center of the historical enterprise, no matter how subtly disguised. Thus we have all sorts of idealist images projected by the masters of medieval studies: whether functional law, or charismatic kingship, or formalist heritages, or popular communities, or perilous journeys of rescue and redemption, or Christ-like steadfastness in holiness. Even Bloch with his autonomous peasant communities and Strayer with his medieval origins of the modern state were also romantic advocates of the Middle Ages. Southern shares with all the inventive twentieth-century masters of the Middle Ages an enthusiasm for a call of the ideal and for assuming the role of illuminator of a glowing dimension in medieval life and culture. There were indeed naysayers, oppositionists, outriders who took a much more negative view of the medieval world and its legacy, and they were in some instances more formidable as thinkers and critics than Frank Barlow, the assiduous collector of gossip and scandal. Yet even these high-profile naysayers about the Middle Ages could not significantly damage the positive belief in the Middle Ages, which was presented in such persuasive and lyrical fashion by Sir Richard Southern.

Another way of developing Southern's highly positive view of medieval creativity was to transpose his hymn of praise for the medieval world into another key, a more secular and materialistic one. This view, which came to the fore in the 1960s and holds a powerful influence today on the younger generation of medieval historians in the United States and Britain, unabashedly applies twentieth-century criteria of progress to evaluation of the Middle Ages. It holds that the Middle Ages were the most dynamically progressive moment in the history of this planet. Borrowing not a little from Pirenne, Haskins, and Strayer, this group makes the concept of social and technological rationality the major motif in its paean to the European Middle Ages. Southern finds much to agree with here, but he gives much greater significance to the emotional strivings and religious insights of medieval people. He also, in his best moments, sees medieval culture from the inside rather than simply evaluates it externally by an anachronistic standard of progressive rationalism.

The materialist progressive school traces a continuous rising stream of rationality from the military advances of feudal technology and the organization of urban commerce in the tenth century, through the classical recovery and dialectical capacity of the twelfth century, to the culminating anticipations of the scientific revolution in the four-teenth century just before the demographic disaster of the Black Death temporarily enervated medieval culture and momentarily halted its progress. But even the loss of more than a quarter of Western Eu-rope's population in the mid-fourteenth century to the plague was in modern hindsight a blessing because it saved this society from being overwhelmed by the uncontrollable population growth that enfeebled the mandarin culture of China, its sole competitor for becoming the foundation of the modern world. Lynn White and Robert Lopez in the United States, Geoffrey Barraclough (who taught at Brandeis University and held a high-level position in UNESCO) in Britain, and Philippe Wolfe in France were enunciating this perspective on the European Middle Ages in the 1960s. They may be seen if not exactly as Southern disciples at least as friendly visiting associates at his round table of celebratory medievalism.

It is my opinion that this straight-line rationalist view of medieval progress detracts from engaging the passionate effects of medieval culture that were its noblest and most subtle moments and takes too mechanical and anachronistic an approach to interpreting the me-dieval world. The persistent spiritual anxieties and destabilizing religious conflicts within medieval Europe are shunted to the back-ground by this social and technological rationalism. White, Lopez, and Barraclough are singing praises for the Middle Ages alongside Sir Richard, but a cognitive as well as aesthetic dissonance disturbs the chorus of adulation by their voicing of a different key. White, Lopez, and Barraclough strike me as a group of pinstripe-suited UN or World Bank observers visiting a third world country and suavely composing a report on whether a grant or loan is merited in light of advancing commerce and technology, conducting this judgmental ac-tivity while sitting serenely in the bar of the country's only three-star hotel.

Sir Richard Southern was a much deeper and more anxious thinker than White, Lopez, and Barraclough. He was not an international bureaucrat or banker generating a scorecard on the natives but a field anthropologist who went into the countryside and immersed himself in both the glory and the mess of medieval sensibility. He placed in the foreground rather than in the margin the religious feelings of the Middle Ages, and as the postmodern era moves into the twenty-first century, the relevance of medieval spirituality rather than rationality will become more meaningful to the survivors of the age of Bush and Gorbachev.

CHAPTER TEN

— ◆ —

OUTRIDERS

JOHAN HUIZINGA, EILEEN EDNA POWER,
MICHAEL MOISSEY POSTAN, CARL ERDMANN,
AND THEODOR ERNST MOMMSEN

I
GORGING OUT

On July 20, 1958, I received a letter from the chairman of the history department at Cornell University in Ithaca, New York. The letter was forwarded to me from Princeton, where I was teaching, to my parents' home in Winnipeg, Canada, where I was visiting with my wife and son. I stood in my parents' dusty backyard under a hot prairie sun and opened the letter. The gentlemanly Cornell chairman regretted to inform me that my teacher and friend Theodor E. Mommsen had died by suicide a few days earlier at the age of fifty-three. He also informed me that Professor Mommsen had in his will left me most of his extensive library. Sure enough, a month later, after I had returned to Princeton, I received a letter from a back-woods attorney in Ithaca confirming this, and five weeks thereafter a diesel truck pulled up in front of my office and delivered three thousand volumes, some of them quite valuable.

I discovered that Mommsen's executor was his friend, another German émigré, Felix Gilbert, who taught Renaissance history at Bryn Mawr College on the mainline of Pennsylvania, and I wrote and asked him if he would share with me the contents of any suicide note or otherwise let me know the ostensible cause of Mommsen's suicide, which was completely unanticipated by me. Visibly Mommsen seemed at the height of his career. He was going off on a year's leave, slated to give a series of endowed public lectures first in the Midwest and then in West Germany. Mommsen, who was a bachelor, was going to be reunited for several months with his brothers, one of them a leading industrialist, another a retired admiral of the German Navy. He appeared to have gained the public recognition and private happiness that had eluded him since he left Germany, in protest against Hitler and anti-Semitism, in 1936. The last time I had seen him was a rainy day in late April 1958 on the Princeton campus, just after he had lunched with his old friend Ernst Kantorowicz at the Institute for Advanced Study. Ted Mommsen seemed in rare good humor, and there was a special softness in his voice that appeared only when he was very happy. Now the suicide.

When I got the bad news, I thought immediately of the expression on the Cornell campus "gorging out," referring to the practice of undergraduates killing themselves by jumping into one of the deep gorges that were located on two sides of the plateaulike campus. Mommsen had killed himself not by jumping but by an overdose of sleeping pills. His cleaning lady had discovered him, still alive, at 11:00 A.M. and called an ambulance, but he was too far gone to be brought around. If she had chanced to turn the lock on his apartment an hour earlier or this had been a decade or two later, when emergency medicine was more advanced, Mommsen would have survived. Now he was gone, my teacher and friend, a man I loved much more than my own father. "Through thee I believe in the great and good who are gone."

Six weeks after I wrote him, Felix Gilbert responded to my inquiry. He could not reveal to me the contents of Mommsen's suicide note. In a memoir published in 1988 Gilbert said he did not know why Mommsen committed suicide. I do not believe him. There was talk at Princeton University, where Mommsen taught from 1946 to 1954, that there had been a woman, the wife of a German classicist at Johns Hopkins, whom he loved. One version was that she had broken off their affair; another that she died. Another story, inevitably, was that Mommsen knew he was dying of cancer and did not want to face another prolonged agony of a sad and disappointed life. I wondered when I started looking through Mommsen's library and found, stuck between the pages of old books, several highly emotional letters from Ernst Kantorowicz to Mommsen whether his suicide was occasioned by the end of a homoerotic relationship.

Ted Mommsen's death signified for me the beginning of the end of a great generation of medievalists who were my mentors and intellectual deities. The generation passed away slowly, it turned out. Knowles died in 1974. Strayer lasted until 1987. Sir Richard South-

ern is still hard at work. But Mommsen's death by his own hand put
the shadow of mortality on the horizon. The giants who invented the
Middle Ages in the mind and sensibility of the twentieth century
would make their departure and leave behind only the dwarfs who
sat on their shoulders. Mommsen's death represented the sign of en-
tropy, a running down, the exhaustion of a great cultural movement
and academic lineage that created and shaped medieval studies. His
suicide meant for me also the frustration and disappointment that
accompanied the process of learned discovery and intellectual creativity, the reluctant but finally decisive realization that the meaning of
the Middle Ages could in the end exceed our mental capacities, could
lie just beyond insight and imagination. There was, after all, a mystery to the medieval world whose accoutrements we would easily perceive, whose main lines of development we could trace, but whose
inner core of fiery truth and reality we could never fully and clearly
comprehend.

Mommsen sensed this limitation very deeply and talked of it many
times. He saw himself personally as a miserable failure, who never
got anywhere close to the academic achievements and renown of his
grandfather, the historian of Rome, after whom he was named in a
moment of rash familial choice, putting too much weight upon him.
He felt additional pressure from his kinship to his uncle Max Weber,
the incredibly prolific sociological theorist. Mommsen sensed, too,
that our profession of medieval studies had failed, had passed its peak,
was marking time, had lost its brilliant expectations of ever-deeper
revelation of medieval realities. Even "Eka" was not the "Eka" who
had written *Frederick II* and set the German intellectual sky ablaze in
1928. Now he was instead a Princeton institute professor who published boring articles with very long, show-off canon law footnotes.
Strayer in Mommsen's mind had become a horror show, with his
harsh American pragmatism and power worship.

The day Mommsen got to Ithaca, to the bleak high precipice over
Lake Cayuga, he was sorry he had come. For long months he was
cut off from the world he knew, from his friends Kantorowicz and
Gilbert at Princeton and Bryn Mawr and others down in Baltimore,
by ice and snow. It was a cold place, this Cornell, this Ithaca, with
its gentlemen WASP faculty. He greatly admired one colleague, the
American historian of slavery, David Brion Davis, of whom he readily predicted great things, which were realized. But the others were
midwestern farmers in Ivy League clothing. I went up to see him

three or four times a year, making a long and tedious trip on the savagely coal-burning Lackawanna Railroad out of Newark, on "the Route of the Phoebe Snow," a late-nineteenth-century adman's fatuous vision. My wife and I drove to Ithaca on our honeymoon in 1957. In those days before the state superhighways went through there, it took eleven hours from Princeton by country road. Mommsen was generous, warm, in greeting us, but very sad. He was dying inside in the Valhalla of the North, just as he believed medieval studies was receding into conformity and routine.

And so he died alone, gorging out as pathetically as those Cornell boys who had been jumping off cliffs there since the 1880s. I remember what Cornell's founding president, Andrew White, said in the 1880s when the captain of the football team proposed that the university provide the funds to send the team to play Michigan at Ann Arbor: "I won't send eleven grown men a thousand miles to kick around a bag of wind." But preserving life and sanity comes from the frivolity of kicking bags of wind. Otherwise you will freeze up and die alone in Ithaca, New York.

From the time of the publication of the first edition of Pollock and Maitland in 1895 to the mid-1960s, there was an integrated era of the intellectual and learned creativity that invented and shaped the contours and character of the Middle Ages in the twentieth-century mind. The influence of these great founders covering three phenomenally creative generations will be carried over past the year 2000, and it is this invented Middle Ages of 1895–1965 that will in the early decades of the twenty-first century be still debated, adjusted, revised, or rebelled against. These are the intellectual fathers of our Oedipal experience. To put it another way, I have examined the formation of a cultural structure that was composed out of learned research, humanistic theory, assumptions about human behavior, and the ever-present ingredient of the personal experiences of medievalists—the ambitions, passions, joys, and sorrows of their lives. Inevitably the personal developments of the medievalist founders were deeply affected by the intellectual and social circumstances that surrounded them.

By the mid-sixties, out of this array of constituents, there was solidified a cultural structure that comprised the fundamentals of the image of the Middle Ages that we read in our textbooks, teach and study in our classes, and disseminate in libraries, museums, and the literary and visual arts. Nothing of consequence from the nineteenth century was found worthy of perpetuation in the way of interpreting and imaging of the Middle Ages. Discovering the meaning of the European Middle Ages is a phenomenon of twentieth-century culture. I have tried to show in the individual instances of the great masters why and how this phenomenon of inventing the European Middle Ages occurred.

We have not dealt with the making of the other Middle Ages—primarily Arab, Byzantine, and Jewish. That is the subject of another inquiry. It is my personal prejudice that while these other medieval civilizations are of enormous importance not only intrinsically but in respect to their impact on the West, for a variety of reasons, including sheer chance, the magisterial intellectual structures that were created to privilege the European Middle Ages in the twentieth century were largely lacking with respect to the conceptualization of these other medieval societies. The great work of masterful interpretations of Arab, Byzantine, and Jewish civilizations has only begun to be entered into since 1965, and the masterworks began to make their appearance only in the later decades of the twentieth century. Putting it brutally, and certainly giving an opinion that will arouse dismay and anger in certain quarters, I believe that while there has been a vast accumulation of information about these three non-Western medieval cultures, no one has yet written a great book on any of them. A Maitland, Schramm, Bloch, Panofsky, Strayer, Knowles, Southern in these fields had not appeared before the mid-sixties, and it is perhaps still too early to tell if one has appeared since then, although I very much doubt it. I would say the first great masterworks of Arab, Byzantine, and Jewish medieval studies will come forward in the first or second decade of the twenty-first century, partly in reaction to the upheavals in the eastern Mediterranean that we are now witnessing.

Turning back to the invention and interpretation of the European Middle Ages, I want to bring this story, insofar as I comprehend it, to a conclusion by looking at those who produced insightful and provocative work that was on the margin of impact and influence. These are scholars who had very important things to say, and their work gained them recognition and academic success by conventional professional standards. But in the creative period through the mid-1960s there was, on the whole, a certain quality of marginality to their reputations and hesitancy about following too closely the lines they set out. They were the outriders among the great medievalists. That may no longer be entirely true in at least one instance, that of Eileen

Power's pioneering woman's history, a field that is now very active, although still somewhat confused and conflicted in its program of action. But in any case these presenters of alternative perspectives, these dissenting voices, deserve at least concise consideration in bringing our intellectual saga of twentieth-century medievalism to a close.

In any humanistic discipline, such as medieval studies, there are special uses to be derived from persuasive expressions of marginality in interpretation. First, these more marginal perceptions provide a breeding ground for revisionist and novel perceptions at a later time and in often updated and revised form a generation or two later move from the periphery to the center of impact and intellectual dominance. The dissenting cultural and theoretical voice of one generation becomes the orthodoxy of a later time. That phenomenon is so well known as to need no explication. Secondly, by looking at first-rate work by brilliant people that retained a character of marginality and experienced a residual quality of reticence in its impact, we can gain further perspectives on the masterworks and socially privileged scholars who prevailed and held the center stage. The difference between academic centrality and marginality in terms of reader response and professional recognition is often small. But that modest difference in located space indicates what the audience wanted and what it considered too bold, difficult, or at least for the moment otherwise problematic and extreme.

"Outriders" is a term used in the natural and social sciences to refer to scattered data that are qualitatively of the same provenance and legitimacy as the rest of the data that have been gathered by experimentation or survey research. But these outriders for some reason (or no visible reason) do not fall within the same pattern revealed by the dominant core of data. The outriding data fall outside the governing paradigm. So it is with certain medievalists of the twentieth century. The implications of their work, their dissenting, negative view of the Middle Ages, lie outside the general pattern of approval and affirmation of the medieval heritage in one aspect or another that distinguishes the work of the mainstream medievalists. These are the dissenters, the eccentrics, the nonconformists. Their status as outsiders does not detract, however, from the intrinsic value of their insights, even if these insights conflict with the standard paradigms.

II
POSTIMPRESSIONISM

Of the prominent medievalists of the twentieth century, only two as of 1989 have left behind autobiographies (it may be anticipated that Dick Southern, so zealous in writing lengthy necrologies of his teachers and colleagues, will also do so). These are David Knowles and Johan Huizinga. We have seen that Knowles's autobiography has been sequestered until 2004. The published autobiography of Johan Huizinga (1872–1945) was written in the last decade of his life, and there is a good English translation. It is quite brief, about two hundred pages, and highly typological: It very consciously attempts to leave in the reader's mind a specific image of the author and his life. The type portrayed is that of the outsider, one might almost say of the joker, the superficially foolish but actually wise Dutch commoner, who seems thoroughly marginal and a failure but is really wiser than the mighty but traditional scholars.

Huizinga, who was the son of a Dutch professor of medicine, tells us that he went to Germany before the First World War to get a Ph.D. in philology but flunked out. Returning to his native Holland, he joined up with an avant-garde group of students and intellectuals. Huizinga lets us know that he was a principal organizer of the first exhibition of the paintings of Vincent van Gogh in his native Holland (Van Gogh never sold a painting in his lifetime). In Huizinga's account, he was therefore one of the first to recognize the importance of postimpressionist art. Slowly Huizinga drifted from philology to (he indicates) the less technical and demanding field of cultural history. After obtaining a doctorate with a dissertation of no great distinction, by his account, he began teaching history at the University of Leyden. According to Huizinga's story, after several years he had published only a couple of insignificant scholarly articles and the head of his department told him that if he did not produce a book soon, he would be let go from his university job. So he retired for a summer to his mother-in-law's farm, sat there in the hot attic with a few writings from the fifteenth century, and wrote *The Autumn of the Middle Ages* (as it was called in the original Dutch edition of 1919 and in the German edition). We know it in the very capable English translation, which appeared in London in 1924 and was done under Huizinga's close supervision, as *The Waning of the Middle Ages*. The change of title was probably made so as to separate it from Oswald Spengler's

Decline of the West, which was a postwar sensation in Germany and which used a cyclical seasonal paradigm.

Thus the avant-garde outsider—the joker, the wise peasant, or artisan—outfoxes the academic establishment and in absurdly quick time, with small effort, produces one of the classic books on medieval history. This is the image that Huizinga seeks to have us retain of him. He later gained further academic success with books on sixteenth-century Dutch history. His collected works in the Dutch edition, about half of which have been translated, run to seven volumes.

In Huizinga's typology, he now becomes the intellectual maverick whom the academic establishment has to recognize and reward, while looking essentially askance and fearfully at what he is doing since he is going down a route where none, or hardly any, can follow—to breakthrough historical sociology of culture. Actually, in terms of the taxological composition of academia, Huizinga was a quite common type in the small countries of Belgium and Holland between the wars and shortly after 1945: a highly original, autonomous scholar who writes for a wide audience and produces generalizing books of provocative nature. Henri Pirenne at Ghent was a prime example. This continued into the post-1945 period with Pieter Geyl, the innovative historian of the Dutch rebellion against Spain, and continues now with the oracular books on medieval law written by R. C. van Caenegem, who holds the chair once occupied by Henri Pirenne. Huizinga's most ambitious work intellectually was *Homo Ludens* (1938), a historical sociology of play, which remains an idiosyncratic outcast in theoretical sociology, now and again arousing comment and interest. Huizinga, a fierce anti-Nazi patriot, was placed in a concentration camp by the occupying Germans and died in 1945 shortly after he was liberated.

The Waning of the Middle Ages, in an American paperback edition, remains one of the all-time best-selling books on medieval history, although today only modestly used in college courses. It is written not out of archival or even documentary material. It relies on Huizinga's sharp eye for the art of the fifteenth-century Low Countries and three or four familiar works of court-sponsored history written in Burgundy (Flanders) during that era. The material he used is easily accessible in any second-rate college library. Obviously this is a highly speculative work, an imaginative exercise, not a work of scholarly research. This genre has always made professional historians and art historians very uneasy. If anyone with a sharp mind and a few standard books can write an important book of humanistic interpretation, the academic guild, behind its defensive walls of immense learning and privileged behavior, is threatened out of its core of livelihood. We have seen that in his immensely learned and magisterially authoritative work on *Early Netherlandish Painting*, Erwin Panofsky ignores *The Waning of the Middle Ages*, a stance derived from contempt and fear—contempt for *Waning's* lack of professional learning and research and fear of its elusive speculative qualities.

Huizinga's book may be seen as an exercise in cultural history of the postimpressionist, protoexpressionist kind of art that Van Gogh himself (along with Cézanne and Gauguin) represented. Huizinga's voice is that of completely autonomous but still highly disciplined personal sensibility, a special vision that aims at universal impact. Huizinga has cause to see himself as the outsider, the joker, the wise fool. He stands quite alone; he had no successors, and the approach he adopted has found no significant imitators. *The Waning of the Middle Ages* is likely to appear on anyone's list of the ten best books ever written on medieval history, and a plausible argument would place it near the top, alongside Southern's *Making of the Middle Ages* and Bloch's *Feudal Society* on the list of paperback hits in medieval history in an American bookstore (Schramm never having been translated and there being no paperback edition of Kantorowicz's *Frederick II*). But Huizinga stands alone and remote from the ongoing dialogues in medieval studies.

Huizinga's thesis on late medieval culture is easily told and comprehended. The main characteristics of medieval culture, he claims, are an overwhelming tendency to "idealism" and "formalism"—to generalizing, symbolic manifestations in all genres and cultural expressions. But in the fifteenth century the vitality drains from this idealizing, formalist, generalizing kind of culture, and it becomes routinized and rigidified: "Every thought seeks expression in an image, but in this image it solidifies and becomes rigid. By this tendency to embodiment in visible forms all holy concepts are constantly exposed to the danger of hardening into mere externalism. For in assuming a definite figurative shape thought loses its ethereal and vague qualities . . . [transl. F. Hopman]."

Huizinga describes a cultural crisis in fifteenth-century Burgundy (Flanders and northern France) that is especially expressed in the new realist, naturalist painting of Jan van Eyck and others and in the extreme, microcosmic detail of court ritual. We encounter, in Durkheim's terms, an anomic situation in which the culture now lacks the absorptive, plastic capacity to sustain itself. Medieval culture is

380 INVENTING THE MIDDLE AGES

passing away because its dynamic symbolic capacity has eroded. The meaningfulness of generalizing, religious-based ideals has emptied and been replaced by intense concentration on the particular, the specific, the tactile, whether in representational painting, court festivals, or religious imagery such as the celebration of the dance of death, a favorite popular motif.

It used to be said that Huizinga was a great opponent of Jacob Burckhardt's *Civilization of the Renaissance in Italy* (1860), which celebrated the postmedieval quality of culture in fifteenth-century northern Italian cities. But Huizinga is not at all contradicting Burckhardt. He is writing about the culture of the Low Countries and northern France, and there he sees a great upheaval coming, only later, and not because of the impact of neoclassical humanism but because of entirely intrinsic cultural forces:

> The fifteenth century in France and the Netherlands is still medieval at heart. The diapason of life has not changed. Scholastic thought, with symbolism and strong formalism, the thoroughly dualistic conception of life and the world still dominated. The two poles of the mind continued to be chivalry and hierarchy. Profound pessimism spread a general gloom over life. The gothic principle prevailed in art. But all those forms and modes were on the wane. A high and strong culture is declining, but at the same time and in the same sphere new things are being born. The tide is turning, the tone of life is about to change.

It is easy to criticize Huizinga. His theory of causation seems to be excessively entropic. Things run down. One culture is exhausted and slowly is replaced by a vital new one. There is no base of causal economic and social forces. Aristocratic culture becomes enervated and rigidified and loses its integrative, symbolic capability. It can be said that Huizinga's argument is tautological—circular, question-begging. He assumes that the Middle Ages ended in 1500, so he looks for cultural change in the previous fifty to a hundred years. The change he pronounces postmedieval and protomodern. Nice, but why are formalism, symbolism, and idealism "medieval" and naturalism, represented in particularism, postmedieval? That is just playing with simplistic definitions, it can be argued. Furthermore, this new naturalism—particularism, in fact—made a powerful appearance in the twelfth century. True, it seems to have spent its force in the later thirteenth and fourteenth centuries, and there was perhaps an idealistic retrogression. But, it may be argued, what you have in fifteenth-century Netherlandish culture is a kind of renewal of twelfth-century naturalism, now better articulated and more consciously and theoretically formulated, with the help of Italian neoclassical humanism. This is actually close to Panofsky's view of what happened.

But none of this distracts from the postimpressionist skill with which Huizinga portrays aristocratic culture in the court of Burgundy in the fifteenth century. That is high art and can scarcely be improved upon. Huizinga was right in subtly bringing attention to a parallel between himself and Van Gogh. They were originally obscure autodidacts, awkward, amateurish at times, but their unique, idiosyncratic art prevails, hauntingly. There is something there that is much better than it ought to be.

Furthermore, Huizinga, it may be claimed, was a great methodological pioneer in bringing attention to the importance of court festivals and the popular culture of death rituals as social events of central importance. In so doing, he anticipated in 1919 the *Annales* school of the 1930s, the post-1945 American school of symbolic anthropology headed by Victor Turner and Clifford Geertz, and the Soviet cultural theorist of the 1930s Mikhail Bakhtin and his Princeton disciple of the 1970s Natalie Zemon Davis. It is not easy, however, fully to sustain these exciting claims for Huizinga. In tone and style, he seems partly a throwback to late romantic historical writing of the nineteenth century (the Age of Burckhardt). Essentially Huizinga is one of those peculiar Edwardian era visionaries, going far on intuitive resources—like Van Gogh, like D. H. Lawrence—rather than a precursor of the 1930s and subsequently. Huizinga lacks the methodological severity and academic arrogance of the Annalists and their epigones. Yet the symbolic significance of ritualized popular culture was certainly a Huizinga perception as early as the second decade of this century and in its time was daringly bold, vanguard thinking. It is much more for this oracular claim of structured ritualism and its social importance than for the dead-end thesis of the entropic decline of the Middle Ages that Huizinga's unique book should be read today.

III

THE PARTNERSHIP

Huizinga dismissed later medieval civilization as enervated and as losing its capacity for collective symbolization. More specific negative assessment of the medieval world was at the foreground of the work of a remarkable couple among the great medievalists, Eileen Power and Michael Postan. They collaborated for about fifteen years in the late 1920s and 1930s. She had a brilliant career before that partnership, and he had four decades of work and great eminence after her premature death. But there is no doubt that they greatly influenced and helped each other. It was a genuine and highly productive partnership in pursuit of understanding medieval economy and society. They both had, like Huizinga, a love of the shock value of the provocative and unconventional.

Eileen Power is the only woman medievalist who belongs in the array of the founders and shapers of our vision of the Middle Ages during the first seventy years of this century. As we look ahead into the twenty-first century, the story will be very different. Indeed, by 2020 medieval studies will be mainly in the hands of women scholars if current trends are sustained. In view of this fact, it is especially appropriate that Eileen Power was not only in the front rank of medievalists but a pioneer of feminism in Britain as well.

Eileen Edna Power (1889–1940) came of mixed English and Irish middle-class ancestry. Her parents died while she was a child, and she and her sister (who became a well-known BBC dramatist and producer) were reared by spinster aunts in Oxford. Power did brilliantly as a student at the state-supported Oxford High School, developing a deep love for medieval literature. She won a scholarship to Girton College, Cambridge, perhaps the leading bastion of British intellectual feminism in the first twentieth-century wave of the women's movement (1900–25), and was graduated with first-class honors in history. She stayed at Girton on a research fellowship and became a tutor there and a lecturer in medieval history in the university. Just before the war Power had a year's training in medieval research at Paris with C. V. Langlois, the social historian of the late Middle Ages and one of Marc Bloch's *bêtes noires*. This encouraged her to begin writing on medieval social history in the personal, presocial science mode that Langlois himself pursued. The result was her two most famous books, *Medieval English Nunneries c. 1275–1535* (1922), the first great work of British feminist history and still the best book on the subject, and *Medieval People* (1926), consisting of subtle and warm portrayals of six medieval personalities, beginning with Bodo, the Carolingian peasant. *Medieval People*, especially in its later Penguin paperback edition, is one of the all-time best-selling books in medieval studies and has gone through more than twenty printings.

Eileen Power was cool toward the war, as were other British feminists of her generation like Vera Brittain, and for the first time she began to take an active interest in current politics and drifted inevitably toward a left-wing position. This brought her into the magnetic orbit of Richard Henry Tawney, the Christian Marxist, guru of the Labour party, and professor of economic history at the London School of Economics (LSE).

After the war Power moved from Girton and Cambridge, where she had become known as probably the best history lecturer on the campus, to the London School of Economics and underwent retraining in economic history from Tawney and another senior professor there. She became Tawney's collaborator in an ambitious project of publishing a three-volume collection of Tudor (sixteenth-century) economic documents designed to sustain Tawney's view of sixteenth-century England as an age of landed capitalist revolution ("the rise of the gentry"). Power was now moving away from the personal, quasi-romantic kind of social history that she had earlier subscribed to and that had made for her an international reputation toward a more highly structured, institutional, and class-focused kind of economic history. She was a principal founder in 1926 of the *Economic History Review*, the journal of the new British economic history of an analytic, impersonal kind, which by 1940 was the best and most influential historical journal in Britain.

Power got a chair in economic history at the London School of Economics, and she became a fastidious and constant traveler. She made several trips to China and also spent time at Harvard and other places in the United States, as well as traveled all over Western Europe. Some of these trips were paid for by foundations. At one point she was the coeditor of a series of commercially published travel books. By the early thirties she was the dominant force in the history faculty at LSE and highly visible in Britain as a whole. She was chosen to be the coeditor of the projected *Cambridge Economic History*, a series with a very high profile and authority in the English-speaking world. By 1930 she was actively engaged, with a group of graduate students and junior colleagues, in thinking about going beyond economic history to a social and behavioral science-based history, somewhat along the lines of the French *Annales* school headed by Marc Bloch and Lucien Febvre, although in practice little progress was made along these lines in Britain before her death.

Tawney's biographer tells us that Tawney's wife was aware of a personal attachment between the socialist guru and his LSE disciple and colleague Eileen Power. But Power soon became emotionally involved with a medievalist younger than she. In her circle at the LSE was a fast-talking, brilliant émigré from East-Central Europe, Michael Postan. He was in turn her student, graduate student, research assistant, colleague, and, as of 1937, husband. They worked very closely together, and the seminal articles that Postan began to publish in the 1930s, which gained for him the chair of economic history at Cambridge in 1938, may very well have been written in close collaboration with Power, who, of course, wanted to advance the career of her husband, ten years her junior. In 1938 Power and Postan moved into a house in Cambridge, she still teaching at the London School of Economics; but now her health rapidly declined, and she died at the height of her career in 1940, the year in which Britain lost another great feminist of Cambridge background, Virginia Woolf.

Eileen Power was an attractive woman who dominated any room she entered, both by her intelligence and sophistication and by her appearance. She was a public speaker of unusual eloquence, who held standing-room-only crowds spellbound with her public lectures. In collaboration with her sister she gave history talks on the BBC to children. She was a great woman as well as an important medievalist, and it is unfortunate that her biography has not been written and that her personal papers, which were moved from the LSE to the Cambridge University Library after the war, appear to have disappeared, possibly destroyed by her widowered husband.

George Macaulay Trevelyan, the best-selling Cambridge author of *English Social History* (1942), suitably dedicated his famous book to Eileen Power. Although Trevelyan's kind of social history, a highly evocative, impressionistic, and personal kind, is now considered obsolete, this change in fashion should not allow us to undervalue Power's two great books of the 1920s. These, along with a strong article on medieval peasants in the *Cambridge Medieval History* (1932) and her lectures on the English wool trade given at Oxford in 1939, when her life strength was already ebbing, which were published posthumously by Postan, are her enduring contribution to the Middle Ages. Postan replaced her as coeditor of the *Cambridge Economic History*.

There are two peculiar aspects to the trajectory of the academic reputation of Eileen Power's student, protégé, and husband, Michael Moissey Postan (1899–1986). First, he was the leading exponent of a subfield of study of the Middle Ages, what is called British economic history, which was and is heavily concentrated in Cambridge University and its satellite programs, with some American colonies. This school—whose journal, the *Economic History Review*, had been mainly founded by Eileen Power and whose ideas and methods she helped define in the 1930s—reached its zenith of influence and prosperity in the three decades after the Second World War. Then British economic history began to experience both inner stagnation and conflict and a steep descent in prestige. Postan's reputation followed this up and down cycle of the school and its methods. A leading member of the British economic history school for the postmedieval era, D. C. Coleman, in a bitingly candid book, has chronicled this roller-coaster story (*History and the Economic Past*, 1987). Postan's image and influence were lower by the time he died at an advanced age than twenty years earlier, and today evaluation of the durability of his contribution is inconclusive.

The second peculiar aspect to Postan's life and career is the personal hostility and contempt he engendered. It was similar to Ernst Kantorowicz's crash at Oxford in 1938 and 1939, although it was much more serious because it was so extended, Postan being the holder of the senior chair in economic history from 1938 to 1966 and a member of the Cambridge community for five decades. One leading Cambridge historian, writing in 1980, while Postan was still alive, remarked that there were things about him that "cannot be reported." Charges of fakery, deviousness, deceit, fraud, with underlying tones of anti-semitism—very much as in Kantorowicz's case at Oxford in 1939—fly fast and furious. Postan was himself partly responsible for all this because he told improbable stories about himself, kept secret his early life before he emerged as Power's student at the London School of Economics, and was even inconsistent about the date of his birth, claiming it was really 1900 after listing it for half a century as 1899 (presumably there are no surviving birth certificates from his place of origin).

According to someone who knew him well, this much is known about Postan's early life. He was born in Bessarabia, on the Romanian borderland between the Russian and Austrian empires and he was a subject of the czar. His parents were Jewish, although now and again, to explain his red hair, he liked to claim a Scottish parent (sometimes the mother, sometimes the father). He was the son sometimes of poor peasants (appropriate for an authority on the medieval peasantry) and sometimes of a well-to-do merchant. The latter seems more likely because he certainly got an early education that would be most unlikely for the son of a peasant before 1914. He fled from Soviet Russia soon after the Russian Revolution, ending up in London by an unknown route. During the Second World War he was declared *persona non grata* by the Stalinist regime (the Churchill government had apparently planned to use him as a contact man with the Soviets), which would indicate that his family was indeed upper bourgeois.

Postan appeared in later years to his Cambridge colleagues to be an incurable fantasizer (he, of course, became old and possibly senile). At his retirement party in 1966 he suddenly announced that in 1916 he had come (at age sixteen) from Petrograd to spend a year at the Rugby School, one of Britain's leading secondary schools, before returning to Petrograd to take part in the Revolution. No one believed a word of this. He announced and in some instances began making detailed plans for projects that were never completed, but he would talk of those projects as though they had. But, says a colleague, "he had a marvelous gift of inspiration and starting others off."

Eventually Postan received the normal kind of high academic rewards in Britain, not only a chair at Cambridge but a knighthood. His second marriage was a happy one. Lady Cynthia Postan, a translator of some of the works of the *Annales* school, keeps the flame of Sir Michael's controversial memory burning brightly. That is not easy to do, not only because of the personal antipathy that he engendered in many quarters but because in fact, he never really completed a project properly. Even his attempt to write a textbook for students summarizing the rural history of medieval England, his main field of expertise, resulted in a confusing and unsatisfactory book. The necessary textbook effectively summing up Postan's lifework in his main field was written by two of his students, Edward Miller and John Hatcher.

Yet there was something refreshing about Postan, especially in his younger days. His extremism, his wild and woolly disposition are in retrospect endearing. In the mid-1930s Sir John Neale, the head of the history faculty at University College, London, was looking for a modern economic historian and heard from Eileen Power about this brilliant young man, starving in a garret while working on the history of the medieval manor. Neale went to see Postan and offered him a job, but Postan, although desperately in need of a steady income, said he was sorry, he could not accept it. The history of the medieval manor was his current vital project, so he could not accept a modern history job. Greatly impressed by this unusual measure of intellectual integrity, Neale promptly created a medieval job and put Postan into it. Of course, half a century later, when Postan died, the history of the manor had still not been written. Stories like this about Postan abound. A colleague who knew him well sums it up: "He was in the main a man who stimulated people into thinking, and as such he was hard to beat, but one always had a sense of a good brain allowed to run to waste."

The fact of the matter is that Cambridge was not a good environment for a man of Postan's tense psychological makeup, which turned toward excitability and fantasizing and was affected by a lifelong concern about his social origins and his adaptability into the difficult upper strata of British life. Postan would likely have been a happier, much more productive, if less glamorous, person in a quiet chair or directing a small research institute in the relaxed atmosphere of a large American state university, like Berkeley or Ann Arbor. Here again, as in the case of his first wife, Postan is a potential subject for a fascinating biography, which again is not likely to get written.

Postan edited and published posthumously Eileen Power's last book, on the English wool trade. Her greatest works, however, were the book on late medieval English nunneries and *Medieval People*, published in the 1920s, which may be called quasi-romantic examples of social history. *Medieval English Nunneries* has long been out of print. It is the most underrated major work in medieval history, at least in the English language. It communicates in searing fashion the distressed, marginal, and anxious world of medieval nuns. The ambience of nunneries is that of impoverished and neglected aristocrats. Power stresses that there were only two thousand nuns in England in the fifteenth century in a population of more than two million. They all came from wealthy families, usually landed; their families had to buy the women's entry into the convents, a form of dowry. Nevertheless, two thirds of the nunneries were poor, and life in them was both physically and psychologically constricted.

What Power does is try to recapture for us vividly the life experience of this peculiar female population. It is not surprising that little rebellions in the form of keeping pets and traveling outside the walls of the convents were frequently noticed and censured. Power is giving us a pioneering work in feminist as well as woman's history—the story of the rebellion of a repressed and marginalized female population within the landed class. This subtle portrayal of the realities of the quiet life of individuals within a complex social situation is done on a broader scale in *Medieval People*, in which six individuals between the Age of Charlemagne and the fifteenth century are intimately examined. What Power is especially good at is communicating the tensions, anxieties, and psychic pain of everyday life without becoming lachrymose about it.

As a forerunner and role model in women's history, Eileen Power was important in two respects. First, she delivered a searing indictment of male chauvinism in medieval civilization. In the aristocratic courts of the French-speaking world of the late twelfth and early thirteenth centuries, there had unquestionably existed a novel feminist consciousness, which is memorialized for us principally in the courtly romances of the era. But by the late thirteenth century male repression and subjugation of women among the nobility had reasserted themselves. Power's account of nuns in late medieval England, the distress and social marginality of their lives, and the lack of care and consideration they received even within the church hierarchy bears testimony to this downturn in the status of women in landed society in northern Europe in the later Middle Ages. It is not surprising that an enthusiast for the Middle Ages like David Knowles passed over the history of women religious very quickly in his monumental four-volume work and had very little to add to Power's definitive account. It is not surprising that Dick Southern never addressed the issue of how modestly women actually benefited in the long run from the Virgin cult and the more humanistic theology of the twelfth century.

Power brought medieval men and their twentieth-century partisans before the bar of moral judgment and found them wanting. Medieval aristocratic nuns were very badly treated. What can be said about the condition of the millions upon millions of less privileged women in medieval society? It was not until the new feminist consciousness of the 1970s penetrated medieval studies that this question was intensely pursued, but Power had essentially made a definitive response to it in 1922. Little attention was paid for half a century to what she was saying.

Called upon in 1926 to contribute an essay, "The Position of Women," to a bumptiously upbeat volume called *The Legacy of the Middle Ages*, which Oxford's Clarendon Press forthwith put through more than nine printings, Power did her best to portray anecdotally the more pleasant and jovial side of the life of medieval women, as the editors demanded of her. But her conclusion is bitter and explicit in its condemnation: "The prevalent [medieval] dogma of the subjection of women, becoming embedded in the common law and in the marriage laws, left to future generations a legacy which was an unconscionable time in dying. It is true that woman was not legally 'a

free and lawful person,' that she had no lot or share then, or indeed
until the twentieth century, in what may be called public as distinct
from private rights and duties, and that the highest grades of education were closed to her." Here, put succinctly, is much of the paradigm of feminist historiography of the 1970s and 1980s, including the
key doctrine of what is now called disempowerment.

Power's other contribution as a women's historian was to serve as
an inspiring role model for a remarkable generation of English women
medievalists who were the product of the first great generation of
British feminism and who emerged in the 1920s and early 1930s. In
retrospect, the most accomplished were the Oxford or Cambridge
dons Helen Maud Cam, Beryl Smalley, Dorothy Whitelock, and
Maude V. Clarke. Clarke, who worked on the fourteenth-century
English Parliament and kingship, was probably the most brilliant of
the group. She died young of cancer. Vivian Galbraith knew her well
and believed that she would have been among the leading medievalists of her generation. It is significant that unlike Power, none of this
group of late 1920s and 1930s medievalist feminists ever married or
were known as other than spinsters. Sexual autonomy was perhaps a
necessary defense for this generation of women medievalists making
their way in a profession that was intrinsically hostile to them and
accepted them begrudgingly and essentially required of them that they
work within the prevailing ethos of a male-dominated medievalist
world. Unlike Power, none of these four formidable women scholars
worked significantly in women's history. So it was really the generation of the 1970s and 1980s that took up the model of women's medievalist that Eileen Power had articulated. They worked on women's
history, many of them, and in most cases they married.

Always in Power's early work a neoromantic sensibility is boldly
combined with bold assessments of the social structure: "It was in the
fourteenth century that there began that steady fusion between the
country gentry and the rich burgesses, which was accomplished before the end of the middle ages and which resulted in the formation
of a solid and powerful middle class. The political amalgamation of
the two classes in the lower house of Parliament corresponded to a
social amalgamation in the world outside." As a matter of fact, this
view of the formation of middle-class solidarity is wrong. The blending of country and urban families sometimes occurred, but it was a
modest and only occasional development. The social amalgamation of
a universal middle class was in fact still going on in the middle decades of the nineteenth century. Power has greatly foreshortened En-

glish social history. But it fitted in perfectly with R. H. Tawney's Marxist paradigm: In order to turn the great rebellion of the 1640s into a bourgeois revolution, Tawney had to get the gentry and the burghers molded into one revolutionary class in the sixteenth century. It was inevitable, therefore, that Power would be his chief collaborator in the 1920s.

Postan had a countervailing and beneficial ideological influence on Power. As a refugee from Soviet Russia he was not enamored of the simple Leninist model of history favored by Tawney. In the late 1920s and early 1930s Postan's influence helped move Power into the third phase of her intellectual development, after quasi-romantic social history and Tawneyite dialectics—into the politically ambivalent and postromantic British economic history school.

Tawney in his historical work had engaged in a moralistic and highly polemical rhetoric condemning capitalism and had used a Marxist model of class struggle. The school of British economic history, which Power and Postan decisively contributed to establishing in the 1930s, whatever the private political commitments of its members, was neutral in the battle between left and right. It tried for a detached analytical approach, showing the development of medieval land tenure and systems of the cultivation and attendant social arrangements, as well, of course, as the later growth of trade and industry. Donald Coleman, a leading practitioner of the school with respect to the modern era and also its best historian, has defined it this way: "The economic historiography which thus throve in Britain, during its rise to respectability [1930–70], was of particular type. From the careful use of primary sources, both literary and numerical, statements were built up which provided a description, partly chronological and partly functional, of a given economic activity in the past. They were placed within a framework derived from the broadest assumptions of neo-classical economics."

This is a good summary of Power's work in the last ten years of her life and of Postan's development of a general paradigm for the whole history of medieval rural England. The problem was that after about 1970 the school of British economic history, along with suffering from rapid overexpansion and complacency, was hit from two sides. On one side, it did not command the sophisticated mathematical and computer-based models of the new American cliometricians such as Robert Fogel, and it was also not sufficiently attuned to new post-Keynesian economic theory. It had never, in fact, even absorbed Keynes very well, being essentially grounded in the theory of mar-

ginal utility offered by the late-nineteenth-century Cambridge economist Alfred Marshall and the population/resources model of the early-
nineteenth-century theorist Thomas Malthus. On the other hand, especially among an emerging younger generation in Britain, there was
a shift in the 1970s back toward leftist polemics and Tawneyite Marxist
dialectics, a neo-Tawneyism that sought support from and established affiliation with the Annalist school, especially in its more blatant Marxist mode under Braudel's leadership.

These radical intellectual departures made Power's work by 1980
doubly old-fashioned—premodern, Edwardian spinsterist feminism,
followed by now-outmoded economic analysis. Postan's work was made
to look impressionistic, unscientific, and idiosyncratic in the eyes of
many in the new generation. The younger economists complained
that Postan's model dealt only with supply (agricultural productivity)
and ignored demand (the nobility's consumer patterns).

By the late 1980s the school of British economic history was in the
awkward position of controlling chairs and institutes at the same time
as confidence in its intellectual foundations was fast eroding. The
solution under the Cambridge statistician E. A. Wrigley—to begin
building huge computerized data bases on population and price
movements—was a partial but far from complete restorative.

Postan's greatest achievement as an economic historian was to articulate a general view of the whole duration of medieval English
rural history, especially in the south-central region, about half the
landmass of England, where intensive grain growing was possible.
Serfdom was shown to be mainly an economic vehicle, whatever its
juristic expression. Manorial serfdom was the way a landlord assured
himself of a continuous supply of labor in a society in which there
was a chronic labor shortage, as was true of England until the late
twelfth century. By serfdom, the peasant and all his descendants were
bound to the land and had to provide labor to the lord and/or share
their crops with the landlord. Serfdom was not cheap because the
peasants had rightful claim to a substantial share of the lord's land
and pasturage. But before 1150 there was no fiscally viable alternative
to serfdom in the grain-growing regions because of labor shortages.
With the tremendous population boom of 1150–1280, serfdom steadily became economically infeasible. It was cheaper to push the manorial peasants off the land (legal manumission means economic
dismissal) and hire laborers on short- or long-term contracts. This
became the halcyon era of medieval English landlords, the age of
"high farming," in which the lord did not share his land with the

peasants but cultivated his own land (demesne) intensely by management through his own stewards and their harsh supervision of paid and contracted labor. By the late thirteenth century, serfdom had all but disappeared, food production had skyrocketed along with the expanding market, and much marginally infertile land had been brought under cultivation.

Eventually, as in all premodern societies (China in the eighteenth century, India in the nineteenth, Latin America and Africa today), by 1280 the English population in Malthusian fashion had outraced food supply. Unusually good weather in the thirteenth century also affected the population and productivity equation. Postan believed that by 1280 the population of England was between five and six million, a level it did not reach again until the Age of the American Revolution. He also believed that even before the Black Death of 1346–48, intrinsic, countercyclical forces (bad weather, food shortage) had begun to drive the population curve downward. After the Black Death (bubonic plague), which eliminated close to 40 percent of the working population, severe labor shortages generated the third medieval English rural system (following the eras of serfdom and high farming): leasehold farming. Because labor was now scarce and expensive, the intensive cultivation of his land by contract labor was no longer profitable for the lord, and late medieval landlords leased (or "farmed") large sections of their demesnes to autonomous peasant families. Here was the basis for the rise of the protocapitalist "yeoman" families, some of which began to move up into the gentry in the late fifteenth century. This form of social mobility from wealthy peasant into gentry families was much more widespread than the earlier Tawney-Power model of the amalgamation of the gentry and bourgeois families.

As in the case of all large-scale generalizations, especially in social history, it is not hard to challenge Postan's triadic model of first serfdom, next high farming, then leasehold farming by close examination of particular estates that turn out to be variants from the pattern he determined. But the important point is that between about 1935 and 1965 Postan did establish the basic pattern to which all subsequent historians of rural England have had to react. He brought clarity and order into a very confused subject, and no doubt Power gave him much good advice.

Postan himself was not much of quantifier. He benefited from the occasional assistance of the statistician William Beveridge, a Labour party economist and friend of Power's (the Beveridge Plan of 1942 established the theoretical basis for the postwar welfare state in Britain). Postan worked mostly in the precomputer age, before the elaborate computer-driven modern refining of vast amounts of data. But it will probably be a long time before an alternative clear and consistent longitudinal model of medieval rural England comes into play.

The account of medieval economy that Postan gives us places it within the gloomy Malthusian paradigm of a premodern society, which still prevails in the less developed third world societies of parts of Africa, East Asia, and Latin America. Greater agricultural yield, generated partly by bringing new, marginal land under cultivation and partly by a long succession of good weather, produced in medieval England a much-enhanced food supply. But with no means of limiting reproduction and with the church in any case opposed to contraception, even though infanticide and abandonment of children were practiced occasionally, the English population at a certain point (c. 1220) escalated rapidly and eventually after several decades began to strain the previously ample food supply. When bad weather, war, endemic crime, and disease afflicted this society, it had no defensive mechanism except a massively accelerating death rate. The population fell once again, by 1400, to where it was in balance with the food supply, but not before this shock had profoundly affected other aspects of the society, its government, religion, law, and family structure.

Postan's view of the medieval world is one of a strictly reactive society incapable of planning and prey to all physical forces. This impotence and terror a modern society transcends. For those who take a positive view of the Middle Ages and the great enterprises of medieval church and state, particularly their learning and spirituality, Postan's unremitting deterministic cycle of rural boom and bust is a chastening lesson.

This bleak message was discomfiting to enthusiasts of the Middle Ages. They wanted to see in medieval government, religion, literature, and art the mainstream of Western civilization coursing into the modern world. Postan was an unwelcome guest at the high table of Oxbridge medievalism. He was that loathsome party guest who in the midst of the elegant festivities keeps pointing to the homeless sleeping on the sidewalks outside and asking rude questions about how the festivity bills are going to be paid when they fall due. It is this naysaying, as well as his occasionally bizarre personal behavior, that earned Postan so much hostility in high academic circles.

Before Postan's revelation of the iron Malthusian cycle of the medieval European economy, the accounts of medieval material development were decidedly upbeat and celebratory. Marc Bloch exulted in the autonomy of medieval peasant communities, which he projected into the durable democracy of modern rural France. Henri Pirenne delighted similarly in the creativity and political power of medieval urban communities led by an entrepreneurial and enlightened bourgeoisie, the putative direct precursors of the solid Belgian upper middle class of the twentieth century. In the first volume of the *Cambridge Economic History*, published in 1941, which Eileen Power had planned and Postan ultimately edited, Richard Koebner, a German émigré who became the distinguished head of the history department at the Hebrew University in Jerusalem, memorialized the skill and courage of medieval landed society, both lord and peasant, in the process of internal settlement and land clearing in medieval Europe, no doubt a heroic and consequential frontier-advancing effort.

But Postan's Malthusian pessimism placed these celebrated aspects of medieval economy in a discouraging and tragic perspective. Not all the labor, enterprise, courage, and freedom of medieval communities would escape the iron law of premodern societies. The very success of these economies inaugurated their descent into misery and disorder because increased food supply generated a population boom within two or three generations, and the resulting demographic explosion could be neither controlled nor serviced by breaking through the rigid technological ceiling on agricultural production. Eventually when all arable land is brought under cultivation and there is still not enough food, bellies begin to knot in hunger, and then pandemics afflict the weakened population, resolving the demographic crisis by a biochemical holocaust.

If we assume that the pattern of the medieval economy that Postan established for England was generally true elsewhere, at least north of the Alps and the Pyrenees, there are some intriguing questions to contemplate about medieval thought and leadership. Why did medieval Europe lose its frequently exhibited capacity to develop new technology and radical novel economic organization somewhere at the middle of the thirteenth century, precisely when the challenge of demographic explosion had to be faced? Why did a society that was so sophisticated in areas like philosophy, theology, and imaginative literature fail to develop a modern type of economic mind? Was this again, like the Roman Empire, a manifestation of aristocratic distaste for material thinking (although not consumption), further reinforced by the revival of Greek thought in the twelfth and thirteenth centuries and the obsessive cultivation of Roman law?

And what of the much-praised medieval state? After developing protomodern techniques of law and taxation, why did it show its only novel managerial capacity between 1290 and 1500 in making war? Why was it incapable of addressing its intelligence and personnel toward economic, social, and public health problems? What was there in the later medieval mind that made it so incredibly sophisticated in some directions (Duns Scotus anticipated much of Wittgenstein's philosophy; *Pearl* is as good a poem as there has been written in the twentieth century) and so impotent and negligible in others? Did the new piety of the eleventh and twelfth centuries that Southern and Knowles admired so much have the calamitous side effect of, after a point, perhaps around 1190, legitimating an antiempirical, asocial way of thinking right in the midst of a critical economic change? Were the kings whom Schramm, Kantorowicz, and Halphen so much admired just narrow, selfish little people decked up in fancy raiments and elaborate rituals, like so many wizards of Oz? In medieval landed society, in spite of Bloch's sentimental effort to antedate the revolutionary peasantry of the Leninist dream, did the nobility gain nearly all the intelligence, and leave the peasants a vast underclass of low reasoning capacity? Postan's model of the medieval English economy inspires these disturbing questions that very few medievalists of his own and the succeeding generation wanted to think about for long.

IV

SAYING NO AND BELIEVING YES

The early work of Eileen Power revealed a previously unspoken shame that clouded the twentieth-century image of medieval culture: its marginalization and deprivation of women, even among the families of the nobility. Power demonstrated this forcefully in her 1922 book on late medieval nunneries. Not until the rise of historical feminism in the 1960s was this line of argument taken up and further pursued. But David Knowles was shrewd enough, after reading Power's book, to deal very succinctly with nunneries in his four volumes on religious orders. The issues of women's mistreatment among religious orders was for him an uncomfortable subject. The repression of women was part of the larger issue of freedom in a medieval culture conditioned by fanaticism arising from the mingling of spirituality with political and military power.

This issue of intellectual and religious freedom in medieval Europe had been noisily highlighted in the late nineteenth century in Henry C. Lea's sprawling volumes on the Inquisition. But in addition to the undisciplined and polemical treatment that Lea gave the subject, the premodern era in which he wrote made his work seem obsolete in light of the highly accomplished authority that began with the work of the great Germans in the 1920s and their positive views of the Middle Ages. Yet the issue of medieval fanaticism lurked on the fringes of twentieth-century consideration of the Middle Ages. Sergei Eisenstein's patriotic historical film *Alexander Nevsky*, made at Stalin's behest in 1938 (the Hitler-Stalin pact of September 1939 led to temporary suppression of the film until the German invasion of Russia in the summer of 1941), is centered on this theme. The film is concerned with the rallying of the Russian people by a heroic czar to repel the German crusading and imperialist order of the Teutonic Knights. In one of the best films about the Middle Ages ever made, Eisenstein coagulates evil in an assembly for battle of the Teutonic Knights, armed like dark forces in heavy armor, and exhibiting the menace rising from the Teutonic order's combination of Roman Christianity with imperialistic militarism.

Fanaticism was unquestionably a central ingredient in medieval culture, and it frequently took the form of attributing sacred qualities to the state and military and political power to the church. This blending of the moral and spiritual on the one side and the political and military on the other inspired key achievements in medieval Europe, among them the conversion of the heathen Germans, the southward drive against Muslim incursions into Europe, the rise of centralized state power, the development of an international papal bureaucracy, and the establishment of the Papal States ("the Patrimony of St. Peter") in central Italy. The blending of the religious and the political in an aggressive fanaticism also gave impetus to the First Crusade of 1095 against Muslim control of the eastern Mediterranean, especially the Christian Holy Land centered on Jerusalem. The medieval intermingling of the political and religious spheres of life also, however, inspired pogroms against Jews, strengthened the legal subjugation of women, motivated repression of dissenting religious groups in the church, and fostered the institutions of what R. I. Moore has recently called a persecuting society.

That medieval church and state were not more oppressive was due to the institutional and corporate pluralism of medieval society (the division of sovereignty among a variety of authorities from emperor down to municipal communes and small feudal baronies) and especially to the technological backwardness of those exercising power and fanatically committed to narrow ideals. By unifying the spiritual and moral with the political and military, the monarchies and papacy of the period after 1050 had an intrinsic proclivity to totalitarianism and elimination of civil society and freedom of thought. But they lacked the means to carry out extensively a totalitarian program, which in many instances would have been their preference.

The modern totalitarian state in Nazi Germany and the Leninist-Stalinist Soviet Union and its satellites was a realization of a medieval nightmare. Norman Cohn has persuasively argued this theme in several books. Now a fanatical, narrow group of power holders, committed to ill-defined but hysterical, hateful ideals, had the technological means to unite all authority in a party and leader, to integrate effectively the moral and spiritual with the political and military, to obliterate all other institutions in society, and to destroy physically minorities it did not want or opposition it encountered. This was called *Gleichschaltung* ("leveling centralization") and the leadership principle in Nazi Germany and democratic centralism and the dictatorship of the proletariat in the Soviet bloc countries. The result was Auschwitz and the gulag, World War II, and the death of at least twenty million civilians at the hand of the Nazi and Bolshevik governments.

The medieval world was spared this magnitude of horror not because of a lack of fanatical hatred and a restraint from a disposition to eliminate all social outcasts and dissenters. Several popes and kings in the high and late Middle Ages had the cast of mind to effect these holocausts. The medieval world was spared by political pluralism and by its technological backwardness, which made mass organization for conformity and genocide too feeble to attain a totalitarian outcome, such as threatened the survival of humanity in the form of Hitlerian Germany and Stalinist Russia. So the indictment against the Middle Ages runs.

There were two young medievalists in Germany in the mid-1930s who saw these comparative situations with piercing clarity and did what they could to resist the onset of medieval nightmare in modern form. They sought to warn, through their writings, of the lessons to be learned from interfacing medieval history and twentieth-century experience. These were the Berlin friends Theodor Ernst Mommsen

(1905–1958) and Carl Erdmann (1898–1945). Their courageous disposition to say no to fanatical bridging of the spiritual and political sides of life cost them dearly in terms of careers and the stability and happiness of their lives. They suffered and were ground up in the maw of totalitarian might.

Nor did the message they communicated really get out to medievalists. Posthumously they are respected but not well understood. These brave dissenters deserve to be remembered, and their message deserves to be reflected on. They were liberal defenders of civil society and daring enemies of totalitarianism in both its medieval and its modern manifestations. They were also naysayers against the overpraisers, the enthusiasts for power and clerical privilege among medievalists. They sensed the problematic nature of medieval culture, particularly the dangers of fanaticism and the blending of church and state.

Mommsen was christened Theodor after his paternal grandfather, the greatest Roman historian of the nineteenth century. He later added the middle name Ernst to avoid confusion with the great man (who looked grimly down on him from a huge portrait in his parents' house; after 1946 this awesome portrait hung in his apartment in Princeton). In 1931, when he was traveling from town to town in northern Italy to do research in archives at the behest of the Monumenta institute in Berlin, Mommsen was greeted in one place, as he got off the train, by a brass band and the mayor offering him the key to the city. Mommsen had written ahead to the archivist to announce his coming, and the archivist had run excitedly to the mayor with the news "the great Mommsen is coming," not realizing that the grand old man had been dead for four decades. After that, Mommsen tried using a middle initial to differentiate himself from his grandfather.

It was a lot of family baggage he carried, growing up in his grandfather's house, which Mommsen's father, a prominent physician, had inherited. His mother was Clara Weber, the sister of Max Weber, the famous sociologist (and Theodor Mommsen the Elder's student in Roman history, initially). When Ted Mommsen went to study for a time in Heidelberg, he stayed at the home of his aunt Marianne Weber, Weber's widow. Mommsen spent the first thirty years of his life trying to escape from his family destiny. He was related to half the illustrious humanist scholars of the German-speaking world, including Adolf von Harnack, the historian of Christian theology. Mommsen's family had decided that he should fulfill his destiny dictated by the famous name he carried. It was not something he wanted.

He loved art and music. He was a gentle, easygoing person with a warm sense of humor. He loved to read newspapers, attend films (Charlie Chaplin was a favorite of his), the theater, and concerts, and gossip endlessly with friends. He would have made a good journalist, perhaps an art or music critic. Instead he was dragooned unwillingly into the academic life. He even tried failing his high school exams, but that only got his graduation postponed for a semester. He then had the idea of escaping to a very recondite branch of humanistic studies and for a couple of years pursued the study of Chinese and Indian civilization in Vienna, where another relative held the chair of East Asian studies. But the language barrier was too hard, and he finally gave up and lapsed into conformity.

Mommsen brushed up on his rusty school Latin and enrolled for a Ph.D. in medieval history at the University of Berlin. He finally received the degree in 1931 under the supervision of the proto-Nazi Albert Brackmann, the enemy of Ernst Kantorowicz, whom Mommsen idolized. To satisfy Brackmann, Mommsen wrote a thesis within Brackmann's paradigm of *Ostpolitik*, the aggressive eastward push of the medieval German peoples. Mommsen was mortified when Marc Bloch wrote a review of his obscure dissertation and denounced its apparently reactionary political tone. Mommsen actually agreed with Bloch's political denunciation of his own dissertation. The formidable director of the Monumenta, Paul Kehr, rescued Mommsen from another psychological crisis by sending him off to work in the Italian archives.

In 1933, on a visit to Germany, Mommsen saw with astonishing clarity what was happening under Nazi rule and was not reticent in expressing his dismay and anger in a private letter: "I don't need to name the specific events. You know what they are, and you will know what my position on them was. They are things about which you can't make any compromise. That is particularly true for the question of anti-Semitism, which has assumed such a massive role in recent events. . . . We have to deal not only with the fiction of a racially purified Germany but with a governmental, social, and intellectual reconstruction of the country. . . . [Transl. Felix Gilbert]."

Mommsen fled back to the more tolerant atmosphere (and much less anti-Semitism) of Mussolini's Italy. He now worked in the rich late medieval archives of Florence, perhaps his favorite city. He visited Bernard Berenson at his villa outside Florence and talked about Renaissance art with him. He attended innumerable concerts and opera performances. He waited for things to improve in Germany, but they got worse. Then, in 1935, Kehr delivered a crushing blow; he said that the Monumenta institute could no longer support Mommsen's research in Italy. Fiscal constraint was the ostensible reason, but politics may have been involved. After a quick visit to Germany to say good-bye to his family, Mommsen headed for England, where he was coldly received and refused an immigration visa. His Jewish friend the classicist Ludwig Edelstein, an authority on ancient medicine, was now a professor at the Johns Hopkins University in Baltimore, whose commitment to medical science stimulated the creation of a faculty appointment for Germany's most distinguished historian of ancient medicine. Mommsen was especially close to Edelstein's vivacious wife. She was probably his private Beatrice.

Edelstein arranged a stopgap fellowship for Mommsen at Johns Hopkins in 1937, and then for two years Mommsen taught European history at Yale. He suffered miserably with the language (to the end of his life he spoke English with a thick foreign accent and had trouble writing clear English prose). In 1940, as the American military draft began, the panicked Yale dean envisaged the loss of many students and fired nontenured faculty all over the place, including Mommsen. For five years, during the war, Mommsen taught Latin at the Groton School, which in his quiet, masochistic manner he enjoyed. His situation had all the irony of someone named Albert Einstein's teaching high school physics. Mommsen now published some important scholarly articles, and in 1946 Joe Strayer rescued him and gave him a tenured appointment at Princeton, where he shared a house with another bachelor, the proud, immensely learned but lazy Renaissance art historian Bert Friend. Mommsen got to know Panofsky, to whom he was appropriately adulatory. He made innumerable trips to Manhattan to attend concerts and operas and visit art galleries and eat in good restaurants. He bought a dachshund, which he named Duffer.

Ted Mommsen was six feet tall, but he didn't seem that tall because he always walked with a stoop and a slouch. His was a very North German face, mixing genetic severity with a distinctive softness and generosity. He was almost blind without his thick glasses and wheezed from heavy cigarette smoking. He wore good clothes in a nonchalant, sloppy manner. He had a large, weird circular office at Princeton in what had been the university library, a late-nineteenth-century Romanesque pile. He sat in an easy chair in the long New Jersey afternoons, holding and stroking Duffer, chain-smoking cigarettes, and talking endlessly with students. Occasionally he sat at his cluttered desk, under a Tiffany lamp, and studied a medieval text. He admitted that he took no pleasure in reading Latin. He took an overbearing interest in his graduate students, discussing intimate family and sexual problems they might have. He went gladly to their ramshackle apartments, carrying bottles of white wine and flowers, and made suggestions on improving their decor, usually quite impractical. He inspected the Graduate History Study Room twice a day, and if one of his students was not there working, he immediately phoned him and inquired why.

Mommsen built up a huge collection of long-playing records, particularly Mozart, and sat for hours listening and reading newspapers. He was one of those displaced, alienated Central European intellectuals, a character in a Musil or Canetti or Nabokov novel. He also brought to understanding of the Middle Ages a rare liberal disposition and an unusual perspective.

What he lacked was not learning or insight or, it may be argued, courage. He lacked an image of himself as a powerful and successful person who could command attention. He lacked a capacity for self-assertion and the urge to use humanistic scholarship in the interest of asserting his personal dominance over others. Even in seminars with students, a brilliant, accomplished report by one of them seemed to depress him after momentary elation and drive him into a defensive and apologetic posture. Mommsen retained the wonderful mental qualities that had distinguished his paternal grandfather and maternal uncle, Theodor, the patriarch, and Max Weber, the ineffable sociologist. What he lacked was their iron capacity to see themselves as leaders, as prophets, as spokesmen not only for the world of learning but for the more liberal sentiments of their generation. Ted Mommsen spoke softly, diffidently. In the presence of dominant figures like Strayer, Panofsky, or even his revered friend and idol Kantorowicz, he was defensive, ill at ease, apologetic. He was not deferential, but he was inhibited from putting up his ideas to challenge theirs. In their imperial presences, he smiled enigmatically and kept quiet, after some marginal comment that did not reveal his underlying resistance or signal his strong dissent from what they were saying.

It was distressing to witness Mommsen's emotional dependence on those for whom he had developed a great admiration and love. He never tired of telling of Kantorowicz's greatness and of how in Germany in 1931 Kantorowicz had demolished the despicable Brackmann, who had been Mommsen's dissertation supervisor. "The Rise of Eka" in the twisted scene of late Weimar Germany took on, in Mommsen's account, an Arthurian legend as told by Bertolt Brecht and Kurt Weill. Gordon Craig, his Princeton colleague, whom he had taught beside at Yale in 1940 until they both were fired with the staffing cutback attendant on the beginning of the military draft, was another object of Mommsen's intense adulation. His faith was not misplaced. Craig had risen to be a tenured full professor on the strength of his dramatic classroom performances and Rhodes scholar penumbra, while having published just a couple of modest articles. "Just you wait," Mommsen told us skeptical and deriding graduate students, "Gordon Craig will be a prolific and eminent scholar." As a matter of fact, that turned out to be true, after Craig had wisely departed for Stanford in the early sixties, several years after Mommsen's death. But some of the time and emotional intensity devoted to defending Craig's reputation would have been better spent in enhancing his own.

Finally, Mommsen fell into the *Mr. Chips/Browning Version* trap of idealizing students and then becoming dependent on them. There was a preciously handsome Princeton undergraduate, whom he singled out as a genius and whom he persuaded to stay on reluctantly after graduation and pursue a Ph.D. under his direction. Mommsen talked to all who would listen of what great things the young student would do, was indeed already doing. As a matter of fact, he turned out to be a respectable, although not phenomenal, scholar with a conventional, solid career in a midwestern university. But when Mommsen left for Cornell in 1954 and in the lonely ice fields of Ithaca, New York, begged him to visit him, his protégé demurred and wounded him deeply.

Carl Erdmann fared less well in the bare externals of his early life and career than his friend Ted Mommsen. He did not have a famous and influential family to fall back on or protect him. He was a brilliant, precocious student, devoted to the intellectual and ecclesiastical history of the Middle Ages. He was a student of Erich Caspar, the half-Jewish historian of the papacy who held one of the two chairs of medieval history, along with Brackmann, at Berlin. When Erdmann presented his *Habilitationsschrift* (second, expanded thesis, necessary for a university job) in 1932, Caspar's future was already cloudy (he died in 1935, after the Nazis removed him). It was obvious that Erdmann was a liberal dissenter and opponent of the Nazis. Paul Kehr, the head of the Monumenta, had helped Mommsen by sending him abroad. Erdmann was similarly sent to Portugal by the astute Kehr to work in the archives, and he stayed on as a tutor to a German business family in Lisbon. When he returned to Germany in 1938, Erdmann could not get a teaching job on political grounds, and he struggled on as an ill-paid researcher at the Monumenta. His health was always delicate, and he had not fought in World War I. By 1942 the Nazis were determined to get rid of him. He was conscripted into the army and sent to the eastern front. He died in a German uniform in Hungary in 1945.

Erdmann's second dissertation was a study, *The Origins of the Crusading Ideal*. It was published in 1935 (English translation, 1977) and was regarded as a work of very superior quality. If it had not been for his political views, it would have soon gained for him a university chair. It is a book written in a totalitarian society in the shadow of political terrorism and is therefore written in code. But its meaning is clear. The title should be "The Crusading Ideal and the Perils of Fanaticism." It is a study of the corruption of high spiritual ideals through their involvement with political fanaticism. It is an account of the perversion of Christianity by transmutation of its missionary impulse into holy war. The lesson for the Germany of the 1930s was obvious, and in spite of the circumspect style and coded reticence, Erdmann did not fool the Nazis. They blocked his appointment to a university job, and in time they got rid of him.

Erdmann's salutary warning not only is relevant to the Germany of today but is a lesson drawn from medieval history for all intellectuals who allow the embedding of noble ideals in a sordid political and military base. It tells how in this iron embrace a destructive culture of terrorist fanaticism is generated. Erdmann is saying no to compromise, careerism, yuppiedom, self-enhancement, eating supper with the devil: "We are concerned with the problem of 'the church and war' and, by the same token, with the historical foundations of the Western ethic of war and soldiering [trans. M. W. Baldwin and W. Goffart]."

In Erdmann's account the most idealistic of medieval popes, Gregory VII (pope from 1073 to 1085), was also the greatest betrayer of the Christian ethic of peace: "The pope harmonized warlike practises with the ethical ideal of the church and gave his wars the spiritual character of crusade. He regretted bloodshed but found it justified at any time for his ecclesiastical aims and for the rights of the papacy. . . . More than anyone before him, he overcame the inhibitions that had once restrained the church from being warlike in preaching and warlike in action. . . . He was as much a warrior as a priest and politician." The result in Pope Urban II's First Crusade of 1095 was the most corrupting amalgam of all, a church-centered imperialism: "Urban II's idea of crusade did not arise from a concern for the Holy Sepulcher and pilgrimages. His original and primary basis was the idea of an ecclesiastical-knightly war upon heathens. . . ." Translating out of medievalist code, Erdmann is also saying: Hitler's aggressive policies are not the result of a professed desire for "living space" for the German people in the East. It is military imperialism pure and simple, using ideology as a cover and force whenever it is not restrained. No human should have such power over other people.

What do we have here? We have a lesson from the Middle Ages applicable to not only the German professors who sold out to the Nazis or the Marxist intellectuals who allowed themselves to be seduced by Stalinist tyranny but to "the best and the brightest," the Harvard and MIT academics who perpetrated the calamity of the Vietnam War. We have the biomedical scientists of today who sell their patents to industry to enrich and empower themselves, while seeking moral cover under the guise of the advancement of science and health and Nobel prizes. We have the moral treason of clerks in all times and places. In the guise of telling the tragic outcomes of the medieval crusading ideal, Erdmann's book carries the message of naysaying to all these dishonesties and moral betrayals.

T. E. Mommsen is one of a short list of people Erdmann thanked in the preface to his crusading ideal book, published in 1935. Mommsen emphatically agreed with its sentiments and urged Erdmann to publish it. At Princeton, in 1952, Mommsen took an inscribed copy of the book off the shelf and remarked that Erdmann had prophesied, in that medieval study, the course of the moral downfall of Germany. Mommsen never forgave his German compatriots and his own relatives for their betrayal of the moral law. Between 1945 and his death he visited West Germany only once, and for a short time. He spoke of his brothers, the admiral and the business executive, with little enthusiasm. They had stayed in Germany and served Hitler. For his cousin Willi Mommsen, a prominent professor of modern European history who had been a blatant collaborator with the Nazis, he had only contempt. Only Brackmann was worse in his eyes.

The Nazi debacle seemed to sour Ted Mommsen retrospectively on his whole illustrious lineage. It is astonishing that I knew him for three years and had had many conversations of a quite personal nature with him, as well as innumerable academic discussions, before he casually mentioned one day that he was Max Weber's nephew. Considering Weber's immense prestige in American academic and intellectual circles in the 1950s, perhaps then at its zenith, Mommsen was depriving himself of much-desired academic luster. But he could not bring himself to think of his famous relatives, not only because of his unhappy family experiences but because Germany was irredeemably condemned in his eyes. I never heard him utter one word of apology for the German people. In his mind there was nothing to say that could mitigate the moral stain upon German culture. In overcompensation he went out of his way to befriend and assist Jewish students. He commented acerbically on the vestiges of anti-Semitism in American universities in the early 1950s—not a popular position to take when the Princeton English department had no Jewish professors and tried hard to avoid admitting Jewish students and when Joe Strayer, who allowed two and a half Jews in the tenured history faculty, was considered a vanguard liberal on the Jewish question.

Living in the United States at its moment of postwar world hegemony, engrossed in the newspapers and very involved in understanding the American political scene, Mommsen also used medieval history to sound a warning to his new compatriots. In a series of brilliant essays published in the 1950s (posthumously collected in *Medieval and Renaissance Studies*) he warned against the consequences of pride and arrogance affecting American society and its ruling group. He did this by undertaking to explain the different ideas of history that prevailed in the Roman Empire of the fourth and fifth centuries, after the triumph of the Christian Church through the conversion of the emperor Constantine in 312.

Bishop Eusebius of Caesarea, the church's leading social theorist in the second decade of the fourth century and the emperor's chief propagandist, identified and united the destinies of the church and the empire. Eusebius claimed that God would reward the Empire for becoming Christian and that the members of the church would enjoy a constantly improving material as well as spiritual condition. This triumphalism Mommsen called "the Christian idea of progress." It was a facile but treacherous doctrine, and when the Empire began to fall apart before the barbarian invaders around 410, when Alaric, king of the Visigoths, held Rome for a time, Christians were bewildered and could not respond to the derisory claims of surviving pagans that Rome had fallen in Christian days. It was in response to these taunts that St. Augustine, bishop of Hippo, in North Africa, started writing

The City of God and developed a Christian philosophy of history to negate the Eusebian idea of progress. Augustine separated the destiny of church and state. Left to itself, he said, what is the state but a band of robbers? It intrinsically has no moral sanction. As for even the noblest Romans of them all, for these pagans even their virtues are only "splendid vices."

In any case, the most important events in history, said Augustine, are internal, mystical, covert—the pilgrimage of the City of God and its struggle against the Earthly City, the spiritual contest between those who love God to exclusion of themselves and those who love themselves to the exclusion of God. This mystical history—until the Last Judgment—is known only to the divine mind. Mommsen wanted his American contemporaries to heed the central doctrine Augustine was expounding: "Augustine did not share the optimism of Eusebius and others; on the contrary, he spoke of his own era as 'this malignant world, these evil days.' " He reminded his readers that, according to Christ's own words, the terminal period of history will not be an era of peace and earthly prosperity but just the opposite. . . . In Augustine's opinion, then, there is no true 'progress' to be found in the course of human history."

There was a crucial lesson for cold war America in this medieval disquisition by Ted Mommsen, and he meant to warn against the troubling consequences of identifying goodness with material power. He wanted Americans to stop believing they were capable of definitively solving the problems of their own society (the welfare and regulatory post-New Deal state) and the problems of humankind (cold war liberalism). Augustinian humility and recognition of the frailty of human nature and the imperfection of human judgment were the cautions he wanted to set before the American ruling class in his explication of the Augustinian as against the vulnerable, triumphalist Eusebian philosophy of history.

Americans did not listen to Mommsen in the 1950s any more than Germans listened to Carl Erdmann in the 1930s. They had to learn the hard way. Joe Strayer, who had been extraordinarily kind to Mommsen in 1946 and rescued him from being a schoolmaster at Groton, by 1954 seemed to Mommsen a figure of evil. Strayer stood for an American Eusebian type, for imperialism and vulgarity. It was no accident that Mommsen submitted his resignation from Princeton and accepted the chair at Cornell in a week when Strayer was rubbing shoulders with Allen Dulles in Virginia at CIA headquarters and planning how the world should be ruled. No human should have this power, Mommsen believed. It was a sin against the Holy Spirit.

The upheavals in his life caused by the Nazi menace, as well as a long series of personal frustrations and disappointments, resulted in Ted Mommsen's essays on early medieval historiography being the main work he left behind. The great general book on medieval historical thought died with him, unwritten, and no one else has written it. We have only these beautiful, imperishable essays on the early period of Eusebius and Augustine. This neo-Augustinianism was Mommsen's legacy to his adopted country. It may seem a small thing, but on reflection perhaps it is more than that. Mommsen's last book (1957) was an edition of the last will and testament of the fourteenth-century humanist Petrarch, whom he so much admired. Petrarch's remarks to his heirs may stand also as Mommsen's: "Now as to the smallness of these legacies, let my aforesaid friends accuse not me but Fortune—if there be any such thing as Fortune."

There is a dissenting, critical attitude that associates Mommsen not only with Carl Erdmann but with those three other outriders among medievalists: Huizinga, Eileen Power in her younger days, and Michael Postan. All five bore an essentially negative attitude to the Middle Ages, rather than being in one way or another enthusiasts for it. Positive identification with one or other facet of medieval civilization characterized all the great medievalists of the twentieth century. Maitland admired its law. Bloch had an emotional attachment to peasant communities; Haskins and Strayer were advocates of medieval government. Schramm, Kantorowicz, and Halphen fastened on kingship in a panegyric vein. The other medievalists we have talked about—Panofsky, Curtius, C. S. Lewis, Southern, Knowles, Gilson—were admirers of medieval culture, whether of its formalist artistic and literary traditions, its imaginative creations, or its clerical traditions.

On the other side, Huizinga argued that medieval culture had been unable to sustain its symbolic integrity, and furthermore, he assumed that this was a fortunate background to modern culture. The aristocratic Middle Ages were over with, and had to be. The young Eileen Power revealed the terrible abuse and disempowerment and loneliness that even women of the landed class suffered in the medieval world. Her account of medieval English nunneries is a bitter indictment of the unfeeling and selfishness central to male chauvinism in late medieval England. Postan placed medieval Europe within the iron

ring of the Malthusian dilemma and thereby called into question what
medieval culture signified. Erdmann soberly explicated the corrupting outcome of intertwining militarism and political fanaticism with
Christian spirituality. His cumulative account leaves an impression of
a debased and suffocating culture. Mommsen tended to agree with
this view and showed that it was founded on a tragic misconception
that moral perfection could be identified with certain political programs, thereby giving religious sanction to the state in a manner that
made it irresponsible and dangerous to freedom, individual autonomy, and moral restraint. Put these dissenting views together, and
the result is a highly unflattering picture of the Middle Ages as a
civilization dominated by an effete nobility that cannot sustain its
symbolic identity or resolve its economic crisis but that goes about
savaging women of every social class and spawns a militaristic state
and collaborationist church that together foreshadow modern totalitarian terrorism.

This bleak picture and anxious nightmare is remote indeed from
the celebrations conducted by Panofsky, Strayer, Lewis, Southern,
and Gilson when they describe facets of the Middle Ages. David
Knowles did not share their optimism about medieval culture, government, and church only because he put up against medieval realities a pessimistic ideal of spiritual perfection that no society can realize.
Therefore, while Knowles was definitely in the camp of the enthusiasts for the Middle Ages, his religious vocation impelled him to sound
a note of limitation on medieval felicity that in the writings of the
five outriders—Huizinga, Power, Postan, Erdmann, and Mommsen—
becomes the dominant motif.

The meaning of this naysaying about the goodness and creativity
of the Middle Ages emerges when we realize that the five were pursuing different agendas from those of the great inventors of the positive Middle Ages. Huizinga was a participant in the intellectual
rebellion of early-twentieth-century expressionism, the most radical
wing of modernism; Power was an advocate and model of women's
liberation; Postan was a Malthusian critic of premodern society; Erdmann and Mommsen were antagonists of nazism and its roots in
mainstream facets of German culture.

Recognition of these distinctive motivations and special agendas
helps account for the failure of the outriders' naysaying to cloud the
positive image of the medieval heritage in a decisive manner. The
work of the great inventors of the Middle Ages and their generally
laudatory constructions of one or other aspect of medieval civilization

endure. What happened after the age of the founders of medieval studies closed in the 1960s was a sharper and closer examination of one or another ingredient of medieval culture and society, but the main lines of portrayal drawn up during the period from 1895 to 1965 persisted.

Huizinga has found no successor. No one has seriously addressed the issue of the late medieval decline of symbolic capability that he raised. There has been a major development of women's history of the Middle Ages, but the feminists have been recently less interested in demonstrating women's mistreatment in medieval times than in highlighting women's creative role in medieval civilization. Even the theology of the church has been found to allow for "Jesus as Mother," for androgyny as well as for the Virgin cult.

The critical stance taken by Erdmann and Mommsen has been tied to a specific moment of lost time and place. The Germans have not been interested in the Middle Ages since the war and the interactive paradigm that Erdmann and Mommsen projected between medieval ideological militarism and modern ones has lost its relevance. It is Southern's sunny view of the Middle Ages that has particularly been in the ascendant recently, and Southern never looked east of the Rhine in any case. Erdmann and Mommsen are just alienated ghosts from a forgotten era, mysterious flying *Deutschers*. It is unlikely that anyone today who wanted to reinvigorate their strictures on the crusading ideal and the medieval idea of progress would even gain a research fellowship in a cow college, let alone an academic appointment.

The great founders of medieval studies from 1895 to 1965, from Maitland to Southern, built well, researched imaginatively and deeply, and wrote persuasively. The Middle Ages they invented prevail, like a cathedral tower shining on the verdant horizon of the placid twelfth-century countryside. The claims against the Middle Ages are not small or light. It may be said with Huizinga that the Middle Ages comprised an aristocratic culture that at a certain time was burned out and lost its plasticity, creativity, and capacity further to articulate itself symbolically. Wherever we are now, we are several centuries into a postmedieval culture. It may be said with Eileen Power that the Middle Ages are morally reprehensible for their abuse and neglect of half the human race, as well as profligate in underutilizing the intelligence of women. The misery that medieval hegemony imposed even on wellborn women makes the Middle Ages irreparably alien to us, it may be claimed. It may be asserted with Postan that the failure of medieval society to break out of the premodern Malthusian cycle brings into question everything else in the medieval world. It may be said with Erdmann and Mommsen that the medieval union of the spiritual, military, and political facets of life makes the Middle Ages protototalitarian and a builder of terrorist systems. Eisenstein's chilly scene of the Teutonic Knights convening (meant in 1938, of course, to represent the Nazi threat) hauntingly freezes this perception of the Middle Ages, and it is no soft or pretty thing.

But these negations have not prevailed. The imaginative constructions of medieval rulership, community, art, and feeling that the great founders of medieval studies devised are too imposing and persuasive to be undone by these dissents. Whatever the merits of the claims against the Middle Ages, the world that the great medievalists portrayed for us—its religion, government, communal organizations, religion, and thought—is too imposing for us and too close to us to do other than convince us that the adoration of the Middle Ages is more compelling than rejection. Believing yes seems much more comfortable and reasonable than saying no to the medieval heritage, after we have read the great texts in medieval studies from 1895 to the late 1960s.

There is something about the Middle Ages that appears integral to the collective memory of Western civilization. There are traces of medieval inspiration and positive reinforcement that lie below the level of consciousness as well as within the received and cultivated heritage of the European world. For any educated person and just possibly archetypically for anyone at all, the Middle Ages are integral to our understanding of people and world and are therefore essentially above reproach. The memory of the Middle Ages endures only to be explored and refined, but never, it seems, to be rejected or forgotten.

In the late 1980s courses in medieval studies exhibited constantly increasing popularity in American colleges. The field of medieval history was one of the first subdisciplines in the academic historical profession to emerge out of the disastrous depression of the 1970s and 1980s. The intrinsic drawing power of medieval civilization courses, as well as the need for colleges to have capable medievalists participate in core curriculum courses in the humanities, necessitated the hiring of new Ph.D.'s in medieval history at every quality level and size of academic institution. Courses in medieval literature and art were immensely popular and often oversubscribed in the late eighties.

This insatiable interest in medieval studies reflects the intrinsic intellectual strength of medieval studies in consequence of the magnificent work of the founders, from 1895 to 1965, and their successors, as well as the archetypical character of the facets of medieval culture in the collective memory of the Western world. The students flocking to medieval studies courses were looking for a message of social salvation and personal satisfaction at a time in the transatlantic world when there was an entropic ending of the cultural age and a yearning for a new system and cultural ideology after the dominant ones of the previous four decades had exhausted themselves. The students were telling us that in medieval studies there lay key ingredients of the new culture of the twenty-first century.

Scarcely anybody believes anymore in capitalism and socialism as value systems. We endure them as ways of social existence, as instruments for physical survival, but we draw no emotional sustenance from them—except for a handful of archaic fanatics or manipulators of vested partisan interest. So we have found our inspiration and teleologies elsewhere, in cultural systems. Since medievalism much more than classicism incorporates the religious faiths of our grandparents, as well as the artistic and erotic sensibilities of our parents' generation, and because of the richness and diversity of the medieval world, wherein anyone can find an aspect of special significance and proximity, medievalism sustains itself and flourishes as the cultural structure of a compelling value system. In the strange world of the twenty-first century, when so much of the ephemeral Victorian and modernist worlds will have been swept away into obsolescence and uselessness, medievalism bids fair to increase greatly its importance in our lives.

Retromedievalism in the twenty-first century will prosper partly because of the vulnerability of alternative systems. For educated people, simple faiths carry no sanction, and its TV preachers inspire derision. Conservative Catholicism of the Cardinal O'Connor variety offers the prospect of slow shrinkage into a sect of Old Believers. The upheavals in Communist countries of Eastern and Central Europe will readily stimulate an effort to revive in the West the militant and frenetic Leninism of the 1960s, and the prominent leftist cohort within the media will play this up noisily. But the fatal flaws, economic and ethnic, in the Soviet bloc, are heavy baggage for the neo-Leninists to carry.

Within the university departments of humanities and social sciences, current confusion and malaise will also slowly deepen into crisis and conflict. A university president today who was an educational visionary, rather than as normally a lawyer or businessman or public relations chief or sports promoter, will begin to disassemble the departments representing disciplines that have lost their rationale and are bared ruined choirs of superseded modernism: anthropology, sociology, much of literary criticism, and conventional history. The wise university president will invest in medieval studies as the focus of a seminal cultural renaissance and retroheuristic movement of the coming century. On the devastated linguistic and semiotic wastes of the future, Eisenstein's clamorous and awesome Teutonic Knights will drop their black visors and win the next time around. Affirmation of the heritage of the Middle Ages is going to be a prominent trend on the academic scene in the 1990s, broadening out into a larger intellectual and cultural movement as we reach the end of the second Christian millennium with the cultures of capitalism and socialism, neo-Victorianism and modernism considered irreparably etiolated and redundant.

The potential of this medieval revival and the cultural and social advantages to be gained from it will be fulfilled only if the *whole* of the Middle Ages is studied, appreciated, and signified. Resistance must be offered to the inevitable efforts to absolutize the Middle Ages on behalf of the Catholic Church or to bring out of the medieval heritage only one strain: romantic gentility for Oxbridge dons or social communalism for French mandarins. A complex Middle Ages with diverse strains and varied ideologies and a broad and subtle set of values— that is what the medievalists of the 1990s and beyond are obliged to set before us if we are to benefit from retromedievalism.

The empowered academic groups will tediously go their accustomed repressive ways and try to filter out the Middle Ages in the interest of a circumscribed portrayal. Intimidation by authority and the seductive screening by hierarchic privilege will again be utilized to censor, filter, and absolutize the medieval past. Not only in the interests of academic truth, but in order that spontaneous student fascination with the Middle Ages be taken advantage of and a neo-medieval-based culture for the twenty-first century be constructed, the Middle Ages must be exhibited in all their glory and terror, in all their joy and distress, in all their harmony and conflict. With respect to the Middle Ages we must exercise what Theodor W. Adorno called negative dialectics; we must never think we have all the answers or even know all the questions. The five most influential medievalists of the past half century in the American context have been Bloch, Curtius, Panofsky, Southern, and Strayer, authoritarian egoists all. We must withstand their reflexive imperial efforts to terminate debate and close down new modes of thinking.

In view of the very few centers of advanced training and research in medieval studies now existing in the United States, antihumanistic rages of the seventies and eighties having taken their rebarbative toll on the American campus, it would be hazardous to predict the outcome in medieval studies. I am most optimistic about the teachers of medieval literature. The art historians seem to have reached a period of intellectual stagnation, circular reasoning, and mind-closing gentility. Social and political history is in need of new questions to contemplate. But still in place are the bases—a handful of great teachers, a dozen superior library collections—for renewal of the creative work of the founders of medieval studies in which the Middle Ages were determined as a cultural structure, moral signification, and therapeutic recourse.

The Middle Ages are a long day in the memory of Western peoples. The memory is not exclusive and varies from people to people as place and circumstance warrant. Obviously the European Middle Ages have modest physical representation in the United States. They exist only in museums or imitative architecture, such as the world's largest Gothic cathedral measured in internal space, the unfinished (appropriately medieval quality, that) Cathedral of St. John the Divine in New York City or the reconstructed Disney-like Cloisters, a transported twelfth-century Spanish monastery on a promontory in Fort Tryon Park in northern Manhattan. But in Europe the immediate physical memory of the Middle Ages is relatively ample and well beyond the classical presence: the great cathedrals like Notre Dame, Cologne, or Durham, thick museum collections, archaeological excavations like the seventh-century site at York, England, and the prodigious holdings of medieval manuscripts, many illuminated, in libraries and archives. Occasionally we can walk down a side street of one of the smaller provincial European towns like Carcassonne, Oxford, or Regensburg and auspiciously sense that this is what it was like in the late Middle Ages. The opening of Soviet bloc countries to the West will make much more accessible the medieval physical heritage of Central Europe.

The memory of the Middle Ages lingers like the air of a clear, windful day in the collective mind of the West. Beautiful and fresh in the morning, hot and placidly rich at high noon, expectant and menacing in the long afternoon reaching into dusk, reverent and brooding in the evening darkness, this is our medieval day.

It was the romantics of the earlier nineteenth century, like John Keats, Sir Walter Scott, Jules Michelet, and Caspar David Friedrich who rediscovered the Middle Ages, after three centuries of neglect. The romantics also had their medieval day. From 1810 to 1840 was the first great age of retromedievalism. The Middle Ages were used to give sanction to the romantics' vision of a particular set of holistic concepts and emotionally charged behavior patterns that they set up in contrast with the chill of the Enlightenment and the terror of the Industrial Revolution. For the romantics, medieval culture was characterized, and legitimated retrospectively, by the more idealistic, passionate, aesthetic, and individuated aspects of thought and life-style. The Middle Ages, in the romantic vision, at the same time was the era of heroic individualism and intense communal and national feeling and action. The violence and cruelty of the Middle Ages, the messiness and disorder, the romantics were vaguely aware of but played down or transmogrified into the magical effects of truth and beauty of a special kind.

We do not, however, need the romantic projection of the Middle Ages. Directly accessible to us is the medieval intelligentsia's perception of its own culture and society. In assessing their own world, medieval intellectuals were heavily conditioned by a persistent idealism that saw in society around them signs of the earthly incarnation of the Heavenly City. The perception of the early-twelfth-century poet Bernard of Morval was the base line medieval social assessment: "God's own nation, God's own congregation. Magnificent towers, fair homeland of flowers, thou country of life [Transl. E. J. Martin]."

The central dogma of the Incarnation likewise governed the social perceptions of medieval people. They were preconditioned by the dogma of the Incarnation, and the philosophy of "realism" that underlies it, to find the ideal within the material, the beautiful within the ugly, the moral and peaceful in the midst of violence and disorder. "The Word was made flesh, and dwelt among us . . . full of grace and truth." Since everything was of divine creation, medieval intellectuals had no doubt that all the pieces would ultimately fit together in an idealistic, morally committed structure. Whatever they saw or experienced was part of a divine manifestation. In the words of the mass for the dead by the thirteenth-century poet Thomas of Celano:

> But thou giv'st leave, dread Lord, that we
> Take shelter from Thyself in Thee,
> And with the wings of Thine own dove
> Fly to the shelter of soft love. [Transl. R. Crashaw.]

After about 1280 medieval intellectuals were painfully aware that there were plenty of wrong and cruel things in their world. They were prolific in condemning what was bad at every level of society, within every major institution. But the more they criticized and condemned, the more zealously they searched for a restorative, integrative force or principle that would serve as God's instrument of bringing peace, justice, and love to the world. Some talked of charismatic kingship or representative government as the solution; others envisioned the breakthrough effects of a small band of saints; others vaguely fell back on the imminent Second Coming of the Lord Himself. But they did not surrender their faith that everything was a divine creation, that Providence dictated unity and integration into a common system, and that no matter how bad the times were now, they were going to get much better very soon.

The greater the pessimism, the greater the optimism. What I particularly enjoy was the Joachimite doctrine, popular in the radical wing of the Franciscan order, that the age of the antichrist had to precede the reign of Christ. The more medieval people talked about materialism, evil, and corruption, the more enthusiastic they were about deliverance by some idealistic force serving as God's instrument. Such inveterate idealism and optimism were the medieval way of thinking. "We know that in everything God works for good with those who love Him." Divine transcendence would somehow overcome the split between the material and spiritual sides of human existence.

There is a thin screen between this way of thinking and our own, although fifty years from now the retromedieval quality of the new culture of the twenty-first century will have mostly dissolved it. For now, however, we are still taught to value provocatively ambiguity and ambivalence, the fragmentary and the discordant, the narcotic gifts of modernism, rather than to focus, as medieval people did, on the transcendental triumph of good over evil and the incarnate absorption of the material into the ideal.

We are capable, however, of appreciating and cultivating specific aspects of medieval civilization. The medieval legacy has conventionally been perceived in many ideas and behavior patterns, among them the unity of European civilization in a Christian framework; the charismatic leadership of saints and heroes; constitutionalism and representative institutions; the synthesis of faith and reason; the continuity of classical traditions; a formalist attitude to art and literature; aristocratic life-styles; the moral sensibility of the common people; clericalism and religious hierarchy; the idea of divine and human love. To me, the medieval heritage and prospective retromedievalism of the end of the twentieth century especially comes down to two things: civil society or privatism and enterprise protected by the rule of law, and tough love or sentimental formalism.

In the model of a civil society, most good and important things take place below the universal level of the state: the family, the arts, learning, and science; business enterprise and technological process. These are the work of individuals and groups, and the involvement of the state is remote and disengaged. It is the rule of law that screens out the state's insatiable aggressiveness and corruption and gives freedom to civil society below the level of the state. It so happens that the medieval world was one in which men and women worked out their destinies with little or no involvement of the state most of the time. A retromedieval world is one that has consciously turned back the welfare and regulatory state from impinging drastically upon, or even in totalitarian fashion swallowing up, society in the corrosive belly of the brackish public whale represented by its self-serving bureaucrats.

The other manifestation of retromedievalism is a symbiotic union of formal cultural and behavior patterns with individual passion, a peculiar temperament of integrated hard forms, persistent traditions, private loves, and idiosyncratic personal attachments. The medieval way is one of hard-edged sentimentality, tough on the outside, soft within the skin of the pearl.

Just as retromedievalism in this paradigm rejects the Leviathan regulatory and welfare state and reasserts the freedom of civil society, so in personal terms it rejects the two polarities of twentieth-century culture: the pitiless demands of institutions, science, and reason (modernism) upon humanity and the irresponsible self-indulgent solipsism of the postmodernist counterculture that rushes destructively downward from the watershed 1960s. Retromedievalism means personal sentiment shaped and controlled by formal traditions as well as institutions and structures that recognize the privilege of private feeling and personal love. This is a narrow target, but in the best moments of the Middle Ages it was secured and valued.

This retromedieval model of our future is possibly threatened by the peril of another manifestation of medieval recurrence. The medieval world in part gained its distinctive texture by the discordance between the mental and material sides of human existence. At one pole the intellectual, religious, and artistic achievements of the Middle

Ages stand preeminent in Western civilization, or at least as remarkable and productive as in any cultural era. At the other pole, however, are their deficiencies and failures in technology and organization. When we reflect on the biomedical, environmental, nuclear, and economic catastrophes that lurk on the horizon of the closing decade of the twentieth century, in the midst of the scientific and artistic triumphs of our day, we cannot repress anxiety about the resurgence of a medieval disparity between the mastery of the intellectual and the downturns of the material side of social existence. We must have faith that God and fortune, as well as reason and the lessons of experience, will avoid these hazards and allow the flourishing of a benign and creative retromedieval moment.

Like the Roman Empire, the modern age will crumble from the crack of inordinate greatness beyond the interest of the many and the desire of the privileged few to sustain, and in the murky streets of ruined cities and meeting grounds of a billion humble habitations, our heroes and saints will show us how to begin history anew.

NOTES

————◆———

The purpose of these notes is to indicate sources and documentation for controversial matters, especially of a biographical nature, to amplify some issues and give additional bibliography beyond what can be provided in the text of the book, and to offer short excursuses on tangential or corollary subjects that could not be explored without breaking into the flow of the book's discourse. Where ample information and bibliography have been provided in the text of the book on a particular subject, it is not repeated here.

CHAPTER ONE: THE QUEST FOR THE MIDDLE AGES

Between Rome and Renaissance. See for general surveys of medieval European history, each with a different focus: Joseph R. Strayer and Dana C. Munro, *The Middle Ages*, 4th ed. (New York, 1959); Norman F. Cantor, *Medieval History: The Life and Death of a Civilization*, 2d ed. (New York, 1968); and Jacques Le Goff, *Medieval Civilization*, rev. ed. (New York, 1990). Strayer's account features political history, Cantor's the church and intellectual development, and Le Goff concentrates on society and economy. For an assessment of the work and influence of Umberto Eco as a medievalist, see Theresa Coletti, *Naming the Rose* (Ithaca, N.Y., 1989).

The First Crusade. While the modern historical literature on the First Crusade is extensive, nothing has replaced the marvelously subtle and evocative narrative of Steven Runciman, *A History of the Crusades* (Cambridge, England, 1951), Vol. I. Runciman was a Cambridge don who came from an aristocratic, extremely wealthy, and politically prominent family. He was a friend and occasional yachting companion of Farouk, the last king of Egypt. Less exciting but providing additional information and insights are Kenneth Setton, ed., *A History of the Crusades* (Philadelphia, 1955), Vol. I, and Joshua Prawer, *The Crusaders' Kingdom* (New York, 1972). Prawer, an Israeli, was trained in Paris and was for many years the head of the history department at the Hebrew University in Jerusalem. His work draws upon the intensive archeological work that Israelis have carried out on the French Christian intrusion into the Arab Near East. The greatest accomplishment of Israeli crusade archaeology was the digging up of the massive crusading castle at Acre, forty miles north of Haifa and the last French citadel in the thirteenth-century Holy Land. I never took the Crusades very seriously until I visited this site in 1981. Its huge circumference and massive walls and vast underground storage rooms would make it a formidable fortress today, and it also signifies what a prodigious effort the Crusades were, whether you regard them as a religious venture or an early act of Western imperialism, or both. See also: Jonathan Riley-Smith, *The Crusades: A Short History* (New Haven, 1987).

Discovery and Learning. There is no general history nor even a comprehensive bibliography of medieval studies. With reference to medieval studies in the United States and Canada, valuable material is found in Francis G. Gentry and Christopher Kleinhenz, eds., *Medieval Studies in North America* (Kalamazoo, Mich., 1982); Lester B. Workman, *Studies in Medievalism* (Holland, Mich., 1982–1990), Vols. I–III; Bernard E. Rosenthal and Paul E. Szarmach, eds., *Medievalism in American Culture* (Binghamton, N.Y., 1989); and the journal *Annals of Scholarships* (New York, 1980–1989, and ongoing), Vols. 1–6. My own discovery of the Middle Ages began in 1949 with Tryggvi J. Oleson at the University of Manitoba and continued from 1951 to 1954 at Princeton University, which then had, between the university and the neighboring Institute for Advanced Study, the greatest collection of medievalists ever put together in one place in the United States or perhaps anywhere.

Tryggvi J. Oleson's premature death from a stroke was a great loss to medieval studies and to Canadian Roman Catholic culture. He was a native of Manitoba's large Lutheran Icelandic community who converted to Roman Catholicism of a particularly militant and conservative kind. This brought him to intense study of the Middle Ages, and he took a Ph.D. in medieval history at the University of Toronto in the late 1940s. His dissertation on the witan (King's Council) in the reign of Edward the Confessor, just before the Norman Conquest, was written under the direction of Bertie Wilkinson, a disciple of the Manchester school of medieval administrative history headed by Thomas Frederick Tout. Oleson's dissertation was published, and it is not without merit, although he felt cramped by Wilkinson's neo-Victorian constitutionalist view of medieval English government. It was the medieval church and ecclesiastical culture that Oleson was really interested in, and he was fortunate to study under two prominent Catholic scholars at the Pontifical Institute in Toronto: the German émigré G. B. Ladner, who later taught at Fordham and UCLA and was an authority on patristic theology and canon law, and G. B. Flahiff, whose important work on medieval ecclesiastical government was cut short by his elevation to the episcopate.

The superstar array of Princeton medievalists of the early fifties consisted of Theodor E. Mommsen (medieval church); Joseph R. Strayer (government and law); E. Harris "Jinks" Harbison (mainly a prizewinning Reformation scholar but with brilliant insights into late medieval intellectual history); Ernst H. Kantorowicz (intellectual history and political theory); Kurt Weitzmann (Byzantine art and civilization); E. A. Lowe (the world's greatest medieval paleographer); D. W. Robertson, Jr. (literature); Erwin Panofsky (art and culture); Albert M. Friend, Jr. (Renaissance art). Of this group, only Robertson and Weitzmann survive. Weitzmann's greatest accomplishment as a Byzantine art historian was in photographing and analyzing the images in the manuscripts from a monastery in the Sinai Desert that was so remote from Constantinople that it was immune from the antirepresentational iconoclastic movement of the eighth century. Weitzmann thereby took the lead in re-creating the pattern of early medieval Byzantine art. He was also an authority on the Macedonian Renaissance of the tenth century, which was distinguished by neoclassical trends in depiction of the human face and figure. A representative Weitzmann work is *Greek Mythology in Byzantine Art* (Princeton, 1951).

Romanticism and History. For a brief introduction, see Norman F. Cantor, *Western Civilization: Its Genesis and Destiny* (Glenview, Ill., 1971), Vol. II, pp. 273–76, with color plates. A subtle and penetrating inquiry into the nature of romanticism is Jacques Barzun, *Romanticism and the Modern Ego* (Boston; 1943). The same author's *Berlioz and the Romantic Century* (Boston, 1950), 2 vols., is much broader in scope than its title implies. The work of the nineteenth-century scholar Georg Brandes, *Main Currents in Nineteenth Century Literature* (London, 1901–1905), 6 vols., remains indispensable. An important recent discussion is Arthur Mitzmann, *Michelet, Historian: Rebirth and Romanticism in Nineteenth Century France* (New Haven, 1990).

On Victorian medievalism, the best studies are Charles Dellheim, *The Face of the Past: The Preservation of the Medieval Inheritance in Victorian England* (Cambridge, England, 1982), and J. W. Burrow, *A Liberal Descent: Victorian Historians and the English Past* (Cambridge, England, 1981). See also N. F. Cantor, *William Stubbs on the English Constitution* (New York, 1966), pp. 1–12.

Humanists. *The American Scholar*, a quarterly published by Phi Beta Kappa, occasionally offers compelling profiles of leading humanist scholars. The most insightful portraits of the pros and cons of humanists' mind and behavior are in C. P. Snow's eleven-volume *Strangers and Brothers* series of novels that had much visibility in the fifties and early sixties and is now neglected. Charles Snow was a Cambridge science don in the 1930s before becoming a civil servant and corporate executive. See especially the novel with the same title as the series; the best-known one, *The Masters;* and *The Light and the Dark*, containing a compelling portrait of a brilliant young Orientalist, who could just as well be a medievalist. Angus Wilson's novel of the sixties *Anglo-Saxon Attitudes* is indeed mainly about a medievalist who can't overcome a block against publishing. For postmodernist trends, see David Lodge's novels *Small Worlds* and *Nice Work* and Stephen G. Nichols, ed., "The New Philology," *Speculum*, Vol. 65, January 1990.

Manuscript Research. Anyone interested in medieval documents should read two masterful German works (unfortunately never translated): Harry Bresslau, *Handbuch der Urkundenlehre* ("textbook of document learning"), 3d ed. (Berlin, 1958), 2 vols.; and Heinrich Fichtenau, *Mensch und Schrift im Mittelalters* ("man and writing in the Middle Ages") (Vienna, 1946). Fortunately a third work by a German master of medieval manuscripts has been translated: Bernhard Bischoff, *Latin Palaeography* (Cambridge, England, 1990). There are two additional important books in English: Michael T. Clanchy, *From Memory to Written Record* (Cambridge, Mass., 1979), a brilliant history of medieval English government from the standpoint of literacy, and the reflective, difficult work of the Toronto scholar Brian Stock, *The Implications of Literacy* (Princeton, 1983). For information on the life of James F. Willard, I am indebted to the information office of the University of Colorado at Boulder, which sent me a file of contemporary press clippings.

CHAPTER TWO: LAW AND SOCIETY

Maitland Biography and General Assessment of His Work. The principal
sources are C. H. S. Fifoot, ed., *The Letters of F. W. Maitland* (London, 1965);
E. L. G. Stones, ed., *F. W. Maitland: Letters to George Neilson* (Glasgow, 1976);
H. A. L. Fisher, *Frederic William Maitland* (Cambridge, England, 1910); C. H.
Fifoot, *Frederic William Maitland* (London, 1971); G. R. Elton, *F. W. Maitland*
(London, 1985); Robert Livingston Schuyler, "The Historical Spirit Incarnate:
Frederic William Maitland," *American Historical Review*, Vol. 57 (1952), pp. 303–
22; H. E. Bell, *Maitland: A Critical Examination and Assessment* (London, 1965);
S. F. C. Milsom, "F. W. Maitland," *Proceedings of the British Academy*, Vol. 66
(1982), pp. 265–81, and Introduction to Volume I of the 1968 reissue of Pollock
and Maitland; James R. Cameron, *F. W. Maitland and the History of English Law*
(Norman, Okla., 1961); R. W. Southern, *History and Theory* (Middletown, Conn.,
1967), p. 111. My account in sections I–III of this chapter, while relying heavily
on the factual material in Fifoot's biography for the life, is an independent assessment based on my reading of Maitland's works and letters and my knowledge
of the field of English legal history. The description of Maitland speaking at a
Cambridge faculty meeting is found in Fifoot's biography. Maitland's principal
works are: Frederick Pollock and Frederic William Maitland, *The History of English Law Before the Time of Edward I*, 2d ed. (Cambridge, England, 1898), 2 vols.;
H. A. L. Fisher, ed., *Collected Papers of Frederic William Maitland* (Cambridge,
England, 1911), 3 vols.; *Domesday Book and Beyond* (Cambridge, England, 1897);
English Law and the Renaissance (Cambridge, England, 1901); *Roman Canon Law
in the Church of England* (Cambridge, England, 1898); and Maitland's edition of
Bracton's Notebook (London, 1987), 3 vols., and *Memorando de Parliamento* (Lon-
don, 1893).

Maitland's Heritage in English Political Historiography. Maitland inaugurated a long-standing school of political history. His thesis on Parliament was
first taken up by an American, C. H. McIlwain, who taught at Harvard for more
than three decades. McIlwain's book propounding Maitland's judicial and royalist conciliar view of the medieval and early modern Parliament was *The High
Court of Parliament* (New York, 1910). In the fifties and sixties this view was
argued polemically as well as eruditely by George O. Sayles alone or in collaboration with H. G. Richardson in several books—e.g., *The Governance of Medieval
England* (Edinburgh, 1963). The recent heirs of Maitland's interpretation of Parliament (which has now become associated with Conservative party politics,
something that might not have greatly pleased Maitland) are Conrad Russell,
Parliament and English Politics 1621–1629 (Oxford, England, 1977); G. R. Elton,
The Parliament of England 1559–1581 (Cambridge, England, 1986); and Jonathan
C. D. Clark, *Revolution and Rebellion* (Cambridge, England, 1986), a brilliant po-
lemical essay. It is my view that the seminal work of Lewis B. Namier, *The
Structure of Politics at the Accession of George III*, 2d ed. (New York, 1957) also
belongs centrally in the Maitland tradition of interpreting English government
and law. See further Norman F. Cantor, *Twentieth Century Culture: Modernism to
Deconstruction* (New York, 1988), pp. 114–15, 234–35.

Maitland's Intellectual Heritage in the United States. This lies in the
functionalist school of legal history, founded in the forties and fifties by J. Wil-

lard Hurst of the University of Wisconsin at Madison. Some of this development
is traced by Harry N. Schreiber, "American Constitutional History and the New
Legal History," *Journal of American History*, Vol. 68 (1981), pp. 337–50. Hurst's
flagship books are: *The Growth of American Law: The Lawmakers* (Boston, 1950)
and *Law and the Conditions of Freedom in the Nineteenth Century United States* (New
York, 1956). Hurst's student Lawrence M. Friedman, in the second edition of
his *A History of American Law* (New York, 1985), has come closest to achieving
the classic functionalist interpretation of American law that Pollock and Maitland
offered for the founding era of English common law. Other prominent works
following in the Maitland-Hurst tradition are: Leonard W. Levy, *The Law of the
Commonwealth and Chief Justice Shaw* (Cambridge, Mass., 1957); Stanley I. Kutler,
Privilege and Creative Destruction: The Charles River Bridge Case (New York, 1971);
and William E. Nelson, *The Americanization of the Common Law* (Cambridge, Mass.,
1975). The Marxist (critical legal studies) work of Harvard Law School's Morton
J. Horwitz, *The Transformation of American Law 1780–1960* (Cambridge, Mass.,
1977), which went through six printings in the decade after publication, is rooted
in the Maitland-Hurst tradition of functionalist legal history, although here reconstructed to suit a Marxist model of capitalist take-over and corruption of the
common law. Interesting recent essays on legal history growing out of the Maitland tradition and toward a legal structuralism are A. W. Brian Simpson, "Common Law and Legal Theory," and David Sugarman, "Legal Theory, the Common
Law Mind and the Making of the Common Law Tradition," in *Legal Theory and
the Common Law*, ed. William Twining (Oxford, England, 1986).

John G. A. Pocock. The work of Pocock referred to in Section IV is *The
Machiavellian Moment: Florentine Political Thought and the Atlantic Republican Tradition* (Princeton, 1975), which brings together several celebrated articles published in the 1960s and early 1970s. Although Pocock (a transplanted New
Zealander at Cambridge, before he moved to the United States) began his work
in the Maitland tradition (Pocock's first, still important book was on Sir Edward
Coke and the seventeenth-century common law), this omnivorously learned,
restless, original mind has emerged as Maitland's most serious opponent in the
interpretation of the English political tradition. Pocock's formulation of a transatlantic ethos of republican virtue, of a positive view of liberty as distinguished
from the conventional common law idea of liberty as due process restraint from
oppressive government, has had a profound impact upon a whole generation of
American scholars exploring the intellectual origins of the American Revolution
and the Constitution, particularly Bernard Baylin, Gordon Wood, Garry Wills,
and Stanley Katz. Central to Pocock's thesis is its secularism—that is, his grounding
of American republican ideas in Renaissance and Enlightenment classical humanism and his downplaying of Calvinism and the evangelical strains of Protestantism. In perceiving the structural cultural plasticity and dynamic capacity of the
common law, which easily made room for the classical republican tradition and
reasserted itself vigorously in the three or four decades after the American Revolution, as represented in the judicial thought of John Marshall and Joseph Story,
I have gained insights from Richard A. Posner, *Law and Literature* (Cambridge,
Mass., 1988); Sanford Levinson and Steven Mailloux, eds., *Interpreting Law and
Literature* (Evanston, Ill., 1988); Stanley Fish, *Doing What Comes Naturally: Change,
Rhetoric, and the Practice of Theory in Literary and Legal Studies* (Durham, N.C.,

1989); G. Edward White, *The American Judicial Tradition*, expanded ed. (New York, 1988); and Robert H. Bork, *The Tempting of America: The Political Seduction of the Law* (New York, 1990). See also Ian Shaporo, "J. G. A. Pocock's Republicanism and Political Theory: A Critique and Reinterpretation," *Critical Review*, Vol. 4, 1990, pp. 433–71.

CHAPTER THREE: THE NAZI TWINS

The Biographical Material. In this chapter information on the lives of Kantorowicz and Schramm is derived heavily from my conversations with Theodor E. Mommsen, Ernst H. Kantorowicz, and Michael Cherniavsky. Fragments of conversation with Ralph E. Giesey, William M. Bowsky, Robert L. Benson, Margery Sevcenko, Vincent Carosso, and Allan E. Gotlieb have also been drawn upon. There is no published memoir or critical assessment of Kantorowicz that is of significant value. These may be cited for bibliographical purposes: Arthur R. Evans, *On Four Modern Humanists* (Princeton, 1970); Ekard Grunewald, *Ernst Kantorowicz und Stefan George* (Wiesbaden, 1982). Kantorowicz's unpublished papers were deposited, after heavy editing by his literary executors, in the Leo Baeck Institute in New York City and are open to the public. The scraps of correspondence there reveal that Schramm sought his help in 1945 when he thought the British were going to purge him from his academic chair. On Kantorowicz's departure for England from Berlin in 1938 with the assistance of Sir Maurice Bowra, there is an account in Bowra's autobiography, *Memories* (Cambridge, Mass., 1967). My description of Kantorowicz's experience at Oxford is partly derived from the reminiscence of his strong critic at that time R. W. Southern. Norbert Kamp, the president of Göttingen University, gave a published lecture on Schramm's life and work in 1987 that is valuable for the early and prewar years: "Percy Schramm und die Mittelalterforschung," *Göttinger Universitätsschriften*, Serie A: Schriften/Band 2 (1987), pp. 344–63. I want to thank Dr. Kamp for sending me this article.

For Schramm's involvement with the Nazis and his notorious 1963 memoir of Hitler, Donald S. Detweiler in 1971 provided a careful, restrained introduction to his good translation of the memoir under the title *Hitler: The Man and Military Leader* (New York). I have gained additional insight into this subject from Francis L. Loewenheim of Rice University. Schramm's extensive private papers are divided between the university in Göttingen and his family home in Hamburg. They are not open, and no one has published a biography based on them—for obvious reasons.

German Universities and Intellectuals and the Nazis. Alice Gallin, *Midwives to Nazism* (Macon, Ga., 1986); Jeffrey Herf, *Reactionary Modernism* (Cambridge, England, 1984); Alan D. Beyerchen, *Scientists Under Hitler* (New Haven, 1977); Walter Struve, *Elites Against Democracy* (Princeton, 1973); Fritz K. Ringer, *The Decline of the German Mandarins* (Cambridge, Mass., 1969).

Nazi Culture: Joachim Fest, *The Face of the Third Reich* (New York, 1970); Ernst Nolte, *Three Faces of Fascism* (New York, 1966); Karl Dietrich Bracher, *The German Dictatorship* (New York, 1970); Robert Jay Lifton, *Nazi Doctors* (New York, 1986); George L. Mosse, *Nazi Culture* (New York, 1966); Robert Wistrich, *Hitler's Apocalypse* (New York, 1985).

Wartime Germany. The endless literature on Germany in World War II, which directly engaged Schramm from 1940 to 1945, has now been capably summed up by John Keegan, *The Second World War* (New York, 1989), Parts I–II, IV–V.

Even though I specify Schramm's record as a close associate of Hitler in 1943 and 1944 and I brand him as a war criminal, some may claim that my portrayal is too sympathetic. This is not only because of my respect for Schramm's unsurpassed medieval learning and my admiration for *Kaiser, Rom, und Renovatio* as one of the best books on medieval history but also because Schramm was personally kind to me. When I published my dissertation on the Anglo-Norman church in 1958, Schramm wrote me a laudatory note about my book that inaugurated an occasional correspondence. This abruptly terminated when I declined to contribute to the volume of papers honoring him on his retirement. Schramm provided extraordinary service to the German Army during the war and to its head, Hitler. But from all I have been able to learn of the man, his judgment on the quality of scholarship was not affected by anti-Semitism, as was the case with some British and American medievalists.

Kantorowicz at Princeton. The circumstances of Kantorowicz's appointment at the Princeton Institute for Advanced Study I learned from conversations with Mommsen and Kantorowicz himself. The institute has not chosen to open to me its director's files from the Oppenheimer era. But I think the account I gave is likely to be borne out by this documentation, if it ever becomes available. Certainly Joseph Strayer believed that Kantorowicz was never in danger of unemployment after he lost his Berkeley job and was annoyed that the institute did not consult him on Eka's appointment, which he would have opposed.

Karl F. Morrison. Although Morrison was Mommsen's last student, collaborated with Mommsen on a book, and envisions himself as a Mommsen disciple, I have placed him briefly at the end of this chapter because he is the purest practitioner of German *Geistesgeschichte* active today in an American university (and probably anywhere). He has a prodigious knowledge of patristic and later medieval thought and is fully cognizant with all intellectual movements in the West right down to the present day. Someone wanting a brief taste of Morrison's thick writing should read "Incentives for Studying the Liberal Arts," in *The Seven Liberal Arts in the Middle Ages*, ed. David L. Wagner (Bloomington, Ind., 1983), pp. 32–54. Morrison's masterpiece is *Tradition and Authority in the Western Church 300–1140* (Princeton, 1969). Another major work is *The Mimetic Tradition of Reform in the West* (Princeton, 1982). Morrison is the greatest medievalist who failed to get tenure at Harvard, where he taught for five years. Harvard medieval studies have not recovered from this error. After being a senior professor and department chairman at the University of Chicago, Morrison now holds a research chair at Rutgers University in New Jersey and also teaches Princeton graduate students.

CHAPTER FOUR: THE FRENCH JEWS

Biography. Necrologies of Louis Halphen were published in *Le Moyen Age* (F. Vercauteren, Vol. 57, pp. 201–04) and *Revue Historique* (E. Perroy, Vol. 206, pp. 189–95), leading Parisian academic journals, in 1951. Aside from their Gallic delicacy about Halphen's Jewish origin ("victim of racial laws"; "subject to vexations and persecutions"), they are well done. Pierre Riché's 1983 synthesis of forty years of research on the Carolingian Empire *(Les Carolingiens)* fully vindicated Halphen's position against his critics Heinrich Fichtenau and J. W. Wallace-Hadrill.

The standard biography of Marc Bloch at long last appeared forty-five years after his death: Carole Fink, *Marc Bloch: A Life in History* (New York, 1989). See also an earlier and a more succinct version by Fink: *Marc Bloch: Historian, Soldier, Patriot* (Smithsonian Institution. The Wilson Center. West European Program. Occasional Paper No. 8). Fink's work is especially valuable for Bloch's often tense relationship with Lucien Febvre, especially in the period 1940–42, and his agonizing over whether to flee to refuge in the United States. Fink's work does not replace the single best essay on Bloch's life and personality by the distinguished historian of modern France, Eugen Weber, in the *American Scholar*, Vol. 51 (1982), pp. 73–82. It is obvious that Weber had access to the gossip network of French academic life that was not as open to Fink. The lengthy review of Fink's book by Natalie Zemon Davis ("A Modern Hero," *New York Review of Books* [April 26, 1990], pp. 27–30) is worth reading, if only to get the official *Annales*-leaning Princeton slant on the subject. A recent article on Bloch in his own *Annales* (Vol. 41 [1986], pp. 1091–1105) by the prominent Polish writer and Solidarity leader Bronoslaw Geremek is merely a panegyric. The critical assessment of his father by Étienne Bloch was originally given as a public lecture at Vassar College in 1986, to a somewhat stunned audience, and privately printed by Vassar History Department in 1987 under the title *Marc Bloch: Father, Patriot and Teacher*. The critical views expressed therein, and quoted here, entirely coincide with the remarks personally made to me in December 1960 by another one of Bloch's sons. Assessments of Bloch's work by two prominent American medievalists, Joseph R. Strayer and Bruce Lyon, are valuable. (Strayer is discussed below in Chapter Seven.) Lyon is an authority on feudalism and the fastidious biographer of Henri Pirenne (Ghent, 1974), and he taught at Brown University. Strayer's ambivalent judgment on Bloch is given in his introduction to the English translation of *The Historian's Craft* (New York, 1953). Strayer's pithy book on *Feudalism* (New York, 1967) is largely a dissent from Bloch's *Feudal Society*, adhering to a political rather than Bloch's social-economic model. Lyon's essays on Bloch are also perceptive: *French Historical Studies*, Vol. 15 (1987), pp. 195–207, and *Journal of Medieval History*, Vol. 11 (1985), pp. 181–91.

The French Academic and Intellectual Tradition. This is brilliantly explicated by the University of Chicago sociologist Terry N. Clark, *Prophets and Patrons* (Cambridge, Mass., 1973), which highlights the complex role of Émile Durkheim. See also Steven Lukes, *Émile Durkheim: His Life and Work* (New York, 1972). On the more recent French intellectual milieu, the most interesting works are Herbert Lottman, *The Left Bank* (New York, 1982); Mark Poster, *Existential Marxism in Postwar France* (Princeton, 1975); Annie Cohen-Solal, *Sartre* (New York, 1987); Deidre Bair, *Simone de Beauvoir* (New York, 1990); and David Pace, *Claude Lévi-Strauss* (Boston, 1983). The anecdotes about André Malraux's and Simone de Beauvoir's behavior during the German occupation are taken from the Lottman and Bair books respectively. On the Nazi occupation generally and the treatment of the Jews, there is a large literature. See especially Robert O.

Paxton, *Vichy France* (New York, 1972); Paxton and Michael R. Marras, *Vichy France and the Jews* (New York, 1981); John F. Sweets, *Choices in Vichy France* (New York, 1986); and F. Malino and B. Wasserstein, eds., *The Jews in Modern France* (London, 1985).

   The Annales School. This is best explored in the writings of its protagonists, in addition to Bloch. Peter Burke has translated a selection of Lucien Febvre's papers and manifestos (*A New Kind of History* [London, 1973]), with a judicious introduction. See also for programmatic statements: Fernand Braudel, *On History* (Chicago, 1980), and Emmanuel Le Roy Ladurie, *The Territory of the Historian* (Chicago, 1979). There are many hyped puff pieces about the *Annales* school. More sober assessments are François Furet, "Beyond the Annales," *Journal of Modern History*, Vol. 55 (1983), pp. 389–410; Peter Burke, "Strengths and Weaknesses of the History of Mentalities," *History of European Ideas*, Vol. 7 (1986), pp. 439–51; Roger Chartier, "Histoire Intellectuelle et Histoire des Mentalités," *Revue de Synthesis*, Vol. 104 (1983), pp. 227–307; and André Burguière, "The Fate of the History of Mentalities in the Annales," *Comparative Studies in Society and History*, Vol. 24 (1982), pp. 424–37. The defection of Furet, originally trained at the Annalist institute, to an anti-Marxist view of the French Revolution in the 1970s and his high academic and intellectual visibility in Paris were a severe blow to the Braudelians and the Bloch-Febvre tradition. With respect to the early years of the *Annales* institute saga, the post-World War II ambience, in which the non-Communist left in Europe materially benefited from the efforts of the CIA and American foundations (sometimes as CIA fronts, sometimes just in parallel), is well described in Peter Coleman, *The Liberal Conspiracy* (New York, 1989). On this subject, see also Edward Shils, "Remembering the Congress for Cultural Freedom," *Encounter*, Vol. 75, No. 2 (1990), pp. 53–65. Essentially what happened as the cold war began was that the American academic and intellectual establishment, in collaboration with the CIA and the State Department, jettisoned the traditional European right (partly because of its discredited association in the thirties with fascism and partly because it was at the time politically impotent) and threw all its support to the non-Communist left. Shrewd leftists, like Stephen Spender and Melvyn Lasky in Britain, Ignazio Silone in Italy, and, perhaps most opportunist and manipulative of all, Lucien Febvre and Fernand Braudel in France, saw a tremendous opportunity in American willingness to subsidize not only the non-Communist leftist parties but also their cultural agencies and affiliates. There was an extended and ironic outcome to all this: By 1970 the Parisian Annalist institute was so rich and powerful that American leftists like Immanuel Wallerstein and Natalie Zemon Davis were looking to Paris for moral and material support. Postwar American cultural imperialism was thus repatriated back to America, with major consequences for American historiography and sociology. On the decline of collective mentalities in France today and the return of individual biography, see Jacques Le Goff, "After Annales," *Times Literary Supplement*, April 14, 1989, pp. 394, 405.

   Radicalization of the Bloch and Annales Heritage in America. Here I drew upon my conversations in 1975 and 1976 with Immanuel Wallerstein and Terence Hopkins, codirectors of the Braudel Center at the State University of New York at Binghamton, and the center's third world-Marxist journal *Review*, as well as my own experiences as a university administrator and teacher. For the leftist trend of the Princeton history department in the 1980s, which greatly pleased Braudel and is reflected in Davis's review of Fink's biography (cited above), see the article by N. F. Cantor in the *New Criterion* (December 1985). The power of the radicalized Bloch-Febvre heritage upon American graduate programs in history in the late 1980s is exemplified by the requirement in the New York University history department, stipulated by the chairman, Thomas Bender, in 1988, that the introductory course for graduate students in medieval history essentially follow and endorse the Annalist position. Of course, such trends are generational (the heritage of 1968) and probably cyclical. From 1986 to 1989, the Cambridge University Press invested heavily in bringing out a three-volume comprehensive history of the Middle Ages, previously published in France by an Annalist group headed by Robert Fossier. The English translation was dressed up with elaborate and expensive illustrations. But the work has not been successful in capturing the American market in medieval studies or even much academic attention, and that failure, along with other indices, suggests that the long reach of Bloch's influence is waning. A critical flaw in the Annalist position on the American scene was always the difficulty in organizing college courses around peasant-centered history. The American undergraduate wants to hear about heroes and saints, not field hands. He or she is normally much more interested in leaders than in "alternative populations."

On the tensions developing in the late 1980s between history and left-wing social theory, see Lynn Hunt, "History Beyond Social Theory," *The States of "Theory,"* ed. David Caroll (New York, 1990), pp. 95–111. On the Furet-led rebellion in French academia against Marxism, see Noel Parker, *Portrayals of Revolution* (Carbondale, Ill., 1990), pp. 210–15. For a critique of the work of Henri Pirenne, see in addition to the 1974 biography by Bruce Lyon cited above: Richard Hodges, *Dark Age Economics: The Origins of Towns and Trade* A.D. *600– 1000* (New .York, 1982). Hodges was the third medieval historian to make his initial reputation largely as a critic of Pirenne, the two others being Robert S. Lopez and Archibald A. Lewis.

CHAPTER FIVE: THE FORMALISTS

Formalism. My own introduction to formalism came from being a student in the seminar of Kurt Weitzmann, the colleague and disciple of Erwin Panofsky, in the spring of 1952. This was reinforced by my being able to do research in the marvelous Princeton Index of Christian Art, set up in iconological fashion according to strictly formalist principles. In addition, in my third year at Princeton, wanting to know what all the fuss was about in consequence of the formalist literary interpretation of D. W. Robertson, Jr., that so upset his gentlemanly colleagues in the Princeton English department, I quietly sat in on Robertson's tempestuous seminars several times and was much more favorably impressed than I expected to be. Formalism is a kind of hermeneutic cult, a private sect in a way, and not easy to explain in expository and comprehensive fashion. I have tried to do so in this chapter. It amazes me that in the long and vehement controversy engendered by Allan Bloom's *Closing of the American Mind*, in the late 1980s, it was not seen how firmly Bloom belongs to the German formalist tradition going back to the 1920s. Bloom's discipleship to his teacher at the University of Chicago Leo Strauss is always mentioned (often making Strauss out to be a Reagan in academic garb), and sometimes the influence of the Johns Hopkins literary theorist Leo Spitzer is mentioned. But no one seems to be able to find the roots of Bloom's cultural conservatism in the formalist tradition of Erwin Panofsky and Ernst Robert Curtius and behind them the seminal figure of Aby Warburg—not even the flagship *American Historical Review* (see the April 1990 issue for a particularly unhistorical article on Bloom). I hope that one accomplishment of this chapter will be to place Bloom in the perspective of the long formalist tradition of Central European thought. A sociological view of formalism would note that its protagonists emerged out of the ethnic and political caldron of *Mitteleuropa*, and formalism may be seen as an effort to find unity and stability in the midst of diversity and disorder.

Erwin Panofsky. Panofsky has fortunately received substantial biographical and critical attention. Shortly after his death his friend and student William Hecksher, at the urging of Panofsky's widow, published a credible brief biography (Princeton, 1969). He provides the description of Panofsky in the early 1920s by Edgar Wind. Panofsky has received close theoretical scrutiny in Michael Prodo, *The Critical Historians of Art* (New Haven, 1982), and Michael Ann Holly, *Panofsky and the Foundations of Art History* (Ithaca, 1984), who also have plenty to say about the whole German art historical movement from Wölfflin and Warburg on down. I do not necessarily agree with all their judgments, but I am indebted to them for thought-provoking and well-informed insights. I have to admit that I must be almost alone in not learning anything important from the writings of Warburg's other famed student, Ernst H. Gombrich, who strikes me as largely a retailer of superficial psychological and aesthetic bromides. (See *Art and Illusion* [London, 1962] and *Norm and Form* [London, 1966].) My views on Panofsky's personality and career have been influenced by the comments about him made by Theodor E. Mommsen, who studied him closely over many years and not always sympathetically. Mommsen thought there was a lot of the show-off and just a bit of the mountebank in Panofsky. I attended two of Panofsky's public lectures, and they were certainly dazzling performances. In rereading his historical writing, I was struck by how much deeper he seemed than I remembered him in the fifties, especially the Renaissance book, which, behind its pretentious facade, exhibits the workings of a first-rate mind. Although Panofsky prospered greatly in America, I do not think the American scene was very good for his intellectual development. He could outflank almost anyone by his erudition and debating capacity, and he was not pushed as hard to do his best as he would have been if Hitler had not happened and he could have stayed in Hamburg. This is shown especially in *Gothic Architecture and Scholasticism* (Cleveland, 1957; original publication 1951), in many ways a wonderful book but not the one he was capable of writing on the subject if he had tried harder. The American academic world is a strange place. There 95 percent of humanists cannot do first-rate work because they do not have the time, leisure, facilities, or income. The other 5 percent get all the plum jam and often don't do their best work because they are not pressed hard enough. Panofsky also enjoyed enormous power of patronage disposal as the senior humanist at the Institute for Advanced Study. Anyone who crossed him was therefore jeopardizing a chance at a year's succulent appointment to the institute. Mommsen had some sharp things to say about

Panofsky, both as a man and as a scholar. I noticed he always lowered his voice when he said these things.

Ernst Robert Curtius. Discussion of Curtius has been greatly facilitated by the exemplary biographical and bibliographical study made by Earl Jeffrey Richards *Modernism, Medievalism, and Humanism* (Tübingen, 1983), drawing in part on the primary biographical research of Heinrich Lausberg (1970). My critique of Curtius's work is, however, based entirely on my own judgment. In this regard, the edition of Curtius's correspondence (Frankfurt, 1980) was helpful.

The Critical Triumvirate. The most influential work of E. Talbot Donaldson was *Chaucer's Poetry* (New York, 1958). Among Donaldson's other accomplishments was the best English translation of *Beowulf*. See also Charles Muscatine, *Chaucer and the French Tradition* (Berkeley, 1957), and Robert W. Hanning, *The Vision of History in Early Britain* (New York, 1968) and *The Individual in Twelfth-Century Romance* (New Haven, 1974).

For Robertson and the Robertsonians, see D. W. Robertson, Jr., *A Preface to Chaucer* (Princeton, 1962), and *Essays in Medieval Culture* (Princeton, 1980).

Medieval Literature. I want to stress that for my understanding of medieval literature and the interpretation of it, I have learned much from friends and colleagues Robert Hanning and Margaret Jennings, with whom I team-taught respectively in 1982 and 1985 a graduate course on medieval literature in the comparative literature department of New York University. In understanding medieval literature, I have benefited from two older books: Karl Young, *The Drama of the Medieval Church* (Oxford, England, 1933), and R. R. Bolgar, *The Classical Heritage and Its Beneficiaries* (Cambridge, England, 1954). Young and Bolgar taught respectively at Yale and Cambridge universities. And I have learned from the recent book of the Duke University Marxist ("New Historicist") critic Lee Patterson, *Negotiating the Past: The Historical Understanding of Medieval Literature* (Madison, Wis., 1987), especially Chapter 1, "Historical Criticism and the Development of Chaucer Studies." This should be read by anyone interested in medieval culture and literature and the way they have been interpreted, whether or not the reader shares Patterson's post-New Left ideology. I thought Patterson's discussion of Robertson was particularly valuable, and it has influenced my account. Alongside Hanning and the deconstructionist Howard Bloch at Berkeley, I would say that Patterson seems like a dominant voice in medieval literary criticism in the United States. I think Margaret Jennings would also be capable of standing in the very front rank if she did not carry an incredibly heavy teaching burden in a small Catholic college.

Medieval Art Historians. Among medieval art historians of the younger generation, the most promising to succeed to Panofsky's throne is Berkeley's James H. Marrow, who was trained at Columbia and London's Warburg Institute. His *Passion Iconography in Northern European Art of the Late Middle Ages and Early Renaissance* (Kortrijk, Belgium, 1979) puts him in the same position as Hanning in literary criticism: formalism softened by some respect for individuation. But Marrow's masterpiece is awaited. It might be noted that Berkeley has Howard Bloch and James Marrow and Columbia Robert Hanning and the well-regarded feminist medieval historian Caroline Walker Bynum. So Columbia and Berkeley are the most likely vibrant centers for generating new views on medieval culture in the 1990's.

CHAPTER SIX: THE OXFORD FANTASISTS

Biographies of Lewis and Tolkien. Their literary celebrity and cult followings, plus the large amount of correspondence they left behind in Oxford libraries, have generated more in the way of biography than is normal for medievalists, but the quality of the biographies is not as high as might be anticipated. In the case of neither Lewis nor Tolkien has a definitive biography, meshing circumstantial life experience, psychological and sociological explanation, and critical insight into their work, yet appeared. The core book remains Humphrey Carpenter, *The Inklings* (London, 1979), artfully dealing with both Lewis and Tolkien and their circle, mainly in the war years. It is highly readable, Carpenter being an experienced professional biographer and literary historian resident in Oxford, but not an academic. There are two recent biographies of Lewis: George Sayer, *C. S. Lewis and His Times* (London, 1989), and A. N. Wilson, *C. S. Lewis: A Biography* (New York, 1990). Sayer's book, entirely ignored by the media in the United States, is idiosyncratic, being a mixture of memoir and biography from sources and sloppily, if engagingly, written. Wilson is one of the most prominent novelists and biographers (nonacademic) among the younger generation of English intellectuals, and his publishers in both London and New York put on heavy promotion for the book, which was supposed to be a blockbuster or at least definitive. It is not, although he did research in the vast Lewis papers in Oxford and therefore has some new scraps of biography to offer (for example, he believes that Lewis had sexual relations with his long-standing dragon housekeeper; I doubt that). Wilson did not, however, use the extensive collection of biographical material on Lewis at Wheaton College in Illinois. (*Chronicles* [June 1990], p. 39). His biography is therefore deficient in basic research. Wilson also attempts a critical evaluation of Lewis's work as a medievalist, which shows both what a quick study Wilson is and how little he knows about the Middle Ages and the modern interpretation of it. There certainly was a heavy turnout in the upscale press on Wilson's biography. *The New York Times Book Review* gave it the special accolade of printing a long prepublication extract in December 1989. But when the book finally appeared a few months later, the reviewers in both New York and London, although generally favorable, didn't know what to say about it because they didn't know much about Lewis and medieval studies, and Wilson had not helped them very much. The most interesting review of Wilson's book was by the veteran critic and poet C. H. Sissons (*London Review of Books* [February 22, 1990], pp. 19–20) who obviously disliked Lewis to start with and was not persuaded in another direction by Wilson, himself extremely ambivalent and indecisive about "Jack." What is really interesting about these many reviews is the cultural gap between the world of 1990 and the culture of the late forties and early fifties with their intense, eccentric, but short-lived Christian revival. No reviewer except Sissons seems to have had a clear idea where Lewis was coming from, and Sissons didn't want to have any part of it. Meanwhile, an earlier review (*Times Literary Supplement* [August 11–17], 1989, pp. 863–6) of the Sayer biography by Claude Rawson is much more assured and engaged in the subject than the Wilson book reviews. Rawson is interested in Lewis's complex psychology, and reviewing at the same time as the Sayer book a volume of some of Lewis' correspondence (ed. Martin Moynihan, London, 1989), he points to sadomasochistic proclivities behind the fantasies (no surprise, of course, to anyone with an elementary knowledge of Freud, but quite a bold thing to say in anti-psychoanalytic Britain).

I patiently made my way through a five-foot shelf of books on Lewis's thought, mostly written by midwestern American admirers and found none that taught me anything. Now that the TV film *Shadowlands*, about Lewis's late marriage, has been turned into a London and Broadway play, presumably a TV sitcom is next (Now! After *L.A. Law*, *Oxford Medieval Studies!* It's got everything: handsome brilliant Oxford don, lovely, caring New York Jewish broad, her two hell-raising sons, muscular Canadian Rhodes scholar students . . .). I can hardly wait.

Biography of Tolkien. Tolkien's biography was written, under the watchful eye of the family, by Humphrey Carpenter (London, 1977). It gives the bare outline of Tolkien's life; it is useful but astonishingly superficial. Carpenter's 1983 collection of Tolkien's letters, edited with the assistance of Christopher Tolkien, a son who is an Oxford literature don, is a wonderful book, much more interesting than the biography, and it greatly raised my esteem for Tolkien. The stress and strains of creation, the tremendous psychic and physical struggle to write *The Lord of the Rings*, and the complex love of the northern medieval world come through immediately. Here is, indeed, material for a very good film or play. Interestingly enough, as befits the great fantasist, some of the best letters (in response to admirers' inquiries, usually from America) were written out fully but never actually sent. Also, Tolkien's memorandums to publishers trying to sell the book, especially to Milton Waldman of Collins Publishers, are stunning pieces of self-criticism. This is a book to treasure and read again. Among the large number of critiques of Tolkien's work, Tom Shippey's *The Road to Middle-Earth* (London, 1985) is the most ambitious. Tolkien remains his own best critic.

Powicke. There is a long necrology by Sir Maurice's student R. W. Southern in *Proceedings of the British Academy*, Vol. 50 (1969), pp. 275–304. It is surprisingly ambivalent about the man and very restrained in praise of the scholarship. Southern admires Powicke's personal qualities and thinks Powicke was a great presence at Oxford while he was there, but it would be hard to say from this lengthy essay exactly what Powicke's impact was on Oxford historiography and what the grand little man represents in medieval studies over the long haul. My account is considerably more positive than that of Southern, who certainly must be credited with frankness. It was he who applied the term "Proustian" to Powicke's view of the thirteenth-century nobility, a characterization I have built upon. A problem with Powicke's legacy in medieval studies is that although he was a prolific writer, there is only one book (*King Henry III and the Lord Edward*) that was durable, and it is far too long and diffuse for even most graduate students today. What needs to be done is publication of a 250-page extract from the magnum opus: "Powicke on the Medieval Nobility." It could be done, and it would be valuable in medieval studies programs and history and possibly sociology and anthropology courses.

Vivian H. Galbraith. Some other Oxford historians were even less enthusiastic about Galbraith's appointment as regius professor to succeed Powicke than Sir Maurice himself. A. J. P. Taylor said of Galbraith in a private letter (and undoubtedly in public, too): "a nonentity who has never written anything, not even academic" (*London Review of Books* [May 10, 1990], p. 12). There was such an outcry over the Galbraith appointment because excellent candidates in modern history (Taylor himself and H. R. Trevor-Roper) had been passed over to maintain the tradition of appointing a medievalist to the regius chair that the next time around Trevor-Roper was appointed (ironically, at the expense of the greatest English medievalist since Maitland, R. W. Southern) and the regius chair at Oxford has gone to a modernist ever since. Galbraith had published little at the time of his appointment because he had slaved away for more than two decades as a head archivist in the Public Record Office, where he did a first-rate job and helped the research of many others. Eventually he published an excellent, if overly concise, book on medieval public records and a surprisingly good study of *The Making of Domesday Book* (New York, 1961). In the latter part of his career he worked for many years to establish the authenticity of an early-fourteenth-century populist treatise called "The Way to Hold a Parliament." There was something quite earthy about Galbraith, and he made no claims to being an intellectual. He swore like a longshoreman, looked like an indigent farmer, and could read not a single word of German. By temperament and archival experience he had the knack of seeing medieval government as a day-to-day process rather than as a set of ideas. He could, however, be cavalier in treatment of students. I think behind all the clowning facade Galbraith was an undereducated, unorthodox, but brilliant medievalist who should have taken himself and his chair more seriously.

CHAPTER SEVEN: AMERICAN PIE

The Wilsonians. There are two good books on the culture of Wilsonian progressivism: Robert M. Cruden, *Ministers of Reform: The Progressives' Achievement in American Civilization 1889–1920* (Urbana, Ill., 1984); and James T. Kloppenberg, *Social Democracy and Progressivism in European and American Thought 1870–1920* (New York, 1986). As the title of Kloppenberg's book indicates, he sees Wilsonianism as part of a tide of liberal-left thinking in the transatlantic world, while Cruden's study focuses on the American cultural and political context. I am inclined to the latter point of view. There is something distinctly American about Wilsonian progressivism, influenced though it was marginally by the European moderate left, especially in Britain. Although Wilson was a Virginian, the roots of his thought (except for his antiblack racism) and those of his disciples lie in New England Protestantism, secularized into pragmatism (Charles S. Peirce, William James, and John Dewey) and Harvard Law School judicial activism (Oliver Wendell Holmes, Jr., Louis D. Brandeis, and Roscoe Pound). Progressivism, in this view, was the intended completion of the transformation of the American Republic that the New England Protestant mind had started earlier in transcendentalism, the abolitionist movement, and the Civil War and Radical Reconstruction. Wilsonian progressivism as the next phase of New England Protestantism was triggered by two social innovations of the late nineteenth century: the expansion of corporate capitalism and the mass immigration from Mediterranean and Eastern Europe. The latter trends produced a kind of apocalyptic fervor in the progressive mind (moving out from New England to the Midwest and California) to control megaton capitalism and ethnic diversity before these changes engulfed and disempowered the Protestant elite for all time. Wilson was neither by background as a southerner nor temperamentally the ideal leader for WASP progressivism, but as a Princeton Presbyterian with distinction as a political scientist and educator he reasonably qualified, and in any case political circumstances and his insatiable ambition made him the center of public life. The progressives had no choice except to adhere to him and indeed to glamorize and canonize him.

Wilson. On Wilson himself, the literature is vast and inconclusive, and some distinguished historians have changed their minds about him several times. That in itself is indicative that there were psychopathological problems at the root of Wilson's behavior. This was identified early by Sigmund Freud himself, who in the early 1920s collaborated with the American diplomat William Bullitt on a psychopolitical study that was so devastating that it was not published until 1967. More recent opinion is given in Edward A. Weinstein, *Woodrow Wilson: A Medical and Psychological Biography* (Princeton, 1981). For the past two decades Princeton's Arthur S. Link has been engaged in editing Wilson's papers and generating a multivolume biography. An early version of Link's laudatory, although not uncritical, view is *Woodrow Wilson and the Progressive Era* (New York, 1954), but the best short biography remains that of John Morton Blum (Boston, 1956).

Haskins. It remains a mystery to me why a scholar and educator of such monumental stature did not receive detailed assessment and circumstantial memoirs, let alone a full-scale biography, after his death in 1937 (he was almost totally incapacitated by stroke in 1931). It is as if Haskins so awed and terrified any who could write of his life and work in detail that they remained silent. Even the obituary notice in the medievalist journal, *Speculum*, that he founded is extremely brief and uncommunicative. Fortunately the Houghton Library at Harvard has a file of Haskins's correspondence, mostly in the 1920s, that, while dealing only with academic matters and nothing of a private nature, does illuminate how he operated as an academic baron and luminary of the medievalist profession. His student and protégé Joseph Strayer, who was closemouthed even about the weather, surprisingly shared with me in the 1950s some of his fond memories of Haskins as a teacher and trainer of research medievalists. The Houghton Library was cooperative in giving me access to the Haskins papers, and I quote from two of these unpublished letters (to Merriam, October 1922, and to Wendell, January 5, 1916). A series of letters shows Haskins in high gear as an academic leader. Determined to further the study of medieval science in the United States, he lobbied to establish a chair at Harvard and handpicked its first occupant, the Frenchman George Sarton. It was a very good choice. Not only did Sarton turn out to be very productive as a published scholar, especially on the key subject of medieval Arab science and its impact on the West, to which he devoted several well-written volumes, but he also exhibited a certain verve and imagination, at the same time being extremely deferential to Haskins, the correspondence reveals. Eventually Sarton made an important addendum to Haskins's negative view of the Italian Renaissance. Sarton claimed that from the point of view of the history of science, Italian Renaissance humanist culture was regressive, substituting literary pursuits for the edge of quantitative-based protomodern science the fourteenth-century scholastics had attained. On Haskins and Norman feudalism: David Bates, *Normandy Before 1066* (New York, 1982), pp. 168–69.

Haskins at Versailles. See E. M. House and Charles Seymour, *What Really Happened at Paris* (New York, 1921), pp. 27–66; C. H. Haskins and R. H. Lord, *Some Problems of the Peace Conference* (Cambridge, Mass., 1920). Although Haskins wrote the first four chapters of the book, on the West European settlement, and Lord the last four on Central and Eastern Europe, it is certain that Haskins endorsed the latter discussion of Poland and the Balkan changes. See also Inga Floto, *Colonel House in Paris* (Princeton, 1980), pp. 200–07, 265, and Arthur Walworth, *Wilson and His Peacemakers* (New York, 1986), pp. 255, 268–69, 272, 274–75, 283, 322–23, 439.

There is a side to Haskins that I have not discussed in the text: whether Haskins was an anti-Semite. He succeeded a Jew in the chair of medieval history at Harvard, Charles Gross, who did good work on merchant guilds and who had been trained in Europe. No Jew again received an appointment in the Harvard history department until Oscar Handlin, the U.S. historian, in 1940. Since Haskins dominated the Harvard department until he was incapacitated in 1931, he must bear part of the responsibility for the Jewish exclusion. Even more significant, Haskins trained a whole generation of American medievalists, possibly as many as two dozen Ph.D.'s; I know of none who was Jewish. This could not be accidental; he must have simply refused to accept Jewish graduate students. This problem, of course, is generational. American medievalists, as American academic humanists generally, from about 1910 to the early 1940s, did not want Jewish students, particularly in the prestigious and influential Ivy League schools. Even if they were not personally anti-Semitic, they were painfully conscious of the difficulty of placing Ph.D.'s who were Jewish in other than New York City colleges or the very bottom tier of state universities. I draw here upon the recollections of Frederick C. Lane, the eminent Renaissance economic historian and department chairman at Johns Hopkins in the 1950s, who got his Ph.D. at Harvard, and of Benjamin Nelson, a fine scholar on the subject of medieval usury. Nelson told me that in 1953, when he received his Ph.D. at Columbia, all his referees, including his dissertation adviser, Austin P. Evans, a vehement advocate of civil liberties and a hostile critic of the Inquisition, sent out letters of recommendation blatantly warning that Nelson was Jewish. Not surprisingly, Nelson ended up in a New York City college when he deserved much better. Columbia itself did not hire a half Jew in its history department until 1945 (Richard Hofstadter) and a full Jew, Richard B. Morris, until 1947. By 1960 Morris was chair of the history department, and more than a third of the Columbia faculty, including myself, were Jewish.

Strayer. He died on July 2, 1987, and my account of his life and work is the only relatively detailed one that has yet appeared. As of August 1989, his papers had not been deposited by his widow in the Princeton University Library. Strayer's second wife and widow, Sylvia Thrupp, is herself a medieval historian of distinction, and possibly she will give us in time a biography of her husband and an edition of his papers. The necrology at Strayer's memorial service was delivered by his student Thomas N. Bisson of Harvard and is published in the *American Philosophical Society 1988 Year Book*, pp. 253–56. It is almost entirely boiler plate. I wish to note an example of Strayer's occasional personal kindness. Hearing from Ted Mommsen in 1953 that I was having fiscal problems, he persuaded the Firestone Library at the university that the medieval collection needed reviewing and appointed me to the job that was thereby created. As a matter of fact, there were no significant gaps in the splendid Firestone medieval collection, but to justify my salary, I ended up ordering about two hundred deservedly obscure European dissertations. There was never the glimmer of a sign that Strayer was ethnically or otherwise prejudiced against anyone. Catholics, Jews, African-Americans, women—they were all OK with him, as long as they met his very high academic standards and were appropriately deferential to him. He was exceptionally kind to John F. Benton, a physically handicapped student, who turned out to be a very good scholar and died prematurely.

The Case for the Anglo-Saxons Against the Wilsonian Normanists. This is summarized by Peter Hunter Blair, *Introduction to Anglo-Saxon England* (Cambridge, England, 1966); Richard Hodge, *The Anglo-Saxon Achievement* (Ithaca, 1990); and, with lots of interesting photographs, James Campbell, ed., *The Anglo-Saxons* (Oxford, England, 1982). Hodge's book makes extensive use of archaeological evidence whose interpretation, in my opinion, is as secure as Samoan ethnography. The affiliation between Anglo-Saxonism and feminism is elucidated by Susan Mosher Stuard in B. Rosenthal and P. E. Szarmach, eds., *Medievalism in American Culture* (Binghamton, N.Y., 1989), p. 76.

CHAPTER EIGHT: AFTER THE FALL

Roman Catholic Views of the Medieval Church. The term "absolutizing of the Middle Ages" is taken from Volume X (*The Church in the Modern Age* [New York, 1981], p. 281, original German edition, Freiburg, 1979) of the multivolume *History of the Church*, edited by Hubert Jedin and published in the late sixties and seventies. This series comprises the definitive post-Vatican II liberal Catholic ecclesiastical history, intended to challenge and replace the multivolume church history edited by Augustin Fliche and F. X. Martin and published in the 1940's. The latter was the work of conservative French and Belgian Catholic scholars who were deferential to papal magisterium and enthusiasts for the centralizing traditions of the Roman Church. Hubert Jedin was a liberal Swiss German Catholic who quickly gained a great reputation both inside and outside the Catholic Church in the 1950's with a beautifully written as well as deeply learned multivolume history of the late-sixteenth-century Council of Trent. In this classic study, Jedin's reformist and ecumenical inclinations were already evident. His view of the Renaissance papacy and its grave shortcomings was scarcely more sympathetic than the opinion of non-Catholics on the pre-Reformation Roman Curia, and Jedin showed that the road that the Catholic Church chose to take at Trent in the face of the Protestant upheaval was not the only conceivable avenue; it might have still been just possible to work out a compromise with the Protestants and reunite the church. Yet Jedin was so subtle and sympathetic in his judgment of the more conservative papalist party that prevailed at Trent and so persuasive in placing the council within the context of a devotional and learned revival in the church that he did not get into trouble with Rome (although like Knowles and Gilson, he became instantaneously so well regarded in non-Catholic academic circles that censure would have been a counterproductive step for the Curia). Jedin flourished in the era of good feelings that for a decade or so followed Vatican II. The three volumes, however, of the Jedin-edited *History of the Church* (there is a somewhat stilted English translation) committed to the medieval church are a quite disappointing work. This is partly because the authors thought they were producing a definitive textbook for advanced students and the work is so freighted with bibliography that it is very hard to read and partly because of indecision and fragmented opinion. Even when its authors are on the reformist wing of the church, Catholic scholarship does have trouble with the Middle Ages, although the Jedin medieval volumes are much better than the comparable relatively partisan "absolutizing" volumes in the Fliche-Martin series, with the possible exception of Fliche's own vigorous volume on the Gregorian reform of the late eleventh and early twelfth centuries. It is, of course, very difficult for believers to write good histories of their own religious communities. Catholics are not the only ones to have this problem. It can be done, however, if one attains a requisite subtle blend of sympathy and critical openness. Owen Chadwick, the Cambridge scholar, succeeded magnificently with his fascinating two-volume history of the Anglican Church in the Victorian era, and the Israelis Gershom Scholem and Rafael Mahler did likewise for Jewish religious history for the period 1500–1800. One subsidiary but real problem that Catholic historians of the medieval church seem to have is an overbearing, compulsive mania for bibliography and documentation. One of the great things about Knowles was his firm dedication to telling the story rather than trying to convince the hypercritical clerics who run the *Revue d'Histoire Ecclésiastique* (a mainly bibliography journal) that he had read every third-rate article ever published on the subject. Prominent Catholic historians of the medieval church (because of their scholarly prowess or visibility among Catholic readers) other than Knowles and Gilson follow, from the more confessional and conservative ("absolutizing" in the Jedin parlance) at the start of the list to the more ecumenical and liberal at the end: Henry Daniel-Rops, *Cathedral and Crusade* (New York, 1953); Augustine Fliche, *La Réforme Grégorienne at la Reconquête Chrétienne* (Paris, 1940); Walter Ullman, *The Growth of Papal Government in the Middle Ages* (London, 1955); Christopher Dawson, *The Making of Europe* (London, 1932); Gabriel Le Bras, *Institutions Ecclésiastiques de la Chrétienne Médiévale* (Paris, 1959); Gerhard B. Ladner, *The Idea of Reform* (Cambridge, Mass., 1957); Stephan Kuttner, *Harmony from Dissonance* (Latrobe, Pa., 1960); J. A. Jungmann, *The Mass of the Roman Rite* (London, 1961); Jean LeClercq, *The Love of Learning and the Desire for God* (New York, 1961); Brian Tierney, *Foundations of the Conciliar Theory* (Cambridge, England, 1955); M. D. Chenu, *Nature, Man, and Society in the Twelfth Century* (Chicago, 1968); Bernard McGinn, *Visions of the End* (New York, 1979). On Christopher Dawson, see the life by his daughter, Christina Scott, *A Historian and His World* (London, 1984).

Bernard McGinn is currently the leading Catholic medieval historian in the United States. He teaches at the University of Chicago. He was the first Catholic to receive an appointment in the Chicago Divinity School. Originally a priest teaching at a parochial high school in New York City, he resigned his order in the dispute over the conservative papal pronouncements on sexuality but has remained a devout Catholic. He studied theology for several years in Rome with the famed Canadian-born liberal theologian Bernard Lonergan and, after getting a Ph.D. under my direction, did postdoctoral work in Germany. His most important work is on Joachim of Fiore and later medieval apocalyptic thought.

Knowles and Gilson Biography. The hostile but well-informed and insightful "memoir" by Adrian Morey—*David Knowles* (London, 1979)—is immensely valuable for Knowles's biography. It draws on materials in the archive of Downside Abbey as well as Morey's and other monks' personal recollections. Brief but characteristically perceptive and honest is the account by Knowles's colleague at Peterhouse College, Cambridge, the conservative historian and theorist Maurice Cowling, *Religion and Public Doctrine in England*, (Cambridge, England, 1980) Vol. I, pp. 129–55. W. A. Pantin, "Curriculum Vitae," in *The Historian and Character and Other Essays* (Cambridge, England, 1963), is now of little value. Alberic Stacpoole, "The Making of a Monastic Historian," *Ampleforth Journal*, Vol. 80 (1975) i, pp. 71–91, and ii, pp. 19–38, offer some insight into Knowles's religious and cultural ambience. The necrology in *Proceedings of the British Academy*, Vol. 61 (1975), pp. 439–77, by Knowles's student and literary executor, the Cambridge professor Christopher N. L. Brooke, is disappointing; it has very little on Knowles's private life, and its critique of his work is superficial. This deficiency is aggravated by Brooke's suppression of Knowles's manuscript autobiography. I have relied not only on my own conversations with Knowles but also on the recollections and opinions of the distinguished British medievalist Geoffrey Barraclough, making allowances for Barraclough's personal animus against Knowles and relish in recounting scandal. Yet Barraclough was extremely well connected (he held chairs at Liverpool, London, and Oxford), and in a position to be well informed on the private life of Father David Knowles, whom he considered something of a hypocrite. My account does not agree with this view of Knowles as an artful deceiver, nor do I assent to Morey's acidulous portrait of a selfish, arrogant person.

All that needs to be known about Gilson's personal life has been narrated at length in somewhat pious fashion by his disciple at the Pontifical Institute, Laurence K. Shook (Toronto, 1989). Shook is a philosopher, and his skill at biographical narrative is not of a very high order, but he must be given full credit for a detailed and thoroughly candid book that makes for fascinating reading. The only thing left out is the sad fact that toward the end of his life, in his mid-seventies, Gilson publicly regretted his close association with Parisian Jewish scholars in the 1920s and 1930s. Let us quietly attribute this to lonely senility rather than the influence on him of the anti-Semitic ambience of the University of Toronto. Shook surprisingly does little in the way of an intellectual biography and critical assessment of Gilson's work. It would be interesting, for instance, to trace the changes in successive editions of Gilson's most widely read book, *The Spirit of Medieval Philosophy*, which first appeared in 1936.

CHAPTER NINE: THE ONCE AND FUTURE KING

Southern. The long quotation from Southern, appropriately the longest in this book, is from N. F. Cantor, ed., *Perspectives on the European Past* (New York, 1971), pp. 194–95. I did a tape-recorded interview with Sir Richard in his rooms at All Souls College over a two-day period in 1968 and edited down the transcript to a hundred pages, which he then revised into more expository prose. The only major work of Southern's that I did not discuss in the text is *Western Society and the Church in the Middle Ages* (London, 1970), which constitutes the second volume in *The Penguin History of the Church*. The Cambridge scholar Henry Chadwick did the previous volume, on the early church, and it is a memorable, delightful, thoroughly idiosyncratic, and very personal statement. Southern tried to do what presumably the series editor, Henry Chadwick's brother Owen, wanted: a consensus overview for students and the general reader. On the whole, Southern succeeded, but in retrospect I wish he had given us the kind of personal statement that Henry Chadwick felt free to do. It would be today a more interesting and valuable work. The merits of the book are evident to anyone familiar with the body of Southern's work. The limitations are that the focus is on the Southern territory—namely, the Anselm/St. Bernard/early Franciscan tradition. It does little on the early medieval church except for appreciation of missionary endeavor, and it characteristically underrates the centrality of heretical movements and separated spiritual groups from the late twelfth century on. Despite the book's sociological-sounding title, it does not explain how the high medieval church actually functioned as an institution. There is lacking a Weberian vision or the kind of thick structural analysis offered up by the French canon lawyer Gabriel Le Bras. Southern in 1990 published another version of his biography of Anselm (Cambridge, Encino). It maintains the interpretation of the earlier version.

Hunt and Galbraith. Because of Southern's reluctance to exercise group leadership and found an institute, the 1950s in the Oxford medieval history scene were in practice unfortunately more the Age of Hunt and Galbraith than, surprisingly, the Age of Southern. I thought this was bad at the time, and I still think so in retrospect, even though when I expressed this opinion in a somewhat jocular article in the *Oxford Magazine* of November 1987, there were several vitriolic responses that truly surprised me. I had forgotten how many British scholars (and American and Canadian ones, too) were beholden to Richard W. Hunt and revered his memory. Hunt, the keeper of the western manuscripts in the Bodleian Library, was in a position as head of the medieval manuscript room to influence research, but he far exceeded this simple mandate. He set himself up as the supervisor of the research to anyone he found working in Duke Humphrey's Library (the manuscript room), especially if he or she was a doctoral or postdoctoral student. Many still see this as reflective of Hunt's innate kindness and generosity. Perhaps, but I also see it as stemming from Hunt's frustration over his own inability to publish. There was a transference effect not only to helping others but also to trying to shape the course and outcome of their work. The very learned Dr. Hunt had strong opinions about medieval culture and especially his own era of high expertise, the twelfth century. I would say that his methodology was 1920s modernism—close textual reading, with a minimum of historical context, and aggressive hostility to anything smacking of a sociological and psychoanalytic interpretation. Therefore, although Hunt was a very learned man and outwardly courteous and friendly, I found him intellectually retrograde and culturally reactionary. I have met many others as well as Southern who think very highly of Hunt, including my friend Margaret Jennings, who did postdoctoral research under his direction on twelfth-century Latin rhetoric. But in my view, while Hunt stood for professional research and expository precision, he was also an obstacle to the productive development of the more interpretive kind of medieval studies at Oxford and in Britain generally. He was for deep psychological reasons the quintessence of that special, dreadful Oxbridge breed, the highly learned anti-intellectual don. Look at the great minds I have discussed in this book. If Hunt could have had his way, he would have excluded from the canon and even the company of medievalists David Knowles and Marc Bloch (they didn't use manuscripts and took the very long view) and Johan Huizinga (he scarcely read documents at all), and as a member of a fellowship or appointments committee I am sure he would have voted against Ernst Kantorowicz and possibly even Panofsky and Curtius. Someone with the set of assumptions Hunt held about what was worthy and unworthy in medievalist scholarship did as much damage to medieval studies as the great benefit he was to Dick Southern and others. In the interest of truth, I will confess (as I did in my *Oxford Magazine* article, but of course, it was overlooked by my hysterical critics) that Hunt hurt me personally by saying (not wrongly) that my weak Latinity made me unfit for medieval studies. It made me unfit for *his* kind of medieval studies, which no doubt is important enough, but there are other kinds. I think that a subtext lurks in Southern's British Academy necrology of Hunt that does not entirely conflict with my hostile judgment upon him.

About Galbraith, the other member of this regnant duo at Oxford in the 1950s, I have written at the end of the note to Chapter Five. Southern's necrology of Galbraith is in *Proceedings of the British Academy*, Vol. 64 (1978), pp. 397–26, and of Hunt in *PBA*, Vol. 67 (1981), pp. 371–98.

Southern's Followers. In addition to the books of Robert Hanning, for which the citations are given above in the note to Chapter Five, major works of those whom I call the knights of the Southern round table are: Maurice H. Keen, *Chivalry* (New Haven, 1989); John Morris, *The Age of Arthur* (New York, 1973); Colin Morris, *The Discovery of the Individual* (London, 1972); Peter Dronke, *The Medieval Lyric* (New York, 1968) and *Poetic Individuality in the Middle Ages* (Oxford, England, 1970); Peter R. L. Brown, *Augustine of Hippo* (London, 1967), *Society and the Holy in Late Antiquity* (Berkeley, 1982) and *The Body and Society* (New York, 1982); Robin Lane Fox, *Pagans and Christians* (New York, 1986); Malcolm Lambert, *Medieval Heresy* (London, 1977); Caroline Walker Bynum, *Jesus as Mother* (Berkeley, 1982) and *Holy Feast and Holy Fast* (Berkeley, 1987); and Frank Barlow, *Thomas Becket* (Berkeley, 1986). The other historians discussed at the end of the chapter: Robert S. Lopez, *The Birth of Europe* (Philadelphia: 1967); Lynn T. White, *Medieval Technology and Social Change* (New York, 1962); and Geoffrey Barraclough, *The Crucible of Europe* (Berkeley, 1976).

CHAPTER 10: OUTRIDERS

Huizinga. Aside from *The Waning of the Middle Ages*, the important works available in English are *Homo Ludens* (London, 1949), *Men and Ideas* (New York, 1959), and *Erasmus of Rotterdam* (New York, 1952). There is a good analytical study: Werner Kaegi, *Das Historische Werk Johannes Huizingas* (Leyden, 1947).

Power and Postan. In 1946, according to the archivist of the London School of Economics, Power's papers, including private material, were sent to the Cambridge University Library from the LSE. The papers were never cataloged (another triumph for British scholarship), and the personal material, according to the Cambridge University librarian, had disappeared by the summer of 1989. On Power and Postan and their place in economic history, there is the concise but very well-informed and frank appraisal of Donald C. Coleman, *The Rise and Fall of British Economic History* (Cambridge, England, 1987). On Power, see the memoir by a leading economic historian of modern Britain and her collaborator in planning the *Cambridge Economic History*, Sir John Clapham, *Economica* Vol. 7 (1940), pp. 351–56. C. W. Webster, the London political historian, wrote an excellent brief biography of Power in *Economic Journal*, Vol. 50 (1940), pp. 561–72. Postan's creative work in medieval economic history is best assessed in two works: *Essays in Medieval Agriculture* (Cambridge, England, 1973) and *Economic Organization and Policies in the Middle Ages* (Cambridge, England, 1963). The necrology of Postan by his student Edward Miller in *Proceedings of the British Academy*, Vol. 69 (1981), pp. 544–56, is boiler plate. I have listed Power's important work in the text. It is to be hoped that her excellent book on late medieval nunneries will be reprinted soon with a suitable feminist introduction.

Feminist Historians of the Middle Ages. Power stood out among the group of feminist medievalists in Britain of the generation of the 1920s.

Helen Maud Cam became highly celebrated in the 1950s, when she taught at Harvard for several years. Cam's vesting of power and decision-making capability in local communities was a conscious effort to revive Stubbs's Victorian populism, which Maitland had negated. Cam may also be viewed as a vanguard thinker from the perspective of today's feminism; her sex-driven communalism represents feminist medievalism's rejection of traditional phallic authoritarianism.

A brilliant woman scholar in the 1930s, who died very young, was Oxford's Maude V. Clarke. Her papers on the politics of the reign of Richard II are still worth reading. It was Clarke who insisted on the authenticity of the early-fourteenth-century populist treatise "The Way to Hold a Parliament," and the researches of V. H. Galbraith have sustained her view.

There was also a group of feminist medievalists in the United States, teaching mainly in the "Seven Sisters" (Ivy League women's colleges). Their lives must have been lonely and difficult. One imagines the patronizing smirks they had to endure at meetings of the Medieval Academy. But they persisted, and one of them, Amy Kelly, eventually published a first-rate book that is still worth reading: *Eleanor of Aquitaine and the Four Kings* (Cambridge, Mass., 1950).

Special recognition should go to Dorothy L. Sayers, who became famous and affluent as a mystery story writer (Lord Peter Wimsey, etc.) but who was a determined medievalist who never got more than visiting appointments (perhaps that is why her vision of Oxbridge is so romanticized in, for example, *Gaudy Night*). Penguin published Sayers's translation of the *Song of Roland*, which, while it has been superseded by a more readable one done by Frederick C. Golden, is meritorious, if a little fustian in its fake medieval language. Sayers also published a translation of *The Divine Comedy*. It is no worse than anyone else's of this untranslatable classic. Recently the Public Broadcasting System has been showing several British TV dramatizations of Sayers's mystery novels, set in the England of the late twenties and early thirties. Since Sayers always imagined herself the heroine of these stories, I watch them not for the story lines (boring) but to catch the pained face of a woman medievalist in the bad old days. I imagine that is the subtext of these things. Poor Sayers lived a quarter of a century too soon. Now she would be lionized and offered university chairs from Berkeley to Princeton (compare the career of the novelist Joyce Carol Oates).

The leading feminist medieval historian in the United States today is Caroline Walker Bynum. There are at least two other formidable ones: Susan Mosher Stuard and Penelope Delafield Johnson.

Mommsen. The letter from Ted Mommsen to his friend Felix Gilbert, written after the Nazis seizure of power in 1933, is quoted from Gilbert's autobiography, *A European Past* (New York, 1988), with his translation. Gilbert devotes several interesting pages to Mommsen in the 1930s. My account of Mommsen's early life is based, however, mainly on his own recollections as told to me.

Alexander Nevsky and Film. Sergei Eisenstein's 1938 film about the Russians repulsing the Teutonic Knights is acted in the German expressionist mode of the 1920's and is not in sync with contemporary taste. But it is withal a superb re-creation of medieval political iconology. *Nevsky* is in my judgment one of the six best films ever made about the Middle Ages, the others being *The Seventh Seal* (Ingmar Bergman's masterpiece set in the Europe of the Black Death); *Ran* (Akira Kurosawa's version of King Lear, set in late medieval Japan and fully capturing the world of aristocratic violence in a way that is also true for Europe); *The Name of the Rose* (based closely on Umberto Eco's novel, and better than the novel, in my judgment). Laurence Olivier's 1944 version of Shakespeare's *Henry V* (as a medieval film, I much prefer this to Kenneth Branagh's 1989 neo-Brechtian version, even though Branagh restored two important cuts that Olivier made because it conflicted with the hyperpatriotic wartime ambience Olivier aimed for. Also, Olivier had the whole Irish army to help him fight Agincourt while Branagh seems to be using six guys he picked up in a local pub); and a little-known 1988 New Zealand film, *The Navigator* (set mainly in a Welsh coal mining village during the Black Death—the most convincing film portrait of medieval peasants; Bloch would have been ecstatic). There have been also some resounding failures at film attempts to depict the spirit of the Middle Ages: *Brother Sun and Sister Moon; Lancelot; Camelot.* A film set in early-sixteenth-century France is worth seeing by students of the Middle Ages: Natalie Zemon Davis's *The Return of Martin Guerre.* The peasants here seem too affluent and articulate, but it is still a most intriguing historical film. If you are willing to go as far as the early seventeenth century, *The Devils,* from the Aldous Huxley novel, will tell you much about medieval witchcraft and reactions to it.

"Retromedieval." I learned this term from the *New Yorker* film critic Pauline Kael, in her review of *Brazil,* a science fiction film set in a horrible "retromedieval" future. I have used the term more positively than did Ms. Kael.

A CORE BIBLIOGRAPHY IN
MEDIEVAL STUDIES

———————•⬧•———————

This is an up-to-date basic bibliography in medieval European studies, listing only books available in English. The citation forms have been reconciled with the Library of Congress data base and double checked against the Princeton University Firestone Library catalog as an aid to librarians. Bibliographic data are taken from the most recent American edition; where this edition is not the first edition published, the original date of publication or in some instances the first English translation is given in brackets at the end of the entry. Most of these books are still in print and can most readily be ordered directly from the publisher. They will be found in any major university library and ought to be in every college library. The aim here is to specify a working core collection, limited to 125 titles. Some famous titles do not appear because they have been superseded by later works.

Abulafia, David. *Frederick II: A Medieval Emperor.* London: Allen Lane, Penguin Press, 1988.

Barlow, Frank. *Thomas Becket.* London: Widenfeld and Nicolson, 1986.

Baron, Salo Wittmayer. *A Social and Religious History of the Jews,* 2d ed. rev. Philadelphia: Jewish Publication Society, 1965 [vols. III–VIII 1957]. Vols. III–IX.

Barraclough, Geoffrey. *The Origins of Modern Germany,* 3d ed. Oxford, England: B. Blackwell, 1988 [1947].

Bartlett, Robert. *Trial by Fire and Water: The Medieval Judicial Order.* Oxford: Clarendon, 1988.

Bischoff, Bernard. *Latin Palaeography: Antiquity and the Middle Ages.* Translated by Dalbhi O. Croinin and David Ganz. New York: Cambridge University Press, 1990.

Blair, Peter Hunter. *An Introduction to Anglo-Saxon England.* New York: Cambridge University Press, 1966 [1956].

Bloch, Howard, R. *Etymologies and Genealogies: A Literary Anthropology of the French Middle Ages.* Chicago: University of Chicago Press, 1983.

Bloch, Marc. *Feudal Society.* Translated by L. A. Manyon. Andover: Routledge, 1989 [1961. Paperback, 2 vols. University of Chicago Press, 1963].

Bolgar, Robert Ralph. *The Classical Heritage and Its Beneficiaries.* New York: Harper & Row, 1964 [1954].

Boswell, John. *Christianity, Social Tolerance, and Homosexuality: Gay People in Western Europe from the Beginning of the Christian Era to the Fourteenth Century.* Chicago: University of Chicago Press, 1980.

Brown, Peter Robert Lamont. *Augustine of Hippo: A Biography.* New York: Dorset Press, 1986 [1967].

———. *Society and the Holy in Late Antiquity.* Berkeley: University of California Press, 1987.

Brucker, Gene A. *Renaissance Florence.* Berkeley: University of California Press, 1983 [1969].

Brundage, James A. *Law, Sex, and Society in Medieval Europe.* Chicago: University of Chicago Press, 1987.

Bury, John Bagnell. *The Invasion of Europe by the Barbarians.* New York: Norton, 1967 [1928].

Bynum, Caroline Walker. *Jesus as Mother: Studies in the Spirituality of the High Middle Ages.* Berkeley: University of California Press, 1982.

Caenegem, R. C. van. *The Birth of the English Common Law,* 2d ed. New York: Cambridge University Press, 1988 [1st ed., 1973].

Cambridge Economic History of Europe. Edited by Michael M. Postan et al., vols. I–II, New York: Cambridge University Press, 1966 [1941, 1952].

Cambridge History of Later Medieval Philosophy: From Aristotle to the Disintegration of Scholasticism, 1100–1600. Edited by Norman Kretzmann, Anthony Kenny, Jan Pinbors. New York: Cambridge University Press, 1982.

Chenu, Marie Dominique. *Nature, Man, and Society in the Twelfth Century: Essays on the New Theological Perspectives in the Latin West.* Preface by Étienne Gilson. Selected, edited, and translated by Jerome Taylor and Lester K. Little. Chicago: University of Chicago Press, 1968.

Clanchy, Michael T. *From Memory to Written Record, England 1066–1307.* Cambridge, Mass.: Harvard University Press, 1979.

Cochrane, Charles Norris. *Christianity and Classical Culture: A Study of Thought and Action from Augustus to Augustine.* New York: Oxford University Press, 1966 [1940].

Cohn, Norman R. C. *The Pursuit of the Millennium,* rev. and expanded ed. New York: Oxford University Press, 1972 [1957].

Contamine, Philippe. *War in the Middle Ages.* Translated by Michael Jones. New York: B. Blackwell, 1984 [1980].

Curtius, Ernst Robert. *European Literature and the Latin Middle Ages.* Translated by William R. Trask. Princeton: Princeton University Press, 1973 [1953].

Douglas, David Charles. *William the Conqueror: The Norman Impact upon England.* Berkeley: University of California Press, 1964.

Dronke, Peter. *Medieval Latin and the Rise of the European Love-Lyric.* Oxford, England: Clarendon Press, 1968. 2 vols.

———. *Women Writers of the Middle Ages: A Critical Study of Texts from Perpetua (203) to Marguerite Porete (1310).* New York: Cambridge University Press, 1984.

Du Boulay, F. R. H. *An Age of Ambition: English Society in the Late Middle Ages.* New York: Viking, 1970.

Duby, Georges. *The Early Growth of the European Economy: Warriors and Peasants from the Seventh to the Twelfth Century.* Translated by Howard B. Clark. Ithaca: Cornell University Press, 1974.

————. ed. *A History of Private Life, Vol. II, Revelations of the Medieval World.* Translated by Arnold Goldhammer. Cambridge, Mass.: Harvard University Press, 1988.

Dawson, Christopher. *The Making of Europe: An Introduction to the History of European Unity.* New York: Meridian Books, 1956 [1932].

Easton, Stewart C. *Roger Bacon and Search for a Universal Science: A Reconsideration of the Life and Work of Roger Bacon in the Light of His Own Stated Purpose.* Oxford, England: B. Blackwell, 1952.

Erdmann, Carl. *The Origin of the Idea of the Crusade.* Translated by Marshall W. Baldwin and Walter Goffart. Foreword and additional notes by Marshall W. Baldwin. Princeton: Princeton University Press, 1977 [1936].

Fawtier, Robert. *The Capetian Kings of France: Monarch and Nation, 987–1328.* Translated by Lionel Butler and R. J. Adam. New York: St. Martin's Press, 1960.

Fichtenau, Heinrich. *The Carolingian Empire.* Translated by Peter Munz. Toronto: University of Toronto Press, 1978 [1st English ed. 1957].

Fletcher, Richard. *The Quest for El Cid.* New York: Knopf, 1989.

Fuhrmann, Horst. *Germany in the High Middle Ages c. 1050–1200.* Translated by Timothy Reuter. New York: Cambridge University Press, 1986.

Ganshof, François Louis. *Feudalism.* 3d English ed. New York: Harper & Row, 1964 [original French ed. 1947].

Gilson, Étienne Henry. *A History of Christian Philosophy in the Middle Ages.* New York: Random House, 1956.

Gimpel, Jean. *The Cathedral Builders.* Translated by Teresa Waugh. London: Cresset Library, 1988 [1963].

Gurevich, Aron. *Medieval Popular Culture: Problems of Belief and Perception.* Translated by James M. Bak and Paul A. Hollingsworth. New York: Cambridge University Press, 1990 [1988].

Halphen, Louis. *Charlemagne and the Carolingian Empire.* Translated by Giselle de Nie. New York: North Holland, 1977 [1949].

Hanning, Robert W. *The Individual in Twelfth Century Romance.* New Haven: Yale University Press, 1977.

————. *The Vision of History in Early Britain: From Gildas to Geoffrey of Monmouth.* New York: Columbia University Press, 1966.

Haskins, Charles Homer. *The Normans in European History.* New York: F. Ungar, 1959 [1915].

————. *Norman Institutions.* Cambridge, Mass.: Harvard University Press, 1918.

Herrin, Judith. *The Formation of Christendom.* Princeton: Princeton University Press, 1987.

Hodges, Richard. *Dark Age Economics. The Origins of Towns and Trade* A.D. *600–1000.* New York: St. Martin's Press, 1982.

Hodgkin, Robert Howard. *A History of the Anglo-Saxons,* 3d ed. London: Oxford University Press, 1967 [1st ed., 1935]. 2 vols.

Howard, Donald R. *Chaucer: His Life, His Works, His World*. New York: Dutton, 1987.

Huizinga, Johan. *The Waning of the Middle Ages: A Study of the Forms of Life, Thought, and Art in France and the Netherlands in the XIVth and XVth Centuries*. New York: St. Martin's Press, 1969 [1924].

Hyde, John Kenneth. *Society and Politics in Medieval Italy: The Evolution of the Civil Life, 1000–1350*. New York: St. Martin's Press, 1973.

James, Edward. *The Franks*. New York: B. Blackwell, 1988.

Jungman, Josef Andreas. *The Mass of the Roman Rite: Its Origins and Development*. Translated by Francis A. Brunner. New rev. and abridged ed. by Charles K. Riepe. New York: Benziger Bros., 1961.

Kantorowicz, Ernst H. *Frederick the Second, 1194–1250*. Translated by E. O. Lorimer. New York: F. Ungar, 1957 [1931].

———. *The King's Two Bodies; A Study in Medieval Political Theology*. Princeton: Princeton University Press, 1957.

Keen, Maurice Hugh. *Chivalry*. New Haven: Yale University Press, 1984.

Kelly, Amy Ruth. *Eleanor of Aquitaine and the Four Kings*. Cambridge, Mass.: Harvard University Press, 1978 [1950].

Kern, Fritz. *Kingship and Law in the Middle Ages*. Translated with an introduction by S. B. Chrimes. Oxford, England: B. Blackwell, 1968 [1939].

Knowles, David. *The Evolution of Medieval Thought*, 2d ed. Edited by D. E. Luscombe and C. N. L. Brooke. New York: Longman, 1988 [1962].

———. *The Monastic Order in England; A History of Its Development from the Times of St. Dunstan to the Fourth Lateran Council, 940–1216*, 2d ed. Cambridge, England: Cambridge University Press, 1963 [1940].

———. *The Religious Orders in England*. Cambridge, England: Cambridge University Press, 1948–1959. 3 vols.

Krautheimer, Richard. *Rome, Profile of a City, 312–1308*. Princeton: Princeton University Press, 1980.

Kuttner, Stephan Georg. *Harmony from Dissonance: An Interpretation of Medieval Canon Law*. Latrobe, Pa.: Archabbey Press, 1960.

Ladner, Gerhart B., *The Idea of Reform, Its Impact on Christian Thought and Action in the Age of the Fathers*. Cambridge, Mass.: Harvard University Press, 1959.

Laistner, Max Ludwig Wolfram. *Thought and Letters in Western Europe*, A.D. 500 to 900, rev. and reset ed., Ithaca: Cornell University Press, 1966 [1931].

Lambert, Malcolm. *Medieval Heresy: Popular Movements from Bogomil to Hus*. New York: Holmes & Meier, 1977 [1976].

Lane Fox, Robin. *Pagans and Christians*. New York: Knopf, 1986.

Leff, Gordon. *Heresy in the Later Middle Ages: The Relation of Heterodoxy to Dissent, 1250–1450*. New York: Barnes & Noble, 1967. 2 vols.

———. *Paris and Oxford Universities in the Thirteenth and Fourteenth Centuries: An Institutional and Intellectual History*. Huntington, N.Y.: R. E. Krieger, 1975 [1968].

Le Goff, Jacques. *Time, Work, and Culture in the Middle Ages*. Translated by Arthur Goldhammer. Chicago: University of Chicago Press, 1980.

Le Roy Ladurie, Emmanuel. *Montaillou: The Promised Land of Error*. Translated by Barbara Bray. New York: G. Braziller, 1978.

Lewis, C. S. *The Discarded Image: An Introduction to Medieval and Renaissance Literature.* Cambridge, England: Cambridge University Press, 1967 [1964].

Lopez, Robert Sabatino. *The Birth of Europe.* Philadelphia: Evans, 1967.

MacFarlane, Alan. *The Origins of English Individualism: The Family, Property and Social Transition.* Oxford, England: Blackwell, 1978; reprinted with corrections, 1985.

Marenbon, John. *Early Medieval Philosophy (480–1150): An Introduction,* 2d ed. London, New York: Routledge, 1988 [1983].

———. *Later Medieval Philosophy (1150–1350): An Introduction.* London, New York: Routledge, 1987.

McFarlane, Kenneth Bruce. *John Wycliffe and the Beginnings of the English Nonconformity.* New York: Collier Books, 1966 [1953].

McGinn, Bernard. *Visions of the End: Apocalyptic Traditions in the Middle Ages.* New York: Columbia University Press, 1979.

McKittrick, Rosamond. *The Frankish Church Under the Carolingians.* New York: Longman, 1983.

Miller, Edward, and John Hatcher. *Medieval England: Rural Society and Economic Change, 1086–1348.* New York: Longman, 1978.

Milsom, S. F. C. *Historical Foundations and the Common Law,* 2d ed. London: Buttersworth, 1981 [1st. ed. 1969].

Mollat, Michel. *The Poor in the Middle Ages.* Translated by Arthur Goldhammer. New Haven: Yale University Press, 1986 [1978].

Mommsen, Theodor E. *Medieval and Renaissance Studies.* Edited by Eugene F. Rice, Jr. Ithaca: Cornell University Press, 1959.

Moore, Robert Ian. *The Formation of a Persecuting Society: Power and Deviance in Western Europe, 950–1250.* New York: B. Blackwell, 1987.

Morris, Colin. *The Discovery of the Individual, 1050–1200.* Toronto: University of Toronto Press in association with the Medieval Academy of America, 1987 [1972].

Morris, John. *The Age of Arthur: A History of the British Isles from 350–650.* New York: Scribner, 1973.

Morrison, Karl Frederick. *Tradition and Authority in the Western Church 300–1140.* Princeton: Princeton University Press, 1969.

Muir, Lynette R. *Literature and Society in Medieval France: The Mirror and the Image, 1100–1500.* New York: St. Martin's Press, 1985.

Munz, Peter. *Frederick Barbarossa: A Study in Medieval Politics.* Ithaca: Cornell University Press, 1969.

Oberman, Heiko Augustinus. *The Harvest of Medieval Theology: Gabriel Biel and Late Medieval Nominalism,* 3d ed. Durham, N.C.: Labyrinth Press, 1983 [1963].

Owst, G. R. *Literature and Pulpit in Medieval England: A Neglected Chapter in the History of English Letters and of the English People,* 2d ed. rev. New York: Barnes & Noble, 1966 [1933].

Painter, Sidney. *The Reign of King John.* New York: Arno Press, 1966 [1949].

Panofsky, Erwin. *Gothic Architecture and Scholasticism.* Latrobe, Pa.: Archabbey Press, 1951.

———. *Renaissance and Renascences in Western Art.* New York: Harper & Row, 1972 [1960].

Patterson, Lee. *Negotiating the Past: The Historical Understanding of Medieval Literature.* Madison: University of Wisconsin Press, 1987.

Peters, Edward. *Inquisition.* New York: Free Press, 1988.

Pierenne, Henri. *Medieval Cities: Their Origins and the Revival of Trade.* Translated by Frank D. Halsey. Princeton: Princeton University Press, 1969 [1925].

Pollock, Frederick, and Frederick William Maitland. *The History of English Law Before the Time of Edward I*, 2d ed. 1898. 2 vols. Reissued with an introduction and select bibliography by S. F. C. Milsom. London: Cambridge University Press, 1968.

Power, Eileen Edna. *Medieval People*, 10th printing. New York: Barnes & Noble, 1963 [1924. The text did not change after the 1924 edition. Paperback edition: Penguin, 1950].

Powicke, Frederick Maurice. *King Henry III and the Lord Edward: The Community of the Realm in the Thirteenth Century.* Oxford, England: Clarendon Press, 1947. 2 vols.

Prestwich, Michael. *The Three Edwards: War and State in England, 1272–1377.* London: Weidenfeld and Nicolson, 1980.

Riché, Pierre. *Daily Life in the World of Charlemagne.* With expanded footnotes and translated with an introduction by Jo Ann McNamara. Philadelphia: University of Pennsylvania Press, 1988 [1978].

Riley-Smith, Jonathan. *The Crusades: A Short History.* New Haven: Yale University Press, 1987.

Robertson, D. W. *A Preface to Chaucer: Studies in Medieval Perspectives.* Princeton: Princeton University Press, 1962.

Robinson, I. S. *The Papacy 1073–1198: Continuity and Innovation.* Cambridge: Cambridge University Press, 1990.

Runciman, Steven. *A History of the Crusades.* New York: Cambridge University Press, 1980 [1951–1954]. 3 vols.

Russell, Jeffrey Burton. *Witchcraft in the Middle Ages.* Ithaca: Cornell University Press, 1984 [1972].

Sawyer, P. H. *The Age of the Vikings.* 2d ed. New York: St. Martin's Press, 1972 [1st ed., 1962].

Southern, Richard William. *The Making of the Middle Ages.* New Haven: Yale University Press, 1953.

———. *Robert Grosseteste: The Growth of an English Mind in Medieval Europe.* Oxford, England: Clarendon, 1986.

———. *Western Society and the Church in the Middle Ages.* Harmondsworth, England, and New York: Penguin, 1970.

Stevens, John E. *Medieval Romance: Themes and Approaches.* London: Hutchinson, 1973.

Stock, Brian. *The Implications of Literacy: Written Language and Models of Interpretation in the Eleventh and Twelfth Centuries.* Princeton: Princeton University Press, 1983.

Strayer, Joseph Reese. *On the Medieval Origins of the Modern State.* Princeton: Princeton University Press, 1970.

———. *The Reign of Philip the Fair.* Princeton: Princeton University Press, 1980.

Stuard, Susan Mosher, ed. *Women in Medieval Society.* Philadelphia: University of Pennsylvania Press, 1976.

Tellenbach, Gerd. *Church, State and Christian Society at the Time of the Investiture Contest.* Translated by R. F. Bennett. Oxford, England: Blackwell, 1959 [1936].

Temko, Allan. *Notre-Dame of Paris.* New York: Viking Press, 1967 [1955].

Tuchman, Barbara W. *A Distant Mirror: The Calamitous Fourteenth Century.* New York: Knopf, 1978.

Ullmann, Walter. *The Growth of Papal Government in the Middle Ages: A Study in the Ideological Relation of Clerical to Lay Power,* 3d ed. London: Methuen, 1970 [1955].

Vinogradoff, Paul. *Roman Law in Medieval Europe,* 3d ed. Oxford, England: Oxford University Press, 1961 [1909. The second edition of 1929 is the definitive text].

Weitzmann, Kurt. *Illustrations in Roll and Codex. A Study of the Origin and Case Method of Text Illumination.* Princeton: Princeton University Press, 1947.

White, Lynn Townsend. *Medieval Technology and Social Change.* New York: Oxford University Press, 1964 [1962].

Whitney, James Pounder. *Hildebrandine Essays.* Cambridge, England: Cambridge University Press, 1932.

Wilson, Christopher. *The Gothic Cathedral. The Architecture of the Great Church 1130–1530.* New York: Thames and Hudson, 1990.

Wolfson, Harry Austryn. *The Philosophy of the Church Fathers,* 3d ed. rev. Cambridge, Mass.: Harvard University Press, 1970 [1st ed. 1956].

Young, Karl. *The Drama of the Medieval Church.* Oxford, England: Clarendon Press, 1967 [1933].

INDEX

Abelard, Peter, 42, 312, 364
academic medievalists:
  costs of intellectualization for, 37–38
  debates among, 19, 28
  humanistic traits of, 36–37
  in literature departments, 38–39
  on relationship and interaction of
    medieval and modern cultures,
    36–37
  research support for, 31–33
  self-criticism among, 38
Académie Française, 334
Ackland, Joss, 213
Acton, John Emerich Edward Dahl-
    berg, Lord, 306
Adams, Henry, 44
Adams, Jeremy duQuesnay, 154
Adler, Mortimer, 215, 332
*Administration of Normandy Under Saint
    Louis, The* (Strayer), 258
Adorno, Theodor W., 143, 145, 412
Adrian IV, pope (Nicholas Break-
    spear), 344
Aeneid (Vergil), 199
Age of Arthur, The (Morris), 361
agriculture:
  in Europe, 21–22
  high farming and, 391–392
  leasehold farming and, 392
  Malthusian pessimism and, 391–394
  serfdom and, 391–392
Ailred of Rievaulx, 312
Alaric, king of the Visigoths, 405
Albigensian Crusade, The (Strayer), 278

Alcuin, 138
Alexander II, pope, 365–366
Alexander VI, pope, 289
Alexander Nevsky, 396
Alfoldi, Andreas, 363
Allegheny College, 250
Allegory of Love, The (Lewis), 206, 217,
    337
Allen and Unwin, 207, 224–225
All Souls College, 102, 123
American Civil Liberties Union, 42
American Civil War, The (Knowles),
    302–303
American Council of Learned Soci-
    eties, 32
American Historical Association, 280,
    283
American Revolution, 73–74
Anglo-Norman architecture, 38
Annales d'Histoire Économique et Sociale,
    133, 139–140, 142–144, 159
Annalist school, 142–144, 148–154,
    386, 391
  on feudalism, 280
  formalists' differences with, 202–203
  Huizinga and, 381
  Marxist interpretive core of, 151–152,
    155, 158–159, 246
  medieval women's history validated
    by, 156
  Power and, 383
  Powicke and, 241
  Princeton and, 284
  transatlantic triumph of, 155–156